AMERICAN EDUCATION

Its Men,

Ideas,

and

Institutions

Advisory Editor

Lawrence A. Cremin
Frederick A. P. Barnard Professor of Education
Teachers College, Columbia University

AMERICAN EDUCATION: *Its Men, Ideas, and Institutions* presents selected works of thought and scholarship that have long been out of print or otherwise unavailable. Inevitably, such works will include particular ideas and doctrines that have been outmoded or superseded by more recent research. Nevertheless, all retain their place in the literature, having influenced educational thought and practice in their own time and having provided the basis for subsequent scholarship.

THE COLLEGE CHARTS ITS COURSE

Historical Conceptions and Current Proposals

BY

R. FREEMAN BUTTS

ARNO PRESS & THE NEW YORK TIMES

*New York * 1971*

Reprint Edition 1971 by Arno Press Inc.

Copyright © 1939 by McGraw-Hill Book Company, Inc.
Reprinted by permission of R. Freeman Butts

Reprinted from a copy in
  The Newark Public Library

American Education:
  Its Men, Ideas, and Institutions - Series II
ISBN for complete set: 0-405-03600-0
See last pages of this volume for titles.

Manufactured in the United States of America

Library of Congress Cataloging in Publication Data

Butts, Robert Freeman, 1910-
    The college charts its course.
    (McGraw-Hill series in education) (American
education: its men, ideas, and institutions.
Series II)
    Bibliography: p.
    1. Universities and colleges--U. S.
2. Education, Higher--Aims and objectives.
I. Title. II. Series: American education:
its men, ideas, and institutions. Series II.
LB2321.B96 1971   378.73   73-165710
ISBN 0-405-03699-X

McGRAW-HILL SERIES IN EDUCATION
HAROLD BENJAMIN, Consulting Editor

THE COLLEGE CHARTS ITS COURSE

THE COLLEGE CHARTS ITS COURSE

Historical Conceptions and Current Proposals

BY

R. FREEMAN BUTTS

Assistant Professor of Education
Teachers College, Columbia University

FIRST EDITION

McGRAW-HILL BOOK COMPANY, INC.

NEW YORK AND LONDON

1939

THE MAPLE PRESS COMPANY, YORK, PA.

PREFACE

The American college presents strange contradictions to students and parents who are faced with the prospect of college education, and to the great majority of youth for whom the possibility of going to college is exceedingly slight the contradictions must seem even more baffling. For those who can go to college a pressing question is, Which one and why? and for those who cannot go to college the question is, Why not? The answer to these questions depends upon the decisions that America must make concerning the aims of college education, the relation of colleges to society, who should go to college, and what kind of education should be made possible after college attendance is achieved. And here the contradictions appear.

When college students ask for training that will help them to make a living, they are often met with solemn advice to "cultivate your intellects." When they ask for a chance to gain a better understanding of the problems of modern living, they are admonished to study "the great books of the past." When they ask for understanding about things that vitally interest them, they are met with stern warnings to study "what is good for you." When they ask to learn more about themselves and their relations with others, it is insisted that college is primarily "a place of the mind."

When the majority of youth of college age wonder, Why can't we go to college? they are faced with elaborate arrangements designed to keep them out and with counsel to go to work—even though there are no jobs for them. When students wish to explore widely in new and exciting areas of knowledge, they are cautioned to specialize in order not to become mere "smatterers," and when they wish to follow an absorbing interest, they are advised to acquire a broad "liberal education" in order not to become mere "specializers." When a great university announces a new course in the art of fishing, it is laughed out of court by academic professors who gained their Ph.D. degrees by counting the number of aorist verbs in Homer. When students become more interested in swallowing goldfish than in the gold standard, the public at large wonders if there is anything good in college education after all.

Yet there are few parents who would not send their sons and daughters to college if they could. And when one wanders on the shaded campuses of a hundred colleges and universities, the appeal of four years in such an atmosphere is undeniably strong and the nostalgic memories of thousands

of graduates are among the most precious they possess.   There are great
strengths as well as great weaknesses in our present colleges.

All these contradictions have strong roots in the history of college
education.   One of the purposes of this book is to bring to light for
examination the arguments that have been formulated in the past in
defense of the traditional type of college and to place over against them
the arguments that are being presented today in favor of changing the
college to make it meet more adequately the social and intellectual conditions of today.   It is assumed that such an examination of college
policies will lead ultimately to fundamental questions concerning the
conceptions of truth and knowledge, how the learning process goes on,
how social and economic conditions affect the college, what human
nature is like, and the relationships of the individual to society and of
man to nature.   Different answers to such problems as these will offer
different answers to the persistent problems of college education.

This book argues that college students present and prospective,
parents present and prospective, and college educators present and
prospective will be better qualified to judge of the claims of college
education if they become more conscious of where our traditional notions
of college education came from, why they are being challenged today,
and in which direction the college of the future should go.   In recent
controversies concerning these questions many outstanding educators
have taken part.   President Hutchins, Professor Dewey, President
Gideonse, and President Neilson, among a host of others, have offered
criticisms and countercriticisms of the college.

In these discussions, however, the illuminating evidence of history
has been largely neglected.   In fact, the whole approach to the problems
of higher education in the United States has for long almost studiously
avoided the historical method.   Each age has assumed that *it* was uniquely a period of "transition" when the college for the first time was
"on trial for its life."   A study of the history of higher education shows
plainly that the issues so hotly contested today are part of long continuing controversies the problems of which were defined in the large more
than a hundred years ago.

Insistence upon the historical continuity of the past with the present,
however, does not mean that the answers to past controversies are
necessarily suitable today.   The "lesson" of history would show rather
that colleges in the past have often changed in order to meet new social
and intellectual conditions.   Then, when the new had won its place and
received the stamp of approval, it often tended to resist further changes.
An understanding of this process can throw light upon similar processes
today.   History can further aid in solving our present problems by
indicating some of the social conditions that have changed so rapidly and

so drastically in recent generations that college education today needs continually to revise itself in order to be appropriate to modern life. New times require new measures—today more than ever—and we need a philosophy of college education that is firmly grounded on that progressive assumption.

This statement should warn the reader at the outset that the author has a point of view. It may be said, indeed, that every writer who deals with historical materials has a more or less well-defined point of view, no matter how much he may profess that he is being "purely objective" or that he is "getting only the facts." Modern historiography insists that facts do not just lie around to be picked up but that facts are ordered and made intelligible by the point of view of the historian. Everything that has ever happened in college education cannot, of course, be gathered and put between the covers of a book or of many books. A selection of materials must be made, and that selection will depend upon the purposes that the writer has in making the study. This does not mean that pertinent and relevant materials may be willfully overlooked or mutilated in order to fit a preconceived notion of what the writer would like to find. The point of view of the historian and of all writers on social affairs must be as fair to other points of view and must be as broad and inclusive as the materials used will allow. With this much warning the reader is referred to Chap. I for a more detailed statement of the author's point of view and his purposes in making this study.

Whether or not there is general agreement with the point of view herein presented, the author hopes that those who are interested in American college education will be prompted to reexamine their assumptions and will find aid in judging which of the current proposals for the reform of the college curriculum are most appropriate to American society. It is hoped that college students, the ones most directly concerned in the process of higher education, will be stimulated to take stock of their college experiences and engage more actively in the formulation of policies and programs that vitally concern them. It is hoped that the general reader will find access in this book to an important phase of the intellectual history of America and that the closer student of higher education will find illuminating material for further study.

A movement is gaining ground to urge college teachers themselves to study more thoroughly some of the major problems confronting higher education. In this movement it seems reasonable to suppose that those now engaged in college teaching or those planning to make college teaching or administration their life work will in the future pay more attention to the historical development of these problems in higher education. If this book makes a contribution toward fulfilling some of these needs, it will more than serve its purpose.

The book is arranged according to the following plan:

1. Part I sketches briefly the origins of the tradition that a liberal education should be predominantly linguistic and literary in character and that such an education can be attained only through a college curriculum that prescribes certain studies.

2. Parts II and III show how the rapidly changing social and intellectual conditions of the nineteenth century weakened this conception of a liberal education in the American college and gave rise to many innovations among which the elective system was perhaps most representative.

3. Part IV indicates the different kinds of proposals and the respective arguments that have been offered in the twentieth century in various efforts to find a remedy for the difficulties that grew out of the elective system and the nineteenth century.

Chapter I will describe at greater length some of the controversies and conflicting points of view that are now besetting college education and will indicate why the story of the rise and decline of the elective system provides an important clue to the study of these problems.

The author would like to make acknowledgment here of some of the debts incurred in the life of this book in its manuscript form. He would like to mention two former teachers, each of whom was uniquely "in" on the conception and birth of the manuscript: Professors Alexander Meiklejohn and Wayland J. Chase of the University of Wisconsin. For special aid in corralling the manuscript in its gangling and unruly days of adolescence the author is especially indebted to President W. H. Cowley of Hamilton College. For helpful criticism in the more mature life of the manuscript he is grateful to Professors Edward H. Reisner, Merle Curti, and Donald P. Cottrell, all of Teachers College, Columbia University. For assistance in a moment of crisis he thanks Mr. Kenneth M. Norberg, and for ministrations in prolonged periods of crisis he owes thanks to his wife, Florence R. Butts.

Acknowledgment is also made here to the following publishers and individuals who kindly gave permission to quote from their respective publications. Credit is given individually to publishers and authors where the quotations appear in the body of the book: The Macmillan Company; D. Appleton-Century Company, Inc.; Harvard University Press; University of Chicago Press; Charles Scribner's Sons; Farrar & Rinehart, Inc.; Columbia University Press; Yale University Press; The New York Times; The Atlantic Monthly; Harper & Brothers; The University of North Carolina Press; Newson & Company; University of Minnesota Press; Longmans, Green & Company; Harcourt, Brace & Company, Inc.; Henry Holt & Company, Inc.; World Book Company; Houghton Mifflin Company; Oxford University Press; The Clarendon

Press; Liveright Publishing Company; Marshall Jones Company; University of Oklahoma Press; Doubleday, Doran & Company, Inc.; Survey Associates, Inc.; Stanford University Press; F. S. Crofts & Company; The Forum; Brown University; The Journal Press; Association of American Colleges; Muhlenberg College; Teachers College, Columbia University; Robert M. Hutchins; Alexander Meiklejohn; William A. Neilson; S. J. Woolf; and Henry M. Wriston.

R. FREEMAN BUTTS.

NEW YORK CITY,
August, 1939.

CONTENTS

PART III

THE ELECTIVE PRINCIPLE WINS THE DAY

PART IV

NEW PROPOSALS FOR PRESCRIPTION

EDITOR'S INTRODUCTION

America's most ancient legend is found in its old tradition of being young and new. This notion is particularly ludicrous in the field of higher education, since the American college is in fact one of the oldest educational institutions in the modern world. It has in full measure, moreover, the appurtenances of advanced age; the myopic, reverent following of time-worn routines, the pious mumbling of old spells and incantations, the supremely naïve faith in its own magic worth.

Occasionally the college stirs uneasily in its senile slumber and announces that it is going to embark upon a new course. Sometimes it actually makes changes in its procedures, but, because these innovations are almost as likely to be retrogressions as advances in any one case, the total picture remains about as dynamic as that of any octogenarian dozing in the sun. Once in a while an individual institution, under the stimulus of a new administration, rises to its feet and makes threatening gestures in the direction of reform, but college administrations wear off, like the effect of drugs, and unlike some drugs they do not commonly appear to be habit-forming in nature. Thus the institution that has lately staggered into changed ways often sinks back to its old repose under the soothing influence of a new administration.

There are various exceptions to this general picture of somnolence, however. Here and there, particular colleges make changes that remain relatively permanent. Administrators and faculty members examine the institution's goals and machinery so critically and revise them so thoroughly that a truly new college to serve contemporary needs is sometimes established.

To college trustees, administrators, and teachers who are interested in the possibility of setting their own institutions on a new road of improved service and heightened significance, the present book will be an indispensable guide. To those who want their colleges to remain sleeping in an uncritical sun of alumni adoration, it may be what the undergraduates of another generation might have called an unpleasant stimulus in the region of the cervical vertebrae. It is not only an outstanding work of interpretive scholarship in history of education—that in itself would not be sufficient to unsettle the minds of academic sun worshipers—but it is also a manual for educational policy making in the college field.   It analyzes the strategy and traces the tactics of opposing forces with which policy makers have to deal.   It does all this with a reasoned fairness to conflicting points of view.   This fairness will commend the book to those who want to make reasoned judgments among the many proposals for building a new and better American college.

HAROLD BENJAMIN.

UNIVERSITY OF MARYLAND,
    August, 1939.

THE COLLEGE CHARTS
ITS COURSE

CHAPTER I

A CLUE TO CURRENT CONTROVERSIES IN HIGHER EDUCATION

A welter of conflicting proposals concerning the American college besieges the earnest student, parent, and educator. One gains the impression that few people are satisfied with what the colleges are doing, yet many have set forth ideas concerning what the colleges *should* do. In order to bring some kind of system into this confused arena, the writer has attempted to list a few of the controversial points of view that are apparent on the current scene. By and large, the criticisms of the American college may be grouped roughly into opposing camps which, for convenience, have been called "conservative" and "progressive." Recognizing that the use of such easy terms may seem to oversimplify the problem, nevertheless the writer believes that the advantages of clarity in a difficult field seem to outweigh the disadvantages of too many equivocal ramifications.

In the interest, then, of cutting through much confused and foggy thinking, a set of conflicting points of view has been devised which will illustrate some of the most important problems in college education concerning which conservative and progressive educators disagree. In proposing solutions for these persistent questions, the educator who tends to be extremely conservative will generally look to the past for his inspiration and will be prone to insist that the traditional aims of liberal education are the best. He will tend to say that the traditional studies are those which will best achieve his aims regardless of social and intellectual changes that have occurred since those aims and studies were devised. In general, the conservative educator often relies for his arguments upon a traditional philosophy, or world view, which has been handed down from the more remote past. Later chapters will try to present a fair picture of the actual content of the conservative intellectual outlook in order to illustrate the values that it cherishes and to show why the conservative position is so strong in American higher education today.

1

In contrast, the educator who tends to be progressive will be likely to emphasize the exigencies of the present and the great changes that have taken place in the social and intellectual world in relatively recent years.   He will insist that the aims of a liberal education and the appropriate studies must take their cue not so much from the past as from a philosophy of science and the dominating social forces of the present. It should be said that, although a few college educators consciously place themselves at one or the other of these extreme positions, *the vast majority remain somewhere between the two extremes,* taking their inspiration now from one side and now from the other.   It is to this great middle group of educators and laymen that this book is especially addressed in the hope that it will aid in clarifying the underlying assumptions upon which conflicting proposals for American higher education are based.   Although the easy bimodal distinction between conservative and progressive may not hold so well today as it did in earlier centuries, it is nevertheless maintained that such a distinction will prove useful in describing the current situation in higher education.

The following list of controveries has been devised to illustrate the conflicting opinions of prominent educators who are active in shaping college policies here and now in the United States.   The controversies will be described quite briefly in this first chapter in order to apprise the reader of some of the persistent issues to look for as he reads the later chapters.   In order to give a sense of the contemporaneous and recent quality of the problems, most of the controversies will be illustrated with headlines taken from the newspaper press of the last year or so.   These headlines are not figments of the imagination but have all been taken *verbatim* from the *New York Times.*   They are not unique with one newspaper, nor are they unique with the times; their equivalent can be found in any number of good newspapers throughout the country, and such issues as they represent have appeared in the past and will continue to appear not only in newspaper headlines but in the pages of professional and serious periodicals the country over.   Some of the controversies illustrate more vividly than others the opposition between conservative and progressive, but the details will be discussed more fully in the appropriate chapters.

Culture versus Cash.   The traditional ideal of the college has often been couched in terms of "culture," and the culturists have opposed vigorously the tendencies of the colleges to stress "practical" or "vocational" studies which directly aid the student to earn a living and make money.   The cultural ideal has its roots deep in the past, and the conservatives stoutly maintain that it should remain at the heart of the liberal college program and should be sharply set off from the more utilitarian type of approach.   The progressives, on the other hand, have insisted that the traditional cleavage between cultural and practical is not appropriate to a democratic society in which the work of the world must necessarily play so important a part in the lives of the great majority of people. Colleges are grappling with this controversy as indicated in the following newspaper headline:

PRINCETON TO TEST
ACADEMIC THEORIES

Symposium to Weigh Conflicting
Views on Values of Cultural,
Practical Studies

In such a controversy, the extreme conservatives would be likely to rule out the practical studies and insist that the proper function of the liberal college is to stress the cultural studies. Usually, "cultural" is defined by them to mean the languages, literature, philosophy, and mathematics of the past. The progressives would likely urge that the traditional conceptions of both cultural and practical values should be redefined and joined to the advantage of both:

NEW COLLEGE LINKS
CULTURE AND TRADE

Goddard, in Vermont, to Train
Students for Participation in
the Administration

TIES VOCATIONAL
TO THE CULTURAL

Dr. McConn Says Best Work Is
Stimulated by Vision of Careers
After College

Here is a conflict that began to appear in the American college as early as the eighteenth century, and it still presses for solution today. Educators and public alike must be prepared to make judgments and frame policies on this problem on the basis of a sounder philosophy of education than ever before.

The Ivory Tower versus the Watchtower. Conservative educators often bemoan the fact that colleges are dealing too much with the affairs of this world, and they urge that the proper collegiate atmosphere is one that shelters the students and provides the faculty with an academic retreat where study and contemplation may go on in restful seclusion apart from the hurly-burly of the everyday world. Progressives, on the other hand, insist that the college must come down from its ivory tower of monasticism and plunge students into activities that will bring them face to face with the realities of the social and economic world:

COLLEGES WARNED ON "MONASTICISM"

Guidance Council Told Youth
Must Not Be Trained for
"Unrealizable World"

COLLEGES URGED TO REVISE ROLE

Dearborn, in N. Y. U. Report,
Urges Them to Take Wider
Community Responsibility

Now, the intelligent citizen must try to decide whether the college of academic retreat is on the right track or whether the college of social responsibility is heading in a direction more appropriate to the social situation in modern American life.

Intellectualism and Book-mindedness versus Intelligence and Personality. Shifting the spotlight of the controversy from the college in general to the individual student, the conservatives argue that their aims can be achieved by stressing "cultivation of the intellect" of the student and by concentrating upon his ability to read books. The progressives, on the other hand, make much of developing in students an effective social intelligence which will aid them in solving actual problems of personal and social life, and to do this they stress the importance of developing all the facets of a student's personality rather than merely his "intellectual" or bookish abilities:

WHAT IS THE JOB OF OUR COLLEGES?

Hutchins Calls for an Intellectual
Discipline; Neilson, Development of Whole Personality

REVIVAL OF ARTS IN TEACHING URGED

Dr. Hutchins Assails System That
Dooms Great Books in
Nation's Schools

A REALISTIC CURRICULUM

Goucher College Trains Girls in
Terms of Life Activities

Now, how is the reader to make sense out of these conflicting statements, and how is he to judge between the relative values of different proposals for the reform of the college? The writer submits that the layman or the educator will be better equipped to make these judgments if he is more adequately aware of where the college is now, how it got there, and what factors should be most urgently considered in deciding where it should go.

Discipline versus Freedom and Interest. The opposing camps also have divergent answers to the question concerning how the college should treat its students. Students must submit to discipline and control by the college, say the conservatives; whereas the progressives urge that students should be given a large amount of freedom in order to share in making the policy of the college and to follow special interests of their own:

ST. JOHN'S HAILS NEW CURRICULM

President Barr of Annapolis College Analyzes Results of 100 Books' Program

ELECTIVE SYSTEM GOES

"Discipline in Liberal Arts" Is Substituted for "Vocational and Cafeteria Courses"

STUDENTS TO SHARE PROBLEMS AT BARD

Equal Numbers with Faculty Will Serve on Committees of Administration

BRYN MAWR GIVING MORE FIELD WORK

Lively Student Interest Aroused by This Causes Expansion of Activity

Here, then, on the one hand, we find a college emphasizing a completely prescribed curriculum of great books in order to revive the discipline of the traditional liberal arts; and on the other hand, we find colleges attempting to give students a greater freedom to work on problems that are of vital interest to them. Different conceptions of the learning process are at work. One believes that students must learn what is good for them; the other, that students learn most effectively when working on projects that interest them.

The Great Tradition versus Experimental Naturalism. Behind the conflicting opinions expressed by different educators can often be discovered different philosophical assumptions. In many cases, the conservatives reveal reliance upon a traditional philosophy of idealism which assumes that truth is fixed and authoritative and that therefore education must also be fixed and authoritative in order to lead the students to the correct conceptions of truth and knowledge. In contrast, the progressives often appeal to a philosophy of experimentalism based upon modern science which looks upon truth and knowledge as changing and flexible and which therefore believes that education must be flexible and change when new conceptions and new ways of doing things are revealed to be effective in solving problems:

Rise in Study of Classics Hailed As a Sign of "Progressive" Ebb

REPLIES TO HUTCHINS ON COLLEGE METHODS

Dr. Fox Opposes Dropping of "Scientific Spirit" for "Authoritarian Finality"

Before support is given to the proposals of anyone, whether in educational, political, or economic matters, his underlying assumptions should be brought to the surface and examined. With particular regard to the college curriculum it is important that we analyze carefully the philosophy of tradition and the philosophy of science to see which is more appropriate in its implications for the college of the present and future in American life.

Traditional Studies versus Modern Studies. Much closer and more vital to the student himself and to his parents is the problem of what he shall study when he goes to college; and the college educator must decide constantly what shall be offered to the student when he arrives. This has been an urgent problem facing institutions of higher education ever since they were first established, and just as urgent has been the struggle of new studies to make their way into the company of the old studies that have taken on the authority of tradition. The new and radical studies of one era have often become the traditional and conservative studies of the next. In recent generations, the most bitter conflict has been the attempt of the classical languages, literary subjects, and mathematics to defend the stronghold of tradition against the onslaught of the physical sciences and the social sciences which claimed that they should have a greater share in the college curriculum because of their greater social usefulness. Thus, we find occasional headlines such as the following:

CLASSICAL STUDIES CALLED SAFEGUARD

Dr. C. B. Gulick, at Radcliffe Exercises, Says They Tend to Combat Ignorance

LINGUISTIC STUDY LURES TRINITY MEN

Classes Read Some Greek at Sight and Revive Latin

A CHECK ON "SWASTIKAS"

But more often we find students and even faculties preferring as "a check on swastikas" the social and physical sciences, the more practical studies, and, in general, the studies that bring students into closer touch with the surrounding world and society:

AMHERST EXPANDS
IN SOCIAL SCIENCES

College of Classical Tradition Adds
New Course to the 14 Previously Offered

PRINCETON'S
NEW TREND

Enrollment Shows Marked Shift
Toward the More Practical
Subjects

HARVARD CHOICES
ATTEST NEW TREND

Freshman Electives for Next Year
Disclose 36 Per Cent Majoring
in Social Sciences

SHARP CUT IN LANGUAGES

Slight Gain Shown for Practical
Subjects

COLLEGES SCORED
AS TOO BACKWARD

Dr. C. M. Hill of Yale Asserts
Women's Institutions Shun
Present-Day Problems

EDUCATORS ARE CHIDED

He Tells Packer Group There Are
Many "Conservative" in a Bad
Sense

So, again, we must decide whether the traditional studies are more appropriate or less appropriate to our times than the recent studies which have grown largely out of our times.

Aristocratic versus Democratic Conception of the College. Traditionally the college has been for the few, especially the few who have had enough leisure and money to spend in four years at college. Today the conservatives still urge that the colleges should be for the few, not so much for the wealthy few as for the intellectually few who are considered capable of profiting from college work. Hence, they urge that the college should rigidly select its students from the relatively small group of young people who have the requisite intellectual capacity. In contrast, the growing progressive point of view insists that democracy should lead the colleges to open their doors wider and wider to the great majority of young people who would be able to profit from college study if it were properly adapted to their needs:

HIGHER STANDARDS
IN COLLEGES URGED

F. H. Dowles of Columbia Warns
Institutions to Restore Rule
of "Selective Admissions"

MASS EDUCATION
IS HELD NEW IDEAL

Old Concept of Schooling for the
Few Is Gone, Says Dr. Luther
Gulick

Before accepting either of these points of view, one should inquire carefully into the assumptions and aims that prompt them.

Religious versus Secular Conception of the College. Time was when the churches had a virtual monopoly on higher education, but the rise of state universities in the nineteenth century and the steady secularization of life have led to a growing division among educators concerning whether college education should be essentially religious or essentially secular in emphasis. The American decision has allowed both types to exist side by side, but parents are constantly faced with the choice as to which kind of college they prefer for their children, and faculty members must decide what part religious training should play in the life of college students. Religious leaders urge that religious colleges are superior in their own right not only because they teach correct religious truths but also because they provide the best civic training for democratic living:

PRESBYTERIANS SET EDUCATION GOALS

Church Seeks $10,000,000 Fund on 150th Anniversary to Strengthen College Work

TRAINED LEADERS NEEDED

Officials Hold Preservation of Democracy Rests on Reviving Interest of Youth

CATHOLIC COLLEGE EXTOLLED AS IDEAL

It Is a Spiritual as Well as an Intellectual Center, Dr. F. M. Crowley Tells Historians

SCHOOL GROWTH TRACED

Students in Higher Institutions Up 63% in Decade, He Says— T. F. Meehan Honored

WARNS LUTHERANS OF COLLEGE CYNICS

Educator Tells Convention That "Godless Professor" Is Christianity's Arch Foe

WORLD DECLARED "HOSTILE"

Support Is Urged for Church's Institutions—Doctrinal Bases for Unity Are Presented

STEADY RISE SHOWN IN STATE COLLEGES

Survey Reveals an Enrollment Increase Seven Times That of Endowed Institutions

BOARD POSES A PROBLEM

It Asks if Greater Reliance Is to Be Put on Public Aid for Higher Education

General Education versus Specialization. The conflict between the demands of general or common values and those of specialized values has come to the fore again in educational discussions of the past few years. It is not a new controversy, but it is one that is all the more vital in the light of the necessities for *common* effort brought about by the social trends of democracy and at the same time the necessities for *specialized* knowledge brought about by the rapid technological advances of a highly industrialized society. The contrast between conservative and progressive attitudes is not so clear in this controversy; but, generally speaking, the conservatives would rule out specialization of a technical sort from the liberal college. The progressives, on the other hand, would seek a newer and closer integration among the common values required by social action, the specialized values required by technological efficiency, and the necessity for the individual to earn a living in a specialized world:

DR. SEELYE CRITICIZES SPECIALIZED TRAINING

Only Liberal Education Turns Out Thinkers, He Says

COLLEGES WARNED TO TRY SPECIALTIES

450 of America's 745 Face Extinction if They Remain "Standard," Says Pitkin

TUFTS HEAD URGES BALANCED EDUCATION

Dr. Carmichael Warns Against Narrow Specialization

In this controversy, as in the others, educators must decide whether the traditional type of liberal and cultural education is the kind of general education that will most adequately serve the common needs of modern democratic society or whether a newer kind of general education or junior college will be more appropriate to newer times.

Elective System versus Prescribed Curriculum. The last of the controversies to be mentioned here centers around the elective as contrasted to the prescribed curriculum. It cannot be said that today conservatives and progressives line up clearly on opposite sides of this controversy. In the nineteenth century, there was a rather clear division, with the conservatives opposing the elective system and the nineteenth century progressives favoring its extension as a means of adapting the college curriculum to the changing times. But now, whereas the conservatives still maintain their opposition to the elective system, the twentieth century progressives have come now also to attack the elective system as it developed but for reasons very different from those of the conservatives.   What is progressive in one day and age may be obliged to change in order to continue to be progressive in another; this is the essence of any point of view that can be called progressive.   In other words, the elective system did not continue to be progressive.   So we find a concert of voices proclaiming the defects of the elective system and proposing some kind of prescription in its stead:

RETIRING EDUCATOR
SCORES COLLEGES

Dr. Smith, 38 Years on Board of Examiners, Says Graduates of Today Are Shallow

BLAMES ELECTIVE SYSTEM

Holds It Has Lowered B.A. Standards

MORE FLEXIBILITY
IN COLLEGES URGED

Dean Hawkes Warns Against Conformity That May Ruin Education of a Boy

YALE TO INCREASE
OPTIONAL STUDIES

Consequently, college educators are trying to find more adequate principles upon which to decide what should be required of students and what should be left to their own choices.   Their decisions upon this question are closely related to their fundamental educational philosophy as expressed in such controversies as have been briefly mentioned above.

This book has selected the elective controversy as being particularly helpful in throwing light upon present-day controversies and as providing a thread with which to trace one's steps through the history of college education in general.   The elective system has been chosen for this task, because it, more than any of the other controversies, has had easily identifiable effects upon the college curriculum.   It is extremely difficult to determine just how "cultural" or just how "intellectual" or "disciplinary" a college curriculum may be, whereas it is relatively easy to see how the prescribed studies gave way to an increasing number of elective studies in the colleges of the country.   In other words, the elective system provides a means of clarifying the meaning of the other controversies, and at the same time it shows most clearly how the conflicting theories have actually been applied in practice to the college curriculum.

Although the elective system may not seem so important to most educators of today as it appeared in 1901 to the writer of the following statement, the issues raised by the introduction of the elective principle into the curriculum of American colleges are still with us:

That the elective system presents the most important and far-reaching problem in American education will hardly be questioned. It is of vital concern to college presidents, superintendents, principals, teachers, pupils, parents,—in a word, to all interested in education. It touches alike, private and public institutions, coeducational and non-coeducational; it involves the relation between colleges and secondary schools, between institutions for general culture and those of strictly professional aims; it involves the relation of society and individual, the question whether one age shall set the standard for another, whether it is the business of education to build on what Nature furnishes or to remedy the defects of Nature. In short, it involves the very aims and ends of education.[1]

We may not argue the merits of the elective system per se with the same intensity that marked the controversies of forty and fifty years ago, but any thoroughgoing study of the problems of higher education today touches in some respect upon the part that the elective system is playing in the college curriculum. A survey of much recent literature in higher education, of which the quoted headlines are an example, reveals that many of the defects of the curriculum and many of the ills of college education in general are still being laid at the door of the elective system. Hence, it has been thought advisable to provide a more secure basis for evaluating the current theorizing and experimentation in higher education by tracing the main outlines of the elective system as it developed in American colleges and universities.

Using the elective system as a guide in traveling the maze of the history of higher education has the great advantage of keeping attention focused upon a coordinating theme in a field whose bounds are so great that no comprehensive history of it has yet been written. Furthermore, the elective system has brought out in the course of its development most of the problems which lie at the heart of any theory of higher education. There is something peculiar in the make-up of educators that rises to the fray when it is suggested that college students should or should not have considerable freedom in determining the kind of studies that they wish to pursue. When two opposing sides are present in such a discussion it is not long before the controversy becomes involved with fundamental points of view concerning what a liberal education should be, what studies are of most value for a college education, what the relation between the college and society should be, what place authority and freedom should have, what the nature of the learning process is, what the nature of knowledge and truth is, and, ultimately, what constitutes the

[1] E. D. PHILLIPS, "The Elective System in America," *Pedagogical Seminary*, 8: 206 (June, 1901).

essential stuff of human nature and reality. In a word, the elective
system as a phenomenon of educational, social, and intellectual development seems uniquely to provide a focal clue for portraying the history of
higher education.

When the prescribed curriculum reigned virtually supreme in the
many centuries prior to the nineteenth century, it seemed to represent
a particular kind of society and intellectual world. When the elective
system began to appear on the college scene, it, in turn, seemed to herald
in its small sphere a quite revolutionary change in the outlook of American
society. As we follow the rise and decline of the prescribed curriculum
and the rise and—shall we say—decline of the elective system, we are
following in miniature form the rise and decline of different world views.
We shall see what kind of collegiate education in the past paralleled what
kind of society and how the insistent demands of changing social environments have constantly changed the college curriculum, even if somewhat
more slowly in some ages than in others. It will be apparent that economic and political drives have exerted persistent pressures upon the
college curriculum, that religious factors have played a tremendous part,
and that the whole milieu of scientific knowledge and intellectual enlightenment has impinged upon the problem. Educational theory has sometimes led and sometimes followed these other forces.

In the thirteenth century, the universities were the leading lights of
civilized activity and were in the vanguard of the cultural life of an age
whose intellectual interests were highly religious. The world was conceived as relatively simple in structure, and as measured by Thomas
Aquinas it was bounded rather easily by the confines of theology and
religious philosophy. But when life began to quicken in many respects
during the Renaissance and Reformation, the universities apparently
were unable to keep pace with the new complexities of life. The new
regard of the Humanists for the individual human being and for his
development as an individual largely left the universities cold; but when
the classical literature that had absorbed the Humanists was finally
accepted, the classics became entrenched in the curriculum and refused
for centuries to be ousted from their place of dominance. The violent
theological debates of the Reformation perforce engaged the interest of
the universities, and it was still with these religious disputations and
theological training that American colleges remained primarily concerned
when the growth of inductive science, the rise of the commercial classes,
and the spread of democracy in the seventeenth and eighteenth centuries
were pointing the way to new social and intellectual worlds.

Finally, as the nineteenth century wore on, the American colleges and
universities gradually began to recognize that a new industrial and
machine age was being created outside their walls; and the strong edu-

cational tradition that had been inherited from earlier times began to be attacked by educational reformers who urged that the colleges must begin to catch up with the increasing tempo of an advancing technological age. The so-called "practical" studies began to edge their way into the curriculum but not without tremendous resistence from the older and more "cultural" studies. An emphasis upon the importance of the individual showed itself in the belief for the first time that the student was capable of deciding what he wanted to make of himself and that he should have freedom to select the corresponding type of preparation. The decline in church dominance was reflected, on one hand, in the attacks made upon the narrowly prescribed curriculum which had long been aimed at training for the ministry and, on the other, by the growth of large, secular, state-controlled, and privately endowed universities. The enormous additions to scientific knowledge forced the expansion of the curriculum to such an extent that no one student could possibly encompass even a small part of the subjects offered. The spread of democracy with attendant increases in per capita wealth and the growth of capitalism with its mercenary ideals sent thousands of new students into the colleges asking for all sorts of training. In all of these ways and in many others, the development of the elective system signalized a new social outlook as the twentieth century began.

To meet these new demands the colleges and universities in America, slowly at first and then more rapidly, tried to add the kind of courses that the public desired and to give almost unlimited freedom to the student in selecting from among them. When at last in postwar days the universities were able to announce that they were meeting the needs of a democratic society whose outstanding characteristics were a rampant individualism and an aggressive capitalistic industrialism, twentieth century critics arose on all sides to attack the "mushroom" growth of the universities and the planlessness of their development. The critics seemed, roughly, to fall into two camps. One group, which for want of a better name has been called "conservative," lamented the passing of the old prescribed curriculum with its well-balanced and "integrated" intellectual fare and deplored the overspecialized and overvocationalized courses of the elective system which had transformed the universities into mere "service stations" for all sorts of industrial, commercial, and agricultural enterprises. They felt that the universities could best serve society by reviving the ideals of the past and by keeping to scholarly pursuits in order to improve the "intellectual" quality of university training. The other group, which has been called "progressive," claimed that the highly individualistic and profit-seeking era was bound to pass out of existence in the face of a growing interdependent society and that therefore the college should place more emphasis upon preparing students directly to live in an interdependent society. They said that modern society was so complex and changing so rapidly that the student needed an "integrating" and unifying experience far different from the isolated prescribed curriculum of the past and far different from the highly specialized and compartmentalized courses of the elective system of the present.

It should be pointed out here that the author of this book believes that the progressive approach in general is the one that holds the more promise for the future of American college education. This does not mean that all that is labeled conservative is bad or that all that is labeled progressive is good. It merely means that any acceptable theory of higher education must be one that most adequately takes cognizance of the best evidence and most thoroughly supported theories of modern society and modern science in so far as they have influenced our conceptions of knowledge, truth, learning processes, social relationships, and human nature. By and large, the conservative point of view looks to the past for its solutions to college problems, whereas the progressive position looks to modern science and modern social developments as beacons along the road that education must travel if it is to improve itself.

The progressive should be identified, not by his adherence to a system, but by his attitude. Two elements that are important in the progressive approach are: A willingness to change educational practices when change is needed, and acceptance for educational practice of the best evidence presented by the study of modern society, modern psychology, and modern science. Although progressive-minded educators often differ among themselves concerning just what the best modern evidence is, they are coming more and more to agree that colleges must lead students to a better understanding of our own society, educate them in the light of the best psychological knowledge of how learning goes on, and try to inculcate respect for and use of the critical methods of science.

History shows that each age has required in its schools those studies which its leaders deemed most important to it. The progressive feels that we should do the same for our age. We should not feel that, just because certain attitudes and studies were developed in the past, they therefore were made good for all time or made in heaven. After all, colleges and courses of study have always been made by human beings for purposes that human beings hold valuable. The progressive attitude says that more and more we must look to our own values, to our own democratic society, to our own psychology, and to our own science to help students arrive at what is most significant in our life. This is what progressive education in various ways seeks *consciously* to do.

Therefore the progressive says that modern education should take its cue from the best that man knows *now* rather than exclusively from the best that man knew in past centuries.   Note that "progressive" is not spelled with a capital P and that it does not necessarily refer to those who profess allegiance to the so-called "Progressive Movement" in education. If a good many of the men who are called progressive in this book also happen to fall within the group loosely known as "Progressives," it merely means that they represent opinions that have a common bond with the interpretations of this book.   John Dewey recently struck a happy note when he cautioned against allying oneself too rigidly with a single point of view:

It is the business of an intelligent theory of education to ascertain the causes for the conflicts which exist and then, instead of taking one side or the other, to indicate a plan of operations proceeding from a level deeper and more inclusive than is represented by the practices and ideas of the contending parties.[1]

If the discussion that follows in this book can set forth fairly and clearly the forces that have been at work to produce the conflicting points of view now expressed in current controversies, it will have made a contribution to the ultimate formulation of a more intelligent theory of college education.

In a discussion of the elective system in college education, it may seem to be starting far afield to consider first some of the remote forces that shaped the traditional prescribed course of study.   Yet, in order to understand more fully the conceptions and practices that have long been at the basis of higher education and to appreciate the confusions and conflicts that beset American higher education today, it seems necessary to unearth as clearly as possible the original factors that determined the long prevailing notion that the college curriculum should be highly literary in quality and that it should be completely prescribed.   In short, to understand more fully why it was that the elective principle came on to the scene to shatter the age-old prescribed curriculum, we need to know what justifications had been established as bulwarks for the prescribed curriculum and what forces were at work to batter down those bulwarks and let in upon the college student a flood of new studies. Since our traditional conception of a liberal education goes back as far as Greco-Roman times, we must trace out briefly the roots of our long reliance upon the past for the aims and content of our liberal education on the college level.

A word should be added concerning definitions and the scope of the book.   The discussion is concerned not with professional training in law, medicine, engineering, business, education, or the like; it is concerned primarily with the "general" or "liberal" education as offered in what

[1] JOHN DEWEY, *Experience and Education* (The Macmillan Company, New York, 1938), p. v

is known variously as the "liberal college," "liberal arts college," "college of letters and science," and "college of arts and sciences," whether it is a separate institution or is the undergraduate college of a large university. The student has always had the right to "elect" which of the professions or technical schools he would enter after he had completed his "general" preparation in the undergraduate college, but he has not always had the right to select among the offerings leading to the baccalaureate degree. Thus, the problem of choice of courses within the professional and technical schools has been considered beyond the scope of this book.

The "prescribed curriculum" in the past referred to the whole course of study that was required *in toto* for all students alike as a prerequisite to gaining a degree. The "elective system" in its most extreme form referred to a course of study in which the student was virtually free to select from among the curricular offerings those subjects which he desired; and he received a degree not for the *kind* of subjects followed but rather for the *number* of subjects. Under the traditional prescribed curriculum, all students of one college class studied the same books at the same time and received degrees only upon completion of the entire required course; whereas under the extreme form of the elective system it was often possible for many students to receive the same degree yet never take any of the same studies that the others had taken. These extreme types of the completely prescribed or the free elective systems are admittedly rare today, but they are described in order to bring out the striking contrasts between the two types of curricular organization. The most common form of curriculum in the college of today is a result of a compromise between these two principles of prescription and election; for a particular degree certain studies or groups of studies are usually required, and the rest are left to the choice or election of the student.

PART I

WHEN THE PRESCRIBED CURRICULUM
REIGNED SUPREME

CHAPTER II

ROOTS OF OUR LIBERAL EDUCATION IN CLASSICAL BOOKS

As certain educators so often point out, our traditional conception of a liberal education has its roots deep in the past. Our most common notions of the ideal liberal education were formulated in the times of ancient Greece and Rome; and then during the intervening centuries the medieval church, the Renaissance, and the Reformation accepted and modified those notions to suit their own purposes. This chapter will trace briefly the high spots in this story down to the end of the fifteenth century, and Chap. III will show how the eighteenth century Enlightenment began to strain at the leash of the predominantly linguistic and bookish conceptions of a liberal education that earlier centuries had found acceptable. Whereas the classical Greco-Roman period had not found it necessary to prescribe very rigidly the studies that it deemed liberal, the decadent days of the Roman Empire produced a series of relatively arbitrary compilations and lists of studies which came to be exclusively identified with a "liberal" education.

The medieval church adapted these lists of books to its own religious purposes and then gave the first real impetus to the idea of a prescribed curriculum. In order to assure itself of the orthodoxy of its clergymen and teachers, the church began to require students of higher education to follow certain specified studies. Interestingly enough, the prescribed studies turned out to be the same ones that the Greeks and Romans had classified as liberal. Prescription was enforced by the practice of granting teaching licenses and academic degrees to show that qualified students had pursued the proper studies. Until the authority of the church and later that of the university faculties appeared on the academic scene, the conception of prescribed studies had not appeared. Ultimately the idea spread that the same liberal studies that were appropriate for clergymen and teachers should also be required for everyone who would like to be considered liberally educated, and the bachelor of arts degree with its prescribed curriculum became the mark of a liberally educated man. The Renaissance promoted the idea that the classical pagan languages and literatures of ancient Greece and Rome should play a greater part in the equipment of a liberally educated man, and the Reformation solidified the classical studies into the prescribed curriculum for its own religious purposes. The real question that faces modern educators is whether

19

or not the traditional conceptions and studies that made up the liberal
education of the past are the best and most appropriate ones for modern
times.

ORIGIN OF THE PRESCRIBED CURRICULUM IN THE "SEVEN LIBERAL ARTS"

Ancient Greece Formulates the Liberal Arts. The ancient Greeks
looked upon a liberal education as that training which would develop
harmoniously all the powers and character of a free man. The man of
action, capable in performing his duties as a citizen, was the ultimate
aim. A liberal education was also conceived by the ancient Greeks in
an aristocratic sense, for "liberal studies" were confined to those fields
of knowledge which involved the political and intellectual life of the free
citizens and did not include those areas of activity which involved making
a living through manual work or subservience to others. So a liberal
education comprised such studies as literature, poetry, and music for
appreciation of epic and drama; rhetoric for affairs of state; mathematics and speculative philosophy for developing the intellect and
satisfying the inquisitive spirit; and gymnastics for developing the body
as an important part in creating a well-rounded citizen and effective
man of action capable of performing his duties.

Historians have often pictured the era of ancient Greece, especially
the Athens of the fifth century B.C., as a time of unparalleled intellectual
freedom, a time when the Greek mind investigated the theory of matter
and of man and speculated upon many branches of philosophy. It has
even been said that science and philosophy were being created—at least
they were being put into such systematized form that they were more
easily taught and handed down than ever before. In such a period of
relatively great intellectual freedom, it may not be surprising that little
prescription was put upon the youth in his search for higher learning.
In fifth century Athens, the young man sought out and sat at the feet of
whatever sophist, or "wise man," he thought could teach him the most;
and the sophist professed to teach anything that anyone wished to learn.
Individualism was the watchword of the day; since man was "the measure
of all things," let him make of himself what he would. A pervading
spirit of informality and freedom militated against the requirements,
credits, and degrees that we have come to associate with higher education;
and a liberally educated man was denoted by his speech, actions, and
abilities rather than by his titles or degrees.

More or less formal institutions of higher education did arise in
Athens, however, during the fourth and third centuries B.C. These
institutions were in the form of several separate "schools of philosophy"
and "schools of rhetoric" to which modern historians have often applied

the misleading term "The University of Athens." The university organization as we know it is essentially a medieval institution, and there was no educational organization in ancient Greece or Rome that approached our use of the term. The schools of philosophy were the Academy of Plato, the Lyceum of Aristotle, the Stoa of the Stoics, and the Garden of the Epicureans, and the rhetorical schools were best typified by that of Isocrates. These schools were private schools, and young men from all parts of the civilized world attended any one or all of them as they desired or as they were attracted.[1]

In Roman imperial times, the emperors often paid the salaries of some of the teachers and granted them immunities and endowments, but apparently no regulations were made concerning what should be taught or what should be learned. The "university" could exert little authority or discipline over the students, for there was no bond among the teachers and no degree to be won:

> One essential difference we see between the ancient university and the modern: in the ancient university there was no governing or examining board—no board which arranged and co-ordinated the studies or conducted examinations and gave degrees. . . . No attempt . . . was made . . . to regulate the kind or the amount of instruction.[2]

Here in Greece we find the young actually being taught by the great thinkers of the day—the philosophers, the scientists, the molders of the intellectual environment. It may be significant that this period which was marked by relatively great intellectual freedom was also marked by relatively great freedom on the part of the student to select what studies he would follow. When limits and prescriptions to study began to be enforced because of limitations put upon intellectual freedom, then the freedom of student and teacher alike began to disappear.

Strong influences were at work, gradually tending to limit the scope of a liberal education and to prescribe only certain kinds of studies as leading to that liberal education. In their educational implications these tendencies were best represented perhaps by Plato. Although students were usually taught what they desired to learn in the higher schools of ancient Greece, Plato was afraid of the individualism and freedom of the Athenian democracy. He tried, therefore, to set up standards of truth and judgment that would be beyond the vagaries and opinions of indi-

[1] See KENNETH J. FREEMAN, *Schools of Hellas* (Macmillan & Company, Ltd., London, 1922), p. 58. Schoolmasters opened private schools, fixing the fees and the subjects to be taught; parents chose what they thought to be a suitable school according to their means, and also they chose the subjects that they wanted their sons to learn. Here is free election.

[2] J. W. H. WALDEN, *The Universities of Ancient Greece* (Charles Scribner's Sons, New York, 1909), pp. 150–151.

vidual men.   His philosophy of idealism has been a source of comfort to authority ever since.   Plato looked upon such concepts as reality, truth, justice, and beauty as essentially fixed, eternal, and unchanging.   The aim of life, then, came to be the discovery and contemplation of these real patterns that lay behind the apparent flux of life.   Whether Plato was essentially a "fascist" or a "communist" (to use the current phraseology of political and social theory), the fact remains that along with his philosophical and social theories went a fixed educational training and a prescribed course of study to prepare the student to live the good life as Plato conceived it.

Therefore in his educational theory, resting upon a philosophy of idealism, Plato prescribed for his prospective "philosopher-kings" a course of study that he believed would best lead them to eternal truth and justice.   According to the plans of his *Republic*, Plato would have required the study first of gymnastics, music, and grammar; then a higher discipline of arithmetic, geometry, astronomy, and musical harmony; and finally the highest study of all, "contemplation of reality" through dialectics or philosophy.   The stress upon mathematics which is evident in this program had long been dear to Plato's heart.   In the subject matter of these studies and in Plato's insistence upon required studies as the means for reaching a fixed and preestablished truth, there is a foreshadowing of the curriculum known as the "seven liberal arts" which later actually came to be prescribed in the schools of the medieval church as the basis for attaining a liberal education.   Plato's separation of ideal truth from everyday practice resulted in a dualism between knowledge and action which has plagued philosophers ever since.

Although Plato's theory was never put into direct practice as such, the subsequent loss of Greek political liberty under the domination of the Macedonian and Roman empires gradually forced the educated Greek to turn from the practical activities that had formerly culminated in statecraft and to lean more and more upon Plato's ideal of education the highest aim of which was taken to be intellectual philosophizing.   The liberally educated Greek became less and less a "man of action" and more and more a "man of contemplation."   Deprived of its political freedom, Greece turned to the development and spread of its "Culture" which emphasized literary, artistic, rhetorical, and intellectual activities more or less divorced from the governing and economic activities of everyday life. As the man of action dropped out of the notion of a liberal education, the aristocratic strain of education for the leisure and wealthy classes gained strength; and it is largely this perversion of the original Greek conception of a liberal education that has been handed down to modern times.

Another voice that spoke with tremendous authority for later ages was that of Aristotle, who, together with Plato, exerted a greater influence upon the thought and educational ideals of Western Europe than that of any other ancient figures.   Aristotle's conception of leisure as opposed to vocational or manual work helped to substantiate the dualism between knowledge and action that Plato had formulated.   Accepting as right and natural that a few free citizens should rest upon the backs of the great mass of slaves who did the actual work of mining, manufacturing, agriculture, and trade, Aristotle insisted that a liberal education was appropriate only to the free citizens who had the leisure to engage in intellectual matters.   Hence, the liberal man must be one who is not only politically and intellectually free but also economically free, which means that he had to be wealthy enough to escape the drudgery of actual work in making a living.   Liberal studies then more than ever became identified with those *books* and intellectual activities with which a leisure class found pleasure in passing the time.   That is not to say that these intellectual studies were not important, but it does mean that for many centuries the more "practical" and vocational activities were rigidly excluded from any education that was called liberal.   Thus, the modern conservatives are on sound historical grounds when they urge a return to the ancient aristocratic cleavage between the intellectual and the practical, but the pressing question is whether or not this historical conception is appropriate to modern democracy.   Modern progressives insist that it is not.

Ancient Rome Compiles Seven Liberal Arts.   Higher education in ancient Rome had apparently been rather highly useful for furthering the arts of practical life until it was shaped by the cultural and literary ideals of a decadent Greek education.   Roman higher education had been marked by the development of such studies as law, agriculture, mechanics, and engineering, and there seemed to be no definite and prevading idea of a rounded curriculum that should be required of all students.   Even when Quintilian was describing the education of an orator, he said:

. . . it is certainly of fundamental importance to distinguish the peculiar gifts of individual pupils.

In the task of training these no one will dissuade us from arranging a definite choice of studies.   One pupil will be better fitted for the study of history, another will have a gift for poetry, another will find the study of law profitable, some perhaps should be sent to work in the fields.   The teacher of rhetoric will separate these gifts just as the trainer we have spoken of will turn out a runner or a boxer or a wrestler or some other type of athlete for the sacred games.[1]

---

[1] William M. Smail, *Quintilian on Education* (Oxford, Clarendon Press, New York, 1938), p. 102.   Translation of Book II, Chap. VIII, sections 6–7 of Quintilian's *Institutes of Oratory*.

The conception of a definitive prescribed curriculum did not seem to be the dominating notion of the educational theorists of Rome, until the Romans became enamored of the culture and education of the Greeks and began to mold their higher education according to Greek patterns. The limitations of liberal studies to what we know as the seven liberal arts came about largely as an accident in the process of this assimilation. When the Romans had done the hard work of conquering an empire, and when the upper classes had acquired adequate leisure, then they turned to absorbing the literary and intellectual culture of the Greeks. The Greek type of gymnastics had never appealed to the Romans who had been too busy with warlike physical education. Thus a liberal education more than ever became associated with nonphysical, noncommercial, and nonpolitical activities.

Certain Roman scholars influenced rather arbitrarily the direction that future liberal education took. In the second century B.C., the Roman scholar Varro sought to establish in Rome a system of education based upon the Greek. To that end he wrote a series of treatises upon nine of the liberal arts of the Greek tradition that he believed should constitute the necessary equipment of the liberally educated man. He expanded Plato's list and named the following studies: grammar, rhetoric, logic, astronomy, arithmetic, geometry, music, architecture, and medicine. His list included most of the subjects suggested by Plato (omitting notably gymnastics), but he included subjects not mentioned by that philosopher. Yet Varro's list did not constitute by any means the whole extent of knowledge known to the Greeks, and it left out such practical arts developed by the Romans as agriculture and engineering. At the outset, the studies that were to become the "liberal arts" of the future were apparently limited to certain fields of knowledge through more or less accidental circumstances.

Varro's selections have been explained by the fact that he was carrying over only those phases of Greek *science* in which Greece was superior to Rome.[1] Greece was not superior to Rome in agriculture, mechanics, and engineering; therefore he did not include those sciences. Varro could find no science in the fine arts of poetry, painting, drawing, or sculpture; therefore he left them out. But he could justify architecture and music, as well as the other seven, on the basis that they had been developed systematically to such a degree that they could be handed down from teacher to student and taught to others. Thus, in Varro's compendium of higher knowledge, we find two principles of limitation at work, namely: (1) Liberal arts were confined to Greek studies, and (2)

---

[1] See H. PARKER, "The Seven Liberal Arts," *English Historical Review*, 5: 417–461 (July, 1890).

they were confined to what Varro defined as Greek scientific studies.[1] But Varro listed nine liberal arts. Why were only seven so important in the Middle Ages?

Further limitation of the scope of the liberal arts was made in the fourth century A.D. by Martianus Capella whose compendium of knowledge happened to be the one that the medieval Christian Church adopted for its own ends.[2] Capella cut the number of liberal arts to seven, naming the trivium of grammar, rhetoric, and logic and the quadrivium of arithmetic, geometry, astronomy, and music. His justification for reducing the number to seven was that he wanted to keep only those arts which would interest a group of celestial beings. Hence he left out medicine because celestial beings had no earthly ills, and he left out architecture because spirits needed no physical habitation. In other words, he did not include the natural or mechanical sciences, as he understood the terms, because they were so closely related to material and mundane interests that they were not suitable for spiritual and, therefore, liberal beings. Music could stay because it was primarily a "pure science" and therefore fit for "supermundane" interests. Capella apparently attached no peculiar importance to the number seven except to keep within the limit of his framework.[3] Thus we find a third principle of limitation of the liberal arts at work, namely, Capella's interest in spiritual rather than in practical or physical things.

Here, then, by the fourth century was a compendium that formulated the liberal arts into seven subjects and that happened to become the heritage of the medieval church. It did not comprise the entire range of cultural subjects known to Greece and Rome, and it did not even reflect actual practice as set up in the pagan schools of the empire. What it did represent was the selective organization and limitation of knowledge for the purposes described above, purposes that more or less by chance came to fix the bounds of the medieval church curriculum in the arts. Thus, at the beginning of the Middle Ages, the liberal arts had been formalized and condensed from the Greek heritage into small literary packets of knowledge, and they had come to be identified with those

[1] Except for architecture and medicine, we should call these studies literary, mathematical, or philosophical. Certainly they were "bookish" when compared with the modern notion of science as an experimental study based upon the observation and experience of the senses as sources of knowledge. Varro's conception of "scientific" comes closer to what we should call organized, or systematic, knowledge.

[2] PAUL ABELSON, The Seven Liberal Arts (Columbia University Press, New York, 1906); see description of Capella's De nuptiis Philologiae et Mercurii, an allegory describing the heavenly wedding of Philology and Mercury with the seven liberal arts as bridesmaids.

[3] Martianus Capella, ed. by Francisous Eyssenhardt (D. G. Teubner, Leipzig, 1866), pp. 332–333.

systematic studies of Greece which had been translated into Latin and which were suited to intellectual and spiritual rather than to material affairs. Here are some historical reasons why a "liberal education" in its traditional form has so often been exclusively literary in quality and has so often been opposed to a "useful" or "practical" education.

The Medieval Arts Curriculum Accepts the Seven Liberal Arts. Intellectually the Middle Ages was distinguished as a period of harmony and unity when the scholars were satisfied that they had solved the major puzzles of the universe. In education, this complacency took the form of simplified compendiums supposedly embracing all unified knowledge and similar to those which we have been discussing. The greatest unifying force of the Middle Ages was undoubtedly the universal church, inasmuch as nearly all phases of life were touched, if not controlled, by the clergy. The pope raised up and lowered emperors; his bishops were powerful feudal lords. The pope received financial contributions from all of Western Europe, and his bishops in an agrarian age were owners of immense tracts of land. In political, economic, and social activities, the clergy ranked along with the nobility as one of the dominating classes of medieval life; but in intellectual and educational endeavors, the clergy ranked alone. Hence intellectual topics were largely confined to religious discourses and within religious walls. So it was with the formal schooling of the times; the teachers were clergymen, and the students were prospective clergymen. The typical intellectual activity of the early Middle Ages has often been characterized by its reliance upon authority; and the curriculum of higher education in the monastic and cathedral schools, which was constructed primarily to maintain the tradition of the church, came to be identified with the pagan seven liberal arts.

Intellectually the medieval church gradually assimilated and reconciled classical thought and literature with religious doctrine; and educationally it adapted pagan education to religious purposes. By the close of the fourth century, the Christian Church had triumphed in the Roman Empire; the pagan schools had declined; and the church needed an education to prepare its clergy for the study of theology. Church fathers were at first skeptical about using the pagan learning, but many of them had received their own intellectual training in pagan schools. Finally, in the sixth century, the clergyman Cassiodorus found sufficient scriptural sanction for the seven liberal arts to fix them securely as the necessary preparation for the study of theology throughout the Middle Ages. The Christian Cassiodorus hated the pagan Capella and set out to write his own book to supersede Capella's compendium which had happened to survive the destruction of the Roman Empire. If Cassiodorus had held his peace, Capella would probably have been forgotten, and his list of liberal arts would never have been known beyond the early Middle Ages.[1]

Medieval ecclesiastics did not like Capella and looked with considerable qualms upon the pagan character of his small compendium. But the notion gradually grew that the spiritual, literary, and philosophical character of the seven studies was so suitable for higher education in the church (coupled with the fact that so little other material was available) that the church eventually appropriated Capella's list as a whole for its monastic and cathedral schools. When Cassiodorus added to this growing feeling the emphatic assertion that the seven liberal arts were specifically justified by the Scriptures, his testimony could not be ignored. He quoted to such good effect the text "Wisdom builded her house; she has hewn out her seven pillars" (*Prov.* 9:1) that the church afterward did not dare to break up the list of seven arts but even accepted them all and sometimes made them preparatory to higher studies.[2] The arbitrary medieval limitation of the liberal arts was thereupon established in fixed form as early as the beginning of the seventh century—long before the rise of the universities—and the seven liberal arts gradually became the minimum requirements for prospective clergymen and teachers.

It must be remembered, however, that continuous changes and adaptations were made in each of the seven arts as knowledge expanded in the various stages of the Middle Ages. The contributions of such scholars as Alcuin, John Scotus Eriugena, Gerbert, Adelhard of Bath, and Sacrobosco were accepted more or less readily into the arts curriculum. Also, in accordance with the varying needs of the times, certain subjects were emphasized over others. Prior to the eleventh century, Latin grammar and literature were emphasized because the scholars needed a thorough grounding in Latin as a preparation for religious study. During the eleventh and twelfth centuries, the study of the classics was promoted especially by such humanistic schools as Chartres and Orléans. Then, during the twelfth century, logic became the predominant study when Abélard made disputes over questions of metaphysics and theology the most engaging topics of the time.[3] Still later, with the incoming of Aristotelian philosophy and science, the interest turned to the mathematical subjects astronomy, arithmetic, and geome-

---

[1] PARKER, in *English Historical Review*, 5: 417–461.

[2] St. Augustine had given the weight of his authority to the liberal arts by writing treatises on all seven of them except arithmetic. Isidore of Seville, Alcuin, Rabanus Maurus, and others all used the term "seven liberal arts" to designate the course of preparatory studies.

[3] See HENRI d'ANDELI, *The Battle of the Seven Arts*, ed. and trans. by Louis J. Paetow (University of California Press, Berkeley, 1914). A poem written in the second quarter of the thirteenth century; the victory of logic and dialectics over grammar and literature is vividly described, pp. 58–60.

try. So it is apparent that the church was by no means hostile to secular literature, for there had been a more or less general interest in the classics all through the Middle Ages.

Rise of the Universities Stresses Prescribed Books. Fostered by the influence of Abélard at Paris; by the influx of the newly discovered philosophy and science of Aristotle[1]; and by the growth of wealth, commerce, and cities, the intellectual activity of the twelfth and thirteenth centuries gave rise to the university type of organization. Despite the secular forces that made the universities possible, they remained largely dominated by ecclesiastical interests, just as the cathedral schools had been. When the number of students and professors at a cathedral school grew to such proportions that the students and teachers found it necessary to organize themselves into a guild or *universitas*, for purposes of mutual welfare and protection, a university may be said to have come into existence. Some of the universities gradually came to include not only a faculty of the liberal arts but also faculties of theology, law, and medicine. Professional, or specialized, studies as well as such practical studies as those of commercial letter writing came to be taught in the universities along with the liberal or general studies of the liberal arts. Some writers even say that it was in the higher development and specialization of medicine, civil law, theology, and philosophy that the university movement broke away from the monkish and medieval system.[2]

With the rise of the university system, an expansion of the liberal arts curriculum followed. To the seven liberal arts were gradually added the newly discovered works of Aristotle on the physical sciences ("natural philosophy"), ethics and politics ("moral philosophy"), and metaphysics ("mental philosophy"). For example, the faculty of theology at the University of Paris was slow to accept the pagan and scientific works of Aristotle, and because they did not seem to fit in with church doctrines the papacy made many efforts to keep them out of the university faculties. The arts faculty, however, was much more receptive to Aristotle's works and welcomed the great mass of new material which it set out to digest and assimilate. In this way, the arts faculty made itself more vital and attractive to students. As Aristotle gradually became "respectable," and as his works were reconciled with church doctrine, particularly through the efforts of Albertus Magnus and Thomas

----

[1] Most of Aristotle's scientific works came to Europe about 1200–1260 in good Latin translations. To his works on logic (*Categories, Analytics, Topics*), which the Middle Ages long used, were added his poetical works (*Poetics, Rhetoric*), practical sciences (*Ethics, Politics*), and physical or theoretical sciences (*Physics, History of Animals, On the Heavens, Metaphysics*, etc.).

[2] See S. S. Laurie, *The Rise and Early Constitution of Universities* (D. Appleton-Century Company, Inc., New York, 1887), p. 214.

Aquinas, the philosophical and scientific studies of Aristotle were pre-scribed along with the traditional seven liberal arts in the arts curriculum. But whence came the power to require these and only these studies for a liberal education?

The origin of prescription as we know it seems to be found in the church's practice of licensing its teachers. Since all teachers in the Middle Ages were clerics, and since it was felt that all clerics should be trained properly in religious orthodoxy as well as in the tools of scholar-ship, the church found it expedient to control entrance into the teaching profession. This was done by granting a license to teach (*licentia docendi*), the condition for receiving which was the successful completion of the course in the liberal arts. Before the rise of the university system, the *licentia* was granted by the bishop or chancellor of the cathedral schools; but with the spread of the university organization, the license, or degree, came to be granted by those who were already professors in the faculty of arts. The gradual winning of the right of autonomy in granting degrees by the university faculties was one of the interesting conflicts between the universities and the papacy. The first complete prescribed curriculum in arts of which we have knowledge seems to have been laid down at the University of Paris in 1215 by the papal legate Robert de Courçon.[1] Graduation was merely the conferring of the right to teach upon students who had attended lectures for a certain period of time, defended a thesis, and passed a more or less difficult examination.

The degrees thus granted varied somewhat from university to uni-versity and from one period to another. Generally speaking, they became fairly standardized by the end of the medieval period, and they were influenced not only by the custom of granting the license to teach but also by the guild organization. When the student had finished the study of some of the liberal arts he was granted the baccalaureate degree (bachelor of arts, or B.A.) which indicated that he was ready to be an assistant teacher. He then studied for some three more years in the higher liberal arts and Aristotelian philosophy, and at the conclusion of these studies he was granted the final license to teach and became a master teacher (master of arts, or M.A.). To get the master's degree the student usually was required to prepare a thesis and defend it against

[1] HASTINGS RASHDALL, *The Universities of Europe in the Middle Ages*, new ed. by F. M. Powicke and A. B. Emden (Oxford, Clarendon Press, New York, 1936), Vol. I, p. 433. The prescribed curriculum was often stated in the form of lists of textbooks that had to be studied. For such lists drawn up before 1200, see C. H. Haskins, *Studies in the History of Mediaeval Science* (Harvard University Press, Cambridge, 1924), pp. 372–376. For a general treatment of the arts course in medieval universities, see S. E. Morison, *The Founding of Harvard College* (Harvard University Press, Cambridge, 1035), pp. 18–35.

disputants in much the same manner that a journeyman presented his masterpiece to the guild members as proof of his qualification to become a master workman.   Although this process was rather general in the universities of Europe, let us look briefly at the requirements found in the English universities which were more directly the progenitors of the American college.

At Oxford, the student followed a four-year course of study under a tutor for his B.A. degree[1]; a first examination included grammar and arithmetic, and a second included rhetoric, logic, and probably music. Then three more years of study beyond the B.A. was required for the M.A. degree during which time the student read prescribed books in geometry, astronomy, and Aristotelian "philosophy" (physical science, ethics, and metaphysics).   Since the curriculum at Cambridge was substantially the same as that at Oxford, we see that in the arts course of the English universities the old seven liberal arts were all present and were all prescribed.[2]   In addition to the seven liberal arts we see that the philosophical studies of Aristotle were also prescribed, for the conception of the liberal arts had expanded as Aristotle had been accepted into the arts curriculum.

Remnants of all these studies will be found in the early American colleges.   The significant thing here is the fact that our traditional notion of a prescribed curriculum grew up because the church desired its clergymen and teachers to be orthodox in belief and educated in the literary and philosophical studies inherited from Greco-Roman culture.   Then, in later centuries, the notion gradually spread that these same liberal arts should be prescribed not only for teachers and professional men but also for all men who would be considered liberally educated apart from their profession or occupation.   Therefore the B.A. degree became in time the denotation of a liberal education.

RASHDALL, op. cit., Vol. III, pp. 152–153.   "In the actual curriculum [of Oxford] we shall find that there was rather more elasticity than at Paris.   The dominion of Aristotle was somewhat less exclusive.   Importance was attached to keeping up the theory that a university arts course included the Trivium and Quadrivium of the earlier Middle Ages, as well as the "three philosophies" introduced by the rediscovery of Aristotle in the thirteenth century.   More importance was attached to mathematics and astrology, and more alternatives were offered to the choice of the individual student."   "Elasticity" and "choice" refer more to medicine, law, and theology than to the arts curriculum.   See LAURIE, op. cit., pp. 281–282, "At every stage of the student's career, text-books were prescribed, and no departure from these allowed." See also RASHDALL, op. cit., Vol. III, pp. 153–156, for a list of the required books for the B.A. and M.A. degrees in the arts.

2 For details of the Cambridge curriculum see Morison, op. cit., Chap. IV. Although Morison says that there was no fixed and rigid curriculum at Cambridge, he means that individual tutors were free to fix the course of study for their students. This was obviously not freedom of election so far as the students were concerned.

It might be noted here that there are other aspects of modern universities than the traditional prescribed curriculum that serve to link modern university organization much more closely with medieval institutions than with the higher education of ancient Greece and Rome. We are peculiarly the inheritors of the medieval tendency to organize and institutionalize. For example, higher schools of ancient times had little conception of the corporate organization characteristic of medieval and modern universities whereby teachers united together in a corporate body and enjoyed more or less autonomy and privilege. Also, the grouping of studies into separate faculties, the requiring of students to confine themselves largely to one faculty, the allotment of a definite period of years to the student's course, the giving of examinations, and the granting of degrees or titles with formality and ceremony are all distinctly medieval in origin. For our purposes, however, the most important characteristic of the medieval university institution was its tendency to mark out a definite line of study based upon the authority of the church and to prescribe only certain books that should be read by the students.[1] Modern faculties have retained for themselves the prerogatives of prescription which the medieval church originated.

In summary, we have attempted to trace briefly the background of the medieval arts curriculum by showing how the liberal arts curriculum was determined and limited by educational philosophers and compilers in ancient Greek and Roman times; how the medieval Christian Church took over this curriculum and made it consonant with religious aims and with theological studies; and how the liberal arts finally became fixed and prescribed as the necessary requirements for receiving a degree in arts or a license to teach.

It seems apparent that the dominating interests of each age determined what should be considered a "liberal education" in that age. When an education was aimed at the practical affairs of life, it was freer and wider than when it was aimed at intellectual and literary "culture" or at religious and otherworldly affairs. When truth was considered to be in a state of flux, a considerable amount of freedom was allowed to teachers and students; witness fifth century Athens. When truth was considered for various reasons to be fixed, eternal, and authoritative, education became circumscribed and prescribed; witness the theory of Plato and the practice of the medieval church. These opposing conceptions of truth and their corresponding conceptions of a liberal education

---

[1] RASHDALL, op. cit., footnote on p. 459. "Prescribed books are a very medieval institution." In addition, Rashdall points out on pp. 456–458 that medieval universities were highly vocational, in the sense that they prepared students directly to engage in the life activities that attracted the greatest number of young men in those days, namely, theology, law, medicine, letter writing, and teaching.

have long struggled for the domination of higher education even down to the present day.

THE RENAISSANCE ADDS THE CLASSICS TO THE PRESCRIBED STUDIES
(ABOUT 1300–1550)

Secularism Rears Its Head. From the time when the university arts curriculum was taking shape, as described in the foregoing pages, to the founding of Harvard College in 1636, a gradual change in the content of the prescribed course of study took place, but no change in the fact of prescription. The seven liberal arts long continued to be the core of the arts curriculum, even after more than a century of existence in the New World, but certain world forces which had their roots in the Middle Ages and which gained increasing momentum through the following centuries eventually wrought changes in the arts curriculum. If any one word could possibly be chosen to describe these movements, it might be "secular." It will be our task to see how the forces of secularism gradually encroached upon the religious domination of the arts curriculum to effect a slow broadening of that curriculum so that it finally lost its rigidity and became more and more flexible. This temper of worldliness which took many intellectual, economic, political, and social forms may be said to characterize the modern world as marked off from the medieval.

The Renaissance and the Reformation[1] mark the real beginnings of the breakdown of established authority, the enunciation of the doctrine of the freedom of the individual, and the scientific emphasis upon present experience rather than upon the absolute authority of the past. Even if these characterizations are taken only as approximations, the secular spirit looms large in all of them, and we must watch their encroachments upon the religious domain. Yet their growth was gradual and difficult; their effect upon education was slow and scarcely perceptible at first. The religious control was extremely tenacious; nevertheless the church was fighting a losing battle for its exclusive hold on higher education. Let us proceed, then, to consider what influences were contributing to an increased secularism and to trace their effects upon higher education during the Renaissance and the Reformation.

Putting the matter more pertinently for our purposes, it may be said that three major forces were striving to dominate life during the four centuries from 1300 to 1700. These claimants for the intellectual energies of men were: (1) the humanistic interest in past Greek and Roman culture, (2) the religious interest in the affairs of the church and the next

---

[1] The terms "Renaissance" (*ca.* 1300–1550) and "Reformation" (*ca.* 1500–1650) are used merely to designate different aspects of life from the fourteenth to the seventeenth century, and they carry no connotation of *sudden* "rebirth."

world, and (3) the secular interest in the affairs of this present-day world.[1] All of these interests had their roots in the Middle Ages, as has been pointed out, and all three were present in greater or lesser degree in the periods under consideration, first one receiving emphasis and then another. We are interested particularly in their influence upon the intellectual temper of the times, but since we are particularly interested in the changes made in the arts curriculum of the universities, we shall describe only so much of the prevailing temper of the times as will illustrate the modifications that occurred in the arts curriculum.

Humanism Captures Educational Theory. By and large, it may be said that the revival of ancient classical learning was the determining educational factor of the Renaissance; that the religious and sectarian temper as shown in theological disputes and in actual warfare dominated the spirit of the Reformation; and that the secular spirit, expressed intellectually in terms of the growth of science, was an essential characteristic of the seventeenth and later centuries.[2] All of these factors, however, were present and playing important parts in the intellectual life of the people throughout the periods involved, but the relative emphasis mentioned seems to characterize fairly the successive changes in the interests of the intellectual classes.

The general efflorescence of life during the Renaissance is often explained largely as a result of the growing secular spirit which had begun to appear in the twelfth and thirteenth centuries and expressed itself in an increased activity in the fourteenth and fifteenth centuries. Commercial and urban life, with its roots in the growth of towns in the Middle Ages, became a more dominant mode of living in the Renaissance. The great creative productiveness in such fields as literature, painting, sculpture, and architecture combined elements of the religious, the classical, and the secular. The breakdown of the authority of the church and the substitution of the authority of classical antiquity had their beginnings in the reform and heretical movements of the Middle Ages and in the "classical renaissance of the twelfth century." The Humanists did not break violently with all of medievalism, but they admired more intensely the classical literature and language and scorned more violently all other authority.

Italy was the first scene of Humanism; and under the leadership of such men as Petrarch, Boccaccio, and Valla, momentum was given to an

---

[1] See WILLYSTINE GOODSELL, *The Conflict of Naturalism and Humanism* (Teachers College, Columbia University, New York, 1910) for a discussion of supernaturalism, Humanism, Naturalism, and pragmatism in their historical relations to education.

[2] It is recognized that underlying economic and social conditions helped to shape the intellectual temper of the times, but no more than brief references can be made here to those important relationships.

emphasis upon the worth of the human individual rather than upon the submergence of the individual to religious authority. The Humanists held up the classical pagan literature of ancient Greece and Rome as expressing the highest and best development of the human individual and human race. The classical literature thenceforth became their authoritative court of appeals for the conduct of life. The spirit of Humanism was spread in northern Europe principally by such men as Erasmus, Agricola, and Reuchlin; in England by Erasmus, Colet, and More (members of the group of so-called "Oxford Reformers"); and in France by Ramus, Francis I, and Budé. The north European Humanism seemed to be somewhat more religious in tone than that of Italy or France and appeared to be particularly interested in the ancient and oriental languages as means of studying more closely the original religious doctrines that were contained in the Scriptures and the writings of the church fathers.

The educational theorists took up the cry of the Humanists that classical Greek and Latin should be substituted for the medieval Latin and scholastic dialectics. In Italy, Vergerius advocated a return to the broad curriculum of the ancient Roman educator Quintilian and illustrated the Humanist's new faith in man by advocating that the natural bent of the student should be recognized and followed in education. Castiglione urged that a broad cultural education for the gentleman be attained through the development of the fine arts and "courtesy," or "courtliness," in addition to classical scholarship and learning. In north Europe and England, Erasmus emphasized the use of the classical languages and literature in the schools and stated the case for the individual choice of subjects with the watchword of observing and following the nature of the students. Vives, believing the human mind to be inclined to freedom, urged not only that the nature of the student should be followed but also that the teacher should try to find what the student's nature was like in order to determine school work in the light of mental development. In England, Roger Ascham and John Elyot expressed the wider conception of "gentlemanliness" and individuality as put forth by Castiglione.

In France, Ramus attacked all Aristotelianism and urged that the schools be freed from religious authority by emphasizing the study of the ancient classics, mathematics, science, and the vernacular languages. Rabelais vigorously attacked the futility and formality of the old studies, appealing to the doctrines of realism, human values, and scientific studies. Montaigne in his outline for the education of a free man or noble gentleman gave a clear recognition to the ideal of freedom as a directing principle of educational activity; in theory, the pupil leads and the master follows, or "trots along," after him, using the student's spontaneous activities as the starting point of education. Thus we see that the

Humanist educators of the Renaissance were enunciating the importance of the development of the individual, of freedom in education, of following the nature of the student, and of giving him "realistic," or scientific, studies to pursue. Significantly enough, they all insisted that the classics were the best means of attaining these educational aims.

The Classics Gain a Place in the Arts Curriculum. The promptings of the Humanists and educational theorists were accepted by many school-masters and professors who attempted to incorporate the new ideas and the new learning into actual school and university practice. In Italy, Guarino da Verona and Vittorino de Feltre set up humanistic schools at Ferrara and Mantua to give youth a well-rounded preparation for service in state and society rather than merely a religious training. They tried to revive the Greek ideal of training the body as well as the mind, but later developments stifled their efforts. The classical learning was promoted largely by court and municipality rather than by church or university, and it made little impression upon the older universities whose conservatism and medieval learning resisted its entrance, accepting it only in a very subsidiary position where it was accepted at all. "In tracing the history of the revival of learning in Italy the great universities may be passed by almost without notice."[1]

In France, the story was much the same: Court and chateau led in the acceptance of Humanism, whereas church and university gave little but opposition. The University of Paris kept aloof from the movement which it rightly considered as a reform that would threaten the vested interests of theology, Aristotelian philosophy, and canon law. It kept to its scholastic ways of thinking and remained engrossed with the ped-antry and subtleties of discussion concerning universal principles instead of admitting the new humanist spirit with its enthusiasm for liberty and beauty. Humanism did gain entrance into some of the higher schools, however; Francis I with the aid of the scholar Budé founded the Collège de France in order to serve better the interests of the state by means of the new learning. Chairs were established for professors of Greek, Hebrew, Latin, French, law, philosophy, mathematics, and medicine. The classical learning was also promoted by such institutions as those set up by municipalities at Bordeaux, Lyons, Orléans, Reims, and Montpellier.

One of the French reformers may be mentioned a little more particu-larly here because of his influence upon the University of Cambridge[2] and, ultimately, upon Harvard. Petrus Ramus had attacked Aristo-

---

[1] LOUIS JOHN PAETOW, *The Arts Course at Medieval Universities* (University of Illinois, Urbana, 1910), p. 61.

[2] J. B. MULLINGER, *History of the University of Cambridge* (Cambridge University Press, Cambridge, England, 1884), Vol. II, p 411 Mullinger says that Cambridge became the great stronghold of Ramism.

telianism and set out to reform each of the liberal arts by improving the material studied and by making the methods of acquisition more simple and easy. His efforts were directed toward a careful systematizing and simplifying of the knowledge of the ancient authors and attempting to do away with the superfluities and intricacies of medieval commentaries. In this way he helped to make knowledge more applicable to actual social use, to free it from ecclesiastical control, and ultimately to clear the way for a new mathematics and science by his emphasis upon these subjects. He wrote new textbooks in all of the subjects of the seven liberal arts, as well as in physics, ethics, metaphysics, and theology, and they gained relatively wide vogue in Germany, Switzerland, at Cambridge in England, and later in colonial America.

Again, in Germany, the story is similar: The courts and schools accepted the new learning before the universities did. Lectures on classical antiquity were attempted as early as the latter part of the 1400's but met with little response by the universities until after 1500. Then, as the religious reformers adopted the new learning, it gradually was accepted by the universities under the leadership of a reform group at Erfurt and Tübingen and especially under the impetus of Melanchthon at Wittenberg and Nuremberg. The predominance of the interest in the "poetical-literary" studies of Humanism over the "theological-philosophical" interests of the Middle Ages was short-lived, however, for the theological disposition of the Reformation tended to subordinate again the classical studies to religious ends.

In England, we find a somewhat different situation. The "Oxford Reformers," a group of orthodox Catholics, aiming at the general reform of church and society as well as of school and university, were aided by Henry VIII and were able to make substantial gains for the new learning in actual educational practice. Colet's grammar school at St. Paul's cathedral represents the growing emphasis upon Greek and classical Latin on the secondary level. Lectures on Greek were read at Oxford by Vitelli, Linacre, Grocyn, and Colet in the late 1400's; but neither Oxford nor Cambridge made official provision for humanistic studies until the early 1500's, when Jesus College began to present the new learning of Erasmus at Cambridge.

Soon the first avowedly humanistic colleges recognizing Greek and Hebrew were founded, namely, Christ's College (1505) and St. John's (1511) at Cambridge and Corpus Christi (1514) at Oxford. Erasmus taught at Cambridge for four years from 1511, and Vives taught at Oxford in 1522. A royal commission appointed by Henry VIII reported in 1535 that

In New College we have stablished a lecturer in Greek and another in Latin with an honest salary and stipend. . . . Wee have set Dunce [Duns Scotus] in

Bocardo [name given to a town prison] and have utterly banished him Oxford for ever, with all his blynd glosses . . . [1]

Even greater advances toward humanistic studies were made at Cambridge at this time when Aristotle began to be studied from the commentaries of the Humanists Agricola and Ramus rather than from the glosses of the medieval schoolmen.   Thus, Humanism steadily gained ground in the subjects of both the trivium and the quadrivium, until finally the founding of Trinity College, Cambridge, in 1546 with its several fellows in Greek along with the regius professorships in Greek, Hebrew, and civil law, appointed earlier by Henry VIII, set the seal upon the transition from the medieval to the humanistic tradition.

Actual modifications in the prescribed curriculum of the English universities meant a decline in the importance of logic or dialectics and a reemphasis upon grammar and rhetoric.   In the hands of the Humanists, grammar lost its purely medieval aspect and expanded to include the grammar and literature of classical Latin, Greek, Hebrew, and other Oriental languages.   Rhetoric also began to receive a greater attention characteristic of the Humanists' interest in the style and form of written and oral speech.   Under the influence of Ramus, logic was simplified and freed of the complexities of scholastic treatment.   The subjects of the quadrivium[2] were changed in so far as the influence of Ramism was felt, and the way was opened especially at Cambridge for the new mathematics and science of the seventeenth century.   Ethics, politics, physics, and metaphysics were also gradually stripped of their medieval garb as the Humanists attempted to study directly the original language and thought of the ancients.   Thus it is apparent that the most obvious effect of the Renaissance upon the arts curriculum was the substitution of ancient classical language and literature in place of the medieval and religious language and literature.   As the classics became "polite letters" particularly suitable for the education of a "gentleman," the Renaissance tended to reaffirm the aristocratic conception of a liberal education which the Greeks and Romans had praised so highly.

Before continuing with the story of what happened to the arts curriculum during the age of the Reformation, it may be interesting to note how the passage of time has reversed the position of educational progressives and conservatives.   During the Renaissance, the Humanists were the progressives, urging that the new and vital humanistic studies should be substituted for the outworn and obsolete studies of the Middle Ages.

[1] Quoted in HASTINGS RASHDALL and ROBERT S. RAIT, *New College* (F. E. Robinson and Company, London, 1901), p. 106.

[2] Along with the most elementary phases of grammar and rhetoric, music began to be put into the grammar schools, or it tended to disappear, as its value in church services waned in the face of a Protestant or secular control of education.

Incidentally, it is the Renaissance historians who largely contributed to the notion that the Middle Ages were barbaric "dark ages" in comparison with the "sweetness and light" of Humanism. The Humanists justified their new studies with such arguments as the following: The development of the individual was of prime importance; the interests and nature of the individual should be considered in education; the student should be given freedom from the obscurantism of medievalism; and the student should pursue more "realistic" studies. The Humanists insisted that the new classical studies of literature and poetry and oratory were admirably suited for attaining these ends.

The curious thing is that in the late nineteenth century these were the very same arguments that were used by the new progressives who were now favoring the elective system as a means of breaking down the very classical curriculum that the Humanists had been at such pains to set up three or four centuries earlier. The Renaissance progressives had become the conservatives of a later date, and these nineteenth century conservative Humanists were now insistently calling upon the Renaissance ideal of culture and the Renaissance conception of a liberal education to bulwark the prescribed curriculum of classics and mathematics against the "barbarians" who advocated the elective system. The answer to this rather common educational phenomenon may be that when the Renaissance was at its height the classical curriculum, in comparison with the medieval curriculum, probably did stimulate the imagination and tend to develop the individuality of students. The point is that as the older social, intellectual, and technological conditions passed out of existence, the older conception of a liberal education was no longer appropriate to the changed situation. The once flexible and liberal curriculum of the Humanists became the rigid and conservative curriculum remote from the realities of a later time. The story of this condition, which sociologists call "cultural lag," will have its share in the chapters to follow.

CHAPTER III

REFORMATION CLASSICS VERSUS ENLIGHTENMENT SCIENCE

THE REFORMATION SOLIDIFIES THE CLASSICS IN LIBERAL EDUCATION
(ABOUT 1500–1650)

We have said that three forces, Humanism, religion, and secularism, were contending for predominance in the life of the four centuries following the Middle Ages, and we have shown how Humanism affected the intellectual ideal of the Renaissance and specifically resulted in adding the Greek and Latin classics to the arts curriculum. In Reformation times, the religious motives, expressed in the warfare of ideas and of arms, so gripped the intellectual interests of the period that definite effects were noted in the universities of the day. The secular trend also received tremendous impetus through advances in scientific, philosophic, political, and economic fields, but it did not make itself felt directly upon the curriculum of the universities for a century or so because of the preoccupation with religious issues. Let us consider first the secular advances, inasmuch as they may help to explain the nature of the religious reformations.

Secularism Becomes More Insistent: Science and Philosophy. The secular temper began to bear fruit in the sixteenth and seventeenth centuries in the tremendous development of the physical sciences, especially in the fields of astronomy, physics, mathematics, biology, anatomy, and medicine. Science has probably been the greatest single molding influence upon modern life and resulted in rapid changes in modern society. The development of political, economic, educational, and religious institutions, as well as that of other fields of thought, philosophy, art, and morals, has depended to a great extent upon the progress of science. Not only has science radically altered techniques in the production and distribution of wealth, but it has altered the whole world view of man which, in the last analysis, is a decisive factor in shaping human life and institutions.[1]

The heliocentric view of the universe, making one of the greatest revolutions in the history of thought and establishing science as an impressive agency for battle with tradition and authority, was elaborated

---

[1] For a good general discussion of the effects of science upon modern culture, see Preserved Smith, *A History of Modern Culture* (Henry Holt & Company, Inc., New York, 1930), Vol. 1, Chaps. II–IV.

through the work of Copernicus, Brahe, Kepler, Bruno, and Galileo. Physics was rather slow to develop until the invention of such new instruments as the thermometer, barometer, and pendulum clock gave impetus to the study of magnetism, optics, mechanics, statics, and hydrostatics. Mathematics helped to pave the way for further scientific work by the elaboration of Arabic notation, decimals, and logarithms and by developments in algebra, calculus, trigonometry, conic sections, and analytical geometry. Other fields of science were being opened by Gessner in biology, Swammerdan in entomology, Malphigi in plant anatomy, and Vesalius and Harvey in human physiology and anatomy. There is little doubt that a scientific revolution was being wrought by a secular temper which was given impetus by a growing urbanization, wealth, leisure, and, above all, the easier storing and dissemination of knowledge resulting from the invention of printing. This scientific spirit developed a sanguine belief in the certainty that knowledge of nature would continue to increase, a belief that looked to the future for authority rather than to the past and that based conclusions only upon what could be observed, collected, verified, and treated mathematically.

Philosophy also took on a secular aspect as rationalism gained ground from the impact of new knowledge of other peoples and as the warfare of the religious sects showed that all religious doctrine might be wrong and that a new way to truth might be needed. Consequently attempts were made to divorce philosophy from religion and inject into it the new scientific and mathematical spirit. Aiming at synthesizing the sciences rather than elaborating religious doctrines, philosophy tended to drop its scholastic form and to become mathematical in form and scientific in content. Bruno, Campanella, and Bacon began the groping that was brought to fruition by Descartes, Hobbes, Gassendi, and Spinoza.

The new science and philosophy did not break into the universities as yet, because the religious elements of the Reformation dominated their energies and subject matter. However, new divisions of subject matter were being made which demanded admission to the curriculum in the eighteenth century. We have seen that the entire round of knowledge that was acceptable to the Middle Ages was set forth in small compendiums containing the seven liberal arts. Attempts were made in the early Renaissance period to do the same sort of thing with all of the new scientific knowledge, but the rapid and enormous increases of systematic learning made impossible such attempts to encompass all knowledge in one volume. Medieval encyclopedism began to give way to many separate subjects. The quadrivium was shown to be woefully inadequate: Algebra and trigonometry broke away from arithmetic; botany, zoology, physiology, and anatomy broke away from Aristotelian treatment; such new subjects as magnetism, mechanics, hydrostatics, pneumatics, optics, chemistry, geography, and geology began to claim separate treatment. But the universities were dominated by ecclesiasticism and were generally hostile to the new sciences and philosophy. The University of Padua had considerable freedom of conscience in the late 1400's and early 1500's under the protection of Venice, but it, like most other universities of Europe, soon declined under the domination of the religious reformations and counterreformations.

Secularism in Capitalism and Nationalism. The sixteenth and seventeenth centuries saw a commercial revolution no less than a scientific one. The explorations of such men as Diaz, Columbus, da Gama, Magellan, Cortez, and Pizarro opened up a new world to the eyes of man and to his acquisitive instincts. Prices went up in the sixteenth century partly as a result of the rapid influx into Europe of silver and gold bullion from America; the avenues of trade shifted from the Mediterranean to the Atlantic and to northern European land routes; banking became centralized and stimulating to industry and commerce. A new type of domestic economy and a rising commercial class, stimulated by the vision of unlimited profits, began to replace the guild economy which had operated under the medieval controls of a "fair price" and denunciations of excessive interest charges. As the new economic horizons unfolded, the "sky became the limit," and profits became the incentive.

A manifestation of the commercial revolution in the field of politics and political theory took the form of a growing sense of nationalism. The merchant class saw benefit to itself if the civil state grew centralized and strong enough to give it protection and subsidy. Strong national governments began to replace the universal authority of the church, and royal justice began to encroach upon feudal and church justice. Politically the rise of the bourgeoisie took the form of despotism in France and Spain but resulted in the formation of republics in England, the Netherlands, and America where the third estate was strong enough to control the government rather than be dominated by it. International law, based on "natural" laws, was being created as Grotius set up rules to guide the nations in their military and commercial competitions for new lands.

The political theories of the English commonwealth were shaped largely by the demands of an ever more powerful commercial class. The republican movement progressed further in the Calvinist lands of Britain, the Netherlands, and New England, because Calvinism, republicanism, and capitalism had become allies. The Puritans tried to find eternal laws to justify their position and found them in the principles of freedom which received enunciation, especially by Milton, in the right to live one's own life, to say what one thinks, and to make and spend one's wealth without unnecessary interference from government. Thus, we see liberty and individualism identified by the Puritans not only with religious freedom but also with political freedom (representative government) and with economic freedom (laissez-faire capitalism).   The secular strains embodied in these economic and political changes of the Reformation had little direct influence upon the curriculum of the universities, but they set in motion the forces of an incipient democracy and capitalism which later had a considerable share in the shaping of higher education.   The universities were affected during the period of the Reformation more directly by the religious activities than by these secular influences.

The Religious Reformations Strengthen the Classics in the Arts Curriculum.   The term "Reformation" is derived largely from the various attempts to reform the Catholic Church first from within and then from without.   Several factors which were so interrelated that they cannot be completely disentangled were contributing to this series of upheavals: There was the *political* factor in the growing centralization of the monarchies which attacked the political and civil power of the church; the *economic* factor showed itself in resentment against payment of taxes to an "ultramontane" authority and in the desire of the commercialized states to appropriate the rich lands of the church; the *humanistic* factor had shown that dogma and theology were not forever fixed but that they could actually be reshaped, and religious practices changed; finally, the genuine *religious* factor appeared in the reactions against the worldliness of the clergy and the formalism of the church.

A combination of these factors, together with the printing press and a wider literacy of the people in the vernacular languages, produced such religious reformers as Luther and Calvin.   Luther set up the Bible as the supreme religious authority in place of the authority of pope or clergy and made salvation rest ultimately upon faith rather than upon mere good works and observance of the sacraments.   He taught that the individual must interpret the Scriptures for himself and that hence he would need to learn to read and to understand the Bible.   Luther came to rely upon the help of the civil state to carry out his reforms and to set up his "Protestant" religion.   Calvin put his emphasis upon the *positive* authority of the Bible and seems to have stressed predestination more than Luther. His was a creed of combat in which the church should control the state and in which the individual must severely discipline himself to be sure of salvation.   The English Puritans embodied the ideas of Calvin and proved themselves to be aggressive, forceful, and energetic molders of secular as well as religious ideas.

In its religious aspects, the Reformation was a period of terrible warfare, cruel persecution, and mad superstition.   There was no decisive victory, and considerable parts of Europe were laid waste before the conflicts subsided, but generally the ground was cleared a little more than previously for the progress of tolerance, reason, and secularism.   The progressive and liberal, the Protestant and heretic, the skeptic and scientist were, by and large, safer in 1650 than they had been a hundred years before. Essentially the religious wars were destructive and reactionary, but eventually the Protestant by the logic of his own thinking had to be somewhat more tolerant than the Catholic had been, although some of the Protestants were often fully as dogmatic and vindictive.[1]

The result upon the universities was largely reactionary. The Italian and Spanish universities lost what freedom they had gained, and the best part of their intellectual life was stifled under the oppression of the Catholic inquisition and counterreformation. In France, Germany, and England, the universities became the centers of theological and ecclesiastical controversy, and the royal power often interfered to make the doctrines of the universities either Protestant or Catholic. The French universities declined into impotency under the oppression of fanaticism and despotism. Henry IV put the University of Paris under civil rule in 1600 and tried to reform the faculty of arts by regulating minutely the order of studies and exercises. But this renovation did not help the university whose whole body lacked life and whose energies during the seventeenth century were largely wasted in fruitless bickering between the Jesuits and the Huguenots. It found no time for the new intellectual spirit of science and was indifferent to the philosophy of Descartes which was the most considerable intellectual influence of the times with its substitution of human reason for religious authority in the search for truth.

In the German universities, the gains of the Renaissance were almost extinguished by the ecclesiastical contests, but a little was saved by Luther and Melanchthon who tried to unite Humanism with Protestant theology. Theoretically, the Protestant position should have been marked by liberty of conscience; but in practice, it developed into a theology virtually as narrow and formal as that of the medieval church. In general, the sixteenth and seventeenth centuries failed to produce the logical results of the idealistic reformers. The Diet of Speyer in 1526 enunciated the doctrine of *cuius regio eius religio* which left to the prince the choice of Lutheranism or of Catholicism for the people of his state. Hence, each prince established a university of his own in order to support the religion that he had selected, and consequently the history of the German universities in the sixteenth and seventeenth centuries is nearly identical with the history of warring theologies. Several Catholic universities and several Protestant universities were thus established, but by the end of the seventeenth century most German universities had sunk to the lowest level of their history under the preponderance of theological interests.

[1] For a vivid picture of Calvinist intolerance, see Stefan Zweig, *The Right to Heresy: Castellio against Calvin* (Viking Press, Inc., New York, 1936).

In England, the story is somewhat similar.[1] The humanistic interest declined and became associated with sectarianism as the various colleges supported different creeds. Humanistic and classical studies were not lost, but they were used as new weapons with which to fight old theological battles. Royal power began to interfere: Henry VIII and Edward VI became hostile to Catholics; Mary drove out the Protestants, who went to Calvinist lands and then came back as Puritans when Elizabeth showed herself hospitable to Protestantism. Magdelene College, Oxford, had become Protestant, and New College, Catholic; other Catholic colleges were founded until in 1575 the Catholics were excluded by Elizabeth, at which time the battles began to be fought between Anglican Protestants and Puritan Protestants. The Puritans went mainly to Cambridge University where endowments had been made favorable to them; and especially they went to St. John's College or to the new Emmanuel College which had been founded in 1584 by Sir Walter Mildmay. St. John's was sympathetic to Puritans, and the charter of Sidney Sussex College was a mere transcript of Emmanuel's. These colleges became the avowed centers of a militant Puritanism from which many nonconformist groups drew their ministers and from which went many of the Puritans who were driven to America by the repressive measures of Archbishop Laud. Theology remained the predominant study, and the required instruction at Oxford and Cambridge was largely aimed at training clergymen who would be well versed in Greek, Latin, Hebrew, and the art of disputation so that they could go forth and defend their church's doctrines against all assailants.

In summary, we have seen first the progress of the secular temper in the rapid development of science and philosophy and of commercial and nationalistic activities, the growing emphasis of which was not able to break into the university curriculum during the Reformation because of the preoccupation with religious questions. We have seen, secondly, how the religious warfare of the Reformation affected the universities, namely, in that the theological disputes led to civil and state regulations designed to enforce respective religious predispositions, and that what remained of the humanistic studies was made subsidiary to religious doctrine, whether Protestant or Catholic.

Thus, in England at the time of the colonizing of America, we find the arts course consisting of (1) the medieval liberal arts (except music which had fallen by the wayside); (2) the reformed philosophy of Aristotle (ethics, politics, physics, and metaphysics); and (3) the Renaissance

[1] See NORMAN WOOD, *The Reformation and English Education* (Routledge, London, 1931), Chap. III, for the religious controversy incident to the introduction of the new learning and for the unique position of the crown in relation to the English universities.

studies of classical Latin, Greek, Hebrew, and other Oriental languages; (4) all studies were more or less subservient to the religious and sectarian aims of the Reformation. Every sect used substantially the same liberal subjects in preparation for their respective ministries, and the study of rhetoric and logic was reenforced by the need for preaching and disputation. When the Puritans set up a college in America, the curriculum was modeled after the Puritan colleges of Cambridge, and the aim was reenforced by the religious zeal of Puritanism.

In view of the fact that the first American college was a copy of the English colleges, it may be well to describe briefly what the term "college" originally meant, and especially what it came to mean in the seventeenth century England. The word is derived from the Latin *conlegium*, or *collegium*, which originally was applied to any company or society of persons who associated together to promote a common purpose. Ancient Rome and the Middle Ages had seen colleges of soothsayers, merchants, choirs, dancers, and priests. The first educational college was founded at the University of Paris in the thirteenth century to provide for poor and needy students a decent place to live. Hence, colleges at Paris sprang up later than and independent of the university proper and were first designed merely as living quarters for poor students with a master in charge to keep the discipline.[1]

Gradually the college masters began to receive endowments to allow them to continue their studies and to take on some of the teaching functions. The university professors at Paris were not given salaries, but usually their incomes were made up from fees paid by the students who attended their lectures. In a sense, therefore, the elective system was present in the *universities* of the thirteenth and fourteenth centuries; but as the *college* became more important from the fourteenth to the seventeenth century, a much greater control was exerted over students' lives, and this came to involve the prescribed curriculum.

In Germany, the early universities were patterned largely after the University of Paris; but from the first, the German colleges were primarily designed to furnish teachers for the university; and from the first, the university professors were paid from endowments and formed a permanent professoriate which controlled the colleges. Thus, the university teachers were also the college teachers, and all instruction was regulated closely by the university. Soon the different subjects were distributed among the professors either by mutual agreement or by supply and demand of students, and one professor began to teach the same subject repeatedly instead of starting a new one each academic year. Much the same sort of evolution took place in the universities of Scotland.

[1] Discipline was generally required because the medieval university student in arts was regularly younger than the modern university student by three to five years.

Finally, as Protestantism destroyed in the universities the old ecclesiastical order with its celibacy and cloister life, the communal college with its dormitory life and monastic seclusion began to disappear. In the German commercial towns of the sixteenth and seventeenth centuries the students began to live about the towns much as other professional men lived.[1]   Much of the arts curriculum had been pushed down into the secondary schools and thus made a longer secondary education necessary, so that most students were now older than students had been in previous centuries when they came to the university.   Since students were more mature (seventeen or eighteen years old), the college as an institution disappeared.

At Oxford and Cambridge, however, the college was not only retained but gradually supplanted the university teaching as the latter tended to become too formalistic.   Since there was no organic relation between the examining and degree authority and the actual teaching in the colleges, the university lectures began to disappear, examinations degenerated into a farce, and the tutorial system became virtually the sole means of instruction.   Ultimately each tutor was made responsible for the entire liberal education and mental and moral discipline of his students.   The college rather than the university was largely the source of the notion of strict *discipline* which later became so important as a justification for the prescribed curriculum in the American college.   The college authorities undertook to determine the whole moral, physical, and intellectual life of the student.[2]

The college in England retained its communal aspect, marked by the "hall" and "quadrangle" in which masters and students lived together, in the effort to give the undergraduate student the "cultural" training that would fit him for service in church and state affairs.   The continued enforcement of celibacy upon masters and tutors also helped to preserve the communal life of the English college long after the Reformation had seen its disappearance in German universities.   Between 1250 and 1550, the educational colleges were not the most important or the most numerous colleges in England, but the chantry acts of Henry VIII in 1545 and of Edward VI in 1548 abolished all but those connected with the universities and with some of the cathedrals.   So the term henceforth became attached mainly to communal groups of students and masters engaged in the pursuit of preparing liberally educated men for church and state.

The American College Appears: Harvard.   This is the sort of college that the Puritans set up in America in 1636 by order of the Massachusetts

---

[1] See FRIEDRICH PAULSEN, *German Universities and University Study* (Charles Scribner's Sons, New York, 1906), pp. 41 *ff.*, 362–363.

[2] See MORISON, *Founding of Harvard*, pp. 35–39, for a good description of the rise of the college.

General Court. Harvard was virtually a copy of one of the many colleges that constituted Oxford and Cambridge, but it happened to follow Cambridge more closely, inasmuch as so many of the early Puritans who came to America had attended Cambridge University. Morison lists approximately 100 Cambridge and 30 Oxford men who had come to American by 1646, and Channing estimates that 1 family in 40 in early New England boasted a college graduate.[1] John Harvard, who gave his name to the young college, was a graduate of Cambridge, and Henry Dunster, the early president of Harvard who formulated the first well-defined curriculum in 1642, was a graduate of Magdelene College, Cambridge.

An inspection of the first Harvard curriculum reveals a striking similarity in content to that already described for the English colleges.[2] Here we find the seven liberal arts (except music); Greek, Hebrew, and "Eastern tongues"; philosophy (physics, ethics, and politics); and divinity. It may appear that metaphysics had been left out, but it is likely that a considerable amount of metaphysics was involved in the study of divinity and other philosophical subjects and especially in the preparation of topics for disputation.[3] History was given an hour on Saturday afternoon in the winter, and the "nature of plants" a similar hour in the summer, but neither appeared in later statements of the curriculum.

Here in the first American college we find a combination of three ideals, or theories, of higher education:

1. The Medieval idea of the seven liberal arts as the entire round of studies necessary for a liberal education and as preparation for later professional study.

2. The Renaissance ideal of classical studies as the best means of arriving at a liberal education whether in church or in state. This included a thorough study of the classical languages and enough of classical literature to indicate a "gentlemanly" education.

3. The Reformation ideal of religious control of higher education for sectarian purposes and for preparation of ministers who would defend and propagate particularized religious doctrine.

[1] Ibid., p. 40 and Appendix B; and EDWARD CHANNING, A History of the United States (The Macmillan Company, New York, 1905), Vol. I, pp. 335–336.

[2] See S. E. MORISON, Harvard College in the Seventeenth Century (Harvard University Press, Cambridge, 1936), Vol. I, Chaps. VII–XIII; or "New England's First Fruits," Old South Leaflets (Boston, 1894), No. 51, pp. 3–5.

[3] A letter written in 1642 describes the first commencement at "which were Latine and Greeke Orations, and Declamations and Hebrew Analysis Grammaticall, Logicall & Rhetoricall of the Psalms: And their Answers and Disputations in Logicall, Ethicall, Physicall and Metaphysicall Questions; and so were found worthy of the first degree, (commonly called Batchelour) pro more Academarium in Anglia," Old South Leaflets, No. 51, pp. 5–6; see also MORISON, op. cit., pp. 252–258.

The medieval conception of a liberal education as subsidiary to theological study was reenforced at Harvard but changed, of course, in the direction of Puritanism instead of Catholicism.[1] It was also enlarged by the Renaissance insistence upon the classical ideal of a liberal education for service in the secular world as well as in the religious world. Even when the religious dominance began to fade, the idea persisted into the nineteenth century that a liberal education and proper mental discipline could be obtained only by study of these same prescribed subjects, and it long held the field against all opponents.

Each of these three ideals of higher education based its conception of a liberal education upon essentially linguistic and literary studies. Each, moreover, sought to educate only the few leaders of church and state. The interplay of the ancient and medieval traditions upon the activities of the Renaissance and Reformation produced the notion that an education through books was the best way to develop a man of action. The books of the past were retained and emphasized because it was felt that the classics had shaped the development of the great men of antiquity and therefore were best suited to developing the great men of the present. The aristocratic conception of a liberal education had been viewed by the Greeks as applying to all free citizens, but it was now taken to mean that only a few men were capable of higher education in literary subjects and thus only a few capable of leadership in society. In these respects, the liberal education of the seventeenth century was founded upon an aristocratic conception of society and upon the scarcity theory of higher education whereby academic degrees and a liberal education were valued because they were relatively rare and thus considered attainable by only a few.

Each of these traditional ideals of a liberal education was also based upon the notion that truth is ultimately a fixed and final thing and that therefore education must be fixed and prescribed completely in order to assure that students arrive at the one and only truth. It is interesting to note that both the Catholic and the various Protestant churches required virtually the same liberal arts in the belief that such studies contributed best to an understanding of their respective doctrines. But the prescribed curriculum still relied upon the belief that truth was fixed and eternal even if conceptions of that truth differed among the various churches. When the Protestant churches grew powerful enough to win some of the

---

[1] Despite the fact that some medieval universities did not give much direct religious training to the majority of their students and that the majority of students never reached the faculty of theology or other higher faculties, the conception remained strong during the Reformation that religion properly should direct the ultimate aims of the universities and that the liberal arts should be the preparation for advanced studies, the highest of which was theology.

freedom that they had demanded, they were likely to become as rigid and unyielding with reference to doctrinal truth and educational prescriptions as the Catholic Church had ever been.

Thus far in our study, we have been tracing briefly some of the influences of society and some of the theories of education that combined to produce the original prescribed curriculum of higher education in America. We have seen that the beginning of college education in America found the theory of a liberal education heavily weighted on the bookish and literary side. In fact, a liberal education largely meant that the student was conversant with more or less of Latin, Greek, mathematics, and philosophy. Our problem from this point on is to trace the forces that began to modify this educational ideal in such a way that many new types of studies were gradually added to the curriculum and eventually the elective principle became a part of the notion of a liberal education. We shall find that the religious-classical prescribed curriculum was extremely tenacious. But it is evident that even before the end of the eighteenth century, certain secular forces had begun to affect the aim and content of college study in such a way that the traditional conception of a liberal education was eventually weakened and the introduction of the elective system made possible.

THE ENLIGHTENMENT HERALDS A MORE PRACTICAL EDUCATION (ABOUT 1650–1776)

The Enlightenment Worships Secularism and Science. Before discussing the outstanding changes that took place in the American college during the Enlightenment, a few words should be said concerning the social and intellectual trends of the age. The term "Enlightenment" is a name often given to that period of history which extends from the middle of the seventeenth to the latter part of the eighteenth century.[1] The keynote of this period was doubtless its unbounded respect for modern science as a standard of value. As the Humanists of the Renaissance had appealed to the authority of the ancient classics, and as the religious reformers of the Reformation had worshiped the authority of the Bible, so the *philosophes* of the Enlightenment worshiped the authority of "natural law" and "human reason." The Enlightenment did not doubt the fixed and absolute quality of logical truth, moral conduct, and aesthetic judgment, as later ages have done, but rather it merely replaced divine revelation with physical science as the standard of appeal. This prevalent confidence in human reason was due largely to the emergence of a new intellectual class whose members often happened to be also

[1] See PRESERVED SMITH, *A History of Modern Culture* (Henry Holt & Company, Inc., New York, 1930), Vol. II, for an able interpretation of the Enlightenment as a whole.

members of the upper middle class who had money to buy books, taste to enjoy them, and the leisure to think about them.   The masses of people were still largely excluded from the expanding cultural and material wealth.

Gradually, the intellectual findings of Newtonian science began to upset the old beliefs which had long commanded such absolute authority. Sir Isaac Newton published his revolutionary work on the mathematical principles of natural philosophy in 1687 and established the law of gravitation as the fundamental basis of astronomy and physics.   His science assumed nature to be ultimately simple, uniform, and completely regulated by mechanical, fixed laws operating in an absolute space and time.   Under the impetus of Newton's discoveries, rapid advances were made in the eighteenth century in the fields of astronomy, mathematics, optics, dynamics, mechanics, and electricity.   In less mathematical sciences, a great mass of facts was gathered, but few laws or theories were developed to bind the facts together into helpful generalizations; chemistry, geography, geology, biology, physiology, and medicine had to await the next century for a Darwin and a Pasteur.

The mathematical principles of Newton were rapidly applied to all other fields of thought in the attempt to base philosophy, politics, economics, religion, education, aesthetics, and all social institutions upon the rule of natural law.   Besides justifying the scientific method in many fields of knowledge, the reformers set out to transform society according to the dictates of "reason."   "The Enlightenment resembled a new religion, of which Reason was God, Newton's *Principia* the Bible, and Voltaire the prophet."[1]   To educate the people in the creed of reason, a great propagandist campaign was carried on by means of books, pamphlets, encyclopedias, newspapers, and journals and through exhortation, argument, satire, prose, and poetry.   The more intellectual classes were also reached by active scientific academies, journals, libraries, and museums.

The spirit of the Enlightenment displayed at least three phases: an extreme faith in the power of science and scientific knowledge; a humanitarian impulse which sought to promote the happiness of the masses of people by remaking social institutions; and an optimistic temper which was fully convinced of the intrinsic goodness of mankind, his indefinite perfectibility, and his ability ultimately to win happiness on this earth. The first two phases began to make an imprint upon the college curriculum during the eighteenth century when utilitarian and scientific studies began to appear in the curriculum.   However, it was not until the third phase blossomed into a virile individualism and capitalism in the nineteenth century that the rigid curriculum began to expand and give

[1] *Ibid.*, p. 21.

way to the insistent demands for differentiated courses of study. But the Enlightenment paved the way for the breakdown of the religious control of the prescribed curriculum by the attempts of its reformers to change institutions according to the dictates of "natural law." They demanded freedom of thought and expression; they attacked irrational religious beliefs and superstitions; and they demanded reform in the laws to make them more humane. As a result of this violent attack upon an established religious tradition, the hold of the churches was considerably weakened, and great strides were made toward secularizing politics, education, and morals through a widespread propaganda for education of the masses. We shall discuss briefly what forms the Enlightenment took in the countries of Europe and its effects upon the European universities before we consider more specifically the effects in America.

Science Enters the Scottish and German Universities. The wars of the eighteenth century witnessed the expansion and consolidation of Great Britain, Prussia, and Russia at the expense and loss of prestige of France, the Netherlands, Austria, Poland, and Sweden. In addition to political changes, there was a shift no less important in the relationships between social and economic classes as wealth and power gradually passed from the landed and military aristocracy and from the clergy to the growing middle class. This shift is indicated by the establishment of parliamentary government in America, a continuing representative government in the Netherlands, and the rule of a wealthy burgher class in Germany and Switzerland. These changes were surface expressions of underlying changes in social, economic, and intellectual forces, which in turn depended upon the advances made in the technical and scientific tools, inventions, and instruments by which man remade his environment. Moreover, these political and economic modifications of the eighteenth century were influenced by forces that had already been in motion for several centuries, namely, the expansion of trade and commerce, a growing spirit of secularism, technical improvements,[1] and the constantly greater dissemination of knowledge through the printing press.

Great Britain probably profited more than any other country from these advances in the eighteenth century as her empire grew in economic, political, and intellectual importance. It is necessary only to mention Newton in science and Locke, Berkeley, Hume, and Hobbes in philosophy and political and economic theory to illustrate Britain's leadership in the intellectual field. In the philosophical conflicts between idealism and materialism that arose from the attempts to shape a philosophy according to the new science, Locke tried to reconcile the two and to defend both

---

[1] Examples are improvements in coal smelting by Darby in 1735; invention of the flying shuttle by Kay in 1738 and of the spinning jenny by Hargreaves in 1764; and improvements in canals, roads, and maritime traffic.

religion and science; Berkeley attacked materialism and even the existence of matter; and Hume ended in a thoroughgoing skepticism which
ultimately aided the cause of materialism.   In the sphere of political and
economic theory, which generally tended to favor the middle class, Locke
defended the Whig revolution, saying that the chief purpose of the government was to protect life, liberty, and property and to allow in all else a
"natural liberty."   Locke formulated the aspirations of the middle classes
whereas Hobbes defended monarchical despotism, but the movement was
away from Hobbes, away from the mercantilist emphasis upon government control, and ultimately toward free trade.

In the field of educational theory, John Locke laid the foundations for
the Enlightenment, as he did in so many other fields.   Although thinking
of the young mind as a blank tablet to be molded by early impressions, he
emphasized the importance of reason as sufficient to discover truth, the
highest possession of man, and wrote his treatise *Of the Conduct of the
Understanding* to show how the rational faculties of man could be strengthened.[1]   The Enlightenment's emphasis upon reason is further exemplified
in education by Isaac Watts, who came out of the dissenters' academies
urging that instruction should appeal to the pupil's understanding and
reason.   The ideals of the leading educational theorists of the period were,
in the main, more scientific, more secular, more democratic, more utilitarian, and more humanitarian than had been those of their predecessors.
As represented by Milton's plans for an English academy, the newer
subjects were given a larger place beside the old classics and catechisms,
and the claims of different kinds of knowledge were given greater recognition in the academies set up by dissenting clergymen in England.

With all the intellectual activity and scientific progress in England
during this period, it might be expected that the universities would have
been radically changed, but tradition and the religious hold established
by Archbishop Laud and by the Restoration kings kept the English universities behind the times throughout most of the eigthteenth century.
Despite a few brilliant names, such as Newton, Gray, and Blackstone, the
favorite studies at Oxford and Cambridge remained the classics, logic, and
philosophy.   One of the reasons for academic torpor seemed to be the
lack of proper salaries for university teachers; and the fact that the tutors
could not teach all the new subjects led them to take refuge in teaching
the elements of the classics and logic which they knew best.   The university examinations had become farces, and the whole state of affairs called

---

[1] Locke is generally credited with a great influence upon American colleges through
his theories of mind which were taken to support the doctrine of faculty psychology
and mental discipline as the proper aims of college education.   Some writers consider
Locke to be inaccurately described as advocating formal discipline, but his influence
in American colleges was doubtless exerted in that direction.

forth the attacks of such disappointed intellectuals as Horace Walpole, Adam Smith, Jeremy Bentham, and Edward Gibbon. The work of the Enlightenment in weakening the Church of England weakened also the English universities which could not break the holds of ecclesiastical domination and civil interference until the nineteenth century.

However, the Scottish universities, which are mentioned here because of their influence upon American colleges, were able to reform themselves by the middle of the eighteenth century. Inasmuch as the original organization of the Scottish universities had been more akin to the German than to the English models, the college teachers were at the same time university teachers; the college as a communal house disappeared sooner; and the assignment of specific subjects to individual professors occurred earlier. So by the middle of the eighteenth century, a great reform movement was under way in the Scottish universities, especially at Aberdeen and Edinburgh. As early as 1708, Edinburgh had abolished the old regency system in favor of the professorship system in which a professor specialized in one or two subjects.[1] By the middle of the eighteenth century, in addition to the separate professors of Latin, Greek, logic, and natural philosophy, there had appeared professors of mathematics and of moral philosophy who gave lectures open to voluntary attendance. "In fact there seems to have been some feeling of reaction at this time against the Procrustean uniformity of the old system, and a good deal of Lehr-und-Lern Freiheit was introduced."[2] By 1741, the course of study in the arts at Edinburgh was far in advance of that in the English universities.

The utilitarian spirit of the reform at Aberdeen is shown in the following excerpts from the resolutions of Marischal College:

That the students may have the benefit of those parts of Education which are not commonly reckoned Academical, such as dancing, writing, book-keeping, French, &c., without losing time in attending Masters at a distance from the College, the Sub-Principal and Regents shall appoint proper rooms in the College, and proper hours when these things may be taught, and shall bespeak Masters of the best characters and qualifications for instructing those who choose to attend them.

[1] Early in the Scottish universities, a system took hold whereby one "regent took the entire instruction of a class, consisting of the men of a single year, through the whole of their four year curriculum. The subjects of each year thus 'rotated' among the regents." As the standard of efficiency demanded of the teacher rose and the area covered by each subject expanded, each regent was fixed to a particular subject. RASHDALL, The Universities of Europe in the Middle Ages (Oxford, Clarendon Press, New York, 1936), Vol. II, p. 321.

[2] ALEXANDER GRANT, The Story of the University of Edinburgh (Longmans, Green & Company, London, 1884), Vol. I, p. 264. For the whole course of study in the arts, see pp. 266 ff.

The Professors of Philosophy, with the concurrence of the other Masters, have unanimously agreed to employ much less time than has been usually done in the Universities, in the Logic and Metaphysick of the Schoolmen, which seem contrived to make men subtle disputants—a profession justly of less value in the present age than it has been in some preceding ones; and to employ themselves chiefly in teaching those parts of Philosophy which may qualify men for the more useful and important offices of society.[1]

Another example of the reform movement in Scotland is a treatise written in 1745 by a professor of philosophy in Marischal College picturing an academy in which free inquiry, debate, and discussion were encouraged.[2] In the proposed institution, each individual followed the method of study most congenial to him, and all subjects were accepted as equally liberal and educative if the individual followed the dictates of nature and of good sense.

Here, then, in the Scottish universities and in the thought flowing from them are early and clear evidences of the impact of the new science upon the arts curriculum; of the notion of "useful," or "practical," subjects as equivalent to the older studies in their value for a liberal education; and of the actual practice of the "voluntary," or elective, principle. We shall note the influence of the Scottish universities upon America during the eighteenth century at the College of William and Mary and more especially at the University of Pennsylvania.

Turning now to Germany, we find that during the eighteenth century the north German states rose to power partly through financial and commercial changes which aided Frederick II and Prussia against Austria and the Hapsburgs. A vital cultural and intellectual life grew up through the efforts of the despotic rulers who professed an "enlightened" care for the interest of the people. Since the Enlightenment was fostered in Germany by the despots, the freedom of intellectual activity was largely confined to science, philosophy, and literature. Professors were not allowed to touch upon political matters or to join in the polemics of the French and English reformers who were attacking entrenched political, economic, and social classes and urging greater privileges for the masses. Thus, under Frederick II, the new science and literature gained favor not only at court but also at the universities, which began to lose their original ecclesiastical character and became more similar to public institutions intended to train the good citizen and the able civil servant.

[1] RASHDALL, *op. cit.*, p. 322, note 1. Rashdall says that every line of these resolutions breathes the spirit of Locke's *Treatise on Education* and of that Scottish "common sense" philosophy whose best representative (Reid) was one of the regents who voted for the foregoing resolution.

[2] DAVID FORDYCE (pseud.), *Dialogues concerning Education* (London, 1745).

In the seventeenth century, as we have seen, the German universities had declined under ecclesiastical control; but in the latter part of that century, the University of Halle was founded (1694) where Christian Thomasius, the rationalist, and August Francke, the pietist, led the revolt against Lutheran orthodoxy. After 1706, Christian Wolff infused the new science and rationalism into Halle, when he insisted upon the right and duty of free investigation. Philosophy became separated from authoritative theology and came to be founded upon human reason and the modern sciences of mathematics and physics. Wolffian philosophy permeated nearly all Protestant German universities in the eighteenth century.

Another step forward occurred when a university was founded at Göttingen in 1734 where the ideas were even more liberal than at Halle which remained the center of a strong religious pietism. The physical and social sciences became the glory of the German universities, although the classics were also ably taught, and almost complete freedom was given to a professor once he had been appointed.[1] The other universities followed the lead of Halle and Göttingen somewhat slowly, but gradually both Protestant and Catholic institutions adopted the new learning. The emancipation of the German universities was connected closely with the rise of the arts faculty from its position as subservient to the faculty of theology to a position as the dominating faculty of the universities and the one in which the public believed the best liberal education in the sciences and literature could be obtained.

Some of the essential changes that occurred in the German universities as a result of the eighteenth century Enlightenment were: The scholastic philosophy of Aristotle was superseded by a more modern philosophy founded upon the principles of the physical sciences and mathematics; the hard-and-fast curriculum was replaced by one embodying the principle of freedom of research and instruction; mere exposition of a canonical text was replaced by the systematic lecture; the disputation was replaced by the seminar; a sound and vital classical scholarship replaced the formal imitation of the classics; and, finally, the German language ousted the Latin as the medium of instruction.[2] We shall see later how the vastly expanded development of science *within* the German universities made the elective system virtually a necessity and how these Enlightenment conceptions of science and elective system were applied to the American colleges in the nineteenth century.

[1] The "liberty of philosophizing," as the corollary of the proposition that universities were dedicated to the search for truth, was demanded by Gundling in an address at Halle in 1711. He said that science can bloom only when professors have freedom of research and instruction in order to follow wherever truth leads.

[2] See FRIEDRICK PAULSEN, *The German Universities and University Study* (Charles Scribner's Sons, New York, 1906), Book I, Chap. II.

Although the "enlightened" despotism of Germany aided the introduction of the new science and philosophy and encouraged academic freedom in the German universities, the workings of despotism in France wrought exactly the opposite effect.   To maintain the glory of the court and the grandeur of the monarchy, Louis XIV and Louis XV had strained to the breaking point the resources and patience of the people by a long succession of disastrous wars, religious persecutions, oppressive taxations, and strict regulation of trade, commerce, and agriculture.   It is no wonder that the French reformers were far more radical in their political and economic doctrines than were the English who had been granted far more tolerance and privilege.   In the field of political theory, Montesquieu attacked the royal despotism and urged greater political freedom, whereas Rousseau expressed the equalitarian doctrines of extreme individualism with only so much control by government as the people granted in the "social contract."   In economic theory, such men as Quesnay, Montesquieu, and Turgot attacked excessive government regulation and advanced the "physiocratic" doctrines that society should be based upon natural laws inherent within itself and should maintain the individual's right of freedom of trade, person, opinion, and property.   Voltaire attacked Christianity with all of the incisive weapons of reason, irony, and wit at his command, and the principles of the new science and philosophy were disseminated through the press, encyclopedias, and salons by such men as Voltaire, Diderot, and d'Alembert.

In the field of educational theory, Rousseau's *Émile* proved to be one of the most influential books ever written.   In his violent reaction against the control of education by the established church with its formalistic programs, Rousseau went to the other extreme to advocate "following nature" to the last detail.   The individual must be free to follow the dictates of his own nature and must not be restrained or repressed (at least to his knowledge) in any way.   Rousseau was not the first to advocate naturalism in education, but he presented it with such vigor that it captured the attention of various educators who attempted in many different ways to put his precepts into practice.   Certainly the elective principle later found great justification in Rousseau's doctrine that each individual should be free to follow his own nature.   But despite the cries of the reformers and the dissemination of the new knowledge, the University of Paris continued to decline, struggling vainly against the oppression of king and clergy, unable to admit the new scientific spirit.[1]   The States-General in 1789 thought that the university could be reformed; but before the turn of the nineteenth century, it had virtually ceased to exist.

[1] Charles Rollin, rector of the University of Paris, tried to modernize the system of studies by introducing the sciences and modern languages, but his Jansenist proclivities led the Jesuits to drive him into retirement.

In summary, then, as the eighteenth century Enlightenment saw the beginnings of a real challenge to the authority of the churches, so it also saw the beginnings of a challenge to the literary and aristocratic conception of a liberal education. As we have suggested, the thinkers of the Enlightenment were greatly impressed by the findings of the physical sciences and began to set up human reason and the "laws of nature" to replace divine revelation as the criterion of truth and of authority in all fields of endeavor. They began to look upon the nature of the individual as inherently good rather than as naturally depraved. The spread of these doctrines and the idea that the individual ought to be free in all of his activities led to a vigorous reaction against authoritarian religious control. The idea of freedom also gave a spurt to the economic desires of the middle classes; and as knowledge was disseminated to an ever expanding audience through the press and popular education, democracy began to emerge as a potent social force.

Each of these growing forces began to affect American life and the American college before the end of the eighteenth century. From England came the new sciences and philosophy which gradually made their way into the American college curriculum despite the opposition of those who favored the linguistic and literary subjects. From England also came political and economic theories of individual freedom which gave ideological justification to the American middle classes in their struggle for power. American colleges also soon felt the influence of the Scottish universities which had accepted the new sciences and had enunciated the doctrine that utilitarian subjects should be admitted to the college curriculum and that students should be allowed to choose some of their subjects.

The influence of the German universities upon nineteenth century higher education in America is virtually immeasurable, and more will be said of it later; but even in the eighteenth century, the hospitality of the German universities to the current notions of freedom was recognized. The older theological and humanistic studies were giving way to the newer physical sciences and scientific philosophy, and the doctrine of academic freedom was getting its first strong endorsement. Professors were allowed to pursue their specialties under the restriction only of a high ideal of scholarship; and the elective principle was involved to the extent that students were allowed to choose almost at will the fields of knowledge in which they desired to specialize. From France came the theoretical doctrines of individual freedom in the realm of politics, economics, and education which affected the social and intellectual temper of America in the decades of the later eighteenth and early nineteenth centuries. Let us now turn to a discussion of the development of the college curriculum in America as a result of the impact of those influences.

CHAPTER IV

THE AMERICAN COLLEGE FEELS THE CONFLICTS OF THE ENLIGHTENMENT

The Colonial Mind Shows a Split Personality. In order to understand the development of the American college curriculum from the founding of Harvard to the American Revolution, we must view briefly some of the important intellectual and social changes taking place in the colonies during the period that roughly corresponds to the Enlightenment. In Europe, we saw the growth of science and the resulting spread of the rationalistic spirit to other fields of knowledge and activity; we also saw a parallel growth in the secular activities of the commercial classes with their emphasis upon everyday affairs and their desires for freedom from despotic control of governmental or religious authority. Science, commercialialism, and individualism went hand in hand in their secular encroachments upon the authority and tradition of religion.

In the American colonies, we find that these secular interests and theories began early to make inroads upon the absolutist theocracy of the Puritans. The strict-constructionist Puritans had set up a social system in which the church exerted virtually absolute control over civil and social as well as religious affairs. From earliest colonial days to approximately the middle of the seventeenth century, Puritanism went fairly unchallenged; but soon its emphasis upon conformity began to weaken in the face of demands for more liberty and democracy.[1] By following in some measure a democratic policy of granting land free to those who would take it, the Puritans planted the seed from which grew an independent, freeholding yeomanry in the hinterlands of Connecticut, Rhode Island, and Maine, where developed a strong democratic and individualistic temper. Power began to slip from the hands of the theocratic clergy when a royal governor was sent to Massachusetts by the English King to take over control of the government and when the property qualification outlasted the religious test for suffrage. The rank and file of the yeomanry began to accept the doctrines of natural as opposed to divine

[1] For elaboration of this view of the Puritans, see V. L. Parrington, *The Colonial Mind* (Harcourt, Brace & Company, New York, 1927), pp. 3–130. For a defense of the Puritans, see Clifford K. Shipton, "A Plea for Puritanism," *American Historical Review*, 40: 460–467 (April, 1935). Shipton says that the clergymen were more liberal than the people and believes that much of their difficulty was a result not of their bigoted views but of too liberal views gained at Harvard which the people would not accept.

rights for either king or clergy. They began to substitute for the traditional absolutism a belief in a democratic church in a democratic state.

The individualism and democracy of the yeomanry were reenforced by commercial advantages after the turn of the eighteenth century when American trade and commerce increased as a result of the extensive warfare being carried on in Europe. American agricultural, forest, and fur products came into great demand; maritime trade prospered; and the new commercial spirit tended to build up a merchant gentry which eventually was to dominate civil and economic policy. The work of Thomas Hooker and Roger Williams in establishing the right of the individual to believe and worship as he pleased received further justification in the principles of John Wise that church control should be more democratic. These principles of individualism and democracy in religious affairs combined with the increasing tempo of economic activities to mark the eclipse of religious absolutism in New England. The cause of freedom, individualism, and democracy was further aided, especially in the central colonies, by the influx of immigrants who were largely attracted by new and free lands. These German Lutherans, French Huguenots, Scotch-Irish Presbyterians, English Quakers, and others swelled the class of farmers who leaned toward the economic individualism that the frontier elicited in the presence of unexploited natural resources; and those who settled in the growing cities joined the free artisans and laborers and eventually added other voices to the demands for democracy and secularism.

Religious zeal, however, was by no means dead, for the middle decades of the eighteenth century saw a "Great Awakening" which demonstrated that religion was still a factor and could sway the emotions of thousands of people in all economic classes. This awakening under the leadership of such men as George Whitefield and Jonathan Edwards swept the length and breadth of the colonies and touched nearly all sects. In many instances, the democratic movement had usually been on the side of increasing secularism (as represented by the interest of the middle classes in science and commerce); but when it came to religious revivalism, democracy parted company with the intellectual forces of science and philosophy as great numbers were converted to the various denominations and scores of new churches were set up to accommodate them. This emotional revivalism which created much hysterical but also much genuine religious feeling among the people sounded the death knell for state churches.

At the same time that religious fervor was sweeping many people into the churches, another prophet in the person of Benjamin Franklin was exerting telling influence upon the economic emotions of the country. Franklin accepted the Enlightenment views of commercial *laissez faire* and extolled the advantages of industriousness and frugality as cardinal economic virtues for every man.   He propagandized through the press, personal correspondence, and farmer's almanacs the practical rationalism and utilitarian ethics of the rising commercial classes.[1]   His secular interests extended to political and educational fields as well as to the scientific fields in which he was the outstanding person in the America of his time.   He aimed at disseminating practical knowledge by means of the societies and educational institutions that he was instrumental in establishing,[2] and he was the apostle of utility in economics, ethics, politics, science, and education.   Franklin was the prime exponent of the profit-seeking motives which have come to be associated with the term "capitalism."

Secularism made advances in the colonies in other intellectual fields besides that of science and economics.   In history, Thomas Prince and Thomas Hutchinson for New England and William Stith for Virginia began to evolve as the basis for their historical writings a more secular reliance upon existing records for evidence rather than upon the workings of a divine providence.   In social economy, the Quaker John Woolman and many others besides Franklin began to discuss pertinent problems of trade, manufacturing, agriculture, money, expansion, and intercolonial union.   The legal profession gradually began to secularize lawmaking and judicial decisions by opposing the claims of the clergy to a voice in the decisions of justice.   The newspaper press, periodical journals, and pamphleteering were quickening by the middle of the eighteenth century, and in these outlets were discussed the affairs of state and society as well as those of religion.   Bookstores and circulating libraries began to disseminate more widely a knowledge of the intellectual, political, and social advances that were being made in Europe and America.   So we see that the essential forces of the Enlightenment were effecting their characteristic influences in the colonies in the forms of an increasing scientific interest, a more utilitarian and individualistic economy, a more democratic form of political and religious institutions, and a wider dissemination of popular knowledge.

ENLIGHTENMENT SCIENCE LIBERALIZES HARVARD'S CURRICULUM

By the turn of the eighteenth century, the liberalism and science of the Enlightenment gradually began to affect the religious outlook· and

---

[1] "The Way to make Money plenty in every man's Pocket," and "Advice to a Young Tradesman," are excellent examples.

[2] "A Proposal for Promoting Useful Knowledge among the British Plantations in America," May 14, 1743. laid down the plans for the establishment of the American Philosophical Society.   Franklin's influence upon educational theory and practice will be discussed briefly in connection with the academy and college in Philadelphia which became the University of Pennsylvania (see pp. 69–70 ff.).

curriculum of Harvard College. As president of Harvard from 1708 to 1724, John Leverett really founded the liberal tradition there by fighting against the attempts of the Mathers to keep Harvard a rather narrow divinity school for the Puritan sect. Then under the presidency of Edward Holyoke from 1737 to 1769, Harvard's Congregationalism began to change from early Calvinism to eighteenth century Deism and Unitarianism. Holyoke's liberalism was enough to make the stricter Calvinists suspect Harvard and to provoke the overseers to try to extract oaths of orthodoxy from the tutors and to censor commencement theses. But despite this inspection and the return to fundamentalism which the Great Awakening sponsored, Harvard maintained its advances over the sectarianism of Yale, Princeton, and other colleges that followed the popular evangelistic trend of the Great Awakening. The liberal trend in religious temper was due, in part at least, to the more urban and commercial nature of life in Boston in contrast to the rural and more isolated character of the communities surrounding Yale and Princeton. Here, again, the secular and commercial interests characteristic of the Enlightenment began to influence college education. Harvard's liberality in religion was officially marked when the Hollis professorship of divinity was established in 1720; and the first incumbent, Edward Wigglesworth, by methods of doubt and inquiry helped to lead New England theology from Calvinism to Unitarianism.

By the end of the seventeenth century, the new Enlightenment science was beginning to creep into the traditional studies of Harvard. Cartesian logic entered alongside that of Aristotle; the geometry of Ramus and the physics of Newton gradually gained a hearing; and the astronomy of Copernicus, Galileo, Kepler, and Gassendi began to replace Aristotle, Ptolemy, and Dante. As early as 1659, Harvard tutors were using Cambridge almanacs which contained some Copernican astronomy; a telescope was presented to the college in 1672; and Thomas Brattle made observations of the Great Comet of 1680 which proved useful to Newton and his writings. Although the great experimental and scientific progress of the seventeenth century was carried on largely outside the universities of the world, natural science at Harvard entered a transitional stage in 1687 when Charles Morton's *Compendium Physicae* was accepted as a text in which a good deal of the new physics had been fitted into Aristotle's categories.[1]

Then as the new science of the eighteenth century was gradually developed in America, it began to make its way slowly into Harvard's program. In 1728, Thomas Hollis established a professorship of mathe-

[1] For an excellent and detailed description of Harvard's curriculum, see S. E. Morison, *Harvard College in the Seventeenth Century* (Harvard University Press, Cambridge, 1936), Vol. I, Chaps. VII–XIII

matics and natural philosophy and contributed books and "philosophical apparatus" which by 1769 included skeletons, globes, microscopes, machines for mechanics, hydrostatics, pneumatics, and optics as well as the transactions of the English Royal Society and the French Academy of Sciences. As the first Hollis professor of mathematics and natural philosophy, Isaac Greenwood wrote books on arithmetic, meteorology, mine damp, and the aurora borealis. He did much to bring the college into closer touch with the practical spirit of the age and to attract to Harvard practical-minded young men who might otherwise have gone to the private schools or into business. His successor, John Winthrop, held the post from 1738 to 1779 and proved himself to be the most accomplished scientific investigator in America next to Benjamin Franklin. At Winthrop's induction, the faculty had supported a liberal board of overseers in forbearing to question his theological position.

By 1743, the Harvard curriculum included more of Enlightenment science and philosophy in the form of Isaac Watts's *Astronomy*, Gravesande's *Natural Philosophy*, Fordyce's *Moral Philosophy*, and Locke's *Essay concerning Human Understanding*.[1] A faint forecast of the elective system was heralded in 1735 when students were sometimes permitted to study the French language which, however, had no official recognition in the curriculum. Such a move was apparently fraught with academic danger, for French was soon withdrawn until 1769, when it was again allowed to the student who obtained the safeguard of his parent's permission to take it. The college was taking no chances of being charged with corrupting its youth.

There was, however, no flexibility in the requirements for the B.A. degree, and everyone was supposed to study the same thing at the same time with his classmates. The religious and bookish character of liberal education remained strong. Since the provision of a learned ministry was a main function of the college, the interests of prospective clergymen were a paramount consideration, but it must be noted that it was assumed in accordance with the Renaissance tradition that a minister should have the same liberal education as any other scholar. The strength of the bookish and literary tradition remained strong, as is indicated in the following description:

> The students compile systems or outlines of the arts, hear *books* read by their tutors, read the same *books* themselves and recite upon them, dispute on questions drawn from these *books*, and declaim orations. There is nothing like a laboratory, or any opportunity for experiments. . . .[2]

[1] S. E. MORISON, *Three Centuries of Harvard* (Harvard University Press, Cambridge, 1936), p. 89.

[2] MORISON, *Harvard in the 17th Century*, Vol. I, p. 166. [Italics mine.] The publication of Morison's proposed works on Harvard in the eighteenth and early

Finally, in 1767, came the greatest change in Harvard's curriculum that had occurred since its founding. The overseers voted to revise the tutorial system so that each tutor would teach only one or only a few subjects to each class instead of teaching all subjects to one class:

For the advancement of learning it is proposed, That one Tutor shall teach Latin; another, Greek; another, Logic, Metaphysics, Ethics; and the other Natural Philosophy, Geography, Astronomy, and the Elements of the Mathematicks. . . . That on Friday and Saturday mornings each class shall be instructed by a distinct Tutor in Elocution, Composition in English, Rhetoric, and other parts of the Belles Lettres.[1]

It is thus apparent that by the time of the American Revolution, Harvard had begun to show a definite interest in the new science and philosophy as well as in the study of English language and literature, but the paramount emphasis remained upon the classical languages and mathematics. Also, the idea of utility does not seem to have appeared; the change was rather from the old Aristotelian science and philosophy to Enlightenment science and philosophy. The aim was still to provide a rounded liberal education to prepare men for aristocratic leadership in church and state rather than for directly earning a living. Furthermore, the college had already recognized along with the German and Scottish universities that the demands of scholarship required the specialization of the teacher in a few subjects. This principle along with the notion that the demands of scholarship required also the specialization of the student in a few subjects laid the foundations for the elective principle, which entered Harvard under the influences of George Ticknor and the German universities during the early part of the next century.

THE GREAT AWAKENING REAFFIRMS THE TRADITIONAL LIBERAL ARTS

The second college to be founded in the American colonies was the College of William and Mary which received its royal charter in 1693 under Anglican auspices. In accordance with the temper of the times, it was founded primarily for religious purposes, namely, to train ministers, to educate youth piously in good letters and manners, and to extend Christianity to the Indians. Its curriculum was similar to that of the Oxford colleges and did not change much during its first 85 years of existence, for when Thomas Jefferson began to reform its course of study in 1779 there were only six instructors: two of divinity and Hebrew; one in logic, rhetoric, and ethics; one in physics, metaphysics, and mathe-

---

nineteenth centuries will be invaluable for illuminating this period in American higher education.

[1] BENJAMIN PEIRCE, *A History of Harvard University* . . . (Brown, Shattuck, and Company, Cambridge, 1833), pp. 245–246.

matics; one in Latin and Greek; and one for teaching Indian boys the elements of religion.

The mathematical and philosophical influence of the Scottish universities may have been strong from the very beginning at the College of William and Mary, inasmuch as James Blair, principal promoter and first president of the college, had graduated from the University of Edinburgh in 1673; and Jefferson had been greatly influenced by a Scottish professor who taught mathematics, rhetoric, ethics, and belles-lettres.[1] That the College of William and Mary was well endowed and taught many of the leaders of the Revolution is undoubted, but the absence of adequate records makes our knowledge of the actual curriculum very doubtful. It is safe to say, however, that for our purposes the greatest change in the curriculum came in 1779 when the efforts of Jefferson marked the first overt recognition of the elective principle as a desirable element in college education to be found in America. Until that time, the curriculum was guided largely by the same interests as at Harvard, namely, to raise up an educated clergy for leadership in the church and state and to provide a liberal education for others who were destined to join in the aristocracy of society.

Yale, the third college in the colonies, was set up in Connecticut in 1701 largely as a result of a conservative reaction against the growing liberal doctrines at Harvard,[2] but its aim remained essentially the same: " . . . wherein youth may be instructed in the arts and sciences, who through the blessings of Almighty God, may be fitted for public employment, both in church and civil State."[3] In 1735, the Connecticut General Court declared anew that the "one principal end proposed in erecting this college was to supply the churches in this Colony with a learned, pious and orthodox Ministry." During most of the eighteenth century, its curricular development largely paralleled that of Harvard; the original course was changed gradually in the direction of the new science and philosophy, but relatively few new studies were added. In 1715, the colonial agent sent to Yale from England a set of approximately 800 volumes of books donated by prominent Englishmen. It included Newton's *Principia* and *Optics* which Samuel Johnson, then a tutor at Yale

---

[1] H. A. WASHINGTON, *The Writings of Thomas Jefferson* (John C. Riker, Washington, D. C., 1853), pp. 2–3.

[2] The Reverend Moses Noyes, a Connecticut minister, writes, "The first Movers for a College in Connecticut alledged this as a Reason, because the College at Cambridge was under the Tutorage of Latitudinarians. . . . " F. B. DEXTER, *Documentary History of Yale University* . . . (Yale University Press, New Haven, 1916), p. 242.

[3] E. P. CUBBERLEY, *Readings in Public Education in the United States* (Houghton Mifflin Company, Boston, 1934), p. 22. Act of the Colonial Assembly of Connecticut, Oct. 8, 1701.

and later president of King's College in New York, tried to teach to the undergraduates. Bishop George Berkeley gave a considerable number of books including some of his philosophical works; and Franklin along with others gave "philosophical apparatus" comparable to that of Harvard. By 1779, Locke's *Essay concerning Human Understanding* and books on algebra, trigonometry, and English grammar had been added to the usual required texts.

The most significant difference between Yale and Harvard up to the time of the American Revolution seemed to be in the methods of instruction and in the strength of religious orthodoxy in controlling the aims and curriculums of the two institutions. Whereas Harvard had changed to a kind of specialization whereby each tutor concentrated on a few subjects and thus paved the way administratively for the introduction of the elective system, Yale retained the traditional methods of instruction whereby one tutor commonly taught all of the subjects to a class or part of a class. Yale's tutorial system did not lend itself so readily to the kind of specialization that seemed necessary before the elective system could flourish.

Another difference that tended to prevent the ultimate acceptance by Yale of the elective system was the whole theory that emphasized the religious nature of college education and the desirability of continuing the prescribed curriculum for religious ends. Whereas the religious position of Harvard had been considerably liberalized, the following statement of President Clap in 1754 illustrates the more traditional position of Yale:

Colleges are *Religious Societies*, of a Superior Nature to all others. For whereas *Parishes*, are Societies, for training up the *Common People;* Colleges, are Societies of Ministers, for training up persons for the Work of the *Ministry*. . . . Some indeed, have supposed, that, the only design of Colleges, was to teach the Arts, and Sciences. . . . But it is probable, that there is not a College, to be found upon Earth, upon such a Constitution.[1]

Here is the typ Reformation attitude which reenforced the classical and Renaissance conception of a liberal education. The aristocratic and religious notions were paramount in the aims of college education which still purported to provide the kind of liberal education suitable to a gentleman. Both Yale and Harvard were generally similar in their loyalty to this tradition and to an emphasis upon the study of divinity, the classics, mathematics, and philosophy, but the greater strength of the religious conception at Yale ultimately worked to keep Yale more loyal to the prescribed curriculum than was the case at Harvard.

[1] THOMAS CLAP, *Religious Constitution of Colleges, especially of Yale-College in New Haven* (T. Green, New London, Conn., 1754), p. 4.

Several other colleges that sprang up during the colonial period followed the traditional attitude of the earliest colleges and were founded largely for religious reasons. The religious awakening in the middle of the eighteenth century had resulted in a great addition to the memberships of the different denominations and prompted many of them to set up colleges of their own in order to prepare ministers to care for their increasing numbers and to provide for their followers a higher education that would be guided by the tenets of their particular belief. In 1746, the Presbyterians founded Princeton (at first called the College of New Jersey); in 1764, the Baptists founded Brown (formerly the College of Rhode Island); in 1766, the Dutch Reformed Church founded Rutgers (Queen's College); and in 1769, the Congregationalists founded Dartmouth. These denominational colleges gradually opened their doors to students of other denominations as the conception of higher education widened and as economic pressure showed the need of admitting more students in order to meet expenses. However that may be, their histories up to the Revolution show little radically different from that of the earlier religious foundations.[1]

A NEW CONCEPTION OF LIBERAL EDUCATION APPEARS

In nearly all of the colonial colleges already mentioned, the aim as expressed in the respective charters indicated the desire to teach the "arts and sciences" or the "liberal arts" as a preparation for the ministry or leadership in civil government. These liberal arts at first were little more than the original seven liberal arts with the addition of Greek, Hebrew, and bits of the newer science and philosophy, all more or less subordinated to the religious temper. With the founding of King's College (Columbia) in New York City in 1754, there was a gradual shading off in the strictly religious aim; and with the establishment of the college in Philadelphia in 1755 (University of Pennsylvania), we find a vastly wider conception of the aim and content of a liberal education. This wider conception of a liberal education implied that college studies should contribute to the commercial and civic usefulness of the many as well as to the religious and civic leadership of the few. The literary and aristocratic conception of a liberal education was challenged, however faintly, by a more practical and democratic conception which was later to produce the elective principle.

---

[1] For early curriculums of Princeton, Rutgers, and Brown, see John MacLean, *History of the College of New Jersey* (J. B. Lippincott Company, Philadelphia, 1877), Vol. I, pp. 140–142, 266; W. H. S. Demarest, *A History of Rutgers College, 1766–1924* (Rutgers College, New Brunswick, N. J., 1924), pp. 133–137; W. C. Bronson, *The History of Brown University* (Brown University Press, Providence, R. I., 1914), pp. 102–129.

King's College represented a new departure chiefly in the fact that the traditional aim to train ministers seemed to be absent and that there was careful provision to tolerate differing religious beliefs. In the advance publicity given to the college in advertisements in New York newspapers, no mention was made of the aim to train ministers, but rather in its place there seemed to be represented the more practical aim to teach students

. . . To know God in Jesus Christ . . . and to train them up in all virtuous Habits, and all such useful Knowledge, as may render them creditable to their Families and Friends, Ornaments to their Country, and useful to the public Weal in their Generations.[1]

With regard to religious toleration, the charter of King's provided that no persons should be denied entrance to the college or be prevented from acquiring a degree or any of the benefits of the college because of his membership in any denomination or because of his particular religious beliefs. Although the college was founded nominally under Anglican auspices, the board of trustees included not only the rector of Trinity Church but also ministers from the Dutch Reformed, Lutheran, French, and Presbyterian churches. Toleration of differing religious beliefs of the students had also been authorized in the charter of Princeton and other colleges, but the aim to provide ministers was uppermost in all but King's and the college at Philadelphia.[2]

With this freer religious atmosphere went a proposal to broaden the liberal arts at King's to include many of the subjects that were useful for the more efficient pursuit of the commercial activities of the time:

. . . a serious, *virtuous*, and *industrious* Course of Life, being first provided for, it is further the Design of this College, to instruct and perfect the Youth in the Learned Languages, and in the Arts of *reasoning* exactly, of *writing* correctly, and *speaking* eloquently; and in the Arts of *numbering* and *measuring;* of *Surveying* and *Navigation*, of *Geography* and *History*, of *Husbandry, Commerce* and *Government;* and in the Knowledge of *all Nature* in the *Heavens* above us, and in the *Air, Water*, and *Earth* around us, and the various kinds of *Meteors, Stones, Mines* and *Minerals, Plants* and *Animals*, and of every Thing *useful* for the Comfort, the Convenience and Elegance of Life, in the chief *Manufactures* relating to any of these Things: And, finally, to lead them from the Study of Nature to the Knowledge of themselves, and of the God of Nature. . . . [3]

[1] Advertisement in the *New York Gazette*, or *Weekly Post Boy*, June 3, 1754; quoted in *A History of Columbia University*, 1754–1904 (Columbia University Press, New York, 1904), p. 444.

[2] MacLean, *op. cit.*, Vol. I, pp. 61, 116, *et passim*. Of the six members of the first graduating class, five became ministers; of the seven members of the second class, five became ministers.

[3] *A History of Columbia University*, pp. 444–445.

The intention that King's College should cater to the more practical pursuits of life was indicated further in letters from George III in 1762 authorizing that funds might be solicited and collected for the colleges in New York and Philadelphia. The statement was made that these colleges had been set up

. . . not so much to aim at any high Improvement in *Knowledge*, as to guard against total Ignorance; to instil into the Minds of Youth just principles of Religion, Loyalty and a Love of Our excellent Constitution; to instruct them in such Branches of Knowledge and useful Arts as are necessary to Trade, Agriculture, and a due Improvement of Our Valuable Colonies; and to assist in raising up a Succession of faithful Instructors, to be sent forth not only among our Subjects there, but also among the Indians in Alliance with us. . . . [1]

Apparently, however, these intentions as well as the proposals noted above in the advertisements formulated by Samuel Johnson, first president of King's, were not yet to be realized. Johnson's predilection for scientific studies had been gained while he was under the influence of Newton's works at Yale, and his desire to make college studies more useful for everyday life was perhaps intensified by his associations with Franklin. He had been offered by Franklin the position of provost of the new college at Philadelphia (a fact that perhaps attested to their similarity of views), but he had refused in order to become head of King's. Also, Franklin had sent him a copy of his *Idea of the English School* which Johnson had commended heartily.

In spite of Johnson's leanings, the literary and classical conception of a liberal education was evidently too strong to permit a radical departure from it so soon, for we find that the curriculum adopted at King's in 1755 and again in 1762 was very similar to those of the traditional colleges with which King's had to compete.[2] The four years of study were heavily weighted with Latin and Greek grammar and literature, rhetoric, ethics, and philosophy; and strict disciplinary control was to be enforced over the minutest details of student life. Thus, although the *conception* of the liberal arts came to be expanded to include scientific and utilitarian as well as the traditional subjects, the actual *practice* at King's did not fulfill the proposals. The elective idea had not yet been overtly formulated on the college level, although it had become a general practice in the private schools which responded more quickly than the colleges to the commercial interests and needs of the time.[3]

---

[1] *Ibid.*, p. 32.

[2] *Ibid.*, pp. 444–456.

[3] See R. F. SEYBOLT, *Source Studies in American Colonial Education: The Private School* (University of Illinois, Urbana, 1925), pp. 100–102. See also SEYBOLT, *The Evening School in Colonial America* (University of Illinois, Urbana, 1925).

It was largely through the influence of Benjamin Franklin that the American colonies became imbued with the secular ideals of freedom, individualism, and democracy; with respect for investigation in the physical sciences; and with utilitarian commercial interests which were so characteristic of the Enlightenment. Five years before King's College opened, Franklin had been instrumental in founding an academy in Philadelphia, embodying the prevailing tendencies of the private schools to offer utilitarian subjects for the commercial classes as well as classical languages for college preparatory needs. Franklin had proposed the academy as early as 1743 but had considered it politic not to press his case at that time. In 1749, his *Proposals Relating to the Education of Youth in Pensilvania* again outlined an academy that was to include three departments: English, Latin, and Mathematics. The famous principle by which he chose the courses of study to be offered to students is indicated in the following statement:

As to their studies, it would be well if they could be taught everything that is useful, and everything that is ornamental: but art is long, and their time is short. It is therefore proposed that they learn those things which are likely to be most useful and most ornamental. Regard being had to the several professions for which they are intended.[1]

That Franklin's ideas were not original but reflected outstanding theories of the times is indicated by his profuse footnotes in the *Proposals* referring to the educational writings of Locke, Milton, Hutcheson (University of Glasgow), and Rollin (University of Paris). Here is a definite channel by which streams of English, Scottish, and French reform flowed into American intellectual and educational ideals. In order to indicate the nature of these suggested reforms and also the extent of the curriculum, it may be well to list some of the subjects that Franklin proposed in addition to the regular subjects of the Latin grammar school and traditional college: writing; drawing; arithmetic and accounts; English language and composition; letter writing; history; natural history (botany); the practice of gardening and agriculture; and the history of commerce, trade, and industry.

His emphasis upon the English branch of the academy was further brought out in a treatise that he wrote entitled the *Idea of the English School.*[2] His idea had been to differentiate sharply between the English and the Latin school by having the English master teach *his* students

---

[1] THOMAS WOODY, *Educational Views of Benjamin Franklin* (McGraw-Hill Book Company, Inc., New York, 1931), p. 158.

[2] Subjects included were English grammar, spelling, reading, rhetoric, composition and writing, history, ethics, geography, logic, English literature, and natural philosophy (physical science).

history, geography, logic, and oratory, while the Latin master taught *his* pupils the same subjects.[1] This would mean that the students were allowed to choose which course they would take. Franklin in another connection brought out even more clearly the fact that the elective idea was implicit in his suggestions: "Each scholar shall pay such sum or sums, quarterly, according to the particular branches of learning they shall desire to be taught. . . . "[2] Referring to the study of languages, Franklin further enunciated the elective principle:

All intended for divinity should be taught Latin and Greek; for physic the Latin, Greek and French; for law the Latin and French; merchants, the French, German and Spanish; and though all should not be compelled to learn Latin, Greek, or the modern foreign languages, yet none that have an ardent desire to learn them should be refused; their English, arithmetic, and other studies absolutely necessary being at the same time not neglected.[3]

Franklin's sponsorship and attendant publicity helped to spread the academy idea throughout America where it dominated secondary education for more than a hundred years.

Franklin's academy was given a state charter in 1753, and that of a college was added in 1755. Reverend William Smith, the first provost, drew up the rather broad curriculum that was established for the college, but the promise of Franklin's notion of voluntary selection of courses was not carried to its logical conclusion on the college level. Of Scottish descent, Smith had attended the University of Aberdeen, and it is possible that his curriculum for the Philadelphia college was framed substantially from the course that had shortly before (1753) been revised at King's College, Aberdeen[4] (see pp. 53–54). Although his Scottish training may have influenced him, Smith was also undoubtedly caught by Franklin's theories and practices which evidently corresponded to those which he may have formulated for himself.

Before he became provost at Philadelphia, Smith had, in 1752, written an article proposing a college in New York City and entitled *Some Thoughts on Education*, in which he said: "I shall only add that Oxford, Leyden, &c., are too complex and large to be any Model for us: the neighboring Colleges of New England, Pennsylvania, &c., may be kept chiefly in our Eye. . . . "[5] Also, in his allegorical treatise entitled

---

[1] *Observations Relative to the Intentions of the Original Founders of the Academy in Philadelphia*, 1789; see Woody, *op. cit.*, pp. 192–228.

[2] WOODY, *op. cit.*, p. 188.

[3] *Ibid.*, p. 173.

[4] T. H. MONTGOMERY, *A History of the University of Pennsylvania* (George W. Jacobson and Company, Philadelphia, 1900), p. 234.

[5] *Ibid.*, p. 187.

A General Idea of the College of Mirania (1753), Smith divided all "Miranians" into two classes, those intended for the learned professions and those intended for the trades, each class to have its own special school. He pointed out that there was little chance for the second class to receive useful instruction, and he proposed a mechanics' school, which he said did not need much explanation because it was so much like Franklin's English school in Philadelphia.[1]

Whatever the source of his ideas, Smith proposed "A Scheme of Liberal Education" which was accepted by the trustees of the college and which embraced the widest course of study and variety of subjects of all colleges in America at the time. It seemed as if he were trying to crowd into the curriculum all the subjects that he had proposed for the Miranians. Under his new plan, the academy was to include only the English and mathematical departments of Franklin's academy, whereas the Latin department was expanded and made into a preparatory department necessary for entrance to the college. Franklin later objected to the fact that the English department from the start had been subordinated to the Latin, but tradition and college entrance requirements had been too strong for him.

Like King's College, the aim of the Philadelphia college was not couched in terms of training ministers but rather to "enrich our country with many *Minds* that are liberally accomplished," and the function of religious study was to "compleat their Wisdom, to regulate their conduct thro' life, and guide them to happiness forever."[2] The college was planned to include three "Schools of Philosophy"[3] in addition to the usual classical and rhetorical studies; and a long list of miscellaneous readings to supplement the required lectures was appended to the curriculum. In this plan, drawn up by Smith, we find the clearest evidence in America that the colleges were accepting the new science and philosophy that the Enlightenment had produced. Its effect was to widen the scope of the curriculum and to extend considerably the conception of the liberal studies that a young man should follow, no matter what occupation he was to enter. Some of the subjects which Franklin's academy and the private schools had offered as specialized studies for utilitarian purposes now entered into the prescribed liberal arts curriculum of this college along with the traditional classical languages and

---

[1] *Ibid.*, p. 187. For a fuller text of Smith's allegory, see William Smith, *Discourses on Public Occasions in America* (London, 1762), Appendix II, No. 1.

[2] Montgomery, *op. cit.*, pp. 240–241.

[3] *Ibid.*, pp. 236–239. The three "Schools of Philosophy" referred to "instrumental philosophy" (logic and mathematics), "moral philosophy" (ethics, history, law and government, trade and commerce), and "natural philosophy" (science). These subjects were taught in the forenoon, and the classical studies in the afternoon.

mathematics.   It is significant that no works relating to divinity, except the Bible itself, appeared in the prescribed curriculum or in the miscellaneous readings.   The plan was designed as a course of three years in which each class progressed regularly at stated intervals of three and four months from one subject to the next.   The only indication of the elective idea was the fact that an occasional classical text could be changed at the discretion of the tutor and that French could be studied if desired in leisure hours; but this was no more than obtained at other colleges.

That Smith thought he had settled for all time the question of a liberal education may be indicated by the following statements included in his original proposal:

Thus we see that this institution is placed on a most enlarged bottom, being one great collection of schools, under a general government; in which all the branches and species of education are carried on that can be conceived necessary for any community, whether in the learned professions, in merchandise, in the mechanic arts, or inferior callings.[1]

As to the plan of education, great care has been taken to comprehend every useful branch in it, without being burdensome or launching into those that are unnecessary.[2]

Although the elective principle was not embodied in this new curriculum, the principle of admitting subjects to the curriculum because of their utility was clearly enunciated; and it was the ultimate overburdening of the curriculum with new fields of knowledge arising out of increasing demands for ever more useful subjects that eventually became a strong factor in the development of the elective practice.

In summary, we have seen that the Enlightenment of the eighteenth century worked only a slight change in the curriculum of the American colleges, especially when it came to adding scientific and commercially useful subjects to follow the trends of the times.   Expansion in scientific knowledge, the refinement of skills needed in trade and commerce, and the prevalence of individualistic ideals of economic gain were responsible for what changes occurred, but the conception still held sway that a liberal education ought to be a complete round of prescribed studies heavily weighted on the linguistic and mathematical side.   The Philadelphia college helped to add the criterion of material success in commercial fields of endeavor to the traditional criteria of religious and civil leadership, but it maintained a completely prescribed curriculum. Although the new science and philosophy may have been added slowly

---

[1] HORACE W. SMITH, *Life and Correspondence of the Rev. William Smith* (S. A. George and Company, Philadelphia, 1879), Vol. I, p. 62.

[2] *Ibid.*, p. 63.   Here is one of the several statements which should make modern educators cautious about asserting that they have the one plan for a fixed prescribed curriculum that will be appropriate for college education at all times.

to the prescribed curriculum of the denominational colleges, they still kept essentially to the conception of a liberal education as embodying a study of Latin, Greek, mathematics, and philosophy as the best preparation for an aristocratic leadership in church and state.   Franklin's theories contained the seeds of the elective idea, and the expanding curriculum supplied fertile grounds for its development, but it was not until the quickening of life following the American Revolution and the infiltration of ideas from abroad that the elective idea received its first explicit formulation; and it was not until the forces of a highly industrial society were at work in the latter half of the nineteenth century that the traditional notion of a liberal education was really put upon the defensive.

PART II
THE PRESCRIBED CURRICULUM WEAKENS

CHAPTER V

THE EARLY NINETEENTH CENTURY SOWS THE SEEDS
OF ELECTION (ABOUT 1776–1860)

European Currents of Thought. Although our attention will be focused principally upon the developments in the United States from this point in our discussion, we shall sketch in enough of the European background to give significance to some of the streams of influence that swept in upon the young republic. After the American Revolution, the United States was taken into the currents of world affairs to assume its place as a new nation of full rank. This greater contact and communication with world powers led America to drop its predominantly English aspect and to develop a complex matrix of thought and culture which not only represented its native temper but also borrowed from France and Germany as well as from England. The ideals of the French Revolution were received with particular sympathy in the new nation which now became attracted to all things French in culture, manners, dress, and intellect. After the turn of the century, however, the Napoleonic wars so wrecked the French dream of equality and democracy that America turned to a Germany that was trying to restore itself by a romantic idealism and nationalism. Meanwhile, English activity in the fields of scientific discovery and invention and middle-class economic theory began to attract the rising industrialism of the new nation. Let us try to distinguish some of the more important of these influences which were finding expression in modified forms in America.

First of all, French humanitarianism which had begun to develop in the social and political theory of the Enlightenment made a real impact upon American life. The French Revolutionists continued to proclaim the equality of man, the essential goodness of man's nature, the indefinite possibilities of his perfectibility, and his "natural rights" of liberty and happiness. Further impetus was given to social theory by the enunciation of the conception of social "progress"; that is, it was felt that man's lot on this earth could continually be improved if organized social institutions concentrated on the subjugation of the material environment in the interests of human welfare. Such theories were possible because of the prevailing climate of secular thought and attitude which had greater respect for human labor and industriousness, more freedom from authority, and reliance upon the "laws of nature" rather than upon the arbitrary interference of an angry God. A still further implication of this humanitarian theory of the rights of man was the doctrine which outlined a state of society embracing universal education, abolition of poverty, reform of criminal laws, old age pensions, and international peace. Thus did the French reformers describe Utopia, and many Americans tried to put it into practice.

Meanwhile, after their defeat at the hands of Napoleon, the Germans set out to create a purely German culture based upon an idealistic philosophy to combat the materialism of French thought. Kant, Schleiermacher, Fichte, Hegel, and Goethe were great names of the day. The French had made "Reason" the tool of knowledge in all fields, including religion and morality. But Kant in his transcendental philosophy set out to separate the realms of reason and faith; thereby he hoped to preserve the conceptions of God, freedom, and immortality from the onslaught of science and reason and reserve them to the realm of faith. The innate worth of man was formulated by the Germans into a metaphysical system of transcendental idealism and nationalism which later appealed to American students and attracted many of them to German universities during the nineteenth century.

In England, the tradition of scientific research which had been given such impetus by Newton and his contemporaries continued to accumulate and finally expressed itself in power-driven machines and many other inventions which produced the "Industrial Revolution." Scientists of all European countries contributed to the advancement of science along modern lines; Rutherford and Priestley in physics, Lavoisier in chemistry, Galvani and Volta in electricity, and Hutton in geology are merely examples. English inventors applied these scientific achievements to produce such technical improvements as Watt's steam engine, Stephenson's locomotive, Arkwright's and Crompton's spinning machinery. Also, the idea of evolution began to make its impression upon intellectual consciousness as a result of the work of Lamarck and Lyell and as a result of the application of the idea of "progress" to plants and animals as well as to man. These currents of thought, along with the romantic movements in European literature sponsored by such writers as Wordsworth, Coleridge, Byron, Keats, Shelley, Scott, and Goethe, were some of the influences that made their imprint upon the intellectual development in America.

The greatest educational activity in Europe during the last quarter of the eighteenth and the first half of the nineteenth century seemed to be taking place in Germany. Attempting to rejuvenate itself along nationalistic lines, Prussia reorganized its educational system from the elementary school through the university under the stimulus of the doctrines of Pestalozzi, Kant, Fichte, Froebel, and Herbart. Germany was the first to adopt the naturalism and psychological methods of the Swiss educational reformer Pestalozzi, who in turn prompted Froebel to put such emphasis upon the play activity of children in his "Kindergarten." Herbart enunciated the doctrine of education for social usefulness and formulated systematic methods of teaching which emphasized the social sciences as the core of the curriculum. Kant, dominating the thought of Germany, elaborated the philosophy of transcendentalism and idealism, which gave further consequence to the power of the human mind and spirit as opposed to theories of human subservience either to material forces or to religious authority. Fichte, believing in democracy, advocated schools free to the masses as the best agencies of social reform.

German Universities Show the Way. In Germany, the universities were making the greatest strides toward freedom for the individual professor and for the individual student. The logical conclusion of the freedom that had appeared in the universities at Halle and Göttingen in the eighteenth century was reached with the founding of the University of Berlin in 1809. Despite reactionary attempts to stamp out liberalism in the German universities, Wilhelm von Humboldt made of Berlin a university of independence and freedom, wherein instruction was carried on not in the form of a prescribed curriculum but in a situation wherein the professor had freedom to teach what he thought best and the student, freedom to study what he desired.[1] The faculty of philosophy now held the place of predominance in the German universities. Next to philosophy the most important studies were the classical humanities, philology, and history, for great contributions were made to scholarship in literary, linquistic, and social studies by the use of the seminar methods of research. The studies of mathematics and natural science began to gain ground soon after the beginning of the nineteenth century; by the end of the second decade, they were flourishing; and after the second half of the century, they took over the leadership as the dominating studies.

In the 1830's, as the interest in speculative philosophy was overshadowed by the great rise of research in the physical sciences, an ever increasing specialization in the fields of investigation took place. Conse-

[1] The famous German expression *Lehrfreiheit und Lernfreiheit* (freedom of teaching and freedom of learning) gained wide currency in the United States during the nineteenth century. It seems scarcely necessary to point out the ironical fact that the birthplace of the modern theory of academic freedom was in those very German universities which today are the tragic examples of the death of all freedom. When G. Stanley Hall was saying at the turn of the century that the German universities were the freest spot on earth, Paulsen remarked with almost prophetic fear, "May the time never come when the German universities will have reason to blush at these words." FRIEDRICH PAULSEN, *German Universities and University Study* (Charles Scribner's Sons, New York, 1906), pp. 227–228

quently, the number of departments increased, and the number of professors in each department multiplied many times. The student was thrown entirely upon his own resources as a free individual. The age of the entering student advanced to approximately twenty years owing to the expanded secondary school; and the greater need of specializing in order to reach a competent degree of scholarship led to the free use of the elective principle. Thereby the student was not required to follow a whole round of studies but was free to select the field of study in which he wished to specialize and to attend what lectures he found necessary in order to attain such proficiency as would enable him to get his degree. The faculties of the German universities were nearly equivalent to what Americans know as the graduate and professional school; the English and American conception of a "college" was no longer known in Germany's university circles. The professor in Germany became a research specialist as well as a teacher, and the universities became the centers of scientific research.[1]

In France, university development took an entirely different course. The University of Paris, along with other French universities, virtually ceased to exist during the French Revolution, and it was not reestablished until 1896, when the separate faculties set up by Napoleon were again combined to constitute the University of Paris. At the time when the University of Berlin was setting out upon a course of freedom, Napoleon founded the "University of France" to include all the educational agencies of the country from the lowest elementary schools to highest university faculties. At the top of the hierarchy were separate technical faculties of letters, science, medicine, and law with strict regulations, a prescribed order of studies, and state examinations at each level of instruction. The entire course of instruction was laid down by the state ministery of education; attendance at lectures and exercises was compulsory; the courses were prescribed for each year; and state examinations had to be passed before the student could be promoted from one year to the next. The active scientific research went on largely outside the faculties and in connection with the Académie des Sciences.

The English universities began to recover a measure of their old vitality with the beginning of the nineteenth century. During the first half of the century, Oxford began to reform from within its examination

---

[1] PAULSEN, *op. cit.*, pp. 4–6, points out that the German universities possessed such leading German scholars as Fichte, Schelling, Hegel, Schleiermacher in literature; Kant and Wolff in philosophy; Wolf, Hermann, and Heine in philology; Ranke in history; Gauss and Helmholtz in natural science; Schiller and Uhland in poetry; and Pufendorff, Thomasius, and Niebuhr in political science. In contrast, the English universities could *not* claim such outstanding English scholars in science and letters as Darwin, Spencer, Mill, Carlyle, Gibbon, Macaulay, Bentham, Ricardo, Locke, Hume, Shaftesbury, Hobbes, and Bacon.

system so that a student needed more adequate preparation for passing his examinations, and "honors courses" became added inducements for the student to attain a high degree of scholarship. The first honors courses were in the classics and mathematics; then with parliamentary acts to reform the universities, other honors courses were added in the second half of the nineteenth century; of these the natural sciences and law and modern history were instituted before 1860. At Cambridge, mathematics continued to gain in importance during the last part of the eighteenth and early nineteenth centuries; it had been the first subject in which a regular "tripos" (honors course examination) was held (1747). Then triposes were added in civil law (1815), classics (1824), moral sciences (1851), and natural sciences (1850). Although this marked an advance over the lethargy of the eighteenth century, the English universities were still far behind the German universities in regard to scientific research and freedom of teaching and learning; courses were still prescribed, and all religions but Anglican were proscribed.[1] Thus, we see that the German universities were the most advanced in the world during the first half of the nineteenth century and were more likely to attract American students than those of either France or England.

Developing Mind of the New Nation. The American Revolution, on the one hand, confused and disorganized the political, economic, and social structure of the new nation and, on the other, brought it into closer touch with the main stream of world affairs. The Revolution had largely been engineered by radical leaders who wanted a loose confederation of states; but lacking British order and regulation, the condition of trade, agriculture, and industry grew more chaotic until the leaders drew up a stronger constitution which the states were finally persuaded to accept. The centralizing measures of Alexander Hamilton on the question of money and a national bank occasioned the rise of an antifederalist, or "republican," party headed by Thomas Jefferson which desired more state autonomy. The French Revolution had flooded the American states with its theories of the natural rights of man and its denunciations of despotic centralized authority, and Jefferson rode into the presidency on a wave of agrarian republicanism. Despite the republican efforts of Jefferson and Madison, they were ultimately carried in the direction of a strong agricultural imperialism in the purchase of the Louisiana territory, the embargo acts, and the War of 1812.[2]

[1] Not until 1871 were the English universities freed from doctrinal tests for all degrees, fellowships, and university and college offices. Prospective clergymen still were required to give evidence of Anglican orthodoxy.

[2] For a more detailed description of this phase of our story, see C. A. Beard and M. A. Beard, *The Rise of American Civilization* (The Macmillan Company, New York, 1937), Vol. I, Chaps. VII–XVI; and V. L. Parrington, *The Romantic Revolution in America*, 1800–1860 (Harcourt, Brace & Company, Inc., New York, 1927).

These events brought the opposition of the merchants and shipowners, but their cause was a losing one until the middle of the nineteenth century. Nine new agricultural states had been added to the union in approximately 30 years of existence; and while the farmers in the West were gaining the privilege of suffrage, the Atlantic states were progressively putting the ballot in the hands of the city mechanics and laborers. These laboring and farming classes joined together in a popular movement that swept Andrew Jackson into the White House where his ideal of democracy was to stay nearly undisturbed until 1860. Meanwhile, the businessmen of the North took up the new technical processes of English and American inventors,[1] collected capital, organized labor forces, and began exploiting the huge natural resources of the land and flooding the markets of the world with American products.

By the middle of the century, the Industrial Revolution was well under way in America. The Lawrences, Lowells, Abbotts, Astors, Brookses, and Vanderbilts were ready to challenge the authority and spokesmen of the agrarian and planter classes. Capital investments in industry, railroads, commerce, and cities exceeded in value all the farms and plantations in the country. Steamboats, canals, railroads, highways, and factories began to destroy the economic basis of Jacksonian individualism and democracy. A laboring class without property began to organize into associations for defense and aggression. The South had also been stimulated by the invention of the cotton gin and spinning jenny to increase production and gain more profits. It was largely this economic conflict supported by the theories evolving from each side that led to the Civil War and finally proclaimed the victory of industrialism over agriculture, rid America of the "romantic imperialism" of a slave economy, and narrowed the potential conflict to the imperialism of Eastern capitalism and Western agrarianism.

Culturally, the floodgates were down after the Revolution, and European intellectual currents swept in. French humanitarianism with its doctrines of democracy, the natural rights of man, personal liberty, progress, and improvability of society was received first into Virginia in the early 1770's where Jefferson became its greatest spokesman and disseminator. French romantic thought spread to the West where it combined with an aggressive individualism already growing on the frontier. It invaded New England and took the garb of Unitarianism to preach human perfectibility so strongly that New England was aroused to several efforts for the reform of man and society. Also, there was the German transcendental idealism which caught the imagination of Emerson, Thoreau, Theodore Parker, and Margaret Fuller in New

---

[1] Examples of such inventions are the power loom, iron smelting processes, mower, reaper, sewing machine, and steam printing press.

England and inspired an intellectual and cultural flowering in the middle decades of the nineteenth century until the triumph of middle-class acquisitiveness stifled it. Along with German idealism went German ideals of academic scholarship which found hospitable reception in the hands of the New England members of the "genteel tradition" and belles-lettres.[1]

The middle classes found theoretical justification for economic aggressiveness in the doctrines of English capitalists who had gained virtual control of the English government and had set up the social ideal in which economic forces were to have free play. The principal instinct of man was considered to be economic acquisitiveness and gain seeking; and individual conduct was supposedly motivated by the desire for profit in an economy in which free trade and exploitation were the aims. Coming to America, this doctrine of capitalism found acquisitiveness already developing, but the great natural resources could not be exploited adequately or quickly by individual effort. Hence consolidation was necessary, and the government was brought in to assist the process of exploitation by granting lands, subsidies, and tariffs and by building roads and canals. Thus, in the latter decades of the nineteenth century, the government was to become the paternal means for aiding strategic groups who claimed that their own prosperity was the best guarantee for the welfare of the masses.

The main intellectual vogue of the young republic was French. Under the influence of visiting artists, engineers, and scientists, proposals were made to establish an American academy of arts and sciences upon the French model instead of the English and to establish a national university patterned after the French higher faculties. The dreams of social progress emerging from France and Europe seemed to be possible of actual fulfillment in America. Jefferson took over Franklin's position as the intellectual leader of the age and outlined his plans for a society based upon agrarian individualism, freedom of the press and religion, humanitarian laws, and a complete system of education from elementary schools to the university.

Secularism continued to make firm its hold upon the political structure and to attack religious authority. The new government was completely and inevitably secular, with few religious qualifications for voting and with its constitutional amendments positing religious, intellectual, and social toleration. With the expulsion of the English official groups, the social classes were pushed upward, and merchants, planters, and even farmers and laborers began to come into positions of dominance. Unitarianism began to challenge and drive out Trinitarianism; deism

[1] For a general picture of this period, see Van Wyck Brooks, *The Flowering of New England* 1815–1865 (E. P. Dutton & Co., Inc., New York, 1936).

attacked all denominational theology. Yet the Methodists and the Baptists arrived to take by storm the masses of the West and Southwest with revivalist meetings somewhat in the temper of the Great Awakening. By converting thousands, these movements continued the democratization of religious organization and accelerated the founding of church-related colleges for religious and missionary purposes.

Science and scientific investigation proceeded apace. Joseph Priestley and Thomas Cooper found haven in America to continue their investigations. Native scientists made outstanding contributions in their special fields; Benjamin Rush in medicine, Nathaniel Bowditch in mathematics and navigation, Benjamin Silliman in chemistry and mineralogy, Louis Agassiz in zoology, Asa Gray in botany are examples. Technical invention received the attention of Americans in the form of Whitney's cotton gin, McCormick's reaper, Morse's telegraph, and Fulton's steamboat. The desire to search out the laws of nature was further evident in the flourishing discussions of the American Philosophical Society and the investigations of other associations and national surveys. The cause of historical scholarship was aided by George Bancroft, George Ticknor, Francis Parkman, and Jared Sparks.

Literary expressions of the early nineteenth century often sided with Jefferson to advocate reform in favor of the rights of the common man against the privileged and wealthy classes. Writers of the middle of the century continued this tendency to the left in the persons of Hawthorne, Whitman, Thoreau, and Emerson; whereas Cooper, Irving, Longfellow, Holmes, and Lowell represented the middle-of-the-road point of view. Radical idealism and communism found expression in the experiments of Brook Farm, Alcott's Fruitlands, and Owen's New Harmony. Even if the drama, opera, painting, sculpture, and drawing showed a cultural lag, many daily, weekly, and monthly periodicals as well as ambitious lyceums and institutes began to carry the knowledge of intellectual and cultural advances to an ever widening audience.

American Education in Theory and Practice. The period from the American Revolution to approximately 1820 was a time of great discussion of educational problems. Scarcely had the Revolution assured the independence of America when the function of education in a republic began to be discussed in a flood of articles, pamphlets, and books. This discussion was further stimulated when the American Philosophical Society offered a prize for the best description of a system of liberal education suited to the genius of the United States. Most of the writers were well imbued with the humanitarian doctrines of the French Enlightenment in their emphasis upon the indefinite perfectibility of man and the possibility of social progress by remaking social institutions. With these philosophical bases for education, various plans were outlined whereby education could be liberalized, democratized, and nationalized. Most of the writers believed that the new education should be highly flexible and accept any new studies (especially scientific) that would better prepare students for life in a democracy. Many also believed that education should be under national control to insure the greatest progress toward social welfare.[1]

Washington urged the founding of a national university for the promotion of the arts, sciences, and American principles of law and order. Benjamin Rush advocated a national system of education, especially emphasizing, as might be expected from his interest in medicine, the importance of scientific studies for their utilitarian value and the necessity of supplanting Latin and Greek in order to remove popular prejudices against higher education. Robert Coram urged that national education should be supported by general taxation in order to provide for the equal opportunity necessary in a democracy. The winners of the American Philosophical Society's contest were Samuel Knox and Samuel Harrison Smith. Knox outlined a complete national system of education consisting of elementary, secondary, and collegiate schools with a great national university at the top to serve as a center of specialized research. Each state was to have a college the curriculum of which would be uniform with that of all other colleges, distinguishing between those students who were to go on to the university and those who would go out into life. The classics were to be emphasized for those who were preparing for the university. Smith introduced most of the current arguments for the attainment of social progress through advancement of the arts and sciences, for utilitarian and democratic education, for national control, and for a national university heading a hierarchy of state schools.

Evidences of French influence were found in the plans for American education drawn up by Frenchmen in America. Lafitte du Courteil's plan for national education emphasized the need for American education to be adapted to agricultural interests, open to all equally, and nationalistic in aim and control. Du Pont de Nemours wrote at the request of Jefferson a plan for a national system of schools and a national university. Quesnay de Beaurepaire tried to establish an American academy of arts and sciences on the scale of a national research foundation, but the fortunes of the French Revolution killed his project. Despite the unanimity of educational theory with respect to national education, the temper of the times was not ready for it. Jefferson with his program of state instead of national control was more in tune, but even he was a half century ahead of his times. However, the ideas were gaining currency that education should be under civil and secular control rather than under

[1] See ALLEN O. HANSEN, *Liberalism and American Education in the Eighteenth Century* (The Macmillan Company, New York, 1926).

religious supervision and that education should be flexible in order to train youth for useful living in a progressive democracy.

All these proposals which helped to lay the foundations for educational development in the middle of the nineteenth century show clearly the continuing influence of Rousseau and Locke, whose philosophies were interpreted by such experimenters as the Swiss Pestalozzi and the German Basedow. From the influence of these latter, the American secondary and primary schools began to expand their curriculum and change their methods in the direction of greater emphasis upon the nature of the child, more activity for his physical senses, and more development of his social senses.[1] From England the idea of education for the masses was given impetus by the importation of Lancaster's monitorial school, Raike's Sunday school, and Owen's infant school. From Prussia came new methods of teacher training and the idea of a centralized system of education under the control of the state. Finally, under the strong leadership of such men as Horace Mann, Henry Barnard, and James Carter the battle was fought and won for state rather than local control of education in order to wipe out inequalities of opportunity, to improve the quality of the educational offering, and to improve the status of teachers.

Despite the active discussion of education in the decades immediately following the American Revolution, the higher education of the United States gave only slight attention to reform, and the academy rather than the college continued to meet the need for a more practical education, until the public high school began to take over some of its functions in the middle decades. However, the general activity in economic and intellectual affairs that appeared in the early decades of the nineteenth century did slowly begin to produce results in higher education. An important United States Supreme Court decision in 1819 held that Dartmouth College could not be taken over by the state of New Hampshire against the will of the trustees, because its charter was a contract the validity of which could not be impaired even by the state.

Private and religious foundations were henceforth secure from encroachment by the state, and many new private colleges were founded. Conversely, the popular movement was now obliged to set up its own institutions of higher education in the form of state universities in the new states of the South and West. Colleges generally continued upon

---

[1] Pestalozzian and Prussian influences were spread through the United States by the reports, articles, and lectures of such men as John Griscom, William C. Woodbridge, Victor Cousin, Calvin Stowe, Alexander Bache, Horace Mann, and Henry Barnard. For Griscom, Stowe, and Cousin, see E. W. Knight, *Reports on European Education* (McGraw-Hill Book Company, Inc., New York, 1930).

their old way; but in the College of William and Mary, in the new University of Virginia, in Harvard, in Brown, and in several other colleges a new spirit began to show itself. Despite the opposition of the more conservative colleges and of strong groups within the advancing colleges, these beginnings flowered during the second half of the century into the most characteristic feature of the modern college curriculum, the elective system.

CHAPTER VI

FIRST EXPERIMENTS WITH THE ELECTIVE SYSTEM

JEFFERSON AND HIS IDEAL OF DEMOCRACY

Thomas Jefferson was one of the first Americans to prepare the ground for the development of the elective system. His educational theories may be seen in sharper outline if they are considered against the background of the current thought patterns of his day. Above all others in the South, Jefferson accepted and spread the doctrines of French humanitarianism, formulating a complete libertarian philosophy saturated with sanctions for "natural rights," theories of social progress, and especially the principle of freedom in thought and action. Evidence of Jefferson's reliance upon various aspects of *freedom* as the foundation of his intellectual position is his own desire that his epitaph read "Author of the Declaration of Independence, of the Statute of Virginia for Religious Freedom, and Father of the University of Virginia."

In 1779, Jefferson drafted a comprehensive social program embodying much of the French humanitarian ideals. He proposed bills to eradicate the exclusive control held by the planter aristocracy over political and economic conditions. He proposed to lay the foundations for a more thoroughgoing democratic government by repealing the laws of entail and primogeniture, allowing religious freedom, abolishing taxation for an established church, and setting up a state system of universal free education. In his education bills, which, however, were not accepted by the legislature, he proposed a series of elementary schools distributed throughout the state, secondary schools for the more intelligent, and finally a reorganized and enlarged College of William and Mary to cap the system as a state university.

The College of William and Mary Germinates the Idea of Election. Jefferson's proposals to expand the curriculum of William and Mary are interesting to us as showing the beginnings of Jefferson's idea of what a university should be. His notion from the very start was to establish a genuine university "where every branch of science" should be taught, for he wished to depart from the traditional notion of college education which was so characteristic of the United States at the time. His outline for William and Mary as proposed in his bill of 1779 included eight broad divisions of study: the ancient languages, the modern languages, mathematics, natural philosophy and natural history, anatomy and medicine, history, law and government, and moral philosophy. The new trends were indicated by the inclusion of the modern languages, history, and law as well as by the greater emphasis given to scientific and medical studies on a par with the classics, mathematics, and philosophy. Outstanding also is the complete absence of religious studies except as history included ecclesiastical history.

It may be that in this first statement of his idea of a university Jefferson was influenced in part by his personal experiences in politics and law as well as by his earlier studies at William and Mary where he had come in close contact with a Scottish scientist, William Small, and with the prominent lawyer George Wythe.[1] Through his whole conception runs the belief in the dignity and possibilities of the human individual and in a broad education for leadership as the best way to maintain and promote political and intellectual liberty in a democracy. This recommendation is the first complete statement of Jefferson's conception of a university and was made before he had traveled in Europe or had been exposed to such educational proposals as those of Condorcet, Talleyrand, Quesnay de Beaurepaire, or Du Pont de Nemours.

That his plans in the proposed bills of 1779 were not idle fancies but were parts of a vital program is indicated by the actual changes that he made in the curriculum of William and Mary when he became a member of the board of visitors in 1779. According to Jefferson's own statement:

. . . I effected, during my residence in Williamsburg that year, a change in the organization of that institution, by abolishing the Grammar school, and the two professorships of Divinity and Oriental languages, and substituting a professorship of Law and Police, one of Anatomy, Medicine, and Chemistry, and one of Modern languages; and the charter confining us to six professorships, we added the Law of Nature and Nations, and the Fine Arts to the duties of the Moral professor, and Natural History to those of the professor of Mathematics and Natural Philosophy.[2]

It can readily be seen that Jefferson, when given the opportunity, actually made use of the principles embodied in his proposals in the bill of 1779. He made no mention of the transfer of William Smith's curriculum from the University of Pennsylvania to the College of William and Mary in 1776, as alleged by Smith's biographer.[3] If such an influence had been felt, Jefferson gave no recognition of it in his writings; and if we may judge from the number of subjects that Jefferson found in the

[1] H. A. Washington, *The Writings of Thomas Jefferson* (John C. Riker, Washington, D. C., 1853), Vol. I, pp. 2–3.

[2] *Ibid.*, p. 50.

[3] Horace W. Smith, *Life and Correspondence of the Rev. William Smith* (S. A. George and Company, Philadelphia, 1870), Vol. I, p. 124.

curriculum before he reformed it in 1779, there is no evidence of radical change since the beginnings of the college in 1693.

Jefferson made no specific reference to the elective principle in any of his writings at this time, but there are several evidences that it was applied in part during this period of reform.   Bishop James Madison,[1] who was president of William and Mary at the time, wrote in 1780 to Ezra Stiles, president of Yale:

The Society at present consists of a President, who is always to be one of the Professors, and is now Prof. of Math. and Nat. Phily., 2 of law and Police, 3 of Chymistry and Medicine, 4 of Ethics and ye Belles Lettres, 5 of Modern Languages. . . . The Prof. of Humanity has been abolished, the Professorship of · Divinity is also abolished.   It was formerly instituted for ye purpose of ye Church of England, wh. was here established, but it is now thought that Establishments in Favr. of any particular sect are incompatible with ye Freedom of a Republic, and therefore, ye Professorship is entirely dropped. . . . The Doors of ye University are open to all, nor is even knowledge in ye ant. Languages a previous Requisite for Entrance.   The Students have ye Liberty of attending whom they please, and in what order they please, or all ye diffr. Lectures in a term if they think proper.

The time of taking Degrees was formerly ye same as in Cambridge, but now depends upon ye Qualifications of ye candidate.   He has a certain course pointed out for his first Degree, and also for ye rest.   When Master of Either, ye Degree is conferred.[2]

Other evidences that some aspects of the elective principle were in vogue at William and Mary are given in the statements of H. B. Adams that a certain amount of election was allowed in the curriculum in 1830[3] and in a report made to the Virginia General Assembly by Professor William R. Rogers in 1845.[4]

We cannot be positive that this beginning of the elective principle was a direct result of Jefferson's reforms or of his ideas, but it so nearly approached the use of the "voluntary" system as instituted 46 years later at the University of Virginia that it may be said to be the logical outcome of his ideas.   Someone, if not Jefferson himself, perceived that if the curriculum were to be shaped by a broad conception of liberty, the student must be allowed some freedom in selecting what courses he

[1] Bishop James Madison was a cousin of the more famous James Madison who later was president of the United States.

[2] Quoted in Louis F. Snow, *The College Curriculum in the United States* (Teachers College, Columbia University, New York, 1907), pp. 74–75.

[3] H. B. Adams, "The College of William and Mary," *U. S. Bureau of Education, Circular of Information*, 1887, No. 1, p. 56.

[4] P. A. Bruce, *History of the University of Virginia* (The Macmillan Company, New York, 1920), Vol. I, p. 331.

desired to take or, if he wanted a degree, in what order and in what length
of time he would take the required courses.

It apparently was no mere accident that the first use of the elective
principle occurred in a college that instituted a considerable expansion
of the curriculum and that had dropped the confining influence so often
exerted where religious studies and the aim to train ministers prevailed.
The application of the elective principle, however, did not approach the
present-day notion that the student may present almost any studies that
he desires for receiving his degree.   Madison's letter shows that the
requirements for a degree remained fully prescribed, but some election was
allowed in the *order* in which studies might be taken and in the amount
of time spent by students in taking the required subjects.   The rigid
four-year class system seemed to have been broken up, and this fact
provided a good entering wedge for the later development of the free
elective system.

Whatever the extent of the elective system at William and Mary
in 1779, it seems to have been considerably wider than that of any other
college of the time and marks the beginning of an explicit enunciation
of the educational policy of allowing students themselves to exercise some
choice in the subjects that they took.   It is significant that this freedom
came only when the rigid class system was broken and when the aim
became the broad one of training for citizenship and leadership in a
democratic society instead of for leadership in an aristocratic church or
state.   In this way did the ideal of democracy, derived partly from
French intellectuals and adapted to suit the American scene, help to
sketch a broader conception of a higher education.

The University of Virginia Brings the Idea to Flower.   As Jefferson
was the guiding light of the reform of William and Mary, so was he instrumental in the founding of the University of Virginia which opened in
1825.   During this period of 46 years, from the time of his proposals in
the bill of 1779 to the opening of the University of Virginia, Jefferson's
conception of a university widened and expanded, but it remained essentially the same as embodied in his earlier principles.   Several writers on the
educational work of Jefferson, especially H. B. Adams,[1] have attributed
his conceptions of a university to the direct influence of French schemes
of education and to the universities of Europe during his sojourn in
France in the 1780's.   Although these may have influenced Jefferson's
general notions of higher education, the fact remains that all during his
stay in France, he considered the College of William and Mary the equal

---

[1] H. B. ADAMS, "Thomas Jefferson and the University of Virginia" *U. S. Bureau
of Education, Circular of Information,* 1888, No. 1, *passim.*   See also WILLIAM T.
FOSTER, *Administration of the College Curriculum* (Houghton Mifflin Company,
Boston, 1911), pp. 38 *ff.*

or superior of any European university for the American undergraduate.[1] Adams makes much of the fact that Jefferson considered the universities at Edinburgh and Geneva the best in the world, but a careful reading of Jefferson's letters shows that his judgment of these universities was influenced as much by his sympathies with their doctrines of political democracy as by their scientific or educational advances.[2]

It is possible, but never mentioned by him, that Jefferson derived an idea of the elective system from its use at the University of Edinburgh. Since the reforms in the curriculum of its arts faculty in 1708 (see page 53), this university had put more emphasis upon teaching and learning than upon graduation; thus the getting of a degree fell into disuse, and the "voluntary" system was widely practiced at the University of Edinburgh:

. . . as soon as graduation fell into disregard no such thing as a curriculum could really continue to exist. The main subjects of Arts teaching were there but each Student attended such classes as he or his friends might think advisable.[3]

Several attempts were made to reinstitute requirements for graduation; but with the absence of church control and the disappearance of the necessity for studying the arts courses as a prerequisite for the ministry, the desire for graduation expired, and attendance upon arts classes became purely voluntary. If Jefferson had been well acquainted with the University of Edinburgh, which seems not unlikely, he probably would have been favorably impressed by the quick acceptance of the new science and philosophy represented by Newton and Locke, by the lack of religious control, and consequently by the freedom of teaching and learning, as well as by the university's proclivities in favor of political democracy. Most speculation as to the sources of Jefferson's ideas must be gleaned from what he probably read and from the people that he knew rather than from what he actually wrote about himself.

By 1800, Jefferson's hopes for making a real university out of William and Mary had disappeared because of the decline of that college owing to financial losses and the removal of the capital of the state from Williamsburg to Richmond. Thenceforth, Jefferson became actively engaged in promoting a separate institution which eventually became the University of Virginia. To aid him in this project, he sought advice from many prominent men concerning the best scheme of organization for his proposed university, which was to be "an institution meant chiefly for use,"[4] "where every branch of science, useful at this day, may be

[1] Washington, *op. cit.*, pp. 466 *ff.*; Vol. II, pp. 175, 192, 427–428.

[2] *Ibid.*, Vol. III, p. 313.

[3] Alexander Grant, *The Story of the University of Edinburgh* (Longmans, Green & Company, London, 1884), Vol. I, p. 277.

[4] Washington, *op. cit.*, Vol. IV, p. 312.

taught in its highest degree."[1] He addressed, among others, the English scientists Joseph Priestley and Thomas Cooper, M. Pictet of the University of Geneva, John Adams, Caspar Wistar of the University of Pennsylvania, and George Ticknor of Harvard. Jefferson was also acquainted with the project of Quesnay de Beaurepaire to establish an academy of sciences at Richmond; with the proposed plan of Du Pont de Nemours for national education; and with the plans of other French, English, Scottish, and American writers on education. However that may be, the degree to which he was influenced by them cannot be certainly ascertained; nor is it possible to trace to any particular source direct evidences of influence upon his final conception of a university.

The course of study as eventually set up at the University of Virginia illustrates Jefferson's conception of a university. The university embraced eight separate "schools," each entirely independent of the others, and they covered virtually the same broad fields of study that Jefferson had proposed for William and Mary in 1779, namely, the ancient languages, the modern languages, mathematics, natural philosophy, natural history (later chemistry only), medicine, moral philosophy, and law. The chief differences were that in 1779 history had been proposed as a separate field, but in 1823 the history of each of the various nations was to be taken up in connection with the respective languages, and two separate schools were provided, respectively, for natural philosophy and natural history.

Students were allowed to choose which schools they would enter, but to get a diploma from a school the student had to take all the prescribed subjects in that school and write a final examination when he was ready. Thus, the student was allowed a certain freedom of choice as to the time and order of taking subjects but none as to the subjects that must be taken in order to get a diploma (general degrees were abolished in favor of specialized diplomas). The extent of subject matter covered by each school was considerably broader and more detailed than it had been 46 years before, but that fact represents not only the increase in Jefferson's conception of scientific knowledge through his study and acquaintance with scholarly men but also the actual increases in knowledge from new researches in many of these fields.

Yet, throughout all the writings of Jefferson during this period of the development of his ideal of higher education, there seems to be no explicit statement of the elective principle until his letter to George Ticknor in 1823:

I received in due time . . . your Syllabus of lectures on Spanish literature. I have considered this with great interest and satisfaction, as it gives me a model

[1] *Ibid.,* Vol. VI, p 356.

of course I wish to see pursued in the different branches of instruction in our University, i.e. a methodical, critical, and profound explanation by way of protection of every science we propose to teach.   I am not fully informed of the practices at Harvard, but there is one from which we shall certainly vary, although it has been copied, I believe, by nearly every college and academy in the United States.   That is, the holding the students all to one prescribed course of reading, and disallowing exclusive application to those branches only which are to qualify them for the particular vocations to which they are destined.   We shall, on the contrary, allow them uncontrolled choice in the lectures they shall choose to attend, and require elementary qualification only, and sufficient age.[1]

No mention of the elective principle had been made in the report of the Rockfish Gap Commission which had been appointed in 1818 by the Virginia legislature to draw up plans for the new university.   Even in the regulations adopted by the board of trustees in April of 1825, after the university had opened, there was no explicit statement of the intention to apply the elective system.

The first suggestion of election as a principle of educational practice for the University of Virginia, beyond the letter to Ticknor in 1823, is found in the regulations of the board of visitors on October 4, 1825, seven months after the university opened:

Each of the schools of the University shall be held two hours of every other day of the week; and that every student may be enabled to attend those of his choice, let their sessions be so arranged, as to days and hours, that no two of them shall be holden at the same time.[2]

Every student shall be free to attend the schools of his choice, and no other than he chooses.[3]

These regulations state also that the student shall receive a diploma for graduation in each school only after passing the requirements of that school and being able to read the "highest classics" in Latin.

It is evident that the modern idea of the elective principle was not formulated in Jefferson's conception of a university.   Whence it came cannot be determined exactly until further evidence is brought to light. For the present, we must say that the special notion of allowing students to choose their subjects was the logical outcome of Jefferson's developing theory of a university rather than the result of an influence proceeding from a particular source (except possibly the University of Edinburgh). The foundations for this conception were firmly laid as early as 1779,

[1] *Ibid.*, Vol. VII, pp. 300–301.
[2] Roy J. HONEYWELL, *The Educational Work of Thomas Jefferson* (Harvard University Press, Cambridge, 1931), p. 270.   This is surely one of the earliest forebears of the modern elaborate "timetables" that universities now devise for their hundreds of subjects.
[3] *Ibid.*, p. 272.

and all of his contacts with the various points of view which have been mentioned merely served to strengthen and broaden that foundation rather than to change it materially.   Every course of study that Jefferson proposed from 1779 to 1824 included the ancient and modern languages, mathematics, scientific studies, philosophy, law, medicine, and history. Jefferson's notions of higher education from first to last seem to have sprung from his general political and social philosophy of freedom and democracy and from his wide interests in science, philosophy, and law.

Jefferson's Theory of Higher Education. Education, Jefferson believed, was necessary for the preservation, welfare, and progress of a democratic society, and higher education must provide leaders for that democracy.   To fulfill its functions, the higher education must develop in the students a sense of freedom, political, economic, social, and intellectual; it must aid each individual in his own peculiar public or personal progress; it must provide subjects useful in preparation for a professional vocation.   Thus, the curriculum of a university must indeed be broad to fulfill Jefferson's aims.   In order to conform to his basic concepts of the function of higher education, the curriculum must allow the student to exercise his freedom, develop his individuality, and increase his usefulness to society.   This could be done most adequately, first, by providing scientific and political studies which would be practical and useful in life as well as providing the traditional linguistic and philosophical studies and, secondly, by allowing the student to enter the course most suited to his requirements.

Jefferson's correspondence was so extensive during the 45 years in which he was particularly interested in higher education that it is extremely difficult to extract essential influences and essential doctrines. It is unsafe merely to say that he derived the elective principle from French educational practice or theory, because that principle was not in vogue in the higher schools of France either while he was in France or when he was gathering data for the new university.   Furthermore, he never mentioned any especial regard for French universities at any time, and while he was in Europe the College of William and Mary appeared as favorably to him as any in Europe.   If he did get the notion of separate faculties or schools from French sources, as is likely, there was nothing in them which necessitated the adoption of the elective principle. Napoleon set up separate faculties of higher study but rigidly prescribed the course of study in each.

Indeed, Jefferson himself allowed election only as among schools and not among subjects within a school, provided the student wished a diploma from that school.   The only exercise of choice that rested with the student was his decision concerning which school or schools he would enter and the order and time in which he took the prescribed courses of that school.   Although this is not the modern form of the elective system, there was accomplished in this way an important preliminary step which was necessary before the elective system could be introduced into any curriculum, namely, the breakdown of the rigid class system in which each member of a class progressed regularly through each subject at the same time with all other members of his class for four years.

The importance of the University of Virginia in the development of the elective principle in the United States is not so much the extent to which the elective system was actually put into practice there but rather the fact that in the United States of those times it represented the broadest conception of what a university should be when based upon a democratic philosophy of freedom, individualism, and usefulness.   The University of Virginia had been widely publicized and consequently occasioned much discussion among the college circles of the day.   It was one of the first state universities set up by the civil states and relatively free from religious or sectarian control.

It clearly stated that democratic leadership was its aim and that useful subjects must be provided in the curriculum.   This meant to Jefferson political and social usefulness rather than vocational usefulness in the industrial or commercial sense, but it was a long step beyond the traditional feeling that literary and linguistic subjects were the best training for leadership in state and church alike.   The belief that what was best for prospective ministers was also best for laymen began to be really challenged.   The fact that after Jefferson's death the new university retreated somewhat from his advanced theories[1] does not destroy its importance in the history of educational theory, for it was widely copied by the colleges of the South after the Civil War.[2]   These colleges usually had the traditional prescribed curriculum and turned to the University of Virginia for guidance when they came to reorganize their courses.   Often this reorganization took the form of a compromise between the traditional prescribed courses and the idea of separate schools; and a certain amount of choice by the student was the outcome.

The direct influence of the University of Virginia in effecting changes in other colleges was confined, however, largely to the South, and for this reason it was perhaps not so noticeable in the general development of higher education in the United States as was the influence of the colleges of the North whose graduates were predominant in carrying their ideals

[1] The M.A. degree was instituted and was granted only after completion of the required courses of five of the schools.

[2] The direct or indirect influence of the University of Virginia was seen in such institutions as Roanoke College, Richmond College, South Carolina College, Randolph-Macon College, and the University of Florida.   See *Bureau of Education, Circular of Information,* 1888, Nos. 1, 2, 3, 4, 7.

to the West. Coupled with this is the fact that under the leadership of Harvard, the elective principle of the Northern colleges was made to apply directly to the traditional prescribed curriculum. The effects of experimentation such as that at Harvard and elsewhere could thus be watched by small traditional colleges which could take similar and gradual steps if desired, whereas the broad scope of the University of Virginia prevented any wholesale following of its example by the small colleges of limited financial resources.

Furthermore, the traditional conception of a liberal education was too strong in the educational theory of the times to allow the wholesale acceptance of the principles of social usefulness and specialization that the University of Virginia had enunciated. Consequently, the influence of Harvard was surer, if very slow, because it attacked more gradually the traditional prescribed curriculum rather than trying to uproot the whole system as Jefferson had aimed to do.

There were other factors that very likely militated against the spread of the influence of the University of Virginia and that are very interesting in the light of modern red-baiting in the universities of today. Conservative educators became quite alarmed at the growing freedom of student life at the University of Virginia which appeared to them to be a "license" brought about as a result of the deplorable abdication of absolute control by the faculty over the life of the students. The overthrow of strict ecclesiastical domination and the introduction of a great deal of physical science into the curriculum also doubtless served to frighten conservative and Federalist parents who were afraid of sending their offspring to be exposed to the "radical" doctrines and practices of French republicanism as represented by Jefferson and his godless university. Jeffersonian democracy, which has so often been invoked in latter days by conservative political orators and writers in the United States, found slow acceptance in American colleges of the early nineteenth century because of its radical nature.

TICKNOR AND HIS GERMAN IDEAL OF SCHOLARSHIP

Liberalism in New England. The currents of social humitarianism and reform were slower in taking effect in New England than in the South. The impress of a middle-class federalism upon patterns of life and thought in New England viewed with anathema the supposedly atheistic and democratic doctrines of French republicanism in the South. After the War of 1812, however, the decline of commercial enterprise following embargoes on American trade gave the intellectual classes a chance to gain the leadership of life and thought again for a few decades before the Industrial Revolution brought the commercial middle class back into dominance. So a renaissance took place in New England arising from the stimulus given by an idealism emanating from England and Germany as well as from France, a renaissance more intellectual and ethical than political or economic and having little in common with the French republican agrarianism that had appealed to the planter South and democratic West. These currents of thought had their own peculiar effect upon the colleges of New England, especially upon Harvard.

French liberalism crept into the theological doctrines of Boston and Harvard in the guise of Unitarianism when strictly theological standards began to relax during the period from the American Revolution to 1820. Unitarianism fostered belief in the inherent excellence of human nature in contrast to the Calvinistic conception of a debased human nature, and by disseminating the currents of French liberalism the Unitarians did for New England something of what Jefferson had done for the South. Unitarianism recovered in large part the original position of New England separatism which had posited belief in the principles of the open mind and free inquiry and which had allowed the individual to go where truth and individual responsibility led him. William Ellery Channing was one of the greatest of these liberal leaders imbued with the doctrine of God's love and man's excellence. Unitarianism captured Harvard, but the conservatives fought back strenuously, and the doctrines of Jonathan Edwards long helped to maintain Calvinism as a force, particularly in Connecticut. Andover Theological Seminary, founded in 1808, and such leaders as President Timothy Dwight of Yale and Nathaniel Walker, professor in Yale's Divinity School, marshaled the conservative forces for combating the Unitarian doctrine.

Along with the full flowering of the New England renaissance went the acceptance of German transcendentalism which virtually asserted that the divine essence was immanent in humanity, a sort of philosophical utopianism and equalitarianism established in metaphysics. When the open mind of Unitarianism had recovered the original Protestant principle of individual freedom and responsibility, idealism could break away from the conservative and federalistic theology of Jonathan Edwards. The young New England intellectuals found glimpses of a better age in Wordsworth and Shelley, Coleridge and Carlyle, Cousin and Madame de Staël, but they also discovered German transcendentalism to add to the beginnings of their Platonic idealism. Transcendentalism provided a metaphysical justification for idealism by routing the sensationalism of Locke and the skepticism of Voltaire and substituting the romantic gospel of a renascent Germany as Kant, Fichte, and Schleiermacher conceived it.

Ralph Waldo Emerson, the greatest proponent of transcendentalism in America, preached the divine sufficiency of the individual, reaching somewhat the same revolutionary doctrine that Rousseau, Jefferson, and Channing had formulated. Especially in his essay on *Education*,

Emerson attacked attempts to produce uniformity in all individuals and urged equality of opportunity for each individual to develop to the fullest his unique possibilities. Emerson felt that this could be done only by adapting education to the needs of each individual. A breadth of outlook through a breadth of studies and the inculcation of a sense of duty should be the aims of education. Emerson thus could be taken by educational theorists as furnishing a philosophical justification for adaptation of the curriculum to the student's needs, and this meant a justification for the elective system to break the lockstep of the prescribed curriculum. Other expressions of the spirit of reform were seen in Thoreau's efforts to find a satisfying life in naturalism, in Theodore Parker's natural religion, and in Margaret Fuller's efforts in behalf of feminism.

A different kind of intellectual activity in New England, not so radical as French or German liberalism, was represented by what has been called the "genteel tradition in letters."[1] It was marked by a refinement, a reticence, and a respect for literary "culture." Superior scholarship and literary excellence were more important ideals than social reform to such men as George Ticknor, Jared Sparks, George Bancroft, Henry Wadsworth Longfellow, Edward Everett, Josiah Quincy, and Francis Parkman. These men turned for literary inspiration partly to England and partly to Germany and for ideals of academic scholarship largely to Germany. It is natural that the German universities with their emphasis upon freedom and scholarship were more attractive to them than the French faculties which had been set up under rigid imperial control or the English universities where tests for Anglicanism were still given as prerequisites for getting a degree.

Largely through the infusion of German academic principles into Harvard by the growing stream of American students to and from German universities, the spirit of reform gained impetus. Out of these reforms grew a conception of scholarship that provided another justification for the use of the elective principle. Strangely enough, the same genteel tradition of letters and linguistic scholarship that long opposed practical studies and today favors a return to the prescribed classical curriculum was a prime factor in the 1820's toward justifying the elective system.

The period from the American Revolution to 1825 was one of gradual expansion for Harvard and of increase of professorships, students, and buildings. The beginnings of a medical school appeared as early as 1782; a botanical garden appeared in 1805; a separate law professorship was established in 1815; divinity was separated from the regular college course in 1819 and flourished during the ascendency of Unitarianism; and

[1] See V. L. PARRINGTON, *The Romantic Revolution in America* (Harcourt, Brace & Company, Inc., New York, 1927), for a general discussion of the intellectual development of this period.

a professorship of mineralogy was established in 1820.   Besides professorships separate from the regular college work, new subjects were added to
the required curriculum until it was nearly as extensive in 1791 as that
which the college of Philadelphia had attempted some thirty years earlier.

Slight evidences of the effect of theological liberalism may be dis-
cerned in the fact that by 1784 all students were no longer required to
take all the divinity offerings.   The divinity teacher evidently preferred
attendance only by those who intended to become ministers rather than
crowding his classes with students who planned to go into law, politics,
or medicine; hence juniors, seniors, and graduates who were not preparing
for the ministry were freed from some of the divinity studies.   Also,
by 1787 Hebrew had so declined in the estimation of the faculty that
French could be substituted for it in certain circumstances.   With these
minor exceptions, the whole round of courses continued to be required
despite the addition of subjects and the increase in amount of subject
matter.   Finally, under the presidency of John Thornton Kirkland
(1810–1828), the first enunciation of the elective principle as a guiding
force in curriculum organization was made by George Ticknor.

Ticknor and the Influence of the German Universities.   George
Ticknor was one of the young intellectuals who had been aroused by the
liberalism of the New England of his day but who leaned more toward a
life of letters and scholarship than to one of social reform.   He therefore
decided to turn to Europe to finish his literary studies and finally picked
out the University of Göttingen in Hanover as being most hospitable to
American students.   Having escaped the depredations of Napoleon's
wars, Göttingen in the early nineteenth century was being made illus-
trious by such scholars as Heyne, Eichhorn, Gauss, and Blumenbach.   In
the spring of 1815, young Ticknor arrived at Göttingen for a stay of 20
months.   He was particularly impressed by the advanced scholarship of
the lectures and by the erudition of his young Greek tutor who astonished
him by the variety, accuracy, minuteness, and readiness of his learning.
Believing that he saw a mortifying gulf between German and American
scholarship, he wrote: "We do not yet know what a Greek scholar is;
we do not even know the process by which a man is to be made one."[1]

In 1815, the University of Göttingen consisted of approximately 840
students and 40 professors (who were paid by the government) and as
many more lecturers.   Each professor gave two courses of lectures a
year (corresponding to our two semesters a year), and in consequence at
least 70 or 80 different lectures were going on all at the same time.
Impressed as he must have been by the size and organization of the

---

[1] GEORGE S. HILLARD, *Life, Letters, and Journals of George Ticknor* (Houghton
Mifflin Company, Boston, 1876), Vol. I, p. 73.   For a description of Ticknor's stay at
Göttingen, see Chaps. IV and V.

university in comparison to the small colleges of America, Ticknor was still more struck with the intellectual freedom of the German professors. He found that the students and faculty in their study of the metaphysical systems of Kant, Fichte, and Schelling were free to accept what they wished. He attributed the inclination of Germans for abstract idealism to two causes. There was, first, an extreme freedom in thinking, speaking, writing, and teaching, extending even to law, politics, and religion: "A more perfect freedom, and in most cases a more perfect use of it cannot be imagined than is now to be found in Germany. . . . "[1] Secondly, the German scholars represented an extreme mental activity, a surpassing desire to understand all systems of philosophy and to write everything in a discriminating spirit on a broad systematic plan.

During a six weeks' vacation in 1816, Ticknor and Edward Everett toured the cities of North Germany, visiting the principal universities and schools. Ticknor made extensive notes in his journal, devoting much space to the universities of Leipzig, Dresden, Berlin, Weimar, Jena, Halle, Wittenberg, and Gotha; descriptions of these were confined largely to impressions and descriptions of famous scholars whom he visited. Leaving his studies at Göttingen in 1817, he spent two years traveling and studying in France, Italy, Spain, and England, returning home to take up his duties as Smith Professor of French and Spanish languages and literature at Harvard in August, 1819.

Imbued as he was with German ideals of scholarship and intellectual freedom, Ticknor found it difficult to come back to Harvard and adapt himself to the old college system of textbook recitation.[2] In less than two years, he was so dissatisfied that he went to President Kirkland to promote a change, but he received no satisfaction. He then approached William Prescott who was a member of the corporation and was asked by him in July, 1821 to write out his ideas for reform. It is significant that these notes furnished the basis for the pamphlet published in 1825 that listed the proposed changes in the curriculum.[3] Prominent among these was the proposal to adopt the elective, or "voluntary," principle in curriculum organization. The corporation issued a circular to the faculty asking them to list all the changes that they desired in the college, but the great majority desired none, so the question of reform was dropped until two years later.

---

[1] *Ibid.*, p. 99. The loss today of the freedom that Ticknor so admired at Göttingen is dramatically illustrated by the refusal of so many universities of the world to attend its bicentenary celebration held on June 30, 1937.

[2] For a description of Ticknor's efforts for reform at Harvard, see *ibid.*, Chap. XVIII.

[3] GEORGE TICKNOR, *Remarks on Changes Lately Proposed or Adopted in Harvard College* (Russell and Carnei, Boston, 1825).

In a club meeting of a few faculty and corporation members, the subject of reform was again discussed, and Ticknor agreed to draw up a paper that he presented at a later meeting in July, 1823, and in which he reiterated and expanded the notes made previously.   The main point seemed to be that it was absurd to make all students attend all the classes of all instructors, for only a very superficial view of important subjects could possibly be gained even by those who were interested; and uninterested students were prevented from studying what would be of more importance and of more interest to them.   The proposal was therefore made that a limited amount of choice be allowed to students by breaking up the old "class" system.   Ticknor believed that there was some merit in the old system for those who were so young that they could not decide for themselves, but he also believed that no parents wished their sons to study branches of knowledge that could never be of use to them in later life:

A beneficial compromise can, however, as it seems to me, be effected between the old system still in operation, and the most liberal concessions that would be demanded by one of the merely free and philosophical universities of Europe.[1]

After Ticknor had read his paper, those present agreed to try to get the board of overseers to take some action; the result was that the board appointed Judge Joseph Story as chairman of a committee to draw up a report which was presented in June, 1824.   This report embodying Ticknor's ideas was incorporated in the new Harvard statutes of June, 1825.   As it was thought advisable to give the public some notice of the changes, Ticknor prepared an article at the instigation of the editor of the *North American Review;* but inasmuch as it was later rejected by that publication, he published it in September as a separate pamphlet.[2] These changes, opposed by an unfriendly faculty from the start and imposed upon them from above, were scarcely given a fair chance by any professor except Ticknor.   Those who were not openly hostile were largely unaccustomed to and unfamiliar with the new arrangements.

Ticknor in his department of modern languages was the only one to continue the new arrangements, and he found them very successful, writing to President Kirkland in April, 1827:

In the modern languages, especially, the operation of the principle of choice was decisive.   The right to choose was presented, it appears, in 240 instances, and was accepted in 227.   That it has been beneficial in this branch I have had full proof, in the alacrity and earnestness with which a very large proportion of those who have been permitted to choose have pursued the studies they have chosen.[3]

[1] HILLARD, *op. cit.*, p. 357.
[2] TICKNOR, *op. cit.*
[3] HILLARD, *op. cit.*, p. 366.

Ticknor also commented on the success of the division of French classes according to proficiency and indicated that the statutes for reform would have been successful in other departments if given a fair chance. There is clear evidence that he worked long and arduously to make his ideas successful in practice and to do the work of instruction as he felt it ought to be done along the lines of German scholarship.

After 1827, Ticknor was allowed to administer his own department in his own manner; and after Josiah Quincy became president of Harvard in 1829, Ticknor received more support and comfort than previously. Part of this was due to the fact that the college recovered under Quincy from some of the financial embarrassments that had resulted from too liberal expenditures of money and from the cessation of the money grants from the state during the administration of President Kirkland. With the help of such coworkers as Judge Story, Quincy was able to get liberal endowments for new professorial chairs and new buildings; all of this expansion was not only helpful but virtually essential to the successful operation of an extensive elective system.

Ticknor's Theory of Higher Education. It may be well at this point in the discussion to describe in some detail Ticknor's plan for the reform of the Harvard curriculum, inasmuch as it was the most complete expression of the theory of the elective principle that had yet been enunciated in the United States, and inasmuch as it presented most of the essential justifications for the elective principle that all later arguments made. Ticknor began the argument of his *Remarks* by listing the grounds for dissatisfaction with the existing state of learning in the college. The most pertinent of these for our purposes concerned the alphabetical arrangement of classes, the lectures, and the recitations. His description of the existing arrangement, known as the "class" system, follows:

The attempt to force together sixty or eighty young men, many of whom have nothing, or almost nothing, in common; who are of very unequal ages, talents, attainments, habits, and characters; and to compel them to advance *pari passu* during four of the most active and valuable years of life, giving to the most industrious and intelligent no more and no other lessons, than to the most dull and idle, is a thing that is unknown to the practical arrangements for education in other countries; that is not attempted in ours either before or after the period of college life; and that has been practiced at college only from adherence to an ancient arrangement, long after the motives for that arrangement had ceased to exist. For though it might be inevitable in the earliest period of the establishment at Cambridge, when there were fewer tutors than classes, and was, probably, less injurious in its operation, while the classes were quite small, and the instruction of their members by a general average not so likely of course to be an injustice to the best of them; yet, after the whole of this state of things was reversed, after the number of instructors was increased, till it amounted to four or five for each class, and the number of students to be taught together had risen to sixty or eighty, and a general average was necessarily become a great neglect and injustice to the most active and able, all ground for continuing the system of instruction on the old alphabetical and arbitrary arrangement of the classes failed. This arrangement, however, exists, in nearly all our colleges, and was continued at Cambridge from one period to another, partly from ancient usage and habit, and partly because it was not thought easy to alter what had been so long established.[1]

The lecture system was criticized because attendance on lectures was required whether or not the students were ready for them and because students were not required to take notes; recitations were inadequate because some classes contained as many as sixty students, all collected on the basis of the alphabet; and real teaching and learning of a subject were subordinated to the superficial scanning of a book.

With these criticisms of the existing conditions as a preliminary picture, Ticknor sketched the changes that had been instituted by the statutes of 1825 based upon Story's report. These reforms, for our purposes, may be classified as follows: opening Harvard to students who did not wish a degree; dividing the instructional staff into separate departments of study, such as Greek, Latin, mathematics, modern languages; allowing a certain amount of choice of studies to students; dividing classes according to proficiency; and, above all, a constant emphasis upon thorough teaching.

Throwing open the facilities of Harvard to all who wished instruction, whether they were seeking a degree or not, was designed to meet the wider demands of the nation for a useful education and especially to meet the competition of rising specialized schools (such as schools of agriculture, law, engineering, and medicine). The reformers evidently thought the increasing number of factories and the development of technical skills required that the college provide more practical instruction to all classes in the community in order to attract more students and increase the good will of the public.   In Story's report to the overseers in 1825, this problem is stated as follows:

With the view of meeting the demands of our country for scientific knowledge in the mechanical and useful arts, [the committee proposed that students not candidates for a degree be admitted] to pursue some particular studies to qualify them for scientific and mechanical employments, and the active business of life.[2]

Opening the college to this kind of student indicated a growing desire to break down the rigid curriculum, and this spirit was realized more

[1] TICKNOR, op. cit., pp. 5–6.
[2] C. W. ELIOT, Annual Report of the President of Harvard College, 1883–1884, p. 25.

particularly in the efforts to allow students to choose for themselves the studies that they desired to follow. The argument ran somewhat as follows: The number of separate studies, originally so few, have become so many and so easily extended that the old principle of requiring every student to pass through the hands of every instructor can no longer be wisely applied, inasmuch as the time for the whole college life has not been increased. With the advance of scientific knowledge and increase in numbers of instructors and students, the students must be permitted, at least within certain limits, to select their subjects.

Therefore, it was recommended that the curriculum be divided into separate departments in order (1) that the professor in charge may be held responsible for his department and turn the capacity of his students to the best account; (2) that each individual according to his capacity may learn thoroughly a systematic subject instead of merely the contents of a book; and (3) that the interest of students may be increased and the knowledge that they obtained made more valuable for their future purposes in life. In Ticknor's words:

And why should not the student or his friends determine in a greater or less degree, what studies he shall pursue, since more may be offered to him than it is possible he should pursue profitably? It were to be wished, indeed, that the choice could be left without limitation, and that the period passed at College could be thus more intimately connected with the remainder of life, and rendered more directly useful to it; but this, perhaps, is not yet possible with us, though it is actually doing in the University of Virginia, and will soon, it is hoped, be considered indispensable in all our more advanced colleges.[1]

Finally, the cornerstone of beneficial reform was considered to be the division of classes for recitation and teaching according to the level of attainment rather than according to the place of the student's name in the alphabet. It appeared a palpable injustice to require the active and brilliant students to go as slowly as the slowest in a class of 60 or 80 members; rather, they should be allowed to go forward as rapidly as their talents and the requirements of a thorough knowledge of the subject would carry them. Running through all the argument was the insistence of Ticknor upon thorough teaching and the attainment of high scholarship. He compared, to the disparagement of the American colleges, their methods with those of the European universities where emphasis was put upon painstaking commentary, explanation, and illustrative material. In concluding his *Remarks*, Ticknor made the plea again that Harvard and the other larger colleges should accommodate themselves more readily to the wants and spirit of the times; otherwise, newer institutions such as the technological schools and the state universities, which could adapt

[1] TICKNOR, *op. cit*, pp. 30 40.

themselves more readily to the needs of the people, would force the other colleges into the rear of the procession on the road to progress.

Summarizing Ticknor's theory of higher education, it may be said that it is strikingly modern in its tone and implications. His picture of a university is remarkably similar to the actual type of American university that finally developed. His ideal, borrowed mainly from the German concept of scholarship and infused into the college curriculum, helped to create a conception of higher education that finally altered considerably the college curriculum as it had originally come from the English universities. The final result was a compromise, and the arts curriculum in the United States became a unique mixture of many ingredients scarcely paralleled elsewhere in the academic world.

Ticknor's efforts for reform at Harvard are exceedingly important, especially in the history of the development of the elective principle, inasmuch as they illustrate some of the causes of the breakdown of the rigidly prescribed curriculum and the substitution of a more flexible course of studies. Paramount among these influences were, first, the demands of a growing capitalistic society that the college offer subjects less literary in emphasis and more useful for making a living; second, the demands of an increasingly democratic society that the aristocratic notion of a liberal education be democratized to include all types of students; third, the necessity of the several colleges to compete for students with each other and with the rising technical schools and state universities; and, fourth, the extension of the scope of the studies themselves until the student could not possibly encompass them all in four years.

Prompted by such causes, Ticknor and his associates introduced the reforms that we have been discussing in order to remedy what seemed to them the outstanding ills of the college curriculum. Dividing the course of instruction into separate departments, allowing selection of studies by students, and classifying students according to their academic progress were the schemes recommended. The advantages that they hoped would be derived from these schemes included: the benefit to society by preparing students to live more successful and useful lives; the economic benefit to the student by giving him a training which would be more valuable to his later life than the traditional academic studies of classical languages, mathematics, and philosophy; the educational benefits to the student by appealing to his interests and adapting the work to his capacities; and, above all, the benefits to scholarship arising from an emphasis upon careful teaching and thorough learning.

This is a remarkable statement of the theoretical justification for elective studies at a time when the prescribed curriculum was accepted so widely throughout the colleges of the period. Its importance looms larger even than the beginnings at the College of William and Mary and at the

University of Virginia, first, because it attempted to revise the actual curriculum from within rather than trying to establish an entirely new organization different from that of the usual college of the day, and, secondly, because the leadership of Harvard was longer and more influential upon the main currents of university development than was that of the institutions of the South.

Writers on the educational influence of Jefferson usually attribute the origins of the elective idea in America to him and to his effect upon Ticknor.[1] Discussion of this debatable issue is not particularly germane to our story but a few points may be recapitulated. Ticknor visited Jefferson in 1815, but there is no direct evidence that anything was said concerning the elective principle at that time. Some letters passed between them while Ticknor was in Europe, but again there is no evidence that Jefferson gave Ticknor any ideas on the subject that Ticknor could not have gathered much more easily from his direct contact with the workings of the European universities. Furthermore, we have shown that Jefferson made no specific reference to the elective principle until his letter to Ticknor in 1823, and we have seen that Ticknor had been working for reform at Harvard along elective lines as early as 1821. Indeed, he wrote to Jefferson in December, 1821:

I am very anxious to hear more about your University, and to learn something of its success. Every day persuades me anew of the truth of *an opinion I have long held*, that at Cambridge we shall never become what we might be very easily unless we are led or driven to it by a rival. I see no immediate prospect of such a rival except in your University, & therefore I long to have it in successful operation.[2]

Ticknor visited the University of Virginia in December, 1824, but that was seven months after Story's report, based upon Ticknor's ideas, had been presented to the Harvard overseers. It even seems likely that Ticknor had as much influence upon Jefferson as Jefferson, in turn, had upon Ticknor—possibly more.[3]

[1] Seee specially WILLIAM T. FOSTER, *Administration of the College Curriculum* (Houghton Mifflin Company, Boston, 1911), Chap. IV. Foster states explicity that Ticknor did not receive his ideals of reform from the German universities but obtained them from Jefferson. There is no direct evidence that Jefferson had formulated explicitly the elective principle before Ticknor had or that Jefferson gave the idea to Ticknor. The evidence seems to indicate, on the contrary, that Ticknor formulated the idea for himself from his German and his Harvard experiences and even may have influenced Jefferson.

[2] *Collections of the Massachusetts Historical Society*, 7th ser., Vol. I, p. 310. [Italics mine.]

[3] See pp. 93–94, where Jefferson shows that he is interested in copying for the University of Virginia the scholarly type of lecture that Ticknor was developing out of his German experience.

Whatever further evidence may contribute to this subject, it seems reasonable to say at present that Jefferson and Ticknor were merely different representatives of a growing intellectual liberalism which had its direct effects upon the college curriculum. Both urged that college studies be made more directly applicable to the daily business of living, but their emphasis was slightly different, and it is possible that they reached similar positions independently and designed their educational reforms in the light of their respective intellectual tendencies. Ticknor seemed to have little conception of Jefferson's emphasis upon the true place of a university in a democracy, and Jefferson seemed to have little notion of Ticknor's penchant for methods of attaining ripe scholarship through college studies. Both had a high regard for the nature and rights of the individual, but for Jefferson this regard was merely a part of his idea of individual freedom extending to all spheres of human endeavor, whereas for Ticknor freedom for the individual and for his interests and capacities was a necessary requirement for attaining a high degree of literary scholarship.[1] Ticknor's ideas exerted more influence upon the history of the American college and university with respect to the elective system, because they were formulated with telling effect and inserted into a college that provided strong support for them later in the century despite several preliminary setbacks. It was Ticknor's plan of allowing choice among several subjects all of which would be satisfactory for a degree that won out as the general type of elective system found in the modern American college.

The Ebb and Flow of Elective Studies at Harvard. The impetus given to elective studies at Harvard by Ticknor and his associates gained rather steadily against determined faculty opposition during the administration of President Josiah Quincy (1829–1846), but then the elective studies declined rapidly under the attacks of the conservative opposition led by Presidents Jared Sparks, Edward Everett, and James Walker, until a revival began again under Presidents Thomas Hill and Charles William Eliot in the 1860's. Ticknor was not alone in his efforts for reform, nor was he the only representative of the ideals of German education. Judge Joseph Story, as we have seen, was heartily in favor of his ideas; and several students, who had gone to Germany to study about the same time that Ticknor had gone, came back to teach at Harvard, notably Edward

---

[1] HILLARD, *op. cit.*, p. 368. Hillard paraphrased as follows the words written by Ticknor on the margin of his pamphlet: "The division of the classes by proficiency he regarded as indispensable, so long as the strictly academic character of the College was to continue; but he supposed that it would fall away naturally when the other important changes had taken effect, and an unlimited choice of studies, as in any university, had been introduced. His pamphlet was written wholly with this ulterior view and hope."

Everett, George Bancroft, and Joseph Green Cogswell. Bancroft and Cogswell became discouraged with Harvard methods during the formative period of Ticknor's reforms and left to set up a school for boys at Round-hill, Northhampton, Mass., based on the theories and methods of the Prussian *Gymnasium*. Ticknor was instrumental in getting appointed to the staff two German scholars, Charles Follen and Charles Beck, who tutored "voluntary" classes in the German language and who joined Ticknor's department of modern languages.

In 1835, Ticknor resigned, convinced that he could go no further along the lines of his reforms. His own statement of his attempts and results are illuminating:

I have been an active professor these fifteen years, and for thirteen years of the time I have been contending, against a constant opposition, to procure certain changes which should make the large means of the College more effectual for the education of the Community. In my own department I have succeeded entirely, but I can get these changes carried no further . . . more than half the instruction I have given has been voluntary. . . . Moreover within the limits of the department I have entirely broken up the division of classes, established fully the principle and practice of progress according to proficiency, and introduced a system of voluntary study, which for several years has embraced from 140 to 160 students; so that we have relied hardly at all on College discipline, as it is called, but almost entirely on the good dispositions of the young men, and their desire to learn. If, therefore, the department of modern languages is right, the rest of the college is wrong; and if the rest of the college is right, we ought to adopt its system, which I believe no person whatsoever has thought desirable, for the last three or four years. . . . [1]

The immediate outlook was not quite so gloomy as Ticknor had imagined. His successor, Henry Wadsworth Longfellow, also trained in Germany, continued Ticknor's policies in the department of modern languages. It is not at all surprising that agitation for the elective system should come first from the modern languages which were struggling for a place in the curriculum, but the cudgel of reform for voluntary studies was even taken up by instructors of the traditional studies—by Beck in Latin, Cornelius Felton in Greek, and Benjamin Peirce in mathematics. This group advocated so effectively the extension of the elective principle, and President Quincy was so successful in obtaining funds for new professors and new subjects, that the curriculum of 1841 showed more elective subjects than at any other time until the time of the most aggressive administrator of all, President Eliot.[2]

---

[1] HILLÁRD, *op. cit.*, p. 400.

[2] See C. W. ELIOT, *Annual Report*, 1883–1884, p. 13; and C. F. RICHARDSON and H. A. CLARK, ed., *The College Book* (Houghton, Osgood and Company, Boston, 1878), pp. 17–18.

The most forward-looking statements with respect to the elective principle at Harvard between Ticknor's period and the Civil War were made by President Josiah Quincy. He set the tone for his administration in his inaugural speech of 1829 in which he defined the function of the college in society. In his view, the college should be the intellectual leader of the community and should free the general mind from its vassalage to special creeds of politics or religion; students should be advanced in college according to their individual powers and acquisitions rather than by classes; special-course students should be given the benefits of higher education, but the standards of regular college work should not be lowered. In the light of our study of Ticknor and his ideas, these are familiar pronunciamentos. Quincy also lived up to the ideals of the advocates for higher scholarship by urging a doctrine very radical for the head of a respectable college of that day, namely, that Greek and Latin should be made elective.

In a pamphlet published in 1841, he set forth the arguments that the arts and sciences had so multiplied that it was impossible for a student to study all of them and that consequently there must be a selection.[1] He showed how a small class of learned men who were in charge of the colleges had long insisted upon the classics as the basis of a liberal education but that the larger and growing class of intelligent wealthy men were becoming less and less sure of the value of a classical education, submitting to it only so that their sons could get degrees. Quincy revealed how low the level of attainment in the classics had become by giving his estimate that a college class would easily be deprived of one-third of its members if a thorough individual examination were given to all. Therefore, he advocated that the classics be made elective subjects so that those who chose them could attain real scholarship in them as attested by an attainment examination and so that those who did not choose the classics would not draw the censure of the community by failing. Ticknor's efforts had not been completely in vain, but the traditional notion that a liberal education must be completely prescribed was too strong, and severe reverses in theory and practice under Quincy's immediate successors cut down virtually all the gains that had been made.

It might be expected that while Edward Everett was president of Harvard (1846–1848) he would have been favorable to the extension of elective studies because of his training in the German universities and his close acquaintance with their methods. Especially would this be expected in the light of his earlier ideas on university education as expressed in 1820.[2] While editor of the *North American Review* he had reprinted

---

[1] Josiah Quincy, *Remarks on the Nature and Probable Effects of Introducing the Voluntary System in the Studies of Latin and Greek* (Cambridge, Mass., 1841).

[2] "University Education," *North American Review*, 10: 115–137 (January, 1820).

Jefferson's prospective plans for the University of Virginia and had used them as an occasion for an extended discussion of what a university ought to be.   Many references were made to European universities, and the contrast was drawn between the German universities and the English or American college systems.   The proper idea of a university for Everett was evidently a place where all the branches of useful knowledge and all parts of a finished education were brought together to illustrate, adorn, and aid each other.   A hint that he might have favored the elective system in the United States was given when he said: "Is it not a defect of our university system, as well as of the English, that no reference is had to the destination of the student, but that he is required to dip into the whole circle of science?"[1]

During his short administration as president some 26 years later, Everett had evidently decided that Harvard must remain an English type of college rather than become a university of the German type, and the elective studies received their first major setback since they had first been introduced.   Everett asked the faculty to give their judgment upon the elective system as it had been working.   The answers varied, those who had used it favoring, and those who had not used it opposing, its extension. Consequently, a new scheme was adopted in December, 1846, which made all subjects again prescribed except three electives each for juniors and seniors.   This plan lasted with minor changes for 20 years.[2]   Everett's influence evidently had been thrown against the elective principle, and the reasons may be brought to light from a study of his inaugural address in which he outlined his conception of collegiate, or "academical," education as opposed to university education.[3]

Everett began his discussion by describing what the word "university" meant in France, Germany, and England and identifying Harvard with one of the colleges of an English university, the aim of which was to provide classical, mathematical, and philosophical training in order to supplement that of the school and to prepare for professional study.   He then listed in ascending importance the three major aims of academical, or collegiate, education as distinguished from those of university education:

1. The acquisition of knowledge in the various branches of science and literature as a general preparation for the learned professions and the other liberal pursuits of life was the least important of his three aims. The difficulty arises, however, in the fact that the fields of knowledge are so extensive that the student covers them only superficially and that

[1] *Ibid.*, 10: 125–126.

[2] WILLIAM R. THAYER, *An Historical Sketch of Harvard University* (Cambridge, 1890), pp. 35–36.

[3] EDWARD EVERETT, *Orations and Speeches on Various Occasions* (Little, Brown & Company, Boston, 1853), Vol. II, pp. 493–518.

much of the knowledge is not directly practical or valuable to later professions. Furthermore, the marked diversity in the taste and capacity of individuals and the consequent variety of pursuits that they adopt must be recognized, as well as the inordinate demands on the time of the student if he is required to devote himself to the whole circle of studies. To meet these circumstances, the elective system had been introduced, and Everett believed that it had helped somewhat to promote the future usefulness of students and that it had fallen in with the tastes or bent of the individual. From the very first, however, he was very cautious about committing himself:

The theory of this system seems reasonable; it has, however, been introduced since my own academical experience terminated, and I have had as yet no means of forming an opinion for myself of its practical operation.[1]

2. The next most important aim of collegiate education was the exercise, development, and training of the intellectual faculties (attention, perception, memory, judgment, abstraction, and imagination). The mental faculties were thought to be in some peculiar manner modified, strengthened, and perfected by special disciplinary subjects which were, of course, the classical languages, mathematics, the moral sciences (philosophy), and astronomy. This approximated the theory of mental discipline which probably stemmed from the philosophy of John Locke and which had been given specific formulation in the report of the Yale faculty some 20 years earlier (see next chapter).

3. The most important aim of academical training was the formation of a "pure and manly character," built upon the moral and religious principle of Christianity. A biographer emphasizes Everett's especial concern for the moral welfare of the student and his efforts to protect students from temptation and bring them under religious influences.[2]

With this picture of Everett's conception of higher education, it appears more reasonable that he should not actively favor the elective principle. First of all, he looked upon Harvard as a college for intellectual and moral discipline rather than as a free university where all branches of knowledge should be taught; secondly, the special efficacy of classical, mathematical, and philosophical studies for mental discipline in his judgment gave them the place of greatest importance in the curriculum, and naturally, therefore, they should be prescribed for all students; and, thirdly, because of the dominance of religious and moral motives, slight importance was put upon the value of material, commercial interests and the physical sciences, which therefore would not be allowed equivalent place in the student's course for a degree. Under these conceptions of

[1] *Ibid.*, p. 503.
[2] R. H. DANA, *Life and Services of Edward Everett* (Cambridge, 1865), p. 43.

collegiate training, Harvard was put off the course set by Ticknor and Quincy toward adopting broad university methods and steered back to the traditional studies of the college.

President Jared Sparks (1849–1853) continued the policy of restriction with regard to elective studies, until by 1850 all studies were again prescribed except that one elective subject of three hours was allowed to juniors and seniors. Sparks's inaugural address[1] showed that he was going to continue the view expressed above that college training should be aimed at discipline, intellectual training, and the development of mental power. He upheld the traditional required courses of four years and even advocated the retention of the class system because it was more democratic than the division of students according to the level of their advancement in a subject. He opposed the elective system as "sacrificing the many to the few." Instead, he urged that the level of scholarship should be raised and the means of education applied to all alike; this he felt was more democratic. Election should apply to the choice of profession or object in life rather than to the strict college discipline that Harvard was attempting to give. Scholarship meant for him acquaintance with all the fields of liberal knowledge rather than being highly accomplished in one field. He contended, too, that the student was not the best judge of what was best for him.

In his report for 1849–1850, Sparks justified as follows his restriction of elective studies:

This system [elective] was attractive in theory, but in framing it the consideration was not sufficiently weighed, that what was gained in one study was necessarily lost in another. . . . The system was subjected, however, to a fair and patient trial. In practice, it never fulfilled all the expectations of its framers, and it soon began to fall into partial disfavor.[2]

It is evident that Sparks and his associates were then determined to include the whole round of studies developed at Harvard as the minimum essentials of discipline and liberal training. However, the apprehension that this restrictive policy could not last for long was indicated by Sparks's own statement in his report of 1851–1852:

The voluntary system, as it has been called, is still retained to a certain extent, rather from necessity than preference. The number and variety of the studies for which the University has provided instruction are so large that it is

[1] H. B. ADAMS, *The Life and Writings of Jared Sparks* (Houghton Mifflin Company, Boston, 1893), Vol. II, pp. 444–446. Sparks received the hearty support of Yale for his position on the elective system. Professor James L. Kingsley wrote to him soon after the inaugural: "Your views on these subjects are precisely my own" (p. 444).

[2] RICHARDSON and CLARK, ed , op. cit., p. 10.

impossible for the student, within the period of four years, to give such a degree of attention to them as will enable him to acquire more than a limited and superficial knowledge from which little profit can be derived.[1]

Nevertheless, fifteen years passed before Ticknor's emphasis upon the elective principle as a necessary requisite for high scholarship was again made the policy of Harvard, for President James Walker (1853–1860) continued Sparks's practices. A vivid picture of methods under President Walker was given by Watson Goodwin, who tells us that the required system was in its typical perfection when he came to Harvard in 1856 as a tutor in Greek and Latin.[2] All subjects were required except that juniors and seniors were allowed one elective. Goodwin favored making Greek and Latin elective because of the benefits to scholarship, inasmuch as under the required system the standard of scholarship was set by the average or slow student instead of the best. His obvious recommendation was division of classes on the basis of proficiency, but the plan had few advocates on the faculty, and President Walker told him severely, when he suggested it, that such a plan was opposed to the established policy of the college.

Goodwin also indicated in his pamphlet that the voluntary system was naturally opposed by the slower students and especially by their parents, inasmuch as it made too obvious the distinction between poor and good students. The argument that scholarship was declining under the old system received further impetus when Goodwin pointed out that, as new subjects were added to the curriculum each year, some reduction had to be made in the time given to the old ones. Even before the use of a generous elective system, the amount of time given to classical studies had to be greatly decreased to give time for each newly prescribed subject. Written examinations also required a higher standard of attainment in each subject, and thus even less time was given for pursuit of subjects that students preferred. Consequently, the raising of the standard of attainment under the required system really impeded scholarship because the overworked student did not have time to do justice to all subjects.

With this somewhat extended discussion of Harvard, we must turn to developments that tended to promote or to hinder the acceptance of the elective principle in other colleges during the period from the American Revolution to the Civil War. This discussion of the ebb and flow of the practice of the elective studies at Harvard has brought out a great many of the arguments for and against the theory of election that were advanced throughout the collegiate world of the day. Among these the ideal of scholarship fostered by the genteel tradition appeared most frequently as justification for the elective principle, and the ideal of mental discipline

[1] THAYER, *op. cit.*, p. 36.
[2] WATSON GOODWIN, *The Present and Future of Harvard College* (Boston, 1891).

and reluctance to change appeared most often in opposition. The theory of mental discipline was by no means originated at Harvard but was inherited from Europe and was given its most forceful statement in America by the Yale faculty at about the same time that the elective principle began to make its way at Harvard.

In the next chapter, we shall examine the doctrine of mental discipline as enunciated at Yale; then, in a succeeding chapter, we shall discuss other efforts for reform of the college curriculum before the Civil War. The aristocratic and linguistic tradition of a liberal education was challenged in theory by Jefferson and Ticknor, but the theory of mental discipline continued to dominate the practice of college education until the last half of the nineteenth century. It was not until then that an aggressive society with a characteristic mixture of democracy and individualism, of industrialism and capitalism, demanded that individual and social usefulness should become the criterion of college curriculum offerings.

CHAPTER VII

THE COLLEGE CONTROVERSIES TAKE SHAPE: CONSERVATIVES

The first half of the nineteenth century was a period of considerable debate and discussion concerning the unique functions of the American college and its fitness to serve American life. The educational fraternity began to divide roughly into two factions: those conservatives who wished to retain the traditional college virtually as it was handed down from the past; and those reformers, or progressives, who felt that the American college was falling too far behind the pace of American life and too much out of touch with the realities of American society. We have discussed at some length the efforts of progressives at the University of Virginia and at Harvard, but it must not be forgotten that the reformers as yet were virtually voices crying in the wilderness of tradition, for the weight of educational judgment and even of public opinion seemed to be on the side of the classical form of a liberal education. The progressives, however, were beginning to be heard, and the entering wedges of such men as Jefferson, Ticknor, and Quincy brought the conservatives to the battle. Numerous speeches, inaugural and commencement addresses, debates and discussions, pamphlets and articles attested to the beginnings of heated controversies which are still going on today.[1]

The demands of a growing industrial society for a practical education and the voice of a democracy which was raised to urge that all youth should have an opportunity to receive an appropriate college education left the conservatives cold. They were certain in their belief that the traditional classical and linguistic education was the best kind of education no matter what kind of society was developing outside college walls. The Reverend John M. Mason was saying in the first decade of the nineteenth century:

Experience has shown that with the study or neglect of the Greek and Latin languages, sound learning flourishes or declines. It is now too late for ignorance, indolence, eccentricity, or infidelity to dispute what has been ratified by the seal of ages.[2]

[1] For an excellent summary of the controversy in the second quarter of the nineteenth century, see George P. Schmidt, "Intellectual Crosscurrents in American Colleges, 1825–1855," *American Historical Review*, 42: 46–67 (October, 1936).

[2] JACOB VAN VECHTEN, *Memoirs of John M. Mason* (Robert Carter and Brothers, New York, 1856), p. 239.

In the *Western Review* of Cincinnati, it was prophesied in 1820:

Should the time ever come when Latin and Greek should be banished from our Universities, and the study of Cicero and Demosthenes, of Homer and Virgil should be considered as unnecessary for the formation of a scholar, we should regard mankind as fast sinking into absolute barbarism, and the gloom of mental darkness as likely to increase until it should become universal.[1]

Not only was scholarship likely to disappear, but the whole future of civilization in general and of the United States in particular was in danger of collapse, so thought Lyman Beecher in 1836, if college men were not trained in Greek, Latin, logic, philosophy, and the Bible.[2]

Thus spake some of the conservatives, and their doctrines were not confined to the traditional colleges of the East but were carried far and wide to the West and to the South. The decades of the thirties and forties saw not only a rapid westward expansion of population and a tremendous spread of religious evangelism, but they also witnessed a marked acceleration in the founding of colleges all over the country by the various religious denominations.[3] Not only were the Presbyterians, Methodists, Baptists, and Congregationalists particularly active in spreading the gospel, but they also concerned themselves with establishing many colleges to aid in the training of devoted and learned ministers to care for the greatly increased numbers of members who were swept into the churches during this second Great Awakening.

As the religious fervor served to combat the rationalism and deism of French philosophy, so the denominational colleges reestablished the religious aim as the paramount purpose of college education and served to entrench still further the traditional notion of a liberal education which had combined religious with literary and linguistic qualities during the Renaissance and Reformation. The missionary zeal of the various Protestant denominations resulted in the spread of denominational colleges through the West and the South as one of the best ways to combat infidels and Roman Catholics. In this way, the religious colleges of the West relied in great part upon the religious culture of the conservative colleges of the East. Yale, the stronghold of orthodox Congregationalism, and Princeton, the stronghold of orthodox Presbyterianism, became notably the greatest "mothers of colleges."

---

[1] FRANK LUTHER MOTT, *A History of American Magazines*, 1741–1850 (Harvard University Press, Cambridge, 1930), p. 146.

[2] LYMAN BEECHER, *A Plea for Colleges* (Cincinnati, 1836) p. 19.

[3] For the detailed story, see Donald G. Tewksbury, *The Founding of American Colleges and Universities before the Civil War* (Teachers College, Columbia University, New York, 1932).

Since it is estimated that Yale and Princeton furnished the largest number of presidents and professors to the colleges of the West and South,[1] it is small wonder that the new colleges looked to the East and saw little but good in the traditional liberal education, despite the exigencies and necessities of life on the frontier. For example, Joseph Caldwell was a graduate of Princeton, and when he went as president to the University of North Carolina (1797–1835) he replaced the somewhat progressive curriculum that he found there with the traditional studies characteristic of his alma mater.[2] Another example is contained in the inaugural address at Randolph-Macon College in 1834 by Stephen Olin, a prominent Methodist clergyman and educator, who rejected the idea of experimenting with the curriculum of a new college as unwise and dangerous.[3]

Suffice it to say here that the traditional point of view remained preeminently strong during the first half of the nineteenth century, and of the statements in its defense there seems to be one that stands out above all the rest. That statement came naturally enough from the faculty at Yale which felt called upon to silence the reformers and doubters once and for all and to assert the essential unity between religious and mental discipline. We have seen how Harvard had returned under Presidents Everett, Sparks, and Walker to the traditional ideals of a liberal education and how the strictly religious aims of college education were again in the ascendancy along with the added support of mental discipline. The Enlightenment psychology of Locke and Watts was taken by American college educators and reconciled with their own religious conceptions of college education to produce the ideal of mental discipline. Religious justification for prescribed studies became intertwined with disciplinary justifications of prescribed studies, and together they contrived to maintain widespread control over the aims and practices of the colleges of America during the first half of the nineteenth century. The most effective statement of the theory of religious and mental discipline was given in the report of the Yale faculty described in the following pages.

THE IDEAL OF MENTAL DISCIPLINE: YALE REPORT OF 1828

Whereas the expanding curriculum at Harvard during the period between the American Revolution and the Civil War had combined with German ideals of scholarship and the genteel tradition to produce alternate advocacy and opposition to the elective principle, Yale held steadily

[1] George P. Schmidt, *The Old Time College President* (Columbia University Press, New York, 1930), p. 96.

[2] Kemp P. Battle, *History of the University of North Carolina* (Edwards and Broughton Printing Company, Raleigh, N. C., 1907), Vol. I, pp. 95 *ff.*

[3] *The Works of Stephen Olin* (Harper & Brothers, New York, 1852), Vol. II, p. 275.

despite its expanding curriculum to a policy of prescribing virtually the complete course of study. In 1828, only a few years after Harvard had first enunciated its theory of elective studies, Yale explicitly and forcefully formulated, in opposition to Harvard's position, the doctrine that a liberal education can be attained only by following a strictly prescribed college curriculum based upon considerations of mental discipline. The course of study at Yale had developed similarly to that of Harvard: Under President Timothy Dwight, chemistry, mineralogy, and geology had been greatly advanced by Benjamin Silliman; mathematics and natural philosophy, by Jeremiah Day; and the ancient languages, by James L. Kingsley.

Soon after Day succeeded to the presidency of Yale in 1817, various complaints, of which Ticknor's was perhaps outstanding, began to be more generally heard that college studies were unprofitable and that they should be altered in order to improve the scholastic attainments of students and to meet the practical and commercial wants of the times. The Yale faculty set out to scotch these complaints and to hold firm to its belief that the methods of university studies should not be extended to college work. In answer to a request of the trustees for faculty opinion on the proposal to make the classics elective along with the modern languages, the faculty set forth its educational creed. They believed that proper college instruction should emphasize the "intellectual ability" of students rather than the amount of knowledge that they acquired, that certain studies were best suited to develop this intellectual power, and that experience had plainly shown that these subjects which were necessary for a liberal education would serve as a preparation for any sort of lifework. The statement of this doctrine of mental discipline was so striking and exercised such great influence upon the educational theory of the American college for several generations that it will be described somewhat at length in the following paragraphs.[1]

The report of the Yale faculty (written by President Day) began by stating that the course of study at Yale had expanded in the past and that it would not remain static in the future but that, on the contrary, it should accede to the demands of society. It was hastily asserted, however, that such accession was to extend only so far as the "proper functions" of a college were not jeopardized. The aim of college education, the report stated, is quite different from that of a university: The aim of the college was clearly the development of intellectual power through mental discipline, and to this end the college should "lay the foundation of a superior education":

---

[1] "Original Papers in Relation to a Course of Liberal Education," *American Journal of Science and Arts*, 15: 297–351 (January, 1829).

The two great points to be gained in intellectual culture, are the *discipline* and the *furniture* of the mind; expanding its powers, and storing it with knowledge. The former of these is, perhaps, the more important of the two. A commanding object, therefore, in a collegiate course, should be, to call into daily and vigorous exercise the faculties of the student. Those branches of study should be prescribed, and those modes of instruction adopted, which are best calculated to teach the art of fixing the attention, directing the train of thought, analyzing a subject proposed for investigation; following, with accurate discrimination, the course of argument; balancing nicely the evidence presented to the judgment; awakening, elevating, and controlling the imagination; arranging, with skill, the treasures which memory gathers; rousing and guiding the powers of genius.[1]

No faculty of the mind may be neglected in a college course, the proper completion of which should bring a student to the full perfection and harmonious balance of all his powers. Thus, there must be a fair proportion between the different branches of the sciences and literature: mathematics to develop the reasoning powers; the physical sciences to promote familiarity with facts and inductive processes; ancient literature to provide the best models of taste; logic and mental philosophy to teach the art of thinking; rhetoric to teach the art of speaking; English reading, composition, and discussion to provide facility in the language of everyday use:[2]

In our arrangements for the communication of knowledge, as well as in intellectual discipline, such branches are to be taught as will produce a proper symmetry and balance of character. We doubt whether the powers of mind can be developed, in their fairest proportions, by studying languages alone, or mathematics alone, or natural or political science alone.[3]

Despite the fact that the college must develop all of the mental faculties through a rounded course of studies, both literary and scientific, the college course should not include all subjects; it must merely lay a foundation and not try to provide professional studies or mercantile, mechanical, or agricultural subjects. These latter must be built upon the foundations of theory and principle common to all pursuits; and the college should not and cannot prepare directly for business, farming, or the professions:

The great object of a collegiate education, preparatory to the study of a profession, is to give that expansion and balance of the mental powers, those liberal and comprehensive views, and those fine proportions of character, which

[1] *Ibid.*, pp. 300–301.

[2] *Cf.* here the recent proposals of Robert M. Hutchins, *The Higher Learning in America* (Yale University Press, New Haven, 1936), p. 33: "The classics provide models of excellence," etc.

[3] "Original Papers," *op. cit.*, p. 303.

are not to be found in him whose ideas are always confined to one particular channel.[1]

As our course of instruction is not intended to complete an education, in theological, medical, or legal science; neither does it include all the minute details of *mercantile, mechanical,* or *agricultural* concerns. These can never be effectually learned except in the very circumstances in which they are to be practised.[2]

The report reaffirms the position that the American college should follow the traditional pattern of the communal English college. Owing to the age of college students, the college must provide a substitute for parental guidance; hence, students and faculty must live together in proper buildings, and tutors must care for the strict surveillance and policing of students' moral and social life as well as the discipline of their intellectual life.

Following to the end the logical conclusions of this conception of a college, the Yale faculty stood directly opposed to the elective principle. The following paragraph contends that the elements of a thorough education have been determined satisfactorily for all time and that none may be omitted or substituted without destroying the whole:

But why, it is asked, should *all* the students in a college be required to tread in the *same steps?* Why should not each one be allowed to select those branches of study which are most to his taste, which are best adapted to his peculiar talents, and which are most nearly connected with his intended profession? To this we answer, that our prescribed course contains those subjects only which ought to be understood, as we think, by every one who aims at a thorough education. They are not the peculiarities of any profession or art. These are to be learned in the professional and practical schools. But the principles of science are the common foundations of all high intellectual attainments . . . so in a college, all should be instructed in those branches of knowledge, of which no one destined to the higher walks of life ought to be ignorant. What subject which is now studied here, could be set aside, without evidently marring the system? Not to speak particularly, in this place, of the ancient languages; who that aims at a well proportioned and superior education will remain ignorant of the elements of the various branches of the mathematics, or of history and antiquities, or of rhetoric and oratory, or natural philosophy, or astronomy, or chemistry, or mineralogy, or geology, or political economy, or mental and moral philosophy?[3]

[1] *Ibid.*, pp. 308–309.

[2] *Ibid.*, pp. 309–310. *Cf.* here the recent strictures on American higher education made by Abraham Flexner, *Universities, American, English, German* (Oxford University Press, New York, 1930), p. 177. Flexner attacks the advent of practical and commercial courses of all kinds in the college which properly should confine itself to the development of "intelligence, capable of being applied in any field whatsoever."

[3] "Original Papers," *op. cit.*, pp. 312–313. Those college educators today who feel that they have the final answer to the college curriculum should note again how such final answers as the foregoing sound in the light of new knowledge and new experiences.

Such a notion was based on the theory that the student should not specialize or avoid certain courses as not fitting his taste or capacity until he had sampled all important fields of a liberal education.   The object of college training was not to give what the Yale faculty deemed a "partial," or "superficial," education (meaning the absence of Greek and Latin), but it was to begin a thorough education and carry it as far as four years would allow.

The report was firm in asserting that the American college should not be modeled after the universities of Europe.   In an unmistakable reference to Harvard's attempts to reform itself on the pattern of German universities the fervent hope is expressed that Yale may be "spared the mortification of a ludicrous attempt to imitate them": A large outlay of money would be required and would not be easily forthcoming; American students were less mature and not so well prepared; and the German universities were really professional schools.   The American college is comparable, so ran the argument, to the German *Gymnasium* rather than to the German university:

It would, in our opinion, be idle to think of adopting in the college, the regulations and plan of instruction in a university; unless the students of the former were advanced three or four years farther than at present, both in age and acquirements.   Would parents in this country consent to send their sons, at the age of sixteen, to an institution in which there should not be even an attempt at discipline, farther than to preserve order in the lecture room?[1]

Even if the surplus funds were available to establish a separate course in arts, along with separate law and medical courses, the college should retain its disciplinary character as preparatory to all further study. Even if time prevents the study of all the subjects desired in a complete and thorough liberal education, the attempt should be made; and the student should set out upon his full course and go as far as time allows, rather than limit his activities in such a way that he will be left with a onesided, or "partial," training.

It is admitted by the framers of the report that there should be no democracy in college education, for all of the population would not be able to benefit from such a thorough course as proposed.   Many must be content with merely an elementary school training or the partial education offered by academies or, again probably referring to Harvard, "in some institutions which furnished instruction in any branch or branches selected by the pupil or his parents."   They admitted that the public is right in insisting that every class of society be provided with appropriate education, but they maintained that it is not the function of the college to make such provision; that should be left to the academies,

---

[1] *Ibid.*, p. 316.

high schools, and technical institutions.[1] The college must maintain the integrity of the bachelor's degree in order to give meaning to a liberal education that is superior to that of the academies or lower institutions. Increasing the numbers of students at the colleges by offering practical courses means nothing if the quality of the degree is lowered; it is more important and ultimately more advantageous for a college to keep its standards high and its degree respected than to stoop to rivalry for large numbers of students. The faculty felt that the elevated quality of the college degree could be maintained only if the college strictly adhered to a policy aimed at "intellectual culture" through a thorough course of study as outlined in the first part of their report.

The second part of the report (written by Professor James L. Kingsley) was concerned more particularly with the place of the ancient languages in a liberal education and defended the insistence upon the study of Greek and Latin in the college curriculum. His arguments are similar to most of the future justifications for setting up the ancient classics as studies superior to all others for purposes of mental discipline and culture. Classical literature as a component part of the college curriculum was defended on the grounds that the state of knowledge and learning in the United States at that time required the continued study of the ancient languages. Students needed classical training to be able to discuss cultural matters on a par with European scholars:

If scholars, then, are to be prepared to act in the literary world as it in fact exists, classical literature, from considerations purely practical, should form an important part of their early discipline.[2]

Apart from these "practical" purposes and upon an independent basis, the classics were considered important for cultivating all the "faculties of the mind," ranging from memory, judgment, and reason to taste and imagination:

Familiarity with the Greek and Roman writers is especially adapted to form the taste, and to discipline the mind, both in thought and diction, to the relish of what is elevated, chaste, and simple. The compositions which these writers have left us, both in prose and verse, whether considered in reference to structure, style, modes of illustration, or general execution, approach nearer than any others to what the human mind, when thoroughly informed and disciplined, of course approves; and constitute, what it is most desirable to possess, a standard for determining literary merit.[3]

[1] *Ibid.*, pp. 317–318. *Cf.* here again the recent arguments made by Hutchins, *op. cit.*, Chaps. I and II, and those of Flexner, *op. cit.*, pp. 37 *ff. et passim.*

[2] "Original Papers," *op. cit.*, p. 328.

[3] *Ibid.*, p. 329.

By analogy, Greek literature furnished models of perfection as Greek sculpture and architecture provided standards of excellence for all time.

Furthermore, the classics were believed to provide the best preparation for the professional studies of divinity, law, and medicine. The modern languages were considered to be distinctly inferior for such professional preparation; and they were also inferior for mental discipline, for the practical pursuits of scholarship, and even for the understanding of English literature: "To establish this truth, let a page of Voltaire be compared with a page of Tacitus."[1] If a course of study were established on the basis of the modern languages, the faculty feared that so many students would enter it to avoid the more difficult work of the classical course that professional and academic levels of attainment would be materially lowered. The modern languages were relegated to be studied as social accomplishments rather than as necessary acquisitions.

The classics could not be required for admission to college, and then a choice allowed, because a large group could complain with truth that the little classical study they had done in preparatory school was worthless and forgotten as soon as learned. Therefore, the argument ran, the classics must be prescribed in the college course. If the classics were done away with or made optional, the value and meaning of the bachelor of arts degree would be gone; and for similar reasons, students who are not candidates for a degree should not be allowed to take courses in the prescribed curriculum along with candidates for the degree. The faculty was certain that the supporters of Yale did not demand change and that there was nothing to be gained in departing from a tradition that had long been tried and found worthy.

The report, by showing how the curriculum had expanded in number of subjects and extent of subject matter from the earliest days of the college to 1828, defended Yale against charges that the colleges of the United States were lagging behind the requirements of a rapidly changing society. Excerpts from Ticknor's *Remarks* of 1825 were quoted to indicate the kind of stricture that was being leveled at American colleges, and Yale was defended from the charges that examinations were farcical and that no thorough teaching was done. It was shown in defense that Yale examined each class (orally) twice a year and that seniors were given examinations lasting three days. To prove that thorough teaching produced real scholars at Yale, appeal was made by the report to "general notoriety."

With this comprehensive statement of the aims and functions of college education to guide its policy for many years, it is no wonder that Yale long continued to hold firm to the linguistic and aristocratic conception of a liberal education and to oppose such "radical" changes in

[1] *Ibid.*, p. 332.

the college curriculum as would admit practical subjects to the curriculum or the hordes of democracy to college halls. Firmly fortified with the doctrines of mental and religious discipline, confident that eternal and fixed educational truth had been found, determined to preserve the *status quo*, and lacking sufficient funds to do otherwise, the attitude of the Yale faculty is represented, in part at least, by the following statement contained in a letter in 1841 from Professor James L. Kingsley to Professor Benjamin Silliman:

This [Harvard's proposed change] is a much more *radical* proceeding than I anticipated. . . . I am not bigoted in my attachment to old plans of study; nor am I disposed to be caught with every novelty. Let them at Cambridge try experiments, and we will try to profit by them. They are better able to experiment than we are.[1]

The ideal of mental discipline was continued at Yale under the presidency of Theodore Dwight Woolsey (1846–1871) who had been professor of Greek and who made the senior year at once the "most laborious and one of the most profitable of the whole college course."[2]   Thus, by virtue of being the largest college in the country, Yale's leadership in formulating the ideal of mental discipline as the proper objective of the American college took on the aura of authority for the conservatives of the country. That is not to say that Yale directly influenced most of the colleges of the time, great as that influence was upon specific colleges such as Western Reserve, Beloit, Illinois College, and the University of Alabama, but the small and conservative colleges found either comfort or a very effective expression of their own ideas embodied in this Yale report of 1828.

BARNARD SUPPORTS DISCIPLINE AND PRESCRIPTION IN THE SOUTH

Frederick A. P. Barnard has the distinction of having been a strong advocate of the prescribed curriculum of mental discipline during the early years of his professional career and of being just as urgent in his demands for the adoption of the elective principle while he was president of Columbia College from 1864 to 1889.   He represents in the development of his own thinking the change from reliance upon the prescribed curriculum to acceptance of the elective system; and to follow the development of his arguments is to gain a valuable insight into the factors at work in this change.   Consequently, he is classed with the opponents of the elective principle in this part of our discussion and with its advocates in the latter part.   He entered Yale in 1824 and was a student there at the time when the report of 1828 was being formulated; he must have

[1] GEORGE P. FISHER, *Life of Benjamin Silliman* (Charles Scribner's Sons, New York, 1866), Vol. I, p. 401.

[2] RICHARDSON and CLARK, ed., *The College Book* (Houghton, Osgood and Company, Boston, 1878), p. 89.

been definitely influenced by it, for his future statements on the college system show a marked resemblance even in wording to this report. In 1838, Barnard was made professor of mathematics and natural philosophy at the University of Alabama.

While he was at Alabama,[1] there was considerable agitation for the "open system" of the University of Virginia so that students might have more choice in the election of their studies. Barnard came out as a determined opponent to the reformers, and considerable publicity was given in the press to the controversy. In 1853, he wrote an extensive report to the board of trustees favoring retention of the prescribed curriculum and supporting his theoretical arguments of the value of a classical course of studies for purposes of mental discipline, with elaborate statistics to prove that the open system was not finding favor at Virginia.[2] Thus, the trustees of Alabama voted in 1854 to keep the prescribed curriculum but to have the hours of recitation so arranged that students who were not members of the regular classes could select those they wished to attend. Later Barnard quoted figures to show that proportionately more students took the prescribed curriculum of classical and mathematical studies at the University of Alabama than elected the arts courses at the University of Virginia where the voluntary system was best known.[3] He quoted further figures from the College of South Carolina, the universities of Mississippi, North Carolina, and Georgia, and from Yale, Harvard, and Dartmouth to show that proportionately more students took the prescribed courses in these institutions than elected the courses in liberal arts at the University of Virginia.

In a speech given in 1855,[4] Barnard summed up his position regarding the college curriculum. He began by stating that the college for 30 years had been the subject of debate and attack in efforts to get more practical studies into the curriculum and to improve the learning of those already there. Practical men, he said, declaimed against the classics and in behalf of the sciences; scholars praised and defended the classics. Some colleges allowed selection; others did not; but the courses of study of all had been considerably broadened, and no one was completely satisfied with the various compromises which gave neither a good practical education nor a good classical one. His suggestions for reform were founded upon the assumption that the colleges had a unique function to perform:

---

[1] For Barnard's position and his part in the controversies at the University of Alabama, see John Fulton, *Memoirs of Frederick A. P. Barnard* (The Macmillan Company, New York, 1896), Chaps. VI and VIII.

[2] *Report on a Proposition to Modify the Plan of Instruction in the University of Alabama* (New York, 1855), or see FULTON, *op. cit.*, pp. 168–192.

[3] HENRY BARNARD'S *American Journal of Education*, 5: 765–766 (December, 1858).

[4] *Ibid.*, 1: 174–186 (January, 1856), and 1: 269–284 (March, 1856).

"This function is the systematic development and discipline of the faculties of the mind, in due proportion and in natural order."[1] He declared that attacks on the colleges have not been mindful of this proper function of the college but have criticized it for failing to keep pace with the progress of knowledge, for taking no account of the prospective pursuits of the students, and for lagging far behind the demands of a utilitarian age.

Barnard defended the college curriculum on the basis that imparting knowledge in new fields was not the work of the college and that subjects should be selected not for their utilitarian or professional value but for their effect upon mental discipline. He showed himself unalterably opposed to lessening the emphasis upon the ancient classics and mathematics and to breaking up the prescribed curriculum by allowing selection or by offering parallel courses. If the college degree is to have meaning, there must be a standard of comparison which he believed could be found only in a completely prescribed curriculum constructed upon standardized principles: First, subjects should be chosen for their value in intellectual discipline; second, no more should be included in the curriculum than can be mastered in four years; and, third, if there is still room in the curriculum, subjects may be added for their value in imparting knowledge but not for their practical utility. It is evident that these arguments smack strongly of the Yale report.

Barnard's suggestions for reform were to enlarge the course; extend the time of college residence; and, in addition, raise the entrance requirements and thereby the entering age of students. If the college course could be extended, the latter part could be devoted to those subjects which were valuable for the knowledge that they furnished (improving the "furniture of the mind"), and the student should be allowed an option to choose among them in order not to fritter away his time upon an endless variety of subjects. Barnard believed, however, that if the course could not be extended or the entrance requirements sufficiently raised, then the disciplinary subjects should be the only ones retained in the college curriculum and that such subjects as natural history, the physical sciences, and the modern languages should be thrown out. These latter could be acquired easily by independent study or in special technical schools. He felt that colleges might be further improved by holding out honors and prizes as rewards for studying, establishing scholarships, giving more thorough examinations, improving the discipline, increasing the punishment for offenses, and improving the system of grading by dividing classes on the basis of comparative scholarship.

Barnard had considerable influence throughout the South before the Civil War in extending the principles of the Yale report and in keeping the colleges on the conservative side against the reforms represented by

[1] Ibid., 1: 177 (January, 1856).

the University of Virginia.   He carried his doctrines to the University
of Mississippi when he became professor of mathematics and natural
philosophy there in 1854 and president in 1856.   Gradually, however, his
strongly conservative position concerning the college and disciplinary
subjects began to change.   In a letter to the trustees in 1858, he proposed
that a postgraduate course granting an M.A. be added to the regular sub-
graduate course which was to grant a B.A. and which was to retain the
strictly prescribed character of the usual college.[1]   The postgraduate
course was to be made up of the scientific and literary subjects that
could not be put into the disciplinary curriculum and that could be
selected by the ambitious student who wished to get a thorough grounding in some subjects of his own selection.   Little came of Barnard's
proposal, but it is interesting as indicating the increasing pressure for
studies other than the disciplinary ones, a pressure that finally led
Barnard to change his position and advocate the elective principle in
the college proper.   His reasons for this change will be presented later.

It would not be possible here to try to trace the spread of the influence
of the doctrines of mental discipline, because they were the dominating
principles of most American colleges before the Civil War.   Suffice it to
say that most of the colleges of the North as well as of the South, whether
influenced by Yale or exerting influence upon Yale, expressed similar
points of view and looked askance, not to say with disfavor, upon the
radical proposals issuing from Harvard, the University of Virginia, and
other colleges.   Besides those examples which have already been given,
the solidity of the conservative position in the South aside from the
University of Virginia is indicated by the authorities who were quoted
by Barnard in his report on the proposition to modify the course of study
at Alabama.   In addition to the Yale report, he cited the opinions of the
presidents of South Carolina College, the University of North Carolina,
the University of Georgia, and Rutgers College, who all seemed unanimous in rejecting the mistaken efforts of the University of Virginia and
retaining the established and well-tried forms of college education.   It
was virtually a solid South for the old guard, and it seemed as if the
progressives had made little headway, for by the middle of the century
the elective system had lost out at Harvard; it was in disrepute as practiced at the University of Virginia; and John MacLean went to Princeton
in 1854 determined that no experiments in education should deprive
students of the mental discipline provided by the prescribed curriculum
or allow them to decide for themselves which subjects they would study
or which neglect.[2]

---

[1] *Ibid.*, 5: 774–780 (December, 1858).

[2] JOHN MACLEAN, *History of the College of New Jersey* (J. B. Lippincott Company,
Philadelphia, 1877), Vol. II, pp. 421 *ff.*

CHAPTER VIII

THE COLLEGE CONTROVERSIES TAKE SHAPE: PROGRESSIVES

Despite the strong hold that the conservative position maintained over the college curriculum during the first half of the nineteenth century, the voices of progressives began to be heard here and there more and more insistently. The intellectual and economic results of the secular trends noted in Chap. V began to receive some recognition by a few educators. As the forces of democracy and industrial capitalism had given impetus to the growth of public, state-supported schools and had prompted more practical subjects in the academies and high schools, so these forces gradually began to affect some of the colleges. We have already seen the effect of reform on the curriculum at the University of Virginia and at Harvard, and we have considered somewhat the nature and hold of the traditional conception of a liberal education upon the conservative colleges. It will be the purpose of this chapter to consider some of the other more or less sporadic attempts to reform the college curriculum that occurred during the first half of the nineteenth century.

Some of the plans for reform were abortive and in the face of determined opposition amounted to little more than a statement drawn up by a board of trustees or a report written by a few progressive faculty members. Other plans were tried halfheartedly for a few years and then given up. Still others which were given a fair trial and favorable conditions served as springboards for further reform when the time was ripe after the Civil War. Although some of the colleges were responding somewhat to the demands of a utilitarian and democratic society, their response was usually slow and grudging. To guide the reader through the many different kinds of proposals for reform, three kinds of development can be identified in this period:

1. *Parallel courses* were set up within the framework of the traditional college to give students a chance to study scientific and "literary" subjects and acquire a bachelor's degree different in kind from that given for the regular classical course.

2. *Independent technical schools* were established in complete isolation from any established college, for example, Rensselaer Polytechnic Institute, Worcester Polytechnic Institute, and Massachusetts Institute of Technology.

3. *Scientific schools* were established alongside some of the traditional colleges to care for "practical-minded" students. Such were the Sheffield

Scientific School at Yale, the Lawrence Scientific School at Harvard, and the Chandler School of Science at Dartmouth.

The most common kind of effort to reform the college curriculum was not so much to change the traditional linguistic curriculum as it was to set up entirely new and separate courses, or schools, parallel to the prescribed classical course. Thus, the integrity of the classical course could be retained and the bachelor of arts degree would remain unimpaired, but there would still be a chance for students who could not or would not appreciate the classical course to get an education in the "scientific" or "literary" course. In these new parallel courses, the classical studies were either diminished, or they entirely disappeared to make way for a greater emphasis upon the physical and biological sciences, history, the modern languages, and the application of science to the trades and industry. In this way, there were attempts in some colleges to make concessions to the "practical" needs of the times; but in most educational and religious circles, the traditional classical course was still looked upon as the only true route to a genuine liberal education. At first, the new courses and schools did not require such high standards for admission as did the classical course; that is, they did not require as much Latin or Greek for entrance. They were allowed to grant not the bachelor of arts degree, which was jealously reserved for the classical course, but only a diploma or, later, such new degrees as the bachelor of science, bachelor of philosophy, and bachelor of letters.[1]

One very compelling reason why the colleges became interested in scientific and practical courses was the beginning of technological education on a high level as represented in the founding of Rensselaer Polytechnic Institute, the first of the independent technical schools. Stephen Van Rensselaer established the school in 1824 with the purpose of " ... affording an opportunity to the farmer, the mechanic, the clergyman, the lawyer, the physician, the merchant, and in short, to the man of business or of leisure, of any calling whatever, to become practically scientific."[2] An "experimental course in the natural sciences" was established, and also a preparatory course for those who did not have the proper background. Emphasis was put upon the fact not only that students would receive literary exercises but also that attention would be given to the proper development of the manual abilities by appropriate muscular exercises. In this way, the student was to become familiar with the most important scientific manipulations and "particularly with

---

[1] For a short discussion of the multiplication of bachelor's degrees, see P. L. Harriman, "The Bachelor's Degree," *Journal of Higher Education*, 7: 301–307 (June, 1936).

[2] From a circular purporting to be the first prospectus of a school of science in the English language, quoted in *U. S. Bureau of Education, Circular of Information*, 1900, No. 3, p. 484.

those which will be most useful in the common concerns of life." In 1833, a new department was established, called the department of mathematical arts, which was to give instruction in engineering and technology; it subsequently gave the degree of civil engineering and became the most important part of the school. Here was a direct menace to and a source of keen competition for the literary colleges, for Rensselaer claims to have trained a majority of the naturalists and engineers of the country before the Civil War.

A few of the older colleges attempted to meet the competition and silence the cries of the reformers by establishing "schools of science" entirely separate from and outside the regular college but administratively associated with it. In this way, the college could retain its classical emphasis and give the traditional training to those students who wished to become ministers, teachers, scholars, or merely cultured persons, whereas the scientific school could give a training to those boys who were intended for the trades or industry. Before 1860, there were three such schools, at Yale, Harvard, and Dartmouth, respectively.

Most of the colleges, however, did not have the financial resources to set up separate institutions. Thus, the result in several colleges was the attempt to establish a new scientific course within the regular college and to give for the scientific or literary course a degree different from that which was given for the classical course. This multiplication of courses and degrees which continued at a much greater rate through the last part of the nineteenth century became one of the most characteristic features of the American college.

BEGINNINGS OF REFORM IN FIFTEEN COLLEGES

The remainder of this chapter will be given to a short discussion of several of the attempted reforms that were taking place principally in the third and fourth decades of the nineteenth century. The elective system as a carefully worked-out principle was not present in most of them; nevertheless the reforms represent an important transition phase between the wholly prescribed curriculum and the free elective system. They show how the rigidly prescribed curriculum began to loosen up; how new subjects began to receive recognition, no matter how slight and grudging at first; and how the traditional classical studies gradually had to accept the sciences, history, and modern languages at first as inferiors and finally as equals in the college curriculum.

The following list of colleges is by no means to be considered exhaustive, but it is presented merely to suggest the kind of thinking that college educators and boards of trustees were doing in the early decades of the century in varying attempts to make the colleges approach more nearly what had been demanded of them by educational reformers, by

the public at large, or by the desire to attract more students.   Some of
these proposals and plans are more germane than others to the development of the theory of the elective principle, but all represent efforts to
give wider choice to students even if that choice were only between two
prescribed courses.   They also represent efforts to provide a different
type of education for those who could not or would not devote themselves
to the classical and literary type of liberal education.

1. *University of North Carolina* (Chapel Hill) in its earliest plans
indicated that greater prominence would be given to the scientific and
practical studies than was common among colleges at the turn of the
nineteenth century.   The preliminary plan of studies drawn up in 1792
included a recommendation that instruction should include not only the
languages, belles-lettres, mathematics, and natural philosophy but also
history (both ancient and modern), botany and the theory of agriculture
best suited to the climate and soil of the state, and the principles of architecture.[1]   One of the members of the committee that drew up this
preliminary plan was Hugh Williamson, who had graduated from the
University of Pennsylvania, taught mathematics there, and gained his
M.D. from the University of Edinburgh.   It may be that the influence
of the University of Pennsylvania was through him brought to bear upon
the young University of North Carolina.   The bylaws adopted in 1795
(the year the university opened) also included the intention to offer
instruction in commerce, arithmetic, bookkeeping, civil government,
agriculture, and architecture in addition to the standard subjects.[2]
According to Battle, an intimation of the elective system is given in
these early bylaws: "Those electing to study the Sciences and the English
language to be formed into a Scientific class, or pursue the chosen subjects
with the Literary classes."[3]

Even more radical was the plan drawn up in 1795 after a year of
experience.   This was largely the idea of General William R. Davie, long
connected with the early days of the university, and Battle indicates that
it anticipates some of Jefferson's plan at the University of Virginia.   A
close inspection of this plan of 1795 will show also that it follows rather
closely the scheme of instruction that Jefferson proposed for the College
of William and Mary in 1779.   Davie proposed that there should be five
professors in the following fields: moral and political philosophy and
history; natural philosophy, astronomy, and geography; mathematics
through arithmetic, algebra, geometry, and trigonometry with electives
beyond these; chemistry, medicine, agriculture, and mechanical arts;

[1] KEMP P. BATTLE, *History of the University of North Carolina* (Edwards and
Broughton Printing Company, Raleigh, N. C., 1907), Vol. I, p. 49.

[2] *Ibid.*, pp. 48–59, gives a full description of these early plans.

[3] *Ibid.*, p. 55.

and languages of English, Latin, and Greek.[1] The practical and vocational import of Davie's plan is clearly indicated in the following excerpt from one of his letters: "The ruling or leading principle in our plan of education is that the student may apply himself to those branches of learning and science alone which are absolutely necessary to fit him for his destined profession or occupation in life."[2] Davie even went so far as to recommend that the B.A. degree should continue to be given to those who study the classics but that an English diploma should be given to those who attain proficiency in the arts and sciences without study of the classics.

Despite these early progressive attempts, however, the University of North Carolina soon returned to the path of tradition shortly after the turn of the century. When Jeffersonian democracy invaded the state in 1805, General Davie was forced to leave, and the dominant control of the university fell into the hands of Joseph Caldwell who was a graduate of Princeton. Caldwell wiped out the nonsense about practical and vocational preparation by granting only the one diploma in the form of the B.A. degree for which both Latin and Greek were required. This state of affairs continued for many years, and it was not until the reorganization in 1875 that other degrees were recognized along with the B.A. The Ph.B. was then given for those who omitted one classical study, and the B.S. was given for those who omitted both classics. By the turn of the twentieth century, the University of North Carolina was following Harvard and Cornell in giving the B.A. without any classical requirement.[3] After a few years of detour in the late eighteenth century, the University of North Carolina was back on the main highroad of conservatism at about the time when a good many other colleges were trying to blaze new trails in college education.

2. *Union College* (Schenectady, N. Y.) was another of the early colleges that attempted to break away from the rigid classical curriculum and to place scientific studies upon a plane of equal dignity with it.[4] President Eliphalet Nott, ably assisted by Francis Wayland as an instructor, was instrumental in making scientific and utilitarian subjects available for those who wished them. By 1828, these studies came to embrace a full scientific course running parallel to the regular classical one.[5] Essential features were the substitution of the modern languages,

---

[1] *Ibid.*, pp. 93–96. For the close similarity with Jefferson's plan at William and Mary 15 years earlier, see pp. 88–91.

[2] *Ibid.*, pp. 97–98.

[3] *Ibid.*, p. 98.

[4] *U. S. Bureau of Education, Circular of Information*, 1900, No. 3, p. 211.

[5] "Historical Sketch of Union College," *U. S. Bureau of Education, Special Report*, 1876, pp. 25–37.

mathematics, and the physical sciences for Greek and Latin and permission to students within certain limits to elect specified subjects.   French and German, for example, were taught to those who elected them, provided the necessary preparation was presented.

Tradition could not be completely defied, however, so the graduates of the parallel course received not the B. A. but merely a diploma stating the amount of work completed.   Union felt the same sting of criticism that other colleges of reform felt, but the alternative course was retained, and, perhaps as a result, Union was the third largest college in the country in 1829 and the second largest in 1839.[1]   That Union College was a center of activity for reform and sent out its influence in the persons of several individuals is further indicated by the fact that it gave training to the first president and several faculty members of Trinity College, to Francis Wayland who became president of Brown University, and to Henry Tappan who instituted effective reforms as president of the University of Michigan.

3. *Trinity College* (founded in 1823 in Hartford, Conn.) had its origin in a strong reaction to the strict Congregationalism in the state and in a desire for more religious and intellectual freedom for its students than was allowed at Yale.   From the very beginning, provision was made to give special studies to those who wished instruction outside the regular prescribed curriculum.   Those who followed a course of their own choosing for at least two years were given an English diploma, and if they continued for another two years on a high level of attainment, they were granted an arts degree.   Modern languages and sciences were strong from the beginning and provided large elements in the practical courses selected by students.   That the faculty was never completely convinced of the value of these "irregular" arrangements is evidenced by a statement in 1878: "The regular course is that which the experience of the past has shown to be the one best adapted to train and to develop all the faculties of the mind . . . and it is to this development and the expansion of the system of study that the efforts of the present faculty will be directed."[2]

4. *University of Nashville* (Nashville, Tenn.).   The president of the University of Nashville for 25 years (1825–1850) was the Reverend Philip Lindsley who had graduated from Yale but who nevertheless set

---

[1] Union was denounced as the "dumping ground of substandard boys" from other colleges and of poor students in general.   *Cf.* C. VAN SANTVOORD, *Memoirs of Eliphalet Nott* (Sheldon and Company, New York, 1876), p. 153.   The *Quarterly Register* of the American Education Society gives attendance figures for 1829 as follows: Yale, 359; Harvard, 247; Union, 227; Amherst, 207; Dartmouth, 137.   For 1839, they were: Yale, 411; Union, 286; Virginia, 247; Princeton, 237; Harvard, 216.

[2] RICHARDSON and CLARK, ed., *The College Book* (Houghton, Osgood Company, Boston, 1878), p. 272.

out to adapt the higher education of Tennessee to the needs of a frontier state.   His general aims and educational philosophy were based upon the belief that if a democracy is to be perpetuated, then all of its citizens must be given the kind of education that they most need.   He ran into the determined opposition of the growing cotton aristocracy of Tennessee and the mushroom growth of the denominational colleges, but he persisted in his belief that "The farmer, the mechanic, the manufacturer, the merchant, the sailor, the soldier . . . must be educated."[1]

His plan as a whole included a university to consist of six separate colleges each with its own land, buildings, staff, shops, gardens, and experimental farm.   The university would thus include not only the regular course but also such other and more practical courses as international law, government, commerce, manufacturing, statistics, agriculture, fencing, riding, swimming, and gymnastics.   Classical studies would not be eliminated but would remain merely as one of several elective courses.   However, the force of tradition, lack of funds, lack of enthusiasm on the part of the people of the state, and the opposition of other colleges prevented Lindsley from realizing his plans.   Nevertheless, some progress was made in bringing college education closer to the people.

5. *Hobart College* (Geneva, N. Y.).   At its opening in 1825, a three-year "English," or scientific, course was proposed and instituted at Hobart.   According to the circular written by Daniel McDonald:

It is proposed . . . to institute . . . a totally distinct course, in direct reference to the practical business of life, by which the agriculturalist, the merchant, and the mechanic may receive a practical knowledge of what genius and experience have discovered, without passing through a tedious course of classical studies.[2]

It was proposed that professors, respectively, of English, mathematics, and chemistry should teach such practical subjects as English grammar, geography, history; geometry, trigonometry, land surveying, and mensuration; dyeing and bleaching.   It was intended that the students in this English course should be classified as usual into classes by years and that they should take the same kind of examinations as students in the classical courses, but they were to get an English diploma instead of a B. A. degree.   President Jaspar Adams, in 1827, commended the course as meeting the needs of the farmers and mechanics of the community, but he could not give it his complete approval and emphasized that it was to be considered as decidedly inferior in value to the

[1] PHILIP LINDSLEY, *Address in Nashville . . . at the Inauguration of the President of Cumberland College* (Joseph Novell, Nashville, Tenn., 1825), p. 16.

[2] *U. S. Bureau of Education, Circular of Information*, 1900, No. 3, pp. 247-248.

regular classical course as a means of attaining a genuine liberal education.[1] He spoke of the desirability of an "aristocracy of talent" and thus indicated, as was true of many other colleges, that Hobart's reform was merely a grudging accession to the demands of democracy and practicality.   It was later admitted by the college that a technical course would cost more money than was available, and therefore the English course became little more than what was left of the classical course after Latin and Greek were omitted and offered a degree of bachelor of letters to those who completed it.

6. *University of Vermont* (Burlington, Vt.). In 1826, the Reverend James Marsh went to the University of Vermont as president and began to infuse new life into a financially weak and small college. He had been influenced by German thought and scholarship and undertook a reorganization which resembled somewhat the proposals of Ticknor. Marsh tried to establish four separate departments: English literature; the languages; mathematics and physics; political, moral, and intellectual philosophy. The student would be allowed to select one or at most two departments in which to concentrate his work; and when he had completed the usual amount of work as measured in hours and courses, he would receive the traditional degree. Here was an attempt to put the newer subjects of English and science on a level of equality with the older studies in ancient language and philosophy and to make the new subjects equivalent to the old for attaining a B.A. degree. Marsh also tried to establish more informal methods in place of the traditional dormitory discipline. He was attempting to open the doors of the university to the large numbers of students who had previously been denied a college education because they were not prepared for or not interested in a classical, linguistic, and philosophical curriculum. Although the university did allow students to pursue single studies in any department, Marsh's plans never went wholly into operation, for by 1829 degrees were given only to those who finished the regular classical and mathematical courses.[2]

7. *Amherst College* (Amherst, Mass.). In 1826, the faculty of Amherst issued a report diagnosing the ills of the American college and emphasizing its lag behind the march of business and industry. As a consequence, the college instituted, in 1827, a "parallel" course of study in addition to the regular classical curriculum. Professor Jacob Abbot and others felt that a more flexible curriculum was needed to give an education to those not headed for the learned professions because of "the inadequacy of the prevailing systems of classical education in this

---

[1] JASPAR ADAMS, *Inaugural Discourse* (Geneva, N. Y., 1827).

[2] *An Exposition of the System of Instruction and Discipline Pursued in the University of Vermont* (Burlington, Vt., 1831).

country to meet the wants and demands of an enlightened public."[1] This equivalent scientific course was designed to be four years in length, taught by as fully capable instructors, and requiring as much hard work and as thorough mental discipline as that of the regular classical course.

Emphasis was to be put upon English literature; substitution of modern languages in place of the ancient languages; "mechanical philosophy," chemistry, and other physical sciences, with their application to the useful trades, inventions, and agriculture; natural history (botany and biology); modern history; and civil and political law. In addition and common to both courses were to be ancient history; geography; grammar; rhetoric and oratory; mathematics; natural, mental, and moral philosophy; anatomy; political economy; and theology. It is interesting to note that a recommendation was also made to establish a new department for systematic instruction in the science of education and a department of theoretical and practical mechanics, neither of which materialized.

The justification for the new parallel course was stated in a pamphlet entitled *An Outline of the System of Instruction recently adopted in the College at Amherst, Massachusetts*, 1827, which indicated that the new course was set up "In consequence of the demand which is at the present made by a large portion of the public for the means of an elevated and liberal education without the necessity of devoting so much time to the study of the Ancient Languages. . . ."[2]

The new plan was discontinued, however, in 1829 for reasons that will sound familiar to innovators in any college: There were not sufficient funds or staff to manage both courses; the Frenchman who taught the modern languages could not keep order in his classes; many of the faculty did not cooperate fully and showed less enthusiasm than did the professor whose favorite scheme it was; and students did not demand the modern languages and sciences to any such degree as had been anticipated because there was not the same prestige attached to the diploma as to the traditional B.A. degree.[3] Although this plan for opening the college to the practical needs of the community was short-lived, it represented another effort on the part of a few bold educators to keep up with the times.

8. *Bowdoin College* (Brunswick, Maine) made a far less successful effort to reform its curriculum in 1827, the same year that Amherst began its new plan and the same year that Yale had fixed, what it thought would be forever, the limits of the college curriculum. The Bowdoin visiting committee in 1827 suggested to the board of trustees that the modern languages might be given a more prominent part in the regular

---

[1] WILLIAM S. TYLER, *History of Amherst College* (Springfield, Mass., 1873), p. 170.
[2] *Ibid.*, p. 172.
[3] CLAUDE MOORE FUESS, *Amherst* (Little, Brown and Company, Boston, 1935), p. 99.

course and that Greek might be made elective: "Whether the courses of instruction ought not to be more of a practical and less of a scholastic character, and to this end whether the study of the Greek language in this college ought not to be optional with the student."[1]   Apparently, the faculty decided against these suggestions, for the next report of the visiting committee stated that no professors of the modern languages had been appointed.

In 1829, the foregoing resolution was again called to the board's attention, and a definite declaration was made in favor of allowing election of studies as between Greek and one of the modern languages and between higher mathematics and a course in moral philosophy. Henry Wadsworth Longfellow was appointed instructor in the modern languages, and students for a time were allowed to choose a modern language in place of the classics and calculus. The doctrine was too revolutionary, however, for a small, conservative college with a president who was strongly partial to the study of the classics, with a natural science professor who was too timid to push forward the claims of the sciences, and with funds inadequate to allow the introduction of many new subjects. Although the modern languages provided the entering wedge for the elective system at Bowdoin as at Harvard, they soon became strong enough to become regular members of the prescribed curriculum where they remained long after the ancient languages had disappeared.

9. *Columbia College* (New York City) in 1830 began to feel the pinch of competition from the proposed New York University and so set up a new course in addition to its existing prescribed curriculum.[2] This was the "Literary and Scientific Course" and was to be open to other than matriculated students, all persons being permitted to attend to such an extent as they saw fit. The new course was abolished, however, in 1843 because it was "apparently in advance of the desires of the community."[3] The "regular" traditional course, however, was retained in full, and all the subjects in it were prescribed.

In 1857, under President Charles King, the regular course was so changed by a college statute that the senior year was divided into three divisions (letters, science, and jurisprudence) among which the student must select one for his work of the senior year. The usual mental discipline of the college course was to be maintained for the first three years; but during the fourth year, the student was to begin to acquire such

---

[1] Louis C. Hatch, *The History of Bowdoin College* (Loring, Short and Harmon, Portland, Maine, 1927), p. 63.

[2] *A History of Columbia University*, 1775–1904 (Columbia University Press, New York, 1904), p. 112.

[3] *Ibid.*, p. 121.

knowledge as would prepare him for life either through the general division of letters or through the special professional training offered in the other two divisions. The Civil War destroyed the efficacy of this statute, but it is further evidence that some attempt had been made to make the curriculum of Columbia College more flexible in the direction of practicality.

10. *New York University* (New York City). Early in 1830, the standing committee that had been formed to organize a new university in New York City issued to the citizens of the community a public appeal in which the principle of election was clearly proposed:

Every person attending the university shall be at liberty to pursue the acquisition of knowledge in the various departments of literature and science according to his own preferences or that of his parent or guardian, having an unlimited choice of the branches taught in the institution.[1]

The elective principle was, however, not used when the institution opened; indeed, despite the efforts of Albert Gallatin and others to establish an English course or English college alongside the classical course the council of the university declined to organize a full college course that would omit the classical languages. The matter was brought before a convention of educators assembled in New York for the purpose of discussing the need of a new university in New York City. The convention appointed a committee which finally decided to give freedom of election only to those students who were not seeking a degree and to reserve the bachelor of arts degree for those who finished "a full classical, philosophical, and mathematical course." It was not until the 1850's that a scientific course (substituting science and modern languages for the ancient languages) was founded which led to the bachelor of science degree. Thus, the promise of the early founders of New York University was not fulfilled, for up to 1894 election was confined to a choice between the classical and the scientific courses; and the old traditions of rhetoric, daily prayers, and moral and Christian training were strictly maintained for all students.

11. *Wesleyan University* (Middletown, Conn.) from its founding in 1831 set out upon a course somewhat different from that of the usual American college. The first president, Wilbur Fisk, put considerable emphasis upon the modern languages and also instituted a scientific course for those who desired a thorough general education but whose preferences or circumstances forbade an extended study of the ancient languages. Furthermore, Fisk desired that all studies be divided into separate departments and that students be classified according to advancement in the various departments instead of according to the time

[1] *U. S. Bureau of Education, Circular of Information,* 1900, No. 3, p. 255.

they had been in college.[1]   The degree was to be granted whenever the student completed the required course of studies, but the plan met with little favor.   Diplomas were actually given only at the end of the college year; students of the same advancement in each department thought of themselves as belonging to the same college class, and they objected to the lack of such class affiliation.   Consequently, the plan of departments was dropped in 1841, and subsequently Wesleyan became an outstanding example of adherence to a classical prescribed curriculum.

12. *Lafayette College* (Easton, Pa.) opened in 1832 with a president, George Junkin, who believed strongly in the manual labor movement that had been gaining ground in the United States during the early decades of the nineteenth century.   His ideal is represented by the following statement:

By a judicious and well-arranged union of the arts of industry with scientific and literary studies in their various departments, Lafayette College now offers to the rising generation as extensive a field for intellectual improvement as any of her sister institutions, while the healthful pursuits of mechanical and agricultural labor preserve the youthful constitution from the wasting effects of mental exertion, and at the same time give to the mind that strength and independence which always result from the proud consciousness of self-support.[2]

An enlarged course of studies in the modern languages was tried, and a teachers' course was established in the college with a model school erected for purposes of practice teaching.   When Junkin left in 1841, however, these "irregular" courses and methods were given up, and "Lafayette became the ordinary small college with a classical course, conspicuous mainly for plain living and thorough work."[3]   Manual labor was too democratic and too menial for the prevailing aristocratic and literary conception of a liberal education.

13. *Oberlin College* (Oberlin, Ohio) opened in 1834 with an emphasis upon the manual labor feature of college work; and by 1837 it had made the startling innovation of admitting women on a level of equality with men.[4]   All of the subjects of the regular college course were open to the women, but it was not expected that many would take the full course. A so-called "Ladies Course" was presented, giving all of the mathematics,

[1] RICHARDSON and CLARK, ed., *op. cit.*, p. 308: "The views of Dr. Fisk in this matter were shared by his friend Dr. Wayland, of Brown, and by President Marsh, of the University of Vermont.   In the latter institution, indeed, the same scheme was for a time in practice."

[2] *Ibid.*, p. 285.

[3] *Ibid.*, p. 286.

[4] See F. J. HOSFORD, *Father Shipherd's Magna Charta; A Century of Co-education in Oberlin College* (Marshall Jones Company, Boston, 1937).

natural science, literature, and philosophy of the college course, with the addition of French, drawing, and a few other special branches, but omitting Greek and Latin or making them optional. This course was expanded as the regular course was extended and was finally made parallel to the regular course so that classes in the same subjects met together.

Women were allowed to take the regular course originally for men or the special course for women or to determine their own special courses as seemed most likely to suit individual tastes and needs. This apparently marked the beginning of admitting women into college courses on an equal basis with men, and their presence from the first required the college to offer special courses for them which ultimately helped to break down the rigid character of the prescribed curriculum. At Oberlin, the democratic movement in higher education seems to have had earlier and more adequate expression than at any other college of the period. Oberlin also gives striking evidence of the way that admission of women as a new clientele helped to loosen the prescribed curriculum.

14. *Norwich University* (Norwich, Vt.), which was chartered in 1835, grew out of the military academy that had been set up by Captain Alden Partridge in 1819 on the basis of certain reforms that he had earlier advocated. In 1820, he had given a lecture[1] in which he listed what he believed to be the outstanding defects of the college system of the day: It was not practical enough or suited to the duties of an American citizen; it neglected physical education; it allowed too much idle time to all and too much money to the wealthy students; it required all students to follow the same course of studies despite the fact that they have different inclinations and capacities and should be permitted to study appropriate subjects; and it prescribed a definite length of time for completing the required course. Partridge proposed his "American Literary, Scientific, and Military Academy" to remedy these defects. The curriculum, as outlined in a prospectus in 1820, was ostensibly very broad and divided the wide range of linguistic and practical subjects into a literary, an engineering, and an agricultural course among which students could select; and a military course, which all took.[2] No specified time was required for completing any course; each student was allowed to progress as rapidly as he could with his studies; and when they were completed, he was given a certificate of graduation. The academy opened in 1820; and when it was chartered as Norwich University in 1834, much the same policy was followed.

[1] G. M. DODGE and W. A. ELLIS, *Norwich University* (The Capital City Press, Montpellier, Vt., 1911), p. 2. See also HENRY BARNARD's *American Journal of Education*, 13: 49–72 (March, 1863).

[2] DODGE and ELLIS, *op. cit.,* p. 170.

Five courses were proposed for the university: the preparatory, collegiate, civil engineering, teacher training, and military. Selection was narrowed after a few years to the collegiate and engineering, because the teachers' course and the preparatory department disappeared, and the military course was required of all. The ancient and modern languages, music, and fencing were elective. Each student was allowed to advance as rapidly as possible in his studies and was graduated when the course was completed. The university was greatly troubled by a series of lawsuits between 1850 and 1860 (it was removed to Northfield, Vt., in 1866); and despite the approach of the Civil War, the public did not like the military aspect of the institution. Hence its influence upon the collegiate curriculum was less widespread than it might have been.

15. *University of Rochester* (Rochester, N. Y.). In a report to the board of trustees in 1850, a committee of faculty and interested members indicated that there was a movement on foot to allow some freedom of choice in the junior and senior years of the college course with a view to the future calling that the student had in mind.[1] In this report, the various proposals for reform of collegiate education were considered, and efforts were subsequently made to loosen somewhat the rigidly prescribed course so that the students who took neither Greek nor Latin for four years would graduate with the same honors as those who did study the classics. To this end, two or three parallel courses were subsequently established which led to the Ph.B. and B.S. degrees; also, the compulsory study of Latin and Greek was terminated after the second year, the study of higher mathematics was not required of classical students, and many studies of the classical course were made optional after the second year. Apparently, by the middle of the century it had become easier to make and to hold gains for a more flexible and practical curriculum.

These short discussions of 15 of the colleges that were attempting curricular reforms in the first half of the nineteenth century may serve to indicate how the traditional prescribed curriculum was being attacked and how the transition was being made from a completely prescribed curriculum to a more elective one. They may also serve to show how tenacious the transitional conception of a liberal education was and with what great difficulty that conception was going to be dislodged from its hold upon the college curriculum, until such a time as social and intellectual conditions more favorable to the elective system should hasten the process. We turn now to two efforts for reform that stand out clearly in the middle of the nineteenth century as fundamentally attacking the problem of revising the college curriculum. Brown University and the University of Michigan held the place in the middle decades that Virginia and Harvard had held in the earlier decades.

[1] *U. S. Bureau of Education, Circular of Information*, 1900, No. 3, p. 291.

WAYLAND MAKES A FUNDAMENTAL ATTACK ON THE PRESCRIBED CURRICULUM AT BROWN

One of the most effective advocates for reform of the American college in the middle of the nineteenth century was Francis Wayland, president of Brown University (1827–1855). Soon after his accession to the presidency, Wayland tried to raise the standard of scholarship and to adapt the course of study to the wants of the community by adding modern languages to the prescribed course.[1] By 1829, he reported to the corporation that several branches of knowledge had been added to the curriculum, and he made strenuous effort to get funds and endowments to improve the library and scientific apparatus. During these early years as president, he believed that the aim of the college should be the discipline of the mental faculties rather than the acquisition of a given amount of knowledge. Despite his connection with the reforms of Union College under President Nott and his acquaintance with Ticknor's *Remarks*, Wayland does not seem to have urged radical reform of the curriculum of Brown until after his visit to Europe in 1840.

He inspected among others the universities of London, Oxford, Cambridge, Edinburgh, and Glasgow; but according to his biographers, their courses of study seemed to him narrow and barren, conferring only a fragment of education rather than an enlarged view of human knowledge and cultivating a narrowness of mind with their endless, fruitless discussions. This view of the effect of the British universities upon Wayland seems a little extreme, inasmuch as he makes many references to them in his reports on the college system and inasmuch as one of the historians of Brown University attributes Wayland's first impulse for reform to the examples of the deep scholarship of the universities of Great Britain.[2] These views may not be so irreconcilable as at first they appear. It is likely that Wayland's first impression of the work done in British universities may not have been so favorable as he had expected it to be; but when proposing changes in American colleges at home, it gave force to his arguments to compare the local colleges unfavorably with those of Europe. As a matter of fact, Wayland did not propose that the American colleges accept the methods of the British universities which, poor as they appeared to him, may still have appeared better than those of the American colleges. Hence, although Wayland did not think highly of the British universities, yet he could easily have been prompted

[1] FRANCIS WAYLAND and HERMAN WAYLAND, *A Memoir of the Life and Labors of Francis Wayland* (Sheldon and Company, New York, 1867), Vol. I, *passim*.

[2] WALTER C. BRONSON, *The History of Brown University* (Brown University Press, Providence, 1914), p. 274.

to seek reform of the American college upon his return to the United States.   Bronson further supports his view with the following statement:

This view, based on Wayland's written or printed words, is confirmed by the opinion of Pres. James B. Angell, a member of the Faculty when the New System went into effect, who in a recent interview attributed Dr. Wayland's discontent with the old system to his study of the universities of Great Britain.[1]

Whatever the incentive for his reforms or the source of his ideas, Wayland began an active agitation for changes in the college system as soon as he returned from Europe.   Besides many speeches advocating innovation, he wrote several articles and pamphlets, the most important of which, for our purposes, were his report to the fellows of Brown in 1841, his *Thoughts on the Present Collegiate System in the United States* in 1842, and his report to the corporation of Brown in 1850.   In his two earlier written statements, Wayland clung to the conservative point of view regarding the requirements for the bachelor's degree, and he did not advocate the elective principle for the regular college course until his report of 1850.   But in all of his statements, he urged that the college should adapt its offerings to those who wished to study mercantile, agricultural, and scientific subjects apart from the required course for the B.A.

Wayland made a rather complete statement of the whole problem of college reform in his pamphlet published in 1842.[2]   In this, he presented a picture of the collegiate system as it existed in the United States at that time, what he considered were its outstanding defects, and his recommendations for improvement and reform. He compared the English college with the American college, showing how they coincided in the following respects: the principle of established classes to each of which a whole year of study was devoted; the fixed course of study for every student; the preparation of every student as a candidate for a degree; enforced residence upon the college premises; and the responsibility of the officers for the moral conduct and life of the students.   The typical college was thus a large boarding school, providing every student with board, lodging, and the proper discipline and obliging everyone to go through the same course of study in the same time and acquire the B.A. degree.   Wayland indicated that some colleges had departed somewhat from this rule, referring doubtless to Harvard which at this time under President Quincy had a fairly wide elective system:

I ought to mention that in some instances of late, the course has been divided. At the option of the student, after the first year, the Modern Languages and

---

[1] *Ibid.*
[2] FRANCIS WAYLAND, *Thoughts on the Present Collegiate System in the United States* (Boston, 1842).

History with some branches of Physical Science may be substituted for the further prosecution of the Latin and Greek Languages and the Mathematics; and students pursuing this latter course are equally entitled to a degree with the others.[1]

Wayland does not indicate at this point whether or not he believes such innovations to be salutary, but his recommendations lead us to believe that at this time he would seek a different way to reform.

The outstanding defect of the college system, as he saw it, was the superficiality of the learning that students acquired in the regular course of study, thereby failing to attain the aims of the college course.   These aims, according to Wayland, were similar to those in vogue at the time; namely, college education was designed to occupy the period between the lower school and the higher profession and was supposed to be sufficient for obtaining the knowledge which society requires of a well-educated man; intellectual discipline should be rigid and vigorous; and the powers of acquisition, investigation, discovery, and communication should be thoroughly trained.

Wayland pointed out, as others had done, that the amount of knowledge and number of courses had doubled or trebled since the colleges were first established and yet that the amount of time allowed for finishing the course had remained exactly the same; thus it had become impossible for young men to acquire all of this knowledge in such a manner as to insure proper mental discipline.   The demands of the curriculum exceeded the abilities of the students to assimilate the material, and consequently some or all of the studies were neglected, the work was imperfectly done, and the knowledge acquired had become superficial.   The students skimmed rapidly over many texts, tended to develop a passive receptivity instead of original and active power, became acquainted with a little of everything, and knew nothing well. The instructors also tended to reduce the content of their courses whenever a new subject was added to the prescribed curriculum, and thus superficiality was increased on the teaching as well as on the learning side.

Wayland's recommendations for reform included not only raising the requirements for admission to college in order to get more advanced students who would appreciate the value of thorough knowledge but also changing the college course in one of three ways: first, by limiting the number of studies so that they could be taught thoroughly and students would attain real scholarship; secondly, by opening the course only to candidates for a degree (this is substantially the Yale position), for if new subjects are to be added to the required curriculum, attendance should be extended to five or six years; or, finally, by making the college resemble a "real" university by offering all the important branches of

[1] *Ibid.*, p. 36.

learning, professional and preprofessional, with one course as usual leading to the B.A. degree and other courses less classical and more practical leading to such degrees as the B.S. or B. Litt.

The third suggestion seemed to fit more nearly Wayland's idea of reform. He wanted to retain the regular prescribed college course of preparation for the professional study in a distinct and thorough manner, emphasizing vigorous mental discipline, but he also wanted to enlarge the system so that the means of education would be open to all who chose to avail themselves of it. He would accomplish this aim by removing compulsory residence, allowing everyone to attend, and establishing courses of lectures that men of all conditions and all classes of society would be interested in attending. Since the farmer, merchant, mechanic, and manufacturer were the backbone of the nation, they should have just as great opportunity to acquire knowledge and intellectual discipline as the lawyer, physician, or clergyman.

Wayland was convinced that the diffusion of scientific principles and the application of scientific knowledge to the arts would aid the progress and wealth of the country as well as improve the level of enlightenment and knowledge of all classes of society. His theories were the most advanced in terms of democracy since the days of Jefferson. Despite publication of this comprehensive statement of the principles upon which reform of the American colleges should be based, Wayland was unable at this time to effect material changes in the curriculum of Brown; and with enrollment decreasing nearly one-fourth from 1835 to 1849, and with income from all courses falling, he tendered his resignation in 1849. It was not accepted, however, and he presented the next year to the corporation a report that embodied many of the fundamentals of the former statements but was much more radical with respect to proposals for breaking up the prescribed curriculum leading to the B.A. and for inaugurating a wide application of the elective principle within the B.A. course.[1]

In this respect, Wayland described a defect in American colleges which he had not mentioned before and which doubtless rose from his experiences at Brown, namely, that American colleges had gradually ceased to be self-supporting because of a decrease in students and in funds. Remedy could be found either in adapting the educational offering to the wants of the community and thereby attracting more student fees or in appealing to the philanthropy of the public for maintaining the traditional type of education. Most colleges had adopted the latter method with disappointing results: " . . . colleges are not filled because we do not furnish the education desired by the people.

[1] FRANCIS WAYLAND, *Report to the Corporation of Brown University, on Changes in the System of Collegiate Education* (Providence, 1850).

. . . Is it not time to inquire whether we cannot furnish an article for which the demand will be, at least, somewhat more remunerative?"[1]

Wayland's new recommendations for adapting Brown to the wants of the whole community were as follows: Abolish the fixed course of four years, and allow the student to carry as many subjects as he chooses; arrange the courses so that every student may study what he chooses and nothing but what he chooses; let every course when begun be continued without interruption until completed; and add to the regular curriculum such courses as the wants of the community require.[2] These reforms, he urged, would attract more students and increase enrollment, inasmuch as the period of preprofessional training would be cut down by one or two years to allow more time for the actual professional study; also, proper teaching could be given for one, two, or three years to young men preparing for any of the active departments of life in addition to those studying for the usual learned professions; and, finally, students would be allowed to study the various sciences as a proper part of a liberal education as well as studying them for their value as applied to industrial and agricultural arts.

Wayland justified such changes on three grounds: (1) They are just—every one has the right to cultivate his mind by discipline and enrich his knowledge by science, and this holds for the farmer, mechanic, manufacturer, and merchant as well as for the lawyer, physician, and clergyman; (2) they are expedient—civilization advances along the lines of the useful arts, and America would have outstripped Europe in all the arts that increase the comforts and refinements of life if a general knowledge of the principles of manufacturing, mechanics, and agriculture had been widely distributed; (3) they are necessary—the colleges must make provision for mercantile and industrial interests, or the businessmen and manufacturers will set up their own private and technical schools to compete with the colleges to the latter's detriment. We have noted that Rensselaer was already offering the competition that Wayland feared.

In this report, Wayland followed out the logical conclusions of his previous position and proposed that the elective principle should be utilized throughout the curriculum. The American colleges had insisted upon requirements never dreamed of in Europe; therefore, they should adopt a system of "equivalents" by which a degree may be conferred for the acquisition of a certain amount of knowledge, although it may differ in kind in different instances. This theory makes all subjects of equal value for attaining a degree and allows the substitution of equivalent subjects for the previously required Greek, Latin, mathematics, and

[1] BRONSON, *op. cit.*, p. 262.
[2] *Ibid.*, p. 263.

philosophy.   Wayland concluded his report on a very practical note by saying:

This college cannot, under any circumstances, be long sustained without large additions to its funds. . . . There is reason to hope that the same amount of funds which would be necessary to sustain the college under the present system, might, if the system were modified in the manner above suggested, add greatly to the number of students, and, at the same time, confer inestimable advantages on every class of society.[1]

As has been indicated, the reforms proposed by Wayland were not entirely new to the colleges of his day or even to Brown itself.   A beginning had been made in the direction of his proposed changes as early as 1830, when students had been admitted to an "irregular" course of study; and in the catalogue of 1847–1848 a new "English and Scientific" course was announced for those who were not planning to enter the learned professions but who desired to prepare themselves "for some of the more active employments of life."   The difference is that the new proposals of Wayland applied directly to the traditional classical course itself and were adopted by the corporation on a much larger scale than previous reforms had been.   They were authorized to be put into force as soon as $125,000 could be raised to finance the "New System."   The funds were soon supplied through the efforts of President Wayland, and then 13 courses were established, enlarging considerably the former curriculum, particularly in science and its applications.[2]

The most radical features of the new program included a change in the requirements for degrees.   The B.A. was to be granted for three years' work in the usual subjects, but a greater freedom of choice was to be allowed; the Ph.B. was to be granted for three years of work that emphasized more of the scientific subjects and their applications to the industrial and agricultural arts; the M.A. was to be granted for a four years' course that was nearly identical with that which had previously been required for the B.A.   Thus, the B.A. and Ph.B. were designed to provide an education for those who did not wish or were unable to take a full liberal course and who desired to prepare for a particular occupation.

Consequently, a scheme for reform that had aimed at raising scholarship actually resulted in degrading the M.A. degree, giving the B.A. for one-fourth less work than previously and granting a new degree that required for entrance to the university little more than a common school education.   Bronson believes that this was done because Wayland

[1] *Ibid.*, p. 266–267.

[2] *Ibid.*, p. 279.   The 13 courses were: Latin, Greek, modern languages, mathematics, natural philosophy, civil engineering, chemistry and physiology, English, moral and intellectual philosophy, history and political economy, didactics, application of chemistry to the arts, and the theory and practice of agriculture.

wanted to spread the benefits of collegiate education more widely among
the people and wanted more students to pay money into the treasury
of the college: "To what extent the democratic motive dominated the
pecuniary it is impossible to decide, but doubtless each was sincere and
powerful."[1] It might be noted here that the new system at Brown did
not last long, for it realized some of the fears of its opponents that
students of inferior preparation would enter the college; and the level
of attainment was low because the range of electives made possible by
limited finances was so narrow that there was no opportunity for students
to progress far enough in one branch of knowledge to become proficient
in it.   Consequently, when Barnabas Sears became president in 1856,
the requirements for entrance and for degrees were raised, and the
elective system was curtailed.

Although Wayland's plans had been too far in advance of the times
to allow vital and continued application of the elective system, his proposals evoked wide attention with much spirited opposition and with
much approval.   Newspapers applauded the new system which was to
reach down among the masses of the people: "Merchants, manufacturers,
farmers, artisans, legislators all saw something worth while in this
practical form of instruction."[2]   The magazines struck a more conservative note and expressed doubts of the practicability of the plan as well as
fears that the traditional cultural course which had proved so valuable
would be neglected.   Whatever the actual results at Brown, Wayland's
effective criticisms of the conventional college curriculum made a vigorous
plea for bringing the American college into closer touch with the material
needs of a new nation faced with the task of developing and exploiting the
enormous resources of a continent.

Whether he intended to be or not, Wayland proved an effective academic spokesman for the aspirations of the middle class of businessmen,
merchants, and industrialists who were gaining power in New England
and who eventually dominated the political and economic policies of the
United States after the Civil War.   Not only did his ideas appeal to the
businessmen, but his democratic proposals to open the doors of the colleges to suit the utilitarian needs of all levels of society received support
from the growing laboring and trades classes.   Thus, Wayland proved
himself to be one of the most forward looking of all those college administrators who were trying to keep their colleges upon a sound financial
footing.   He saw, as Ticknor had seen, that the curriculum must be
adapted to meet the needs of all classes of society, or the college would
lose essential patronage and support to the technical schools.   He saw,

---

[1] *Ibid.*, p. 283.   For an extended discussion of the effects of Wayland's report, see
ibid., pp. 274–278.

[2] *Ibid.*, p. 275.

as Jefferson had seen, that everyone in a democracy had a right to an education; and he saw, as did his contemporary Quincy, that additional funds must be obtained for the college if it were to be reformed along these lines.   In these respects, his arguments gained greater importance in the light of the developments that followed the Civil War, for they were incorporated in the position of President Eliot of Harvard and of President Barnard of Columbia, who came to support the elective system largely because it proved to be an effective means of attracting more students and of competing with the more progressive colleges, academies, and technical schools.

TAPPAN ATTEMPTS TO "PRUSSIANIZE" THE UNIVERSITY OF MICHIGAN

Another outstanding and distinctive attack upon the question of college reform was started before the Civil War by Henry Tappan, who was president of the young University of Michigan from 1852 to 1863. In his attempts to introduce the German idea of a university into the American college, he harked back rather to the scholarship ideals of Ticknor than to the democratic and practical ideals of Wayland.   Getting his degree from Union College in 1825, Tappan was acquainted with the new streams of thought that were beginning to make themselves felt there under the influence of President Nott.   After holding a position for some time as professor of moral and intellectual philosophy at New York University, Tappan resigned and wrote extensively on philosophy, traveled in Europe, and became imbued with the Prussian ideals of state school systems and university scholarship.

In 1851, Tappan published his first treatise upon college reform entitled *University Education* in which he outlined the essential features of the Prussian system of state-supported secular schools extending from the elementary level to the university.[1]   He believed sincerely that a real university could exist only as a component part of a complete system of education arising from and built upon the successive stages of lower training.   Only in this way could a university offer facilities for the most thorough scholarship and research in every branch of knowledge. Perhaps it was the desire to establish this sort of university that led him to accept the presidency of Michigan.   There he saw a young state and a new university which did not have the hampering traditions of the older colleges and which perhaps could be integrated with the whole public school system.   Such integration had been impossible in the older states, because the colleges had been largely denominational or privately endowed, and Tappan believed that financial support by public taxation was the only means whereby an institution large enough to be called

[1] HENRY P. TAPPAN, *University Education* (G. P. Putnam's Sons, New York, 1851).

properly a university could be maintained.   Furthermore, he found that
the state of Michigan had already been committed to a program similar
to the Prussian system by the state constitution of 1835 which had been
influenced by Victor Cousin's report and by the first superintendent of
public instruction, John D. Pierce, who had formulated a plan for a
university to crown the educational system of the state.[1]

Tappan began immediately to advocate the building of the Michigan
school and university system upon Prussian lines.   In his inaugural
address, he gave credit to the first superintendent and others who had
paved the way for a complete system of state education and outlined
plans for realizing Prussian ideals in practice.   He indicated that American collegiate education as it was then organized on the basis of mental
discipline was comparable to the German *Gymnasium* (secondary school)
rather than to the German university.   Thus, the college curriculum
must be amplified by scientific and other studies if it were to be raised
to the level of a university properly so-called.   To accomplish this the
prescribed course of study must be broken up so that:

. . . we shall also be under no temptation of pressing the student with overmuch
study and thus inducing superficial scholarship.   The university will then be
ever before him with its ample preparations, inviting him to a ripened scholarship
in whatever department he may select.[2]

With this ultimate aim in view, Tappan carried into effect an act of the
legislature in 1851 providing a course or courses for such students as did
not desire to follow the usual collegiate curriculum, admitting them without examinations in the ancient languages.   To this end, the college
curriculum was broken up into three courses: the usual classical course
of four years ending with the bachelor of arts degree; a scientific course of
four years ending in the bachelor of science degree with emphasis upon
engineering, astronomy, and the application of chemistry to the arts as
well as upon other sciences; and an "optional," or "partial," course.   In
the university catalogue of 1852–1853, the optional course was described
as follows:

Those who do not desire to become candidates for a degree may be admitted
to any part of the classical or scientific course, for such length of time as they may
choose. . . . [3]

[1] See CHARLES KENDALL ADAMS, *Historical Sketch of the University of Michigan*
(Ann Arbor, 1876).

[2] H. B. ADAMS, "The Study of History in American Colleges and Universities,"
U. S. Bureau of Education, Circular of Information, 1887, No. 2, p. 90.

[3] ELIZABETH FARRAND, *History of the University of Michigan* (Register Publishing
House, Ann Arbor, 1885), pp. 99–100.   For details of the classical and scientific
courses in 1853 and 1863, see *ibid.*, pp. 102–110.

In Tappan's own words:

The optional course was intended to meet the wants of those who aimed at special acquirements; and of those the inequality of whose preparatory studies in the different branches required for admission, whether in the classical or scientific course, demanded special arrangements.[1]

The university not only offered students a choice among the three courses, but by 1856 several subjects had been made elective in the scientific courses as well; these were history, astronomy, chemistry, zoology, botany, geology, German, philosophy, Greek, and Latin.

Tappan's reasons for establishing the scientific and optional courses illustrate the close relationship to the interests of the people of the state that was maintained by the state universities of the Middle West from the very beginning of their histories.   Catering to the material wants of the people in new and undeveloped states led the state universities to expand their curriculums with subjects designed to be more useful to the public and later provided an incentive to the older colleges to do the same sort of thing in order to meet the competition.   The reasons given by Tappan for adopting a scientific and optional course in addition to the classical course are as follows: Too many students had been excluded from university work because of the scarcity of adequate classical preparatory schools of the young Northwest states; Tappan felt that it was easier for a student to pursue scientific subjects without preparatory studies in science than it was to study the college classics without previous preparatory work in them; and the natural prejudice of a new and rapidly improving region in favor of mechanical and useful arts rather than the classical studies demanded the establishment of such courses.[2]   It is interesting to note here, again, that it is these very responses to practical needs that are deplored by such recent critics of university education as Abraham Flexner and Robert M. Hutchins.

Besides these changes in the college courses, Tappan began, in 1858, to offer what he called "university courses" to graduates in an effort to make a "real" university out of the college in line with the arguments of his treatises on *University Education*, his inaugural, the catalogue of 1852–1853, and other publications and speeches.   The university courses were lectures rather than recitations and were given as higher courses offered in each department to students who had the bachelor's degree; and a master of arts or master of science degree was to be given after the completion of a year's work in two subjects each semester, an examination in three of the subjects, and the presentation of a thesis.   Despite the

---

[1] *Review by Rev. Dr. H. P. Tappan of his Connection with the University of Michigan* (Detroit, 1864), p. 6.
[2] *Ibid.*, pp. 5–6.

fact that these beginnings were very slight and developed very slowly, Tappan had begun to actualize his ideal of a German university. Illustrating these ideals of freedom, research, and thorough scholarship in an address which he gave to the Michigan Christian Library Association in 1858, he said:

Freedom—this is the grand characteristic of University Education, as it is the essential attribute of manhood. . . .

How simple the idea of a university! An association of eminent scholars in every department of human knowledge; together with books embodying the results of human investigation and thinking, and all the means of advancing and illustrating knowledge.

How simple the law which is to govern this association!—That each member as a thinker, investigator, and teacher shall be a law unto himself, in his own department.[1]

In an effort to realize these ideals, Tappan not only established university lectures but abolished the dormitory plan of the college to do away with the English idea of a communal, disciplinary institution, and he turned over the dormitory buildings to laboratory and classroom use.

To summarize President Tappan's university policy of reform, it may be said that his primary aim was the transformation of the existing small college with its narrow disciplinary curriculum into the genuine university contemplated by the pioneer statesmen of Michigan and modeled after the German university ideal. To this end, the first condition of success was the selection of faculty members upon the basis of their accomplishments as thorough scholars and original investigators in their specialized fields of study. Tappan immediately began to select such men, and among them were Andrew D. White and Charles Kendall Adams, who are important for our purposes because of their later connection with Cornell University and their effective advocacy of the elective principle both at Michigan and at Cornell.[2]

President Tappan's administration was also significant for the changes made in the college course. He realized from the beginning that, because of the inadequate preparatory schools in the Middle West, he could not alter it radically. Consequently, the "gymnasial" course of the college, with its prescribed curriculum of four years and its schoolmaster methods and discipline, had to be retained until such time as this work could be adequately done by the secondary schools of the state. The close integration of the University of Michigan with the school system of

---

[1] HENRY TAPPAN, *The University* . . . (S. B. McCracken, Ann Arbor, 1858), pp. 6–7.

[2] Adams also provided effective leadership while president of the University of Wisconsin (1892–1901) in developing the resources and facilities of that university.

the state provided an example to other state universities. Meanwhile, Tappan believed that the college course should gradually be changed with the introduction of more useful courses and the introduction of university methods of lecture, research, and freedom for the student to follow what courses he would. Another objective was that requirements for admission to the college and professional work should constantly be raised until all departments of the university admitted students of relatively equal attainment and learning.

In advocating and effecting this program, Tappan roiled the waters of nationalism and brought upon himself and upon the university a flood of abuse and censure from the press of the state which charged him with trying to "Prussianize" the school system by his "un-American" doctrines and methods.[1] During his term of office, however, he had the support of most of his faculty[2] and went ahead with his program of reorganizing the university until he was forced out after 11 years of service. His aims are so effectively presented in his own words that they deserve quoting at length:

First. To adapt the University to the present wants of the community. To this end a *scientific* course was organized, in distinction from a *classical* course; a school of civil engineering was instituted; a laboratory and observatory were erected; and an agricultural school, and a school of military engineering, were sought to be created. The University, as at present developed, is in part composed of the intermediate or pre-disciplinary course common to our colleges, and to the gymnasia of Germany; and in part of that which belongs to a University properly so-called. And this must remain until all the parts of a just system of public education are fully developed in their order and relations. When this is accomplished, the University can become purely a University—an institution for professional study, for the culminating studies in science and literature and for manly self-development. Hence my aim was,

Secondly. Through the graduates of the University to perfect the intermediate and common schools. . . .

Thirdly. My aim was to keep the idea of a University constantly before the public mind; to make the young men educated at the University thoroughly to

[1] A sample of the attack upon Tappan by the press is given by the *Lansing Journal:* "Of all the imitations of English aristocracy, German mysticism, Prussian imperiousness, and Parisian nonsensities, he is altogether the most un-Americanized—the most completely foreignized specimen of an abnormal Yankee, we have ever seen." Quoted in CHARLES M. PERRY, *Henry Philip Tappan* (University of Michigan Press, Ann Arbor, 1933), p. 202.

[2] E. O. HAVEN, *Increased Mental Activity of the Age* (Ann Arbor, 1854), a speech by Professor Haven before the Literary Societies of Michigan, in which he described the stimulation of intellectual activity in the United States and the demand for experiment incident to the development of the great resources of the country; there was consequently great need for the adoption of the best of the Prussian university methods, with their great resources for research in all branches of knowledge.

comprehend it; and to engage the best efforts of the Regents and the Professors for its realization.

Thus, I hoped, that while wisely meeting present exigencies, we should still be pressing forward to the great end of developing a University worthy of the name, and of perfecting our entire system of education.[1]

Despite his earlier aristocratic ideals of scholarship and his enthusiasm for Prussian universities, and despite the attacks upon him by the democratic state of Michigan, Tappan persevered. He thus helped to lay the theoretical foundations for the development of the Western state universities which were shaped, as we have seen, not only by the democratic and practical needs of the frontier but also by the aristocratic and scholarly models of the German universities. Both influences tended to emphasize specialization rather than breadth in the student's college course, and hence both influences helped to pave the way for the widespread introduction of the elective system into the college curriculum.

Thus, even before the Civil War, the lines of educational battle were clearly drawn between the conservatives, who wished to hold to the traditional college, and the progressives, who wished to reform it. Although most of the essential theoretical arguments for broadening the notion of a liberal education and for introducing the elective system into the college curriculum were made before the Civil War, it was not until the last half of the nineteenth century that economic and intellectual forces had advanced far enough to allow the theory to be put into actual widespread practice.

[1] *Review by Rev. Dr. H. P. Tappan of his Connection with the University of Michigan*, p. 5.

PART III
THE ELECTIVE PRINCIPLE WINS THE DAY

CHAPTER IX

THE LATER NINETEENTH CENTURY REAPS THE HARVEST
(ABOUT 1860–1910)

Economic and Social Trends Nourish the Elective System. The quickened life in the United States during the period from the Civil War to the turn of the nineteenth century wrought drastic economic and intellectual changes which, in turn, profoundly affected education from its lowest to its highest levels. Economic movements which had been set on foot before the war were hastened to fulfillment in the later decades of the century. Along with the amazing growth of machine technology and large-scale industry, the exploitation of the West proceeded more rapidly than ever; and the dominance of the business and manufacturing classes in American life was assured. "Triumphant business enterprise," with its ostentatious display of riches and its bitter struggles with organized labor, gave the dominant tone to the intellectual and moral temper of the later decades. As Beard puts it, this acquisitive order had a simple philosophy: The state and society mean little; the individual means everything.[1] And the basic urge of the individual was conceived to be his desire to acquire money, wealth, and property. Man works best, said capitalism, when he is spurred by the desire and hope for profits. So the rationale of gain seeking became the foundation for a whole philosophy of economic individualism.

This philosophy of capitalism was not long confined merely to the wealthy class, but it soon permeated the professional, "white collar," and working classes as well. Most people, indeed, became imbued with the idea that the individual could get on if he merely made use of his talents and if he were not hindered by interference from the government. Demands grew that education of all levels should become more practical and train more directly for the industrial and business pursuits that were obviously so profitable.

Another side of the picture of economic acquisitiveness was the fact that the growing national wealth made more funds available for the expansion and improvement of public education. Common schools were greatly multiplied; public high schools increased in number and began to

---

[1] For a vivid picture of this period, see C. A. Beard and M. R. Beard, *The Rise of American Civilization* (The Macmillan Company, New York, 1937), Chaps. XIX–XXV.

take over much of the elementary work of the traditional college. The number of students grew enormously: The United States commissioner of education reported in 1900 that the *percentage* of students in the total population of the United States who were studying college preparatory and equivalent subjects had more than tripled from 1878 to 1898.[1]

These economic forces also had their effects upon higher education. Public and private funds were increasingly made available for founding and enlarging both state and private universities. Prompted by growing wealth and the desire for educational opportunity on the part of greater numbers of people, state legislatures increased their grants to state universities. Through the land grants of the Morrill acts, the federal government made possible many agricultural and engineering schools which were set up either as separate institutions or connected with established state or private universities. Profiting from public generosity were many such institutions as Cornell and the state universities of Michigan, Wisconsin, Minnesota, and California. Increasing wealth among the capitalist group also permitted private donors to endow with munificent foundations such institutions as Cornell, Johns Hopkins, Chicago, Stanford, and Tulane. The older institutions such as Harvard, Yale, Columbia, and Princeton were also able to obtain generous grants from wealthy alumni and friends. Thus, colleges and universities grew further and further away from religious control as public funds were increasingly poured into institutions of higher education and as administrators appealed to business enterprise rather than to church denominations for support.

In the last quarter of the century, the number of students going to college more than doubled.[2] This increase in numbers of students going to college was not only a result of the democratic movement which sent a great influx of men and women into higher institutions, but it was also a result of the greater demand by more men and women for higher training to prepare them for the various professions, trades, and businesses that required specialized training. More and more young people wanted to go to college, and more and more now could actually go. Many new occupations began to open up not only to young men but also to young women,

---

[1] *National Education Association, Journal of Proceedings and Addresses,* 1900, p. 199. In 1876, 2,150 students per million of total population were working on college preparatory and equivalent studies; in 1897–1898, there were 7,630 per million. In round numbers, this increase was from approximately 175,000 to 600,000.

[2] *Ibid.* The number of students in higher institutions increased from 598 per million of total population to 1,215 per million. In other words, the increase in round numbers was from approximately 50,000 to 100,000 students in collegiate departments. In 1900, the enrollment in all kinds of higher institutions was nearly 240,000 according to the "Biennial Survey of Education, 1932–1934," *U. S. Office of Education, Bulletin,* 1935, No. 2, p. 9.

and they made their wants felt by demands upon the high school and university curriculum. Women had been admitted to Oberlin and Antioch in the first half of the century; the state university of Iowa proclaimed the equality of the sexes at its opening in 1856; and women were gradually being admitted to other state and private universities, especially those of the West, such as Wisconsin and Michigan. Some of the older colleges set up coordinate colleges for women, for example, Barnard at Columbia and Radcliffe at Harvard; and long before the close of the century, women had obtained special colleges of their own in such institutions as Bryn Mawr, Mount Holyoke, Smith, Vassar, and Wellesley.

Expansion was the keynote not only of American economic life but also of the development of higher education during this period. The more students that went to college the more the resources and curriculum expanded. Colleges needed more professorships, more funds, more buildings, and more equipment; they also needed more subjects and more courses to meet the demands for subjects concerned with industrial, business, and agricultural pursuits. All of this expansion resulted in overcrowding the curriculum and greatly expedited the need for and the introduction of the elective system. The rush to the colleges was not merely to take vocational and professional courses, however; the notion began to circulate that even the liberal arts course would be financially worth while in the business world. The reply of a student at Harvard to Henry Adams in 1871 that "The degree of Harvard College is worth money to me in Chicago" represented the widespread faith of Americans in college education no matter what was taught.

Besides the changes in economic and social ideology that greatly affected university education in the United States in the last half of the nineteenth century, there were also important intellectual movements which influenced the theory and practice of higher education in the direction of the elective system of studies. The three most important intellectual influences for our purposes were: (1) the continued achievements in the field of the physical and biological sciences and the formulation of the peculiarly American philosophy of pragmatism; (2) the beginnings of an experimental psychology that threatened to destroy the theoretical bases of mental discipline; and (3) the highly controversial discussions concerning, in general, the nature and functions of higher education and concerning, in particular, the relative advantages of the classics and literature versus the sciences.

Influence of Science: Evolution and Pragmatism. The continuing advancement of the physical and biological sciences and the enrichment of such studies as history, economics, politics, and sociology were instrumental in adding many new subjects to the liberal arts curriculum and showed the necessity for specialization in the undergraduate college if the student were to progress very far into any field.   The rapid developments in many fields of science, such as bacteriology, physics, and electricity, are too numerous and too well known to require more than mention here.   It is enough to say that during the last half of the nineteenth century, "science" came to be applied to nearly all bodies of knowledge that had been classified, systematized, and recorded, and the universities came more and more to play a part in the creation of these bodies of knowledge.

As a result of the influence of German methods of research and of the renewed attempts to apply scientific methods to other fields of knowledge than the natural sciences, the curriculum of higher education by 1910 had been increased enormously by additions to the established sciences and by the introduction alongside the older studies of such new "sciences" as those of language and philology, history, economics, politics, sociology, anthropology, archeology, music, psychology, education, and religion. The sheer fact that a tremendous amount of new knowledge was gradually being made available in the curriculum of higher institutions represented one of the greatest differences between the old college with its narrow curriculum and the new university with its greatly enlarged courses of study.

Another way in which science fundamentally influenced higher education was the increasing impact of the theories of evolution and pragmatism upon the intellectual consciousness of the country.   Evolution and pragmatism joined forces in challenging the older religious and scientific notions of the eighteenth century which held that truth was a fixed and eternal body of knowledge which could be reached only through a set of carefully prescribed studies.   From the time when Darwin's *Origin of Species* was published in 1859, the theories of natural selection and mutability of the species served to increase the activity in the biological and social sciences as well as to stimulate a furious controversy in the intellectual life of the later nineteenth century.   The most obvious impact of the theory of evolution was upon the religious conception of authority which was the bulwark of theology.   Much of religious authority and theology centered about the Old Testament doctrines that the world and man were specially created by divine intervention and that by virtue of his immortal soul the human species is a distinctly different form of living being from the rest of nature.

In direct opposition to the religious doctrines came the startling theories of evolution which said that the earth was not created all at once but millions of years old, that by natural processes the simpler forms of life became more complex, and that man and all living things were branches of a common stock of life.   Thomas Huxley and Robert Ingersoll carried the war into the theological camps, and Herbert Spencer applied the evolutionary concepts and the doctrines of the survival of the fittest to the fields of ethics, politics, history, economics, and social development in general. Thus, the authority of religion was challenged in the intellectual field, and the authority of the religiously sponsored liberal education of a classical and linguistic kind was bound to be challenged by scientific studies that clamored for a place of dignity in a liberal education.

Not only was the religious control over colleges challenged by science, but the whole philosophical position of idealism and the "genteel tradition" was attacked by the new and uniquely American philosophy of pragmatism. The original tradition of Calvinism in America and the early nineteenth century influence of German idealism had led most American philosophers to envisage a monistic universe in which everything had a fixed place in relation to the whole and in which truth was looked upon as uniform, fixed, and eternal. Such a view of truth had supported the classical notion of a liberal education; for inasmuch as truth was always the same, a single group of unchanging studies could always be prescribed as the best means of arriving at that truth. The prevailing conditions of American frontier life, however, with its wilderness to be conquered and its dangers, uncertainties, and constant struggle for existence, had shaped an "American mood" which was out of sympathy with the finalities of philosophic idealism; established order, routine, and finality became less vital to Americans than initiative, enterprise, and innovation. From the temper of American life and from the example of Darwinism and the sciences, Charles Peirce and William James formulated a pragmatic philosophy which they felt was more appropriate to the changed conditions of life.

Pragmatism looked upon the universe as essentially incomplete and changing; the varieties of existence and of experience were set over against the organic unity and homogeneity of idealism. The appearance of novelty was considered to be a genuine fact of experience, and belief in the immediate experience of human beings rather than appeal to the remote authority of a religious or philosophical kind was considered the court of last resort in validating ideas. In other words, truth was not a single and closed body of knowledge which held good despite all the experience of men; truth was viewed as depending upon the consequences that occurred when men acted in certain ways. Truth became plural and became subject to change whenever better methods of acting and thinking were devised to meet the exigencies of life.

Inasmuch as law, religion, government, art, and science were looked upon as receiving meaning and value from what they accomplish, it was a short step to look upon the college curriculum as valuable only in so far as it accomplished what was desired. Those who justified the traditional prescribed curriculum on the grounds that only the classics, mathematics, and philosophy as they had long been taught would lead to the fundamental and fixed truth were hard put to defend their position in the face of pragmatism. After the turn of the century, John Dewey and his "instrumentalism," which was a philosophical descendant of the pragmatism of Peirce and James, made it even more difficult for advocates of a completely closed body of truth and of a completely prescribed curriculum to hold their own.

Decline of Faculty Psychology and Rise of Experimental Psychology.
The gradual acceptance and spread of the elective system was aided not only by the theoretical arguments of the period under consideration and by the force of economic events but also by the development of a newer psychology which emphasized the study of the individual and his capacities. Mental, or "formal," discipline had received its psychological justification in the doctrines of "faculty psychology," according to which the mind was conceived as consisting of separate, independent, and ready-made capacities, or faculties, such as memory, judgment, reason, will, imagination, and taste. These faculties were looked upon as distinct powers of the mind; hence they were considered to be merely potential until brought into actuality by training or practice, and the exercise of one faculty was thought to transfer beneficially to other faculties. Development of the powers of the mind had been set up, especially by the Yale report of 1828, as the supreme aim of college training, and the classics and mathematics had been looked upon as the best means of bringing about this development of the intellectual powers. For the exercise of the faculties, the form of studies was considered more important than their content. Thus, when the older studies of the college curriculum were attacked for the reason that they were not practical or useful enough, their supporters defended them with the doctrines of faculty psychology. They said that the classics and mathematics should retain their position of importance in the curriculum because the form of their subject matter was more valuable for mental discipline than that of such so-called practical studies as the physical sciences and modern languages.

So long as faculty psychology remained the dominating theory of the learning process, the defenders of mental discipline and of the traditional prescribed studies held their position rather securely. Even some of the advocates of the newer subjects and of the elective principle often used the doctrines of formal discipline to support their own theories by showing that, since the value of studies was measured by the way the work was carried on and not by the content of the subject matter, all subjects could be equally valuable for mental discipline. Therefore, the doctrine of "equivalence of subjects" was often advocated in order that students might be allowed to select among a large group of studies, provided those studies were all taught with the same thoroughness and difficulty.[1] But more often the advocates of the newer subjects and of the elective principle attacked the classics, mathematics, and traditional philosophy because they were not sufficiently adapted to the varying interests, capacities, and prospective pursuits of the students. This latter view was increasingly supported by the theories of a newer psychology as the nineteenth century drew to its close and as faculty psychology lost its dominance in the field of the theory of the mind.

Several phases of the development of the newer psychology tended to cause the decline of faculty psychology. There had been the growth of the so-called "associational school" of psychology in England which declared that, in the classification of the processes of the human mind, faculty psychology had distinguished too minutely among different mental powers that actually were not mutually exclusive or independent of one another. Associationism tried to reduce all mental processes to the single process of association. The mind was looked upon by this new psychology as made up of groups of ideas that had become associated in different ways and with varying emphases. From Hobbes and Locke to Hartley and Mill, the various elements of sensation and perception were conceived to be associated somehow into mental movements or ideas. Thus, memory, reason, emotion, and invention were conceived not as independent faculties but merely as different ways in which simple perceptions had become associated with other perceptions to form more complicated perceptions and ideas. In Germany, Herbart also attacked faculty psychology on somewhat the same grounds. He said that ideas followed one another and competed for recognition until some became associated together into what he called the "apperceptive mass" which then helped to determine what new ideas would be associated with old ones in the learning process. Thus, it was believed that *specific* ideas rather than independent mental faculties determined an individual's memory and reason.

Another type of newer psychology which tended to weaken faculty psychology was the development of experimental method in psychology and the recognition that psychology was based upon physiological and neurological processes of the human organism.[2] Wilhelm Wundt in his

---

[1] See, for example, "Report of the Committee of Ten on Secondary School Studies," *U. S. Bureau of Education*, 1893, p. 52, and "Report of the Committee on College Entrance Requirements," *N.E.A.*, *Proceedings*, 1899, pp. 632–811.

[2] Johannes Müller represented this attitude neatly when he said, "No one can be a psychologist who is not a physiologist." Thereupon, psychologists turned to the measuring of motor reactions, nerve impulses, binocular depth perception, eye muscles, kinesthetic sense, auditory mechanics of speech and music, vision and hearing, tactile senses of skin, weight, etc.

laboratory at Leipzig was an influential factor in emphasizing the conception that sensory, motor, and physiological processes greatly affected mental development.   The mental faculties gradually came to be looked upon as valuable merely for descriptive and classificatory but not for explanatory purposes.   (This school of psychology is sometimes called "structuralism.")   The tendency to pay closer attention to physiological factors in psychology was further supported by the development of an experimental psychology in the United States in which the doctrines of biological evolution were applied to psychology.   As a result of the influence of the laboratory methods of Wundt, the theory of evolution, and actual experiments with animals by E. L. Thorndike, the notion grew that mind, far from being a separate entity, or faculty, was really the functioning of the organism in adjusting its behavior more adequately to its environment.   (This school of psychology is sometimes called "functionalism.")   In the field of learning, "behavior" became more important than "consciousness," and William James said at Harvard that mind was in what it does.

Furthermore, experimental psychology was supported by studies in heredity and original nature conducted by such men as Francis Galton, J. McKeen Cattell, and E. L. Thorndike.   The startling findings as to "individual differences" as early as the 1880's led progressive educators gradually to emphasize the differing capacities of different individuals and to recognize the need for taking account of these varying abilities and interests in the learning process.   In these ways, the traditional conception that the minds of all men were essentially alike and that the human mind was made up of separate faculties which should be exercised by certain formal studies gradually gave way to the notion that the mental make-up of different individuals required special treatment and that the content of different subjects was appropriate to different individuals. Thorndike's *Educational Psychology* in 1903 called particular attention to individual differences; and from that time on, the differences of individuals came to be stressed much more emphatically than ever before.   Thus, by the turn of the century there was psychological evidence for the argument that all studies were of more or less equal value for a liberal education but that some studies were merely better for one individual and others better for another.

As the theories of mental discipline and transfer of training began to be suspect by the new experimental psychology (see pages 263–264*ff*), the nature of each individual was looked upon as worth developing in its own way for its own sake; and since the nature of each individual had been found to differ from that of every other, the notion gained strength that each individual should receive special attention through special studies if education were to be adapted to differing individuals.   Another factor of importance was the decline of Latin as the universal language of scholarship and the rise of the modern languages as effective instruments of research. As long as every scholar needed Latin in order to conduct advanced research, the prescription of Latin held on tenaciously; but when considerable scholarly material was written in the modern languages, the feeling grew that the study of Latin and Greek was of no more special value in the learning process or in a liberal education than was the study of German or French. With greater attention being given to the needs and capacities of students by psychology as well as by the economic philosophy of individualism which had permeated political and intellectual fields, the elective system in varying forms became the predominant characteristic of curricular organization by the turn of the century.

European Controversies Concerning the Aims of Higher Education. In Europe, the controversy over the functions of universities took two forms: debates concerning the relative value of science versus literature as the main subjects of study; and wholesale criticisms of the established university systems, especially as developed in England. The most insistent British advocates for a greater emphasis upon scientific studies were Spencer and Huxley; outstanding defenders of literature, and especially of the literature of ancient Greece and Rome, were John Stuart Mill and Matthew Arnold. In his famous essay *What Knowledge Is of Most Worth?* Spencer insisted that the physical sciences provided the knowledge that was most valuable for the guidance and conduct of life as well as for mental discipline.[1] He advocated that science should be given a greater place in education, because it was so much more efficacious than the classical literature for the main functions of human living which, according to him, included self-preservation and bodily health, the gaining of a livelihood, activities of parenthood and citizenship, and the relaxations and pleasures of leisure and art.

By means of speeches and writings, Huxley carried the banner of scientific studies through the British Isles and the United States. In a speech "On the Educational Value of the Natural History Sciences" in 1854, he pointed out that the biological and physiological sciences should have as much emphasis as the chemical-physical sciences and the social sciences; he eulogized their value as subjects for promoting mental discipline as well as for the practical information that they conveyed.[2] In *Science and Culture*, Huxley pointed out how the introduction of the scientific studies had met the continued opposition of the classicists and even of the businessmen at first, but he argued that neither the sub-

---

[1] See HERBERT SPENCER, *Education* (D. Appleton-Century Company, Inc., New York, 1912), pp. 1–87.

[2] THOMAS H. HUXLEY, *Science and Education* (D. Appleton-Century Company, Inc., New York, 1914), pp. 38–65.

ject matter nor the mental discipline afforded by the classics justified the expenditure of time usually made upon them and that for real culture an exclusively scientific education was as good as an exclusively classical one.[1] He denied the right of the classicists to confine a liberal education to the study of literature, but he contended that both literary and scientific studies were needed to prevent undesirable mental twists in the educated man.

Classical studies were especially defended by Matthew Arnold.[2] Arnold was the most vigorous opponent of Huxley and Spencer, and in speech and essay he attacked the notion of allowing utilitarian aims as embodied in scientific and practical subjects to gain dominance and drive out the aims of "true culture." He represented the viewpoint of Humanism in looking upon man as a moral and spiritual being who was different in kind from animals, whereas Huxley and Spencer represented the naturalistic position which looked upon man as an animal different only in degree from the rest of the natural world. Arnold defended the classical languages and literature as the best means to develop the spiritual and moral qualities of man and to arrive at his famous ideal of culture—"to know the best which has been thought and said in the world"—but he did not deny the important place that the writings on modern science should have in education.[3] He merely deplored the great emphasis upon utilitarianism and the neglect of the ancient classics. Arnold and Huxley were really much more in agreement than is usually recognized, for each admitted the validity of the other's arguments, but neither wanted his own favorite to be neglected. The counterpart of this controversy in England over the place and functions of science versus the classics was carried on in a great many articles and speeches in America.

Another means by which the ideal of university education received more explicit formulation both in Europe and in America was the great amount of general criticism that was being leveled at the universities and the various suggestions for reform.[4] Cardinal Newman joined hands with Arnold and Huxley in criticizing the English universities. In lecture and essay, Newman formulated his idea of a university which he believed

---

[1] *Ibid.*, pp. 134–159.

[2] See also J. S. MILL, *Inaugural Address delivered to the University of St. Andrews,* Feb. 1, 1867 (London, 1867), for a defense of classical studies.

[3] A. L. BOUTON, ed., *Matthew Arnold, Prose and Poetry* (Charles Scribner's Sons, New York, 1927), p. 55, from Arnold's "Literature and Science," an address given in America. For recent expositions of the Humanistic point of view, see Norman Foerster, *The American State University, Its Relation to Democracy* (University of North Carolina Press, Chapel Hill, N. C., 1937), and *The Future of the Liberal College* (D. Appleton-Century Company, Inc., New York, 1938).

[4] See, for example, MARK PATTISON, *Suggestions on Academical Organization, with especial reference to Oxford* (Edmonston and Douglas, Edinburgh, 1868).

should be a place for teaching universal knowledge and aiming at "intellectual culture." In a liberal education, the knowledge should be acquired for its own sake with no ulterior motive; whereas in a professional or useful education, the knowledge is acquired with the aim of teaching or turning it into revenue or social service. The university should disseminate knowledge of the liberal sort only and thereby aim to cultivate the intellect: "It educates the intellect to reason well in all matters, to reach out toward truth, and to grasp it."[1] Newman felt that the universities as they were then constituted emphasized too much the acquirement and attainment of knowledge as mere information or as aid to expertness in particular pursuits or in moral and religious proficiency rather than as means to freeing and developing the intellect. "Intellect" was thus viewed as something apart from conduct in everyday matters.

Huxley formulated a quite different idea of a university in his inaugural address as rector of the University of Aberdeen.[2] In this address, he described a university as he believed it should be: "In an ideal University, as I conceive it, a man should be able to obtain instruction in all forms of knowledge, and discipline in the use of all the methods by which knowledge is obtained."[3] He then outlined the various fields of knowledge that he would include and among which there would be no question of relative importance or superiority. It is very evident, however, that he proposed much more for the scientific subjects than was the custom in the English universities of the day. In his address on university education given at the inauguration of Johns Hopkins University, he touched upon the elective system by saying: "It is obviously impossible that any student should pass through the whole of the series of courses of instruction offered by a university."[4]

Arnold also criticized the narrowness of the English university curriculum; and despite his pleas for literature, he recommended that greater scientific research and more advanced instruction be attained in the English universities:

The idea of a university is, as I have already said, that of an institution not only offering to young men facilities for graduating in that line of study to which

---

[1] JOHN HENRY, CARDINAL NEWMAN, *The Idea of a University* (Longmans, Green & Company, New York, 1927), pp. 125–126. *Cf.* again Hutchins' theories and the belief of both Newman and Hutchins that truth is a fixed and eternal thing which can be reached for and grasped. See ROBERT M. HUTCHINS, *The Higher Learning in America*, (Yale University Press, New Haven, 1936), pp. 62–67. Hutchins quotes Newman on pp. 63–64 to show that the intellect must not be useful in any "low, mechanical, mercantile sense."

[2] HUXLEY, *op. cit.*, pp. 189–234.

[3] *Ibid.*, pp. 204–205.

[4] *Ibid.*, p. 243.

their aptitudes direct them, but offering to them, also, *facilities for following that line of study systematically, under first rate instruction.*[1]

Arnold had made a study of the educational systems of the Continent, and his recommendations for the English universities were that they should follow, in general, the example of the German universities with their freedom of teaching and learning, their state control, and their emphasis upon systematic research in all fields of knowledge.

Newman, Huxley, and Arnold are merely examples of the wide interest and the wide discussion concerning university education that took place during the last half of the nineteenth century in both Europe and America. Gradually, the notion gained currency that a true university was one in which all branches of knowledge were taught and investigated, the teacher had the freedom to follow the truth wherever it led him, and the student had the freedom to study whatever pleased him or best suited his needs and capacities. As has been pointed out earlier, the German universities were the models for this conception of a university, as opposed to the narrower English and American colleges with their restricted curriculums which aimed at mental discipline rather than at extended knowledge.

Paulsen gives a good picture of the freedom of the student in a German university as it existed in the nineteenth century:

Aside from a fixed period of study, almost everything is left to individual choice; there is no prescribed course of study, with intermediate examinations, as at the French faculties; each student selects the branches which he wishes to study in each semester, and attendance upon the lectures depends solely upon his own volition; the freedom of learning is so extensive that it actually includes the freedom not to learn or to do anything.[2]

The French universities, or rather, until 1896, the French "faculties," had promoted scientific research and had extended the branches of higher education to include nearly all of the fields of knowledge, but strict government control had prevented any such freedom of teaching or learning as had developed in the German universities. The latter therefore provided the major stimulus both to England and to America for the reform of higher education.[3]

[1] MATTHEW ARNOLD, *Schools and Universities on the Continent* (Macmillan & Company, Ltd., London, 1868), p. 287. In this connection, Arnold said of the English universities, "It is science (in the German sense of *Wissenschaft* or systematic knowledge) that we have most need to borrow from the German universities. The French university has no liberty, and the English universities have no science; the German universities have both.

[2] FRIEDRICH PAULSEN, *German Universities and University Study* (Charles Scribner's Sons, New York, 1906), p. 283.

[3] See B. A. HINSDALE, "Notes on the History of Foreign Influence upon Education in the United States," *U. S. Commissioner of Education, Report,* 1897–1898, Part I,

The following chapters will describe in more detail the explicit influences that these economic and intellectual forces exerted in the development of higher education in the United States, with special reference to the acceptance in theory and practice of the elective system. In the statements of educational leaders is found a heightening of the controversies between conservatives and progressives. The progressives demanded a more democratic and "practical" education; and the conservatives, the retention of the classical and "cultural" education. The progressives proposed to expand the college upon the model of German universities and to offer more freedom to students and more research for teachers; the conservatives defended the traditional, narrow curriculum of the English-type college with its emphasis upon mental and moral discipline. The progressives advocated a secular education which tended to look upon the student as capable of guiding his own destinies, and the conservatives extolled a religious education which looked upon the student as needing careful supervision and discipline.

pp. 591–629, for a list of some of the American students who went to German universities and brought back German conceptions of university study.

CHAPTER X

PLANS FOR CHANGING COLLEGES INTO UNIVERSITIES

ELIOT'S IDEAL FOR A UNIVERSITY AT HARVARD

Among American institutions of higher education in the later nineteenth century, Harvard seemed to be responding most effectively to the outstanding social and intellectual trends described in the preceding chapter. After a period of nearly 20 years of strict limitations, the elective principle was again made the basis of curricular policy there during the presidencies of Thomas Hill and Charles William Eliot. In its own internal history, Harvard gives a good example of the general development that took place in the colleges throughout the United States, a development that saw the increase in the theory and practice of the elective system running parallel to the growing acceptance of the ideal of a broad and liberal university as opposed to the narrow and disciplinary college. The elective system was one of the principal means by which colleges were converted into universities.[1]

The administrations of Kirkland and Quincy at Harvard had seen considerable increase in the number of professorships and courses, and the elective system had reached its greatest development prior to Eliot. Then Presidents Sparks and Walker concentrated upon the undergraduate college as the most important part of the university, and they consequently put great emphasis upon mental discipline and the narrow prescribed curriculum. President Cornelius Felton (1860–1862) as a professor had favored the elective principle and had shared with other progressive professors the ideal of a university, but his administration as president was too short to make substantial gains, except to add a few elective studies to a list that grew rapidly from that time on.

President Thomas Hill Starts the Ball Rolling. The period of President Hill's administration (1862–1869) witnessed a gradual change in the ideal of a university at Harvard. From the conception of an undergraduate college with professional schools as isolated appendages, the

---

[1] "College" is meant to apply to institutions which emphasize general or liberal training in the arts, letters, and sciences; "university" applies to institutions which also offer professional, technical, and specialized training in the advanced branches of knowledge. As university work was taken on, colleges tended to adopt the elective system and to allow more specialization in the undergraduate courses of study.

idea grew that Harvard should be a fully coordinated university which would add to the body of human knowledge by research as well as by dissemination. Consequently, the elective principle received warm advocacy during these formative years, but the financial resources of the college were as yet too inadequate and the opposition still too strong to allow more than a formulation of the doctrine and the beginnings of the elective system on a scale larger than ever before. To make possible a vital and complete use of the elective system, the work of these preparatory years needed not only the impetus given by the growth of prosperity following the Civil War but also the energetic and effective administrative leadership that President Eliot later contributed.

Thomas Hill was too mild mannered to be a strong administrator; but with the aid of Professor Louis Agassiz, he set Harvard upon the course toward becoming a real university in which all the branches of knowledge would be taught and investigated through original research. In 1861, Agassiz had proposed a plan for advanced lectures to be open to all members of the university and to outsiders; this laid the foundation for the university extension system, of which Agassiz said: "In this way . . . I would break open the class system which is too exclusively adhered to in the University, and initiate a freer system of elective studies outside of the undergraduate department."[1]

This plan together with Agassiz's museum of comparative zoology formed the basis for the development of graduate instruction and for the opening of courses to students in departments other than the one in which they were enrolled. In turn, the way was opened for the replacing of recitations by lectures and for reviving the elective system in the undergraduate departments. The effect of graduate instruction upon the undergraduate departments can be seen in virtually all of the colleges of the United States. As specialized graduate courses were increasingly offered, the undergraduate courses increased in number, became more specialized, and eventually were opened alike to graduates and undergraduates, so that the elective principle necessarily came into wider and wider use.[2]

That President Hill's administration was a period of transition from emphasis upon the college as a place of mental discipline to the idea that individual capacities should be recognized through the use of the elective system may be seen in the development of Hill's own thinking on the subject from before his inauguration in 1862 to the end of his administra-

[1] WILLIAM G. LAND, *Thomas Hill* (Harvard University Press, Cambridge, 1933), p. 140.

[2] For example, the dean's report in *Annual Report of the President of Harvard College*, 1877–1878, p. 71, shows that the increasing number of graduate students made necessary the establishment of many new specialized courses.

tion in 1869.   In an address delivered before the Phi Beta Kappa society
of Harvard in 1858, he presented the thesis that a perfectly trained man
must have all of his powers cultivated.[1]   This was essentially the position
of mental discipline, but it is unique in that Hill omitted the ancient
classics as essential parts of that training.   He believed that the five
great departments of thought which were essential parts of a unified
whole and which the student must study in consecutive order were mathematics, natural history, history, psychology, and theology.   He felt that
a student must acquire the essential principles of each of these in order to
become a liberally educated man.

In his inaugural address five years later, Hill still asserted that a
liberal education depended upon the extent and solidity of general attainments, but he also pointed out the desirability and necessity of specialized
study in order to develop the student's particular talents and genius to the
highest degree.[2]   The capacity for profiting from this specialization
depended upon developing all the mental faculties; thus, he advocated an
"integral education" aimed to develop harmoniously all the powers of
the individual and to give him an adequate knowledge of the principles of
each great department of thought, at the same time aiding him to acquire
special proficiency in the particular departments of learning most applicable to his professional needs.

Following Agassiz's lead and his own developing notions, Hill suggested in his report of 1863–1864 that specialized graduate instruction
and research should be recognized along with dissemination of knowledge
as aims of the university.   As a preparation for the more advanced and
specialized work of graduate instruction, the undergraduate needed to
specialize in greater degree, with the consequent need for selection of
particular courses in the college instead of touching upon each of a complete round of studies.   Such a change in Hill's thinking is shown in his
paper "Studies in Harvard College," probably read in 1866 to the
committee on reform.[3]   From this report, it is evident that the function
of the undergraduate department was still envisaged as the training of
the powers of the student but particularly in such a way as best to
fit him for any special pursuit that he might choose.   And the minimum
number of studies that the liberally educated man needed to study was
reduced from the five great fields of knowledge noted in his address in
1858 to history, political economy, and philosophy.   This reduction in the
amount of required study would leave greater freedom for selection of
courses for specialization:

[1] Thomas Hill, *Liberal Education* (Cambridge, 1858).
[2] Thomas Hill, *Inaugural Address* (Cambridge, 1863).
[3] Land, *op. cit.*, p. 144.   Land says that Hill initiated discussion of the elective
studies in a report to the academic council in 1865, but the paper is lost.

What should we do with the [freshman] Class when it had entered? . . . It appears to me desirable to give them still for three years a compulsory course in American History and Political Economy, in Mental and Moral Philosophy, and the practice of writing. In regard to other matters allow them a free choice, only requiring the student to take studies enough to occupy his time.[1]

Hill had not surrendered his conception of an integral education aimed at wide and general study, but he now believed that much of the essentials of a liberal education should be acquired in the preparatory schools and in collateral reading so that the student would be able to choose more intelligently a specialty suited to his aptitudes and inaptitudes. He was able to enlist the support of the majority of the faculty, and the elective principle was applied to a much larger number of studies in 1865 and again in 1867;[2] thus was started the development that was brought to its ultimate conclusion under Eliot. The time was not yet ripe in the 1860's for complete election of studies, because the finances were too insecure to allow expansion of courses and increases in numbers of professors, but progress was soon possible because the college had been committed to the policy of wide election, parents were complaining that the traditional course was outworn and inadequate,[3] and opposition among faculty members was gradually lessening.

President Eliot Carries the Elective System to Its Ultimate Conclusion. During the forty years of his administration (1869–1909), President Eliot supplied a long continuing advocacy of the elective principle and an energetic administrative leadership which enabled Harvard eventually to boast of the freest elective system known to the American college. Eliot took up the plans of Hill's administration to make of Harvard a "real" university, and he carried them forward by means of a most effective administration policy and by advocating forcefully the new ideal of a university which embodied a drastic change in the traditional theory of a liberal education. As a student and as a professor at Harvard, Eliot had been particularly interested in the mathematical and scientific subjects; he had been a professor of chemistry at the Massachusetts Institute of Technology when called to the presidency of Harvard in 1869; and, moreover, he had seen in Europe outstanding universities and technical schools in operation. These experiences impressed upon him the necessity for a redefinition of the meaning of a liberal education and the necessity for giving a greater amount of freedom to the student.

[1] *Ibid.*, p. 146.
[2] WILLIAM R. THAYER, *An Historical Sketch of Harvard University* (Cambridge, 1890), p. 36.
[3] LAND, *op. cit.*, p. 150

Eliot was not captivated by the constitutional pattern of the German universities or of the French faculties, but he was impressed by the range and variety of subjects offered to the student for his choice.[1] He thought that he saw a connection between this abundance of courses and the more highly developed cultural and technical efficiency of France and Germany; and he wanted America to emulate the quality and variety of instruction afforded in the continental universities as a means of improving the intellectual and technological standards of America. Before he became president of Harvard, Eliot advocated such reforms in two periodical articles on "The New Education," in which he evinced a desire for more ample provision for individual needs, a more reasonable preparation for practical and useful pursuits, and the need for more advanced study beyond graduation from the college.[2]

In his inaugural address, Eliot stated emphatically that the current controversy over whether literature or science was more important for a general education should have no place at Harvard, because it was the duty of a university to provide instruction in all of the main subjects of interest, general and specialized.[3] To accomplish this ideal, Eliot set out upon an effective campaign to get funds for the college in order to increase the number of professors and the number of courses offered. That he was eminently successful is indicated by the fact that during his administration the number of faculty members increased from 60 to 600 and the institution's income-bearing funds increased from slightly more than two million to twenty million dollars.[4] The tremendous growth of Harvard, aided by the increasing wealth of the country and by the efforts of Eliot, was accompanied by an increasing number of elective studies. All requirements for particular subjects were abolished for seniors in 1872, for juniors in 1879, and for sophomores in 1884; then requirements for freshmen were reduced in 1885, and only English and a modern language were required after 1894.[5]

[1] HENRY JAMES, *Charles W. Eliot* (Houghton Mifflin Company, Boston, 1930), Vol. I, p. 137.

[2] C. W. ELIOT, "The New Education," *Atlantic Monthly*, 23: 203–220 (February, 1869), and 23: 358–367 (March, 1869).

[3] C. W. ELIOT, *Educational Reform* (D. Appleton-Century Company, Inc., New York, 1898), pp. 1–38.

[4] *Dictionary of American Biography*, 6: 71–78.

[5] The gradual development of the elective system at Harvard and the problems incident to its growth may be traced in detail in the *Annual Reports of the President and Treasurer of Harvard College*, published by the university. For a concise statement of the history of the elective system at Harvard prior to 1884, see Eliot's *Annual Report of 1883–1884* (Cambridge, 1885), pp. 5–30; and for a general picture of the elective system at Harvard since 1869, see S. E. Morison, *The Development of Harvard University* . . . 1869–1929 (Harvard University Press, Cambridge, 1930), pp. xxxix–li.

Besides these actual evidences of his ability to get funds[1] to expand the university and to apply the elective principle in practice, Eliot was very effective in his many public statements concerning the theoretical justification for the elective system. In speeches, debates, articles, pamphlets, and books, he advocated for 40 years the elective principle so forcefully that he not only received much support but also provoked the determined opposition of educators from many quarters. For our purposes, his utterances deal principally with (1) his ideal of what a university should be; (2) his redefinitions of a liberal education; and (3) his advocacy of greater freedom in education for the student. Eliot's statements were not strikingly new or original; most of his ideas may be found in the writings of Ticknor, Wayland, or Tappan; but the material and economic advancement of the country had so progressed and he was so effective in his advocacy of the elective doctrines during his long presidency that the whole aspect of the American college was radically changed during the last half of the nineteenth century. Among Eliot's numerous utterances are five statements of educational theory that are particularly related to our problem: the articles on the New Education in the *Atlantic Monthly* in 1868; his inaugural address in 1869; a paper in 1884 entitled "What Is a Liberal Education?";[2] an address in 1885 entitled "Liberty in Education";[3] and a chapter in his book on university administration written in 1908.[4]

In his early magazine articles on the New Education, Eliot followed the usual theory of the time and advocated the separation of those liberal studies which should be offered in the regular college from those technical or practical studies which should be offered in the polytechnical school. His contention was that the distinction between liberal and technical subjects is not one of subject matter but of aim. In a college, a student seeks to attain the highest culture and the best formation and information of his mind, and he engages in study for its own sake and for the love of the knowledge to be obtained, with no reference to ulterior motives; whereas in the technical school, although exactly the same subjects may be taught, the student aims at a practical preparation for a particular occupation. The technical school training is by no means inferior to that of the college; it is merely different. Thus spoke Eliot one year before he became president of Harvard.

---

[1] Illustrative of Eliot's efforts is the story told by Charles Kendall Adams in *The Chronicle*, (February, 1885): "I remember a few years ago it was said that whenever a rich man of Boston saw President Eliot coming, he reached for his check-book and anxiously asked: 'and how much must it be?'" p. 13.

[2] C. W. ELIOT, *Educational Reform*, pp. 89–124.

[3] *Ibid.*, pp. 125–150.

[4] C. W. ELIOT, *University Administration* (Houghton Mifflin Company, Boston, 1908), Chap. IV, pp. 131–173.

According to Eliot's first principle of collegiate reform, therefore, a real university should be built which would include all of these aims and all courses that could be taught in the most advanced manner. At that time, however, Eliot felt that there was no real university in the United States and that therefore the discussion was idly theoretical rather than of practical importance. He criticized such attempts as those of Union College, Brown University, and the University of Michigan to establish scientific courses parallel to the regular classical course. He was not opposed to scientific or technical training as such—in fact, the articles were written to stimulate further activity along these lines—but he did believe that both types of higher education should not be carried on within the college as it was then organized. He would have allowed scientific subjects to be taught in the undergraduate college, but they must be taught as the means to a liberal education and not for vocational purposes. Then, as Eliot's theories matured, he looked upon a genuine university as one that included not only the undergraduate college for liberal education but also all sorts of coordinate schools for technical, graduate, and professional training; all were to be unified into one strong institution.

After fifteen years of experience as president of Harvard, Eliot in his paper on "What Is a Liberal Education?" elaborated his second principle of reform, namely, that the traditional conception of a liberal education should be expanded to include the modern subjects. He definitely stated that the significance of the bachelor of arts degree, which was the usual evidence of a liberal education, should be enlarged in the light of the growth of knowledge and the rise of the great mass of new literature, arts, and sciences that had been accumulating during the preceeding 250 years. He described at length how long it had taken during the Renaissance for Greek and the newer mathematics to gain a place along with the seven liberal arts and Aristotelian philosophy as suitable subjects for a liberal education; and he indicated that the time had now come for increasing again the circle of subjects that should receive equal attention and carry equal weight in preparation for a liberal education. Announcing the good progressive doctrine that the best intellectual and moral materials of the day should be made the substance of a liberal education, Eliot urged that the following subjects should be given equal rank along with the ancient classics and mathematics: English language and literature, French and German, history, political economy, and the natural sciences.

Eliot continued in this article by showing that the corollary of widening the circle of equivalent subjects for a liberal education must be a greater amount of freedom for the student to choose his subjects and to choose them at an earlier age than had been the practice. One person could not possibly encompass all of these subjects and acquire a thorough knowledge of any, so the student must be allowed to select those to which he would devote himself. All the subjects in the college should be "liberal" and should promote mental discipline, but freedom of choice could still be justified, because even mental discipline must take account of the differences in student capacity and taste, and the value of any study as a discipline changes as knowledge accumulates. Eliot pled for the enlargement of the circle of liberal studies on the ground also that the interests of higher education and of democratic society demanded it; the professions needed men with a liberal education broader than that afforded by the classics, and the growing population and wealth of the country required that the narrow courses be expanded.

Besides his attempts to clarify the ideal of what a university should be, and besides his efforts to redefine the traditional conception of a liberal education, the third of Eliot's fundamental principles of educational reform that led to the justification of the elective principle was his insistence upon greater freedom for the student to develop himself as his individual traits directed. In his inaugural address, Eliot stated that the college must attend to the individual characteristics of different minds. After the boy has dipped into the major fields of human knowledge in elementary and secondary schools, he should know as a youth of eighteen or nineteen what he likes best and what he is best fitted for. The individual requires concentration upon a given field in order to bring about the highest development of his own peculiar propensities; and society requires a variety of intellectual specialists each well versed in his own field. The intention to continue the elective principle for these purposes was indicated in Eliot's inaugural as follows:

The elective system fosters scholarship, because it gives free play to natural preferences and inborn aptitudes, makes possible enthusiasm for a chosen work, relieves the professor and the ardent disciple of the presence of a body of students who are compelled to an unwelcome task, and enlarges instruction by substituting many and various lessons given to small, lively classes, for a few lessons many times repeated to different sections of a numerous class. The College therefore, proposes to persevere in its efforts to establish, improve, and extend the elective system.[1]

In 1885, Eliot devoted a whole speech on "Liberty in Education" to the specific means by which a college with one uniform curriculum could be transformed into a university with no prescriptions by granting a larger measure of freedom to students.[2] Freedom could be attained by allowing greater liberty in the choice of studies; by giving to students

[1] ELIOT, *Educational Reform*, p. 14.
[2] *Ibid.*, pp. 125–150.

the opportunity to win academic honors in specialized fields of study; and by permitting them, in the main, to govern themselves. He justified greater freedom in selecting studies with the argument that it would be impossible in four years to take more than one-tenth of the instruction offered; 80 teachers gave 425 hours of instruction a week without repetition, and it would take an industrious student some 40 years to cover the fields of knowledge if they were all prescribed.

Another justification for freedom was the psychological argument that the American youth was fully capable of choosing for himself by the time he was eighteen or nineteen years old. Eliot believed that the American boy was more mature than the European boy who goes to the universities between seventeen and twenty years, that the change from school to university should be made when the boy is ready to associate with older instead of with younger boys, and that the boy will more rapidly take on responsibility if it is expected of him earlier than heretofore. By eighteen years of age, the temperament, physical constitution, mental aptitudes, and moral growth of individuals are well determined, and their unique capacities evident; external and compulsory discipline, is no longer so suitable for motivation as prizes or rewards; and the well-instructed youth of eighteen can select for himself his course of study better than anyone else can. He will naturally seek aid from his teachers and friends and, contrary to many fears, will probably be intensely conservative. Since every individual differs in inherited traits, environment, emotions, desires, and intelligence, uniformity should end and diversity begin at college. After the elements of reading, writing, and ciphering have been acquired in the elementary and secondary schools, the elective system should be instituted as the best means of developing the differing tastes, inclinations, and special capacities of each individual. Thus, if the student is to be allowed freedom at all, it must come between the ages of eighteen and twenty-two, for he will be obliged to submit to a greater amount of prescription in professional or technical study than in college.[1]

Student freedom should be promoted not only by allowing greater choice of studies but also by a chance to win academic honors. In this way, specialization and advancement in single lines are promoted, as well as a healthy competition among the departments to stimulate both teachers and students. Election of subjects is a necessary requirement for such specialization. Furthermore, freedom must not only be allowed with regard to college studies but must be allowed in extracurricular affairs as well. There must also be a larger number of students enrolled in a university in order to fill the specialized courses and to get the advantages of wide contacts; and a large city with its opportunities for highly cultivated society is thus the best location for a university. Consequently, the

[1] See also *ibid.*, pp. 325–327, "The Unity of Educational Reform."

university cannot deal with students in seclusion or mechanically protect them from temptations. It should rather give them a sense of personal freedom and responsibility, training them in self-control, self-reliance, self-government, and independence: "The *in loco parentis* theory is an ancient fiction which ought no longer to deceive anybody."[1] All of these arguments came into conflict with the conservative notions that the college should be small, disciplinary, secluded, and traditionally situated in a small town.

The mature judgment of Eliot as to the objectives and advantages of the elective system is set forth in his book on university administration which was published near the close of his presidency. In this statement of his position, Eliot showed that he was convinced that the elective principle had been worked into a definite system with a well-ordered series of consecutive courses in each large department of instruction; and these courses were open to the choice of students under "rules partly artificial, but chiefly natural and inevitable."[2] Many arguments for the elective system that have already been discussed were included, but Eliot added one that has not been touched upon, namely, that the elective system was valuable because it mixed graduates and undergraduates together in the same classrooms and brought into contact persons of widely differing ages and academic status. This he believed was an unqualified advantage for increasing intellectual stimulation and thus broadening social intercourse.

In his long advocacy of the elective system, Eliot was confronted with many arguments intended to point out its weaknesses and disadvantages. Paramount among these were the arguments that the significance of the B.A. degree would be lost, that Greek and Latin would be subordinated to less valuable studies, that mental discipline was more important than individual development, that students could not select wisely for themselves, and that the lazy or indifferent student would select easy courses of little value to himself. The many arguments pro and con will be discussed at greater length in a later chapter, but the essence of Eliot's position may be pointed out here. Eliot granted that the B.A. degree would no longer mean that every holder of it had progressed through the same subjects and would no longer indicate a knowledge of Greek and Latin, but he said it was enough for the degree to mean that a student had spent a certain number of years in liberal studies and pointed to the German Ph.D. as the most significant and valuable arts degree in the world, though it did not represent any particular studies. As for Greek and Latin, he said that they should be able to stand upon their own merits and not be supported by an outworn prescription. It

[1] *Ibid.*, p. 147.
[2] ELIOT, *University Administration*, p. 131.

was not intended to substitute the new subjects for the old but merely to offer both and allow students to choose.

Eliot believed that the lazy, indifferent, or careless student would certainly receive no worse treatment from the elective system than he had received under the prescribed curriculum in which no effort was made to adapt subject matter to individual inclinations. Under the elective system, however, he would select courses that would appeal to him more than the prescribed studies had done, and he would be obliged to attain a certain level of scholarship as set by examinations; and there was always the chance that a spark of interest could be elicited by subjects of his own choosing. In his annual report of 1876–1877, Eliot gave evidence to support his contentions that students could select with wisdom and advantage to themselves.[1]

In a speech in 1885, Eliot described how as a student and as a professor at Harvard he had seen the prescribed system at work and how he had helped to change it gradually to a free elective system. His observation was that the varying needs of students had always been satisfied more adequately by their own selections than by the prescribed curriculum. After 40 years of watching the elective system, he said that there was little extreme specialization and that students on the whole chose wisely and did not take the easy courses.[2] Eliot's final conclusion may be indicated as follows: " . . . the permanence of the elective system is assured by the demonstrated fact that it provides on a large scale an invaluable addition to human freedom. . . . "[3]

Eliot believed that the pressure of public opinion could be brought to bear in order to enlarge the curriculum and thus meet the competition of the technical schools through the demands of parents upon the trustees and through the conditions laid down by benefactors for the disposal of their funds. His idea was to change the small college into a large university by introducing the elective system directly into the college course of study, by raising the standards of admission, and by shortening the period of college residence for those students who could finish the college course in less time by using the elective principle.

Here in Eliot's long administration was a most effective frontal attack upon the traditional aristocratic, linguistic, and classical conception of a liberal education. Eliot saw clearly the direction in which the winds of public opinion and of industrial activity were blowing, so he opened the doors of Harvard to meet the demands of democracy and of industry for more specialized and professional training. He took advantage of the tremendous financial resources that became available to him as a

[1] *Annual Report of the President of Harvard College*, 1876–1877, pp. 61–69.
[2] ELIOT, *University Administration*, pp. 155–161.
[3] *Ibid.*, pp. 172–173.

result of the vast fortunes created under the new industrial capitalism and so built up the foundations of Harvard. He found Harvard a small and unorganized group of loosely affiliated schools, and hence he startled the faculty of medicine when he appeared at its faculty meeting and asserted that he was president not only of Harvard College but of all of the schools that were gathered about the college.

He did much more than promote the elective system; he was one of the most outstanding educational spokesmen for adapting the American college to the forces of modern America. He represented in his career the changing status of the college from an institution of strict discipline over the religious, moral, and intellectual life of students to an institution that boasted of its secular character and the great amount of freedom allowed to the activities of its students. Not only was Eliot an outstanding factor in effecting these changes through his advocacy of the elective system, but also for the first time in American history he was able to gather enough support to put the educational conservatives upon the defensive.

IDEAL FOR A UNIVERSITY AT CORNELL

While Eliot was effecting the transformation of Harvard from a college into a university during the last half of the nineteenth century, several other distinctive contributions were being made to the development of higher education in the United States, contributions that had definite influence upon the theory and practice of the elective system. Five outstanding plans for the creation of genuine universities are of particular interest as indicating the various forces that were at work to establish more firmly the dominance of the elective principle in the college curriculum. At Columbia University, Frederick A. P. Barnard gradually became convinced that the elective principle should be applied to the last two years of the college course in order to effect real university training. Under the guidance of Andrew D. White, Cornell University instituted from the beginning a broad elective system. Although Johns Hopkins University was intended as a distinctly graduate institution, Daniel C. Gilman found that a collegiate division was necessary which would embody a considerable amount of election in order to give proper preparation for the advanced work of the university. Stanford University under the leadership of David Starr Jordan opened with a broad elective system; and the new University of Chicago under William R. Harper presented a unique application of the principle.

These institutions, along with Harvard, Brown, and Michigan, represented the outstanding leaders in the growing movement to convert colleges into universities. The efforts of other institutions in the United States were of great importance, but in their details they were largely variations on these patterns. For example, much further attention might be given to the development of the University of Michigan in the last half of the nineteenth century when James Burrill Angell was president from 1871 to 1909. Angell had been a student and later a professor of modern languages at Brown under Francis Wayland and had assimilated some of the new ideas being promulgated there. From 1866 to 1871, Angell was president of the University of Vermont where he received valuable training in the art of canvassing for money and in arousing the people of the state to an interest in their state university.

When Angell went to the University of Michigan, he immediately appealed to the people of Michigan in his inaugural address to support his plans for realizing his ideal of a university.[1] His plans were brilliant and effective, but they were clearly in line with the ideals that Tappan had previously advocated, namely, to establish facilities for advanced research and to cement a closer connection of the university with the school system of the state. Angell could make more progress than Tappan had been able to, because the social conditions were more ripe and because Angell's personality and abilities were such that he was more able to bring many of his plans into actuality. He had in mind a university in the broadest sense—a college, professional schools, and a graduate school. To this end he broadened the college curriculum, enlarged the range of electives, made possible a college education for those who did not have classical preparation, and established certification of high school graduates under the inspection of the university. It is apparent from this short summary that the work of Angell and of other progressive college educators is worthy of more detailed study, but there was so much similarity of opinion and so much repetition of arguments during this period that it seems advisable to deal only with such old or new institutions as have not been discussed so fully in previous chapters.

President White and the Cornell Idea. A chance for a distinctive contribution to the development of higher education in the United States arose out of the circumstances that brought together the endowments of Ezra Cornell, the grants of the federal government contained in the Morrill Act of 1862, and the educational leadership of Andrew Dickson White. The result was the cementing of a closer relationship between the university and the needs of the people and represented, in general, the development of the state universities of the Middle and Far West. Another result was an extensive use of the elective system which elicited imitation through the admiration of other institutions or through the necessities of competition. White had been a student at Yale from 1850 to 1854 and had thoroughly disliked there the system of a fixed course in the classics

---

[1] J. B. ANGELL, *Selected Addresses* (Longmans, Green & Company, New York, 1912), pp. 3–33.

and mathematics "through which all students were forced alike, regardless of their tastes, powers, or aims."[1]

In his autobiography, White tells of the evolution of the Cornell idea in his own thinking.[2] As early as his undergraduate days at Hobart College in 1850, before going to Yale, he had read Newman and Huber on the English universities and had dreamed of an ideal university on a large scale like that of the English universities but different in that it would provide for such studies as the modern languages, English, and history as well as the classics and mathematics. Later, while in Europe, he visited Oxford and Cambridge; then at the Collège de France in Paris he saw "the university lecture system, with its clearness, breadth, wealth of illustration";[3] and finally the University of Berlin appeared to be his dream wrought into reality.

Upon returning to Yale for graduate study, White discussed the problem of the college course with Daniel Gilman and Noah Porter; but reaching no conclusions and hearing Francis Wayland state in a commencement address that the greatest opportunity for graduate study in the United States was in the West, he decided to go to the University of Michigan when offered the opportunity by President Tappan. At Michigan, White's ideas of a university took further shape under the influence of Tappan's adaptation there of Prussian ideals, and he was convinced that a university should be nonsectarian and should break up the "one simple, single, cast-iron course."[4] A further influence was Herbert Spencer's treatise on education which, as we have seen, advocated that scientific studies should receive more emphasis than usual in the college course because of their practical value.[5]

With these ideas of university education already developing in his thinking, White was called in 1865 to help organize the new Cornell University and eventually to become its first president from 1868 to 1885. Combined with White's leadership were other influences that contributed to the development of the Cornell idea. These were, first, the provisions of the Morrill Act to offer instruction in the agricultural and mechanical arts without displacing scientific and classical studies; and, secondly, the desire of Ezra Cornell, the founder, to foster agricultural and industrial studies because they were closely related to his personal experience as timberman, farmer, carpenter, machinist, engineer, and electrician. In accordance with all of these interests, White submitted to the board

[1] *Autobiography of Andrew Dickson White* (D. Appleton-Century Company, Inc., New York, 1905), Vol. I, p. 289.
[2] *Ibid.*, pp. 287–293.
[3] *Ibid.*, p. 291.
[4] *Ibid.*, p. 272.
[5] *Ibid.*, p. 363.

of trustees in 1866 a report[1] in which he outlined a plan for dividing the university into two great divisions, the first to consist of separate departments devoted to such special sciences and arts as agriculture, mechanics, engineering, commerce and trade, mining, medicine, law, history and political science, and education; the second to be made up of several departments of general literary and scientific subjects among which the student was to have a wide liberty of choice to suit his tastes and the amount of time at his disposal for an education. In these earliest plans for the university, the intention was clearly to do away with the traditional prescribed curriculum and to offer the student a considerable number of opportunities to get the sort of education that he desired.

The more matured theory of higher education to be followed at Cornell was enunciated in the statements of White and Cornell at the inaugural ceremonies when the university was opened. President White summarized his ideas as follows: The university should foster the close union of liberal and practical studies, should forever be under nonsectarian control, and should develop a close relationship with the school system of the state. The heritage of the University of Michigan may readily be seen in these ideals. Furthermore, there should be perfect equality among the different courses of study with no special privileges for particular subjects and with greater emphasis than previously upon scientific, political, historical, and modern literary subjects; also, an opportunity for the student to select the courses in which he desired to specialize. The ultimate aim of the university was the development of the individual in all of his intellectual, moral, and religious powers and the bringing of these powers thus developed to bear upon society and its welfare—"the adaptation of the university to the American people, to American needs, and to our own times."[2]

Ezra Cornell supplemented White's statements with some remarks that indicate his ambition that the university really meet the needs of the working classes and provide opportunity for them to seek higher education by combining study with manual labor. He wished to found an institution

. . . which will place at the disposal of the industrial and productive classes of society, the best facilities for the acquirement of practical knowledge and mental culture, on such terms as the limited means of the most humble can command.

I hope we have laid the foundation of an institution which shall combine practical with liberal education, which shall fit the youth of our country for the professions, the farms, the mines, the manufactories, for the investigations

[1] *Report of the Committee on Organization, presented to the trustees of the Cornell University,* October 21, 1866 (Albany, N. Y., 1867).

[2] *U. S. Bureau of Education, Circular of Information,* 1900, No. 3, p. 399.

of science, and for mastering all the practical questions of life with success and honor.

I believe we have made the beginning of an institution which will prove highly beneficial to the poor young men and the poor young women of our country . . . as will enable any one by honest efforts and earnest labor, to secure a thorough, practical, scientific or classical education.[1]

How far the ideal of a university had progressed from the days when the aim was to train ministers and the curriculum was strictly prescribed for all students is shown in Cornell's declaration of purpose which came to be placed upon the seal of the university: "I would found an institution where any person can find instruction in any study."[2]

In an effort to bring this ideal into realization, President White devised a broad curriculum for the university upon the basis of his first plan in 1866 and made provision for three types of courses: academic courses in arts and sciences; technical and professional courses; and graduate courses. Originally, he planned five parallel academic courses in the arts and sciences; the studies of four of these were to be prescribed, and the studies of the fifth were to be open for free election. These general courses were designated as: (1) the arts, or classical, course, requiring Greek and Latin; (2) the philosophical, or literature, course, requiring Latin and a modern language; (3) the science course, requiring modern languages, mathematics, and science; (4) the science and letters course, requiring modern language, literature, philosophy, and elementary mathematics and science; and (5) an elective, or "optional," course which did not prescribe specified studies. Here, again, is a feature reminiscent of Tappan's optional course at Michigan. This fifth course was in existence only about ten years, but the original announcement regarding it stated that any student might choose all of his work for himself, subject only to the conditions that he be fit to pursue the studies and that he attend three exercises daily. The announcement read: "These elective courses are intended to give to the student full and entire freedom in the selection of his studies—a freedom every way equal to that which prevails in the universities of continental Europe."[3]

A degree was to be conferred upon the student when he had completed a course equivalent to the general courses, and the degree was to correspond to the nature of the work pursued. In the announcement of 1873–1874, a more guarded statement appeared· and in 1875–1876, the

[1] The Cornell University; Account of the Proceedings at the Inauguration, October 7, 1868 (Ithaca, N. Y., 1869), p. 4.

[2] Autobiography of White, op. cit., p. 300; also A. D. WHITE, My Reminiscences of Ezra Cornell: An Address delivered before the Cornell University on Founder's Day, January 11, 1890 (Ithaca, N. Y., 1890), p. 9.

[3] U. S. Bureau of Education, Circular of Information, 1900, No. 3, p. 263.

student was plainly told that if he intended to graduate with a degree he
" . . . should by all means select the course that leads to the degree he
expects to take, and follow it in the order laid down; the disadvantages of
doing otherwise are so great as to render success almost impossible."[1]

By 1878–1879, even the possibility of graduating by way of the
optional course disappeared, and the term optional came to mean merely
that the student so designated was not a candidate for a degree. Such
was the fate of free electives at Cornell for some 20 years. Tradition and
the demand for a degree of known ingredients were too strong even in
this new institution; but the doctrine had been enunciated; and after
1896, all specified courses were abolished, the free elective system was
applied to the whole curriculum, and the B.A. degree was given to all
who finished the required number of hours of study.

Except for dropping the optional courses, the essential characteristics of the opening plan of studies were retained throughout President
White's administration (1868–1885). The significance of his presidency
in the development of higher education lies in the greater number of
parallel courses open to selection by students, the growing number of
elective studies within the separate courses from 1874 on, the equal
importance of practical and liberal studies, and the direct attempt to
fashion educational offerings to meet the needs of the industrial classes.

During the administration of Charles Kendall Adams (1885–1892),
the separate courses were simplified, and electives in each were extended,
as well as more adequate provision made for graduate studies. In his
inaugural, Adams indicated that he would strive to extend the parallel
course system rather than introduce the Harvard type of free elective
system.[2] He also intimated that he would prefer to extend the traditional disciplinary subjects to the end of the second year, but the Morrill
Act and the state legislature rather prevented such action because they
had committed Cornell to the policy of providing agricultural and mechanical subjects along with the classical. Perhaps this attitude of President
Adams helps to account for the fact that the free elective system was not
given complete sway until after the end of his presidency.

[1] *Ibid.*

[2] *Proceedings and Addresses at the Inauguration of Charles Kendall Adams to the
Presidency of Cornell University*, November 19, 1885 (Syracuse, N. Y., 1886), pp.
51–76.

CHAPTER XI

PLANS FOR CHANGING COLLEGES INTO UNIVERSITIES
(Continued)

PRESIDENT BARNARD AND THE COLUMBIA IDEA

The experience of Frederick A. P. Barnard at Columbia is very instructive as to the compromises that conservative educators were forced to make in the face of influences demanding greater use of the elective system. We have seen that Barnard was a determined opponent of the elective system as applied to the regular college during his years at the universities of Alabama and Mississippi, and there is no evidence in his inaugural address as president of Columbia College in 1864 that he had changed his conception of college aims.[1] He insisted that the main function of the college was to train young minds by strenuous discipline as preparation for any pursuit to which they might afterward be called, and he deprecated attempts to sacrifice this aim to one of greater utility. His idea of the way to build a university at that time consisted in the setting up of technical and professional schools outside the regular college. In his annual report of 1866, he showed that he favored this same method as the best way to solve the problems of decreasing enrollment.

During the next few years, however, Barnard's position concerning the value of the elective system began to change; and by 1870–1871, he was strongly advocating its use in the undergraduate college. In 1867, he went to Europe and saw there the arrangements for teaching the practical sciences in London and Paris where the modern languages were used extensively as tools for the study of technical subjects. Upon his return to Columbia, he found that Harvard had just put French and German into the required curriculum of the first two years and that Greek and Latin had been made elective along with Spanish and Italian. The Harvard plan commended itself to him, and he began to believe that this move to increase the number of elective studies was the path along which all colleges must sooner or later go. He came to the realization, as had many others, that the number of subjects had grown so large that the college could no longer require every student to take everything that

---

[1] JOHN FULTON, *Memoirs of Frederick A. P. Barnard* (The Macmillan Company, New York, 1896), pp. 343–361. For a general view of Barnard's ideas on the elective system, see Chaps. XV and XVI, pp. 379–423.

the college was prepared to teach.   He now believed that the use of the elective system was the only way in which a student could become a respectable classical scholar, because the student could not be required to study the whole range of scientific studies without sacrificing the attainment of thorough knowledge.

In 1870, Barnard presented a report to the trustees of Columbia in which he exhibited statistics to show that the desire for modern languages and scientific studies was rapidly growing and that the proportion of students who sought a purely cultural education was decreasing.[1]   He declared that from 1826 to 1838 the number of young men going to the colleges had been steadily increasing but that after 1838 the demand for a college education had dropped and the demand for practical scientific training had increased as evinced in the growth of technical and professional schools.   Barnard, therefore, recommended that, without putting aside the classical subjects, the colleges should throw open their doors more widely than was customary to students who had scientific as well as literary aspirations.   Barnard believed that Harvard's growth in numbers was a result of this policy and advocated that Columbia proceed along similar lines in order to stimulate enrollment.

Barnard's own statements are so pertinent and illustrate so well the administrator's dependence upon enrollment that they deserve quotation:

. . . but it is extremely questionable whether the popular favor which seems now to distinguish that venerable institution [Harvard], is not owing to her having substantially abandoned the collegiate system as it has always been understood until our day, and thrown into the hands of the student the selection of his own course of instruction. . . . I have nothing at all at present to say as to the wisdom or unwisdom of the view which the governing authorities at Cornell University and at Harvard have adopted as their guide.   I say only that those views are evidently well adapted to catch at this time the wind of the popular favor, and that they have been the undoubted reason why an institution the newest in the country . . . has been able, at the very outset, to take precedence of nearly every competitor in the contest for numbers; and why another, the oldest of all, after having, for nearly two centuries, held only, in respect of numbers, a secondary rank, has at length succeeded, in a few years, in placing herself foremost of all.[2]

The college [Columbia] therefore cannot grow, or cannot at any rate grow rapidly . . . unless it shall, at least to some extent, modify its plan of instruction in a more or less distant imitation of that of Harvard or of Cornell University.

[1] Quoted in WILLIAM F. RUSSELL, ed., *The Rise of a University*, Vol. I, *The Later Days of Old Columbia College* (Columbia University Press, New York, 1937), pp. 66–92. Barnard's thinking on higher education as expressed in his annual reports can be traced in detail in this book.   For the elective system as a means of changing a college into a university, see in particular Chaps. III and IV, and all of Part IV.

[2] F. A. P. BARNARD, *Analysis of Some Statistics of Collegiate Education* (New York, 1870), pp. 21–22.

That such a modification *would* bring additional numbers there can be little doubt, inasmuch as there are now not infrequent applications for admission to an elective course.[1]

Barnard followed up this report with a much more extensive one in 1871 in which he marshaled many more statistics to prove that the number of students who followed a strictly collegiate course was diminishing whereas the demand for scientific education was everywhere increasing.[2] In this statement, Barnard did not relinquish his view of the value of the usual disciplinary studies, but *he frankly admitted that in the long run the popular judgment of a system of education must prevail.* His argument ran somewhat as follows: If the system of education is not adapted to the exigencies of life, the people soon detect such failure and avoid such systems of education; it is idle to try to prove to the people that they ought to prefer a system that they unquestionably do not like. The examples of Cornell, Harvard, and Michigan prove that they like the elective system, and the decline in numbers of students at Yale and at other colleges that hold to the old collegiate curriculum shows that they do not like the traditional studies. Therefore, Columbia should adopt the elective system in order to attract more students and to meet the competition.

In this report of 1871, Barnard presented in justification for adopting the elective system several arguments with which we are familiar, but he added one concerning the influence of the academies that is noteworthy. He offered the psychological argument that the increase in age of college students owing to improvements in the secondary schools no longer required the mental discipline for a young man of seventeen or eighteen years that was necessary for boys of thirteen and fourteen. Another argument was that the elective principle should be adopted because it was no longer practicable to retain the required curriculum which had grown too crowded; students were getting neither a disciplinary nor a utilitarian education, and the elective system would at least allow one or the other. A third argument was to the effect that the college was the only institution in the United States that could ever give advanced training comparable to that of the European universities, and this was possible only if students could become highly proficient in a given field of knowledge through the use of the elective principle.

Barnard also indicated that the colleges must broaden their curriculums in order to meet the competition of the academies which allowed unlimited choice to students in the courses which may be taken and in the number of

[1] *Ibid.*, p. 24.
[2] HENRY BARNARD's *American Journal of Education*, 22: 435–452; quoted also in RUSSELL, *op. cit.*, pp. 92–114.

years that a student may attend.   The academies offered not only a
secondary education but the opportunity for a higher culture which had
all the aspects of the college course of study with the added advantage of
the elective system.   He said of the academies:

The existence of a class of schools of this high character, in which perfect
freedom is allowed in the choice of studies, cannot but have something to do in
turning away students from the colleges. . . . It is in this manner only that a
satisfactory explanation can be found of the fact that the State of New York
furnishes to the regular colleges of the country a very exceptionally small number
of undergraduate students in proportion to the aggregate population.[1]

Barnard also discussed economic considerations which made it evident
that only those colleges that could increase their financial resources sufficiently to install a wide elective system would become the real universities
of the United States, whereas the others would either remain as preparatory institutions for the universities or disappear.

Under this strong advocacy of the elective principle at Columbia, the
course of study was gradually opened to wider and wider selection by
students.   A moderate and tentative amount of choice was given to
seniors in 1870, and Barnard reported in 1872 that it was working successfully and that students chose wisely and did not pick out the easy
courses.   In 1874, he suggested that a scientific course be established
parallel to the regular course in order to meet the growing demand for
scientific studies which seemed indicated by the large percentage of
students who took the scientific courses at New York University and at
the College of the City of New York.   In 1876, he again reported that the
elective system was operating satisfactorily and recommended that it be
extended to juniors and perhaps to sophomores.   He had revised his
notion of liberal studies and indicated that the free elective system should
be instituted after the student had taken a very few minimum requirements.   Only in this way could Columbia become a real university, for he
pointed out how the "close" system of Yale which had been justified by
the theory of mental discipline 50 years earlier had gradually been revised
along the lines of Harvard's leadership.

In 1879, Barnard again advocated the extension of the elective system
in order to fill in the gaps of the curriculum which left it short of the level
desired of a graduate institution.   He believed that such subjects as the
modern languages, calculus, botany, physiology, Hebrew, Sanscrit, and
Arabic should be offered to students who desired them.   He gave an
effective argument for the elective system as promoting higher scholarship for both teachers and students:

[1] HENRY BARNARD'S *American Journal of Education*, 22: 446.

The principle of elective study is the key which solves the whole difficulty. By limiting the student to a certain number of subjects, sufficient time may be allowed him to perfect himself in each, and sufficient time may be allowed the teacher to do his subject justice.   The college may at the same time enlarge the scope of its teaching, and embrace in its general scheme of instruction every subject of literary or scientific interest, without in any degree diminishing the thoroughness with which each branch is taught.   And it is only in this way that, in the present age, any college can hope to secure and maintain a really high character as an institution of learning.[1]

In 1880, Barnard continued his insistence that the elective system be extended to the junior and senior years as the best way to provide proper preparation for genuine graduate work and to make of Columbia the great university that would be appropriate to the city of New York.

Finally, the elective system was extended in 1881 to both the senior and the junior years, and the modern languages were made elective for all years.   Barnard's report of 1882 expressed his satisfaction with the working of the system, for he now felt that most students obtained the greatest profit from the studies in which they found the greatest pleasure, but he declared that it was evident that many students needed the aid and guidance of teachers in electing their studies in order not to waste their time and energies in unprofitable combinations.   Again, in 1882, Barnard noted that the level of scholarship had increased materially as a result of the introduction of the elective system, but he again warned that it would be better to arrange several definite courses of study with due regard to the interrelationships of topics and the logical order of sequence and allow the student to choose among them.   He believed that the most disciplinary value could be obtained by thus choosing a group of studies instead of single unrelated subjects.   During the presidency of Seth Low (1890–1901), this plan was substantially carried out; freshmen were divided according to their entrance offerings, and each group was provided with a different set of prescribed and elective studies, depending partly upon their professional and vocational intentions.

The report of 1883 was Barnard's last communication to the board of trustees concerning the elective system; and when his administration ended in 1888, Columbia had evolved a distinctive theory of higher education based upon the elective system.   Harvard had introduced the free elective system into the college and had tried to keep all of the collegiate subjects within the term liberal.   Cornell had set liberal and technical courses alongside each other and had gradually increased the amount of election within each course.   Columbia retained more of the traditional curriculum than either of these and tried to compromise by extending the elective system only halfway down into the college cur-

[1] FULTON, *op. cit.*, p. 393.

riculum. In reaching this compromise, the desire to retain as much disciplinary value as possible during the first two years of the college course was combined with the desire to prepare students adequately to increase the level of their scholarship and to enter more easily upon higher professional courses.

Thus, Columbia was brought to expand its curriculum and introduce the elective system through the demands of popular favor for the newer and more utilitarian subjects, the demands of scholarship and of professional and graduate study, and the necessity of meeting the competition of other institutions. These are not new reasons for the development of the elective system, but they are particularly well illustrated in this development of one of the largest universities in the United States. Barnard's conception of a university and the way it was to be brought about are illustrated in these two statements from his annual reports of 1879 and 1883:

> The adoption of a liberal system of elective study . . . prepares a college to rise naturally and easily to the higher level of postgraduate instruction.[1]
> . . . by the multiplication of the subjects taught in our College, by the establishment of professional schools, and of a Department of Graduate Instruction, and by the very great increase in the numbers of students matriculating in the different departments, our College had taken on the functions and assumed the character of a proper university.[2]

DANIEL C. GILMAN'S GROUP SYSTEM AT JOHNS HOPKINS

Daniel Coit Gilman had the opportunity to plan a new institution of higher education without the usual ties to tradition, and the result in 1876 was a graduate institution modeled upon the European type of university. He soon found, however, that a collegiate department was necessary, because so many American students were not adequately prepared for graduate work; so an undergraduate college was organized in order not to leave the university suspended in the air. Although Johns Hopkins was designed essentially as a graduate institution, it had considerable effect upon the development of the elective system in the American college. What the effect was may be brought out more clearly if we discuss briefly Gilman's ideas of a college as distinguished from those of a university.

During his seventeen years of association with Yale University, Gilman had been thoroughly imbued with the idea of mental discipline and the desirability of the prescribed curriculum for students in the college as a necessary preparation for the wider freedom that should be allowed in the

---

[1] W. F. RUSSELL, ed., *The Rise of a University*, Vol. I, *The Later Days of Old Columbia College* (Columbia University Press, New York, 1937), p. 342.
[2] *Ibid.*, p. 370.

university, but he tempered his notion of the requirements of the college with advice that individual differences should be taken into account. His attitude as represented in his inaugural address as president of the University of California was as follows:

We distinguish the requirements of young scholars, like those who have just left the high school and the academy, from those of advanced students, whose tastes, talents, and wants are specialized. Give the former prescription; give the latter freedom; but let the prescription vary with the varying peculiarities of individuals, and let the freedom allowed be the freedom which is governed and protected by law. College work for college boys implies daily guidance under prescribed rules; professional work implies voluntary, self-impelled enthusiasm in the acquisition of knowledge.[1]

Indicating that he would make a sharp distinction between college and university work, Gilman expanded this idea in his inaugural address as president of Johns Hopkins University. He defined a university as a place for the advanced and special instruction of youth who had been prepared for their freedom by the discipline of a lower school; and the college as an institution which stands *in loco parentis*, implying restriction instead of freedom, tutorial rather than professorial teaching, and residence within college halls. The college should provide a rather narrow scope of studies but should give a liberal and substantial foundation upon which university instruction may be built. That he intended Johns Hopkins to be a university rather than a college is indicated in the following:

I see no advantage in our attempting to maintain the traditional four-year class system of the American colleges. . . . If parents or students desire us to mark out prescribed courses, either classical or scientific, lasting four years, it will be easy to do so. . . . Moreover, I would make attainments rather than time the condition of promotion; and I would encourage every scholar to go forward rapidly or go forward slowly, according to the fleetness of his foot and his freedom from impediment. In other words, I would have our university seek the good of individuals rather than of classes.[2]

Elaborating the university idea further along lines which imply the use of the elective system, Gilman said that his aims were:

. . . the most liberal promotion of all useful knowledge; the special provision of such departments as are neglected elsewhere in the country . . . the encouragement of research . . . and the advancement of individual scholars, who by their excellence will advance the sciences they pursue and the society where they dwell.[3]

[1] D. C. GILMAN, *University Problems in the United States* (D. Appleton-Century Company, Inc., New York, 1898), p. 167.
[2] *Ibid.*, pp. 33–34.
[3] *Ibid.*, p. 35

The methods of the university would be:

Liberal advanced instruction for those who want it; distinctive honors for those who win them; appointed courses for those who need them; special courses for those who can take no other; a combination of lectures, recitations, laboratory practice, field-work, and private instruction; the largest discretion allowed to the faculty consistent with the purposes in view. . . . [1]

If a university were to be built that would be free from partisan or sectarian control and that would promote all branches of knowledge through original research and the most thorough, advanced, and special instruction, then

. . . great freedom must be allowed to both teachers and scholars. This involves freedom of methods to be employed by the instructors on one hand, and, on the other, freedom of courses to be selected by the students. [2]

Other statements of the aims and functions of university and college education, substantially along these lines, were made by Gilman during his long career as an educational leader in the United States, but they do not add materially for our purposes to the ideas contained in the two inaugurals. [3]

Gilman was generous in giving credit to the many influences that helped to shape the idea of the university in Baltimore. In his inaugural in 1876, he indicated that Johns Hopkins would reap the benefits of the early lessons of Jefferson, Nott, Wayland, Quincy, Agassiz, Tappan, Mark Hopkins, and Woolsey and would be aided by the contemporary controversies being carried on by Eliot, Porter, Barnard, White, Angell, and McCosh. In another connection, Gilman stated that when the idea of Johns Hopkins was still being formulated Eliot, Angell, and White had been asked to give advice and that the writings of Cardinal Newman, Matthew Arnold, and other European thinkers had been consulted. [4] Also, Gilman had traveled widely in the United States and in Europe visiting several universities and conversing with such men as Jowett, Spencer, Huxley, and James Bryce.

Borrowing from such of these sources as Gilman thought applicable to the American situation and to the resources of the institution, Johns Hopkins was opened in 1876 for advanced study with opportunities for library, laboratory, and seminar work which was soon among the most outstanding in the country. Graduate instruction throughout the United

---

[1] *Ibid.*, pp. 35–36.

[2] *Ibid.*, p. 33.

[3] See *ibid.*, pp. 289–312, especially pp. 294, 298, 307, also pp. 45–78, 79–108. See also D. C. GILMAN, *The Launching of a University* (Dodd, Mead & Company, Inc., New York, 1906), pp. 255–280.

[4] GILMAN, *The Launching of a University*, Chap. I, pp. 19–24.

States took many cues from the example of this new institution where fields of study became ever more specialized and scholarly. The Ph.D. degree was given there only after a minimum of three years of study beyond the B.A., the passing of written and oral examinations, and the presentation of an original piece of research reported in a dissertation. Moreover, the publications of the university set a high standard for scholarly work in disseminating the results of scientific and technical research.

In the undergraduate department, the B.A. degree was the only one given, because it was felt that too much confusion had resulted from the multiplication of baccalaureate degrees in many of the colleges. The undergraduate degree at Johns Hopkins was intended to denote a liberal education which was defined as meaning a prolonged and systematic study of the five major branches of knowledge, namely, languages, mathematics, science, history, and philosophy, all combinations of which were supposedly of equal difficulty and honor. Gilman was not yet ready to adopt the free elective system; and in an attempt to arrive at the best elements of the prescribed and elective systems, seven combinations or groups of studies from the foregoing fields of knowledge were arranged.

Students were allowed to choose one of these seven different lines of study; but once they had selected a course, they were obliged to follow the prescribed sequence of subjects. Such courses were outlined as: the classics; Latin and mathematics; mathematics and physics; chemistry and physics; modern languages; prelegal; and premedical. Common to every course was the requirement of the study of French and German and at least one branch of laboratory science. The departure from the old college curriculum was great indeed when the modern languages and science came to hold the prominent place among the few remaining fixed requirements.

In reviewing the growth of the American universities during the last half of the nineteenth century, Gilman noted that the outstanding developments had been the great support given to scientific, historical, and modern language studies; the increasing value of a liberal education as a preparation for higher and special studies as well as for the duties of a business life; and the opportunity for selection by students of the course of study that they would like to follow.[1] The influence of Johns Hopkins upon these currents of development was undeniably strong. The example of pursuing advanced scientific and historical studies through extensive use of research in laboratories and seminar was followed in the graduate departments of many universities, and ultimately this greater specialization on the graduate level required earlier and more intense specialization

[1] GILMAN, *University Problems in the United States*, pp. 1–6, 145–158; also GILMAN, *The Significance of a Liberal Education* (Richmond, Va., 1907).

on the undergraduate level in order that students might be better prepared to take up without loss of time the advanced work of graduate study.

Thus, the professional and graduate schools forced courses in the undergraduate college to become ever more specialized and more numerous, until a considerable amount of election was allowed to students. In its undergraduate college, Johns Hopkins tried to retain as much as possible of its original plan for a liberal education by offering several equivalent prescribed courses instead of opening up the curriculum to free election of individual subjects; nevertheless, in pursuance of this plan, it offered more separate courses leading to the B.A. degree than any other university or college had offered, and consequently it aided in spreading the notion that many subjects besides the classics and mathematics were worthy to be presented as requirements for the time-honored arts degree.

DAVID STARR JORDAN'S MAJOR-MINOR PLAN AT STANFORD

That the developing idea of a university as a higher institution of research and of advanced instruction in all branches of knowledge had taken firm root in the theory of higher education in the United States was indicated by the founding of Leland Stanford Junior University in 1885 and the University of Chicago in 1891. The munificence of Leland Stanford and of John D. Rockefeller provided the necessary financial resources, and David Starr Jordan and William Rainey Harper provided the necessary educational leadership to make universities of the first magnitude out of Stanford and Chicago in a relatively few years. The elective principle found freer use at Stanford than at Chicago, owing perhaps to the experience of Jordan and also to the fact that Chicago, like Johns Hopkins, was intended to concentrate upon the attainment of scholarship in the graduate departments and hence was not so interested in allowing free election in the undergraduate college. The history of the elective system has shown that when emphasis is placed upon directly reforming the undergraduate college as the nucleus of the desired university, as at Harvard, the elective system is given more attention than when the college is regarded merely as subsidiary and preparatory to the more specialized work of the graduate schools.

During his student days at Cornell from 1869 to 1872, under the presidency of Andrew White, Jordan had been favorably impressed by the elective system which had put all students and all studies upon a plane of academic equality. In describing these days, Jordan applauded the fact that each student was not driven over the same course but was rather given access to that form of training which was most enriching and strengthening to his own life:

The important thing was the recognition of 'the democracy of intellect,' the solid basis of the elective system. Then for the first time in the history of education, perhaps, the aristocracy of discipline was officially and successfully challenged.[1]

Carrying this admiration for the elective system with him when he went to the University of Indiana as a professor, Jordan tried to introduce elective subjects into the University of Indiana as early as 1881. Believing that every course of study should have one special line of work as a backbone but believing also that the classics should not be the only studies so distinguished, he tried to get the biological sciences accepted on an equal basis with the classics as studies for specialization. The best justification for the elective system, he believed, was the necessity that the student's work be thorough and advanced in fields that have a direct relationship to the student's own life and to his dynamic volitions. The duty of the college teacher was to adapt the work to the student and not the student to the work:

Higher education should thus foster divergence instead of conformity, its function being not to bring youths to a predetermined standard, but to help each to make the most of his inborn talents. A prearranged course of study is like ready-made clothing, fitting nobody in particular; it is the acme of educational laziness.[2]

Upon becoming president of the University of Indiana in 1885, Jordan began to institute changes aimed at allowing the student to specialize in a line of study of his own choosing. Consequently, in an effort to frame an individual course in so far as possible for each student, the elementary studies were relegated to the first two years. Then at the beginning of the third year the student was required to choose a specialty, or "major study," upon which he would concentrate a major amount of his work. Meanwhile, Jordan was busy writing articles and making speeches advocating the elective system as a remedy for the evils of the required system and as a means of adapting study to the needs of the individual.[3]

When Leland Stanford was looking for a man to become the first president of his new university, Andrew White recommended Jordan. Stanford wished to found in memory of his son a university that would foster the mechanical arts and the applications of science to industry as

[1] DAVID STARR JORDAN, *The Days of a Man* (World Book Company, Yonkers-on-Hudson, N. Y., 1922), Vol. I, p. 80.

[2] *Ibid.*, p. 237.

[3] *Ibid.*, pp. 323–325, an address entitled the "Evolution of the College Curriculum," given in 1887.

well as the usual cultural studies and that would be open equally to both sexes, all classes of people, and all religious denominations:

I am particularly anxious that the young men who are by thousands graduated from the colleges of the land and sent forth weaponless, so to speak, shall here find an opportunity to take up some specialty. We shall teach the classics, in fact everything beginning with the kindergarten, but we shall also teach the specialties so that young men and women will not be without knowledge of a specialty at graduation. We will fit all the students for some active calling in life.[1]

Jordan's ideas fitted in admirably with those of Stanford, who approved, in general, a plan of organization for the university that Jordan presented in his *Circular*. In this preliminary announcement, Jordan proposed to appoint faculty members who were noted for their high scholarship and who were also original investigators. Work in applied science was to be carried on side by side with work in the pure sciences and humanities; eighteen departments of instruction were to be provided; large liberty of substitution and election was to be allowed; and no fixed curriculum of any sort was to be set up.

Jordan instituted his "major study" scheme by which students were to select during their first year a major professor under whom they would do the amount of work necessary for fulfilling the requirements of specialization. By a later plan, students were not required to choose a major professor until their third year. As to "minor," or elective, studies, all subjects were to be open alike to any student who was intellectually ready for the work. The bachelor's degree was to be given when enough work had been done to satisfy the major professor and enough other work had been done to fill the usual four years of residence. Thus, the results of the working of democracy and industrialism at Stanford made serious inroads upon the traditional conception of a liberal education. It was hoped that practical and manual work would become as respectable as bookish work; that the sciences would be on a par with the classics; and that the major-minor system would deal a death blow to the four-year prescribed curriculum.

WILLIAM RAINEY HARPER'S JUNIOR COLLEGE AT CHICAGO

In his plans, which were adopted by the board of trustees in 1890, William R. Harper proposed many innovations for the new University of Chicago of which he was to be president. For our purposes, most important of his proposals was the separation of the last two years of the under-

---

[1] GEORGE T. CLARK, *Leland Stanford* (Stanford University Press, Stanford University, Calif., 1931), p. 417. See Chap. XII, "The University and Educational Ideals," pp. 380–425, for Stanford's ideas.

graduate college into a "senior college" which was to allow large freedom of election as distinguished from the first two years of the "junior college" in which the course was to be largely prescribed. A concentration of the students' attention upon a few studies at a time and emphasis upon graduate study and research in order to establish not merely another college but a genuine university were other phases of Harper's proposals.

The undergraduate plan called for a four-year course granting the regular bachelor's degree and a two-year course granting the title of "associate" in the university. The two-year course was designed to meet the needs of those students who could not afford to stay for a longer term of residence and to take care of those who, in the judgment of the officials, should not be allowed to take a longer course. The four-year course was designed to meet the needs of the average student, and special provisions were made for those who could finish in three years and for those who needed or wished five. In these ways, Harper hoped to meet the varying needs of individuals and to satisfy the demands for specialization. By separating the junior from the senior college, specialization could be postponed until the last two years, and the use of the elective system would also be relegated largely to the last two years.

In his written and spoken statements concerning the theory of higher education, Harper was more temperate in his advocacy of the elective system than were some of his more ardent contemporaries. He had a somewhat Jeffersonian conception of the university, believing that the university should act as a spokesman and interpreter of democracy.[1] In this sense, the university should be the philosopher of democracy, formulating its principles and theories and furnishing opportunity for study of the problems arising from democracy. With respect to the current controversies over the curriculum, Harper struck an intermediate position between those who advocated a required curriculum emphasizing the ancient classics and those who demanded that science and the modern subjects be substituted for the classics. Harper believed that all persons should not be required to know Latin but that all, especially the scientist, needed to know something about the heritage of the past through the study of history and literature.[2] He would therefore replace the requirements in ancient languages with requirements in history.

He would allow the use of the elective system, but he believed that it should be used carefully and with greater knowledge of the student's needs than had previously been the custom. In a speech at Brown University in 1899, Harper indicated that individualism as distinguished from collectivism was the greatest contribution of the nineteenth century

[1] WILLIAM RAINEY HARPER, *The Trend in Higher Education* (University of Chicago Press, Chicago, 1905), Chap. I, "The University and Democracy," pp. 1–34
[2] *Ibid.*, Chap. XVII, "Latin versus Science," pp. 285–293.

to higher education and that one of the outstanding applications of the doctrine of individualism had been seen in the introduction of the elective system into college courses of instruction.[1] He believed, however, that, by means of a scientific study of the student's character, intelligence, social nature, special aptitudes, capacities, and tastes, greater steps should be taken to prevent students from abusing this freedom. Only on the basis of such a careful diagnosis could the student be adequately and safely guided in the selection of his studies.

A distinctive justification for the elective system was given by Harper when he pointed out that it was as necessary that students be allowed to select their instructors as that they be permitted to choose their studies. He felt that a close relationship between student and teacher can be reached and maintained only when they have interests in common, and it is just here that the principle of election plays its part in changing the relationship from that of task setting to that of fellow guidance and stimulation. The opportunity to elect certain subjects allows the student to place himself in close relationship with those instructors who have interests similar to those of the student: "The principle of election, then, has made student-fellowship between officer and pupil possible; nay more, it has made any other relationship impossible."[2] Thus, the influence of Harper and of the University of Chicago was ranged on the side of the reformers. It was tempered, however, by a caution which hesitated to meet wholeheartedly the democratic and industrial currents in the country to the same degree that Harvard or Cornell had done. By the same token, Chicago was less free in introducing elective courses but preferred to stand with Johns Hopkins in giving more attention to the graduate levels of study which were considered to be more appropriate than the undergraduate college for proper university education.

The detailed discussion of the several plans for "university building" as related in this chapter may have seemed somewhat repetitious, but it was necessary to present enough evidence to show clearly what the progressive educators of the later nineteenth century were thinking and doing. It now seems advisable to indicate briefly some of the outstanding ideas expounded by these educational statesmen who were crusading for the reform of the college in accordance with the new social and intellectual conditions of America as they found them. Taking up the theoretical arguments of the earlier reformers, these men were now able to put theory into practice. For our purposes, their collective contribution to American higher education was to lead the way in *actually transforming the character of college education* in the following ways:

[1] *Ibid.*, Chap. XX, "The Scientific Study of the Student," pp. 317–326.

[2] *Ibid.*, p. 333; Chap. XXI, "The College Officer and the College Student," pp. 327–337.

1. The narrowly prescribed curriculum of a few subjects gave way to a large elective curriculum of many subjects.

2. The conception of a liberal education (as represented by the B. A. degree) was widened to include on a level with the traditional subjects such new studies as English, the modern languages, the physical sciences, and the social sciences.

3. The bookish and linguistic character of a liberal education began to be challenged by the notion that motor and manual skills should be developed as well as reading and mental techniques.

4. The ideal of the small undergraduate college began to lose ground in favor of the German ideal of a large graduate university where all branches of knowledge could be taught, investigated, and extended. The lecture and laboratory systems began to encroach upon classroom recitation as methods of instruction.

5. The so-called cultural studies (classics, mathematics, and philosophy) which had long monopolized the prescribed curriculum now had to make way for scientific and technical subjects which were useful as preparation for specialized careers in the professions, business, industry, or academic worlds. Specialization in the graduate courses required more and more specialization in undergraduate courses.

6. The notion of mental discipline or development of "intellectual power" through the particularly efficacious study of the ancient classics and mathematics gave way to the notion that knowledge of subjects especially appropriate to each individual was the paramount aim of college education.

7. The practice of treating all students alike in the learning process gave way to the increasing attempt to provide for differing interests, abilities, and future occupations of different individuals.

8. The religious tone of college education began to lose ground to the advancing secular aim to prepare for citizenship or occupation and to an increasingly secular curriculum.

9. The close and strict supervision of all phases of student life by the college administration began to weaken in favor of a greater freedom for the student to develop his own sense of responsibility and self-reliance.

10. The aristocratic nature of higher education as represented in the scarcity value of a college degree began to give way to the democratic notion that college education should be open to all classes of society and should try to develop civic responsibility and social understanding as well as occupational efficiency among the majority of young men and women.

CHAPTER XII

THE CONTROVERSIES HEIGHTEN: WHAT SHALL BE THE NATURE OF COLLEGE EDUCATION?

From the amount of space that has been given in the foregoing chapter to the college reformers, it might be suspected that they were having everything their own way and that the conservatives had given up the fight. Such, however, was far from the case, for there was still a large and powerful group of conservative educators who lined up in opposition to those who were trying to reform the college curriculum in the ways that have just been mentioned. The controversies that had begun to take shape in the earlier part of the nineteenth century reached a crescendo in the later decades of the nineteenth century. That the ideals of the progressives did not go unchallenged in circles of higher education in the United States can be dramatically illustrated in the many forms of polemics and pamphleteering that appeared during this period.

The periodical literature was full of the discussion; scores of controversial pamphlets were widely circulated; the inauguration of a new college president seldom passed without a challenging reexamination of the aims of higher education; baccalaureate and commencement addresses were full of references to the conflicting ideas of the function of higher education; speakers before all sorts of literary and scientific assemblies touched upon the question; debates and forums were held specifically to present the opposing points of view; and educational associations and teachers' meetings were very often concerned with the controversies. The amount of literature on this subject is so extensive that little more can be done than to cite some material that will be representative of the type of argument involved and to give something of the flavor of these colorful controversies.

The controversies included several aspects of the general question What is the aim and function of the college in American life? For purposes of clarity, it may be well to summarize here some of the ways in which that question was answered with reference to the extension of the elective system. First of all, as was indicated in earlier chapters, considerable attention was given to the question whether or not the German university ideal should be applied to the American college. Generally speaking, those who favored the university ideal also favored the elective system, and those who favored retention of the traditional English conception of the college were likely to favor the prescribed curriculum. Another point of attack was the question whether the college was to emphasize freedom or discipline for the student. Those who favored the college of freedom usually favored the extension of the elective system, whereas those who held to the notion of the college of discipline usually favored the prescribed curriculum. A third area of discussion was concerned with the validity of faculty psychology and mental discipline as over against the newer individual psychology that was being developed. Those who held to mental discipline generally opposed the elective system, whereas the newer psychology was usually brought in to support the extension of the elective system.

A fourth kind of discussion concerned the question whether or not a liberal education could be attained through practical studies as well as through the traditional cultural studies. A fifth phase of the controversy which was often closely associated with this practical-cultural discussion and which evoked many heated debates was the question of the relative prominence of the classics versus the modern subjects in the curriculum. In most cases, although not always, those who advocated that more attention should be given to the practical and modern subjects were also supporting the elective system; and those who defended the preeminence of the cultural subjects and the classics were opposing the elective system.

A sixth problem which was discussed extensively was the question whether the colleges should open their doors to the pressure of democracy and admit all kinds of students, including women, or whether they should preserve their privileges for those destined to become members of the intellectual aristocracy. The division here is less clear-cut than in other arguments, but it may be said that those who presented the argument of democracy were most often on the side of the elective system. A seventh phase of the controversy had to do with the question whether the college should retain its religious character and aims or should become an increasingly secular and nonsectarian institution. Here the division is least clear, but it may be said that, more often than not, those who were most emphatic that the college must retain its religious functions were also most in favor of the prescribed curriculum, whereas those in favor of secularizing college education were more often than not advocating also the elective system.

There was, of course, a final phase of the college controversies which referred directly to the extension or curtailment of the elective system itself. When writers or speakers were either defending or attacking the elective system, they would usually bring evidence to support their respective positions from one or several of the points of view outlined above. It may be emphasized here that the separation of the controversial subjects into eight classifications is an entirely artificial grouping and is done solely for purposes of analysis to show that the problem of the elective system was bound up with many other collegiate problems and that it was being approached from several different points of view.   Some educators emphasized one aspect of the problem in order to support their positions, and others would emphasize other aspects to suit *their* purposes. Attention will be given in the following pages to each of the eight phases of the controversy as outlined above.

UNIVERSITY IDEAL VERSUS THE COLLEGE IDEAL

As we have indicated in previous chapters, the spreading influence in the United States of the university ideal which came especially from Germany was very instrumental in aiding the progressives to justify the elective system in American colleges.   Outstanding in support of the university ideal were such leaders as Eliot, White, Gilman, Barnard, Jordan, and Harper,[1] but there were also many others who advocated that the university should be an institution wherein all subjects known to man should be taught, investigated, and extended.   There were many in addition to the foregoing who may have been less well known but who were nonetheless very influential in the spread of the notion that the university should be a place of freedom, specialization, and research. For example, John W. Burgess was urging in 1884 that the American college should adopt the German ideal, with its lecture system, its seminar, and especially its elective system whereby the student could make his own selection of studies in order to form a combination of subjects that most nearly suited his needs.[2]

In 1893, President Seth Low of Columbia University stated that the elective system was the American expression of the German emphasis upon "freedom of learning"; and although he was not ready to allow free election to freshmen in the college, he did recognize that Harvard and Johns Hopkins with their emphases upon university scholarship and specialization had been the most influential factors in the American college for 20 years.[3]   This side of the controversy also appeared prominently in the deliberations of the National Education Association where, in

---

[1] In his pamphlet *The Prospects of the Small College* (University of Chicago Press, Chicago, 1900), Harper cited some of the forces working against the small college; he named the high school, demand for specialization, decline of the sectarian ideal, increase in professional schools, the university idea, the state universities, and the small college's lack of adequate financial resources and personnel.   He felt that the future of the small college was secure only if some were strengthened and adopted specialties and if others became academies or junior colleges.

[2] JOHN W. BURGESS, *The American University.   When Shall It Be?   Where Shall It Be?   What Shall It Be?*   (Ginn and Company, Boston, 1884).

[3] SETH LOW, "Higher Education in the United States," *Educational Review*, 5: 1–16 (January, 1893).

addition to Eliot and White and others, even some of the more conservative educators were recommending that the elective system be introduced into at least the last two years of the college in an effort to make those two years take on the aspect of a real university.[1]

As Harvard was the leading light in reform, so was Yale the leading opponent of the elective system, and thus it was appropriate that one of the most outstanding opponents of the progressives and the most vigorous advocate for the retention of the traditional type of college should be Noah Porter who was president of Yale from 1871 to 1886. Porter presented the conservative position in the most glowing terms in his book entitled *The American Colleges and the American Public;* here he set forth most of the current arguments against the elective system and in favor of preserving the traditional college.[2] He vigorously defended the long emphasis of the traditional college upon a prescribed curriculum, with its prevailing classical and mathematical studies and its fundamental assumptions of mental discipline.

Porter defended the English type of communal college which had spread through America, with its dormitory and "class" system, because he felt that such a college had made more effective a strict supervision over the life of the student and more possible the dominating religious character of the institution. He believed that the college as thus evolved had most adequately met the needs of the American public, and he was confident that the public was satisfied with it as it was already functioning and therefore did not desire radical changes. Thus, Porter was a constant and effective opponent of introducing the ideals of the German university and the elective principle into the undergraduate college. He attacked the progressives in his inaugural address[3] and in many articles, addresses, and appearances before literary and educational groups. He was carrying on the Yale tradition which had been formulated in the Yale report of 1828, and he was quite effective in preventing the rapid spread of the elective system in Yale and in the colleges that attempted to emulate Yale.

As might be expected, Noah Porter had many faithful adherents as well as many ardent opponents. His successor as president of Yale, Timothy Dwight, showed in his inaugural address that he would willingly

---

[1] See J. H. WRIGHT, "Original Research in College Education," *N.E.A., Proceedings,* 1882, pp. 91–115; and ELI T. TAPPAN, "The University; Its Place and Work in the American System of Education," *ibid.,* pp. 3–7.

[2] NOAH PORTER, *The American Colleges and the American Public* (Charles Scribner's Sons, New York, 1878). An earlier edition was published in 1870 by C. C. Chatfield and Company, New Haven, and a later edition in 1890 by Charles Scribner's Sons, New York.

[3] *Addresses at the Inauguration of Noah Porter as President of Yale College* (New York, 1871), pp. 28–65.

adhere to Porter's ideals and that he would change the character of Yale slowly and with great respect for the past, but Dwight also showed himself fearful that the twentieth century might force Yale to change its course in the direction of more election just as the nineteenth had forced the admission of limited elective studies.[1] An article in ·the *Nation* entitled "Yale and Harvard" indicated that the editors felt that the Yale system was becoming outmoded, for it was predicted that the ideals of Porter would ultimately be obliged to give way and that the college of the future would follow Harvard's example of free election rather than Yale's emphasis upon prescribed courses.[2]

A more direct opponent of Porter was Charles Phelps Taft, who pointed out the meritoricus advances in scholarship, specialization, and freedom of teaching and learning made by the German universities and denied Porter's contention that American colleges were not ready to be made into recognizable copies of such universities.[3] Finally, testimony that Yale was not being completely able to hold to its traditional path despite the intention of its leaders is given in an article by President Charles Kendall Adams of the University of Michigan, who was describing the effectiveness of Michigan, Harvard, and Johns Hopkins in making universities out of colleges: "Even old Yale, that stronghold of everything conservative in education, has been obliged to yield to the demand for electives. . . . "[4]

Despite attacks and counterattacks, the conservative view of the college had many loyal followers; and in point of fact, the conservative view of college education probably commanded the loyalty of the majority of college educators up to the close of the nineteenth century. For example, when the Reverend Asa D. Smith was being inaugurated as president of Dartmouth College in 1863, he emphasized his belief that the whole tone of the college should be conservative.[5] In 1869, an attack was made upon the *Atlantic* articles of President Eliot of Harvard by Israel W. Andrews who believed that the college should continue to concentrate upon general education through prescribed studies, for he believed

[1] *Addresses at the Induction of Professor Timothy Dwight as President of Yale College* (New Haven, 1886), pp. 17–45.

[2] "Yale and Harvard," *Nation*, 34: 50–51 (Jan. 19, 1882). A month later, a correspondent to the *Nation* deplored the elective system because it destroyed the value of the B.A. degree; see "The American Colleges versus the European University," *ibid.*, 34: 142–143 (Feb. 16, 1882).

[3] C. P. Taft, *The German University and the American College* (Robert Clarke and Company, Cincinnati, 1871).

[4] C. K. Adams, "The Part of the University of Michigan in the Work of Higher Education," *The Chronicle*, February, 1885, pp. 7–8.

[5] A. D. Smith, *An Address Delivered at the Inauguration of the Author as President of Dartmouth College* (Hanover, N. H., 1863).

that there could be no real university in the United States until an institution could embrace only graduate students.[1] When Franklin Carter was inaugurated as president of Williams College in 1881, he affirmed that the New England college should hold to the prescribed curriculum of tradition and of discipline even if other institutions wished to change themselves into universities for individual freedom.[2] Alexander Winchell stated in his inaugural as chancellor of Syracuse University that the communal life and class system of the college was more important for American society than the dispersion of student life that occurred in a large university in a city.[3]

Caleb Mills, a professor of Greek at Wabash College, even went so far as to thank God in his attacks on the progressives that the "ravages of the optional fever" were not so extensive in rural as in metropolitan institutions, and he commended the wisdom—or perhaps it was the poverty—of the small colleges that kept them holding to the prescribed curriculum.[4] A final example here of the affinity of college educators for the traditional college is given in the article written by John J. Stevenson for *Popular Science Monthly* in 1904 attacking some earlier articles in the same magazine by David Starr Jordan.[5] Stevenson did not believe that the American student was ready for the university ideal that Jordan advocated, and he urged that the only corrective for the evils of college education was to return to the college of 25 years earlier, with its four-year prescribed course and its greater severity of training and discipline.

FREEDOM VERSUS DISCIPLINE

A great many other college educators concentrated their attention upon the question whether or not the college should give increasingly more freedom to the student in choosing his studies for specialization and in developing his own sense of responsibility and self-control in the general conduct of his college life. The progressives were most often in favor of greater freedom for the student, but the conservatives were more likely to stress the fact that students were too young or too inexperienced to choose for themselves. It were much better, said conservatives, that students should be directed carefully in their mental and moral life by the close supervision of the college administration. They felt that students

---

[1] I. W. ANDREWS, *The American College* (Marietta, Ohio, 1869).

[2] *Williams College, Inauguration of President Franklin Carter* (Williamstown, Mass., 1882).

[3] *Inauguration of Alexander Winchell as Chancellor of the Syracuse University* (Syracuse, N. Y., 1873).

[4] CALEB MILLS, *New Departures in Collegiate Control and Culture* (New York, 1880).

[5] J. J. STEVENSON, "The College Course," *Popular Science Monthly*, 64: 202–209 (January, 1904); also D. S. JORDAN, "University Building," *ibid.*, 61: 330–338 (August, 1902), and "University Tendencies in America," *ibid.*, 63: 141–148 (June, 1903).

must be disciplined to obey others before they could be expected to control themselves and ultimately to direct others.   Thus, it was really a deep-seated conflict over the question of authority in college education: Progressives suggested that the college relinquish some of its authority over the life of the students, whereas conservatives insisted that strict control and supervision should be maintained.

As early as 1866, Dr. F. H. Hedge in an address to the alumni of Harvard had deprecated the excessive coercion present in the traditional college because it stifled opportunity for the student to develop his own self-determined activities through voluntary study.[1]   In commenting with approval upon Hedge's address, the *New Englander* urged that all colleges should allow more freedom to the student, do away with police requirements, and extend the elective system, but the writer cautioned that most reforms proceeded from an overestimate of the value of knowledge as such and from an underestimate of the value of training.[2]   In commenting upon the results of the elective system, a Harvard professor in 1889 made the point that it had improved the relation between the student and the teacher, for now the teacher did not look after the conduct of the student but concentrated his energies upon guiding him in the pursuit of intellectual and other desirable aims.[3]

The most effective proponent of the doctrine of freedom was, of course, President Eliot, and the most dramatic expression of the opposing points of view was given in a debate scheduled to be held between Eliot and James McCosh, president of Princeton, before the Nineteenth Century Club in New York City on February 24, 1885.   Eliot made the point that the student should be given more freedom in three areas of his college life: in choosing his studies, in choosing a specialty, and in governing his own social and religious life.   McCosh attacked each of these points in turn.[4]   He believed that the student should not have freedom in choosing his studies but rather should be made to pursue certain required subjects if he were to be granted a B. A. degree.   McCosh felt also that voluntary attendance upon classes was a mistaken notion of student freedom and that all students should be required to attend all classes and recitations.   To Eliot's second proposal for freedom, McCosh replied that, although the student should be allowed a limited choice of electives beyond the requirements, the choice of a specialty should not

[1] F. H. HEDGE, "University Reform," *Atlantic Monthly*, 18: 296–307 (July, 1866).

[2] "Dr. Hedges' Address to the Alumni of Harvard," *New Englander*, 25: 695–710 (October, 1866).

[3] N. S. SHALER, "The Problem of Discipline in Higher Education," *Atlantic Monthly*, 64: 24–37 (July, 1889).

[4] See ELIOT, "Liberty in Education," *Educational Reform*, pp. 125–148; and JAMES McCOSH, *The New Departure in College Studies; Reply to President Eliot's Defense of It in New York, Feb. 24, 1885* (Charles Scribner's Sons, New York, 1885).

come until he had finished prescribed studies in various fields. As to Eliot's third proposal, McCosh denied to students the right to determine their own self-government with such freedom that they would miss definite moral and religious training. That the religious and authoritative character of the college should be maintained was one of the cornerstones of the doctrines of this Scotch-Presbyterian minister.

It was not unnatural that Princeton under the tutelage of McCosh and later presidents should follow a course similar to that of Yale and stand rather firmly for the traditional type of college and for the prescribed curriculum. To be sure, McCosh in his inaugural had pointed out that some election was necessary if newer studies were to be admitted to the curriculum without excluding the older studies, but he was confident that no choice should be allowed until the student had been introduced to all the major groups of studies, namely, ancient languages, mathematics, physical sciences, and mental and social sciences.[1] When Francis L. Patton was inaugurated, he indicated that he would hold to the Princeton tradition of prescribing fully the first two years and allowing limited election in the last two.[2]

Another outstanding defender of the Princeton position was Andrew F. West who was for many years dean of the graduate school. West was particularly active in defending the high place accorded to the ancient classics in the college curriculum, and he made particular attacks upon Eliot's annual report of 1884–1885 which presented a description of the workings of the elective system at Harvard.[3] West was frankly skeptical that the freedom of the elective system at Harvard was doing all that Eliot was claiming for it, and he reaffirmed his faith that the Princeton type of disciplinary college was far more effective for the true education of college students. A final example of the Princeton opposition to the kind of reform that was issuing from Eliot at Harvard was an article in the *Princeton Review* by Lyman Atwater who stood firmly on the ground that students should not only be required to take certain subjects but should be strictly supervised by the college officers and should be compelled to attend chapel.[4]

It is perhaps needless to say that, although Yale and Princeton felt called upon to be the major antagonists against Harvard, there were many other institutions the leaders of which felt just as strongly as did

[1] *Inauguration of James McCosh as President of the College of New Jersey*, Princeton (Robert Carter and Brothers, New York, 1868).

[2] *The Inauguration of the Rev. Francis Landey Patton as President of Princeton College* (Princeton, N. J., 1888).

[3] A. F. WEST, *A Review of President Eliot's Report on Elective Studies* (New York, 1886). Reprinted from *The Independent* (May 6 and 13, 1886).

[4] L. H. ATWATER, "Proposed Reforms in Collegiate Education," *Princeton Review*, 10: 100–120 (July, 1882).

the leaders of these two powerful colleges. Perhaps the most vitriolic of all attacks upon Harvard's elective system was the broadside launched at Wabash College by the professor of Greek who has already been mentioned.[1] Professor Caleb Mills was positive that optional study was merely a "current hobby of the day" and a "marauding fancy" which foolishly maintained that a "namby-pamby diet of modern languages" was as valuable as a disciplinary course in Greek. Mills sought to annihilate with a flood of invective the "false" assumption that the student could select his studies as well as the wise men who had put into the college curriculum the combined experience of the past.

The question of college discipline also appeared in the form of a controversy over whether or not the college was to exert the same authority over its students that parents exerted over their children when they were at home. The conservatives often justified their pleas for discipline with the argument that the college should stand *in loco parentis*. A series of articles and correspondence in the *Nation* represent the kind of arguments carried on in this phase of the controversy. The editors pointed out to some of its correspondents that the doctrine of *in loco parentis* no longer existed, but their correspondents continued to insist that the character of youth was such that they needed strict discipline from parents and from the college authorities.[2]

EXPERIMENTAL PSYCHOLOGY VERSUS FACULTY PSYCHOLOGY

Closely associated with the problem of freedom and discipline was the question concerning how the learning process was carried on to the best advantage. The progressives were usually quite insistent that the best learning occurred when the particular interests, aptitudes, and capacities of each student were taken into account by the course of study. The argument then went on to show that individual differences were not adequately cared for by the prescribed curriculum or by a linguistic training that compelled every student to take the same subjects irrespective of his interests. Therefore, the progressives advocated the elective system as a proper way to allow students to select subjects that most nearly approached their special needs. They began to support their arguments with the evidence of the new experimental psychology described on pages 164–167.

On the other side, the conservatives insisted that the formal faculties of the mind were essentially the same for every human being and that effective mental discipline should therefore be the fundamental aim of the

---

[1] CALEB MILLS, *op. cit.*, pp. 28–32.

[2] "The American Colleges versus the European Universities," *Nation*, 34: 142–143 (Feb. 16, 1882), and correspondence in *ibid.*, pp. 143–144.

colleges. The argument very often indicated that intellectual training was more important than the specific kind of knowledge acquired and that therefore all students should study those studies which were peculiarly suitable for mental discipline. It is obvious that this argument fitted in nicely with all the other phases of the controversy, for the conservatives could point out that college training as opposed to university study had the unique function of disciplining not only the social and moral character of students but also their intellectual capacities. In this way, it was thought that undergraduate students would have a rounded, harmonious, and general training as the best preparation for the later specialization of university study.

Some of the implications of a psychology of the individual were set forth by reformers as far back as Ticknor and Wayland, not to mention the theoretical suggestions of the individualism of the Renaissance and the Enlightenment, but the applications of the psychology of individual differences in terms of the elective system did not really gain substantial headway until late in the nineteenth century. Aside from such men as Eliot, Barnard, White, and Jordan, there were many others who were beginning to use psychology as a justification for the elective system. In 1865, Jacob Bigelow advocated in an address at the Massachusetts Institute of Technology that the student should select a special pursuit and follow it in his college studies so that his learning would be of most value to him: " . . . education to be useful must . . . be made simple, limited, practicable, acceptable to the learner, adapted to his character and wants, and brought home to his particular case by *subdivision* and *selection.*"[1]

From the same institution in Boston came the arguments of William P. Atkinson a few years later that the prevailing conceptions of a liberal education must be modified inasmuch as the progress of psychology had tended to discredit the notions of mental discipline. Hence, the emphasis in learning upon purely linguistic activities should be reduced in favor of the physical sciences, with their greater emphasis upon motor and manual activities.[2] Near the end of the century, an editorial in the *Educational Review* summed up the attitude of the progressives so neatly that it deserves quoting:

That the principle of individuality is the only rational basis of educational activity was made clear by psychology some time since; and it is entirely proper to attack the rigidly prescribed curriculum of the old-fashioned American college

[1] JACOB BIGELOW, *An Address on the Limits of Education read before the Massachusetts Institute of Technology* (E. P. Dutton & Co., Inc., New York, 1865), pp. 13–14.
[2] W. P. ATKINSON, *The Liberal Education of the Nineteenth Century* (D. Appleton-Century Company, Inc., New York, 1873); also *N.E.A., Proceedings*, 1873, pp. 141–163.

from this point of view. . . . The elective system is the scientific, the psychological system of education. . . . [1]

On the side of mental discipline there was so much literature during this period that in an unselected group of commencement or inaugural addresses the chances were about three or four to one that the author would be quoting the doctrines of mental discipline or of "intellectual development" as justification for continuing the prescribed curriculum of classical and mathematical studies. There is so much material from which to choose that it is difficult to single out a few arguments, but some of the most representative attitudes have been selected to give something of the flavor of the controversy on this aspect of the problem of what college education should be.

It might be well to mention here that even some of the advocates of the newer subjects and of the elective system found it expedient to justify the introduction of the newer subjects into the curriculum on grounds of mental discipline. They would say that, since the difficulty of a subject rather than its content was the criterion of value for mental discipline, then the newer studies of English and physical sciences could be taught with such difficulty and thoroughness that the aim of mental discipline would be served. For example, William LeRoy Broun of Vanderbilt University, in a speech before the National Education Association in 1877, defended the entrance of the physical sciences into the curriculum because of their unique value in training the mental faculties of observation and inductive thought.[2] A few years later, Albert S. Bolles was defending the modern languages on the grounds that they were just as valid as the ancient languages for mental discipline, for developing the powers of the mind, and for improving expression of thought in speech and writing.[3]

However, from the time of the Yale report of 1828 to the end of the century, most of the advocates of mental discipline as a fundamental aim and practice in college education were on the side of the conservative opponents of the elective system.[4] The inaugural address of James McCosh at Princeton has already been mentioned in another connection, but his fundamental thesis was expressed as follows: "I do hold it to be the highest end of a university to *educate;* that is, draw out and improve the faculties which God has given."[5] Likewise, the inaugural of Noah Porter

[1] *Educational Review*, 6: 199 (September, 1893).

[2] W. L. Broun, "The Elective System," *N.E.A.*, *Proceedings*, 1877, pp. 87–95.

[3] A. S. Bolles, "What Instruction Should Be Given in Our Colleges?" *Atlantic Monthly*, 52: 686–694 (November, 1883).

[4] An occasional exception to this generalization could be found in scholars who held to the doctrine of mental discipline through the classics yet favored the elective system in order to give those who selected the classics a real chance to acquire a fair amount of disciplinary value from them. For example, see E. S. Joynes (Washington and Lee University), "Classical Studies," *N.E.A.*, *Proceedings*, 1873, pp. 131–140.

[5] James McCosh, *Inauguration*, p. 40.

at Yale indicated the same adherence to the doctrine of mental discipline: "Two principles must be regarded as unquestioned: The higher education should aim at intellectual culture and training rather than at the acquisition of knowledge, and it should respect remote rather than immediate results."[1] In another connection a few years later, Porter felt confident that the disciplinary value of the traditional subjects was the only justification needed for them: "The very fact that he [the student] is to make no direct or conscious use of these studies may be the best evidence that these studies will be the most useful."[2]

Besides these two powerful leaders in higher education, the United States Commissioner of Education William T. Harris was publicly taking a stand in favor of mental discipline and against the elective system.[3] Apparently, that aspect of the German philosophy of absolute idealism which Harris embraced was putting its weight upon the side of "spiritual" activities and the formal training of the subjective powers of the mind. In the same year, another Harris was making even more explicit the religious connotations of idealism. Samuel S. Harris, a bishop in Michigan, told the graduating class at the University of Michigan that man was essentially a "spirit" endowed with faculties to perceive, remember, combine, imagine, think, and reason; therefore, a complete education for man would develop all of these faculties and would give him moral and emotional as well as intellectual training.[4]

The final examples of the argument for mental discipline will be taken from the proceedings of the annual meetings of the National Education Association where the controversy was bitterly carried on for many years in the last three decades of the nineteenth and the first decade of the twentieth century. In presenting a report of the committee on higher education of the National Council of Education in 1888, S. H. Peabody indicated that the studies in college should be disciplinary rather than pleasant for the students. The implication was, of course, that if studies were hard and disagreeable, the student would benefit more than if the subject were interesting to him; therefore, the report opposed the elective system as bad educational practice.[5] In 1896, John E. Bradley stated explicitly that students should be required to do things for which they have no taste merely in order to train their will.[6] When the conservative educators were reduced to the argument of difficulty merely for the

---

[1] NOAH PORTER, *Inauguration*, p. 41.

[2] NOAH PORTER, "The Class System," *N.E.A., Proceedings*, 1877, p. 104.

[3] W. T. HARRIS, "Equivalents in a Liberal Course of Study," *N.E.A., Proceedings*, 1880, pp. 167–175.

[4] S. S. HARRIS, *Complete Education* (Ann Arbor, Mich., 1880).

[5] S. H. PEABODY, "The Elective System in Colleges," *N.E.A., Proceedings*, 1888, pp. 268–275.

[6] J. E. BRADLEY, "The Higher Life of the College," *N.E.A., Proceedings*, 1896, pp. 428–438.

sake of mental discipline and of disagreeableness merely for the sake of improving the other mental faculties, their cause was on the brink of disaster.

PRACTICAL VERSUS CULTURAL CONCEPTION OF A LIBERAL EDUCATION

In his crusade for widening the scope of the conception of a liberal education to include the practical and utilitarian values of the modern age, President Eliot was running up against one of the most impregnable strongholds of the traditional education. It is true that Eliot received the support of capable men from bo ɩ the educational and the lay fields, but their position was so contrary to the long held belief that a liberal education should be "cultural" and should be pursued for its own sake that headway was made but slowly. Reference has already been made to the advances made along this line not only by Eliot at Harvard but also by White at Cornell and by some of the larger of the state universities.

In addition to these men and institutions, the technological schools and noneducators often raised their voices in protest against the exclusive hold of "education for its own sake." William P. Atkinson of the Massachusetts Institute of Technology has been mentioned as urging that the conception of a liberal education be expanded in order to admit the physical sciences on a level of equality with other subjects and to undermine the ancient languages which claimed to be the sole foundation of a liberal education.[1] Another commanding voice on the side of the reformers was that of Charles Francis Adams, who came from outside the ranks of professional educators to attack the purely cultural emphasis of a liberal education. In his Phi Beta Kappa address at Harvard in 1883, Adams declared himself enough of a practical man to believe that the demands of a scientific and utilitarian age would not and should not forever be sacrificed to the dead languages.[2]

The conservatives quickly rallied to the fight and defended with all the power at their command the traditional meaning of a liberal education. The favorite defenses centered around three or four main types of argument. There was, first of all, the type that viewed the traditional classical education as the "best expression of the eternal spirit of man" and as the best way to elevate man "to the highest and best ideals of human life." In this vein, E. R. Sill and E. E. White attacked Spencer's "useful" education through science because it did not aid man to search out the higher and richer planes of the intellectual life or to develop the "culture of man as man."[3] White specifically stated that scientific knowledge

---

[1] W. P. ATKINSON, op. cit.

[2] C. F. ADAMS, A College Fetich (Lothrop, Lee & Shepard, Boston, 1883); for a specific reply to Adams, see D. H. CHAMBERLAIN, Not a "College Fetish" (Willard Small, Boston, 1884).

[3] E. R. SILL, "Herbert Spencer's Theory of Education," Atlantic Monthly, 51:

which was necessary for guidance in the duties of life was of distinctly lesser importance than cultural study.

A second type of argument emphasized that the true liberal education was sought for its own sake and would be destroyed if utilitarian values were inserted into it. For example, Theodore Dwight Woolsey had asserted emphatically when he became president of Yale University that a liberal education must be valued not as a means to practical ends but solely for its own sake and that the true college would resist altogether the effort to introduce professional or practical studies into the college course.[1] Likewise Taylor Lewis, who was for long professor of Greek at Union College, insisted that a liberal college should embrace only those fields of knowledge required for "man as man" and should shun knowledge that was useful as preparation for a business or profession.[2] Yet despite many such arguments, it appears that even the conservative denominational colleges began to give more attention to vocational aims in the latter nineteenth century. A recent investigation has found not only that *statements* of vocational aims increased during this period but also that the actual offering of vocational subjects far exceeded the explicit statements in college catalogues and other literature.[3]

A third phase of the argument stated that a liberally educated man should be acquainted with all of the principal fields of thought before being allowed to specialize. Only in this way could there be a common background among educated persons. This point of view was often expressed by many educators; but if anyone could be picked out who best represented the others, it might be Noah Porter, who announced in nearly all of his public utterances and writings that the specialist needed a well-rounded general education as a background in order that he would not become narrow in his point of view and interests.[4]

A fourth type of expression commonly found in support of the traditional liberal education was the argument that the meaning of a liberal education and the integrity of the bachelor of arts degree must be maintained by keeping out of the course of study any practical or utilitarian studies. Thus, when Thomas W. Bickrell was making the presidential address before the National Education Association in 1884, he attacked

171–179 (February, 1883); and E. E. WHITE, "Election in General Education," *N.E.A., Proceedings,* 1897, pp. 373–384.

[1] T. D. WOOLSEY, . . . *Inauguration as President of Yale College* (New Haven, Conn., 1846).

[2] TAYLOR LEWIS, "The True Idea of a Liberal Education," *Proceedings of the Meeting of the Officers of Colleges and Academies* (Albany, N. Y., 1863).

[3] LESLIE K. PATTON, *The Purposes of Church-related Colleges* (Teachers College, Columbia University, 1939).

[4] See NOAH PORTER, *Inauguration;* and "The Class System," *N.E.A., Proceedings,* 1877, pp. 95–105.

the elective system because it was destroying the meaning and confidence in a liberal education.[1] Two years later, William A. Mowry was insisting before the same association that the B.A. degree must be reserved for the classical course and that if other courses were to be offered they should grant the B.S. or Ph.B. degree.[2] What the conservatives really meant by preserving the meaning of a liberal education was plainly stated by William G. Frost, a professor of Greek at Oberlin College, when he insisted that a harmonious liberal education could be gained only when the *classics* were at the center of the course of study and that the B.A. degree should not be granted unless the student had studied the ancient classics.[3]

More influential in this respect than anyone else, perhaps, was Andrew F. West, dean of the graduate school at Princeton. For over 40 years, West carried on the battle to keep Latin and Greek as prescribed studies in the course that led to a true liberal education. In 1884, he wrote an article entitled "Must the Classics Go?" in which he decided that Greek as well as Latin should be kept in the college curriculum if the true scientific and cultural spirit was to be kept alive.[4] He cited the types of persons who objected to the classics: men of action; those who had never studied the classics; those imbued with the spirit of money-making; those who disliked a severe mental training; those who believed that the modern languages were more adequate; those who advocated the physical sciences; and those who had suffered from poor teaching in the classics. That was an admirable analysis of the type of person that was rapidly becoming a most important influence in all of American life. West defended the classics against this sort of person by quoting John Stuart Mill at length on the positive value of the classics for mental discipline and literary culture. He concluded by deciding that Greek must be kept as well as Latin because the two together were better than just one, because Latin would be hurt by the separation, and because there was ample time for both in the curriculum of four years.

In 1886, West replied to Eliot's report on the elective system by stating that Harvard students were specializing prematurely without proper common liberal education and that Harvard's B.A. degree had dissipated and disintegrated the true meaning of a liberal arts degree.[5] West would admit other degrees for other subjects, but he felt that the disciplinary

---

[1] T. W. Bickrell, "Annual Address of the President," *N.E.A., Proceedings*, 1884, pp. 52–59.

[2] W. A. Mowry, "The College Curriculum," *N.E.A., Proceedings*, 1886, pp. 358–368.

[3] W. G. Frost, "Greek among Required Subjects," *Bibliotheca Sacra*, 42: 327–350 (April, 1885).

[4] A. F. West, "Must the Classics Go?" *North American Review*, 138: 151–172 (February, 1884).

[5] A. F. West, *A Review of President Eliot's Report on Elective Studies.*

and cultural connotation of the traditional B.A. degree should not be touched. In 1903, West was still viewing with alarm the "perils to a liberal education" which he identified as the spirit of commercialism; the lack of appreciation for good literature; the disposition to do the pleasant rather than the hard thing; and finally, of course, the acceptance of the free elective system.[1] West is perhaps one of the best examples of the conservative educators who identified a liberal education with study of the classics.

THE CLASSICAL CONTROVERSY: NEW STUDIES VERSUS OLD STUDIES

All of this chapter might have been called "The Classical Controversy," for we have discussed at least indirectly most of the arguments that were brought to bear for and against the classical studies. They were most often defended because of their unique connection with higher education since the days when Latin and Greek were the universal languages of scholarship; because of their efficacy for moral and intellectual discipline; and because they had long been looked upon as the very heart of a liberal education. The justification for making a separate section for the classical controversy is merely to draw special attention to the fact that nearly all of the different kinds of arguments in higher education in the latter part of the nineteenth century were concerned in some respect with opposing or defending the study of the classics.

When Charles Francis Adams was talking about a "college fetich," he was challenging the right of the classicists to say that *their* path was the only one to a liberal education. He ridiculed their theories which described the benefits of the classics in terms of an "impalpable-essence-and-precious-residuum," and he quoted the rest of the members of the Adams family to show that they had thrown away the study of Greek because it was useless. When F. H. Hedge was speaking to the alumni of Harvard on university reform, he was attacking the classicists for failing to realize that the preemptive hold of the classics upon world literature had passed with the passing of the Renaissance and Reformation. When Bigelow was speaking to the Massachusetts Institute of Technology, and when Atkinson was redefining the conception of a liberal education for the nineteenth century, they were trying to assert the claims of modern languages and physical sciences to a place of equal rank in a course of liberal education.

Likewise, when a long list of conservative educators was speaking and writing on the subject of higher education, it was with the explicit or

[1] A. F. WEST, "The Present Peril to Liberal Education," *N.E.A.*, *Proceedings*, 1903, pp. 54–60. As late as 1932, Dean West indicated that the classics should still play a large part in general education; see his *American General Education* (Princeton University Press, Princeton, 1932).

implicit intention to justify continuance of the classical studies as the paramount subjects in a college education. Reference has already been made to the arguments of such men as Porter, McCosh, West, W. T. Harris, Mills, Sill, Frost, Lewis, and Chamberlain. Rather than overburden an already long survey with repetitions of the arguments of these men, only one more statement on each side of the classical controversy will be mentioned here. A little book written by George Frederick Mellen in 1890 summed up many of the reasons for the decline in the study of the classics: Entrance requirements in Latin and Greek had been relaxed; the curriculum of the secondary schools had been overcrowded with nonclassical studies; the elective system in colleges had tempted students to select easier subjects; the establishment of scientific and technical schools had attracted great numbers of students; teachers and students were apathetic toward general culture; and the idea was beginning to prevail that students should follow only those subjects which would lead directly to mercenary gain.[1] Mellen was convinced that the debt of civilization to Greece and Rome was too great to allow the decline in classical studies to be more than temporary, and he quoted Harris, Porter, Matthew Arnold, and the examples of the German *Gymnasium*, the French *lycée*, and the English public school to emphasize his points. His conclusion was that all levels of general education, including the college, should foster study of the classics, raise requirements, and stiffen up the work.

On the other side of the argument, a most vigorous and colorful attack was made upon the classics by a prolific writer Montague Leverson, a lawyer by profession who boasted both the Ph.D. and the M.D. degrees. Leverson held up to ridicule with a scathing scorn all of the common arguments in favor of the classics.[2] He stated that the classics had never been able to define with any precision what they mean by "intellectual training." He criticized the arguments made by such men as Mill and Gladstone and suggested that they became great in spite of rather than because of their study of the classics. He quoted statements made by a clergyman, Howard Crosby, in the current report of the New York Regents and labeled tham as pompous, ex cathedra falsehoods.

Leverson used the quite unusual argument against the classics that they instilled immoral ideas among youth, portrayed lewd and licentious living, praised the glories of war, and eulogized the Greeks and Romans who were essentially "robber" nations. For these reasons, he denied that the classics could provide the best means for arriving at the true, the good,

---

[1] G. F. MELLEN, *Popular Errors concerning Higher Education in the United States and the Remedy* (Gressner and Schramm, Leipzig, 1890), especially pp. 23–24.

[2] MONTAGUE R. LEVERSON, *Thoughts on Institutions of the Higher Education, with a Chapter on Classical Studies* (S. and D. A. Huebsh, New York, 1893).

and the beautiful. He issued a call to the people of the country to eradicate the classics from higher education and to lend their support to a new type of university which would emphasize the physical, political, and legal sciences. His rousing arguments doubtless alienated many sincere opponents of the classics, but they are interesting as illustrating the extreme lengths to which the reaction against the classics could go.

Much more important than such arguments as those of Leverson in the campaign against the classics was the growing amount of literature in the newer fields of knowledge. Numerous articles and books began to portray the advancements being made in such newer fields of study as the modern languages, English, biology, physical sciences, history, economics, political science, sociology, and anthropology.[1] This growing amount of literature in the younger fields of knowledge indicated that they were coming to maturity in the organization of subject matter and in methods of teaching. The scientific discoveries of the seventeenth and eighteenth centuries were becoming more teachable in the nineteenth century, and the newer social sciences were becoming more specialized and exacting. They were consequently challenging the classics on all of the grounds upon which the classics had ever been justified; they were asserting that they could discipline the mind and provide just as much "culture" as the classics could.

Moreover, the modern subjects were insisting that they were even more adequate than the classics, because they dealt with more recent materials and embodied the "best that had been thought and said" within the last hundred years. They were therefore appealing to students on all the familiar grounds and were adding for good measure the arguments that they were up-to-date, practical, and interesting. Thus, the newer subjects continued to shoulder their way into the liberal arts curriculum and to make more impossible than ever the continuance of the completely prescribed curriculum. As the newer subjects began to win the day, and as the elective system was extended to make way for them, the worst fears of the classicists became literally true. The traditional meaning of a liberal education was lost; that is, a liberal education no longer necessarily meant the study of Greek and Latin.

SHALL THE COLLEGE BE SECULAR OR RELIGIOUS?

Often combined with these other approaches to the problem of higher education, many discussions were specifically concerned with the question whether the college should be nonreligious and nonsectarian or remain essentially religious in tone. Although a generalization in this respect is somewhat difficult, it may be said with some caution that the progressives

---

For specific descriptions of the social sciences, see H. E. Barnes, ed., The History and Prospects of the Social Sciences (Alfred A. Knopf, Inc., New York, 1925).

were often in favor of making the college a secular institution, especially with reference to the growing state universities, whereas the conservatives were usually hesitant to give up the traditional religious character of college education.   Jefferson and Tappan had been especially outstanding in fighting the religious conception of the college in the earlier part of the nineteenth century, and Eliot and White were perhaps leading the antireligious crusades of the latter half of the nineteenth century.

It may be more than a coincidence that the large universities put less emphasis upon the religious conception of higher education than did the small colleges.   There seemed to be something inherent in the idea of a large university with its hundreds of students, often living in a large city, that militated against the continuance of the strong religious influences that had been so characteristic of the small, rural, and denominational college.   City life seemed eventually to be an enemy of religious colleges, just as it seemed to weaken the hold of the churches upon urban community life in general.

Be that as it may, the large and progressive universities appeared to be ranged against the small and conservative colleges with reference to the question of religious dominance of higher education.   Harvard, Cornell, Johns Hopkins, Chicago, and the state universities seemed to break away from the religious and disciplinary conception of higher education sooner than did Princeton, Yale, the New England colleges, and, of course, the smaller denominational colleges wherever they were found.   One of the most dramatic instances of this conflict was the controversy between Eliot of Harvard and McCosh of Princeton, wherein Eliot stood out clearly for a greater secular emphasis in college studies and a discontinuance of compulsory chapel, and McCosh maintained just as firmly that college training should be essentially religious in character.[1]

Lyman Atwater, writing in the *Princeton Review*, provided more good evidence that the officials of Princeton were determined to keep within the traditional religious fold of Presbyterianism.[2]   The inaugurals and other pronouncements of Woolsey and Porter at Yale showed that they, too, were resolutely on the path of religious control of college life.[3]   The inaugurals of Seelye at Amherst and Bartlett at Dartmouth indicated that they

---

[1] See the debate between Eliot and McCosh mentioned on page 210 above.   Voluntary chapel was instituted at Harvard in 1886, a move which was vigorously criticized by the more conservative colleges.   See S. E. MORISON, *The Development of Harvard University Since the Inauguration of President Eliot* (Harvard University Press, Cambridge, 1930), pp. li–lviii.

[2] L. H. ATWATER, "Proposed Reforms in Collegiate Education," *Princeton Review*, 10: 100–120 (July, 1882).

[3] T. D. WOOLSEY, *Inauguration*, pp. 89, 96; NOAH PORTER, *Inauguration*, p. 47: "We cannot, if we would, avoid the ethical and religious aspects of the higher education."

felt the Christian religion to be the topstone of college education and the inculcation in students of reverence and mental docility to be a paramount aim of college training.[1] Without going into further detail, it seems apparent that where the conception of a liberal education was firmly grounded upon religious and intellectual authority and discipline, the prescribed curriculum was more likely to be maintained longer against the inroads of the elective system with its attendant doctrines of freedom and flexibility.[2]

To be sure, some of the church-related colleges began to admit the scientific and newer studies into their curriculum, but it was usually upon a decidedly inferior basis. For example, some of the denominational colleges began to provide scientific courses, but often their catalogues warn students against enrolling in such courses unless their financial status will not allow them to pursue the traditional classical course:

While the laws of the college permit this fourth, *irregular* [scientific] course, it is felt to be due to the cause of thorough education, to discourage all students from entering upon it whose pecuniary ability or age will possibly permit them to take the regular course. Long continued experience teaches that but few select the irregular course, except those who wish to avoid hard study; and yet without this hard study thorough mental training is never attained.[3]

Apparently the religious college felt that mental and moral discipline could not be properly instilled outside the prescribed classical course, and thus the true intellectual elite was limited largely to economically privileged persons:

The Trustees, therefore, in maintaining a Department in which the Course of Instruction is confined to the English Language, have no intention to lower the standard of liberal education, or in the least to depreciate the Classics. They simply design to bring the advantages of a scientific and English education at once systematic and thorough, so far as it goes, within the reach of a class of young men who desire such an education, and yet are hindered by their circumstances from attempting to explore a field so vast as that to which the study of the Classics is designed to introduce the student.[4]

[1] J. H. SEELYE, *Inauguration;* S. C. BARTLETT, *Exercises at the Inauguration of Samuel Colcord Bartlett as President of Dartmouth College* (Concord, N. H., 1877).

[2] Although all references to date have singled out Protestant institutions, it should be noted that Catholic colleges maintained a similar if not, indeed, even more strict conception of the prescribed curriculum as the only proper route to a liberal and religious education; see, for example, W. H. HILL, *Historical Sketch of St. Louis University* (P. Fox, St. Louis, 1879), p. 154, for the view that the prescribed curriculum comprised adequately the entire range of human knowledge, the ultimate crown of which was theology.

[3] *Catalogue of Mississippi College* (Clinton, Miss.), 1857, p. 12.

[4] *Catalogue of Illinois College* (Jacksonville, Ill.), 1860, pp. 14–15.

The growth of secular education was alarming to many of the church colleges, and some of them gave solemn warning to parents not to allow their children to be exposed to the dangers of a nonreligious education. One of the best examples of this attitude is described below:

The Christian religion we endeavor to make the basis on which our system of education rests. All that is truly noble and substantial in human character must rest on this basis; and we make constant efforts to bring our students to a saving knowledge of the truth as it is in Christ Jesus, that they may early in life be established upon this immovable foundation. Take care not to send those who are most dear to you to schools in which the Christian religion is openly attacked, or even ignored, lest while their intellects are being developed and furnished, the foundations of their religious life should be rudely torn up and the darkness and desolation of skepticism take the place of the light and comfort of the faith you taught them at home. See to it that the mother's religion, the father's faith, the sweet influences of the pious home, are not discredited by the "philosophy, falsely so called," of the arrogant professor. Put your son into the care and keeping of Christian teachers, if you value his soul.[1]

Along with the determination to place college education upon a classical and religious foundation, many church colleges aimed at a very strict control of the details of the daily life of the students. Many catalogues listed detailed rules of prohibitions and admonitions. The catalogue of Shurtleff College (Alton, Ill.) in 1863 contained a pledge of obedience in which the student promised to obey all the rules of the college and promised not to drink, play cards, swear, or join secret societies. Saint Vincent College was very strict about letter writing:

Unless there are extraordinary reasons, letters may be written only on Saturdays and Sundays, and must invariably be handed unsealed to the Director. Such as fail to comply with this rule are suspected of unlawful correspondence, and may, according to circumstances, be expelled.[2]

Although such strict conceptions of the disciplinary function of the college have largely been relaxed, some colleges still maintain rules virtually as severe (see pages 312–313 below).

SHALL THE COLLEGE BE DEMOCRATIC OR ARISTOCRATIC?

The question of the democratic versus the aristocratic conception of the college in the latter nineteenth century is more difficult to document than is the question of the religious versus the secular college, for it was not until the turn of the twentieth century that the problem became more

---

[1] *Catalogue of Central College* (Fayette, Mo.), 1891, under "General Information, The Christian Religion."

[2] *Catalogue of Saint Vincent College* (Latrobe, formerly Beatty, Pa.), 1903–1904, p. 13.

explicit in educational literature. The great influx of students into institutions of higher education after the turn of the century, and especially after the World War, and the rise of the testing program which showed the glaring differences in mental ability among students helped to make the question of democracy in college attendance something more than implicit references in the literature of higher education.

It may be said with some assurance, however, that those conservative college educators who held rigidly to the traditional aristocratic conception of a liberal education to be attained only through certain prescribed subjects were likely to say also that those who could not complete successfully a classical and mathematical curriculum should not be called liberally educated and should not be granted a B.A. degree. This implied that a liberal education was intended only for an "aristocracy of the intellect" and helps to account for the strong feeling still held in many quarters that the B.A. degree somehow represents an education superior to that represented by a degree in science or modern literature or any of the more "practical" subjects of home economics, agriculture, business, or education. The whole trend of multiplication of degrees in order to maintain the meaning of the B.A. degree might be interpreted in the light of the continuing strength of the aristocratic conception of a liberal education.

Again, with caution as to the validity of such generalizations, it might be said that, with the exception of the larger institutions of the East, the democratic movement in higher education gained its most rapid headway in connection with the state universities of the Middle West and Far West; whereas the aristocratic conception of higher education remained longer and stronger in colleges of the East, where the traditional notions of a liberal education had been so thoroughly ingrained in the culture of the people. One phase that this controversy took was the question whether or not women should be allowed in the colleges and universities on a level of equality with the men. It seems significant that women were accepted earlier and more generously in the colleges and universities of the West, where coeducation still finds its stronghold, than in the East, where the education of women on the college level was accepted more grudgingly and where it often had to find outlet in separate colleges for women when it did come. The psychological literature of the period is especially interesting for the many attempts that were made to prove that the mental equipment of women was not equal to the tasks set down in the best of the colleges for men.[1]

Notwithstanding the theoretical arguments to the contrary, when the time was ripe economically and culturally, the floodgates were opened,

[1] For opposition to coeducation, see L. H. Atwater, *op. cit.* For a detailed bibliography on the controversies over coeducation, see Thomas Woody, *A History of Women's Education in the United States* (Science Press, New York, 1929).

and all kinds and classes of students, both men and women, began to pour into the colleges and universities. With such expansion in numbers went necessarily a great expansion in studies and courses which ultimately destroyed the unity and strength of the traditional prescribed curriculum. In spite of the opposition of conservative educators, the public at large began to respond enthusiastically to the wider opportunities for higher education that the state universities began to present. President James Burrill Angell of the University of Michigan made a plea in 1879 that higher education should be made accessible to all economic levels in a democratic society, and the public increasingly came to believe that he was right. Angell made it clear that it was better for society and better for the individual if the higher education was not left to an aristocracy of the rich but responded to the demands of all those who could profit from it.[1]

Near the turn of the twentieth century, the University of Wisconsin became one of the outstanding institutions in attempting to put into actual practice the theory of democratic higher education. Not only were the doors of the University of Wisconsin opened wider for all kinds of students to enter, but it made genuine efforts to carry the work of the university directly to the people of the state through its extension division. By means of correspondence courses, public debates, discussion groups, and traveling libraries, the university attempted to carry practical and cultural knowledge to the very homes and local communities throughout the state: "The increasing spirit in Wisconsin demanded that the university should serve the state and all of its people and that it should be an institution for all the people within the state and not merely for the few who could send their sons and daughters to Madison. . . . "[2]

Perhaps the most farsighted statement on many of the controversies cited above was made by Wisconsin's great president Charles R. Van Hise, in his inaugural address in 1904. One of the best ways to summarize the progressive position in this period of the latter nineteenth century is to describe his point of view with reference to the university ideal, the practical and cultural ideals, the place of the newer physical and social sciences, and the democratic theory of higher education. Van Hise took his stand firmly on the ground that a state university should be for *all* the people:

Until this movement of the state universities had developed, the advantages of all educational institutions of the highest rank in all countries had been restricted to one sex, and even now it is practically impossible for the sons of artisans and laborers to enter the doors of many. In state institutions, where

[1] J. B. ANGELL, *The Higher Education* (Ann Arbor, Mich., 1879).
[2] CHARLES McCARTHY, *The Wisconsin Idea* (The Macmillan Company, New York, 1912), p. 132.

education is maintained by the people for the good of the state, no restriction as to class or sex is possible. A state university can only permanently succeed where its doors are open to all of both sexes who possess sufficient intellectual endowment, where the financial terms are so easy that the industrious poor may find the way, and where the student sentiment is such that each stands upon an equal footing with all. This is the state university ideal, and this is a new thing in the world.[1]

President Van Hise clearly recognized that the great increase in enrollment resulting from such a theory of higher education was likely to jeopardize the values of communal living that the English conception of the college had made possible through residential halls, commons, and student unions. He therefore insisted that the large university must not only meet the demands of democracy by admitting the masses of young people of a state but must also try to preserve the advantages of the small college by providing adequate housing and recreational facilities for students. Likewise he urged that the state university must also adopt the university ideal of Germany with its emphasis upon advanced research in all areas of knowledge. Thus, the state university must not only provide a general education for the undergraduate, but it must also provide the best facilities for higher study for the most advanced student. It will perform its function best by being both a college and a university.

Van Hise pointed out that the state university began to exert its real progressive leadership when it adopted even more quickly than the institutions of the East the study of modern science. Whereas the eastern colleges admitted the sciences grudgingly and often put them into schools of science outside the liberal arts college, the Western state universities admitted the sciences directly into the liberal arts college, and the B.A. degree was given for study of the sciences along with other liberal studies:

In the state universities where the college and the school of science were never made separate foundations, and where with the great increase in number of subjects, freedom of election has been introduced, it has become recognized either that there should be a separate degree for every group of studies, or else one degree for any group of liberal studies. This latter alternative has been accepted by the leading state universities. . . . No one now doubts the right of pure science to full admission to the list of subjects which may be pursued for a liberal education. Not only so, but it is recognized that the scientific spirit has permeated and vivified the studies of the old college course.[2]

Van Hise likewise indicated that the newer *social* sciences should find an adequate expression in a forward-looking university:

Scarcely less noteworthy than the winning of a place for pure science in the university has been the rise of the great groups of studies classified under political

---

[1] *Inaugural Address of Charles Richard Van Hise* (Madison, Wis., 1904), pp. 13 14.
[2] *Ibid.,* p. 20

economy, political science, sociology, and history. From a very subordinate, almost insignificant, place in the curriculum they have risen to a place not subordinate to classics or science.[1]

Next, Van Hise made a most effective plea for practical studies in his argument for greater attention to "applied knowledge." In other words, the university quite properly should expand its functions to include studies that will be directly useful to the individual and to the affairs of the state:

After science found its way into the universities, a natural, indeed an inevitable outcome of its admission into the institutions supported by states demanding both culture and efficiency was the rapid growth of the applied sciences, of which the more important are agriculture, engineering, and medicine. The people of the west went even further than this and demanded that *language, mathematics, political economy, and history should be taught so as to serve the man of affairs,* and thus there arose here the first strong course in commerce in the United States. . . . Whether one deplores or approves the rise of applied knowledge in the universities, it is an inevitable movement which, for my part, I expect to see extended.[2]

I unhesitatingly assert that there is no investigation of matter or force or mind to-day in progress, but tomorrow may become of inestimable practical value. . . . It is easy to show that the discoveries at the University of Wisconsin bring vastly more wealth to the state each year than the entire expenditure of the institution. . . . [3]

Finally, Van Hise made a notable forecast of the "watchtower" conception of the university which was later to gain such a large place in the progressive theory of higher education in the following decades of the twentieth century. He made it clear that the genuine university should take more and more responsibility for the social affairs of the state both in the training that it gives to students who go out to take their places in society and in the activities of the professors who remain at the university but who also engage actively in helping to solve important social problems:

In the university men are trained to regard economic and social questions as problems to be investigated by the inductive method, and in their solutions to *aim at what is best for the whole people rather than at what is favorable to the interests with which they chance to be connected.* . . . Already men who have studied history, economics, political science, and sociology in the universities have achieved large results in the formulation and enforcement of the written law, and in the growth of a healthy and powerful public sentiment. Soon such men will be found in every city and hamlet, leading the fight against corruption and misrule, and, even more important and vastly more difficult, *leading in constructive advance.*

[1] *Ibid.*, p. 20.
[2] *Ibid.*, p. 22.   [Italics mine.]
[3] *Ibid.*, p. 25.

In these men lies, in great measure, the hope of a peaceful solution of the great questions deeply concerning the nation, some of which are scarcely less momentous than was that of slavery.[1]

Van Hise had great faith that the fruits of research could be used directly for the solution of social problems; in effect, there should be no gap between knowledge and action:

It would be easy to show that the qualities of mind gained by such work [research] are those which best fit him for the struggle of life—which best fit him to handle difficult business, social, and economic problems. . . . University professors are asked to serve on tax commissions, in the valuation of the railroads, and in various other capacities. Within the next half century the number of such men in these and similar positions will increase many fold. The college-trained man, and especially the university-trained man, is, directly or indirectly, to control the destinies of the nation.[2]

With this remarkable hope and prophecy for what the state university might and should become, President Van Hise proved himself to be one of the most able American spokesman for the progressive and democratic theory of higher education. The fact that the University of Wisconsin became one of the leading universities of the country in the early decades of the twentieth century is a tribute to his ability to put theory into practice. His contribution to the controversies noted in these pages aimed at the inclusion of the best features of the English system, with its dormitories, commons, and union; the liberal and fine arts along with the sciences and applied sciences; and the best features of the German ideal of advanced scholarship and research. In this way, Van Hise hoped that the colleges of liberal arts, applied science, and creative research would so interlock that students with primary interests in any one field could profit from close association with the others.

This inaugural address by Van Hise, written 35 years ago, is so appropriate to the modern scene that it deserves to be revived and reread by college educators throughout the country. This is the excuse for quoting so extensively from it here. The following words set up an ideal for a university that could well be adopted as a goal for higher education today:

I, therefore, hold that the state university, a university which is to serve the state, must see to it that scholarship and research of all kinds, whether or not a possible practical value can be pointed out, must be sustained. A privately endowed institution may select some part of knowledge and confine itself to it, but not a state university. A university supported by the state for all its people, for all its sons and daughters, with their tastes and aptitudes as varied as man-

---

[1] *Ibid.*, pp. 20–21. [Italics mine.]
[2] *Ibid.*, pp. 24–25.

kind, can place no bounds upon the lines of its endeavor, else the state is the irreparable loser.

Be the choice of the sons and daughters of the state, language, literature, history, political economy, pure science, agriculture, engineering, architecture, sculpture, painting, or music, they should find at the state university ample opportunity for the pursuit of the chosen subject, even until they become creators in it.   Nothing short of such opportunity is just, for *each has an equal right to find at the state university the advanced intellectual life adapted to his need.*   Any narrower view is indefensible.   The university should extend its scope until the field is covered from agriculture to the fine arts.[1]

In the light of such a democratic conception of a university, the present-day advocates of an aristocratic "intellectual" and disciplinary education seem narrow and shortsighted indeed.

In fact, the conservatives of the latter part of the nineteenth century are the lineal ancestors in educational theory of those conservatives of today who decry a "practical," or "*ad hoc*," education in the colleges and who long for a return to the tried and tested curriculum of sound classical training and thorough intellectual development attributed to the past.[2]   It is essentially the age-old argument of the value of tradition against the argument of adapting the college curriculum to the changing demands of the social situation.   As a result of the intermingling of these two opposing theories of higher education and of the corresponding compromises worked out between the ideals of election and prescription, of university and college, of old and new, of cultural and practical, the customary types of college curriculum of today exhibit varying amounts of prescribed and elective studies.   The modern college curriculum has developed more as a result of the pulling and hauling between many interests and groups in conflict than of a well-considered, inclusive theory of college and higher education.   Something of the controversy that centered specifically around the elective system near the turn of the present century will be the concern of the next chapter.

---

[1] *Ibid.*, p. 28.   [Italics mine.]

[2] Abraham Flexner, Robert M. Hutchins, and Norman Foerster have been mentioned earlier as representing the kind of approach that has been made recently in this respect.

CHAPTER XIII

THE VICTORY OF THE ELECTIVE PRINCIPLE

It is beyond the scope of this book to trace in detail the fortunes of specific elective subjects in the colleges and universities of the United States. The interest here is rather to trace the general development of the ideas underlying the elective system as portrayed by its leading proponents and opponents and thereby to throw the light of history upon some of the controversies and problems confronting higher education today. The first part of this chapter will be devoted to a discussion of the controversy that arose when educators came to evaluate the workings of the elective system, particularly as it had been instituted at Harvard, Michigan, and other institutions. In this discussion, emphasis will be upon those arguments and points of view that have not already been discussed in previous chapters.

The second part of the chapter will be devoted to a description of those studies of an investigative nature which tried to determine more accurately how widespread the elective system had actually become by the turn of the century. The last part of the chapter will summarize some of the types of curriculum that were devised through compromises effected between the principles of election and of prescription. It has been thought that such a treatment would be of more value to the general student of higher education than a minute and statistical treatment of the development of elective studies as portrayed in the catalogues of specific institutions. In this way, the reader may be spared the tedium of a narrative that was more or less similar in its general outlines throughout the country, and yet those who are interested in pursuing the subject in more detail will find sufficient factual data to provide opportunity for further study.

As indicated earlier, Yale and Princeton may serve as the archetypes of the conservative position held by many such colleges as Wesleyan, Williams, Hamilton, Colgate, Rochester, Rutgers, Syracuse, Amherst, Bowdoin, and Dartmouth. Inaugural addresses and other pronouncements of the college officers, as well as the reluctant admission of elective studies into their curriculums, indicate how conservative their positions actually were. On the other hand, colleges that more quickly tried to adopt "university" methods were represented by such institutions as Harvard, Cornell, Columbia, Michigan, Northwestern, and Stanford.

Between the extreme of theoretical free election as represented by Harvard and the extreme of prescription as maintained by Yale and Princeton, all varieties of intermediate positions were devised as a result of compromises made between the principle of free election and prescription. As already indicated, those compromises were reached largely as a result of academic politics which usually took the form of conflicts between the older and more conservative professors and the younger or newer professors who represented the more modern subjects. The colleges in which the more conservative professors and presidents maintained their control were more likely to refrain longer than the others from introducing the free elective system; but by the turn of the century, nearly all colleges were allowing some measure of election. The educational literature of the period clearly shows this change.

In the middle of the century, the controversy had centered largely about whether or not the elective principle should be admitted to any extent in any of the four years of college life. As the century drew to its close, however, the working of the elective system became more familiar, and the demands of the newer subjects and of the public for more practical training became more insistent. Newly founded institutions like Cornell, Johns Hopkins, Chicago, and Stanford adopted different forms of the elective system, and the more conservative colleges ultimately were forced by competition to admit of some election in their curriculums. Thus, the literature of the latter part of the century was concerned not so much with the merits of the elective system as such (which were granted to a certain degree even by the most conservative) but with the question as *to what extent* the elective principle should be admitted and *at what point* it should be introduced into the college curriculum. The conservatives gradually began to admit elective studies into the last two years of college life as a supplement to prescribed studies, but they usually demanded that virtually full prescription be maintained in the first two years.

THE ELECTIVE CONTROVERSY GROWS HOTTER

We have seen in previous chapters that the elective system was defended and attacked in theory for several different reasons; in this section, we are concerned only with the controversy as it actually operated in various institutions. Thus, it should be kept in mind that we are dealing here as far as possible with arguments that have not been touched extensively before and with persons who have not been mentioned in detail before. It should be reiterated, however, that supporting arguments on one side or the other were drawn largely from the type of argument presented in the previous chapters. In commending the results of the elective principle as it had been introduced especially at Harvard, the proponents of the elective system were most often anxious to show that it had actually improved the scholarship of students who had studied under its operation and that teaching had thereby also been improved considerably over the conditions present under the prescribed curriculum. Its opponents, on the other hand, were most often at pains to show that it had created by-products that destroyed its effectiveness. They were concerned that students did not choose wisely, that they selected courses because they were easy rather than because of their value to the student; and moreover they believed that the prescribed curriculum itself could produce all of the values of scholarship and teaching claimed for the elective system.

Although President Eliot was perhaps the most consistent and the most able defender of the Harvard "new education," there were several others who rallied to his defense when he was bitterly assailed by the opponents of the elective system. For example, a letter to the *Nation* written by W. G. Hale in 1882 defended the system on the grounds that it had wrought results better than the prescribed curriculum could do in terms of scholarship and needed specialization.[1] Hale also pointed out that, owing to the helpful advice and guidance given to them by the faculty, students had been prevented from making unwise choices. A few years later, another letter to the *Nation* from W. H. Pettee testified to the success of the elective system as it worked at the University of Michigan and, by comparing it with the program at Harvard, concluded that both institutions were more adequately meeting the varying interests and professional needs of students.[2] After the turn of the century, the *Nation* commented editorially several times to the effect that, although the elective system was not perfect, it was still far better than the traditional prescribed curriculum and should continually be improved.[3]

The most conspicuous defender of Harvard's new departure in education, aside from Eliot himself, was perhaps Professor George Herbert Palmer, who published a series of articles in the *Andover Review*[4] which evoked spirited replies in the pages of the same magazine from George Trumbull Ladd of Yale and G. H. Howison of the University of California. Palmer pointed out that the Harvard faculty had become convinced of the worth of the elective system and that he himself had been

[1] W. G. HALE, "The Working of the Elective System at Harvard," *Nation*, 34: 314–315 (Apr. 13, 1882).

[2] W. H. PETTEE, "The Elective System at the University of Michigan," *Nation*, 42: 403–404 (May 13, 1886).

[3] "The Elective System Again," *Nation*, 77: 47 (July 16, 1903); and "The Problem of Electives," *ibid.*, 84: 426–427 (May 9, 1907).

[4] G. H. PALMER, "The New Education," *Andover Review*, 4: 303 107 (November, 1885).

persuaded of its worth over a period of years. He insisted that it was not merely an opportunity for "roving study" but had been so organized into a comprehensive system with its own bonds of authority that its essence had become "a fixed quantity and quality of study with a variable topic."

Palmer pointed out further that the use of the elective system had begun to flower into definite improvements in the life of the students: More manly character was emerging; better discipline and scholarship had been maintained; teaching had been improved; classroom interest was raised; and general behavior had changed for the better. On top of that he believed that the amount of funds given to the college had increased and the number of students had mounted largely because of public approval of the elective system. Palmer maintained that the evils of free election had been checked by careful faculty deliberation and advice, by the exercise of the consent of the instructor, and by outlining certain prerequisites for advanced work. He defended the extension of the elective system to the freshman year on the grounds that it gave the young students the training in character, manners, and scholarly disposition that they needed at the age of eighteen.

Two months later, Professor Ladd of Yale replied point for point to Palmer's article and in general showed himself to be opposed to a considerable expansion of the elective system.[1] His position was that Harvard's experiment was not yet old enough to be judged adequately; and, whereas he admitted of the validity of the elective system to a limited extent, he saw no reason why it should be good for students in large doses merely because it was good for them in small doses. In comparing Harvard as representing the new with Yale as representing the old education, Ladd indicated that traditional methods at Yale had done quite as well, if not better, all that the elective system was supposed to have done at Harvard. He showed that general deportment and "manly culture" had also improved at Yale along with better scholarship; that Yale's funds and numbers of students had likewise increased greatly; and that, in addition, Yale could boast a much better record of attendance in class than could Harvard.[2] He hit especially at the effort of Harvard to put the choice of

---

[1] G. T. LADD, "Education, Old and New," *Andover Review*, 5: 1–18 (January, 1886). Palmer replied to Ladd in two more articles in which he outlined desirable ways in which to improve the elective system; see "Possible Limitations of the Elective System," *Andover Review*, 6: 59–60 (December, 1886), and 7: 1–18 (January, 1887).

[2] Palmer later retorted that the Charlestown Penitentiary had also solved its attendance problem as well as Yale had done, the implication being, of course, that intellectual or moral growth did not take place where there was no freedom and no chance for choice in action. Forty years later, Palmer was making the same point with reference to religion and education: Just as God lets human beings develop self-reliance by making mistakes, so does Harvard let students flounder so that they will become men of independent intelligence: "Our Father in heaven had been using the

subjects into the hands of freshmen and sophomores, because he felt that he himself was much better off for having been obliged to study things that he did not wish to study.

A few months later, G. H. Howison of the University of California also advanced to the attack and denounced Palmer because, in his opinion, the elective system was destroying the notion of a liberal culture.[1] Howison admitted the need of the elective studies in principle, but he was objecting to their timing in the curriculum; in other words, the power to choose should be greatly limited at first and then increased gradually as students progressed through the four years, because too much election produced soft, onesided, and limited minds.   He believed on top of it all that whatever benefits had come to Harvard in recent years had come from other causes than and in spite of the elective system; and he mentioned as examples the increased age of students, better teachers, and the long tradition that had attracted the best students to Harvard.   These, he believed, accounted for the improvement of scholarship at Harvard rather than the elective system.

The *New Englander* also showed itself very interested in the elective controversy of this period.   It followed carefully the arguments presented by Palmer and Ladd[2] and quoted at length from a speech given by Samuel Brearley before the Harvard Club of New York City in 1886.[3]   Brearley was a Harvard man who did not agree with the "open system" being extended at Harvard; he felt that the opportunity for election was being given too early to students and in too large doses.   He thus gave notice that all Harvardians were not in complete agreement with Eliot and the Harvard administration.   The pages of the *New Englander* were soon hot again with withering blasts directed at Eliot and the elective system as delivered by D. H. Chamberlain, who believed that the elective policy was hostile to all of the better ideas of a university throughout the world.[4] He did not believe that Eliot's statistics were accurate, and he was confident that merely crowding into the course of study shreds and patches of new knowledge would not make college education more useful.   Ladd struck the same note some time later when he asserted that social demands

---

elective system long before we discovered it."   See G. P. ADAMS and W. P. MONTAGUE, ed., *Contemporary American Philosophy* (The Macmillan Company, New York, 1930), Vol. I, p. 52.

[1] G. H. HOWISON, "The Harvard 'New Education,'" *Andover Review*, 5: 577–589 (June, 1886).

[2] "The 'New Education' at Harvard and Yale," *New Englander*, 45: 264–272 (March, 1886).

[3] SAMUEL BREARLEY, "The System of Instruction and Government at Harvard College," *New Englander*, 45: 359–372 (April, 1886).

[4] D. H. CHAMBERLAIN, "The Elective Policy," *New Englander*, 45: 459–461 (May, 1886).

to make the curriculum more adaptable to modern life did not mean the use of the elective system; they merely meant more of the modern languages and sciences and less of the classics and mathematics in the prescribed course.[1]

Although the decade of the '80's and '90's may have seen the height of the elective controversy, the arguments were still being waged heatedly at the turn of the century. For example, Edward Channing of Harvard was saying before the National Education Association in 1895 that experience seemed to show that the elective system had led to great improvement in the work of the teacher and the student, for elective courses demanded more of the students and made them feel as if they were really learning something.[2] Channing insisted that the "soft snap" course did not exist, because students were limited in their choices by advice and prerequisite requirements. As far as he could see, the only valid objection to the elective system was that it required an increased expenditure of money, and he was therefore willing that it should be confined to such institutions as Harvard, Chicago, and Columbia which could afford it; but he pertinently suggested that this real reason be given for opposition rather than hiding behind the arguments of mental discipline and other objections.

On the other hand, Dean LeBaron R. Briggs of Harvard, in 1900, showed again that the whole administration and faculty of Harvard was not completely convinced of the value of the free elective system.[3] Dean Briggs wondered if election was not begun too early and whether or not merely catering to the whims of students was a sufficient reason for giving them a choice of studies; he was also fearful that the free elective system meant that Harvard was rushing from a servitude to prescribed studies into a new servitude to specialization and smattering. Paul H. Hanus, in 1901, gave in effect an answer to Dean Briggs by saying that the extension of the elective system was justified because it helped to organize the dominant interests and capacities of students and that students could learn to choose wisely only when they made actual choices

[1] G. T. LADD, "The Disintegration and Reconstruction of the Curriculum," *Forum*, 33: 164–178 (April, 1902).

[2] EDWARD CHANNING, "Conservative View of College Electives," *N.E.A.*, *Proceedings*, 1895, pp. 657–661.

[3] LeBARON R. BRIGGS, "Some Old-fashioned Doubts about New-fashioned Education," *Atlantic Monthly*, 86: 463–470 (October, 1900). Dean Briggs represented a strong faction at Harvard which had opposed the extension of the elective system. From 1886 on, they had lost ground, but they still had the sympathies of conservative educators. In May, 1886, the presidents of eight New England colleges urged Harvard not to destroy the meaning of the B.A. degree by allowing students to graduate without taking Latin and Greek. The signers of the statement presented to the Harvard Overseers were the presidents of Yale, Brown, Dartmouth, Wesleyan, Williams, Trinity, Amherst, and Boston University.

repeatedly with guidance.[1] Then John Corbin entered the fray to point out that administratively the offer of electives was specious, inasmuch as a student, because of conflicts in hours, examinations, and in general the weight of machinery as represented by the growing complexities of college catalogues, could not really choose what subjects he wished.[2] The recurrence of such jockeying of arguments gave evidence that the elective controversy had not lost vitality after the turn of the century.

One aspect of the elective controversy that has not yet been mentioned in particular was the question that came up especially in the nineties and after the turn of the century concerning whether or not the college course should be shortened to less than the customary four years by allowing students to choose their subjects and advance as rapidly as they could. The leader in proposing that the college course should drop the traditional class system of four years was, of course, President Eliot, who threw the subject into meetings of the National Education Association and thereby stirred up a hornet's nest of debate on the question. The lines of controversy on this subject shaped up in much the same way as they did in other aspects of dispute. For example, in 1877, William LeRoy Broun of Vanderbilt University stated in an N.E.A. meeting that one of the advantages of the elective system was that it helped to destroy the class system which no longer had any value for college education and no counterpart in the proper organization of the course of study. He felt that it was unwise to force students to go through all four years in an artificial arrangement whereby they were required to advance each year with the same group of students with whom they had entered college.[3]

In reply to Broun, a defender of the class system immediately arose in the meeting in the person of President Porter of Yale, who stated his belief that mental discipline and culture were better imparted by the class system than by the elective system. To the participants, the seriousness of the question is indicated in the following statement by Porter:

> The writer holds that it is vitally important to the culture of this country, he would almost say to the existence of this country as a country, that the American College with its class system, its fixed curriculum, its generous and earnest common life, and its enforced discipline, should be retained and re-enforced. . . .[4]

The controversy over the length of the college course heightened in the nineties when Eliot, Angell, Gilman, and others pressed for the adoption of the elective system in order to cut the course to three years for those

[1] P. H. HANUS, "Two Contemporary Problems in Education," *Popular Science Monthly*, 58: 585–590 (April, 1901).

[2] JOHN CORBIN, "Is the Elective System Elective?" *Forum*, 31: 599–608 (July, 1901).

[3] W. LeR. BROUN, "The Elective System," *N.E.A.*, *Proceedings*, 1877, pp. 87–95.

[4] NOAH PORTER, "The Class System," *ibid.*, p. 100.

brighter students who could do the work in that amount of time. The amount of work was not to be decreased, and nothing was to be left out, but the better students would merely be allowed to advance at their own rate and select the necessary courses instead of being required to spend four years in college no matter what their ability and interests.[1] The type of reply that the conservatives made to such proposals is represented by that of John M. Coulter, who pointed out that proper intellectual training required the full four years, because mental development at college age was rather slow and there was too much haste in the first place.[2]

The controversy was continued in the meetings of the N.E.A. in 1903, when a round-robin discussion was held on the subject of how long the baccalaureate course should be in relation to preparation for the professional schools.[3] In that discussion, Eliot proposed again that there should be no reduction in the amount of work but that the elective system should be used by students in order to finish the work more quickly; President Butler of Columbia felt that the four years should be kept, since that was not too long a time to require for a boy of seventeen years to acquire a liberal education; President Harper of Chicago was not in favor of cutting the four-year course for the B.A.; and Dean West of Princeton stated that four years was a result of wide and long experience and tradition and thus should not be given up lightly. It might be mentioned incidentally that President Butler had earlier been in favor of the three-year baccalaureate course in order to shave a year off of the long preprofessional training required of students and that President Harper in another connection had stated that the college course should be three, four, or five years depending upon the aptitude of the student.[4]

Thus, the controversy was waged back and forth. It seemed as if the heart of the conflicting theories of higher education was centered about the value of the elective system. Certainly, the best effort of the outstanding educational leadership of the period was vitally concerned with the theory and practice of elective studies and with the part that they

---

[1] For the position of Eliot, Gilman, Angell, White, and others, see "Length of College Curriculum," *U. S. Commissioner of Education, Report*, 1889–1890, 2: 799–813, and 1902, 1: 927–948. See also D. C. GILMAN, "The Shortening of the College Curriculum," *Educational Review*, 1: 1–7 (January, 1891); and R. H. JESSE (president of the University of Missouri), "University Education," *N.E.A., Proceedings*, 1892, pp. 120–127.

[2] J. M. COULTER, "Should the College Course Be Shortened?" *N.E.A., Proceedings*, 1891, pp. 696–701.

[3] "Length of the Baccalaureate Course and Preparation for the Professional Schools," *N.E.A., Proceedings*, 1903, pp. 489–516.

[4] N. M. BUTLER, "Shortening of the Undergraduate Curriculum," *N.E.A., Proceedings*, 1898, pp. 717–718; and W. R. HARPER, *The Trend in Higher Education* (University of Chicago Press, Chicago, 1905), pp. 88–89.

should play in the future of American higher education. Before summarizing some of the actual changes that the principle of election made imperative in the college curriculum by the early decades of the twentieth century, and before continuing with the more recent vicissitudes and criticisms of the elective system, it seems advisable to indicate other sources of evidence (for those students of higher education who wish to go into the problem more fully) that the elective principle had actually won for itself a permanent place in the college curriculum by 1910.

THE TIDE OF OPINION RUNS IN FAVOR OF THE ELECTIVE SYSTEM TO 1910

Up to this point, we have been concerned principally with the theoretical arguments of educators who have favored or opposed the extension of the elective principle in undergraduate education, and it now seems appropriate to supply some of the evidence that was being collected by "fact-finding" investigations concerning the actual spread of the elective system as a part of the accepted procedure in building and administering the collegiate course of study in the United States. The most obvious conclusions of all the investigations of prevailing opinion and practice of the elective principle seemed to be that it had entered in some form the great majority of American colleges by 1910 and that the form in which it appeared was exceedingly different from one college to another. The actual expansion of the elective system may be traced by inspecting a series of studies made when the interest in the elective controversy was running highest during the years from approximately 1870 to 1910.

A chart showing the increase in elective studies in fifteen New England colleges from 1875 to 1885 was included in the article written by Palmer when he was explaining and defending the use of the elective system at Harvard.[1] After the 1880's, the detailed extension of elective studies can be traced in the annual reports of the United States Commissioner of Education in which the elective system was commended as a valuable method of curricular procedure. In the one for 1888–1889 is a list of the subjects taught in 101 American colleges and universities, with the elective subjects written in italics.[2] In 1897, Albert Perry Brigham published a report in which he had studied the catalogues of 25 colleges for 1895–1896 to determine the extent of the acceptance of the elective system, and his most obvious conclusion was that there existed a tremendous variety of practice.[3] Brigham found the 25 institutions to be divided roughly into

[1] G. H. PALMER, "Possible Limitations of the Elective System," *Andover Review*, 6: 581 (December, 1886).

[2] See *U. S. Commissioner of Education, Annual Reports*, 1881, p. clxi; 1882–1883, p. cxliii; 1883–1884, p. clviii; 1888–1889, 2: 1224–1361.

[3] A. P. BRIGHAM, "Present Status of the Elective System in American Colleges," *Educational Review*, 14: 360–369 (November, 1897).

four groups: Those requiring the greatest number of subjects, especially in the freshman and sophomore years, were Yale, Williams, Hamilton, Colgate, Rochester, Rutgers, Columbia, and Union; those allowing a considerable amount of election were New York University, Pennsylvania, California, Northwestern, Michigan, and Chicago; and those allowing the greatest amount of election were Harvard, Cornell, and Stanford.

In 1901, Professor E. D. Phillips of the University of Denver made what was the most exhaustive investigation of the spread and extension of the elective system up to that time.[1]   Philips based his conclusions on the inspection of over a hundred college catalogues, on 97 questionnaires filled out by college presidents, and on considerable direct correspondence with colleges throughout the country.   He found such a great variety of arrangements among the different institutions that he was prompted to remark that we should speak not of "an elective system" but of "elective systems."   He gave a detailed description of the different forms that the elective principle had taken and singled out especially the "major-minor" and "group" systems.   He also indicated that the most customary practice for the smaller and weaker colleges of the South and West was to multiply their courses, keep all of them highly prescribed, and give other degrees for the nonclassical courses in order to maintain the dignity of the original classical course and the B.A. degree.

The main body of Phillips' study dealt with the summaries of answers made by the 97 college presidents in reply to his questionnaire in which he had asked a series of questions concerning the present extent of the use of the elective system, how long it had been in use, and whether or not it was workable and advisable as a part of college education.   The most important result for our purposes was his estimate that out of 97 institutions, 34 had more than 70 per cent, 12 had between 50 and 70, and 51 offered less than 50 per cent elective studies.   Princeton and Brown were the most striking of the better known colleges that had remained largely conservative; and the lowest ebb of the elective system was reached in the South.

Although a few presidents felt that the elective system was still in the experimental stage, only five spoke disparagingly of it as an undertaking, and the overwhelming majority believed that it was workable and advisable.   All in all, the study prompted Phillips to conclude:

The elective system is a fixture as far as our colleges are concerned.   The tendency is more and more toward free election.   There is no indication as to whether colleges will ever settle upon a small but central core of subjects for all students.   Certainly there must be a "golden mean" somewhere between the

---

[1] E. D. PHILLIPS, "The Elective System in American Education," *Pedagogical Seminary*, 8: 206–230 (June, 1901).

prescribed four years of classics and mathematics and four years of elective laboratory courses, shop work, dentistry, drawing, music, etc.[1]

Phillips implied that he felt that a "central core" of subjects would be desirable in the college curriculum, and he explicitly stated this point of view in his study of the elective system in secondary schools which was also included in the report. In this respect, he was estimating rather closely what later actually happened.

Another type of investigation popular at this time was a study of the opinions and reactions of students and graduates who had been exposed to the workings of the elective system. In 1902, Paul Hanus made a study of the opinions of Harvard alumni as to the value and efficacy of the system as they had been acquainted with it in their undergraduate days.[2] Hanus indicated that the replies seemed to substantiate the theory of its advocates that the elective system was beneficial for developing in the student a higher standard of scholarship, increased interest in his work, more responsibility and thoroughness, and a greater ability to solve problems for himself. His report also testified that students did not select merely the easiest courses. Another investigation was made the next year at Harvard to determine the variety of courses that students selected for themselves, and an inspection of 448 senior programs convinced the investigator that on the whole students chose rather wisely and tended to avoid extreme specialization or extreme smattering.[3] A year later, a committee that included Professor A. Lawrence Lowell sent a questionnaire to students, and the replies convinced the committee of just the opposite, so the point of view of the investigators apparently had something to do with the results.[4]

President Boone indicated with gratification that after six years of the elective system at the University of Indiana, there seemed to be no significant change in the proportion of time given by students at large to the various subjects; in addition, he found improved scholarship and teaching and an obvious tendency toward democracy and obliteration of class

[1] *Ibid.*, p. 218.

[2] PAUL HANUS, "Graduate Testimony on the Elective System," *Harvard Graduates' Magazine*, 11: 530–534 (June, 1903).

[3] CHARLES S. MOORE, "The Elective System at Harvard," *Harvard Graduates' Magazine*, 11: 530–534 (June, 1903).

[4] "Report of the Committee on Improving Instruction in Harvard College," *Harvard Graduates' Magazine*, 12: 611–620 (June, 1904). As early as 1887, Lowell had given notice that he opposed the elective system on the familiar grounds that some subjects should be prescribed because they were of more value than others for mental discipline and for a liberal education; see also A. LAWRENCE LOWELL, *At War with Academic Traditions in America* (Harvard University Press, Cambridge, 1934), pp. 3–11.

distinctions.[1]   In 1905, James H. Canfield reported to the National Education Association a compilation of replies received from several colleges and universities in answer to the question whether or not wide election and narrow courses tended to weaken the undergraduate course by too much specialization.[2]   He estimated that a few were for wide election and cited Harvard, Cornell, Stanford, Michigan, Nebraska, and Oregon, but he found that the great majority were opposed to excessive free election and were in favor of some sort of prescribed arrangement in connection with it, usually the group system.   Among the latter, he listed Columbia, Pennsylvania, California, Dartmouth, Ohio, Clarke, Chicago, Northwestern, Syracuse, Williams, Pennsylvania State, Knox, and Beloit.

Two more published investigations remain to be mentioned in this short survey.   The first of these was made by George Ordahl, who studied 78 college catalogues for 1904–1905, classifying them into six convenient groups for purposes of comparison.[3]   This study found the New England colleges to be the most conservative as a group, for they had the highest average of prescribed courses of all the groups and retained the greatest emphasis upon the classics.   Then, in the order of increasing use of the elective system were listed the state universities of the South; the women's colleges; the small state universities of the West; the large privately endowed universities; and, most liberal of all, the large state universities of the West.   It was pointed out that where the traditional cultural conception of a liberal education was strongest and where the financial resources were weakest, there were found the most conservative courses of study; and where the financial resources were largest and the response to practical needs the greatest (as in the large state universities of the West), there the courses were the most liberally sprinkled with elective studies.

Finally, a recheck of the same institutions in 1910 showed that the elective system had gained much ground in all sections of the United States; no one subject was regarded by all institutions as essential to a liberal education; and the old four-year college course was increasingly breaking up and leaving the last two years for specialization in technical or professional schools.   Ordahl recognized the trend which was to become more pronounced as the twentieth century wore on; he saw that it was necessary to group elective studies into broad fields and to give more opportunity to students to see the interrelationships between subjects

[1] R. G. Boone, "Results under an Elective System," *Educational Review*, 4: 53–73 142–156 (June, 1892).

[2] J. H. Canfield, "Wide Election and Minute Courses," *N.E.A.*, *Proceedings*, 1905, pp. 494–501.

[3] George Ordahl, "The College Curricula: A Study of Required and Elective Courses in American Colleges and Universities," *University of Nevada Studies*, Vol. II, No. 2 (Reno, Nev., 1910).

through the development of courses in "general science," "general mathematics," "general history," and so on.

The most extensive investigation of the elective system was made by William T. Foster, president of Reed College, as a part of his book, published in 1911, on the administration of the college curriculum.[1] President Foster devoted a part of his book to the historical development of the elective system as one of the most important phases in the development of the American college and the major portion to a critical study of some of the problems that the elective system had raised for the college administrator.   Foster presented a mass of detailed information concerning such problems as the varying requirements for the B.A. degree in institutions throughout the country, the various systems by which the student may acquire "concentration and distribution" of studies, the relation of the subjects taken in college to later success in life, attempts to base graduation upon the quality of work done in courses as well as the accumulation of a certain number of quantity points, and the necessity of distributing college grades on a more "scientific" scale.

All in all, President Foster ranged himself with the progressives in the history of the elective system, and he was convinced in 1911 that the elective principle was here to stay, provided the students were required to do a considerable amount of creditable work in whatever field they chose.   President Foster's study of the history of the elective system made him farsighted in many respects, for he made short shrift of those who had attempted to prescribe in detail the essentials of a liberal education, but he did not himself go so far as to see that the elective system itself needed to be reformed in the direction of integrating the experience of the student so that he might bridge the gaps among many separate and unrelated subjects.   Foster was too much a part of the victory of the elective system.

TYPICAL COMPROMISES BETWEEN ELECTION AND PRESCRIPTION

It is apparent from the foregoing that the elective principle was appearing in many different forms throughout the country, and it is perhaps needless to point out that there had been many, many advocates of compromise who tried in several different ways to reconcile the need for election with the need for prescription.   As a matter of fact, it was largely through the attempts to retain the alleged advantages of the traditional prescribed curriculum and yet accede to the alleged necessities of the more flexible arrangements of the elective principle that the modern curriculum of most American colleges was developed.

[1] W. T. FOSTER, *Administration of the College Curriculum* (Houghton Mifflin Company, Boston, 1911).

The liberal college was caught between the pressure from above for more specialization in the undergraduate college (a pressure exerted by the professional and graduate schools) and the pressure from below for increasing the number of possible courses that students might take as they came up from the expanding high schools. As a result, the college arts curriculum began to take on as much of the university methods of specialization and freedom of choice as the varying financial resources and the varying educational philosophies of the administrators and faculties of the different colleges would allow.

Some of the compromises that represented the most common types of college curriculum up to the end of the first decade of the twentieth century are summarized below, but it must be remembered that any given college was likely to vary in some respect from any other given college, although they may be roughly grouped in the same general classification. One of the safest generalizations that can be made concerning the development of the college curriculum is that no two colleges were exactly alike in their development, and the range of variations was as great as the number of colleges. For the sake of discussion, however, it may be said that by 1910 there were roughly five types of compromise between election and prescription which would cover most of the colleges of the day:

1. There was, first, a curriculum that was mostly prescribed and that adhered most closely to the traditional curriculum of the early American college, with its emphasis upon the classics and mathematics and philosophy. The small New England and Southern colleges were most representive of this type of curriculum which allowed only a minimum of elective studies. Also, many small religious colleges in 1910 still maintained virtually a completely prescribed curriculum; among these were Boston College, Holy Cross, and St. Anselm, all Catholic institutions. Lack of funds for expansion and the maintainance of strong religious authority were largely responsible for keeping the colleges of this type away from the elective system and close to the inherited cultural education of their forefathers.

2. A curriculum in which approximately half or more of the studies were prescribed was probably the most common type in the United States by the turn of the century. Most often, the half-and-half arrangement meant that the first two years were largely prescribed and the last two, largely elective. This was the type of curriculum that most of the large endowed colleges had adopted by the end of the century; Yale, Princeton, Columbia, Chicago, and many others were representative. A. T. Ormond pointed out in 1897 that Princeton's ideal of a university had been to provide mental discipline in the first half of the college course

and for research in the last half,[1] and President William DeWitt Hyde of Bowdoin stated on different occasions that the policy of the small college should be to prescribe most of the first half of the course and allow enough election to provide for proper concentration in the last half.[2]

3. A third general type of compromise was often called the "major-minor" system in which the student was usually required to take a certain amount of prescribed work in several fields during the first two years and then was required to specialize somewhat in a "major" subject and to a lesser degree in one or more "minor" subjects during the last two years of his college course. In this way, it was hoped that the student would get the advantages both of a well-rounded education and of a certain amount of specialization. Some form of this type of curriculum was adopted by several institutions of which the outstanding were perhaps the state universities of Indiana, Wisconsin, Michigan, Nebraska, Colorado, and California. Richard G. Boone of the University of Indiana was especially favorable to this scheme which had been instituted there under David Starr Jordan.[3]

4. A fourth type of curriculum closely associated with the major-minor system was the so-called "group" system in which studies were classified into a few, well-defined large fields of knowledge such as "science," "language," "history," and "philosophy."[4] Thus, the student was required to take a certain number of "credits" in each of the large groups, but he was allowed to select among different subjects within the groups. This was another attempt to insure that the student would at once have a well-rounded education and know something of all the great fields of knowledge and yet have an opportunity to take studies within those fields which were appropriate to different individuals. (The group system gradually became very popular as a means of limiting the free elective system's evils of smattering and specialization,)especially after Harvard, in 1909, under its new president A. Lawrence Lowell, retreated from the free elective system and set up an arrangement whereby the student was required to "concentrate" and "distribute" his studies in proper amounts (see below).

[1] A. T. ORMOND, "University Ideals at Princeton," N.E.A., Proceedings, 1897, pp. 346–373.

[2] W. DeW. HYDE, "The Policy of the Small College," Educational Review, 2: 313–321 (November, 1891).

[3] R. G. BOONE, "Results under an Elective System," Educational Review, 4: 53–73, 142–156 (June, 1892).

[4] Not to be confused with Gilman's group system at Johns Hopkins where different fully prescribed courses all led to the B.A. degree. The Johns Hopkins arrangement was a distinctive contribution to solving the elective problem, but it never became very widespread in the United States.

5. The fifth type of curriculum, which, however, never attained much favor among the great majority of colleges, was the free elective system whereby students could select virtually at will among the subjects in the curriculum, all of which were looked upon as equal in value for a liberal education. Harvard (before 1910), Cornell, and Stanford most nearly approached this type. These institutions had been very influential in persuading and impelling other institutions to adopt some form of the elective system, but only a few were financially able to provide the extensive number of studies requisite for such a system and willing to depart in their educational attitudes so far from the traditional conception of a liberal education.

It is apparent from the foregoing pages that some form of the elective system was being accepted by most colleges and universities in the United States during the last part of the nineteenth and early years of the twentieth centuries. It is also apparent that along with acceptance of the elective principle went a good deal of hesitation with respect to departing completely from the prescribed curriculum inherited from the past. Thus, while colleges were admitting the elective principle in greater or lesser degree, they were still trying to hold on to as much of the ideal of a well-rounded education as they could, and the various types of compromises listed above were the result.

The signal that the free elective system had perhaps reached its height and that later decades of the twentieth century would see further limitation of it was given when Harvard, long the radical reformer, changed its stand under President Lowell to assume a modified form of the group system. As stated previously, Lowell had been on a committee which sent a questionnaire to 1,757 undergraduates concerning their courses of study, and the committee felt that students were dissipating their energies in too many different fields or were specializing too exclusively in one narrow field.[1] It was also stated that students studied approximately only $2\frac{1}{2}$ to $3\frac{1}{2}$ hours a week in each course and that they chose subjects haphazardly, especially with reference to convenient hours and "snap" subjects.

Thus, Lowell led a movement to reform the courses of study so that notoriously easy subjects might be stiffened and students discouraged from rushing through the curriculum in three years and encouraged to work harder in order to gain "honors" at graduation. In his inaugural address, Lowell later indicated that he would proceed to limit further the free elective system by requiring the student to specialize more thoroughly in one field and at the same time to take a certain amount of work in each of several other fields.[2]

[1] *Op. cit., Harvard Graduates' Magazine*, 12: 611–620 (June, 1904).
[2] See A. L. Lowell, *At War with Academic Traditions in America* (Harvard Uni-

Consequently, in 1910, Harvard's famous plan of "concentration and distribution" went into effect, whereby all undergraduate subjects were classified into four large fields: arts of expression (language, literature, fine arts, and music); natural sciences; social sciences; and mathematics and philosophy. In order to provide for concentration, the student was required to take at least six of his sixteen elective courses within one of these divisions; and to provide for distribution, he must divide another six courses among the three remaining fields. In this way, Lowell and his committee hoped that students' choices would secure for them a more systematic education, based upon the principle that a liberally educated person should know a little of everything and something well. Lowell also aimed to encourage students to plan their courses seriously and to plan them as a whole. With this change in the policy of Harvard, which had supported so long and so strongly the principle of free election under President Eliot, a definite phase in the history of the elective system appeared to be ended.

The principle that *some* election on the part of the student was desirable had been firmly established in most institutions by the end of the first decade of the twentieth century; and in that sense, the victory of the elective principle had been made virtually complete. But there was another sense in which the very fact that the elective principle was accepted so widely meant that thenceforth it would be limited more and more in one way or another. The evidence presented in all the foregoing chapters of this book indicates that the elective system had met with continuing criticism and opposition; and in many colleges where it was accepted at all, it was accepted with limitations and reservations. That criticism and limitation have continued to increase up to the present time, but there seems to be at least one very significant difference between the criticisms of the period before and those of the period after 1910.

Before 1910, the numerous limitations of the elective system were essentially concessions between hostile camps, and nearly all of the compromises assumed the adequacy of separate, discrete, and specialized courses or studies. There was little or no attack as such upon the fact that the curriculum was made up of many distinct, compartmentalized subjects. What attack there was centered upon the fact that students were not required to study a sufficient *variety* of such subjects to a sufficient degree or that they did not study *certain* subjects long enough. It was felt that a well-rounded education could be acquired merely if students were compelled to take enough different subjects in enough different fields.

---

versity Press, Cambridge, 1934), pp. 32–45; or S. E. MORISON, *The Development of Harvard University* (Harvard University Press, Cambridge, 1930), pp. lxxix–lxxxix.

The criticism after 1910, however, and increasingly in the 1920's and 1930's, took on a different aspect by pointing out the necessity of reforming the college curriculum in such a way that the student would acquire a better understanding of the relationships existing between different subject-matter fields.   Thus appeared a type of course that aimed to give to the student an understanding of the interrelationships among subjects, and we see the emergence of survey courses, orientation courses, reading for honors, and other such arrangements.

Only a few educators in this period before 1910 began to see that reform of the elective system should take not merely the form of a compromise with the principle of prescription but rather that the narrow, compartmentalized subjects must give way to larger fields of knowledge which cut across the artificial barriers of the specialized courses.   One of those who began to see the problem in the new light was James Harvey Robinson, professor of history at Columbia University, who wrote a short article on some of the historical aspects of the elective system.[1]   He mentioned some phases of the problem (which have received detailed attention in foregoing chapters here) and then noted that there should be a greater attempt to bring out more clearly the interrelations and interdependence among the various subjects and to redefine what the liberally educated man needed to know.

Another who saw even more clearly in 1901 the direction which the problem of the elective system should take, and which, in fact, it did take, was John Dewey in the addresses included in his book *The Educational Situation*.[2]   As Dewey viewed the current controversies in higher education, he felt that the problems had been misstated and that the constant wrangling over practical versus cultural, science versus classics, freedom versus discipline, and election versus prescription would not lead to the proper solution of the problem.   In other words, he believed that the problem was to join the culture factor (a well-rounded and symmetrical education of the best that has been thought and said and done in the past) with the practical, or social, factor (adaptation to the present).

Although the college had often been more remote from the people and closer to the cultural tradition of the past, it should, Dewey thought, conserve the past only to put its resources more effectively at the disposition of the present.   Since the multiplication of studies in the college curriculum was really a reflection of the multiplication of knowledge in the various fields of activity, it was useless to argue over whether the sciences *or* the classics should be uppermost, because *both* were

[1] J. H. Robinson, "The Elective System, Historically Considered," *International Quarterly*, 6: 191–201 (September–December, 1902).

[2] John Dewey, *The Educational Situation* (University of Chicago Press, Chicago, 1902).

illustrative of essential human activities.   Furthermore, it seemed to Dewey a lack of sanity to assume that subjects were in a settled and fixed condition and that ready-made standards existed by which to measure the claims of the various studies.   All were in a process of formation and development and should be used by the college in the degree that they contributed to better social and individual life.

With reference to the problem of discipline, Dewey indicated that *absolute* standards of discipline or training were harmful to a true understanding of education, because *each generation must redefine for itself* its aims of character, discipline, information, and culture.   The assumption that training and discipline were good only to the degree in which they were good for nothing in the practical sense was to Dewey an assumption that could be grounded on no adequate philosophical basis.   He believed rather that all training and all discipline must ultimately be measured in terms of social availability; to be trained is to be trained *to* something and *for* something.

Too often, Dewey felt, traditional education had been founded on a dualism of mind *or* matter, culture *or* occupation, aristocracy *or* democracy, dualisms that stemmed from an age when education was the exclusive acquirement of an aristocratic, nonworking, leisure class. Social democracy meant to Dewey that we abandon these dualisms and recognize the common heritage, common work, and common destiny of all the people.   Therefore, he felt that the business of the university should be more and more to supply the specific knowledge and training that would fit the individual for his calling in life.   In fulfilling this aim, the first two years of college would appropriately aid the student to become oriented in the world; become acquainted with the universe in its mânifold phases; and, in general, come to an increasing knowledge of himself in his individual and social relationships to the needs of life about him; then the student would be ready to go on to his special training.

It is along these lines that the controversies have continued into the twentieth century and to the present day.   Criticism of the elective system has continued, on the one hand, in the same vein in which the conservatives have pursued it for a hundred years, but a growing criticism of a different and more progressive type has also developed along the lines laid down by John Dewey.   Today, conservative opponents of the elective system wish to go back to a limited and prescribed curriculum which would restore the "cultural and intellectual" qualities that they see slipping out of the colleges; and present-day progressive opponents of the elective system wish to reform it in such a way that the student will become better oriented in the world in which he will live.

Dewey put his finger upon the direction that progressive reform of the elective system should take when he said that the discussion should center not around "election versus prescription" but around an elastic and flexible curriculum versus a rigid and static one and that elasticity was possible only where there was breadth. Thus, the elective system enlisted the efforts of the progressives of the nineteenth century because it was more elastic than the prescribed curriculum; but after the turn of the century, the system itself became rigid, and the new progressives have been devoting their attention to providing more flexibility by reforming, in turn, the elective system. Some indication of the directions taken by the various efforts for reform of the elective system during the twentieth century will constitute the last part of this book.

Dewey proved himself a remarkably accurate prognosticator when he said in 1901:

In the future it is going to be less and less a matter of worrying over the respective merits of the ancient and modern languages; or of the inherent values of scientific *vs.* humanistic study, and more a question of discovering and observing certain broader lines of cleavage, which affect equally the disposition and power of the individual, and the social callings for which education ought to prepare the individual. It will be, in my judgment, less and less a question of piecing together certain studies in a more or less mechanical way in order to make a so-called course of study running through a certain number of years; and more and more a question of grouping studies together according to their natural mutual affinities and reinforcements for the securing of certain well-marked ends.[1]

Dewey's prediction with reference to the elective system was extremely accurate, because he judged so correctly the direction in which social and economic events were moving in the United States and because he devised a social and educational philosophy that was so influential in guiding the thinking and acting of educators throughout the country. Through his effective interpretations of society, knowledge, and education for some fifty years, Dewey has literally seen his predictions come true.

[1] *Ibid.*, p. 71.

PART IV
NEW PROPOSALS FOR PRESCRIPTION

CHAPTER XIV

THE TWENTIETH CENTURY REQUIRES NEW MEASURES
(ABOUT 1910 TO PRESENT)

As the twentieth century opened, the elective system appeared to be firmly seated in the saddle of collegiate education. It seemed to be the proper answer to the demands of the prevailing isms of the day—industrialism, capitalism, and individualism. Apparently, it had solved the difficult problems raised, on the one hand, by the tremendous additions to knowledge achieved by the physical and social sciences and, on the other, by the growing demands of a young democracy that more and more youths should be given the advantages of higher education. The bulk of the evidence presented by the various fact-finding studies cited in Chap. XIII seemed to indicate that it was here to stay. Despite the stout opposition of the conservative educators, who defended the traditional conception of college education, the trends of social and economic forces, scientific investigation, educational theory, and public opinion seemed to be against them. The colleges and universities of the twentieth century continued to change rapidly in the ways that were summarized on pages 202–203. However, the final answer was not yet.

As the colleges and universities expanded to meet all kinds of practical needs, twentieth century critics arose to attack the universities for what they were doing. These criticisms took myriad forms, and the literature increased steadily in volume from the early decades of this century to the present time, until today the conscientious reader of criticisms of higher education would have a full-time job on his hands to keep up with the monthly and weekly protests.

In an endeavor to provide a more adequate thread through the maze of controversy, it is the purpose of Part IV of this book to view present-day discussions of higher education against the perspective of past discussions. That is not to say that present controversies are merely repeating the arguments of the past, for that is quite evidently not true. But it is nevertheless true that there is a great amount of continuity between certain arguments of the past and the present, especially on the side of those who defend and reaffirm the principles of the "Great Tradition." Hence, at the risk of oversimplification, but with the hope of gaining more understanding, it is suggested that, in general, all critics of the universities and colleges during the twentieth century again seemed to range themselves into two opposing groups which for the lack of better terms we have called the conservatives and the progressives.

The conservatives form an unbroken link with the scholarly traditions of the past, and they wish to preserve as far as possible the ideals of the traditional conception of a liberal education. They claim that the universities have degenerated into mere "service stations" for all sorts of industrial, commercial, and agricultural enterprises. They insist that the university must return to its proper function of improving the "intellectual" quality of university training. On the other hand, the progressives say that modern society is so complex and changing so rapidly that the college must give the student an integrating and unifying experience in order to prepare him more directly for living in an interdependent society.

Although the elective system may have met definite needs in the American life of the nineteenth century by adding technical and "hand-minded" subjects to the curriculum, it now appears that it has become inflexible, out of touch with more recent social trends, and encumbered with almost meaningless requirements as to hours, credits, prerequisites, and degrees. Since the highly specialized and unrelated subjects of the elective system do not give the needed integration to students, the progressive educators feel that new courses and new colleges should be devised which would attempt to do so. So it seems that the rule of the elective system was not to go unchallenged, and here are two widely differing proposals for the way that it should be reformed.

It is the argument of the last part of this book that those interested in higher education can better judge the validity of these differing conceptions of college education by seeing them in their historical setting and by seeing which conception seems to fit in most adequately with the social and intellectual trends that promise to be the dominating factors in American life of the future—at least the near future. To this end, the remainder of the chapter will mention some of the outstanding changes that have taken place in the social and intellectual life of the United States in the twentieth century and which, in turn, have given rise to new psychological and educational theories. The remaining chapters of the book will then discuss the renewed attack upon the elective system made by the advocates of tradition and the different kind of attack made by the progressives who have come armed with new psychological and social theories.

Social and Economic Developments Require New Solutions. Anything approaching a detailed discussion of the social backgrounds of twentieth century America is of course beyond the scope of this book; hence, we shall merely point to some trends that seem to have significance for the development of college education. It is a commonplace to say that life has become much more complex than in earlier times and that conditions have changed so rapidly that people are left bewildered at what seems to be the chaos and confusion of modern life. It is also a commonplace to say that much of the complexity of modern life grows out of the increasing use of the machine in its many forms, so that our time has been described variously as the "Machine Age," or the "Power Age." The main trends that seem to be of great significance in the social and economic life and therefore in the educational life of the United States in the twentieth century may be indicated somewhat by the terms (1) industrialism, (2) democracy, and (3) capitalism. Conflicts among the fundamental assumptions and practices of these three forces have led to a great many of the confusions and complexities of modern life.

The tremendous impact upon American life that industrial technology had begun to make in the nineteenth century was widened in scope and increased in activity during the opening decades of the twentieth century. The story of mass production of manufactured goods; increased invention; improved and astounding advances in the means of transportation, communication, and power production is too familiar to warrant retelling. American life was undergoing fundamental changes as a result of the application of science to all phases of our economy. Among the many implications that students of American society have drawn from the fact of this application of technology to our culture, at least two or three warrant mention here.

There was, first, the recognition that when technology was at work it involved careful use of precise and exact measurements in constructing machines, a definite need for careful planning, and considerable reliance upon experimentation to devise those instruments which would work best in a given situation. Secondly, it was recognized that the earlier emphasis upon rapid expansion and rapid building was no longer so important as the need for consolidating the gains that had been made and designing an economic and political system that would make the most efficient use of the new industrial plant. In other words, our economic plant now has the possibilities of producing an abundance of things for everyone, but the great need is to make it work to the best advantages of all. Finally, it has been recognized that the boundaries between city and country and between different regions of the nation have been so obliterated that all areas of life have become highly dependent upon all other areas. No longer can the self-sufficient farm or family or community get along in isolation from other parts of the economy.

Besides the rapid growth of industrialism, a second authentic strain in American life has been gaining strength during the early twentieth century, namely, the trend toward greater political and social democracy. The voices of the farmer, the industrial worker, and the social theorist began to challenge the exclusive dominance of political and economic arenas by conservative industrialists who played up the role of the individual and played down that of the state and society. Gains were made for greater popular control of the political scene through such reforms as the civil service, secret ballot, direct primaries, initiative, referendum, recall, direct election of senators, and universal suffrage for women.

Gains were made for greater control of big business by the government through such agencies as the Interstate Commerce Commission, antitrust acts, the Federal Trade Commission, federal conservation of natural resources, Federal reserve bank loans to farmers, and income taxes. Tremendous grants were given to the states for general welfare in forestry, highways, public health, and educational services in agriculture, trades, industry, home economics, and child hygiene. Finally, gains were made for the greater expression of the popular voice in economic affairs through the advances in organized labor; the formation of Social Democratic, Farmer-Labor, and Progressive political parties; the increase of women in industry; and legal provisions for maximum hours of labor, minimum wages, and workers' accident and unemployment insurance, compensation, and pensions.

In such ways as these, democracy served notice that it was a force deeply rooted in the American tradition and one that was to be reckoned with in the future developments of social and educational life in the United States. In such ways as these, expression was given to the guiding conceptions of democracy which had come, in part, from the thought of the Enlightenment and, in part, from the indigenous conditions of American frontier and social life. In essence, the democratic conception expresses a regard and respect for the fundamental dignity, worth, and personality of the individual; it posits the inherent equality of all men; it demands liberty of action and thought in order that the individual may develop freely his inherent capacities; and it demands that political, economic, and social affairs shall rest upon the active consent of the governed in order that decisions may rest upon the use of intelligence rather than upon force or mere drift. These are some of the liberal and democratic conceptions that American life at its best partially succeeded in realizing and at its worst tended to deny while still paying lip service to democracy.

The third strong element that continued to express itself in the American life of the early twentieth century was what may be called capitalism. As has often been noted, capitalism rests upon a rationale of money-making or gain seeking which assumes that the "acquisitive instinct" is the basic drive of man. A whole theory of life and economics had been built up on the assumptions of the sanctity of private property, individualisic enterprise, and a "natural" economic order in which the state must not interfere with the "natural laws" of economics. As capitalism became associated with the control of machine technology, and as industrialists became political as well as economic and social spokesmen for the nation, the liberty of the individual in the democratic tradition came to mean "every man for himself." As the businessman became supreme, individualism became more "rugged," the tempo of life increased in its demands for big things, efficiency, service, and immediate profits.

The spirit of making money was, of course, not confined to any one area of American life. Although more millionaires than ever were being created during boom times, many more people were also pouring into the middle-class occupations of selling; advertising; commercial pursuits; and professions of law, medicine, teaching, and preaching. As wages and prices rose, farmers and laborers were also deeply affected by the spirit of acquisition and spending, and the ranks of absentee stockholders knew no class boundaries. The desire to get on was even more prevalent than in the "gilded age" as new thousands poured into schools and colleges before and after the World War. Along with the prodigious accumulation of wealth went also a prodigious capacity to spend and to give to charitable and educational agencies; hundreds of millions of dollars were showered on universities, colleges, schools, and health and welfare agencies.

Social Theory Blazes New Trails. As a result of the increased activity in the areas of industrialism, democracy, and capitalism, and particularly as a result of the thoroughgoing self-criticism that was prompted by the depression following 1929, new social and educational theories were formulated in an attempt to revaluate those elements in the American tradition which needed revision in the light of the changed conditions of the twentieth century. There was a growing recognition that industrialism was here to stay and that society should make more adequate provision for it. Many believed that democracy *should* be here to stay but that society must make much more adequate provision for its expression in many more areas of life. Such an analysis meant as a corollary that the capitalistic emphasis upon rugged individualism and money-making must somehow be limited in order to give more concrete expression to the need for planning and precision that industrial technology required and to make more adequate provision for popular consent in social affairs as the principles of democracy required.

In other words, it was apparent that the economic plant was not producing at peak efficiency and that the distributing system was woefully inadequate. At one end of the economic scale, unemployment and impaired purchasing power increased the insecurity of the worker in contrast to the increasing concentration of wealth in a few hands at the top of the economic scale. All this pointed to a revision in our traditional conceptions of every man for himself. Somehow, the system of economic production and distribution should be so planned and so controlled, if necessary, that the welfare of the total population is placed above that of those individuals who have been accustomed to exploiting for private profit. Just how this was to be done engaged the attention of an increasing number of persons in the New Deal administrations and among professional students of American society.

On the one hand, it seemed clear that the necessities of an industrial and interdependent society required a greater integration and consolidation of social and economic affairs; but on the other, it seemed clear that the values of the democratic ideal should not be lost in the process. An increasingly important answer seemed to rest in a reinterpretation of democratic liberalism whereby the tradition of individualistic and laissez-faire liberalism should be minimized and the collectivistic and humanitarian phase of traditional liberalism should be emphasized. This means that the whole people operating through the state have the right to use their collective powers to provide the conditions whereby all the people may reach a higher standard of economic security and a greater opportunity for expression of individuality.

Such proposals for the reformulation of social theory recognized not only the necessity for planning and for changing plans when conditions warrant change but also that the democratic process must play a strong part in making plans and meeting change. Thus, the traditional reliance upon the consent of the governed must come to mean not merely the opportunity to vote for political officers but also an ever more active participation by ever larger numbers of people in the control of those things which concern them. Hence the range of active discussion, cooperation, and consent must be extended to the economic and social as well as to the political spheres.

As the alternative to the use of force or casual improvisation, the democratic process must judge ideas on their merits through the greatest possible use of free intelligence and social experimentation in the realm of planning. Likewise, the conception of equality must mean that ever larger numbers of persons must be given equal opportunity to participate to the fullest of their abilities in political, social, economic, and educational activities. The conception of liberty must decrease the freedom of persons to act merely as they please regardless of the effects upon others and must emphasize the humanitarian aspect of freedom whereby everyone will have greater freedom of social action. Finally, the conception of individualism must lose its connotation of excessive and "rugged" individualism and must mean a reassertion of the conception of individual worth and dignity which can find its most adequate and useful expression through the democratic social process.

It is recognized, of course, that great difficulties lie in the path of such social theory in the form of privileged groups, widespread resistance to change, the desire for profits, and the demand of extremists for immediate and thoroughgoing changes. But it is felt that if the best values of the democratic conception are to be preserved, the attack upon economic insecurity must be at once decisive and yet through democratic means. The indicated methods, therefore, consist of a much more concerted effort at economic and social planning through the cooperative consent of the governed; a more thoroughgoing use of the technical advice of experts, who nevertheless should be held to strict account by the people; and the more thoroughgoing use of education of all the people as a means of developing understanding of social problems and intelligent habits in actually dealing with decisions concerning industrial and social planning.

In general, then, it may be pointed out that the new social theory emphasizes the conflicts between industrial democracy, on one hand, as opposed to capitalism, on the other. Capitalism assumes individualistic action as opposed to the interdependence created by industrialism; private ownership of the tools of production as opposed to the social operation and social use of such tools and their products; the planless character of capitalistic competition as opposed to the planful and precise nature of industrial technology; the private interest of capitalists as opposed to the public interest of democracy; and the operation of "natural" law assumed in capitalism as opposed to the conscious aspiration for social good through democratic social control. Thus, the new social theory which looks to the best interests of the whole people and which deals realistically with the conditions of industrial life will require much less emphasis upon the competitive and individualistic nature of the inherited capitalistic society and much more upon integration of the social life through planning for industrial welfare and through participation of the people in planning for democratic welfare.

Intellectual Trends Point Toward Modern Science. Just as twentieth century social and economic developments required new social theories, so have twentieth century scientific and intellectual developments required new intellectual adjustments and new theories of man in relation to nature. Again, we cannot hope to describe the trends of the physical sciences in any adequate sense; all we can do is point to some of the outstanding developments in knowledge and some of the most general implications. The first thing that may be said is that the Newtonian conception of a mechanical universe operating according to simple laws was severely jolted by investigations in the realms of astronomy and physics. The traditional dualism between mind and matter seemed to be obliterated as the scientist came to believe that the ultimate force in the physical world is energy and that matter is merely its manifestation. Whatever else the doctrines of relativity meant, they seemed to indicate that older conceptions of absolute and unchanging laws of motion, time, and space were no longer tenable as they had been for centuries. Motion was now viewed as relative to the observer; time became a kind of fourth dimension of space; and the law of gravitation became merely a property of matter. Likewise, the secrets of the atom were being revealed even to the point of questioning the fundamental law of cause and effect in the microscopic world. All in all, the universe of our sun and world seemed to shrink in comparison with the cosmos as a whole.

Not only the results of investigations in the physical sciences but also those in the biological and social sciences seemed to indicate that the traditional conceptions of complete and fixed knowledge were no longer tenable. In other words, the doctrines of pluralism and pragmatism seemed to be confirmed by actual investigations, despite the protests of modern exponents of the Great Tradition, who look for inspiration to Plato, Aristotle, Aquinas, Enlightenment science, and the traditional liberal education of the nineteenth century. During the twentieth century, the evolutionary process as a description of organic life was elaborated and vindicated by testimony from biology, anthropology, and sociology until it took an almost undisputed place in the intellectual equipment of the educated person.

The social sciences dropped their earlier preoccupation with classification, definitions, and dogmatic laws. History became more concerned with the growth of all human institutions; sociology turned to a realistic analysis of actual social processes and institutions; anthropology began to give a realistic picture of primitive life; economics described the growth of economic institutions; and political science turned to the analysis of actual institutional influences upon political life. In all of the social sciences, there was first the urge to "get the facts" which resulted in the amassing of great accumulations of "scientific" data and knowledge; but now the emphasis seems to be more in the direction of *interpreting* social change, its causes and its control. In effect, the social sciences came into their own as they created great new bodies of knowledge and as they became more and more closely related to the actual realities of life. Although this process had been well under way before 1929, the ensuing depression stimulated and released a great flood of new creative students in science, history, economics, political science, and the other social sciences.

Nearly all of the trends mentioned, social, economic, and intellectual, had their effects upon the secularization of life, so that, despite great gifts to the churches, more than half of the gentile population is estimated to have been outside the pale of organized religion before the depression began. Religion lost more and more of its authoritative control over greater numbers of people as a steady stream of evidence from scientists and historians further weakened traditional religious beliefs. Perhaps even more important than all the arguments of the skeptics in weakening the hold of the churches over the social activities of people have been the automobile, radio, movies, and other recreational facilities.

Despite these secularizing trends, however, the twentieth century has seen a popular fundamentalist movement, with strict adherence to the Biblical story, gain in strength and culminate in the famous Tennessee evolution trial of 1925. Also, the intellectual movement that became known as the "New Humanism" defended and relied upon traditional religious beliefs in many of its aspects. On the whole, religious interests were being crowded out by other more secular interests, but there remained strong religious movements ranging all the way from the completely orthodox who denied the findings of science to the advanced modernists who tried to assimilate modern science. In general, the masses of people connected with the churches were either unaware of or passed over the conflict between religion and science.

A word should be said concerning the conflict in the realm of literature and the arts between the exponents of the "genteel tradition" and the modern realistic writers. Increasingly between 1910 and 1930, a whole younger generation of writers tried to separate themselves from what they felt were the bloodless and overrefined attitudes of the genteel tradition and to express the sweep, strength, beauty, ugliness, and actual life of America. Such were Dreiser, Sinclair, Brooks, Sandburg, Anderson, Mencken, Lewis, O'Neill, Cabell, Dos Passos, Faulkner, and Hemingway. Whereas gentility stood for Victorian and Puritan denial of the life of the body and of practical concerns, the moderns were candidly sensual and even praised sexual freedom; whereas gentility was optimistic and saw only the bright side of life, the moderns were antioptimistic and painted sin, tragedy, and despair; whereas gentility centered on the eastern seaboard and looked to the refined and bloodless "culture" of England, the moderns were rooted in the Middle West and South and looked either to a strictly American tradition of populism or farmer-labor democracy or to the socialism or Freudianism of the Continent.[1] The trends since 1930 are not so clear, but the popularity of historical novels and the attention being paid to social themes and the interests of the common people seem significant.

[1] For an extended discussion of this conflict, see Malcolm Cowley, *After the Genteel Tradition; American Writers since* 1910 (W. W. Norton & Company, Inc., New York, 1937).

A reaction against the social and mechanistic interpretation of literature which gained some strength in the twenties has already been identified as New Humanism.   Outstanding spokesmen for this position were Irving Babbitt of Harvard and Paul Elmer More of Princeton, who seemed especially interested in restoring the classical languages and literature as a means of disciplining the mind and morals and denying the cult of the natural or the spontaneous.   They seemed determined to keep literary criticism and literature free from the unpleasant and disturbing realities involved in social reform.   In a sense, they represented a revival and resurgence of the genteel tradition, but their position is so laden with philosophical, psychological, and educational implications for higher education that they will be discussed at greater length in the following pages.   Let it suffice to say here that not only literature but the drama, plastic arts, the dance, music, and architecture also gave evidence of the struggle between the old and the new, as the moderns in each of these fields attempted to slough off the conventions and accouterments of traditional forms and strip down to what they felt were the essential, or appropriate, or "functional," characteristics of their respective art forms.

The last type of trend to be mentioned here includes the developments in philosophy and psychology that led to revised conceptions of human nature and the relation of man to his surrounding environment.   Here, again, there has been considerable conflict between what may be called the Great Tradition and the position sometimes known as "experimental naturalism," or merely "experimentalism."   For purposes of convenience and discussion, the Great Tradition is taken to cover those various philosophical and psychological views which are largely inherited from the distant past.   This would apply to those positions which hold strongly to the classical idealism of Plato and Aristotle as represented by the New Humanists or to the scholastic philosophy of Thomas Aquinas as represented by Roman Catholic colleges and universities or to the Germanic idealism and Hegelianism which still attracts enthusiastic disciples in academic circles.

On the other side, with quite different conceptions of the nature of knowledge and truth and human nature, is the position of experimentalism which has attempted to incorporate the methods and evidence of science into a progressive philosophical approach more appropriate to the twentieth century.   This position has received its most effective and characteristic formulation at the hands of John Dewey who has attempted to make philosophy conform more closely to the requirements of an age committed to machine technology, democracy, and science. These opposing positions will not be discussed in more detail at this point, for the following chapters are given over to them in turn with an attempt to show some of their respective implications for the theory and practice of college education.

In the field of psychology, the development was so tremendous that only one or two generalizations can be made here. The experimental and scientific methods that had been envisioned and started in the latter nineteenth century developed with enormous rapidity in the twentieth century in the many different fields of learning, instincts, individual differences, and emotions. E. L. Thorndike made devastating inroads upon the introspective and "faculty" psychology of an earlier day. At Teachers College, Columbia University, he was virtually creating "educational psychology" as he attempted to apply the methods of the exact sciences to certain educational problems. With the publication of his three monumental volumes entitled *Educational Psychology*, in 1913, attention in America began to turn more and more to an "objective" psychology for the answers to problems of original nature, learning, and individual differences.

By his insistence that learning was highly specific, Thorndike made a frontal attack upon the doctrines of mental discipline which had long held that certain studies were uniquely valuable for "training the mind" so that it could transfer its operations to any field whatever. Thorndike attacked this doctrine by asserting that the reflex arc was the hereditary unit of behavior rather than a group of untrained "faculties" and that learning depended upon the number and ease with which bonds of connection were established in the synapses of the nervous system. Learning consisted not in a general training of unformed faculties but in the formation of specific bonds of connection between a situation S and a response R. These S-R bonds were established in two major ways according to Thorndike's famous laws of learning: by exercise and by satisfying effect. According to the law of exercise, connections were strengthened the more they were used, and they were weakened when not used; other things being equal, the more frequently and the more recently the bonds were practiced the stronger would be the connections and hence the more effective the learning. According to the law of effect, connections tended to be stamped in when the learning was satisfying and pleasant for the learner, and bonds tended to be weakened when the result was unsatisfying or unpleasant; other things being equal, connections were established more easily when the action system was ready and less easily when not ready to act.

Thorndike's psychology has changed considerably in recent years, but for our purposes the important thing is that mental discipline received a major setback, especially in the elementary and secondary-school practices of the United States. Thorndike pointed out that transfer occurred only when the content or the method of a school subject was

similar to the use to which it was to be put; in other words, if students
were to be educated for specific ends, they should study those subjects
which would contribute directly to those ends.   This theory gave great
comfort to the new scientific and social studies for which there was a
growing demand throughout the country.   Hence, specialized studies
entered more easily into the elementary and secondary schools of the
United States, but they were not accepted so readily into the traditional
liberal arts courses of colleges which held more stubbornly to the doctrines
of discipline.   In the chapters to follow, the more recent efforts of certain
college educators to revive mental discipline as a predominate aim in
college education will be discussed in some detail.

The testing movement in the areas of native intelligence and achievement in the various school and college subjects went so rapidly ahead
that "standardized tests" were perhaps the most characteristic features
of educational procedure in the 1920's.   Tests widened their scope to
include all sorts of special aptitudes, from music and Latin to character
and vocations.   A characteristic development of the twentieth century
was the creation of applied psychology to deal with industrial and
educational   problems   of   guidance,   personnel   selection   and   training,
advertising appeal, and other phases of human relations.   Clinical, or
abnormal, psychology grew in proportion to deal with variants from
the average type of mental adjustment; psychiatry was developed to
deal more directly with the physiological bases of psychological phenomena; psychoanalysis called attention to the influence of subconscious,
or inner, motivations and desires which when inadequately expressed
result in detrimental complexes, or defense mechanisms; and social
psychology gained recognition by studying specifically the relation of the
individual to his complex social situation.

Of recent years, there has been increasing discussion of a psychological
position known as "organismic" psychology which is not so much a
special school as it is a general point of view, drawing evidence from
such sources as scientific investigations in biology, physiology, endo-
crinology, neurology, Gestalt psychology, and Dewey's experimentalism.
Organismic psychology may be as good a term as any to use in describing
the psychological position that has tried to incorporate the findings of
new social theory and of science into a new formulation of human nature
and human behavior.   This position will be discussed at greater length
in the following chapter as a contrast to the traditional Humanism, and
therefore little will be said here concerning its specific ideas.   Suffice
it to say that organismic psychology grew up partly in reaction to the
mechanistic position represented by "behaviorism" and other "con-
nectionist" approaches to psychology which were so popular in the 1920's.
Whereas the behaviorists had described learning in terms of stimulus-

response bonds, the organismic approach would expand that conception to include stimulus-organism-response activities.

In other words, life is viewed as a continual interactive adjustment between an active environment and an active living organism. Behavior arises when a condition of equilibrium between the organism and the environment has been upset, causing tension or disturbance in the organism which seeks to restore the equilibrium by acting upon the environment. In this behavior, the organism acts with certain *purposes*, and it acts as a *whole* so that the whole organism responds to the upset; the organism thereby is changed by its behavior, and the environment is also changed by its behavior. The aim of individual behavior is thus viewed as the continual attempt of the individual to become integrated with respect to his social and physical environment, and the aim of social behavior is viewed as the continual attempt of society to integrate its activities with respect to the greatest welfare of all the individuals. The following chapters will deal with the implications of these twentieth century trends in industry, democracy, science, social science, philosophy, and psychology as they have contributed to new conceptions in educational theory which have, in turn, affected elementary, secondary, and higher education.

Trends in Higher Education Raise Persistent Problems. The machine era of the twentieth century served to strengthen and hasten the tendencies toward expansion of the educational population and curriculum that had begun in the later nineteenth century. The rapid increases in total population, urban population, and compulsory attendance laws poured thousands of new students into the high schools of the country and thus provided a much larger potential clientele for the colleges. While the total population of the United States was roughly doubling between 1890 and the present, the number of high school students was increasing more than fifteen times and the number of college students was increasing more than eight times.[1] Some colleges with two or three hundred students in 1890 had grown to institutions of ten or fifteen thousand students in 1939. Thus, the proportion of students in high school or college in relation to the total population has made astounding advances since the turn of the century and has made necessary some far-reaching adjustments in educational aims and procedures.

As a result of this new kind of student clamoring for education, and as a result of steady increases in the bounds of knowledge from the

---

[1] The number of students in higher institutions has grown from approximately 150,000 in 1890 to 1,250,000 in 1938–1939. After the decreases in 1933 and 1934, enrollments have gone to new highs in 1939. For recent statistics, see Raymond Walters, "Statistics of Registration in American Universities and Colleges, 1938," *School and Society*, 48: 765–786 (Dec. 7, 1938).

physical and social sciences, the curriculum of the high schools and colleges continued to expand enormously in terms of new subjects and new courses of study. Industrial technology increased the demand for technical and practical studies; the conceptions of democracy led to demands for "education for all"; and the desire to make money led to demands for increasingly useful and vocational subjects. Schools or departments of business, journalism, engineering, architecture, pharmacy, dentistry, agriculture, mining, forestry, household arts, applied arts, library science, and education were added to large institutions that had already included colleges of liberal arts, medicine, law, and theology.

As a result of the expansive notes of the twentieth century, it was only natural that the elective system should continue to expand and widen. Courses of instruction were divided, subdivided, and multiplied until a subject for a year or half year of study often narrowed down to a very small division or segment of knowledge in its respective field. Too often, a department of instruction looked upon all of its students as potential specialists in its field and constructed its courses as if a student were going to take all of them, as a result of which students who took only one or two courses in a given department came away from their study with a very narrow and superficial knowledge of the field as a whole. College catalogues took on the size of mail-order catalogues and the complexity of railroad time tables, listing their subjects in alphabetical order from art to zoology and representing the lack of a guiding philosophy of higher education except that which had been used to support the extension of the elective system. The most frequent terms that came to be applied to this state of affairs indicated that the curriculum was too "compartmentalized" and too often encouraged the student to engage in too much smattering or too much specialization.

A fairly recent study shows dramatically how far the liberal college curriculum has departed from the traditional conception of a liberal education by allowing wide election of studies from the offerings of all other professional and technical courses in the institution.[1] According to this study, all but one of 42 universities allowed a wide variety of elective courses both from within and from without the liberal arts college; 97 per cent allowed the election for the B.A. degree of courses classified as "vocational." In fact, it appeared that nearly all of the

---

[1] EVELYN TRUTH BIXLER, *A Study of Electives in the Liberal Arts Colleges of Certain Universities in Forty-two States*, (M.A. thesis, University of Maryland, 1933). Courses accepted in the liberal college were classified under three heads: *professional* (education, medicine, law, dentistry, pharmacy, nursing, and veterinary medicine); *vocational* (agriculture, home economics, forestry, fine arts, music, arts, architecture, business and commerce, religion, journalism, library science, and physical education); and *technical* (engineering, mining, and military science).

institutions were more willing to allow outside electives to be submitted for the B.A. degree than for the B.S. degree.

This situation certainly represented a great departure from the position of the conservatives in the nineteenth century who were trying to keep the validity and meaning of the B.A. degree from being impaired by the encroachment of practical and utilitarian subjects. Thus, the most common practice with regard to the elective system even today seems to consist of setting up different courses of study with a certain amount of credits required from specified groups of studies (majors and minors) and with provision for electives to be chosen to fill out the required number of credits for graduation. It should be mentioned here that despite the emphasis during the rest of this book on the reform of the elective system, it still is apparent that the most common feature of the usual college curriculum is a combination of a relatively few required subjects along with a considerable amount of election.

In general, then, it may be said that college education developed so rapidly in the first decades of the twentieth century that there is little wonder that a growing chorus of criticism has appeared in recent years to lament the planlessness and confusion in college education. Despite the growing rigidity of mechanical requirements concerning credits, prerequisites, entrance requirements, and degree requirements, there was enough flexibility, diversity, and freedom to admit of considerable self-searching and self-criticism. Not only laymen but college educators themselves came more and more to realize that something should be done to revise and reform the college in general and the elective system in particular. The first attempts seemed to be somewhat similar to the "scientific" and measuring movement which was sweeping elementary and secondary schools. Great emphasis was put upon objective tests to improve grading, upon entrance examinations and requirements to improve the "quality" of college students, upon standardization of secondary and college offerings and teaching, upon guidance and counseling techniques to provide better selection of courses for individual students, and upon curriculum revisions and techniques to provide better approaches to study in the light of the new thousands who had flocked to the colleges.

Then, in the last decade or so, there has been a concerted effort to attack more fundamentally the problems created by the elective system. In this concerted attack, two quite distinct and divergent trends of opinion appeared. On the one hand, the so-called "progressive education" movement has tried to incorporate into educational theory and practice the most valid evidence derived from modern social and scientific trends. On the other, a definite revival of the conservative educational position, which has its roots deep in the traditional liberal education of the past, has proposed a type of reform that also attacks the elective system but for reasons very different and toward ends far different from those represented in the new progressive and general education. Thus, the battle between conservatives and progressives continues, but it is proceeding along somewhat different lines from those laid down in the nineteenth century. A further discussion of these opposing points of view and of their respective implications for the college curriculum and for the elective system will be the subject of the following chapters.

CHAPTER XV

OPPONENTS VIE IN ATTACKING THE ELECTIVE SYSTEM

No sooner had the principle and practice of elective studies become a widespread feature of college education than the pendulum of educational criticism began to swing in the opposite direction and to direct its efforts upon reforming and limiting the elective system. As the twentieth century wore on, it became increasingly apparent that criticism was taking quite different forms. The conservative criticism seemed to be a direct continuation of the type of attack that had been made all through the nineteenth century upon the expansion of the elective system. The philsophical and educational assumptions underlying such criticism were largely a direct heritage from the traditional conception of a liberal education. At the other extreme, criticism was gradually turning for comfort to the assumptions of the new progressive education movement which grew largely out of the experimental philosophy of John Dewey and other progressive educators. Between these extremes can be identified all kinds of compromises, and most educators took their cues now from one side and now from the other. Let us look first at the underlying philosophical assumptions of the conservative position.

UNDERLYING ASSUMPTIONS OF CONSERVATIVES

The twentieth century saw a continuation of the same kind of arguments that the conservatives of the nineteenth century had used to oppose the elective system when it was gaining ground under the stimulus of Eliot and others. If anything, this kind of argument came more into the open then ever before, for the traditional conception of a liberal education was embraced by a revival of the genteel tradition which called itself the New Humanism. Inasmuch as the New Humanism had a special vogue during the decade of the twenties and continues today in the arguments of outstanding educators in higher education, this position will be described as representing the extreme opposite to that represented by experimental naturalism and progressivism.

Although there are, of course, differences in the position of those who call themselves Humanists, nevertheless there are certain fundamental assumptions which they all accept sufficiently to warrant grouping them together. Inspiration for the Humanist position stemmed in the early decades of the twentieth century from the work of Charles Eliot Norton

269

of Harvard and Stuart P. Sherman, and it has been advocated in America more recently by Irving Babbitt of Harvard, Paul Elmer More of Princeton, and Norman Foerster of the University of Iowa. Recent voices from England representing this position are those of Phillip S. Richards in philosophy and T. S. Eliot in literature and criticism.

In general, the New Humanism has involved a defensive reaction against the upsetting implications of modern social and scientific theories as formulated in experimentalism. In social theory, it has reasserted the claims of an aristocratic and social conservatism against the humanitarian demands of the Enlightenment and experimentalism which insist that society should reshape and modify the environment in the interests of the masses of the people. Babbitt stated explicitly that Humanism is interested in the discipline of the few rather than in a benevolence toward all men and that Humanism is interested in the perfection of the individual rather than the elevation of mankind as a whole. Witness the following statement:

The eager efforts of our philanthropists to do something for the negro and the newsboy are well enough in their way; but a society that hopes to be saved by what it does for its negroes and newsboys is a society that is trying to lift itself by its own boot-straps. Our real hope of safety lies in our being able to induce our future Harrimans and Rockefellers to liberalize their own souls, in other words to get themselves rightly educated. Men of heroic capacity such as Messrs. Rockefeller and Harriman have in some respects shown themselves to be are, of course, born, not made; but when once born it will depend largely on the humaneness of their education whether they are to become heroes of good or heroes of evil.[1]

"Heroes are born, not made," is the age-old argument of those who build up philosophical arguments to support their unwillingness to trust in the present or possible intelligence of the great majority of people. Aristocratic theories of society and of human nature lead to aristocratic theories of education.

Morally and intellectually, the New Humanism has shuddered at the advances of an industrial society that has brought so much confusion, chaos, despair, noise, disillusionment, and futility into the life and into the modern literature of America. It reasserts the claims of Puritan restraint and discipline as against the cult of freedom of expression and of action which it identifies with Rousseau's "natural man." It has demanded a renewed effort of the ascetic qualities of "intellectual discipline" to control moral conduct more severely so that it will not get out of hand in the direction of spontaneity and naturalism. Intel-

---

[1] IRVING BABBITT, *Literature and the American College* (Houghton Mifflin Company, Boston, 1908), pp. 70–71.

lectually, the New Humanism repudiates the leadership of the natural and social sciences in the affairs of life and reverts in essence to the traditional philosophy of idealism as represented best in the humane letters and literature of the past; it draws for philosophic inspiration from Plato, Aristotle, medieval Scholasticism, and even, in the case of some Humanists, from Indian theosophy and Buddhism. All in all, the trend seemed to indicate a further retirement from the pressing affairs of this world in the direction of greater contemplation of the more fixed and eternal world of the supernatural.

Among the most extreme of the Humanists (but implicitly represented in all), the most fundamental postulate of this position is the reaffirmation of the essential dualism between man and nature. They believe in an *absolute* distinction between man and the world of nature, and they believe that man has certain universal and eternal qualities that prevent him forever from partaking of any of the qualities of lower forms of life. In other words, the extremists deny the essential implications of the evolutionary doctrine that the natural and social sciences have been at such pains to establish, and they assert that man is a "Real Kind, meaning that all men possess an identical human nature, in virtue of which we call them all men."

Attend to the words of one of the recent Humanists:

The issue between Humanism (as we may, for the sake of brevity, call the traditional Belief in Man) and its opponents resolves itself into the question whether or not there is in man anything that essentially distinguishes him from the rest of Nature, anything that separates him from the other animals by an impassable gulf. . . . It is the theory of evolution, and nothing else, which has turned the tide of opinion decisively in favour of Naturalism. . . . Unless this assertion [of the continuity of nature] can be discredited, the cause of Humanism is already lost.[1]

And again, the Humanist asserts that the question of dualism cannot be determined by the evidence of the natural sciences but only by philosophy or metaphysics:

In short, we must accept the duality of mind and matter, with the concomitant mystery of their interaction, as one of the insoluble data of experience, because we can neither express one in terms of the other nor find an element of identity between them.[2]

Thus, in its fundamental approach to the problem of man and nature, the Humanist position is poles apart from that of experimentalism. Humanism denies the postulates of science with regard to the continuity of nature, whereas experimentalism assimilates them into its position.

[1] PHILLIP S. RICHARDS, *Belief in Man* (Farrar & Rinehart, Inc., New York, 1932), p. 3.

[2] *Ibid.*, p. 10.

The Humanist view of human nature follows logically from the assumptions of dualism. Human nature is looked upon as a unique, unchanging, and absolute quality of man which sets him off from the rest of nature. Here the Humanist approach closely parallels the traditional faculty psychology, for the Humanists speak of human nature as if it were a separate substance or entity as opposed to the body of man. The faculties that distinguish man from lower animals are usually described in terms of inherent qualities of morality, reason, sense of art and beauty, and religion.

The Humanist insists that moral conscience is a part of man's original endowment and that it does not admit of degrees, for it is absolute; reason is a universal ability to draw distinctions and form judgments; man's sense of beauty is curiously independent of time and sets him immeasurably above the rest of the animal world; and, finally, for some Humanists, the religious instinct is considered universal in man.   In sum: " . . . man, wherever he is found, is essentially the same: a moral and rational being, with a sense of beauty and a natural propensity for religion."[1]   The assertion is made that these qualities of human nature cannot be described by the scientific method; but rather it is expressly asserted that this conception of human nature has come down to us as a result of ancient classical thought which has been supported by the Christian religion and medieval thought.   The expressed implication is also that the best way to revive and rehabilitate this conception of universality is by an increased study of the ancient classics.

These assumptions of Humanism have specific implications for distinctive conceptions of knowledge, truth, and human values which, in turn, have definite implications for the theory of learning and the college curriculum.   Whereas the experimentalist philosophy looks upon knowledge, truth, and values as arising from experience and from the social situation, the Humanist believes in absolute and even supernatural standards of value whereby the knowledge or truth of a situation may be tested.   In other words, values for the Humanist are somehow related to a sphere of existence that is above and beyond nature and that gives to knowledge and truth an unchanging and authoritative character. Knowledge, then, takes on the character of a rather fixed body of true principles which are to be handed down as the heritage of the race, and thus it is divorced from experience and from human action as such:

Truth, whatever else it is, undeniably consists in a relation between the mind and reality.   If there is no permanence on either side of that relation . . . then knowledge is impossible.[2]

[1] *Ibid.*, p. 117.
[2] *Ibid.*, pp. xiii–xiv.

It is, as I have said, definitely and eternally impossible to introduce order into this [intellectual] chaos on any naturalistic principles.   The order must come into the world of knowledge from *outside*, *i.e.*, from the world of values.   The sciences, which deal with fact and not with value, must all recognise some supreme value. . . . [1]

Stemming from this desire to introduce order into the chaotic world of society by appealing to a higher and fixed realm of values which lies behind the flux and flow of experience, the Humanist's conception of learning and of the curriculum takes form.   It is evident to the Humanist that learning has to do with the unique part of man that is his "mind" as opposed to the activities of his body which are "natural" and therefore less "human" than mind.   Learning has to do especially with that faculty of human nature which is termed reason, or intellect, and the main aim of the higher learning is thus viewed as the discipline and development of the intellectual powers of discrimination and judgment.

The Humanist argument follows that the studies that best present the enduring principles of absolute truth and that most effectively develop the intellect are contained in the great literature of the past.   Best of all are the ancient classical studies for these purposes.   So we return to the problem of the elective system which continues to be under fire as it was in the past because it allowed scientific, vocational, and practical studies to crowd out the literary and linguistic studies handed down by the Great Tradition.   In other words, the scientific and practical studies are less human in the Humanistic definition of the word, and they therefore should be minimized or eliminated from the college curriculum to make way for a revival of Humanistic studies which will provide that common fund of knowledge and ideas which has been lost with the coming of the elective system.   In the words of Paul Shorey the main issue in liberal education

. . . is the survival or the total suppression, in the comparatively small class of educated leaders who graduate from high schools and colleges, of the very conception of linguistic, literary, and critical discipline; of culture, taste and standards; of the historic sense itself; of some trained faculty of appreciation and enjoyment of our rich heritage from the civilized past; of some counterbalancing familiarity with the actual evolution of human man, to soften the rigidities of physical science, and to check and control by the touchstones of humor and common sense the *a priori* deductions of pseudo-science from conjectural reconstructions of the evolution of the physical and animal man.[2]

The Humanist position has been used at this point to represent the conservative side of the argument, but the following chapters will show

[1] *Ibid.*, p. xvii.
[2] PAUL SHOREY, *The Assault on Humanism* (Atlantic Monthly Press Publications, Boston, 1917), pp. 73–74.

that many educators who do not profess to be Humanists nevertheless belong in the conservative camp. The group that has associated itself with President Hutchins, Mortimer Adler, Stringfellow Barr, and Scott Buchanan are certainly akin in spirit if not in name to the Humanists. Likewise, conservative religious groups, notably Roman Catholic educators, show themselves to be closely associated with other conservatives in their common opposition to the experimental and progressive position. In his preface to a recent book that attacks naturalism from the dualistic Christian point of view, Professor Louis Mercier of Harvard welcomes the support of the Catholic point of view by such Humanists as Babbitt, More, and Foerster; by such eminent educators as Charles H. Judd, William C. Bagley, and Nicholas Murray Butler; and by such dualistic critics as Mortimer Adler and President Hutchins.[1]

UNDERLYING ASSUMPTIONS OF PROGRESSIVES

The significant thing about the development of the progressive educational position is that it has attempted to devise a theory of education that will adequately assimilate the new social and intellectual trends mentioned in the previous chapter. New trends demanded new theories of society, of human nature, and of human learning; and it was apparent to the progressives that an adequate theory of education must take account of the best evidence that has been presented by modern natural science, social science, and psychology. Since modern America was moving into an ever more interdependent status where planning and cooperation were more necessary than ever before, it seemed logical that education must try to make its activites lifelike and help students not only to understand but also to engage more effectively in solving the problems present in American society.

The expression of these ideas apparently gained ground first in the elementary and secondary schools; but by the 1920's and increasingly during and after the depression in the 1930's, the demand was made that college courses, too, must become much more interested in the problems and activities of modern society. The narrow, specialized, and compartmentalized courses of the elective system were criticized because they did not help students to become aware of the society in which they would live or help them to thread their ways through the complexities and confusions of modern life. A term that gained currency in expressing this need was "integration," indicating the need for students to see life "whole" and to see life's problems as interrelated.

[1] GEOFFREY O'CONNELL, *Naturalism in American Education* (Benziger Brothers, New York, 1938), pp. x–xi. The nonsectarian case for Christian theology as the organizing force in higher education is stated by W. A. Brown, *The Case for Theology in the University* (Princeton University Press, Princeton, 1938).

Besides the emphasis upon relating college study more closely to the needs of present-day society and upon giving students a more integrated approach to their study of modern life, there was the realization that if democracy were to be made more effective it must encourage the more active participation of greater numbers of people in the democratic processes. And it seemed only proper that experience in actually engaging in the processes of democracy should be a great part of the college experience of all students. Also, if democracy were to be served properly by higher education, the college should throw off its traditional aristocratic air and admit an increasing number of students. The standards of college admission and graduation were attacked as artificial and as not meeting the needs of the great masses of American students. In these ways, the pressing needs of a new industrial technology and of a democracy that had been put upon the defensive in the world scene were translated into new educational theory.

The other side of the progressive picture was a tremendous movement on all levels of education to give much more attention to the individual student and to his personal development than had been possible in the large impersonal lecture courses and lecture methods of the mature elective system. The converse of the demand of democratic higher education was that the individual should not be lost in the masses of new students who swept into the colleges. Here it was that the new conceptions of science and psychology contributed to a changed conception of human nature and of individuality. Earlier in the century, the so-called scientific movement in education had stressed objective tests as a means of measuring student abilities in an attempt to standardize as well as to individualize instruction; but in more recent years, a changed conception of what human experience is like and how the learning process is carried on most effectively has somewhat dimmed the testing movement as a cure-all in itself. To adopt a term that is being used increasingly to identify this approach, it will be called hereafter experimentalism.

Whatever the name given to this position, it has developed largely out of the philosophy of John Dewey and has tried to incorporate recent findings of physiology and psychology. In general, experimentalism denies the traditional distinctions or dualisms that have divided man from nature, mind from body, individual from society, and knowledge from action. On the contrary, it interprets the findings of science to mean that man is essentially a part of nature and, in common with other organisms, lives in constant interaction with his physical and social environment. Man's mind is thus looked upon not as a separate spiritual entity but as the tool, or means, whereby he adjusts and controls his environment to solve his difficulties and accomplish his purposes.

Man's intelligence is looked upon as the means of "reconstructing" or remaking experience whereby he is able to meet novel situations and effect real changes in the sequence of events to a degree that makes him *superior to but not different in kind from* other living organisms. On this basis, the individual is not something discrete and separate from society, but he develops his own unique individuality and personality as a result of his participation in and through the social situation. In other words, human nature is viewed not as something fixed and eternal from all time but as a mode of reaction which is affected by and which affects the surrounding culture. Differences in the pervading culture of an individual produce such differences in the way people react that we *may not* say that human nature is the same everywhere in spite of its surrounding social environment.

From this point of view emerge new conceptions of knowledge and truth and learning. Knowledge is not considered as something connected with the unchanging material contained in books as distinct from the actions that men carry on. Knowledge is thought of as organized plans of action and refers to active understanding of the conditions and consequences of events. Knowledge is thus constantly changing and closely linked to action. Truth, or true knowledge, is not a fixed and closed set of eternal principles but changes as the consequences of actions are verified in actual experience. Thinking is not merely a spectator which tries to find out what principles have already been established; thinking reflects the scientific method of problem solving by viewing the possible ways of resolving a disturbing situation, selecting what seem to be appropriate ways of acting (hypotheses), and then actually testing out the hypotheses to see if they solve the problem.

Ideas are thus not absolute principles to be handed down or discovered but are those tentative plans of action which are considered true when they show that they make good when tested in consequences. As a corollary, the learning process becomes not a matter of memorizing or acquiring a preestablished body of materials but the means whereby the student acquires ever more adequate ideas or effective plans of action and thereby becomes more qualified in remaking his experience in terms of his purposes. Learning becomes not a matter of the mind as separate from the body but a matter of what the whole organism brings away from a problem or situation in terms of knowing, thinking, and feeling.

Some of the implications for educational practice that arise out of this position and that are beginning to affect the college curriculum may be stated briefly. From the social approach, it is apparent that education must stress much more the vital connection between the college and the surrounding community and larger society. The student must gain a much more genuine understanding of the problems of society, and therefore he must give much more time to the study of society. Studying must mean a far greater reliance upon the use of all kinds of materials and activities in order to see the relationship of one problem to other problems and to make preliminary efforts at solving the problems. Such solving must place more and more reliance upon the cooperation of students in carrying on social activities together and at arriving at group decisions based not so much upon authority or majority voting as on a genuine consensus reached through discussion and working together. "Social integration" is a term used to describe this social process which looks to the problems outside the college and tries to make the solution of social problems a matter of actual activity within the college.

From the point of view of the individual, the implications of the experimental position are fully as far-reaching. The conception of *growth* in education resulted in a much greater respect for the individual student and for his development as a unique individuality. Education came to be visualized in terms of the physical, intellectual, emotional, and moral growth of students rather than in terms of the discipline of fixed faculties. Furthermore, the conception of the *active* character of experience proved to be very fruitful for educational theory and techniques. Since experience is the interaction of the organism and environment, then knowing and meaning arise only when there is an active response on the part of the individual. That learning is viewed as best which encourages the learner himself to take the initiative in planning, carrying out, and judging his own activities. Learning is best when students themselves have the freedom to carry out those activities which seem to be in line with their own genuine purposes and interests. The test of learning thus becomes not the ability to recite in class or write an examination so much as it is the ability to act intelligently in subsequent experiences.

Besides the conceptions of growth and activity, a third implication of the experimentalist approach is the conception of *wholeness*. The whole organism contributes to the responses that the individual makes, so that learning becomes not a matter merely of a mind as opposed to a body but a matter of all that the student brings from a situation in terms of physical, mental, and emotional attitudes as well as the intellectual meanings. Hence bodily, manual, and creative activities of all sorts become fully as important as purely mental activities. From the point of view of the individual, wholeness, or integration, of response is achieved when the individual makes effective adjustments within as he faces the situation without. If the learner faces effectually a sufficient variety of situations, he integrates himself as a personality; but when a number of such interactions are sufficiently inadequate to upset the normal balance of the individual, then incipient maladjustments follow. From the point of view of the college curriculum, wholeness, or integration, is aided when the constant attempt is made to see whole situations and problems in relation to each other.

Steps in this direction are indicated by the growing emphasis upon broader fields of study to cut across narrow subject lines or upon the study of a whole civilization in order to see the whole picture from different angles or upon the individual and social interests of the students themselves as a basis for building ever wider experiences. Thus, whether from the point of view of society, of the individual, or of the curriculum, the emphasis implied in the experimental and organismic approach seems to point to integration which has become more and more a byword in progressive educational circles. As the conception of integration gained currency, it meant that the elective system would come in for more and more criticism because it had resulted in such narrow subdividing of the curriculum that it prevented adequate realization of all three kinds of integration that the experimentalist position found necessary. The elective system reflected too faithfully the confused and compartmentalized state of a profit-seeking society, and it prevented too effectively the desirable integration of social, individual, and curricular activities.

We have presented these two opposing positions of experimentalism and Humanism in as extreme form as possible but also with as close approximation to fairness as possible in order that we may describe in bold outline the different kinds of philosophical approach being made today to the question of college education. If these two positions are taken to be at the opposite extremes of an imaginary scale, most college educators could be placed at some intermediate point on the scale.

The main hope from this discussion is that all who are interested in college education may have a more adequate basis for analyzing and judging the arguments that have been presented in the past and that will doubtless be presented in the future concerning college education. Despite the discussion's inadequacies, it seems evident to the writer that, as the theory of college education attempts to take adequate account of the pressing trends of modern social and scientific theory, it will tend to approach the experimentalist position and to leave the Humanist position.

THE GREAT TRADITION VERSUS EXPERIMENTAL NATURALISM

The opposing points of view in philosophy and psychology which have been mentioned above have had clearly recognizable counterparts in the theory of college education. As the twentieth century has witnessed an increasingly sharp clash of philosophical positions, it has seen also an increasingly sharp antagonism between conflicting philosophies of education. In other words, the opposing educational points of view have been making greater efforts to support their respective positions by developing elaborate intellectual justifications and by formulating more thoroughgoing underlying philosophies. Although this trend is sometimes difficult to trace, the broad outlines of the controversy stand out rather clearly.

Those educators who favored the traditional type of college education have tried to support their views with traditional types of philosophy and psychology; and the more progressive educators have gradually tried to formulate an underlying philosophy that would be more consistent with modern principles of science and psychology. This meant that the elective system in college education was attacked on all sides because it represented no well-defined or guiding philosophy of education. The suggestions for reform of the elective system have led in different directions, and the direction has often depended on the underlying philosophy of the educator who was pointing the way.

Although all educators were not always clearly aware of their fundamental assumptions, a careful analysis of a great deal of literature reveals that many college educators can be divided into opposing *educational* camps which roughly correspond to opposing *philosophical* and *psychological* positions. In general, the conservative plans for reform of the college resemble a plea for retirement to the ivory tower of academic retreat where the pressing problems of everyday life can be shut out and the select group of teachers and students can pursue "intellectual" and "scholarly" studies in the best tradition of the past. The conservative most often appeals to the absolutistic and dualistic principles of philosophical idealism and rationalism, to the things of the mind as separated from the things of everyday life, and to a kind of psychology that harkens closely back to the traditional faculty psychology.

On the other hand, progressive plans for reform of college education resemble a demand that the college take on the aspects of a watchtower where teachers and students can become most alert and sensitive to the pressing problems of present-day life and where they can jointly gain necessary and helpful practice in solving those problems. The progressive position most often appeals to a philosophy of scientific and experimental naturalism which denies a cleavage between intellectual and social concerns and embraces an organismic psychology devoted to developing in students a greater ability in dealing with social affairs of a democratic society.

In order to make these opposing positions clearer, and to illustrate them from the works of educators who can be considered to embrace in whole or in part the respective positions, the rest of this chapter will be devoted to a more detailed description of the Great Tradition versus experimental naturalism. It should be remembered that the educators who are discussed in the following pages represent the most extreme or the most vocal examples of each position.

In defining what they conceive to be the proper form of college education, conservative educators often appeal to the Great Tradition of the past as the essential element in college education. Reference is constantly made to the philosophy, art, literature, and religion of the past and to the great part that they have played in our heritage. Education is identified with a knowledge and mastery of the elements of the past, and reform of the elective system is found to lie in the reestablishment of those studies which deal principally with the past. In keeping with philosophical idealism, it is thought that there are certain eternal and absolute elements in the past that every liberally educated person should know, and the assumption is made that the world and man are essentially dualistic in nature. Many conservative educators have firmly expressed their allegiance to these two characteristics of *absolutism* and *dualism* in the tradition of Western civilization, and it is in adherence to them that the essential nature of college education is found.

President Nicholas Murray Butler of Columbia University has been outstanding in his affirmation of the importance of tradition and in his criticism of more recent philosophical positions that do not seem to fit in with the Great Tradition. In his annual report for 1925–1926, he stated clearly his adherence to philosophical idealism and his opposition to the philosophy of science and experimentalism when he said:

It is plain enough that the most popular of present-day philosophical teachings do not aid us when we reflect upon these great questions [such as the nature of truth]. But these pseudo-philosophies are having their little day and will shortly pass. The Great Tradition will again assert itself and the current of intellectual and spiritual understanding and appreciation will be found to flow unbroken from the classic springs and sources of insight and interpretation down to the time in which we live, and once again to assert its commanding power and to make manifest its lofty inspiration.[1]

In another connection, President Butler expressed his scorn of a philosophy that tries to accept modern science:

The problem is gravely complicated by the odd-assortment of anti-philosophies which, attempting to wear the garb of philosophy and using its nomenclature, just now occupy a considerable portion of the academic stage. These anti-philosophies are the product of minds that have never really grasped the meaning of the word philosophy or the significance of philosophy itself. They either confuse philosophy with psychology, after the fashion of John Locke or William James, or they look upon it as a more or less ornamental appendage of the natural

---

[1] EDWARD C. ELLIOT, ed., *The Rise of a University*, Vol. II, *The University in Action* (Columbia University Press, New York, 1937), p. 32.

and experimental sciences. They appear to have no conception of the fundamental fact first discovered and made irrefutably clear by Plato and Aristotle nearly twenty-five hundred years ago, that there are three distinct stages or orders of thinking manifested by man.[1]

When President Butler goes on to say that the three levels of thinking are common sense, the science of change, and the philosophic view of the world as totality, he reveals that he believes philosophy proper has to do with those eternal and absolute principles so long represented by Plato and traditional idealism. Thus, the liberally educated man, according to President Butler, is one who identifies himself with the philosophical idealism of the Great Tradition rather than with the "pseudo-philosophies" of experimental science.

Other forthright expressions of loyalty to tradition are found in the writings of such professors as Albert Jay Nock (formerly of Columbia) and Hartley Burr Alexander of Scripps College in California. On the lecture platform, Professor Nock has reiterated his conviction that the college should emphasize the Great Tradition for those few students who are educable:

We can do nothing for the Great Tradition; our fidelity to it can do everything for us. Creatures of a day, how shall we think that what we do or leave undone is of consequence to that which abides forever? . . . The Great Tradition is independent of us, not we of it.[2]

Although Professor Nock is rather pessimistic about the return of American society to the Great Tradition, his allegiance remains strong to the eternal and absolute verities that it can convey to any contemporary society that will nourish it.

In a symposium on higher education published in 1930, Professor Alexander stated clearly his confession of faith in the culture of Europe.[3] He pointed out that Scripps College was founded in 1927 to make more familiar the sense of the Tradition and to keep strong the "linkage with the sustaining Past." He believed firmly that the Tradition, that is, humane letters, cannot be displaced without lapsing into barbarism:

. . . there is an imperishable center [of learning] Classical and Biblical, Medieval and Renaissance, whose forgetting means our present relapse into barbarism; and at all costs this is to preserve . . . [4]

[1] *Ibid.*, p. 325.

[2] ALBERT JAY NOCK, *The Theory of Education in the United States* (Harcourt, Brace & Company, Inc., New York, 1932), pp. 155–156.

[3] PAUL ARTHUR SCHILPP, ed., *Higher Education Faces the Future* (Liveright Publishing Company, New York, 1930), p. 31.

[4] *Ibid.*, pp. 45.

Two more very recent statements will suffice to illustrate the respect held by conservative educators for the authoritative, controlling, and unchanging character of the tradition.   President Henry M. Wriston, formerly of Lawrence College and now of Brown University, cautioned in his recent book against taking change and experiments too seriously, for he felt that change is too much with us.   Modern methods of communication merely make the *appearance* of material change more pronounced, whereas, "On the other hand, changes in the nonmaterial, in the intangible, in the mental and spiritual life, cannot be so rapid."[1]

In other words, President Wriston believes that practices change but principles abide and that therefore the liberal college should hold to relatively unchanging principles and theories and discard the blueprints of social planners who are concerned more with materialism as a philosophy of change than with idealism as a philosophy of permanence:

The prophets of change speak almost wholly in terms of a raw materialism. It is under the impulse of materialism that they would turn education away from the discipline of the mind, the cultivation of the emotions, and the freedom of the spirit to training in techniques.[2]

In repudiating the philosophy of change, President Wriston points to the past to show that Dewey does not surpass Socrates as a teacher, no one approaches Jesus as an ethical leader, no poetry or art is so good as that of the Greeks, and no modern logician has reasoned so clearly or cogently as Aristotle.   Therefore, he reasons, "These instances remind us that there are certain unchanging fundamentals in education."[2]

Professor Norman Foerster of the University of Iowa is perhaps the most outstanding recent exponent of the doctrine of New Humanism, and he presents a clear-cut expression of faith in the unequivocal authority of tradition and of the philosophical position of dualism in education:

The background of the old American liberal education, *and of any new liberal education we may hereafter seek to set up*, is the humanistic and religious tradition which governed the culture of Europe prior to the seventeenth century and then gradually declined in prestige, though to this day it retains a vitality that is commonly underestimated.[3]

It is clear that Professor Foerster looks to the past and that he rejects the philosophy of science and experimental naturalism: "Liberal

---

[1] HENRY M. WRISTON, *The Nature of a Liberal College* (Lawrence College Press, Appleton, Wis., 1937), p. 129.

[2] *Ibid.*, p. 140.

[3] NORMAN FOERSTER, *The American State University* (University of North Carolina Press, Chapel Hill, N. C., 1937), p. 202.   [Italics mine.]

education cannot be achieved by naturalism."[1] He admits that liberal education based upon Humanism and tradition is far stronger in Europe than in the United States, and it is also evident to him that it will be difficult to revive in America.[2]

Foerster also follows in the tradition of Irving Babbitt, Paul Elmer More, and other Humanists when he stoutly affirms the duality of existence. In 1930, Foerster edited a symposium on Humanism in which Irving Babbitt among others not only paid his respects to the Great Tradition but also expressed his faith in the supernatural as more important than the natural world. Babbitt stated that Humanism clashes with naturalistic philosophy because the Humanist

. . . requires a centre to which he may refer the manifold of experience; and this the phenomenal world does not supply. In getting his centre the humanist may appeal primarily to tradition, or as I have said, to intuition.[3]

For my own part, I range myself unhesitatingly on the side of the supernaturalists.[4]

Paul Elmer More, in his book published in 1936, called upon Humanism to do battle with naturalism and to emphasize the fact that man has faculties of human nature such as free will and conscience that are superadded and set him off generically from the animals.[5]

Foerster himself states the position of dualism with great clarity in his recent book:

. . . humanism is content to accept, without explanation, the "doubleness" of human existence, experience shared with nature and experience not shared with nature. It is willing to acknowledge two realities, the reality of nature and the reality of the human spirit, without subsuming either under the other. . . . The reality of nature and of man in his purely corporeal existence is suited to scientific investigation; the reality of the human spirit, as we know it in normal experience, is in a realm to which science, because of its initial assumptions, has no access. Today, as in the past, humanism can only accept the paradoxical terms on which

[1] *Ibid.*, p. 244.

[2] A striking example of the continued prominence of Humanism as the guiding philosophy of secondary education in France was given by Célestin Bouglé, director of l'Ecole Normale Supérieure of the University of Paris, when he gave the Julius Sachs lectures at Teachers College, Columbia University, in April, 1938; see Célestin Bouglé, "The French Conception of 'Culture Générale' and Its Influence upon Instruction," *Teachers College Record*, 39: 685–700 (May, 1938).

[3] NORMAN FOERSTER, *Humanism and America* (Farrar & Rinehart, Inc., New York, 1930), p. 32. For an effective refutation of this volume, see the symposium edited by C. Hartley Grattan, *The Critique of Humanism* (Brewer, Warren & Putnam, Inc., New York, 1930).

[4] *Ibid.*, p. 39.

[5] PAUL ELMER MORE, *On Being Human* (Princeton University Press, Princeton, 1936).

we live. . . . To study man as a purposive being by the methods of physics or chemistry is about as inept as to study atoms or elements by the methods of ethics or aesthetics.[1]

For example, Foerster regrets that the study of science has led so many professors and students to the acceptance of naturalistic philosophy, for he does not believe that acceptance of scientific assumptions and methods necessarily lead to naturalism: "A professor of physics or biology, if he is a dualistic Christian, for example, can certainly believe in the supernatural as well as the natural."[2] What all this emphasis upon dualism means for the college is clearly stated by Foerster when he urges that truly liberal studies must be reinstated in the college, and by "truly liberal" he means those studies which the Humanist believes minister to man's inner, spiritual side rather than to his outer, natural side. Those studies which are liberal to the Humanist are, naturally enough, heavily weighted with literary and nonscientific studies of the past.

Although Foerster says that there should be no hostility to science as an expression of the human spirit, nevertheless he makes his major intent clear when he states that the college must stop looking upon man as the mere flux of nature and reassert the inner life of values through the aid of Humanism:

We shall turn to the studies most useful in the furtherance of human as opposed to scientific knowledge. . . . The proper study of mankind is still man, not man as known through a naturalistic psychology (which, so far as it is positive, is really physiology), or through a naturalistic sociology (which views human society as merely a form of animal society), but man as known directly, in his inner life and its manifestations in social and political history, in literature and the arts, in philosophy, in religion.[3]

Foerster makes it further evident that the inner life of values is unchanging because human nature does not change and that therefore humanistic studies that nourish human nature need not change:

Through the ages of recorded history the unity of human nature is so marked that we commonly say there is nothing new under the sun. Those who assert

---

[1] FOERSTER, *American State University*, pp. 216–217.

[2] *Ibid.*, p. 120.

[3] *Ibid.*, p. 243. Attention should be called to the fact that several Humanists have objected to the extreme position of More, Babbitt, and Foerster and have urged that science should not be separated from humanistic studies but that science and scientific studies should be recognized as playing a major role in humanistic thought and education; see, for example, two recent books written for this purpose: George Sarton, *The History of Science and the New Humanism* (Harvard University Press, Cambridge, 1937), and Cassius Jackson Keyser, *Humanism and Science* (Columbia University Press, New York, 1931).

that human nature is going to be different tomorrow are nearly always deficient in knowledge of the past.[1]

Another recent book by Foerster is principally a restatement of his position in which he carries the attack directly to John Dewey and Teachers College as outstanding representatives of all that he considers to be bad for American education and the American college:

I propose to consider the college in relation to the conception of life now dominant in our society, which I take to be materialistic and humanitarian, and in relation to our prevailing philosophy of education, for which John Dewey and Teachers College are largely responsible. In consequence of these forces, as I conceive, the liberal college is threatened with extinction.[2]

Foerster condemns the basing of educational philosophy upon a social philosophy of experimentalism and humanitarianism, and he condemns the program of planning suggested by *The Educational Frontier* (written in part by Teachers College professors). In fact, he states clearly that the college must rigidly forsake all of the important social trends of the last two centuries and return, as a good conservative should, to the great classical and religious tradition of earlier times:

The truth of the matter is, I think, that the liberal college is, with the whole force of its tradition, conservative, out of sympathy with all the extremist tendencies of the present century.[3]

In contrast to the Humanists and other conservatives who have put so much emphasis upon the absolute and stable character of past tradition, the twentieth century witnessed the vigorous statements of progressive-minded educators who have put great emphasis upon the fact of cultural change and the need for flexibility in institutions and outlook. Whereas the conservative educators rested their case upon an underlying philosophy of idealism and dualism, the progressives tended more and more to rest theirs upon a philosophy of scientific and experimental naturalism which posits the essential continuity between human nature and the rest of nature. This position has been discussed at some length in the preceding sections, and greater attention will be devoted to it in following chapters. Hence, reference will be made at this point merely to a few outstanding individuals who have gradually gained a following among American educators. These educators have been constantly looking more to the present than to the past, and they have looked upon the past tradition not so much with reverence for its authority as for

---

[1] FOERSTER, *American State University*, p. 219.

[2] NORMAN FOERSTER, *The Future of the Liberal College* (D. Appleton-Century Company, Inc., New York, 1938), p. v.

[3] *Ibid.*, p. 4

its use in helping to explain our culture and to help in guiding the revision of our institutions and beliefs.

Professor John Dewey of Columbia University has undoubtedly been preeminent in his leadership in this direction from the turn of the century to the present time. Attack upon absolutes and upon the dualisms has been a part of Dewey's educational program from the time of the publication of his influential *Democracy and Education* in 1916 down to his recent books *Experience and Education* and *Logic, the Theory of Inquiry*, in 1938. His famous dictum that "education is life" and that students must be concerned with present-day life rather than solely with the past or with the future indicates his revolt against the authority of tradition in education and his insistence upon flexibility and change in educational as well as other social institutions. He has emphasized many times over that education is a continuous reconstruction of present experience and not merely a preparation for the future or a mere unfolding of the individual's powers or external formation of his powers through discipline or a recapitulation of the past.[1]

Besides his attacks upon the absolutisms of the past, Dewey has constantly attacked the traditional dualisms that have tended to interfere with necessary revisions of educational practices. Many times he has pointed out how the class distinctions of ancient Greece and Rome tended to solidify dualisms between intellectual and manual activities, between leisure and labor, and between cultural and vocational activities. As these social dualisms carried over into the realms of knowledge, truth, beauty, and reality, there arose the long continuing dichotomies between theory and practice, between fixed, absolute truth and the flux of things and the whole separation of reality into a higher realm of spirit and mind and a lower realm of matter and body. Dewey has long been insistent that these dualisms no longer should have a place in a world that has developed such intellectual tools as science for dealing with all kinds of problems and that has developed the ideal of democracy where no class barriers should prevent the free flow of ideas and interest among the whole population.

The conception of *continuity* has therefore been developed to combat the traditional conception of duality. Intellectual concerns must no longer be merely "things of the mind" but must be used as tools for the betterment of social relationships and social institutions. The progressives believe that evidence from biology and psychology make it no longer tenable to speak of an absolute separation of mind *from* body, man *from* nature, and ideas *from* practical experience. What all this means for the liberal college can best be made clear in the second part of the next

[1] JOHN DEWEY, *Democracy and Education* (The Macmillan Company, New York, 1916), Chaps. I–VI.

chapter, where it will be pointed out that students must constantly be grappling with present-day problems and trying to solve them with all the techniques and evidence available to modern man.

Although many other educators could be cited here,[1] attention will be called only to one more whose influence has been great and whose recent statement is so timely and pertinent here. Professor Boyd H. Bode of Ohio State University has recently published a book entitled *Progressive Education at the Crossroads* in which he urges the progressive education movement to become the explicit exponent of the democratic way of life. Bode finds the most characteristic element in democracy to be its constant opposition to absolutes of all kinds. He points again to the historical cleavage between intellectual and practical affairs which arose out of aristocratic class conceptions wherein the leisure class tried to justify its absorption in nonpractical pursuits by referring to absolute and final Truth. He serves notice on progressive education that it must forsake the absolutism and aristocracy of tradition and become the proper educational system for democracy.

This means, among other things, to Bode that values must not be considered as fixed and as handed down from the past but must be centered in the improvement of human living through the constant widening of common concerns and common interests and through the continuous and frequently extensive reconstruction or revision of traditional beliefs and attitudes in accordance with growing insight and changing circumstances. It means also that man's future lies in his own hands and that ethical and aesthetic principles have not been irrevocably deduced from the inherent structure of things but are created and recreated by man himself. When Bode suggests that it is no wonder that college students have not been interested in the musty smell of "intellectual" interests that do not relate to life, his implication is, of course, that college education should be more closely related to life and to present-day living. This point leads us directly into the next type of controversy.

---

[1] See especially JOHN L. CHILDS, *Education and the Philosophy of Experimentalism* (D. Appleton-Century Company, Inc., New York, 1931).

CHAPTER XVI

INTELLECTUALISM VERSUS INTELLIGENCE

Just as the conservative followers of the Great Tradition have adhered to an underlying philosophy of idealism, so have they adhered to a theory of knowledge and a psychology that, if not identical with the traditional faculty psychology of discipline, at least tends to emphasize the intellectual function as something distinct from the other activities of human beings. Of the two realms of life that dualism posits, the conservatives definitely prefer the realm of mind as opposed to that of body or matter; they identify education with development of the mind and tend to neglect the other aspects of human activity. Their psychology prompts them to extol the benefits of such activities as "intellectual training," "cultivation of the intellect," "intellectual power," or "mental discipline." In their writings, there is much emphasis upon return to "first principles," or "fundamental concerns," and closer investigation usually reveals that they are implying studies that are highly traditional and highly bookish.

There seem to be three crucial points at which the conservative emphasis upon "intellectualism" differs from the position of the progressive reliance upon an experimentalist theory of knowledge. (1) The intellectualists appear to hold that there is a separate faculty of intellect, or reason, which is somehow capable of reaching out and grasping truth. (2) Truth in its ultimate form is considered to be absolute and fixed and serves to give order to such lower forms of knowledge as scientific knowledge of the physical world and empirical knowledge of practical affairs. (3) In their adherence to fixed truth of an intellectual character, the intellectualists stoutly maintain the superiority and purity of intellectual affairs and maintain that intellectual matters in the college should remain free of defilement by worldly matters. Hence, the intellectualists definitely deprecate the knowledge to be attained through the natural sciences.

On the other hand, the experimentalists hold that the natural sciences, the experimental method, and the role of experience must be at the very center of any adequate theory of knowledge. Hence, they deny the notion of a separate faculty of intellect and deny the notion of a fixed truth. They believe that all knowledge or truth worthy of the name is attained by human "intelligence" which grows out of the scientific method; reliance upon "operational" truths; and a close connection between knowledge and practical, active affairs. The conservatives say that the college should develop the powers of the intellect, whereas the progressives say that the college must aid students to develop a "problem-solving" technique closely akin to the scientific method. In both cases, the elective system comes in for criticism.

"INTELLECTUALISM" AND PRESIDENT HUTCHINS

The most forceful and outstanding exponent of the position of intellectualism in the last few years has been President Robert M. Hutchins of the University of Chicago. Through many written and oral utterances, President Hutchins has insisted that the way out of higher education's chaos and confusion is a return to the fundamental principles and truths of the intellect: "A university education must chiefly be directed to inculcating the intellectual virtues, and these are the product of vigorous intellectual effort. Such effort is the indispensable constituent of a university course of study."[1]

President Hutchins has spoken much of the intellectual virtues, but he has not defined them very closely except in the series of lectures given at Yale University in 1936 and published in his book entitled *The Higher Learning in America*. In that book, he analyzes what he believes are the faults of higher education. First, an "anti-intellectualism" grows out of an excessive love of money and leads to reliance upon the tricks of the trade of a trivial vocationalism; second, a false theory of democracy believes that everyone has the ability to be educated; and, third, a false notion of progress believes that science and technology can point the way to social improvement:

At last the whole structure of the university collapsed and the final victory of empiricism was won when the social sciences, law, and even philosophy and theology themselves became empirical and experimental and progressive. . . . We begin, then, with a notion of progress and end with an anti-intellectualism which denies, in effect, that man is a rational animal.[2]

Inasmuch as an anti-intellectual university is a contradiction in terms, Hutchins argues that we must set up a general education which will embrace the years now devoted to the last two years of secondary school and the first two of college. This general education will combat specialism and give a common intellectual training and a common stock of fundamental ideas to all by cultivating the intellectual virtues. To

[1] ROBERT M. HUTCHINS, *No Friendly Voice* (University of Chicago Press, Chicago, 1936), p. 30.

[2] ROBERT M. HUTCHINS, *The Higher Learning in America* (Yale University Press, New Haven, 1936), p. 26.

define the intellectual virtues, Hutchins quotes approvingly the definitions given in the thirteenth century by St. Thomas Aquinas in the tradition of Aristotle.   In other words, Hutchins says that there are three virtues of the *speculative intellect* in the order of ascending importance: intuitive knowledge to develop the habit of induction; scientific knowledge to develop the habit of demonstration (which thus excludes experience and practice); and, the highest of all, philosophical wisdom or metaphysics to achieve first principles and first causes.

Hutchins also refers to the two virtues of the *practical intellect* which are definitely in a lower order of things and which receive their authority from the higher intellectual virtues; these practical virtues are: art, which is the capacity to make according to the true course of reasoning; and prudence, which is right reason with respect to action.   That Hutchins deprecates the natural and social sciences and the whole realm of experience is indicated in the latter part of his book, where he indicates that the natural and social sciences are subordinate to the first principles of speculative philosophy and metaphysics and derive their theoretical principles from metaphysics.[1]

After establishing what he means by the intellectual virtues, President Hutchins goes on to illustrate how they can be translated into college education so as to cultivate the intellect and, incidentally, reform the elective system.   His own words are so vivid and to the point that some of them will be quoted in order to bring out his conceptions of a fixed human nature, fixed truth, and consequently a fixed and permanent course of study which should be required of all students in college. Opposition to the progressive notions of operational truth, of close relation of knowledge to practical and social affairs, and of a flexible curriculum are revealed at many points.

To help controvert the arguments of progressives who stress social change and the necessity of educating students for change, President Hutchins quotes not only St. Thomas Aquinas but also Plato, Aristotle, Cardinal Newman, and the humanist Paul Shorey to show that fixity and permanence are the rules of intellectual and proper college affairs:

One purpose of education is to draw out the elements of our common human nature.   These elements are the same in any time and place.   The notion of educating a man to live in any particular time or place, to adjust him to any particular environment, is therefore foreign to a true conception of education. . . . Education implies teaching.   Teaching implies knowledge.   Knowledge is truth.   The truth is everywhere the same.   Hence education should be everywhere the same. . . . I suggest that the heart of any course of study designed for the whole people will be, if education is rightly understood, the same at any time, in any place, under any political, social, or economic conditions.   Even

---

[1] *Ibid.*, pp. 100–108.

the administrative details are likely to be similar because all societies have generic similarity. . . . If education is rightly understood, it will be understood as the cultivation of the intellect. The cult of the intellect is the same good for all men in all societies.[1]

President Hutchins' disdain for things practical and his isolation of intellectual matters from everyday life are indicated as follows:

In general education, therefore, we may wisely leave experience to life and set about our job of intellectual training. . . . If there are permanent studies which every person who wishes to call himself educated should master, if those studies constitute our intellectual inheritance, then those studies should be the center of a general education.[2]

Notice his recommendation that permanent, prescribed studies should take the place of elective studies and his condemnation of the doctrine of student interests:

But educators cannot permit the students to dictate the course of study unless they are prepared to confess that they are nothing but chaperons, supervising an aimless, trial-and-error process which is chiefly valuable because it keeps young people from doing something worse. The free elective system as Mr. Eliot introduced it at Harvard and as Progressive Education adapted it to lower age levels amounted to a denial that there was content to education. Since there was no content to education, we might as well let students follow their own bent. . . . It cannot be assumed that students at any age will always select the subjects that constitute education. . . . In any field the permanent studies on which the whole development of the subject rests must be mastered if the student is to be educated. . . . If we are educators we must have a rational, defensible one. If that subject matter is education, we cannot alter it to suit the whims of parents, students, or the public.[3]

President Hutchins goes on to define what he believes the permanent studies to be, and in the process he reveals again his reliance upon the seven liberal arts of the Middle Ages, the rationalistic idealism of the Great Tradition, and a faculty psychology of formal discipline. The permanent studies consist of the reading of "classic" books of the past and the study of formal grammar, rhetoric, logic, and mathematics:

They [permanent studies] are in the first place those books which have through the centuries attained to the dimensions of classics. Many such books, I am

[1] *Ibid.*, pp. 66–67. Professor Mortimer Adler has supported these conceptions of human nature and knowledge in his book *What Man Has Made of Man* (Longmans, Green & Company, New York, 1938) and in his article "The Crisis in Contemporary Education," *Social Frontier*, 5: 140–145 (February, 1939). For an effective reply to Adler, see John Pilley, "The Liberal Arts and Progressive Education," *Social Frontier*, 5: 211–216 (April, 1939).

[2] HUTCHINS, *The Higher Learning in America*, p. 70.

[3] *Ibid.*, pp. 70–73.

afraid, are in the ancient and medieval period.   But even these are contemporary.
A classic is a book that is contemporary in any age.   That is why it is a classic.
. . . Such books are then a part, and a large part, of the permanent studies.   They
are so in the first place because they are the best books we know. . . . In the
second place these books are an essential part of general education because it is
impossible to understand any subject or to comprehend the contemporary world
without them.[1]

In order to read books one must know how to do it. . . . Grammar is the
scientific analysis of language through which we understand the meaning and
force of what is written.   Grammar disciplines the mind and develops the logical
faculty.   It is good in itself and as an aid to reading the classics.   It has a
place in general education in connection with the classics and independently of
them.   For those who are going to learn from books learning the art of reading
would seem to be indispensable.[2]

I add to grammar, or the rules of reading, rhetoric and logic, or the rules of
writing, speaking, and reasoning.   The classics provide models of excellence;
grammar, rhetoric, and logic are means of determining how excellence is achieved.
We have forgotten that there are rules for speaking. . . . Logic is a statement
in technical form of the conditions under which reasoning is rigorously demon-
strative.   If the object of general education is to train the mind for intelligent
action, logic cannot be missing from it.[3]

It remains only to add a study which exemplifies reasoning in its clearest and
most precise form.   That study is, of course, mathematics, and of the mathematical studies chiefly those that use the type of exposition which Euclid
employed.   In such studies the pure operation of reason is made manifest.   The
subject matter depends on the universal and necessary processes of human
thought.   It is not affected by differences in taste, disposition, or prejudice. . . .
Correctness in thinking may be more directly and impressively taught through
mathematics than in any other way.[4]

One final quotation is given to summarize Hutchins' proposals and
to indicate his belief that this curriculum will fulfill all the aims of general
education in the United States:

We have then for general education a course of study consisting of the greatest
books of the western world and the arts of reading, writing, thinking, and speaking, together with mathematics, the best exemplar of the processes of human
reason.   If our hope has been to frame a curriculum which educes the elements
of our common human nature, this program should realize our hope.   If we wish
to prepare the young for intelligent action, this course of study should assist us;
for they will have learned what has been done in the past, and what the greatest
men have thought.   They will have learned how to think themselves.   If we
wish to lay a basis for advanced study, that basis is provided.   If we wish to

[1] *Ibid.*, pp. 78–79.

[2] *Ibid.*, p. 82.

[3] *Ibid.*, p. 83.   Notice the great similarity of thought and even of language
between the foregoing statements and the Yale Faculty Report of 1828, pp. 118*ff.*

[4] *Ibid.*, pp. 83–84.

secure true universities, we may look forward to them, because students and professors may acquire through this course of study a common stock of ideas and common methods of dealing with them. *All the needs of general education in America seem to be satisfied by this curriculum.*[1]

Through these lengthy quotations, President Hutchins surely reveals himself ranged upon the side of the conservatives who partakę of a strong tradition in American education and who look steadily to the distant past for philosophical, psychological, and educational guidance. One cannot refrain from commenting here that if President Hutchins and his intellectualistic followers had looked more carefully at the more recent past of college education, they would have found sufficient warnings against the tendency to set up for all time a fixed college curriculum to suit all the needs that they can forsee. The controversies of the eighteenth and nineteenth centuries which have been discussed in earlier chapters have given adequate warning that social trends do not respect the desires of conservative-minded college educators.

"INTELLIGENCE" AND THE EXPERIMENTALISTS

Attention must now be given in more detail to the progressive philosophy of experimentalism which President Butler has termed "pseudo-philosophy," President Hutchins has condemned as "anti-intellectual," and President Angell has found "feeble and unpromising." The position of experimentalism has constantly grown in influence and in ability to combat the conservative philosophy of rationalism, largely through the growing adherence of more and more educators to the leadership of such men as John Dewey, William H. Kilpatrick, John L. Childs, and Boyd H. Bode. Many other individuals could be cited, but only those will be selected who seem to have particular pertinence for the field of college education. Although differences of viewpoint are found among the educators in the progressive camp (as is also the case within the conservative group), certain general ideas run through nearly all of the statements of their philosophy and serve to illustrate their common opposition to the conservative notions that have been described above.

Professor Dewey has been the spearhead of attack throughout the period of the twentieth century with which we are concerned here, and his statements have been so voluminous that only a few can be selected for citation here. In his widely influential book *Democracy and Education*, published in 1916, Dewey emphasized the importance of science and of scientific method as central in the governing of human affairs of all kinds. In the scientific method, he found principles of procedure that gave him a clue to a conception of experience, knowledge, and thinking widely at variance with the notion of a separate faculty of intellect

[1] *Ibid.*, p. 85. [Italics mine.]

held by the conservatives.   His theory closely associates knowledge and
thinking with action and with the consequences of action; knowledge
and action are definitely not separated into two antagonistic spheres, as
in the intellectualistic doctrine.   Knowledge does not become the grasping of *a priori* principles fixed in advance but consists in understanding
the conditions and consequences of events of all kinds.   Truth, or true
knowledge, is not merely recognition of eternal general principles but
depends upon the verification of consequences.   Ideas are not something separate from action but are tentative hypotheses or plans of action
to be tested by their ability to make good through the consequences of
acting upon them.

Translating these notions into a specific theory of knowledge, Dewey
arrived at a description of thinking that rests upon the scientific method
of problem solving.   In other words, problem solving becomes the method
of human *intelligence* in the conduct and control of human affairs as
opposed to the intellectual methods which the conservatives identify
with distinctively "human" qualities.   Mind becomes not a separate
faculty for dealing with "Ideas" but the name given to human activities
that approach experience intelligently with the intent to remake human
experience and to accomplish real changes in events with the purpose
of improving and enriching human life and enjoyment.   Thinking as
problem solving thus takes on the famous formulation that Dewey gave
it.   It involves four steps: a sense of a disturbance, or *problem*, to be
solved; *observation* of the conditions surrounding the problem; formulation of suggested *hypotheses*, or *plans of action*, with their possible consequences if acted upon; actual and active experimental *testing* to see if the
hypotheses when acted upon give the desired consequences.[1]

Then, basing educational method upon the process of thinking, as
outlined above, Dewey comes to the following implications for education:
The student must be in the center of genuine situations of experience
and continuously engaged in activities in which he is interested when
the *problem* appears to confront him as a genuine stimulus to thought.
He must possess or obtain the proper information to make *observations*
that are necessary for dealing with the problem.   Suggested solutions,
or *hypotheses*, must occur to him, and he must be responsible for developing them in an orderly way.   Finally, he must have the opportunity
and the occasion to *test* his ideas by applying them in practice in order
to make their meaning clear and to discover for himself their validity.
Thus, educational method really consists of the method of thinking made
conscious and realized in action.   Just as the experimental method of
thinking links theory closely with action and insists that thinking is a

[1] John Dewey, *Democracy and Education* (The Macmillan Company, New York,
1916), Chap. XI.

process of intelligently remaking experience, so education becomes a process that links theory closely with action and insists that educational method and subject matter are not distinct but are closely unified in the process of remaking experience.[1]

Dewey indicated the implications of this method of experimental thinking, for the curriculum in general and for reform of the elective system in particular, in his Inglis lectures at Harvard in 1931. One of the alternatives to the organization of subjects according to the traditional divisions and classifications or knowledge is the so-called "project," or "problem," or "situation" method mentioned above. In the traditional procedure, a relatively fixed and isolated body of knowledge is assumed in advance; whereas in the project, "material is drawn from any field as it is needed to carry on an intellectual enterprise."[2] The central question, or problem, acts as a magnet so that material is drawn from a variety of fields when needed, and educational organization consists in noting the bearing and function of the things acquired in much the same way that things are studied outside college or school. In contrast, the traditional organization of the elective system consists of formal requirements within a particular field as devised by the expert who has mastered the subject.

Furthermore, intellectual activity does not consist of memorizing bits of ready-made subject matter that are handed out but of reaching out and returning with whatever is relevant to the problem in hand, of making constant judgments to detect relationships, and of absorption of an eager kind to assimilate the knowledge found and to get the problem solved for purposes of action. In this way, the student is often overtly active in applying his knowledge, constructing things of all kinds, and expressing himself in new ways:

The outcome is continuously growing intellectual integration. . . . He puts his knowledge to the test of operation. Naturally, he does something with what he learns.[3]

Dewey sees these elements in the project method as the indispensable aims in all study and believes that they are desirable objects of experimentation in secondary school and college.

Besides the experimentalist's critique of conservative notions of knowledge and fixed truth as outlined above, the experimentalists made a frontal attack upon the theory of the separation of knowledge from action as held by the conservatives. This attack culminated in 1933 in a book written by several experimentalists and edited by Professor

[1] *Ibid.*, Chaps. XII–XIV.
[2] JOHN DEWEY, *The Way Out of Educational Confusion* (Harvard University Press, Cambridge, 1931), p. 32.
[3] *Ibid.*, pp. 34–35.

William H. Kilpatrick of Teachers College, Columbia University. Particularly in the last chapter, which was written jointly by Professors Dewey and John L. Childs, traditional philosophies of idealism and rationalism are criticized because they have isolated knowledge from action and practice:

Speaking in general terms, life is characterized by a gap between knowledge and conduct, by separation between theory and practice. This divorce between the two is "rationalized" in the philosophies which have hitherto been most influential in thought. These have glorified knowledge as an end in itself, something divine, superior to the vicissitudes of experience, while at the same time they have depreciated the importance of action, connecting it with a realm of existence which is transitory, related to the body and material interests rather than to mind and ideal things, connected with mundane affairs instead of with pure truth.[1]

Dewey and Childs go on to indicate how modern science has provided a method of knowing and acting that unites knowledge with action and does away with the dualisms of the traditional philosophies:

The development of the natural sciences since the seventeenth century has demonstrated the falsity of the idea that reason and thought apart from action can issue in valid knowledge. The primary bond of union of thought with existence or "reality" is action. These statements do not rest upon opinion but upon the observed fact that the progress of natural knowledge has been made constant and secure only by the adoption of the experimental method. Thought *suggests* a course and way of acting so as to effect a change of conditions. The execution of the procedure which is suggested effects consequences which enable the validity of the idea to be judged and which bring about its further development. In this way thought is converted into authentic knowledge.[2]

In this view, ideas do not become general principles which are merely there to be grasped by the intellect but are framed in a form that points to acts to be performed and interpretations to be put upon the consequences of those acts. In this way, the criterion for the operation of thinking and the development of ideas is not the position of fixed ideas in a hierarchy of values with metaphysics at the top and action at the bottom but consists in the relevancy of ideas for use in action:

Think in terms of action and in terms of *those* acts whose consequences will expand, revise, test, your ideas and theories. This is the first commandment of the experimental method. It is by observation of this commandment that thinking, inquiry, observation, and interpretation have been rendered fruitful in progressive knowledge of nature.[3]

[1] W. H. KILPATRICK, ed., *The Educational Frontier* (D. Appleton-Century Company, Inc., New York, 1933), p. 299.
[2] *Ibid.*, p. 305.
[3] *Ibid.*

The experimentalists point to the progress of inventions and technology as evidence of the practicability of the experimental method in control of nature, and they urge that something of the same sort should be extended to the area of social and human affairs. Although they recognize marked differences between the experimental method in physical and that in human affairs, the experimentalists believe that the method of defining a problem, observing pertinent conditions, suggesting hypotheses, and testing of the hypotheses will prove the most profitable for revising and improving traditional beliefs in social and educational affairs that man has yet devised.

To sum up this discussion of the progressive approach to the question of intelligence, attention is called to the most recent restatement of the progressive philosophy by Professor Dewey. In the Kappa Delta Pi lectures for 1938, published under the title *Experience and Education*, Dewey calls attention to the controversies that have been raging between traditional and progressive education, and he reasserts his faith in an education based upon a well-defined philosophy of experience:

I assume that amid all uncertainties there is one permanent frame of reference: namely, the organic connection between education and personal experience; or, that the new philosophy of education is committed to some kind of empirical and experimental philosophy.[1]

Whereas traditional education has relied upon such terms as "culture," "discipline," and "heritage" to cover up its reliance upon custom and existing practices, Dewey firmly believes that progressive education must formulate a social philosophy of education based squarely upon experience. Only in this way can human intelligence be adequately released through education to deal with the pressing problems of society.

Dewey attacks not only the traditionalists who have expressed too great reverence for the past but also the extremists among the progressives who tend to ignore the past.   To be sure, he makes it clear that we must study the past but says we must study it in such a way that it contributes to our understanding of the present.   Intelligence is not developed by starting with the past and selecting traditional subject matter on the basis of the judgment of adults as to what will be useful for the young in the future.   Intelligence can be developed only by starting with the experiences of the young and leading them to a study of the past as the best means of understanding and approaching the problems of the present:

. . . the achievements of the past provide the only means at command for understanding the present.   Just as the individual has to draw in memory upon his

[1] JOHN DEWEY, *Experience and Education* (The Macmillan Company, New York, 1938), pp. 12–13.

own past to understand the conditions in which he individually finds himself, so the issues and problems of present *social* life are in such intimate and direct connection with the past that students cannot be prepared to understand either these problems or the best way of dealing with them without delving into their roots in the past.[1]

To the extremists who would ignore the past, Dewey replies by insisting that the nature of economic, social, and political problems cannot be understood except as we know how they came about; but to the reactionaries who would say that the main business of education is to transmit the cultural heritage, Dewey also replies by insisting that the past must be used merely as a means for knowing the present better: "The way out of scholastic systems that made the past an end in itself is to make acquaintance with the past a *means* of understanding the present."[2]

Referring directly to the reactionary requirements of the traditionalists who would go back to the intellectual organizations of an earlier era, Dewey states that unless the problem of intellectual organization can be worked out on the basis of experience, the reaction will be able to grow and to impose upon education the external methods of organization of the past. Our only alternatives, according to Dewey, are either a return to the intellectual methods and ideals of the centuries before science was developed or else a direct use of the scientific method. He recognizes that appeal to the past is great during times of insecurity and desire to lean on authority, but he says:

Nevertheless, it is so out of touch with all the conditions of modern life that I believe it is folly to seek salvation in this direction. The other alternative is systematic utilization of scientific method as the pattern and ideal of intelligent exploration and exploitation of the potentialities inherent in experience.[3]

Dewey criticizes the traditionalists for saying that science does not deal with "Ideas"; for he believes that if the nature of ideas is understood correctly, the scientific method will be found to put more reliance upon them than any other method. If ideas are looked upon as hypotheses to be tested, then ideas and the testing of ideas will be most jealously guarded in the hands of science. In concluding *Experience and Education*, Dewey once again expresses his reliance upon the methods of science as "the only authentic means at our command for getting at the significance of our everyday experiences of the world in which we live."[4] Dewey finds both the radicals and the conservatives dissatisfied with

---

[1] *Ibid.*, p. 93.
[2] *Ibid.*, p. 94.
[3] *Ibid.*, p. 108.
[4] *Ibid.*, p. 111.

modern education, but they propose different ways out: "The educational system must move one way or another, either backward to the intellectual and moral standards of a pre-scientific age or forward to ever greater utilization of scientific method in the development of the possibilities of growing, expanding experience."[1]

THE HUTCHINS CONTROVERSY

Although Dewey does not, in *Experience and Education*, refer by name to any of the "traditionalists," there is unmistakable evidence that his argument pointed to the position of President Hutchins. In fact, he had replied specifically to Hutchins at an earlier time; carrying the argument directly into the field of college education, a spirited controversy was waged for two or three years following the publication, in 1936, of Hutchins' book. Among the many replies that were made to the conservative position of President Hutchins (see also pages 345 *n.* and 376 *n.*), the one offered by Professor Dewey himself and another by a member of President Hutchins' own faculty at the University of Chicago, Professor Harry D. Gideonse, are most pertinent here.

In the columns of the *Social Frontier* from December, 1936, to March, 1937, Dewey and Hutchins carried the controversy back and forth in such a way that the opposing views met head on with an impact seldom found in educational discussions. Dewey began the discussion in the first article by pointing out the differences between the conceptions contained in Hutchins' *The Higher Learning in America* and those contained in the *Retreat from Reason* by Lancelot Hogben, an English scientist. Dewey indicated that whereas Hutchins looked to Plato, Aristotle, and Aquinas for his conceptions of reason, Hogben looked to the activities of experimental science to discover its nature.[2]

Dewey then went on to show what implications these differing conceptions of reason had for three important aspects of higher education: the constitution of human nature, the relation of theory and action, and the methods of operation of reason. Whereas Hutchins looked upon human nature as fixed, constant, and the same at any time and place, Hogben found the common qualities of human nature in human *needs;* and although such needs as food, shelter, and reproduction are the same in the abstract, they always change in the concrete, and the means of satisfying them change with every change in science, technology, and social institutions. Whereas Hutchins looked upon reason as related to pure theory and hence undefilable by the action involved in technical and vocational education, Hogben believed that reason, knowledge, and

---

[1] *Ibid.*, pp. 113–114.
[2] JOHN DEWEY, "Rationality in Education," *Social Frontier*, 3: 71–73 (December, 1936).

science must be put into useful action in order to serve human needs, and he quoted such men as Francis Bacon, Robert Boyle, and Thomas Huxley to indicate the usefulness of science in action.

Finally, whereas Hutchins conceived of *the* truth as somehow *there* merely to be apprehended and learned by the intellect as embodied in permanent as opposed to progressive studies, Hogben conceived of truth and knowledge as constantly being worked out in the framework of socially useful action.   Thus, Hogben believed that students would obtain more knowledge in a significant way and have a better grasp of truth if the facts acquired in school and college had some intimate connection with basic social needs, with the resources available for satisfying those needs, and with an understanding of the reactionary forces that prevent these resources from being used.   So he called for *more science* and *better taught science,* inasmuch as the very methods of getting knowledge are best exemplified in such progressive studies as the natural sciences and the scientific advances made in the course of human history.

In his second article, Dewey concentrated on Hutchins' position and stated many of the criticisms that have already been indicated in the previous pages devoted to the progressive position. He found that Hutchins' belief in fixed and eternal principles that are not to be questioned and his insistence that higher education should remain aloof from contemporary social life lead to an authoritarian position which distrusts freedom and which makes it pertinent to ask who shall decide what the first principles are. Dewey believes that it is not enough to say that Plato or Aristotle or the Church has already worked out the principles, because, although they may have worked out creative solutions for their own times, their solutions are no longer applicable to ours. Higher education rather should do for our present confused society what Plato and Aristotle and Aquinas did for theirs; but we cannot accept their solutions as suitable for our society, because science has changed so much within itself and in our civilization. Further, the Hutchins position is weak logically and psychologically because students do not learn so well when acquiring pre-existent truths as they do when they are making truths over for themselves. Dewey decided that: "President Hutchins' contempt for science as merely empirical perhaps accounts for his complete acceptance of the doctrine of formal discipline."[1]

In addition to Dewey's criticisms of Hutchins, the most direct frontal attack upon the philosophical implications of Hutchins' conserva-

---

[1] JOHN DEWEY, "President Hutchins' Proposals to Remake Higher Education," *Social Frontier*, 3: 103–104 (January, 1937). Hutchins replied to Dewey in the February issue of the *Social Frontier*, 3: 137–139, but Dewey felt that the reply had so far evaded the fundamental points raised that he concluded his final article in March, 1938, with the question, "Was President Hutchins Serious?" 3: 167–169.

tive position came from Harry D. Gideonse who was professor of the social sciences in the college of the University of Chicago. In 1937, Professor Gideonse published a book entitled *Higher Learning in a Democracy* in which he insisted that American higher education must not return to the intellectual position of the Great Tradition but must be based upon the modern mind, for the absolutism of traditional philosophy and logic is what modern science revolted against. The metaphysical tradition of the past is alien to the dominant currents of American life and philosophy, whereas intelligent action demands that the best tools at hand must be used; hence, general education cannot be the same at all times and all places, for modern life requires the use of modern science. Gideonse stated that Hutchins is responsible for the rumor, if there is such a rumor, that " . . . the higher education in America is to forsake the path of science and humanistic concern for a democratic society and to return to the Ivory Tower of absolutistic metaphysics."[1]

Gideonse made it plain that Hutchins' proposals to create order out of social chaos through sheer intellectuality are not at all in line with the direction that the Chicago College plan has been taking since 1934. He insisted that the Chicago College has stressed the "whole man"; has eschewed the isolated and exclusive cultivation of the intellect as such; and has tried to produce well-rounded persons who will be good knowers, doers, and appreciators equipped with the soundest methods of investigation, reflection, and social understanding that the twentieth century can provide. This means a considerable emphasis upon the various modern sciences.

A sound general education, according to Gideonse, should introduce the student to the main fields of knowledge (physical sciences, living organisms, human society, and ideas and ideals as expressed in art and literature). Other things being equal, the test for inclusion of any study in the college curriculum must be its significance for living the life of our society, and thus it is difficult for Gideonse to see any justification for the central position assigned by Hutchins to the classical books of the past. In the following statement, Gideonse illustrates clearly the fact that progressives agree with conservatives in condemning the elective system, but he has given evidence that he differs with Hutchins as to the direction that that reform should take: "This program is based upon a rejection of the same excesses of elective freedom which Mr. Hutchins criticizes so sharply."[2]

Gideonse makes common cause with Dewey and other progressives in his attack upon the separation of theory and practice that Hutchins

[1] HARRY D. GIDEONSE, *The Higher Learning in a Democracy* (Farrar & Rinehart, Inc., New York, 1937), p. 10.
[2] *Ibid.*, p. 15.

proposes and in his attack upon the resulting overemphasis upon books. Gideonse sees the paramount job of education to consist in making evident the connection between theory and practice: "Liberal education has always aimed at both theory and practice with the dominant concern of making theory available for practice, and of correcting and fertilizing the theory by the practice."[1] Gideonse thus finds that Hutchins, by separating general and theoretical from practical and vocational education, not only makes an unproved assumption concerning the transfer of learning from theory to action but also exalts to an unwarranted extent the place of books in college education: "'Books were put in the place of things'—this is not only the thesis of this essay but it is an historical evaluation that is perhaps the final comment upon an educational proposal to substitute the classics of the Western world for scientific training in our modern society."[2]

In concluding his assault upon Hutchins' position, Gideonse asserts again that modern higher education must put its main emphasis not upon the metaphysical orientation of the classical academy, not upon the theological orientation of the medieval university, not upon the literary orientation of the Renaissance university, but squarely upon the methods of modern science: "Instead of stressing the Truth enshrined in books . . . it [science] stresses the methods by which new truth is established and ancient truths are corrected."[3] In other words, if method instead of final results is the emphasis, then the conflict between Ideas and Facts drops away, and the problem-solving, or experimental, method becomes paramount.

Order is to be made out of the chaos not by authority from above but from the creation and sharing of values by the people concerned; and integration comes not from permanent prescribed books but from the use of the experimental method as a technique for dealing with the problems of man and society and for creating shared values and clarifying them. The true scholar must integrate his own work with other bodies of knowledge and with the values of society, or else the totalitarian *Weltanschauung* of metaphysical first principles will do the integrating. Gideonse sums up by saying that Hutchins' proposals were born in authoritarianism and absolutism, the twin enemies of democratic society. Truth is never single, complete, and static; it is rather multiple, fractional, and evolving. The true scholar and student must find their unifying principles in the methods of science.

Mention should be made of at least one more educator who has engaged in a long fight against the dualisms and intellectualisms of the

[1] *Ibid.*, pp. 25–26.
[2] *Ibid.*, p. 23.
[3] *Ibid.*, p. 28.

conservatives and who has constantly urged the development of experimental intelligence to aid in governing human affairs of all kinds. In his *Conflicting Psychologies of Learning*, published in 1929, Professor Boyd H. Bode of Ohio State University directed fire at the dualisms handed down from an earlier era; and he advocated the pragmatic, or experimental, point of view as the way out. The flexibility that individuals have developed for dealing with new situations is human intelligence, and thinking is not purely intellectual but a method of procedure in achieving aims. Thus, education is a continuous process of reconstructing or reorganizing experience.

In the first chapter of *The Educational Frontier*, published in 1933, Professor Bode returned to this theme with considerable force. He pointed out how American society and the liberal college had accepted different and opposing elements in our tradition without reconciling or assimilating them. This resulted in a rather thoroughgoing compartmentalization of ideas and attitudes out of which grew conflicts that people did not recognize because they avoided them. The conflicts in the tenets of religion and business or politics were avoided by keeping them separate. In like manner, the colleges tried to absorb all the elements of traditional culture, piety, literary appreciation, scholarship, scientific knowledge, and pecuniary utility; when all of these elements did not fit in with each other, they were merely put into compartmentalized and isolated departments, or courses, and the result was the elective system: "In brief, the basic trouble with the modern college is that, like Stephen Leacock's horseman, it rides off in all directions at once. If the college of liberal arts is to survive, it must recognize that it is confronted by a problem that is essentially new."[1] In other words, the college must strive to assist every student to develop an independent philosophy of life which will help him to solve these inherent conflicts in our society, and this means a "kind of social gospel for the remaking of the world."

Bode considered some of the various attempts being made to reexamine the whole conception of general or liberal education, and he found that the so-called "scientific education" and the "analysts" were not attacking the fundamental problem of compartmentalization but were merely devising techniques for making it work better. Bode found in Progressive Education a more thoroughgoing attempt to escape from compartmentalization, but he insisted that it must put more emphasis than it has in the past on progressively remaking the social order. We cannot begin to operate with fixed principles, or there is trouble ahead; we must focus attention upon the basic conflicts that are to be found in every

[1] W. H. KILPATRICK, ed., *Educational Frontier* (D. Appleton-Century Company, Inc., New York, 1933), pp. 15–16.

major area of life and become more sensitive to the need of reexamining our national and philosophical tradition. By getting the school and college to relate their activities more closely to the concerns of the larger social order, and by aiding students to develop independent philosophies of how to remake the social order, we can begin to break down compartmentalization and restore to students the sense that education is a way of life. In developing this way of life, the student will get a sense of integration in modern life to replace that which traditional education gave for an earlier society.

Bode's more recent statement of educational philosophy, already referred to, is contained in *Progressive Education at the Crossroads* in which he joins direct issue with President Hutchins' conceptions of thinking. Bode points out that the rise of the common man and his influence upon the college have been one of the disturbing factors in American education. As a result, the colleges have begun to offer technical and vocational subjects alongside the older humanities; their loyalties are divided, and they do not know which way to go. Hutchins suggests one direction, namely, a return to the four-dimensional realities of Plato; a devotion to eternal truth in the supersensuous world; and a return to "basic principles," which, Bode believes, Hutchins never adequately describes. Bode suggests that the other direction and the one that the colleges must take is to accept the implications of modern science and view theories as "operational" concepts. In this way, science becomes recognized as the refinement of the procedures of the practical man; it shuts the door on absolutes and makes all truth, goodness, and beauty subject to the test of usefulness for democratic living: "All learning is a matter of making over experiences in terms of what we can do with things and situations or in terms of what they will do to us; and so this conception of learning links up directly with the doctrine of 'operational concepts,' which is a denial of all absolutes."[1]

TRANSITION FROM "INTELLECTUALISM" TO "INTELLIGENCE"

Numerous other educators could be cited to illustrate the reliance of the progressives upon development of intelligence for the solving of practical problems rather than upon an intellectual power apart from actual practice. However, only one more educator will be mentioned, and he has been selected because of his unique service and intimate connection with efforts for reform of the liberal college in the United States since the beginning of the twentieth century. Alexander Meiklejohn has been dean at Brown University, president of Amherst College, and more recently chairman of the Experimental College and professor of

---

[1] B. H. Bode, *Progressive Education at the Crossroads* (Newson and Company, New York, 1938), p. 42.

philosophy at the University of Wisconsin. He is of particular interest at this point in the discussion, because he has held vigorously to an underlying philosophy of idealism; nevertheless his actual influence has been predominately in the direction of reform that can be called in the best sense progressive.

Meiklejohn's inaugural address as president of Amherst in 1912, which has often been quoted as an outstanding statement of the aims and nature of the liberal college, contains references to the intellectual function of the liberal college, but a careful reading of that statement shows that Meiklejohn's conceptions of intellect are much nearer to the progressive use of the term intelligence than to Hutchins' conception of "cultivation of the intellect." In fact, 20 years later, in his masterly statement of college education contained in *The Experimental College*, published in 1932, he used the term intelligence to indicate the primary aim of college education. Despite his underlying philosophy of idealism, Meiklejohn's efforts have been in the direction in which progressives have wished the colleges to go. Although it may appear that his case tends to invalidate the pattern of opposing views that this book has been attempting to describe, yet it must be remembered that these patterns have never been represented as absolute or rigid categories to encompass all educators. The positions of many men will shift back and forth on different questions of controversy and at different times in any single controversy.

Meiklejohn is a fine example of an educator who has been pushing out the frontiers of college education while holding to an underlying philosophy that was current in the days of his earlier development. He saw that the philosophy of idealism must so adapt itself that it could grapple with the pressing problems of man and society rather than remain in its ivory tower of seclusion. It may be that in so far as the philosophy of idealism comes down to deal with practical affairs of man, it begins to make itself vulnerable to the attacks of a progressive philosophy.

It may be that Meiklejohn's experience indicates that social philosophy is more influential than metaphysics in determining an educational point of view. In any case, the patterns of opposing views that have been set up in this book were intended to be used only pragmatically and only in so far as they helped to give *some* aid in guiding us through the maze of thought and literature on the American college. Although they seem to help in a great many cases, they do not seem to be so satisfactory for such men as Meiklejohn, whose social philosophy is much closer to that of the experimentalists than to the traditionalists. Be that as it may, Meiklejohn's influence has been on the side of the progressives with reference to the question of intellectualism versus intelligence and with reference to the next controversy to be discussed, namely, discipline versus freedom and interest.

That Meiklejohn represents a transition from the conservative position can be shown in his inaugural address as president of Amherst College. When he says that the college must be essentially a place of the mind, he sounds like Hutchins, or rather Hutchins sounds like him.[1] But when Meiklejohn comes to interpret the meaning of the intellectual function of the college, he approaches the progressive notion that knowledge is for actual use in solving social problems. According to Meiklejohn, knowledge and thinking are not only good in themselves but help attain other values which would be impossible otherwise; in the long run, this conception rests on the belief that living will be better if men analyze, study, and understand what they have done and are trying to do. The liberal college should take no special field as its sphere of action but should take human activity as a whole, in order that students may understand human activities in their relations to one another.[2]

Meiklejohn insists that the aim of the college as thus defined is "avowedly and frankly practical" and that the intellectual and practical are not opposed but are closely related:

> Knowledge is to be sought chiefly for the sake of its contribution to the other activities of human living. . . . The issue is not between practical and intellectual aims but between the immediate and the remote aim, between the hasty and the measured procedure, between the demand for results at once and the willingness to wait for the best results.[2]

College teachers have too often hidden and denied the practical results of intellectual efforts, whereas we must aggressively assert that knowledge is justified by its results. Thus, Meiklejohn departed from the traditional intellectual conception of the college still proposed by Hutchins, and he tended toward the progressive notion of the college as proposed by Dewey. When it is remembered that he was enunciating these ideas as early as 1912, his forward-looking leadership becomes more easily recognized.

Meiklejohn goes on in his inaugural to touch directly upon the elective system; and in his suggestions for its reform, he again shows himself to be trying to reconcile the absolutistic doctrines of idealism with the demands for socially useful knowledge made by the progressive point of view. He says that teachers have too often considered all parts of knowledge to be equally useful and that this attitude shows that they have not defined a sound principle for the selection of studies but have

---

[1] ALEXANDER MEIKLEJOHN, *The Liberal College* (Marshall Jones Company, Boston, 1920), p. 30.

[2] *Ibid.*, p. 38.

[3] *Ibid.*, pp. 38–39.

become too immersed in their own specialties and isolated from other fields of knowledge. This is the same lament that Hutchins is making 25 years later, and both men decide that the elective system must be reformed to allow the introduction of a more adequate curriculum. But whereas Hutchins would introduce a prescribed curriculum that looks essentially to the past and to the study of books of the past, Meiklejohn recommends prescribed studies that will enable the student to deal more adequately and directly with his own social situation. Meiklejohn points out that the elective system is usually justified on the grounds that it arouses the interests and enthusiasms of the student: "But if the special interest comes into conflict with more fundamental ones, if what the student prefers is opposed to what he ought to prefer, then we of the college cannot leave the choice with him."[1]

In the light of the tremendous additions to knowledge that were apparent to Meiklejohn in 1912, he felt that the college must assume leadership in the attempt to think through human knowing and to synthesize and unify modern knowledge so that it makes some sense for the intelligent and socially responsible person. This means that the elective system cannot be allowed to continue to isolate and separate our knowledge so that it remains largely unintelligible and relatively useless to modern society.

Meiklejohn mentioned the areas of human knowledge, which, if required of all college students, would help them to see life whole and to become integrated in the social situation. He listed five fields: *philosophy:* acquaintance with the fundamental motives, purposes, and beliefs that underlie human experience; *science of man:* study of social institutions such as property, church, courts, family, factory, and their contributions and failures to contribute to human happiness and welfare; *natural science:* the physical conditions surrounding human life and determining it; *history:* development of motives, institutions, and natural processes as springing from the past and changing in the process of time so as to throw light on present problems, tools, and opportunities; and *arts and literature:* concrete representations of life as depicted by artists and writers. It is evident how much broader and more inclusive this proposal of 1912 is than that of President Hutchins some 25 years later.

Two years after Meiklejohn's inauguration, Amherst established in 1914 a survey course "Social and Economic Institutions," usually considered the first of the survey courses that have become so popular in recent years as a means of giving students a unified picture of civilization as a whole or of some broad field of knowledge. Meiklejohn was insistent from the first not only that students should be given a fair understanding of human experience in its broader relationships but also that all students,

[1] *Ibid.,* p. 42.

even freshmen, should come to grips with the pressing social situation and social problems of mankind.

The intellect would thus not be a mere spectator of "pure reality" but would grapple with human problems and try to make better human living out of life as we find it:

> I should like to see every freshman at once plunged into the problems of philosophy, into the difficulties and perplexities about our institutions, into the scientific accounts of the world especially as they bear on human life, into the portrayals of human experience which are given by the masters of literature. . . . Let him once feel the problems of the present, and his historical studies will become significant.[1]

Meiklejohn worked as steadily as he could for the next 15 years to put these ideals into practice, but his most conspicuous opportunity came when he went to the University of Wisconsin to become chairman of the Experimental College which opened in 1927. Among the many problems that were opened up during the five years of that institution's existence, one of the most important for our discussion here was that of reconciling a prescribed curriculum with freedom for the individual in the methods of teaching. This question of freedom as opposed to discipline is one of the ways in which the Experimental College showed itself to be going more in the direction proposed by the progressives than in the direction of discipline and compulsion proposed by the conservatives who cling to the disciplinary ideal. The solution of this problem of freedom as stated in Meiklejohn's book, entitled *The Experimental College*, comes very close to the solutions that progressive educators have been working out in recent years to overcome the *overemphasis* that the "Progressive Movement" put upon student interests and student freedom in the early days of the reaction against discipline. This controversy leads us into the next chapter.

[1] *Ibid.*, pp. 48–49.

CHAPTER XVII

DISCIPLINE VERSUS FREEDOM

We come now to several points of contrast between the opposing positions with regard to the methods by which the respective theories of knowledge can be put into practice. Conservatives suggest strict *discipline* of the mind as the best way of developing intellectual power, whereas progressives make much of the fact that learning proceeds most effectively when students have considerable *freedom* to follow well-directed *interests* of their own. The long and intense struggle between the ideals of discipline and freedom that has been noted in earlier chapters is still being vigorously waged. Another point of difference has to do with the activities in which students are to engage. The more extreme of the conservatives say that since the college should be devoted to intellectual matters, it should encourage primarily those activities which have to do with *books*. Somehow, the intellect has been closely associated traditionally with "book-mindedness."

In opposition to this view, the progressives put great store in a far wider variety of activities in order that students may develop *well-integrated personalities* through "hand-minded," physical, and social activities as well as through the reading of books. In general, then, the conservatives object to the elective system because it does not develop the intellect, and they recommend required reading courses as a means of reform. The progressives likewise object to the elective system, but their objection rests on the basis that it does not give students scientific habits of procedure or adequate freedom to develop their interests; they therefore recommend several new kinds of teaching arrangements as means to reform.

IDEAL OF DISCIPLINE IN MODERN DRESS

It is significant that the old controversy that has been waged for well over a century concerning the disciplinary nature of the college is being revived today. Some eminent educators still cling to a position that the conservatives of the nineteenth century were upholding in their insistence that the college retain its disciplinary function and eschew freedom for the students. A few examples will be cited to indicate that the torch of discipline is still being kept lighted by votaries of the tradi tional college. Although a great many college educators today still subscribe to the vocabulary of discipline, yet only a few can be selected as representative of the last three decades of the twentieth century.

Humanists like Irving Babbitt and Norman Foerster have kept hammering at President Eliot's ideals of "service and power" as expressed in the elective system and have kept extolling the virtues of discipline and restraint to be achieved mainly through the classics. From the time of his book entitled *Literature and the American College* in 1908 down to the symposium on higher education edited by P. A. Schilpp in 1930, Babbitt insisted that the college should be disciplinary. Professor Foerster has been a close second in his long allegiance to Humanism and the disciplinary conception of the college as indicated by his most recent books *The American State University* and *The Future of the Liberal College.*

In another symposium on the American college which appeared in 1915, President William F. Slocum of Colorado College proudly stated his belief that the small colleges of the West were holding out against the scientific and practical demands of the times and were remaining loyal to the traditional ideal of intellectual and moral discipline as the prime aim of the four-year college. He cited such colleges as Beloit, Carleton, Colorado College, Grinnell, Oberlin, Pomona, and Whitman to indicate some that were holding true to the conception of "learning for its own sake" to be attained through the study of literature, poetry, art, philosophy, ethics, and, most of all, religion.[1]

In 1917, a conference was held at Princeton to prove by piling up extensive testimonial and statistical evidence that intellectual discipline and transfer of training were sound educational conceptions and that the classical studies were the best means of developing moral as well as mental discipline. Dean Andrew F. West of Princeton, who had been so effective as an opponent to Eliot in the latter nineteenth century, wrote the introduction for this classical symposium in which he pointed to many signs of attack upon the traditional notion of a liberal education and to at least one sign of encouragement. Indifference to mental training as an ideal and the elective system as a general practice had weakened the traditional notions, but Dean West saw the World War and its requirements for discipline as factors that might help the disciplinary conception of the college to revive:

Yet one fact of power and encouragement has already appeared. The war, with its clamorous call to duty and discipline, is producing a revulsion of feeling which may bring in its train a beneficent and lasting influence. . . . The "free elective system" is dead and the war has buried it.[2]

[1] *The American College* (Henry Holt and Company, New York, 1915), pp. 138–143.
[2] ANDREW F. WEST, ed., *Value of the Classics* (Princeton University Press, Princeton, 1917), p. 7.

In his annual report of 1917–1918, President Butler was also impressed by the fact that the war might help to reaffirm the principle of discipline and dissipate the laxity arising from progressive philosophies which emphasized freedom and interest:

For instance, the war has brought back to the American people, and in some degree to the schools and colleges, the spirit of discipline which had been almost lost. The sentimental imitations of philosophy which have been spread out before teachers for a generation past have decried discipline as something unnatural, abhorrent, and to be avoided.[1]

President Butler lashed out against "Progressive Education," which he termed the "New Barbarism" because it was making us an uncultivated and undisciplined people. Children were being given full and free expression of their own individualities instead of being guided and disciplined by their elders:

This decline in educational power is primarily the result of a widely influential and *wholly false philosophy of education* which has operated to destroy the excellence of the American school and college, as these existed a generation ago, without putting anything in its place.[2]

These new and numerous Philistines are concerned with displacing discipline for indiscipline, scholarship for deftly organized opportunities for ignorance, thoroughness for superficiality, and morals for impulsive and appetitive conduct.[3]

Coming to another symposium on college affairs in 1928, we find Dean John R. Effinger of the University of Michigan mincing no words when he demanded that colleges must stick to the narrow path of discipline and make students work harder "even to the extent of using uncouth and drastic methods." His suggestions for reform are summed up when he said: "Better mental training, harder study, less superficiality, are what young America needs."[4]

A similar note was struck in the symposium of 1930, mentioned earlier, when Professor William C. Bagley of Teachers College, Columbia University, attacked the elective system and "progressive education" for disrupting the coherence and standards of value represented by the older college curriculum. Professor Bagley deplored the fact that the selective function and high standards of earlier colleges had been relaxed through the upward expansion of democratic and mass education. He further deplored the fact that "progressive education" had helped to push the conceptions of drill and effort into the background by justifying the path

[1] EDWARD C. ELLIOTT, ed., *The Rise of a University*, Vol. II, *The University in Action* (Columbia University Press, New York, 1937), p. 120.

[2] *Ibid.*, pp. 110–111. Annual report of 1919–1920. [Italics mine.]

[3] *Ibid.*, p. 119.

[4] ROBERT L. KELLY, *The Effective College* (Association of American Colleges, New York, 1928), p. 15.

of least resistance through emphasis upon natural growth, initiative from the learner, and reliance upon the needs and right of the learner to make free choices. He was sorry that the disciplinary ideal was being discredited, and he spoke out clearly in favor of developing a new discipline to replace the new freedom.[1]

President James Rowland Angell of Yale University also has spoken out recently in favor of discipline in terms that hark back strongly to the days over a century ago when the Yale Faculty Report was inveighing against the progressives of that day and the time a half century ago when President Noah Porter was standing out against the progressives who favored the elective system. In an address at Bryn Mawr College in 1935, President Angell pointed out that the progressive colleges had appeared along with the vocational ideal to challenge the liberal college of discipline. He reminded the audience that by their insistence upon the interests of students, these colleges had called down upon themselves the most critical and uncharitable scorn of the conservatives—and he showed himself by and large on the side of the conservatives. President Angell summed up the conservative estimate of the progressive colleges as follows:

> To the conservatives . . . the whole process appears to involve asking young people to do only what they most wish to do, knowing full well that they are highly unlikely to choose anything which they find very difficult and that they will consequently be deprived of the discipline which flows from mastery of the distasteful and hard, to say nothing of any probable expansion of the boundaries of their native intellectual provincialism . . . . for a hard-bitten world, where sturdy human fiber is needed, fiber toughened by struggle with difficulty and adversity—for the requirements of such a world, the program seems feeble and unpromising.[2]

Although most of the foregoing discussion refers to "mental" discipline, a good deal of evidence could be cited to show that many colleges still conceive it to be their duty to stand in the place of parents with regard to instilling obedience and exerting close inspection of the details of the student's life. The older disciplinary college undertook to train not only the intellectual faculties but the moral habits as well by requiring strict observance of the college regulations. And some colleges of today

---

[1] P. A. SCHILPP, ed., *Higher Education Faces the Future* (Liveright Publishing Company, New York, 1930), p. 149. It is interesting to note in this connection that Professor Bagley was one of several educators who have come out recently in favor of stressing the "essentials" in education. Since the convention of the American Association of School Administrators in Atlantic City in 1938, the term "essentialist" has been used to describe a movement in elementary and secondary schools that is roughly similar to the conservative position in college education.

[2] JAMES R. ANGELL, *American Education* (Yale University Press, New Haven, 1937), p. 153.

still supervise closely the activities of their students, even in the realm of what many have come to believe are very personal matters.   To quote from a 1937 college catalogue:

The regulations of Saint Michael's College are similar to those which obtain in the conservative American Catholic college. . . .

It is a grave misdemeanor to be absent from the grounds without due authorization from the Prefect of Discipline, and a student so acting is liable to suspension at the discretion of the authorities.   Leaving the grounds at night without permission renders one liable to suspension on the first offense.

Letters, books, and packages are subject to inspection at their arrival and departure.   They must be prepaid.   No book, newspaper, or periodical may be circulated in the College without approbation of the disciplinary authorities.[1]

FREEDOM AND INTEREST GAIN IN THEORY

When the twentieth century progressives were first emerging as a distinctive "Progressive Movement" in education, crystallizing in the formation of the Progressive Education Association in 1918, they put great stress upon the growth of the student and upon freedom to follow his interests wherever they led.   The reaction against the discipline and external compulsion of the traditional methods led the progressives to the other extreme of freeing the student from virtually all compulsion and authority from the outside.   This tendency, of course, led to charges of "license" and "triviality" from the conservative corner, and it also soon disturbed a good many of the adherents of a genuine progressive point of view who felt that some of the more irresponsible followers of the movement had let teachers abrogate all functions whatsoever.   Hence, during the last 10 years or so, and especially since the beginning of the 1930's, the progressives themselves have been putting more and more emphasis upon the social responsibility of education and the greater part that the teacher must play in helping students to realize significant problems while at the same time not giving up the advantages of reliance upon student freedom and activity.

The reemphasis upon the social responsibility of teachers and students in working out their problems of freedom and interest is one of the most significant developments in progressive theory.   Dewey had never enunciated the doctrine that children's interests should be the *sole* criterion of educational method, for in *Democracy and Education* he notes that interest and discipline are really correlative aspects of any activity having an aim.   Interest identifies the person with objects that seem to him important and significant and that furnish means and obstacles to the realization of the aim.   The difference in time between incomplete and complete realization of the aim requires effort and

[1] *Catalogue of St. Michael's College,* 1937–1938 (Winooski Park, Vt.), p. 19.

continuity of attention and endurance; this effort and attention result in a *discipline* that is self-imposed and self-realized as necessary to attaining the more important end in which the person is interested.

In an address before the annual convention of the Progressive Education Association in 1928, Professor Dewey indicated that the first phase of progressive education which had exalted the individual student and his interests was passing and should be replaced with a second phase which would recognize the teacher as directing, taking part in planning the course of study, and giving suggestions of what to do in order that the student's experience might become no mere succession of unrelated activities. The task of the progressive teacher is not to impose tasks for which the student sees no value but to create an environment and determine surroundings that will help him build a coherent and integrated self within the framework of socially significant problems.

When Professor Meiklejohn followed Dewey with an address before the Progressive Education Association the next year, his problem went back to the one already mentioned, namely, how to devise a *coherent* plan of studies while at the same time allowing students to work from their own initiative, with a sense of freedom in arranging their experiences and with a desire to study without fear of compulsion. Meiklejohn resolves this problem by finding relatively common and permanent elements of coherence within the progressive method of teaching itself. The two elements that he found were summed up in terms of "the *growth* of the individual" and "the *freedom* of the individual." He believed that attention to the growth and freedom of students would inevitably lead them to a study of significant problems of self, society, and the natural world.[1]

When Meiklejohn gave the foregoing address, he and his staff were struggling with the problems of freedom and prescription in the Experimental College; and when he came to write up the story of this experiment, he came to a slightly different emphasis. He and his staff resolved the apparent paradox of how to fit a required curriculum to the freedom of the individual in teaching methods through a reemphasis upon the conception of democracy and intelligence. Democracy was conceived as a society in which people live freely by their own determinations and in such a way that they not only do not interfere with the free living of other people but actually aid other people to live freely for themselves. In a democracy, students must be so educated that they not merely play their own parts but, by mutual understanding and cooperative agreements, help to plan, organize, and administer a social order in which people may do what they wish as long as they take responsibility for

[1] SCHILPP, *Higher Education Faces the Future*, pp. 303–304.

the social order.   Now, a method of teaching emphasizing freedom must contribute to democratic living, and it was felt in the Experimental College that the best way to develop a sense of social responsibility along with the cultivation of individuality was to plunge students into situations in which they must exercise responsibility as a result of their freedom.   Release from formal and external restrictions was felt to be a stimulus to responsibility, for the student would be guided by the social situation and by the teachers in the form of the general pull of the community rather than by arbitrary regulations and discipline.

The attempt was made to approach the student with the intention not of obliging him to accept a certain point of view but of having him formulate his own point of view and standards of criticism.   Indoctrination and compulsion were not used, because they were felt to be inefficient and to defeat their own ends when they try to compel students to be free. Students cannot be compelled or induced to be free by secondary motives of fear or punishment, because that does not produce the kind of people or the kind of society that we want.   We must rather stimulate the ability to make intelligent choices, for a person is free only when he can make deliberate judgments for himself.

But freedom in teaching was not taken to mean mere appeal to student interests with no criticism of him.   It was rather felt that there are certain fundamental and important things with which a young man ought to be acquainted; that he must be led to understand these things by his own self-effort and self-direction; but that if he strays from important things, he must be led back by guidance of the teacher and by the pull of the social group to see his mistakes.   Individual guidance through small group discussions and individual conferences with the teacher was the keynote of the actual practice used in the Experimental College for creating in students the desire to understand and deal with important problems of man, society, and nature.[1]   In the nineteenth century, the progressives were linking freedom and interest to the elective system; in the twentieth, strong efforts were being made to root out the elective system and still hold on to freedom and interest for the student.

That Meiklejohn and the Experimental College were going in a direction close to the conceptions of freedom that the progressives have been developing in recent years is indicated in two statements of progressive theory made in 1938, one by Bode and the other by Dewey.   In *Progressive Education at the Crossroads*, Bode sharply criticized progressives who cling too closely to a kind of mystical reverence for the student's immediate interests, for he urged that it must be remembered that the physical and social environments affect interests as much as does the

[1] For elaboration of this position, see Alexander Meiklejohn, *The Experimental College* (Harper & Brothers, New York, 1932), Chaps. VIII and IX.

learner himself. The upshot is that students must be given a whole way of life as an all-embracing interest and that this must lie in the path of democracy. Yet the democratic way of life must not be imposed authoritatively as totalitarian ways of life are being imposed in Germany, Italy, and Russia. It must derive its warrant from the students' own intelligence; and when interests collide, settlement must be based on intelligence and must make progress toward cooperation for common ends. This is the democratic way: Education must try to aid the youth to emancipate himself from dependence on immediate interests, or else he remains a baby and subservient to others as well as to himself.

Bode also attacked the earlier reverence of progressive education for the "felt needs" and growth of students. He pointed out that needs cannot be considered to be inherent in the nature of the individual in the sense in which Rousseau stated the case; rather must they be considered as determined by the ends to be achieved and by an inclusive scheme of values. It is silly to try to discover needs by examining students themselves, for needs must be determined with reference to the way of life that is adopted, and this must be democracy. Thus, the "child-centered school" must give way to the "democratic school" which knows that students develop through their social relationships and that growth is directed not from within the individual but by the patterns of the social order. These patterns must be constantly revised in a democratic social order, and this issue of democracy versus tradition must be the central concern of the democratic school.

With reference to the problem of freedom versus discipline, Bode states that freedom is gained through intelligence, not intelligence through freedom. Freedom through intelligence has its center in the ability to go through with an undertaking by the discovery of appropriate means, by surmounting obstacles, and by modifying original plans or conceptions in the light of new facts. This calls for *sustained effort* in the face of distractions and exercise of discrimination and constructive imagination—in short, real thinking. This, apparently, is Bode's definition of discipline as related to freedom. We must rely not upon the free development of student needs to go in any direction they please but upon the development of free intelligence which can face problems in any field whatever, political and economic as well as scientific.

The student must be taken into the logical organization of subject matter, and he must go beyond it if intelligence is to be freed to the point where it can use science in the battle with the absolutes. If scientific thinking is trustworthy as an example of the way thinking goes on " . . . the possession of a body of scientifically organized matter is of inestimable value, not only as a resource in later life, but as a basis for present thinking."[1] Bode is confident that when such organized subject matter is missing, we are prone to rely on guesswork and random experiment instead of thinking. It is the thinking that is important rather than a freedom that may result in poor or faulty thinking. The example of adult education shows that holding people responsible and accountable is an aid to learning.

The chief defect in American education is thus seen as the lack of a program and the lack of a sense of direction. Bode believes that science, intelligence, and democracy must join together to provide such a social program and sense of direction. Although progressive education has recognized the social factor in learning as represented by emphasis upon student planning, group projects, and socialized recitation, still there is a failure to develop adequate criteria for distinguishing between desirable and undesirable social relations. Bode finds this standard in a democracy which promotes continually expanding and consciously shared interests for greater numbers of people and allows the fullest and freest interplay with other forms of association. Here is Bode's guide and direction for education in social relationships. In its war upon absolutes, democracy will not become an absolute itself so long as it does not let authoritative commands come from outside the social situation but rather sets up a social situation in which individuals have a chance to grow to their fullest stature with no fixed and final claims upon them except the claim of increasing social advantages to greater numbers.

Dewey has added his voice to that of Bode in decrying the practices of some professedly "Progressive" educators who, Dewey thinks, have never properly understood his conception of interest and freedom. In his book *Experience and Education,* Dewey has made an effective restatement of his philosophy of experience and has taken both the traditionalists and the extreme progressives to task. He believes that just as the traditionalists have assumed a false doctrine of discipline, so have some progressives assumed a false conception of freedom. To arrive at a proper conception of freedom, Dewey believes that education must recognize both of the aspects of an educative experience, namely, the qualities of *continuity* and *interaction.* Here Dewey relies upon what has been described earlier as an organismic rather than a disciplinary approach to education.

The principle of continuity implies that every experience that one undergoes tends to modify and change the one who acts and also affect the quality of subsequent experiences. Thus, if education is carried on according to this principle, the individual must be engaging in experi-

[1] B. H. BODE, *Progressive Education at the Crossroads* (Newson and Company, New York, 1938), pp. 98–99.

ences that will constantly aid him to broaden into new avenues of development. In other words, *educative* experiences are those which lead to ever wider and higher qualities of experience, whereas *miseducative* experiences tend to restrict and contract the area of possible experiences. Hence, the educator must know which experiences and attitudes are conducive to growth and expansion and which are detrimental to growth; and he must know how to recognize and how to utilize surroundings conducive to such growth.

The second principle of experience implies that every situation of experience is one of *interaction* between the outer, objective conditions and the inner, individual conditions. The mistake of traditional education was to emphasize the outer conditions to the neglect of the individual; that of the earlier Progressives was to emphasize the inner urges of the individual to the neglect of the objective conditions of natural and social life. A real philosophy of education, according to Dewey, must consider both. It should be indicated here that this point is to be found in the earliest of his writings on educational theory.[1] Continuity and interaction are not to be considered separate from each other, for they intercept and unite in the flow of experience. As situations succeed one another, something is carried from the earlier experience to the later ones, and what the individual has learned in earlier situations becomes the instrument for understanding and dealing with those which follow. When the successive experiences fit in with one another to make understandable wholes, *integration* is taking place; when successive experiences do not fit together but come into conflict, divided personalities—and even insanity—are being created.

The educator is primarily concerned with the situations in which interaction between the individual and surrounding conditions takes place, especially in those situations in which the objective conditions of environment can be regulated and manipulated. He must so regulate conditions that they will meet the existing capacities and needs of those who are being taught, and worth-while subsequent experiences will follow. A good deal of the trouble with traditional education, Dewey believes, was that it did not consider the powers and purposes of those being taught, and it assumed that *certain* conditions were desirable no matter how they affected the students.

In the following passage, in which he denies the validity of permanent studies, Dewey eloquently expresses himself on such proposals as that of Hutchins for permanent prescribed studies:

[1] See, for example, such writings of Dewey as *Interest and Effort* (Houghton Mifflin Company, Boston, 1913), *The School and Society* (University of Chicago Press, Chicago, 1900), and *Democracy and Education* (The Macmillan Company, New York, 1916).

There is no subject that is in and of itself, or without regard to the stage of growth attained by the learner, such that inherent educational value can be attributed to it. Failure to take into account adaptation to the needs and capacities of individuals was the source of the idea that certain subjects and certain methods are intrinsically cultural or intrinsically good for mental discipline. There is no such thing as educational value in the abstract. The notion that some subjects and methods and that acquaintance with certain facts and truths possess educational value in and of themselves is the reason why traditional education reduced the material of education so largely to a diet of predigested materials.[1]

If the foregoing quotation and the following one are read in connection with Hutchins' plea for permanent and fixed studies quoted on pages 290–293, the reader will get an enlightening contrast between the two opposing positions:

In addition, the field of experience is very wide and it varies in its content from place to place and from time to time. A single course of studies for all progressive schools is out of the question; it would mean abandoning the fundamental principle of connection with life-experiences.[2]

The point of all this discussion for the problem of freedom is that, although the interests and purposes of the student must be the starting point of the educational situation, nevertheless the educator has the responsibility for taking the future into account, for making intelligent plans, and for manipulating the objective conditions of instruction so that the student does not remain on the level of his first interests and purposes but proceeds to broader and more socially useful ones. The principle of *continuity* requires that the future be taken into account and that the student derive from his present experiences all that there is to be obtained from them. Dewey believes that this is the only way to prepare for doing the same thing in the future. Thus, the educator must give great care to arranging conditions so that *present* experiences will have a worth-while meaning and thereby subsequent experiences may be expanded and enriched. Hence, the students cannot merely be left to their own devices, and the teacher must no longer abdicate the duty of the mature which is to see the connection between present and future and institute conditions that will have a favorable effect upon the future. On the other hand, the principle of *interaction* requires that the interests and abilities of the student be free at the outset to interact with the determining conditions. If this is not done, Dewey believes, modern education will fall into the errors of traditional education which

---

[1] JOHN DEWEY, *Experience and Education* (The Macmillan Company, New York, 1938), pp. 45–46.

[2] *Ibid*, p 95.

required certain doses of subject matter and held the student at fault if he did not swallow them:

The principle of interaction makes it clear that failure of adaptation of material to needs and capacities of individuals may cause an experience to be non-educative quite as much as failure of an individual to adapt himself to the material.[1]

When Dewey comes to describe more closely the nature of freedom according to his conception of experience, there is a good deal of similarity between his position and those of Bode and Meiklejohn. All of them find the essence of freedom in the development of a free intelligence which can delay judgments until worthy ends and actions can be brought together. Real freedom of action arises when the individual has developed his intelligence to the place where he can exert self-control and evolve the ability to frame worthy purposes and achieve them:

The only freedom that is of enduring importance is freedom of intelligence, that is to say, freedom of observation and of judgment exercised in behalf of purposes that are intrinsically worth while.[2]

Dewey asserts that the common mistake of the extreme Progressives is to identify freedom with outward, overt physical movement and activity and to treat such activity as an end in itself. He believes that increased outer movement, the mere doing of things, is not an end in itself but only a *means* to greater freedom of intelligence. To be sure, increased outward activity does aid the teacher to learn more about the individual student, and it is advantageous in helping him to carry deliberately chosen ends into action and to judge them, but the amount of needed outer activity varies among different individuals, and it decreases with maturity:

For freedom from restriction, the negative side, is to be prized only as a means to a freedom which is power: power to frame purposes, to judge wisely, to evaluate desires by the consequences which will result from acting upon them; power to select and order means to carry chosen ends into operation.[3]

Hence, the student must be free to start with his own experiences and with his own interests; but to reach a genuine freedom of action, he must develop a high degree of self-control:

Natural impulses and desires constitute in any case the starting point. But there is no intellectual growth without some reconstruction, some remaking, of impulses and desires in the form in which they first show themselves. This remaking involves inhibition of impulse in its first estate. The alternative to

[1] *Ibid.*, pp. 46–47.
[2] *Ibid.*, p. 69.
[3] *Ibid.*, p. 74.

externally imposed inhibition is inhibition through an individual's own reflection and judgment. . . . Thinking is thus a postponement of immediate action, while it effects internal control of impulse through a union of observation and memory, this union being the heart of reflection.[1]

Dewey is not retreating from the position that the interests of students must be given free play in the educative process; he is trying to make that position really educative:

There is, I think, no point in the philosophy of progressive education which is sounder than its emphasis upon the importance of the participation of the learner in the formation of the purposes which direct his activities in the learning process, just as there is no defect in traditional education greater than its failure to secure the active cooperation of the pupil in construction of the purposes involved in his studying.[2]

It can be seen from this discussion that Dewey is holding steadfast to his opposition to the traditional conception of discipline, but he is urging that the conception of educational freedom be defined a little more closely. He comes out strongly for recognition of student freedom but also for a greater recognition of the importance of guidance and planning on the part of the teacher. Education must start with the experiences of the student, but the student must be led by the teacher through orderly development toward the expansion and organization of subject matter. Education must not be merely a matter of new experiences but must consist of experiences that lead ever toward new problems and, while related to older experiences, toward still better organization of ideas and facts:

Anything which can be called a study, whether arithmetic, history, geography, or one of the natural sciences, must be derived from materials which at the outset fall within the scope of ordinary life-experience. In this respect the newer education contrasts sharply with procedures which start with facts and truths that are outside the range of the experience of those taught, and which, therefore, have the problem of discovering ways and means of bringing them within experience. . . . The next step is the progressive development of what is already experienced into a fuller and richer and also more organized form, a form that gradually approximates that in which subject-matter is presented to the skilled, mature person.[3]

Too often, the newer education has emphasized starting with student experiences and has neglected the development into organized subject matter, whereas the traditional subject matter has too often been selected

[1] *Ibid.*, p. 74.
[2] *Ibid.*, pp. 77–78.
[3] *Ibid.*, pp. 86–87.

by adults on the basis of their own judgment of what would be useful for the young in the future; and thus the material was settled outside the experience of the young and looked to the past.

Hence, Dewey is urging progressive educators to put more emphasis upon intellectual organization of subject matter as a means of developing free intelligence and the disciplined mind. He hastens to insist, however, that the intellectual organization must not be imposed externally but must have the flexible nature of *scientific method* and *scientific organization:*

No experience is educative that does not tend both to knowledge of more facts and entertaining of more ideas and to a better, a more orderly, arrangement of them. It is not true that organization is a principle foreign to experience.[1]

Education must move from a social and human center toward a more objective intellectual scheme of organization, but it must always be borne in mind that intellectual organization is not an end in itself, as it seems to be in the hands of the intellectualists, for intellectual organization of the scientific kind is the best means by which social relations may be better understood and more intelligently ordered:

When education is based in theory and practice upon experience, it goes without saying that the organized subject-matter of the adult and the specialist cannot provide the starting point. Nevertheless, it represents the goal toward which education should continuously move.[2]

Thus, Dewey finds discipline in education to arise from a rigid adherence to the scientific method and to a progressive philosophy of experience. In this sense, discipline arises when the individual is in the midst of a genuine situation of experience of his own making wherein he must solve problems of importance to him in resolving the difficulties of the situation. Freedom arises when the student attains some mastery and ability in solving important problems. The scientific method not only requires the formulation and testing of hypotheses, but it demands the keeping track of ideas, activities, and observed consequences. Keeping track is a matter of reflective review and summarizing in which there is both discrimination and recording of significant features of a developing human experience:

To reflect is to look back over what has been done so as to extract the net meanings which are the capital stock for intelligent dealing with further experiences. It is the heart of intellectual organization and of the disciplined mind.[3]

There is no discipline in the world so severe as the discipline of experience subjected to the tests of intelligent development and direction.[4]

[1] *Ibid.*, p. 102.
[2] *Ibid.*, p. 103.
[3] *Ibid.*, p. 110.
[4] *Ibid.*, p. 114.

Conservatives and progressives alike would see importance in discipline, but their conceptions of what discipline means are far apart. The conservatives think of discipline in terms of an older faculty psychology and appeal to tradition for authority. The progressives think of it in terms of modern psychologies of learning which stress interest, freedom, and the scientific method of thinking.

BOOK-MINDEDNESS VERSUS DEVELOPMENT OF WHOLE PERSONALITY

An interesting conflict, which has often been aroused as a result of the problem of discipline and freedom, revolves around the part that books shall play in the college curriculum. The traditional conception of intellectualism has tended over long periods of time to identify the "cultivation of the intellect" with the study of books; and, the argument runs, since the college is the prime agency for the cultivation of the intellect, therefore the study of books must be the primary activity of the college. A large share of the thesis of previous chapters has been devoted to tracing the development of this emphasis upon language and books. It has been pointed out how the dualistic conception of mind as a separate entity from the time of Plato to the present has fostered this prevailing respect for the materials contained in books. However, the twentieth century has developed a conception of mind and human nature that has tended to connect much more closely the activities of the mind with all the other functions of the human organism. The result has been an organismic conception which has put much more emphasis upon the development of the whole personality as a primary aim of education.

More recent evidence from the fields of psychology and physiology has stressed the fact that human organisms act as "wholes" and that the human organism is so interconnected and interdependent that changes in any part bring about correlative changes in other parts. In other words, there seem to be at least four aspects of this wholeness: a *physiological* level of activity where internal glandular secretions and chemical changes are most important; a *physical* level involving neural and larger muscular activity; an *emotional* level which involves feelings and emotions in relation to changed physiological and physical states; and a *mental* level of activity having to do with the quality of thinking. All of these four levels of activity affect each other so closely that changes in one effect changes in others. For example, it is now common knowledge that disturbed glandular or nervous or emotional conditions have a decided effect upon the mental and intellectual activities of human beings. Therefore, the college can no longer afford to act as if the intellectual sphere were its only proper province and to ignore the important areas of human activity that so vitally affect human welfare and intelligence.

It might also be said that there is still another level of human activity which may be called the *social* sphere which is also closely interwoven with all of the others as the individual interacts with his social environment made up of other people, institutions, customs, beliefs, laws, and systems of ideology. Thus, progressive educators are urging that the college must more and more take account of all of these factors in order to promote most effectively the whole personal and social development of the individual. As a result, development of the "whole personality" or of an "integrated personality" has become one of the watchwords of progressive education.

This means that the college must be on the alert to give students opportunity to develop their abilities in many different ways in order that they may become well-integrated individuals. They must have opportunity and help in developing strong and healthy bodies through physical activities. They must have an opportunity for emotional expression through various artistic and social channels. They must have opportunity to develop high qualities of personality and character through various group activities of social life. The exercise of intelligence and judgment and thinking cannot be sharply divorced from these other more "active" activities which have come to play such a large part in the American school and college, especially through extracurricular activities, in contrast to the European secondary school of the traditional type. Here, then, is the conflict: Shall the college concentrate on books for intellectual development alone, or shall it foster a wide variety of activities, including the reading of books, in order to develop well-integrated personalities? The answer of the intellectualist and traditionalist often favors emphasis upon books, and that of the progressive is likely to emphasize a good many other activities in addition to the reading of books.

This particular controversy received a nice definition in the *New York Times Magazine* for March 7, 1937, in an article entitled "What Is the Job of Our Colleges?" President Hutchins presented the case for intellectual discipline through the study of books, and President William A. Neilson of Smith College presented the argument for development of the whole personality through varied activities. A good deal of President Hutchins' argument will be familiar to readers of these pages; but thrown against the background of previous chapters, it stands out clearly on the side of tradition and intellectualism.

The point of his article that concerns us here is that the college should be primarily for the reading of books and should accept into its halls only those who are "book-minded." Those who are merely "hand-minded" should not be admitted to the college but should go elsewhere for their training:

For that large proportion of the youthful population which can profit from the reading of books we should establish a new kind of college, primarily devoted to the cultivation of the intellect. For those less able to profit from reading we could create, for the parallel years, a series of technical institutes of subprofessional or homemaking nature. As we learn how to teach this group how to read, its course of study should approach more nearly that of those who are now able to read. It is even possible that we could then get along with only one type of educational unit at this level.[1]

And again:

We have a great many hand-minded boys in the colleges and I should not be surprised if we had some book-minded boys in the CCC. Perhaps we might arrange an exchange. Then we might have an undergraduate population who really want the kind of education the college is prepared to give.[2]

Hutchins goes on to state explicitly that physical and social activities have no place in the college as he conceives it:

So I come to the conception of certain permanent studies which we shall teach in our new type of college, and which will not be expected to develop the body or the character, to give social grace or impart a utilitarian skill. These things can be learned as ancillaries or elsewhere.[2]

Although President Hutchins seems to imply that ruling out physical and social activities would create a "new type of college," it is evident that he would in fact attempt to recreate the traditional type of college which was long in existence before modern conceptions of personality were devised.

President Neilson is keenly aware of this fact and indicates some of the areas of activity into which the better liberal colleges of today are entering. He believes that a single, simple, and unified curriculum such as President Hutchins recommends would not be appropriate for the many different kinds of persons found in college today. President Neilson would defend the right of a variety of young people to be in college and not shuttled off to a technical institute if they happen to be hand-minded. Since so many young people have gone to college in recent decades, a great variety of educational program is demanded, for the intellect cannot be cultivated on the assumption that all intellects are the same, and a purely intellectual education would be too bleak and too devoid of concession to individual taste or capacity. President Neilson finds the good liberal college of today giving intellectual training a central but not exclusive place, and he commends the effort to provide physical,

[1] *New York Times Magazine* (Mar. 7, 1937), p. 2.
[2] *Ibid.*

recreational, and social activities which will develop bodily and emotional health, artistic expression, and social responsibility:

Whereas he [Hutchins] excludes development of the body, they [good liberal colleges] seek to teach the laws of health and to encourage their application in the practice of proper diet and exercise. Whereas he excludes the development of character, they seek to create an atmosphere in the class room, the dormitory and on the playing fields that will favor the growth of worthy personal and social conduct.

Dr. Hutchins ignores the music of the ancient curriculum. The modern college more and more is affording opportunities for the development of insight and capacity for enjoyment of art, not only by the departments of music and the fine arts, literature and the drama, but by the increasing beauty of its landscape and architecture . . . and all of them see in the varied activities of the campus an opportunity for training in citizenship and life in a civilized community.

The training of the intelligence goes on in all these fields as well as in others excluded by President Hutchins, such as foreign languages, and it is more, not less, effective because it is approached through a variety of avenues. If, as we agree, the student is to be trained to understand the past and his fellow-men and to deal intelligently with the future, his development on the physical, moral, spiritual, esthetic and social sides as well as the intellectual is an essential part of this training. And this development is the common and well understood aim of scores of American colleges of liberal arts today.[1]

Evidence that these aims, noted by President Neilson, are, in reality, a part of the college aims at the University of Chicago in President Hutchins' own institution is given at length by Professor Gideonse in his book already cited, *The Higher Learning in a Democracy*. Gideonse reports that the aim of the new Chicago college plan was to develop the "whole man" and to produce well-rounded persons as knowers, doers, and appreciators. A great deal more literature could be cited to support President Neilson's description of the direction that colleges are taking, but a good deal of it is common knowledge. Suffice it to quote one paragraph from the annual report for 1936–1937 of Dean Herbert E. Hawkes of Columbia College:

The "whole man" is admitted to college, and the College accepts the responsibility for knowing and offering opportunity for the development of each aspect of the individual just so long as he seems to be educable at the College level. In the first place the entire personality of the student, his mind, temperament, emotional and physical make-up, and ethical attitude, each and all present opportunities for education. This principle accounts for our development of the program of social events, of sports both intercollegiate and intramural, the encouragement of the religious activities, and our liberal attitude toward all

[1] *Ibid.*, p. 25.

sorts of organizations and movements. Whole human beings have all of those vital interests and activities.[1]

Whereas the "intellectualists" deny that the college should concern itself with the recreational, physical, or "social" activities of its students, many institutions are giving increasing attention to the problem of making extracurricular activities more profitable as well as more pleasurable. This movement is being focused at several colleges and universities in the student union centers which provide a headquarters for the recreational life of the student body. Outstanding pioneers in this field are the Memorial Union at the University of Wisconsin and Willard Straight Hall at Cornell University. In these and other unions, the universities are taking official responsibility for providing expert leadership and guidance in making recreational, creative, and artistic activities an integral part of the whole college experience.

In such union centers, students may have greater opportunity for developing their own talents in music; drama; the dance; literary and newspaper activities; handicraft work in clay, wood, and metal; and painting and sculpture. They also receive valuable and practical experience for later use in their own community life by promoting and managing lectures, concerts, social dances, games, and informal sports both indoor and outdoor. Thus, the aim of the more forward-looking union centers is to take advantage of the great interest that students have in these activities and to recognize that guided activities can and should be as effective for the whole educational development of the individual as work done in classroom and library. The University of Wisconsin has recognized this point of view by making the director of the student union a member of the teaching staff in "social education" so that students may get as much credit for work in the field of community recreation as in language or history or chemistry.

The newer and more progressive colleges are also particularly anxious to develop all sorts of physical, creative, and social activities as an essential part of the learning process for the modern student. Bennington, Sarah Lawrence, and Bard have tried to increase the educative value of the whole curriculum by absorbing the extracurricular activities into it. The Experimental College of the University of Wisconsin was a good example of a program that set out to emphasize the study of books and yet found it advisable to develop a thoroughgoing program of "activities" of all sorts. In Chap. III of Professor Meiklejohn's book *The Experimental College,* he sets forth the ability to read books intelligently as the primary method by which the college develops a sense of responsibility in young persons:

[1] Columbia University, *Report of the Dean of Columbia College for the period ending June 30, 1937, p. 3.*

The college does not build up maturity by the same methods as those employed in a mill or an office. Its chosen material is literature; its chosen instrument is the book. . . . To put the matter sharply, we may say that the only really significant question to be asked concerning the graduate of a college as such is, Does he in his living depend upon books and does he use them effectively? Does he know what are the significant values, the significant problems, of his civilization; does he follow these as they are recounted and considered in newspaper, in magazine, in books ranging from fiction to scholarly and technical discussion? Is he an intelligent reader?[1]

That the Experimental College by no means confined itself to this aim of reading books, the writer can give testimony from personal experience both as student and as adviser there. One had only to see the tremendous enthusiasm aroused over a well-developed program of intramural games of all sorts; the dramatic productions entirely created, produced, directed, and acted by the students themselves; the varieties of hand-mindedness being displayed in the workshop; the intensive study of community life in all its aspects; the vigorous discussion groups on a great variety of subjects; and such activities as the complete building to scale of a model of the Parthenon in substitution for written papers to realize that books were not playing the whole part in the learning process. That Professor Meiklejohn and his staff recognized the validity of these observations is shown in Meiklejohn's book in the paragraph immediately following the one quoted above:

As one looks back upon the statement just made, one is uneasily conscious that it is, or seems to be, badly over-intellectualized. Practice in the arts and crafts and games, as well as in the reading of books, can be used as an instrument of liberal education. For example, the activities of dramatics and dancing are at times startling in the richness of their contribution to the development of a student. And it is equally clear that both creative and receptive experiences in music, in painting, in sculpture, in architecture, in games—all these in significant and valuable ways play their parts in that enriching and strengthening of the human personality which we call liberal education. That the Advisers have accepted these statements will be clearly seen in the later chapters of this report. When then we say that "books" are the chosen instrument of the college, the term must be used to cover, in some sense, the appreciative and active as well as the intellectual activies in the narrow sense.[2]

Despite the progressive emphasis upon activities, most colleges still, of course, put their major stress upon the study of books. The problem remains as to whether they will move in the direction of making the study of books instrumental in the solving of present problems or will strive

[1] ALEXANDER MEIKLEJOHN, *The Experimental College* (Harper & Brothers, New York, 1932), pp. 34–35.
[2] *Ibid.*, pp. 35–36.

more and more to study the books of the past with a good deal of reverence for their own sake as representative of the best that has been thought and said in the world. Humanists have criticized the elective system because it has allowed students to escape from reading the "human masterpieces" of the past. Thus, for example, Norman Foerster assures us that humanistic education should lead students to assimilate "what is best in the past and present" through the study of great books:

. . . the "best" is composed of what G. R. Elliott has termed "human master-pieces"—the great human persons, and the great human works of literature, art, science, history, philosophy, and religion that are competent to transmit to the future the knowledge and wisdom and beauty of the past and present.[1]

Furthermore, Hutchins' proposals for permanent studies have largely taken the form of prescribed books, the majority of which were written in the ancient, medieval, and early modern periods; and the new program of St. John's College in Annapolis, Md., is attempting to put such a program into practice. A good many of the reading courses, honors courses, independent study plans, and even survey courses such as the new course in the Humanities at Columbia College have stressed the reading of selected books of the past.

The question that progressive educators would doubtless ask as to the validity of such reading courses is whether the reading of books is made a matter of academic retreat from the world for purposes of individual "culture" or is made a part of a larger program to enable the student to grapple with the pressing problems of the present and to get him to develop a keen sense of social responsibility or esthetic appreciation for the knowledge that he is acquiring. This leads us into the controversies of the next chapter.

[1] NORMAN FOERSTER, *The American State University* (University of North Carolina Press, Chapel Hill, 1937), p. 255. For other proposals that the core of college study should be great books of the past, see G. R. Elliott, "President Hyde and the American College," *American Review*, 2: 143–169 (December, 1933); and Robert Shafer, "University and College," *Bookman*, 73: 225–240, 387–400, 503–521 (May, June, July, 1931).

CHAPTER XVIII

THE IVORY TOWER VERSUS THE WATCHTOWER

One of the most difficult problems that the modern college has to face is whether to look upon itself as a monastic retreat where scholars and students can retire for quiet contemplation apart from the rapid tempo of society or try with all the means that it can devise to provide students and teachers with the best materials for the study and actual practice of living in the society that they serve. In other words, is the college to be an ivory tower of academic retreat or a watchtower where an eye may be kept out for changing social conditions and to give aid in the solution of those problems which changed conditions make necessary? The nature of college education depends a good deal on the answer that colleges make to this question.

A closely related problem has to do with the question whether the college shall be aristocratic in nature or democratic in aims and function. In other words, is the college to be a selective institution, as it has been in the past for the training of the few and the "best" who are destined to be leaders in our society; or shall it take as its province the education of the vast majority of young people who will make up the active citizenry of the present and future? The rest of this chapter will be given to a discussion of the differing answers that college educators have given and are giving to these questions.

ACADEMIC RETREAT VERSUS SOCIAL RESPONSIBILITY

In general, it may be said that those educators who look upon the college as a place for handing on the Great Tradition, for developing intellectualism and discipline among the book-minded, also look upon it as a place primarily devoted to knowledge as separated from action. "Knowledge for its own sake" is a motto with a long tradition behind it and a good many advocates today. Many educators believe that colleges and universities should emphasize the transmission of knowledge and scholarship apart from and unsullied by the pressures and confusions of present-day society. Although the term "ivory tower" has been applied to the college in this position, the figure might very well be changed, as one college president puts it, to "cyclone cellar." President Wriston of Brown University believes that the college should be sensitive to its environment but not controlled by it; if necessary, the college must provide a cyclone cellar, or place of retreat, quiet, rest, and thoughtfulness apart from the hurly-burly of the market place and business. In other words, the college must not become a "service station."[1]

The American Humanists have long been attacking the idea that the college exists to serve society in any immediate or practical way. They have been attacking the notion of "service" ever since President Eliot and the state universities made it a familiar term in higher education; and they have been resenting the notion that the higher education should be useful, or utilitarian. Rather have they insisted that the college must continue to transmit the "wisdom of the ages" which, of course, is locked in the books of the past and thus is peculiarly appropriate to the "inner," or "spiritual," life of man. Thus speaks Irving Babbitt:

. . . President Eliot's attack in the name of the elective system on the traditional college curriculum will be found . . . to involve a clash between a familiar type of naturalistic philosophy and the wisdom of the ages; for nothing is more certain than that this wisdom has been neither utilitarian nor sentimental, but either religious or humanistic.[2]

In other words, the college is not to minister to the utilitarian needs of common humanity but should devote itself to cultivating spiritual matters in the Greek tradition of a liberal education for those who have a freedom based upon leisure:

At the bottom of the whole educational debate, as I have been trying to show, is the opposition between a religious-humanistic and a utilitarian-sentimental philosophy. . . . It will be found to be no small matter whether our higher education is to have enshrined at its center the idea of leisure in Aristotle's sense, or the idea of service in the sense given to the word by President Eliot and the humanitarians.[3]

One of the most incisive critics of the American college and university on this matter of social usefulness has been Abraham Flexner whose book *Universities, American, English, German* caused a considerable stir in educational circles when it was published in 1930. By his caustic criticism of the American universities, Flexner made the term service station almost a byword for those who wished to attack them for their attempts at popular and useful education. We are concerned here with Flexner's conception of the social responsibility of institutions of higher education. His criticism of vocational, or *ad hoc*, training on the university level will be discussed in the next chapter.

Whereas the Humanists such as Babbitt and More said that the colleges should concentrate on knowledge for its own sake and should

[1] H. M. WRISTON, *The Nature of a Liberal College* (Lawrence College Press, Appleton, Wis., 1937), p. 23.

[2] IRVING BABBITT, "President Eliot and American Education," *Forum*, 81: 2 (January, 1929).

[3] *Ibid.*, pp. 9–10.

eschew the study of present problems in relation to their solutions for modern society, Flexner says that the universities must study present social problems but that they have no obligation to accept responsibility for translating their solutions into social action. He conceives of the university as a place where a community of scholars and scientists study the problems of society objectively and apart from the exigencies of social affairs:

The university must shelter and develop thinkers, experimenters, inventors, teachers, and students, who, *without responsibility for action*, will explore the phenomena of social life and endeavor to understand them.[1]

In his assumption that knowledge must be separated from action, Flexner approaches the intellectualistic position of the ivory tower. The major concerns of a university, according to him, are the conservation of knowledge and ideas, the interpretation of knowledge and ideas, the search for truth, and the training of students who will carry on these functions. The university must have original thinkers and investigators who create knowledge; and teachers who gather, generalize, and interpret knowledge; but none is to be responsible for what the student or society does with the knowledge:

I have been urging that universities maintain contacts with the actual world and at the same time continue to be irresponsible.[2]

With respect to the study of social problems through the social sciences, Flexner makes even more apparent his assumption that knowledge and action should be separated:

The social sciences must be detached from the conduct of business, the conduct of politics, the reform of this, that, and the other, if they are to develop as sciences, even though they continuously need contact with the phenomena of business, the phenomena of politics, the phenomena of social experimentation.[3]

That Flexner's position is quite representative of the outlook of a great many college educators could be supported with much evidence, but only

---

[1] ABRAHAM FLEXNER, *Universities, American, English, German* (Oxford University Press, New York, 1930), p. 10. [Italics mine.] The whole issue of the *Journal of Higher Education* for October, 1931, was given over to reviews of Flexner's book. Reviews were written by Kilpatrick of Teachers College, McConaughy of Wesleyan, MacCracken of Vassar, Bode of Ohio State, Coffman of Minnesota, and Cowley of Ohio State. Most of the reviews were largely unfavorable.

[2] *Ibid.*, p. 15.

[3] *Ibid.*, p. 17. This problem naturally brings up the question of academic freedom which is beyond the scope of this book. A good many progressive educators, however, would contend that genuine academic freedom must allow faculty and students freedom not only to formulate and interpret knowledge but also to make appropriate efforts to put such knowledge into practice.

one or two will be cited here.   A good example is found in *Higher Education and Society*, a symposium of speeches and papers given at the Southwestern Conference on Higher Education held in November, 1935, to celebrate 10 years of progress at the University of Oklahoma.   A general theme found in this book sounds almost exactly like Flexner.   Colleges and universities must carefully avoid partisanship and must not take sides in social and moral affairs; they must merely provide the factual basis and knowledge that others can somehow use to solve the problems. In other words, "facts" and knowledge can be created without regard to the assumptions or theories or bias of the scholar, a conception that modern progressive sociology and historiography has come to challenge, as we shall see in the next part of this chapter.   In the words of Professor Isaac Lippincott of Washington University, St. Louis:

. . . it is not within our province to attempt to fabricate systems of social order based upon our concepts of right and wrong, beauty or ugliness, harm or good. We observe the data, whatever the source, and describe what we have discovered. We leave it to others to make use of the data.   This all means that there is a clear demarcation between the disciplines engaged in discovery and experiment and those engaged in the applications of the findings.[1]

Another example is found in the recent humanistic point of view represented by Norman Foerster:

The state university is, properly, free to exercise the dispassionate pursuit of knowledge; it is not free to apply its knowledge to the practical direction of affairs.   Its function is intellectual, not political.[2]

Thus, we find these particular representatives of the state university flying in the face of the theories and practices that have made such state universities as Wisconsin, Minnesota, Michigan, and Professor Foerster's own Iowa great forces in the higher education of twentieth century America.   The intellectualist and the Humanist would revoke the principle that there should be close practical union and cooperation between the state university and the state for whose welfare it exists.

If, then, this position would renounce the theory that the university should serve directly the needs of the community, how can the university perform its obligation of social responsibility?   The answer of the intellectualist is clear.   The university should confine itself to "training the minds" of the students and in this manner develop individuals who will be good citizens.   The best society comes from good individuals, and the moral character of individuals is developed best by cultivating

---

[1] *Higher Education and Society: a Symposium* (University of Oklahoma Press, Norman, 1936), pp. 176–177.

[2] NORMAN FOERSTER, *The American State University* (University of North Carolina Press, Chapel Hill, 1937), pp. 164–165.

their minds and intellectual qualities. As President Hutchins would put it, intelligent social change can best be brought about not by leading students into the actual problems of society but by training their minds. In this way, *mirabile dictu*, the intellectual content of higher education will transfer most adequately to social problems only if the educator is careful that the student is *not* concerned too directly with the present social problems:

If the object of general education is not scholarly, professional, or vocational; if its primary purpose is not the development of character or personality; if it should not be composed of current information about the *status quo* or imaginary information about the future, what is its object and of what should it be composed? Clearly, the object of general education is the training of the mind. Clearly, too, the mind should be trained for intelligent action. Or, to put it another way, the object of general education is to produce intelligent citizens. Facts, data, and information, present and prospective, cannot be ignored. But the emphasis must be on the training of the mind. . . . A program of general education resulting in trained minds will facilitate social change and make it more intelligent. The educational system cannot bring about social change. . . . But the educational system can facilitate social change; it can make it more intelligent.[1]

As Professor Foerster would put it, social progress and change arise not by a humanitarianism that would try to improve the condition of the great majority of people but by a Humanism that would concentrate on developing superior individuals. The properly cultivated individual will automatically become the most socially minded person:

All men who have attained a high degree of inner order and justice and peace will tend to produce, in their social relations, outer order and justice and peace. Self-cultivation is the root, social harmony the fruit. Self-control precedes any desirable form of social control. The sound individualist, beginning with himself, progressing toward self-fulfillment, will become the social man.[2]

In another connection, Foerster deplores and ridicules the humanitarian movement which, since the eighteenth century, he believes has become too much concerned with physical comfort and the avoidance of physical pain and suffering. After all, he points out, the glory of Greece and Rome was not cleanliness or bodily comfort, and a civilization based on avoidance of suffering is empty and hollow. It is the spiritual and ethical values that are important. Whereas the old Humanism started rightly with the individual person, the new humanitarianism is too prone to start with society and blame the environment for the ills of the world; and thus Foerster believes that it is the individual who is at fault and that it is with the individual that social reform must start. The best

[1] HUTCHINS, *No Friendly Voice*, pp. 130–131.
[2] FOERSTER, *op. cit.*, p. 227.

way to reform society is merely for individuals to become good examples for others to imitate:

Thus every person, as father or mother, friend or citizen, renders his most fundamental service to society by being, so far as he can, an example that others may safely follow.[1]

In a word, then, the social philosophy that Foerster approves for the college rests upon a highly individualistic basis, a scorn for movements that attempt to alleviate the suffering of the masses of the people, and may be summed up in the highly significant sentence: "It is something, *but not much*, to feed men."[2]

Thus, when the conservatives come to describe the kind of training for individuals that will produce the best type of social-mindedness, they usually fall back upon "character training" or "intellectual training" as the best methods of moral and social responsibility. Foerster indicates that general "culture of mind" as developed by the traditional liberal education will exert the most profound influence upon the moral nature of individuals and produce qualities of probity, veracity, equity, benevolence, and fairness. In other words, mental discipline produces good character.[3] Hutchins indicates that, although the college cannot develop character directly, it does influence character through the best means at its command, namely, mental discipline: "A peculiar possession of the college of liberal arts, is its influence upon character. . . . Hard intellectual work is doubtless the best foundation of character, for without the intellectual virtues the moral sense rests on habit and precept alone."[4]

A final statement of this point of view will suffice to illustrate the reliance of the intellectualists upon mental discipline for developing character and social responsibility: "It is not explicit moral training and discipline that we are considering, but the bearing of the *intellectual* activity, in which universities are rightly engaged, upon moral advance individual and social."[5] The circle of the conservative argument for academic retreat is complete: The colleges and universities should retire from active social problems in order to study and create pure knowledge apart from action; they fulfill their social obligations not through service to the community and study of the present but through "cultivation of individuals," mental discipline, and study of the past.

[1] FOERSTER, *Future of the Liberal College*, p. 18.

[2] *Ibid.*, p. 19. [Italics mine.]

[3] *Ibid.*, p. 203. Foerster adds that the complete development of the moral nature is possible, however, only through religion.

[4] HUTCHINS, *op. cit.*, p. 93.

[5] *Higher Education and Society* (University of Oklahoma Press, Norman, 1936), p. 51. [Italics mine.]

Ideal of Social Responsibility Urged by Progressives. Progressive college educators have struck out against this conception of academic retreat and individual cultivation that has been described above and have urged that the college identify itself much more closely with the social needs and demands of a changing civilization. This position received dramatic formulation recently when a great many leading scientists and educators formed the American Committee for Democracy and Intellectual Freedom. Its chairman, Professor Franz Boas of Columbia University, has stated that scientists and educators must recognize the fact that they have a moral obligation to society, and they must exert their influence in a positive program for democracy. Here is one phase of the watchtower ideal.

Furthermore, in so far as the experimentalist point of view has come to represent progressive college theory, there has been a growing insistence that knowledge must be conceived in close union with action and that therefore the college must use its knowledge in social action or take responsibility for so using it. In other words, the college and university as an institution must directly serve the community and must give students by *direct* means a better understanding of the problems of modern society and an opportunity to work *with* the community and *in* the community in the solution of its problems. Good citizenship and good character are developed by actual participation in a social situation and in group cooperation.

Up to the turn of the twentieth century, the most customary statement of the aims of education was in terms of the harmonious development of all the powers of the individual. After the turn of the century occurred the beginnings of an increased emphasis upon social aims and upon social forces as means of attaining these aims. It was recognized by Dewey and others that education should enable students to take a greater and more active part in the solution of problems arising out of an industrialized and changing society. They continually emphasized the idea that the school and college should come into closer union with the community life, until the *social* emphasis became a prominent part of progressive educational thought of this century. However, the effects of the boom days of the twenties, a resurgence of Humanism, and the great popularity of "scientific" testing and measurement tended to exalt once more the individual and his needs in the educational process. Thus, the progressive education movement in its early days found itself stressing development of the individual to the neglect of social values. After the climax and decline of the individual aim in the economic world as represented by the depression following 1929, the progressive educators who had long been raising their voices in favor of social aims once more began to be heard; and the decade of the thirties has seen a steady growth in the influence of the theory of social aims in education.

One of the outstanding expressions of this reemphasis upon social aims in education was contained in the volume entitled *The Educational Frontier* written by a group of progressive educators in 1933. It is expressly stated therein that our educational philosophy must be based upon a social philosophy and that therefore education must refer directly to the needs and issues of our generation. As stated by Professors Dewey and Childs, education must be closely related with the social demands of the time:

An identity, an equation, exists between the urgent social needs of the present and that of education. Society, in order to solve its own problems and remedy its own ills, needs to employ science and technology for social instead of merely private ends. This need for a society in which experimental inquiry and planning for social ends are organically contained is also the need for a new education. In one case as in the other, there is supplied a new dynamic in conduct and there is required the cooperative use of intelligence on a social scale in behalf of social values.[1]

This view implies that education involves a definite moral and social outlook:

Education, as we conceive it, is a process of social interaction carried on in behalf of consequences which are themselves social—that is, it involves interactions between persons and includes shared values.[2]

This emphasis upon social values has been attacked by Humanists and intellectualists on the grounds that it does not adequately serve individuals, but the progressives reply that true individuality can be developed only in relation to a social situation. Therefore, to develop integrated individualities there must be an integrated form of social organization within which such an individuality can be developed:

Social cannot be opposed in fact or in idea to *individual*. Society *is* individuals-in-their-relations. An individual apart from social relations is a myth— or a monstrosity. . . . Education is the process of realization of integrated individualities. For integration can occur only in and through a medium of association. Associations are many and diverse, and some of them are hostile to the realization of a full personality, they interfere with it and prevent it. Hence *for the sake of individual development*, education must promote some forms of association and community life and must work against others.[3]

Since individual development is so closely related to social affairs, education, according to this view, must be concerned with the kind of social organization that exists and that may exist:

[1] W. H. KILPATRICK, ed., *The Educational Frontier* (D. Appleton-Century Company, Inc., New York, 1933), p. 64.
[2] *Ibid.*, p. 290.
[3] *Ibid.*, p. 291.

Admit that education is concerned with a development of individual potentialities and you are committed to the conclusion that education cannot be neutral and indifferent as to the kind of social organization which exists. Individuals develop not in a remote entity called "society" at large but in connection with *one another*. The conditions of their association with one another, of their participation and communication, of their cooperation and competition, are set by legal, political, and economic arrangements. In the interest, therefore, of education—not of any preconceived "ism" or code—the fact is emphasized that education must operate in view of a deliberately preferred social order.[1]

Inasmuch as this position believes that education must make choices concerning the type of society it deems best, it becomes evident that the college and university cannot and in fact do not isolate themselves from the surrounding social situation as the intellectualists and Humanists desire. In other words, higher education cannot deal with facts irrespective of their implications for social action. Knowledge cannot be separated from action; for knowledge always has implications for action. Scholars and scientists in their seclusion cannot create knowledge of objective facts, as Flexner proposes, because whether they profess it or not, the facts that they discover and formulate really depend upon the point of view of the one who does the discovering or the formulating.

Facts do not just lie around to be picked up; facts and knowledge depend upon the choices, convictions, and interpretations of the discoverer. Facts do not order themselves but are ordered by the historian, scientist, or investigator in any field whatsoever in accordance with his fundamental assumptions and theories concerning the organization of nature, society, and human values. Social knowledge, thought, research, and the investigator himself are influenced by the social situation, interests, biases, values, loyalties, and the whole "scheme of reference" in which that knowledge is created. Therefore, according to this point of view, colleges and universities cannot create knowledge apart from its social implications, and college and university teachers must accept responsibility for what they profess as truth and knowledge. Knowledge cannot be separated from action.[2]

On the basis of this progressive philosophy of the close union of knowledge with action, the progressive college and university have developed a theory and practice of social responsibility that is at variance with the intellectualistic conception of academic seclusion and irresponsibility and has led some colleges and universities into closer cooperation with the surrounding community in two general ways: (1) the direct

---

[1] *Ibid.*, p. 291.

[2] For further elaboration of this point of view in modern sociology and historiography, see Charles A. Beard, *The Discussion of Human Affairs* (The Macmillan Company, New York, 1936), and Karl Mannheim, *Ideology and Utopia* (Harcourt, Brace & Company, Inc., New York, 1936).

participation of the university as an *institution* through the activity of its scholars and scientists who give direct aid and guidance to the community in the solution of its problems; and (2) the specific intention of the college and university to train its *students* directly for more intelligent participation in the affairs of the community both before and after they graduate. These two methods of increasing the social responsibility of higher education are not entirely separate but merely represent different types of emphasis. Some institutions have emphasized one type; some, the other; and some have emphasized both types.

The state universities have been outstanding in their efforts to increase their social usefulness in both ways; and outstanding in the formulation of this philosophy of social service in the early years of the twentieth century was the University of Wisconsin. When the elder Robert M. La Follette was directing the political and social destiny of the state of Wisconsin, and when Charles R. Van Hise was directing the University of Wisconsin from 1903 to 1918, a very close union and cooperation developed between the state and the university in the solution of the state's political, economic, social, and educational problems. The "Wisconsin Idea" as developed particularly by these two men led the way for the country in realizing how socially useful the university could be. The university professors engaged actively in aiding farmers to solve their pressing agricultural problems; university economists aided in devising tax structures and in solving urgent labor and industrial problems; and university political scientists gave direct aid to the state legislature in effecting needed political reforms which helped to make of Wisconsin one of the leading political and social laboratories for the nation. Direct service to the commonwealth became the watchword for a university that would become the watchtower for the state.[1]

The ideal of the university as a great aid in social planning for social betterment spread rapidly to other state universities, and the visions of early state university builders from Jefferson and Tappan through White and Adams were finally coming to fruition. A particularly appropriate statement of the university's obligation to the social order was made in 1920 by Professor Jay William Hudson of the University of Missouri:

By the Obligation to the Social Order is meant the obligation of academic experts to use their special knowledge to its utmost to solve the more pressing

[1] For further description of the Wisconsin Idea, see Charles McCarthy, *The Wisconsin Idea* (The Macmillan Company, New York, 1912), Chap. V; this indicates in a general way how a university actually serves a state by offering practical courses dealing with all aspects in the life of the state. In the Appendix, pp. 313–317, is a list of approximately 45 professors who served both the university and the state in various capacities during the year 1910–1011.

concrete social problems of the day, and to teach others to solve them. They are to do this as a business, not as a side issue. They are to do it themselves.[1]

Here is no mincing of words as to the social responsibility of colleges and universities as institutions.

A more recent advocate of this same view of the state university has been Lotus D. Coffman, former president of the University of Minnesota. He has stated not only that the state university can serve the state by developing an intelligent spirit of cosmopolitanism among its students but also

There is another way in which a university may serve the community, and that is by assisting it in solving its problems.[2]

And President Coffman specifically mentioned such assistance as investigations into better ways of mining ore; fighting wheat rust; making sirup from corn; improving roads and water supply; giving advice to engineering, judicial, and medical groups; and stimulating cooperation of all kinds.

President Coffman also made a frontal attack upon Flexner's conception of a university soon after Flexner's book appeared. Writing on "Flexner and the State University" in the *Journal of Higher Education* for October, 1931, he stated:

. . . I believe that the university which he [Flexner] longs for does not exist, never has existed, and never will exist. Certainly no state university can, nor is it ambitious to dwell in the realm of intellectual exclusiveness. Being earthly, these institutions to some extent smack of the earth. Being creatures of democracy, they possess the strengths and weaknesses that democratic institutions ordinarily have.[3]

In answer to Flexner's argument that the university should not concern itself with the practical vocations of a changing social order, Coffman insisted that the state university should change its offerings in the direction of greater social usefulness when the needs of the people so direct:

. . . the entire history of university education has been in the direction of greater practicality. Almost every expansion of the curriculum has arisen out of some social need. The "liberal" studies of each age have been the practical studies of that age. These studies differ from age to age. New studies have come in because new needs have arisen, and old ones have disappeared when old needs have become obsolete. Universities will teach what the people want. . . . Universities, certainly state universities, are not merely places for the living of

[1] J. W. Hudson, *The College and New America* (D. Appleton-Century Company, Inc., New York, 1920), pp. 36–37.

[2] L. D. Coffman, *The State University, Its Work and Problems* (University of Minnesota Press, Minneapolis, 1934), p. 22.

[3] *Ibid.*, pp. 157–158.

an intellectual life; they are definitely designed and maintained to train practitioners for higher levels of service.[1]

In the same article, Coffman quotes approvingly from another article
in the *Journal of Higher Education* for April, 1931, entitled "Town and
Gown Today," written by President William A. Neilson of Smith
College. President Neilson makes the same point that state universities
are a great source of expert knowledge and should not limit their functions
to intellectual matters, as Flexner desires: "The professors of classics
are not seriously disturbed in their philological labors because a colleague
in the agricultural department gives advice to farmers on the best breeds
of cattle for milk or beef. . . . "[2]

Finally, Coffman, in another connection, made a well-known statement which evoked the scorn of the Humanists and intellectualists:

> The state universities hold that there is no intellectual service too undig-
> nified for them to perform.[3]

He warns that the acceptance of the intellectualistic conception of a
university will mean the decay of the university's social leadership in
modern life:

> The chief danger inhering in university circles is that they will become intel-
> lectualized and standardized and that in consequence their pliability and useful-
> ness as educational institutions will be diminished, if not destroyed. . . . But
> it is certain that any university which loses step with current movements, which
> fails to give consideration to the sweeping changes that are occurring in every
> part of the world, will soon become archaic and incompetent to educate youth
> for the exercise of leadership.[4]

The other way in which colleges and universities could increase their
social responsiveness, namely, through giving students a more direct
training in social problems, is beginning to receive more general attention
by institutions of higher education. The agitation to give students a
more acute sense of social understanding and responsibility has usually
taken the form of urging that the curriculum be brought up to date so
that they could study vitally important problems of present-day society.

In addition to the study of present problems, progressive educators
have insisted that students can acquire a genuine social responsiveness
only when they actively engage in the solution of social problems in a
social situation. This means that they should not only try to make
their activities within the college as lifelike as possible but also actually

---

[1] *Ibid.*, pp. 159–160.
[2] *Ibid.*, p. 160.
[3] *Ibid.*, p. 205; he said this at the Conference on the Obligation of Universities to
the Social Order, held at New York University in 1932.
[4] *Ibid.*, pp. 206–207.

go into the surrounding community while in college in order to understand more clearly the real problems with which the community is wrestling. In other words, it is held that students will not develop into good citizens merely by "disciplining their minds" but that good moral character can be developed only by practicing socially useful acts in a group situation both within and without college walls.

Of recent years, the statements of college aims as formulated in college catalogues and in surveys of college aims show that the colleges are beginning to lay greater stress upon social-mindedness, but progressive educators are convinced that not enough is being done along this line. In 1921, Koos and Crawford collected 27 statements of college aims from material published in the period 1842–1876 and compared them with 40 that appeared in the period 1909–1921. They found that only approximately 25 per cent of the earlier statements included the aim of civic and social responsibility, whereas 75 per cent of the later ones included this aim.[1]

This type of survey was brought up to date in 1937, when investigators for the North Central Association found considerable mention in the literature of college education of such terms aiming at social competence of students as "social leadership"; "high social ideals"; "spirit of useful citizenship"; "training for life"; "social resourcefulness"; "intelligent, effectual, and loyal participation in the life of home, community, and state"; "service to humanity"; "affect cultural tone of community"; and "coordination of life-activities."[2] The surveyors point out, however, that these terms along with a great many others are often too vaguely defined and too intangible to give real aid to the educational process. Yet they do represent the recognition of a need that progressive educators are anxious to translate into more effective educational content and procedures.

Since the early years of the century, when John Dewey began his long fight to have education recognized as a social function,[3] progressive educators have been urging colleges to come to closer grips with the pressing social problems that all too often impinge too slightly upon the college curriculum. In 1916, James H. Baker, president emeritus of the University of Colorado, was urging that universities ought to reform themselves in order to meet the new needs of the day. They must utilize to the fullest the new sciences in order to be of more public service and of more usefulness to universal welfare; and they must utilize more fully

[1] L. V. Koos and C. C. CRAWFORD, "College Aims Past and Present," *School and Society*, 14: 399–509 (Dec. 3, 1921).

[2] MELVIN E. HAGGERTY, *The Evaluation of Higher Institutions*, Part III, *The Educational Program* (University of Chicago Press, Chicago, 1937), p. 40.

[3] See, for example, JOHN DEWEY, *Democracy and Education*, Chap. II, and Chap. VII.

the new political, economic, and social sciences (especially sociology) in order to prepare students for more practical efficiency in municipal, industrial, and other social affairs.[1]

In 1920, Professor Jay William Hudson of the University of Missouri was insisting that the college must take the American social order for its province and train students to understand and cope with whatever was most important in American social life: "The purpose of the college must be coincident with whatever is the supreme moral obligation of the age."[2] Here is one of the most succinct and pertinent statements yet made of the progressive doctrine that the college aims must change with social conditions.

On all sides and in greater volume in the years following the World War, progressive educators kept insisting that colleges should adapt their programs of study to include—even in a dominant position—the study of problems created by the new scientific and industrial society. In 1924, James Harvey Robinson, famous Columbia University historian, was lending his efforts to a campaign to bring vital social knowledge into the daily experiences and thinking of more and more people. He was trying to popularize knowledge, in the best sense of that phrase, and he felt that this was, in the last analysis, the real aim of schools and colleges. To do it properly, the colleges should make their knowledge much more relevant to the vital social issues of the day:

Education ought to be largely devoted to the issues upon which the young as they grow up should be in a position to form an intelligent opinion. They should understand that scientific advance has greatly altered, and promises still further to alter, our environment and our notions of ourselves and possibly the expediency of existing moral, social and industrial standards.

We should have a dynamic education to fit a dynamic world. The world should not be presented to students as happily standardized but as urgently demanding readjustment.[3]

College students were quick to agree with Robinson, if the contest and symposium conducted by the *New Republic* for the expression of student opinion, is a valid criterion. A recurrent refrain running through most of their essays embodied a revolt against the musty textbook and an urgent desire for colleges to deal with real life problems and experiences and abandon the all too prevalent academic hash and rehash.[4]

[1] JAMES H. BAKER, *American University Progress and College Reform Relative to School and Society* (Longmans, Green & Company, New York, 1916).

[2] HUDSON, *op. cit.*, p. 75.

[3] JAMES HARVEY ROBINSON, *The Humanizing of Knowledge* (Doubleday, Doran & Company, Inc., New York, 1923, 1926), pp. 68-69

[4] *The Students Speak Out!* (New Republic, Inc., New York, 1929).

An interesting attempt of a college to reform itself along progressive lines is recorded in *Modernizing the College,* published in 1926 by A. Monroe Stowe. Here Professor Stowe tells the story of the struggle to inaugurate in an unnamed college a progressive program emphasizing the study of modern social problems. It is a striking example of the way in which traditional and progressive forces came into conflict within an urban institution that was trying in the decade following the World War to develop socially efficient American citizens who would be alive to economic and civic problems and prepared to help solve them. The obscurantist methods of the traditional bloc on the faculty of this college are revealingly discussed by Professor Stowe, and his own predictions of what the college of tomorrow will be like are surprisingly close to many efforts being carried on today to develop men and women "for intelligent participation in the activities of life." In an introduction to the book, Chancellor Samuel P. Capen of the University of Buffalo registers his belief that the modern college must meet modern demands:

The old ways must go, unless they can justify themselves as appropriate to modern demands. The touchstone for determining the validity and the importance of college studies and college methods is the intellectual environment of the present, not the intellectual environment of the Reformation, or even of the Victorian Age.[1]

Many other college educators are on record in favor of bringing the college curriculum into closer touch with the realities of social life, but only a few more will be mentioned here to show their opposition to the purely academic conception. President Ernest Martin Hopkins of Dartmouth College has registered his opposition to the conception of knowledge for its own sake. The college "must relate thinking to the realities of life. The possibilities of thought for thought's sake alone are soon exhausted. This notion is early to be consigned to the limbo of useless, if not degenerate, things."[2]

In the same symposium, President Norman Frank Coleman of Reed College, Portland, Oregon, listed as one of the "finger posts" of college progress the development of social understanding in students whereby ancient tradition and academic seclusion are overcome and students are put in close contact with the industrial and social problems of our modern life.[3]

As early as 1912, President Meiklejohn of Amherst was urging that college students should be plunged into the study of social problems; and in 1932, his report of the Experimental College showed that the

[1] A. MONROE STOWE, *Modernizing the College* (F. S. Crofts and Company, New York, 1926), p. viii.

[2] SCHILPP, ed., *Higher Education Faces the Future,* p. 160.

[3] *Ibid.,* Chap. XVII.

curriculum was so planned that students would be obliged to come to grips with the important problems of modern society.   Finally, Professor Gideonse of Chicago has insisted that a sound general education should introduce the student to the main fields of human knowledge and that, other things being equal, the test for inclusion of material in the college curriculum must be its significance for living the life of our society.   A more detailed statement of some of the plans for achieving these ends, particularly as they imply reform of the elective system, is presented in Chap. XXI.

This conflict between the ivory tower and the watchtower conceptions of the college will continue to be one of the hottest educational issues in American education as long as the state of national and international crisis is prolonged in economic and political arenas.   As long as the future of democratic institutions is challenged by extreme reactionary and radical movements, the question of what to teach about controversial social issues will be a difficult one for American schools and colleges.   Conservative educators tend to dodge the issue by taking refuge in "objectivity" and academic retreat as discussed above, whereas progressive educators are urging that colleges must come more directly to grips with the problem in a democratic fashion.   One is tempted to say that conservative educators are using traditional notions of the ivory tower to defend a conservative political and economic point of view, but that is a generalization which should be checked by further investigation which is beyond the scope of this book.   From the evidence submitted, however, it does seem safe to say that a conservative educational position often reveals a conservative political and economic position and that a progressive educational position tends to reveal a more progressive and liberal social philosophy.[1]

ARISTOCRATIC IDEAL VERSUS DEMOCRATIC IDEAL

The problem of who should go to college has become a particularly thorny aspect of the more general question of social responsibility for colleges and universities.   Especially in the years following the World War, college educators were faced with thousands of new students

[1] For example, Humanists like Babbitt and Foerster reveal an underlying individualistic and conservative economic and political philosophy in the quotations on pp. 270 and 334–335.   The position of President Hutchins has been attacked as "fascist" by Theodore B. Brameld, "President Hutchins and the New Reaction," *Educational Forum*, 1: 271–282 (March, 1937).   In reviewing a book by W. A. Brown of Union Theological Seminary entitled *The Case for Theology in the University* (University of Chicago Press, Chicago, 1938), Frank H. Knight says, "What the propaganda represented by Drs. Brown and Hutchins obviously means in political terms is a theocratic-ecclesiastical dictatorship"; see Frank H. Knight, "Theology and Education," *American Journal of Sociology*, 44: 676 (March, 1939).

clamoring for higher education; and out of the varying responses to the problem that these students presented two rather well-defined and opposing points of view developed.   In general, those who advocated the ivory tower conception of college were also in favor of an aristocratic ideal which they believed fitted in with the traditional conception of a liberal education as it had been developed in earlier days.   They stoutly maintained that the liberal college should admit to its halls only the "best" students who could profit from the traditional type of education and were destined to be the "leaders" of the coming generation.   Thus, they looked upon the college as a selective institution whose standards of admission and graduation should remain rigidly high so that those of lower intellectual ability would be kept out.

These conservatives ranged in their attitudes all the way from some Humanists who denied the democratic ideal altogether to others who professed allegiance to democracy but who said that it would be served best by the colleges if they concentrated on training *leaders* and disavowed any attempt to educate the great majority of youth.   Still others emphasized the selective function of the college but insisted that selection should be based upon intellectual qualities alone and that greater attempts should be made to give intellectually qualified youth from the lower economic classes a chance at higher education.   In general, this position tended to eulogize the independent liberal arts college of the traditional type and to urge that it retain relatively unmodified its narrow and limited curriculum of literary and philosophical studies despite the changes demanded by a changing society.

On the other hand, the more liberal and progressive educators who visualized the college as a watchtower for the benefit of society began to make their voices heard more insistently in favor of admitting and educating the great masses of youth, or at least the majority, who were being graduated from the high schools.   They looked upon the college not only as a place for training leaders but also as a place that would aid social democracy and raise the general level of intelligence in the community by educating greater and greater numbers of youth.   Whereas the conservatives had assumed that their standards were perfectly all right and that the great majority of young people were not intellectually qualified for college education, the progressives began to criticize collegiate standards as too rigid and too selective.   Consequently, the progressives insisted that the colleges should adapt their curricular offerings to meet the needs of a much more heterogeneous student population and that the curriculum should be changed whenever social conditions warranted.

Furthermore, the progressives insisted that colleges should not only change in these ways in order to fulfill the democratic ideal in college education but should also give conscious and direct attention to training students for life in a democratic society. This meant, in its extreme form, that students and faculty alike should have a much greater voice in the shaping of the curriculum and the educational policy of higher institutions. This problem of the aristocratic versus the democratic conceptions of higher education has been made all the more pressing in recent years in view of the attacks made upon democracy in Fascist, Nazi, and Communist countries and upon academic freedom both abroad and at home. In contrast to the conservative assumptions of social duality and educational rigidity, the progressive assumptions of social fluidity and educational flexibility have appeared all the more marked.

Aristocratic Conception of the College Reaffirmed by Conservatives. To give a little more substance and color to the generalizations made above, a few educators will be mentioned who illustrate the conservative and aristocratic notions of college education. We shall begin with one or two professed Humanists who have rejected altogether the ideal of democratic higher education. Professor Irving Babbitt has stated explicitly that Humanism is interested in perfecting individuals rather than in the elevation of mankind as a whole. In his view, traditional *humanitas* should be applied only to the select few; it is thus aristocratic and does not imply a general benevolence toward all men or toward democracy.

Babbitt believed that the humanitarians and democrats were on the wrong track when they thought of democracy as the uplift of the many and of the college as something for everybody; the college should rather return to its former estate, when it was a careful selection for the social elite and a thorough training for the few:

The democratic spirit that the college needs is a fair field and no favors, and then the more severe and selective it is in its requirements the better.[1]

Another statement which shows the Humanist's denial of the democratic ideal follows:

In one sense the purpose of the college is not to encourage the democratic spirit, but on the contrary to check the drift toward a pure democracy. If our definition of humanism has any value, what is needed is not democracy alone, nor again an unmixed aristocracy, but a blending of the two—an aristocratic and selective democracy.[2]

Finally, Babbitt decided that the colleges should concentrate on a small number of standardized subjects which the Great Tradition has found valuable for training the select few:

[1] IRVING BABBITT, *Literature and the American College* (Houghton Mifflin Company, Boston, 1908), p. 78.
[2] *Ibid.*, p. 80.

There is another aspect of the democratic spirit—the tendency, namely, that the elective system has fostered in the college toward a democracy of studies; and this can be refuted in the name of a higher democracy. Assuming that the selection of studies in the old curriculum was purely arbitrary, that the respect accorded to certain studies over others was superstitious, there would be, even then, a great deal to be said in its favor.[1]

Another Humanist who has rejected the democratic conception of the college as represented by the state universities has been Norman Foerster, a professor in the State University of Iowa. Foerster has lamented the fact that the state universities became an expression in higher education of Jacksonian democracy and the humanitarian movement and that they became forces for direct democracy, social leveling, applied science, material success, and the training of men for their present and appointed tasks.   Rather than opening their doors wider and wider, extending their services in all directions, and offering something for everyone who comes, the state universities should select rigidly on the basis of "quality" rather than "equality," and Foerster echoes Babbitt's sentiment:

A truly democratic idealism would seem to involve, not lowering the standard so that everyone could find some interesting means of securing a diploma, but rather giving everyone a chance to measure up to an exacting standard.[2]

Foerster neatly classified everyone into three groups according to his abilities at the age of twelve years: those who have reached the limits of educability and for whom any further education is a waste, those who can proceed further under authoritative indoctrination to be prepared for some adult job or useful vocation, and those who are capable of active assimilation and expression of mind and personality. Naturally enough, Foerster believes that only the third, and smallest, group should be admitted to college, for that is the only group that can profit from a liberal education.   The state may provide other institutions for the first two groups, but the university must be reserved for selecting and training an aristocracy of intelligence and character if democracy is to continue.

Foerster agrees with Babbitt that training of individuals in an aristocratic minority is the hope of democracy and social progress.   Hope does not lie in dictators or in social groups who identify their rights with the general welfare or in the average man and woman who do their best under leaders no better than themselves or in political machinery designed to run well no matter who runs it:

[1] *Ibid.*, p. 82.
[2] NORMAN FOERSTER, *The American State University* (University of North Carolina Press, Chapel Hill, 1937), pp. 177–178.

Whatever progress may be possible for a society . . . depends, then, on the leadership of a persuasive minority composed of men of intelligence and character. . . . Once we have sound leaders, we may safely intrust to them the administration of our economic, social, and political arrangements.[1]

Thus would Foerster set up an aristocracy of Plato's philosopher-kings.

This aristocratic conception of college education has been by no means confined to acknowledged Humanists but rather has become the most common stock in trade of most college and secondary school educators of the postwar period up to the depression of the early 1930's. In a symposium of the papers and addresses delivered at the annual meeting of the Association of American Colleges in 1928, President Frank Aydelotte of Swarthmore College was disturbed because the colleges in the twentieth century had responded too quickly to the tides of public demand, when it were far better for the colleges to give students what they need rather than what they want. He was pleased that the race of colleges for greater numbers of students was over and the race for quality had begun. He found the clearest signs of progress for the colleges in the fact that they were beginning to limit their numbers, admit only the best, and be proud of the multitudes that they were turning away. He believed that they should concentrate in the future only on the best and give more attention to the brilliant student.[2]

In 1929, Dean Max McConn of Lehigh University published an amusing little book entitled *College or Kindergarten?* in which he insisted that only those should go to a real college who have superior intellectual ability or genuine interest in the culture purpose of colleges. He cited Meiklejohn and the Wisconsin Experimental College as the best examples of the democratic ideal in college education; but he found it inadequate because he was sure that the colleges have discovered that the masses cannot think, inasmuch as college students became flippantly and irresponsibly "collegiate" when the masses were admitted.[3]

The widespread currency of the aristocratic conception was invading even textbooks for courses in education. According to Chapman and Counts in 1924, the aim of the college was definitely to train leaders, and therefore the college must select for admission only the highest intellectual group who would go on to advance the intellectual tradition or go into the professions; and in order to raise the intellectual tone, the college must eliminate more rigidly than ever those who could not profit from the vigorous discipline that it offers.[4]

[1] *Ibid.*, p. 231.

[2] KELLY, ed., *The Effective College*, Chap. I.

[3] C. M. McCONN, *College or Kindergarten?* (New Republic, Inc., New York, 1928), Chap. II.

[4] J. C. CHAPMAN and GEORGE S. COUNTS, *Principles of Education* (Houghton Mifflin Company, Boston, 1924), Problem 21.

Although their institutions have not always practiced exactly what they preached, leaders in some of the largest private universities in the country have often demanded stricter entrance requirements and the weeding out of all but the most superior students. At Columbia, President Butler has not hesitated to say that from some points of view too many young people are going to college. In an interview in the *New York Times Magazine*, he is quoted as follows: "There is no more reason why every one should attend a university than why every one should learn to fly an airship."[1]

A former professor at Columbia, Albert Jay Nock, has insisted that our historical conceptions of equality and democracy have been misconceived, because everyone is not educable and only relatively few are structurally capable of education and maturity. This is evident, Nock says, from the fact that when everyone was pushed into the studies of the Great Tradition through mass education, the whole thing failed. Therefore, his argument goes, since studies of the Great Tradition embody education, and since everyone cannot be so educated, the majority must be kept out of college. Nock even notes that one college in desperation admits that it proposes to make a special curriculum for each individual, a proposal he believes to be the preposterous result of a preposterous conception of equality and democracy.[2]

From the University of Chicago has come the voice of President Hutchins deploring the false notions of democracy and progress that have weakened the universities. To him the heart of the problem is one of selection. Inasmuch as more and more youth will doubtless need some kind of education beyond high school in the future, the colleges must see to it that only the proper students (book-minded) are admitted to the college and that all others go elsewhere for a vocational, or useful, training:

I believe such a plan would come closer to true democracy than the present system of opening the doors of higher education practically to all comers . . . and then adjusting the quality of education to the quality of the student. We do not create centers of learning in any such fashion. We come close in some instances to creating centers of anti-intellectuality.[3]

At Yale, President James R. Angell said that education for leadership and selection of students were the prime purposes of higher institutions

[1] S. J. WOOLF, "Butler Gives a Definition of Education," *New York Times Magazine* (Jan. 3, 1937), p. 16. (One is prompted to wonder whether the time may not be rapidly approaching when everyone *should* learn to fly an airplane if the conditions require it.)

[2] ALBERT J. NOCK, *The Theory of Education in the United States* (Harcourt, Brace & Company, Inc., New York, 1932).

[3] ROBERT M. HUTCHINS, "What Is the Job of Our Colleges?" *New York Times Magazine* (Mar. 7, 1937), p. 2; or *Progressive Education*, 14: 312 (May, 1937).

in a democracy;[1] whereas at Harvard, President A. Lawrence Lowell was saying that universities must raise their level of scholarship by raising their standards and remorselessly dropping those who did not live up to the high standards and show aptitude for study of university grade.[2] As Lowell's successor at Harvard, President Conant has suggested that there are far too many students in the professional schools of the university, because they cannot all get jobs, and that therefore the numbers admitted should be cut down by one-fourth or one-half. By providing more scholarships for less wealthy students, Conant believes that the universities can fulfill both the aristocratic and the democratic strains in our tradition of higher education.

Many other college educators have rung the changes on this aristocratic conception of college education, but only a few more will be mentioned here. E. H. Wilkins, president of Oberlin College and formerly dean of the College at the University of Chicago, stated the matter bluntly in 1927: "Every potential leader, then, and no one else, should go to college."[3] Dean J. B. Johnston of the University of Minnesota classified all American people into six categories, ranging from those who could not progress beyond the mental capacities of infants to those of unusual intellectual endowments, and said that only the highest two categories should be admitted to college.[4]

President Wriston of Brown University is confident that not everyone should go to a liberal college but only those who have the proper amount of " . . . time, the intellect, the character, the sensitive emotional organization, the philosophical potentialities, and the spiritual resources to find life, as such, an absorbing and thrilling experience."[5] Finally, President James L. McConaughy of Wesleyan University indicates unwillingness to let the lower types of students into the traditional four-year liberal college when they can profit only from the practical courses of state universities which must respond to the professional and practical demands of the public and of the taxpayers. Meanwhile, the independent liberal college should be left to its own devices so that

---

[1] JAMES R. ANGELL, "Some Reflections on Democracy and Education," *Yale Review*, n.s., 14: 417–432 (April, 1925); also *American Education* (Yale University Press, New Haven, 1937).

[2] A. LAWRENCE LOWELL, "Universities and Colleges," *Yale Review*, n.s., 32; 301–308 (Winter, 1934); also *At War with Academic Traditions in America* (Harvard University Press, Cambridge, 1934).

[3] E. H. WILKINS, *The Changing College* (University of Chicago Press, Chicago, 1927), p. 75.

[4] J. B. JOHNSTON, *The Liberal College in a Changing Society* (D. Appleton-Century Company, Inc., New York, 1930), Chap. II.

[5] H. M. WRISTON, *The Nature of a Liberal College* (Lawrence College Press, Appleton, Wis., 1937), p. 32.

. . . it can concentrate on literature, philosophy, and art while the legislature grants increases to the state university for courses in hotel management, and for the development of the shorthorn herd. If the college is bold enough, it can refuse to admit students of low intellectual promise, who are, too often, eligible for admission to the state institution by legislative decree, and who will often profit by attendance at practical courses even if intellectually incompetent for liberal arts study.[1]

Thus does the aristocratic liberal college conceive its function to be different from that of the state university or democratic college.

Democratic Conception of the College Hailed by Progressives. The assumptions underlying the democratic philosophy of higher education differ considerably from those of the aristocratic philosophy. Whereas the latter assumes that only a small minority of the population has a native ability that will permit it to profit from college education, the former believes that democracy rests its case upon the ability of the great majority of citizens to solve or at least aid in the understanding and solution of the major problems confronting the people of a democracy. In other words, intelligence is not to be taken as an innate ability that cannot be altered or merely as the ability to pass intelligence tests. Intelligence is considered to be the ability to meet novel situations and to solve practical problems with the aid of suggestions from experts and leaders in various fields of activity. In this sense, it can be developed and increased in the masses of the population through education.

Thus, education through the college level not only should be open to all the people of a democracy but must direct its efforts to raising the level of intelligence of the whole people. Therefore, it can no longer be identified with the traditional college studies, as the intellectualists would have it, but must be defined in terms of any activity that will develop intelligence and the ability to solve practical and social problems; and the advocates of the democratic philosophy of higher education believe that the vast majority of people in a democracy *are* capable of developing such intelligence and of profiting from the proper kind of college education.

A good many of the state universities and some of the more recent progressive colleges have attempted to put this democratic philosophy of college education into practice. They have taken a cue from Frederick Jackson Turner's conception that the state university has responded in the past and should respond in the future to the needs of the whole people: "Nothing in our educational history is more striking than the steady pressure of democracy upon its universities to adapt them to the requirements of all the people . . . all under the ideal of service to democracy

---

[1] WILLIAM S. GRAY, ed., *Current Issues in Higher Education* (University of Chicago Press, Chicago, 1937), Part II, p. 34.

rather than of individual advancement alone.''[1] Some of the state universities were beginning to admit more and more students before the World War, and some of their spokesmen were justifying such admissions in terms of democracy.

In 1916, President Emeritus James H. Baker of the University of Colorado was making a plea that Humanism should admit new subjects, study the problems of the present, and drop its aristocratic and exclusive air, a plea that self-styled Humanists apparently still disregard. Baker insisted that the university should be democratic and should serve the state through its common people as well as through its leaders:

> The new humanism has for its basis a knowledge of sociology, politics, philosophy, history, literature, and art. It centers its interest in the needs of the present. We have already referred to the fact that the Greeks related their education to their own time and country. Philosophy must have an immediate vision; psychology and literature must deal with the urgent hunger in the soul today; sociology must strike a chord of sympathy. Humanism will have an insight into man's nature as conditioned by the present. Whatever of the exclusive and aristocratic has been contained in it will be eliminated.[2]

Baker expressed a faith in democracy and the hope that

> The college will be broad enough, not only for cultured leisure and the need of the learned professions, but for business, and for the average citizen in whatever occupation.[3]

One of the most effective and brilliant expositors and practitioners of the democratic philosophy of higher education has been Alexander Meiklejohn. In his annual report for 1918 as president of Amherst College, he insisted that the greatest need of the colleges was not to devise means for eliminating poor students or to concentrate on the best but to devise means for making effective citizens out of the average youth the country over.[4] Again, when the Experimental College at the University of Wisconsin was opening, Professor Meiklejohn was particularly concerned that it should be a democratic college representing a cross section of the general run of students and not a highly selected few. He felt that, among other things, it must try to answer the question whether or not young people as a whole could be liberally educated.

Inasmuch as our whole democratic society is built on the theory that the masses of people are capable of understanding and thinking for them-

---

[1] F. J. TURNER, *The Frontier in American History* (Henry Holt & Company, Inc., New York, 1920), p. 283.

[2] J. H. BAKER, *American University Progress and College Reform* (Longmans, Green & Company, New York, 1916), pp. 45–46.

[3] *Ibid.*, p. 46.

[4] MEIKLEJOHN, *The Liberal College*, p. 153.

selves, Meiklejohn felt that the colleges must try to do their part in developing the ability to think among the great majority of people. He asserted that no one had the right to say that average people could not think, because general education and the colleges had not yet given the average person a fair chance:

> We wish to experiment on the general run of students. It seems to me that the vital social question in American education today is not, How well can we do with specially qualified groups of students? but rather, Can our young people as a whole be liberally educated? Must we accept the aristocratic division of people into two classes, one of which can be trained to understand while the other is doomed by its own incapacity to remain forever outside the field of intelligence? . . . For the present our primary task is that of taking all types of young people and discovering their powers.[1]

Finally, when the Experimental College had run its course, Meiklejohn was more than ever of the opinion that democratic college education *is* possible, for he found that the greatest progress had been made by those very students who at the outset were uncultured; unlettered; often awkward; and, all in all, quite average.[2]

Another and most effective exponent of the theory of democratic higher education has been President Coffman of the University of Minnesota. Speaking before the Department of Superintendence of the National Education Association in 1928, President Coffman stated explicitly and forcefully that the state university was definitely not for the aristocracy of wealth or for developing an aristocratic leadership of the intellectually elite. It was therefore not to be rigidly selective or proud of its high mortality rate. He admitted, of course, that the university should keep out those who could not do the work, but he insisted that the range of work should be expanded widely and that slowness in getting the work done should be no bar. Inasmuch as education for followership was fully as important as education for leadership, Coffman urged that ever greater numbers of students should be allowed to enter the university and that it should serve the state in every way needed. He thus took his stand on the side of ever wider opportunity for college education for the people of the state.[3]

In other connections, Coffman reiterated his stand that the state universities should increase their availability and usefulness to the youth and adults of the state: "They [universities] will undertake to raise the cultural level of all the people as well as the cultural level of those who

[1] ALEXANDER MEIKLEJOHN, "Wisconsin's Experimental College," *The Survey*, 58: 269 (June 1, 1927).

[2] MEIKLEJOHN, *The Experimental College*, pp. 198–204.

[3] COFFMAN, *The State University, Its Work and Problems*, Chap. III, "The State University: Its Relation to Public Education."

are to assume leadership among the people."[1] In commenting on the effects of the depression of 1929 upon higher education, Coffman indicated that the state universities were increasingly recognizing "the tendency as well as the necessity of higher education to spread so as to include the great masses of youth not now being reached."[2] In line with this philosophy, the University of Minnesota established its General College to carry out these democratic aims which Coffman so effectively enunciated.

College educators other than those connected with state universities have also attacked the aristocratic emphasis upon leadership. President Hopkins of Dartmouth expressed himself as skeptical of the aim of leadership unless it was interpreted as broadly as President E. A. Birge of the University of Wisconsin had interpreted it in one of his baccalaureate addresses. Birge had said that leadership is developed when the university fits all of its students for service in all fields through work well done in the community. In the following statement, Hopkins showed his suspicion of aristocratic leadership:

It seems clear that we must distrust the validity of much that has been said in regard to its being the function of higher education to train for leadership. We must revise this statement to say that the first function of the college is to educate men for usefulness.[3]

Professor Donald P. Cottrell of Teachers College, Columbia University, struck the same general note when he stated that the college should be for the majority, not for the minority, of young people. He criticized colleges that try to select their students too rigidly and stated that selection is proper only when the college defines its position clearly and when there is a state university available to students to fill in all of the gaps that the differentiating institutions leave open.[4]

The problem of admission to college on a democratic basis has been effectively summarized from the historical and critical point of view in a recent book entitled *Democracy Enters College* by R. L. Duffus of the *New York Times*. Duffus was given a grant of money by the Carnegie Foundation for the Advancement of Teaching to study different systems of admission throughout the country, and his findings fit in admirably with the democratic theory of higher education as described here. Duffus shows how the unit system of admission to college grew up as a corollary of the expansion of the curriculum and the elective system in the high

---

[1] *Ibid.*, p. 162.

[2] *Ibid.*, p. 277.

[3] SCHILPP, ed., *op. cit.*, Chap. VII, pp. 162, 167.

[4] DONALD P. COTTRELL, "The Liberal Arts College Problem," *Teachers College Record*, 32: 457–462 (February, 1932).

school and college. He also points out how the unit system has been reformed and modified in order to individualize standards of admission and to meet more adequately the needs of the greater number of students who have flocked to the colleges and universities of the country.

Duffus found that the state universities were not nearly so selective in their admission requirements as were the more conservative private colleges and that therefore the state universities were able to raise noticeably the level of civilization and intelligence throughout the various states. He found also that the more progressive colleges were discarding the rigid unit system and making admission an individual matter; in other words, they—for example, the General College of the University of Minnesota—are beginning to ask, "Can we do anything for this student?" rather than, "Can he meet our standards?"

Duffus found in his study of admission requirements a remarkable parallel to the findings of this book concerning the college elective system:

We have seen, in the course of this present survey, that the old pattern of college education broke down as new subjects forced their way into the curriculum; that the result of this breakdown was a period of educational anarchy in which it became almost impossible for educators to agree on the content or objectives of a college course, and in which educational standards were threatened because no one could define them; that the next step was an attempt to reduce education to mathematical units; that this attempt failed because it was found that units, hours and credits did not and could not measure the student's achievement or present worth; and that the current tendency is toward the evaluation of the individual student and the use of that evaluation as a basis for his further education.[1]

One final point concerning the democratic theory of college education should be made. Not only do its advocates believe that the principle of democracy requires that more and more students should have an opportunity to gain a college education and be trained in the practices of democracy, but they are beginning to recognize also that the teachers and students alike should be given more voice in the direction of college policy and curriculum development, as at Black Mountain College, Bard, and Goddard. Some progress has been made along this line by the attempt of some progressive colleges to have students cooperate in planning the curriculum and fit it to individual needs. Several have appointed student committees which have reported their suggestions.[2]

---

[1] R. L. DUFFUS, *Democracy Enters College; A Study of the Rise and Decline of the Academic Lockstep* (Charles Scribner's Sons, New York, 1936), p. 234.

[2] For a summary of some of student reports, see LESLIE K. PATTON, "Undergraduate Student Reports," *Journal of Higher Education*, 3: 285–293 (June, 1932).

Progress has also been made in giving faculty members a larger share in the conduct of the affairs of various colleges. Professor J. E. Kirkpatrick traced the development of administrative control of colleges in the United States and showed how legal control had slipped from the hands of the faculty into those of the boards of trustees. He urged that faculties be given once again their ancient right to direct college policy legally as well as actually.[1] Several reports of the American Association of University Professors contain statements of varying degrees of progress made in various colleges along this line of development.[2]

The experience of Wisconsin's Experimental College pointed to the advisability of small faculties wherein each member could have his say in the direction of college policy through discussion and cooperative effort.[3] Finally, the most recent gains for democratic control of college administration have been made in the colleges of New York City. There the Board of Higher Education passed a bylaw (effective September 1, 1938) giving more power to a faculty council that includes teachers of instructor's status and giving to faculty members the power to elect deans, heads of departments, and new faculty members.[4]

This controversy between aristocratic and democratic conceptions of the college is, of course, one of the most crucial issues facing democracy and the college today. The conservative conception of the college as a place for the few is historically an anachronism inherited from the days when an aristocratic conception of society was thought to be perfectly natural. It now appears that the democratic conception of the college must take greater precedence if the ideal of democracy is to be genuinely achieved in our society. Time was when democratic elementary and secondary education was thought to be too radical for the good of society, but the battle for democratic schools was fought and largely won in the nineteenth century. It now seems reasonable to suppose that the same historical forces that made democratic schools necessary in the nineteenth century are making democratic colleges a like necessity in the twentieth.

[1] J. E. KIRKPATRICK, *Academic Organization and Control* (Antioch College Press, Yellow Springs, Ohio, 1931).

[2] *American Association of University Professors, Bulletin*, March, 1920; April, 1928; March, 1936.

[3] MEIKLEJOHN, *The Experimental College*, pp. 250–253.

[4] News stories, *New York Times*, Apr. 13, 1938; June 21, 1938.

CHAPTER XIX

CULTURE VERSUS CASH

One of the oldest controversies concerning the nature of higher education and one that still evokes considerable debate is the conflict between cultural and liberal as opposed to practical and vocational education. This has plagued higher education ever since the days of Plato, Aristotle, the Medieval Church, the Renaissance, and the founding of Harvard in America. It is a conflict that has been traced in this book in so far as it has affected the fortunes of the elective system in American colleges. It is a conflict that is still being debated in higher educational circles today and helping to shape the American college of the future. With some notable exceptions, the battle lines have been drawn with surprisingly great similarity to those of other controversies already discussed.

In fact, the quarrel over cultural and practical is largely another aspect of the general conflict between conservatives and traditionalists as opposed to progressives and experimentalists. For example, a great many of the educators who affirm the cultural ideal are the same ones who base their arguments on the philosophy of the Great Tradition, intellectualism, discipline, academic retreat, and aristocratic notions of the college. Conversely, the educators who say that college education should become more practical and useful are mainly those who have supported a philosophy of experience, scientific intelligence, freedom and interest, social responsibility, and democratic ideals.

This chapter, then, will deal as briefly as possible with four aspects of the college controversies that have emphasized cultural versus practical arguments. In the first place, the controversy has been waged by conservatives in favor of a cultural aim which seems to emphasize non-vocational elements and remote values having to do with leisure and recreation, "gentlemanly" manners and taste, and a maintenance of the traditional meaning of the Bachelor of Arts degree. In opposition, the progressives have tended to emphasize more immediate practical values of a political and social nature as well as the more specifically economic value of training for a vocation and making a living.

Secondly, the conservatives have felt that cultural values can best be served by concentrating upon the traditional liberal arts of language, literature, philosophy, mathematics, and especially the classical languages and literature. The classical controversy is by no means dead. In opposition, the progressives have been insisting that college education can be made more practical and useful by a greater recognition of the more modern studies, such as the physical sciences, scientific method, the social sciences, and in some cases the modern as against the classical languages.

A third aspect of the controversy has been a conflict between those who wish to keep the four-year liberal college intact as the best means of attaining a cultural education and those who see no particular sacredness to the four-year program and would substitute a more flexible scheme such as the junior college or other arrangements that allow more attention to the practical studies.

Finally, evidence exists that the religious and denominational conception of the college has maintained greater allegiance to the cultural ideal, whereas secular colleges have professed to be more ready to embrace practical and vocational aims.

CULTURAL VALUES REAFFIRMED BY CONSERVATIVES

The cultural aim of the college has not been changed much by its adherents since the controversial days of the nineteenth century. Many of the arguments and phrases used today remain virtually the same as they have been for several generations. The word cultural is usually interpreted in a rather narrow sense and is often identified with the traditional literary and philosophical heritage with which an educated person is presumed to be familiar. Hence, a sharp division is usually made between liberal and cultural as opposed to the vocational and technical studies which are assumed to be nonliberal and noncultural. Often the definitions of cultural are no more exact than merely to say that cultural means nonpractical. In any case, there seems to be an assumption of a definite cleavage between the two, a pronounced preference for the cultural, and an urgent plea that colleges eschew all that smacks of the practical, or vocational. Most college educators can be found at one time or another to be using such terms as cultural, liberal, "taste," and "manners" with a glib and sometimes mystical significance which carries great effect but often little specific meaning.[1]

The Humanists, of course, have been in the forefront of the protest against practical and utilitarian values in college education, and they have set the tone for many of the arguments that have urged the college to remain true to its cultural and liberal aims. For example, Irving

[1] See, for example, three studies of college aims made in the last 20 years: Koos and CRAWFORD, "College Aims Past and Present," *School and Society*, 14: 499–509 (Dec. 3, 1921); FREDERICK J. KELLY, *The American Arts College* (New York, 1925), Chap. II, "Summary of Aims"; MELVIN E. HAGGERTY, *The Evaluation of Higher Institutions*, Part III, *The Educational Program*, Chap. I, "The Purposes of Higher Institutions."

Babbitt fought a long fight against the "pure utilitarians" and "scientific radicals" whom he considered the common enemies of literature and humanistic education, the only true cultural education. Typical of his attitude is the following statement:

> In other words,—and this brings us once more to the central point of our discussion,—even if we sacrifice the letter of the old Bachelor of Arts degree, we should strive to preserve its spirit. This spirit is threatened at present in manifold ways,—by the upward push of utilitarianism and kindergarten methods, by the downward push of professionalism and specialization, by the almost irresistible pressure of commercial and industrial influences.[1]

A more recent Humanist, Norman Foerster, has been carrying valiantly forward the fight against allowing students to study vocational courses in the undergraduate college. Foerster would go so far in the other direction toward humanistic education for leisure purposes that he admits: "The vocation of being a gentleman, even a merely ornamental gentleman, may be more valuable to society than many another occupation."[2]

The presidents of several of the largest and most influential universities in America have put the weight of their influence on the side of the cultural approach to college education. President A. Lawrence Lowell of Harvard University gave much attention in the many public utterances of his long career to defining the cultural aims of the college in an attempt to keep out the useful and vocational values. Even before he became president of Harvard, he differed from President Eliot on this question and urged that students be not allowed to select courses with a view to a future vocation or profession:

> . . . I understand it [the object of an undergraduate education] to mean a general training of the mind as distinguished from the acquisition of specific information which is expected to be of any definite use in later life.[3]

Then, soon after he was elected president of Harvard, he indicated that by culture he did not mean the command of the tools of one's trade but rather an attitude of mind:

> . . . enjoyment of things the world has agreed are beautiful; interest in the knowledge that mankind has found valuable; comprehension of the principles that the race has accepted as true.[4]

---

[1] IRVING BABBITT, *Literature and the American College* (Houghton Mifflin Company, Boston, 1908), pp. 115–116.

[2] NORMAN FOERSTER, *The American State University* (University of North Carolina Press, Chapel Hill, 1937), p. 67.

[3] A. LAWRENCE LOWELL, *At War with Academic Tradition in America* (Harvard University Press, Cambridge, 1934), p. 5.

[4] *Ibid.*, p. 117.

In his annual report of 1915–1916, Lowell indicated that he was quite pleased that Harvard in contrast to other universities had sharply divided a general and cultural education from a technical and professional one by keeping the respective faculties and student life separate. A little later, Lowell reaffirmed his belief that the college must hold to the cultural ideal that enlarges knowledge, aids students to think clearly, and stimulates their imagination rather than aiming at the practices of a definite occupation. In other words, the students of a liberal college must study the philosophy, literature, art, and science that has occupied the greatest minds on earth without regard to any definite use:

The thesis I desire to maintain about the future of the American college, as thus defined, is that its aim must be . . . of a cultural rather than a vocational type.[1]

Finally, as Lowell laid down the reins of administration at Harvard in 1932, he stated in his last annual report his belief that the college was properly becoming less vocational:

The trends in the College have been toward a less vocational objective, a greater correlation of knowledge, a recognition of the principle of self-education, and a stimulation of more vivid intellectual interests. . . . "Less vocational" means regarding the purpose of college education less from the standpoint of its direct utility in a future career, and more from that of developing the faculties of the student; building the mind rather than storing it with special knowledge; teaching young men how to think accurately and comprehensively about large subjects, rather than how to use the tools of a restricted field.[2]

President James R. Angell of Yale University is another college administrator of great influence who has maintained in many of his public utterances that the college should definitely not try to emulate the trade or technical school. In his address before the Department of Superintendence of the National Education Association in 1928, President Angell stated that, although the public institutions of higher education may have aimed more directly at training for occupations, the privately endowed institutions had rightly aimed at liberal culture.[3] Then, in a commencement address at Swarthmore in 1930, Angell quoted approvingly the Yale Faculty Report of 1828 in which the aim of the college was stated in terms of intellectual culture and discipline and cultivation of taste. He believed these aims worthy but that colleges had not adequately attained them.[4]

[1] R. L. KELLY, *The Effective College* (Association of American Colleges, New York, 1928), p. 281.

[2] LOWELL, *op. cit.*, p. 344.

[3] J. R. ANGELL, *American Education* (Yale University Press, New Haven, 1937), pp. 27–41.

[4] *Ibid.*, pp. 63–72.

While the presidents of Harvard and Yale were declaring their allegiance to the cultural ideal, President Nicholas Murray Butler of Columbia University was making several declarations to the same effect. It is interesting to note that whereas a former president of Columbia, F. A. P. Barnard, started out with an inclination toward the cultural conception of the college and then shifted his ground in favor of the elective system to allow greater specialization and vocational study, the evolution of Butler's position took the opposite form.

In his annual report of 1903–1904, Butler spoke approvingly of the tendency to allow professional and technical courses to be submitted for credit in the liberal arts college:

> The College, and the University as a whole, will gain, not lose, by adhering to the policy of permitting undergraduate students to choose professional courses in law, medicine, technology, teaching, or fine arts, as part of a curriculum leading to the degree of bachelor of arts.[1]

A more striking note in favor of joining liberal and vocational education was struck by Butler again in the early days of his presidency (1908), when he was fighting with White and Eliot for the elective system as a means of building a great university out of a small college:

> It is a grave error, therefore, and one which gives rise to many misconceptions and many mistakes of judgment, to set vocational training and liberal training in sharp antagonism to each other.[2]

Despite, however, his earlier statements and work in behalf of recognizing vocational studies as a part of liberal education, President Butler later tended to retreat from his former attitude and to urge that vocational studies were the greatest enemy of truly cultural and liberal education. As early as his annual report of 1911–1912, he showed that he had begun to change his attitude with reference to the relation between cultural and vocational education:

> Without knowing just whither they were going, the colleges have followed the trend of the time toward a slackening of discipline . . . toward that confusion between general training and vocational preparation which is for the college a painless but sure form of suicide. . . . We need at Columbia more men, not fewer, who pursue a college course with no vocational aim in view, but who wish to furnish the mind for enjoyment, for happiness and for worth in later years.[3]

[1] E. C. ELLIOTT, ed., *The Rise of a University*, Vol. II, *The University in Action* (Columbia University Press, New York, 1937), p. 163.

[2] N. M. BUTLER, *The Meaning of Education* (Charles Scribner's Sons, New York, 1915), p. 124.

[3] ELLIOTT, *op. cit.*, Vol. II, pp. 167–168.

In the same report, Butler lamented the fact that the colleges had lost so many of the old so-called culture courses; and he insisted that despite the two-year courses, the real aim of the college is to train "citizens who will be educated gentlemen" or "liberally educated gentlemen."[1] A little later, in 1921, Butler repeated that one of the most important causes of wastefulness and inefficiency in education was the doctrine that the college should be dominated by an immediate and narrowly economic aim rather than moral purposes.[2]

The clearest statements of the present state of President Butler's thinking on this controversy have been made in recent years. In his report for 1934–1935, he insisted that vocational education laid too great stress on the profit motive in American life and that it must be weeded out of a truly cultural and liberal education:

The tendency to lay emphasis upon vocational preparation is the greatest enemy which liberal education has to face. . . . Vocational preparation is all well enough in its way, but it is always and everywhere of secondary importance.[3]

In 1937, as he looked back upon his 35 years as president of Columbia, Butler decided that the vocational influence had been definitely bad for college education:

These [changes] have been due primarily to the pressure of new subjects of instruction claiming a place in the program and to the pressure to make school and college training increasingly specific and vocational. The combined influence of these two movements has brought great changes in the schools. The good old-fashioned education which I myself had in the public schools in Paterson and in old Columbia College is no longer possible. I do not think that which has taken its place is half so good.[4]

In his more positive statements of what he believes a cultural and liberal education ought to be as opposed to a specialized and vocational education, President Butler has emphasized the qualities of gentlemanly manners and taste and knowledge of the fundamental facts of history, morals, art, literature, science, and politics. An aristocratic note also creeps in as he proclaims, in the tradition of Plato and Aristotle, that

A liberal education is one that is fit for a free man who is worthy of his freedom. Such an one must be intellectually, morally and economically free as well as in enjoyment of that freedom which is strictly political.[5]

[1] *Ibid.*, p. 167 *ff.*
[2] *Ibid.*, pp. 134–135.
[3] *Ibid.*, pp. 178–179.
[4] S. J. WOOLF, "Butler Gives a Definition of Education," *New York Times Magazine*, (Jan. 3, 1937), p. 16.
[5] ELLIOTT, *op. cit.*, p. 324.

In another connection, President Butler has again indicated his sympathy with the gentlemanly humanistic and literary ideal of such men as Erasmus, Matthew Arnold, and other conservative advocates of the traditional type of a liberal education:

What one misses today is that background of good manners, of correct and cultivated speech, of high standards of appreciation in art and in letters, that general and kindly acquaintance with all that is best in literature, in the fine arts and in reflective thought, which has always constituted the tie that binds together the men and women of genuine educational insight and competence.[1]

Butler has also deplored the lack of knowledge of the classical and modern languages among present-day students and by implication regrets that teachers are no longer entirely recruited from professional classes— from among lawyers, clergymen, physicians, men of letters. His faith in the cultural conception of college education may be summed up as follows:

A neat and well-kept person, good manners, cultivated speech and some appreciation and understanding of the best that has been said and done in the world would constitute a high but practicable ideal for the education of American youth in this twentieth century.[2]

Although the influence of the Humanists and of some of the presidents of large universities has doubtless been great in favor of cultural as opposed to vocational aims, far greater and more unanimous has been the opinion of presidents and educators connected with the smaller liberal arts college. The names of such educators have been legion, and they can be found almost everywhere that college issues have been discussed in the last generation, but only a few recent examples can be mentioned by name here.

In his penetrating and incisive book *College or Kindergarten?* Dean C. M. McConn of Lehigh University came out strongly in favor of the college of culture. As a result of thousands of interviews with parents and students, Dean McConn found the three most important purposes with which students went to college: the "bread-and-butter" purpose to earn more money and make a better living, the "superkindergarten" purpose of those on the higher economic levels to attain greater pleasure from recreational and leisure pursuits, and the culture purpose of the earnest students who wish to promote the intellectual life through non-utilitarian activities. Dean McConn found these incompatible aims all worthy ones, but he felt that they should not exist side by side in the same institution, so his suggestion was that the professional and vocational courses which clutter college curriculums should be separated into sepa-

[1] *Ibid.*, p. 327.
[2] *Ibid.*, p. 328.

rate schools of education, journalism, and home economics for the lower income groups. Likewise, there should be established a "Gentleman's College" for the wealthier students; finally, the "Real College" should be maintained for scholars and those interested in the cultural and intellectual purposes of knowledge, enjoyment, freedom, disinterested thought, and spiritual ideals.[1]

More recent statements of the same general tone have been made by the presidents of Lawrence College, Appleton, Wisconsin and Wesleyan University, Middletown, Connecticut. Henry M. Wriston, when president of the former, insisted that a liberal education should be valuable in itself at the time, so that if a student were to die at commencement time, his liberal education would have been worth the living: " . . . there is no quarrel here with vocational, technical, or professional training. They have an indispensable function. The point insisted upon is that schools devoted to these subjects are not liberal colleges, and that colleges which imitate such schools lose their liberal character."[2]

In a recent symposium on the current issues in higher education, President James L. McConaughy of Wesleyan insisted that the college of liberal arts should divest itself of training for professional and vocational livelihoods and should concentrate on the cultural subjects of college education. He agreed with Hutchins that the desultory attention given to the liberal arts college is to be deplored and that colleges should provide a fundamental intellectual training rather than give training for making a living. McConaughy would differ with Hutchins as to the methods of attaining this goal, but they would agree on the fundamental opposition between cultural and vocational education.[3]

Perhaps the most insistent proposal that colleges should slough off their vocational courses and aims came from Abraham Flexner in his oft quoted book on the universities. His book is filled with devastatingly ironical examples of the way in which modern universities and colleges have acceded to practical demands by cluttering up their offerings with trivial courses (the word "trivial," incidentally, seems to be the estimate of recent times upon the fate of the medieval trivium to which many modern educators would like to return). Flexner extended his philippics to denounce all sorts of "wretched *ad hoc* courses" which were extolling vocational virtues in schools of education, journalism, business, optometry, and hotel management. He felt that many people were attending colleges but few were getting educated, because so much money was

---

[1] C. M. McCONN, *College or Kindergarten?* (New Republic Inc., New York, 1928), Chap. II.

[2] WRISTON, *The Nature of a Liberal College*, p. viii.

[3] W. S. GRAY, ed., *Current Issues in Higher Education* (University of Chicago Press, Chicago, 1937), pp. 25–35.

being spent for incidental and unnecessary vocational work and too little for philosophy, art, literature, and other scholarly, cultural subjects. The case for the inclusion of courses, or faculties, in a college must be based upon their "inherent and intellectual value"; and if they have merely practical value, they must be excluded: "Practical importance is not a sufficient title to academic recognition: if that is the best that can be said, it is an excellent reason for exclusion."[1]

It should be noted, however, that Flexner has not always been so adamant in his opposition to courses with a practical and vocational purpose. In 1923, he was urging that the college might introduce more purposiveness into the undergraduate curriculums by prescribing sets of courses looking forward to the vocational aims of students. Thus, he proposed that definite objectives leading to engineering, law, medicine, ministry, business, journalism, and teaching might be introduced into the college course in order to make the student more thoughtful of his future at an earlier date. In other words, the college might " . . . after careful analysis of the situation, offer a group of studies adapted to the future needs of the prospective business man or journalist."[2]

It is wholly evident, then, that the traditional cultural objectives of the college have played a major role in determining the dominant conception of college education down to the present day. Even students have assumed in their written statements of college aims (if not in the courses that they have selected in the last 30 years) that the college should be for cultural rather than vocational purposes. In 1932, Dean Leslie K. Patton of Emory University made a survey of 17 reports written and published by student committees in several universities. In his summary statement, he said: "Without quoting from each report, it may be justifiable to state that students hold that the college should be distinctly cultural rather than vocational; it should teach one how to live, not how to make a living . . . "[3]

Even while students were aping their elders in their formulated statements of the aims of college education, in actual practice they were choosing courses largely for their practical and occupational advantages. In 1931, a study was made of students' reasons for the selection of their

---

[1] ABRAHAM FLEXNER, *Universities, American, English, German* (Oxford University Press, New York, 1930), p. 27.

[2] ABRAHAM FLEXNER, *A Modern College and a Modern School* (Doubleday, Doran & Company, Inc., New York, 1923), pp. 34–35. This book, by the way, stirred up a substantial controversy over the merits of making school and college education more practical through a greater emphasis upon scientific studies. In this instance, Flexner was on the side of the progressives and under attack from the Humanists and traditionalists who favored the classics and literary subjects.

[3] LESLIE K. PATTON, "Undergraduate Student Reports," *Journal of Higher Education*, 3: 288 (June, 1932).

courses in 10 liberal arts colleges of different size, location, and control. These revealed, first, the obvious fact that they were required for a degree or a major study; but the second greatest number of courses was selected for vocational and occupational reasons.[1] The cultural reason was only fourth in popularity and was considerably below the vocational motive. A recent study of the church-related college shows that, although college educators still predominately avow the cultural aim, even the conservative religious colleges are giving more vocational courses than ever before.[2]

The cultural motive seems to be strongest, too, with those who have been making surveys of higher education. At least, the investigators in a recent survey of the institutions of the North Central Association voice their fears that the occupational motives have hurt the traditional liberal arts colleges:

> How far the human mind can depart from the stream of knowledge represented by these subjects [traditional liberal arts], how far it can penetrate into the newer and marginal areas of learning without losing the ancient character of the liberal arts, is a problem yet unsolved. It is clear that departure from the traditional subjects is frequently accompanied by an attenuation of content that leaves little of the constructive power of true knowledge. Such a result is a loss in educational values for which there appears to be no compensation, not even that offered by facility in occupational skills.[3]

PRACTICAL AND VOCATIONAL VALUES REDEFINED BY PROGRESSIVES

Despite the opposition of conservatives to what they have disparaged as practical, vocational, occupational, useful, utilitarian, technical, and professional training, there is little doubt that these values have steadily grown in the twentieth century as a part of the collegiate curriculum in the United States. The great emphasis that American culture has put upon profit-seeking and making of money has carried over into the college through pressure to add courses that will train students more directly for making a living in the rapidly increasing number of occupations for which training can be offered.

Furthermore, even if the urge to make money is discounted, the great strides toward the use of machines and development of an industrial and

[1] HELEN FOSS WEEKS, *Factors Influencing the Choice of Courses by Students in Certain Liberal Arts Colleges* (Teachers College, Columbia University, New York, 1931), pp. 52–53.

[2] LESLIE K. PATTON, *The Purposes of Church-related Colleges* (Teachers College, Columbia University, 1939). Patton gives impressive lists of vocational subjects offered by a high percentage of the church-related colleges for occupational preparation, Chaps. IX-X.

[3] MELVIN E. HAGGERTY, *The Evaluation of Higher Institutions*, Part III, *The Educational Program* (University of Chicago Press, Chicago, 1937), p. 30.

technological society have made necessary a much more elaborate system of occupational training for hundreds of new vocations for millions of workers. For example, Professor Harold Clark of Teachers College, Columbia University, has insisted that nearly the whole range of 30,000 identifiable occupations in our modern technological world now require technical training beyond that of the high school. He estimates that out of the 80 or 81 million workers in the United States there are approximately 75 or 76 million people who need at least two years of training in addition to high school in order to cope adequately with the technical problems of farming, household, office, transportation and communication, and industry. In other words, it simply is not true that most occupations require only a mental age of five or six years for proficiency, and Professor Clark estimates that in the future only about 2 million of the 80 million workers can reasonably be expected to stay in repetitive work that does not require much special training. Thus, the capitalistic and industrial development of the country has forced upon the college a great deal more useful type of study than ever before.

Various studies of the aims, courses of study, and catalogues of the American colleges have shown that the occupational motive has been strong in the past and has grown stronger in recent years. The survey made by Koos and Crawford in 1921 shows that colleges were recognizing to some degree as far back as the period 1842–1876 such aims as "domestic responsibility," "occupational training," "training for life's needs," and "opportunities for specialization." It shows also that every one of these aims had increased in influence and importance in the later period from 1909 to 1921.[1] When Dean F. J. Kelly of the University of Minnesota made his survey of the arts colleges in 1925, he found that the vocational objective was present in all the colleges along with the preparatory and cultural aims. He made it evident that he did not believe the vocational aim was an intrinsic part of the liberal arts curriculum, but he could not deny that it was strongly present in the colleges that he studied.[2]

These earlier surveys have been reenforced by later studies and notably by the survey of college literature and practices directed by Melvin Haggerty of the University of Minnesota. Dean Haggerty stated the case clearly as follows:

Whichever route the investigator takes, he soon comes upon one incontrovertible fact, namely, that higher education in America is saturated with the purpose of preparing men and women to be competent in the work of the world. Higher education in America has from the very beginning been characterized by a

[1] L. V. Koos and C. C. CRAWFORD, "College Aims Past and Present," *School and Society*, 14: 499–509 (Dec. 3, 1921).

[2] F. J. KELLY, *The American Arts College* (The Macmillan Company, New York, 1925), Chap. II.

vocational purpose, and occupational fitness has always been a desired outcome of a college education.[1]

Although Haggerty believed that such occupational training should perhaps be given in specialized institutions rather than in liberal arts colleges, nevertheless the survey revealed that vocational aims existed in a great majority of all types of institutions studied and admitted that this practical conception of college education certainly fitted the American culture that supported it. In the specific study of North Central institutions, the survey found that 59 claimed to give training in approximately 160 different occupations discrete enough to be given different names. Also, although some institutions expressed hostility to occupational aims, they nonetheless gave such training, and even the denominational colleges offered many occupational curriculums. All in all, the survey found that vocational preparation was generally accepted as a legitimate aim by the North Central institutions.

Traditionalists who have opposed the introduction of occupational aims into college education have forgotten how genuinely practical higher education has often been in the past. President Hutchins; Abraham Flexner, and others who found so much to admire in the medieval universities did not care to point out that these same medieval universities were highly professional and vocational in character with reference to the society that they served.[2] These conservatives were not willing to admit that the liberal arts of an earlier day were highly vocational and practical, training for the professions of law, medicine, theology, and teaching in the days when these were the only vocations for which systematic training had been developed. They were not willing to admit that new types of courses should be added to the college curriculum when the technological conditions of society created new vocations for which the colleges could also give training. It is upon this latter point that progressives insist. The progressives of the twentieth as well as those of the nineteenth century have responded to the changed conditions of American life by urging that the college should change too and should give the kind of education that is appropriate to new industrial and technological vocations.

The progressives, however, have not always agreed as to just how the college should change to meet these new needs. Some represent a transition position from the extreme position of the conservatives who would keep liberal studies separated from vocational studies and admit only liberal studies into the college. Thus, for example, Alexander Meiklejohn would keep the liberal studies in the liberal college for develop-

[1] HAGGERTY, op. cit., p. 15.
[2] HASTINGS RASHDALL, Universities of Europe in the Middle Ages (Clarendon Press, Oxford, Clarendon Press, New York, 1936), Vol. III, pp. 453 ff.

ing general intelligence and yet have the college become much more practical in its efforts to make students more intelligent participants in modern technological society. In this way, he would segregate vocational and professional studies into separate professional and technical schools in order to give the specialized training necessary for the new types of occupations, but he would reserve the college for general and liberal studies leading to practical intelligence in the society of today.[1]

Another statement that represents the transition from the extreme conservative to the extreme progressive position was made in 1918 by Professor Henry Waldgrave Stuart of Leland Stanford University. Stuart believed along with the conservatives that a sharp distinction should be made between liberal and vocational studies, but he approached the progressive position when he insisted that *both* types should be offered in the college of liberal arts. His interpretation was that the controversies of the nineteenth century between the values of science and those of literature had now been realigned and taken the form of the controversy between liberal and vocational studies. As Stuart viewed the problem, he found that both liberal and vocational studies were necessary for modern life; in other words, the student needed a capacity for contemplation, criticism, and trained enjoyment of life as well as for constructive participation in the activities of modern life. Just as vocational education is incomplete in itself, so is a purely liberal education incomplete in itself. A complete education must recognize one's vocation as a perfectly natural characteristic and one of the universal and necessary interests and activities of man along with the activities of politics, religion, philosophy, and art.[2]

It is now common knowledge that most colleges have developed in just the way that Stuart advocated. Along with the spread of the elective system went the custom of allowing liberal arts students to elect technical and vocational courses in fulfillment of some of their requirements for the B. A. degree. In 1933, Bixler's study of liberal colleges in universities of 42 states showed that 40 or 41 out of 42 colleges allowed students to submit professional, technical, and vocational courses to a greater or lesser extent for the B.A.[3]

The more extreme progressive position would not agree with either Meiklejohn or Stuart that there should be a sharp distinction between liberal and vocational studies. The more characteristic proposals of the

[1] MEIKLEJOHN, *The Liberal College*, Chap. I; and *The Experimental College*, Chaps. I, II.

[2] H. W. STUART, *Liberal and Vocational Studies in the College* (Stanford University Press, Stanford University, Calif., 1918).

[3] EVELYN T. BIXLER, *A Study of Electives in the Liberal Arts Colleges of Certain Universities in Forty-two States* (unpublished M. A. thesis, University of Maryland, Baltimore, 1933).

progressives urge that the college must revise its conceptions of both liberal and vocational studies and must not separate them as has been done in the past or as the conservatives would still do.   John Dewey, of course, has led the progressive attack upon the older dichotomy between these two types of study.   As early as 1916, Dewey insisted that the term vocational was usually defined too narrowly, particularly by the conservatives who favored the cultural type of education.   He felt that the term should be applied to man's callings in many fields, such as family, friendships, and politics, as well as to one's occupation: "A vocation signifies any form of continuous activity which renders service to others and engages personal powers in behalf of the accomplishment of results."[1]

Dewey warned in 1916 (just a year before the Smith-Hughes Vocational Education Act was passed by Congress) that the movement for vocational education at that time would tend to harden even further the dichotomy between liberal and vocational studies by reserving the traditional liberal and cultural education for the few of the upper economic classes and give merely a narrow and specialized trade training to the masses of people.   He felt that this would help to perpetuate the older social, intellectual, and moral dualisms which had produced the liberal arts in the first place: "In general, the opposition to recognition of the vocational phases of life in education (except for the utilitarian three R's in elementary schooling) accompanies the conservation of aristocratic ideals of the past."[2]   Dewey's recommendation at that time was that democracy could best be served by joining together the liberal and vocational studies and introducing into education a good deal more scientific and practical study in order to work toward modifying the socially obnoxious features of the industrial order.   In this way, he would hope to broaden the conception of vocational education so that industrial workers would be able to find more meaning in the mechanical features of production and distribution through a larger share in social control, and so that the more privileged economic groups would gain a greater sympathy for labor and a greater sense of social responsibility.

Dewey returned to this subject many times during the ensuing years but never more forcefully than in the Inglis lectures at Harvard in 1931. In those lectures, he devoted considerable attention to the conflict between the practical aim and the liberal, or cultural, or humanistic, ideal.   He referred unmistakably to Flexner as one of the conservatives who had questioned the legitimacy of adding to the universities and colleges such practical schools as journalism, commerce, engineering, teaching, dentistry, pharmacy, agriculture, forestry, library science, and

[1] JOHN DEWEY, *Democracy and Education* (The Macmillan Company, New York, 1916), p. 373.
[2] *Ibid.*, p. 373; see all of Chap. XXIII, "Vocational Aspects of Education."

domestic and household arts.   Dewey insisted that the only difference between these vocational schools and the traditional "trinity" of learned professions (theology, law, and medicine) is that the vocational schools are *newer* than the traditional trinity which themselves were once in the position of vocational schools with no background.

The point is that these newer vocational or semivocational arts were not in existence or were in the apprenticeship stage when the trinity made its way to the status of "learned professions," but now the arts and technologies of life have become so advanced that methods of apprenticeship no longer serve.   Thus, instruction must be so organized concerning them that they too may be taught legitimately in colleges and universities.   This is not to say, Dewey urged, that vocational subjects have not often been superficial and thin but that when well taught they are socially necessary:

> But the ultimate point is that instruction of this kind, but of a better type, is *socially* necessary, and that until it is properly given in educational institutions, the practical activities carried on in society will not be liberalized and humanized, to say nothing of being most efficiently conducted.[1]

In other words, Dewey rejected the notion that the cultural and liberal must be separated from the practical, and he believed that the only way to arrive at a genuinely vital culture for the masses of people is to recognize that a genuine development of cultural and liberal outlook can be achieved in intimate connection with the practical activities of life.   To be sure, practical courses must remedy their defects of narrow specialization and thinness and superficiality, but this is not to be done by separation but rather by providing them with a larger outlook and a fuller background of the liberal ideal which views knowledge in its relation to the sciences, history, and society.   In the following words, Dewey summed up his view that liberal and practical can be made fruitful only by a vital connection with each other:

> Conflict between the cultural, or liberal, and the practical will continue with result of confusion as long as both of them are narrowly conceived.   I can hardly go into the philosophy of American life, but I do not see how anyone can doubt that as long as the humanistic is set off as something by itself, apart from the interests and activities in which the mass of men and women must perforce engage, it will grow thinner, more and more merely reminiscent, a struggling survival of what Santayana calls the "genteel tradition."   It is equally true that as long as the actual occupations of men, with the exception of a few professions labelled "learned," are not affected by the larger outlook and the fuller background presented by the ideal for which the liberal in education stands they will

[1] JOHN DEWEY, *The Way Out of Educational Confusion* (Harvard University Press, Cambridge, 1931), pp. 22–23.

be narrow and hard, tending not merely to the "utilitarian" in its restricted sense, but even toward the brutal and inhuman.[1]

A good many other progressive educators have taken up the gauntlet flung down by such conservatives as Flexner and Hutchins, but only one or two can be mentioned here. The reply of President Coffman of the University of Minnesota to the conception of a university presented by Flexner has already been cited in previous chapters (see pages 340–341), and much of what Coffman said applies to this problem of cultural versus practical in college education. Suffice it to say, that he believed that the history of higher education shows a perfectly justifiable trend toward greater practicality and that colleges and universities would be remiss in their function if they did not respond to the social needs for better practical knowledge.[2]

Professor Harry D. Gideonse has not only lashed out against the intellectualistic doctrines of President Hutchins because they deny the legitimate claims of practicality (see pages 301–302), but he has also found much to criticize in Flexner's diatribes on the vocational tendencies of modern universities. In his review of the latter's book, he admits that Flexner presents a good deal of material that is of "absorbing and humiliating interest" but finds that Flexner is not always accurate in his criticisms of the universities. One of the most fundamental errors in his thinking, Gideonse believes, is his whole conception that universities should be cultural and not vocational or practical in nature:

Flexner begins with preconceived notions of what universities should be— and never have been—and then derives a great deal of pleasure from a conclusive demonstration that they vary widely from his ideal. . . . A study of the institutions in terms of their own objectives, and the financial and social difficulties which they encounter, might have thrown a wealth of light on many of the practices which the author derides, but it would also have deprived his indictment of much of its vigor.[3]

Writing in 1927 before the most recent attacks of the conservatives upon vocational education, Boyd H. Bode recognized that the ideal of culture in a democratic society must be revised to fit the needs of democracy and that education must train for both culture and vocation. Bode discovered a desirable means of orientation to this problem by doing what this book has tried to do in considerable detail, namely, look closely at the history of culture and its educational correlative, the traditional liberal education. He found that the modern development of democracy

[1] *Ibid.*, pp. 26–27.

[2] COFFMAN, "Flexner and the State University," *Journal of Higher Education*, 2: 380–383 (October, 1931).

[3] HARRY D. GIDEONSE, "Review of Flexner's *Universities*," *American Journal of Sociology*, 37: 1013 (May, 1932).

has revolted against the aristocratic and fixed conceptions of culture whereby the ancient Greeks and Medieval Church had divided irrevocably the free from the slave and had reserved "culture" only for the free.

Nevertheless, Bode indicated, the cultural notion prevailed for long despite the democratic movement, and vocational education became merely a tool for getting ahead and making money. Consequently, cultural education took more and more pride in retiring from earthy things and seeking seclusion in a realm of spirit where no one digs ditches or works with his hands. Despite the reticence of the cultural motive, however, the forces of democracy pushed on, and a great variety of vocational and elective courses forced their way into the high school and college curriculum in order to bring education as much as possible into direct contact with everyday life:

> The general trend of this development is clear enough. It is away from the separation between "practical" and the "cultural" and toward a type of education that will combine the two. This new educational ideal we indicate by such terms as "citizenship" and "social efficiency."[1]

Democracy, therefore, requires a new conception of culture considerably broader than that proposed by the traditionalists. Culture must mean the capacity of the individual person to change and to reorganize his own world, to which process a vocation can contribute as well as science, literature, and art. Bode quotes approvingly Dewey's conception of culture as the "capacity for constantly expanding in range and accuracy one's perception of meanings."[2] But the trouble with the new vocational courses was that they had no sense of direction, and all subjects began to claim to be as cultural as all the rest.

The only way out of this confusion, Bode believed, was for all subjects to be revised so that they contributed more genuinely to increasing the individual's personal and social capacities:

> As I suggested previously, the social changes that are going on are making for a new ideal of culture. The development of science and industry in particular has shown impressively the possibilities of cross-fertilization between vocation and the life of social and intellectual interests. Vocation is becoming a gateway to participation in all the major interests of the race. The traditional opposition between vocation and culture is beginning to disappear. We are learning to think of culture not as a possession but as a way of life, an expression of the whole personality in everyday occupation.[3]

[1] BOYD H. BODE, *Modern Educational Theories* (The Macmillan Company, New York, 1927), p. 251; see whole Chap. XI, "The Ideal of Culture in a Democratic Society."

[2] DEWEY, *Democracy and Education*, p. 145.

[3] BODE, *op. cit.*, pp. 264–265.

In view of the strength of the traditional conception of culture, it may seem that Bode's prediction for the success of the newer democratic conception of culture was overly optimistic, but there is considerable evidence that the movement that he cites is gaining steadily, not only in the lower schools but particularly in some of the more progressive colleges of the country.

Of recent years, the movement to introduce into the actual college curriculum some measure of the progressive theory of union of cultural with practical studies has gained headway. One of the outstanding new expressions of this point of view, which Andrew D. White formulated so clearly at Cornell in the 1870's, was made in the report of the conference held at Rollins College in 1931. John Dewey was chairman, and a variety of college educators attended, including Professor Goodwin Watson of Teachers College, Columbia University; W. S. Anderson, dean of Rollins; J. P. Gavit; J. K. Hart; Hamilton Holt, president of Rollins; A. E. Morgan, president of Antioch College; Professor James Harvey Robinson of Columbia University; Constance Warren, president of Sarah Lawrence College; and C. M. McConn of Lehigh University. The report took its cue from an article by Goodwin Watson in which he proposed that the colleges should be reorganized into seven departments to represent actual life experiences. Watson proposed that the studies of the newer college should center around such life interests and activities as those of health, homemaking, purchasing and consumer activities, leisure-time experiences, vocation, citizenship, and philosophy of life.[1] It is evident that this list is weighted on the side of the practical rather than the cultural studies, breaks down the traditional separation of these two types, and departs radically from the old system of prescribed studies.

The Rollins report itself took its stand squarely in favor of combining cultural with practical studies, and it proposed a new type of college that would provide an integrated curriculum beginning with the last two years of high school and continuing through the completion of professional preparation. In this way, cultural courses would extend throughout the whole course, and professional and vocational studies would come in whenever the student was ready for them by virtue of his maturity and clear realization of his vocational aim. The report criticized the traditional college in the following terms:

One of the limitations of the liberal arts college has been a tendency to deny worth to economic and other practical issues and to assume the old classical attitude that usefulness and dignity are in conflict. For the liberal arts college to survive it must recognize the unity and equal dignity of all necessary human concerns, and must endeavor to include and synthesize them all. This is the

[1] GOODWIN WATSON, "What Should College Students Learn?" *Progressive Education*, 7: 319–325 (November, 1930), and 7: 399–403 (December, 1930).

lesson the liberal arts college must learn from the institutions which seem to threaten its existence.[1]

The point is made again in this report that in simpler days, when most occupations involved only the rule of thumb which could quickly be learned by apprenticeship, there was some excuse for considering vocations as illiberal; but this is no longer true, since science and the arts have been applied to the various vocations in such a way that they now involve a scientific search for general principles. In this part of the report, which Dewey attributes to President Morgan of Antioch, the progressive position is summed up as follows:

In so far as the liberal arts college stands for a perpetuation of the traditional conflict between vocation and culture, it seems doomed to play a constantly decreasing role in education. In a day when most of the occupations of men involved little more than manual skill and the repeated application of a few rule-of-thumb formulae, the concept of vocation as illiberal may have had some basis. With the modern applications of all the sciences and arts to vocations, and the successful search for principles within the operations and purposes of the vocations themselves, it is no longer true. It is rapidly becoming a fact that study within one's vocational preparation is an important means of freeing and liberalizing the mind. This being true, the inevitable trend in education is toward the rapid thinning of the traditional educational wall between vocational and cultural. The liberal arts college will survive and render service in proportion as it recognizes this fact and brings its course of study and administrative set-up into effective conformity with it.[2]

This question of relating the functions of colleges and universities closely to vocational activities was given wide publicity in 1936 when the position was defended by the eminent scientist Alfred North Whitehead, in the pages of the *Atlantic Monthly*. President Hutchins replied to Whitehead in the same magazine, and the controversy was on from many quarters.[3] Writing with reference to the tercentenary of Harvard University, Professor Whitehead made the general point that universities should relate knowledge closely to action: "Thus unapplied knowledge

[1] *Rollins College, The Curriculum for the Liberal Arts College* (Winter Park, Fla. n.d.) p. 9.

[2] *Ibid.*, p. 9.

[3] See, for example, R. M. HUTCHINS, "Reply to Professor Whitehead," *Atlantic Monthly*, 158: 582–588 (November, 1936); A. W. LEVI, "Problems of Higher Education: Whitehead and Hutchins," *Harvard Educational Review*, 7: 451–465 (October, 1937); H. W. CHASE, "Hutchins' Higher Learning Grounded," *American Scholar*, 6: 236–244 (Spring, 1937); C. M. PERRY, "Education: Ideas or Knowledge," *International Journal of Ethics*, 47: 346–359 (April, 1937); C. E. CLARK, "Higher Learning in a Democracy," *ibid.*, 47: 317–335; "University of the Future Envisioned; Hutchins and Whitehead Debate Intellectual vs. Vocational," *Literary Digest*, 122: 24–25 (Nov. 7, 1936).

is knowledge shorn of its meaning. . . . The careful shielding of a university from the activities of the world around is the best way to chill interest and defeat progress. Celibacy does not suit a university. It must mate itself with action."[1]

Focusing his general principle upon the problem of vocational studies, Whitehead commended the tendency of universities to bring their theoretical activities into close association with such vocational and professional schools as law, religion, medicine, business, art, education, government, and engineering. He intimated that universities should lend their best efforts to giving systematic understanding to these practical affairs of life. He pointed out that earlier universities had maintained just such close relationships with the important practical affairs of their own days; and he insisted that the withdrawal of universities from close association with the practice of life was a modern phenomenon, culminating in the eighteenth and nineteenth centuries and heralding the decay of a cultural epoch. Disagreeing fundamentally with the position of such men as Flexner and Hutchins, Professor Whitehead pointedly stated: "It is mid-summer madness on the part of universities to withdraw themselves from the closest contact with vocational practices."[2]

Such statements as these have found concrete expression in several kinds of actual college courses. The best known, perhaps, is the cooperative plan worked out several years ago at Antioch College whereby students work six weeks on their studies at the college and then go for six weeks to work in actual industrial or business jobs throughout the country. In this way, it is hoped that they will be able to relate their college studies more vitally to the problems of earning a living and to the more general economic and social problems that face our society. Another approach has been the "self-help" colleges which give students a chance to pay part or all of their college expenses by working on college farms and in college shops to provide the daily necessities of food, clothing, and shelter as well give actual experience in the activities of making a living. A good many such colleges have been established throughout the country, notably, Berea College, Berea, Ky.; Blackburn College at Carlinville, Ill.; and Madison College, near Nashville, Tenn.

Attempts to solve the problem of the union of liberal with vocational studies have been made not only by colleges that appeal to the less fortunate economic groups but also by progressive colleges the clientele of which comes largely from the higher economic stratum of society. Such a progressive college is Bennington, in Vermont, whose president, Robert D. Leigh, effectively stated the case against separation of the

---

[1] A. N. WHITEHEAD, "Harvard: The Future," *Atlantic Monthly*, 158: 267 (September, 1936).

[2] *Ibid.*, p. 268.

cultural from the vocational.   Bennington was founded upon the premise that the student's work should center around a major interest wherever that might lead:

The field of major interest in practically every case will be broader than any single academic department.   It may be organized round a present interest leading to a future adult activity.   Bennington has no sympathy with the false antithesis between vocational and liberal studies.[1]

Since it is difficult, stated Leigh, for the student or for the college to know whether the preparation of a particular student will ultimately be for a vocation or for an avocation, the program must include not only a broad liberal background but also the training for techniques that may be required for entrance upon a vocation:

For example, stenography and typewriting can be pursued as incidental parts of undergraduate work in the case of those young women who plan definitely to enter the secretarial field after graduation.   The type of intellectual asceticism which fears that contact with practice or reality will destroy the field for culture will be studiously avoided at Bennington.   Breadth and thoroughness of work requiring sustained intellectual effort, whether directed toward a vocation or as preparation for leisure, will be the test of success rather than a program distinguished by its isolation from practical usefulness.[2]

In these ways, then, would the progressives try to break down the opposition between cultural and vocational that the conservatives have been at such pains to maintain.   When the conservatives charge that vocational courses are inspired by the desire to make money, the progressives reply that college education must face the realities of modern life and cannot shut out pressing economic and occupational problems. The progressives, too, deplore the profit-seeking motives that have prompted so many of the usual vocational courses; they charge, however, that the way to solve the problem is *not* by shutting out such courses but by trying to broaden and liberalize them so as to make them serve socially useful rather than selfish personal ends.   When the conservatives maintain that the superficiality and narrow specialization of vocational courses make them unworthy to be called "education," the progressives reply that the vocational courses have had no other recourse, because colleges have attached a higher value to culture and to academic courses. The progressives urge that the way out is to unite the liberal and vocational ideals in a joint effort to improve individual and social welfare and, incidentally, to improve the college offerings.

[1] *The Educational Plan for Bennington College* (New York, 1931), p. 11.
[2] *Ibid.*, pp. 11–12.

CHAPTER XX

THE OLD VERSUS THE NEW

TRADITIONAL VERSUS MODERN STUDIES

Another form that the "culture versus cash" controversy has taken is the conflict of opinion over what kinds of study are most important in the college curriculum. When one listens closely to these conflicts, one hears the undercurrent of earlier clashes not yet settled. In other words, the classical controversy is still alive in the twentieth century. As a matter of fact, when the proponents of the Great Tradition, of intellectualism, of discipline, and of culture bring themselves to outlining the course of study that will achieve their aims, they lay a surprisingly great emphasis upon the values to be derived from the study of the classical languages and literature, "classical" books, mathematics, and traditional philosophy.

When the progressives get down to citing specific examples of the way in which students can achieve intelligence, freedom, social responsibility, integrated personality, and practical experience with social problems, it is evident that the main emphasis revolves around problems that appear in the physical sciences, the scientific method, and the social sciences. Thus, the persistent battle between traditional or older and the newer or more modern studies still rages today as it has raged in the past. Shall the college concentrate on study of the past or study of contemporary problems?

A great part of conservative opinion in favor of the classical studies as an indispensable core of a liberal and cultural education has taken its cue from the Humanists who have perhaps been the most extreme claimants in behalf of the classics. All through the writings of Irving Babbitt, there is bountiful evidence that he would prefer the older studies to the newer ones as a center for the college curriculum. He even went so far as to urge the claims of the classics not only against the physical and social sciences but also against the modern languages which he felt could never take the place of the classics, because modern literature "merely encourages sentimental and romantic revery rather than to a resolute and manly grappling with the plain facts of existence."[1]

Babbitt was sure that modern literature was unfit for young minds because it lacked discipline and sobriety and that its very escape from

---

[1] IRVING BABBITT, *Literature and the American College* (Houghton Mifflin Company, Boston, 1908), p. 173.

discipiine was what made it so popular, whereas the classical literature
provided all the qualities necessary for a truly humanistic education:

> Classical literature, at its best, does not so much tend to induce in us a certain
> state of feelings, much less a certain state of nerves; it appeals rather to our
> highest reason and imagination—to those faculties which afford us an avenue of
> escape from ourselves, and enable us to become participants in the universal life.
> It is thus truly educative in that it leads him who studies it out and away from
> himself. The classical spirit, in its purest form, feels itself consecrated to the
> service of a high, impersonal reason. Hence its sentiment of restraint and dis-
> cipline, its sense of proportion and pervading law.[1]

Paul Shorey often proclaimed that the study of language and literature was indispensable to a truly liberal education. He felt that language
study was perfectly secure in the college curriculum, because it provided
the tools for attaining knowledge of all kinds and was somehow peculiarly
bound up with the higher intellectual functions and thus good for mental
discipline. Serious study of great literature was considered by him the
only sure way to develop and refine those human sensibilities which
science leaves cold and to correct the claims of inchoate and pseudo
sciences.[2]

Norman Foerster followed in the footsteps of his eminent Humanist
forebears when he spoke out against "scientism" and the scientific
method in the college and in favor of the traditional studies: "We shall
turn to the studies most useful in the furtherance of human as opposed to
scientific knowledge."[3] Although disavowing any hostility to science,
Foerster's general emphasis was to deprecate the physical and social
sciences and to praise the studies that will reveal " . . . man as known
directly, in his inner life and its manifestations in social and political
history, in literature and the arts, in philosophy, in religion."[4] Foerster
thus disparaged the argument that the social sciences should be developed
in order to aid in the control of society and of man, for he believed that
social knowledge of an economic and sociological and political kind can
never give us a science of man because the essential nature of man is too
complex and intangible: "The control of man is concerned with values
rather than actualities, with what ought to be rather than what is—with
what humanly ought to be rather than what naturally is."[5]

---

[1] *Ibid.*, pp. 173–174.

[2] *The American College*, p. 35; see Chap. II, "The Place of Languages and Literature in the College Curriculum."

[3] NORMAN FOERSTER, *The American State University* (University of North Carolina Press, Chapel Hill, 1937), p. 243.

[4] *Ibid.*

[5] *Ibid.*, p. 240.

The Humanists, of course, were not the only ones to extol the virtues of the classics; even they could not outdo the teachers of the classics or the various symposia that appeared in the second and third decades of the twentieth century on the value of the classics in secondary schools and colleges. Space will permit the mention of only two or three of many volumes and articles published at this time. In 1911, Francis W. Kelsey edited a symposium on the value of the classical and humanistic studies for a liberal education.[1] In addition to the familiar arguments written by the editor himself, the book included articles by R. M. Wenley of the University of Michigan on the nature of the cultural studies and their relation to the elective system; the case for the classics by Shorey; defenses of the doctrine of formal discipline by James Rowland Angell and Charles Judd of the University of Chicago; and testimonials from a good many quarters on the value of the classics for future training in law, medicine, theology, business, and practical affairs.

Another influential symposium was edited by Andrew F. West of Princeton who earlier had fought President Eliot over the elective system. This symposium, published in 1917, contained a report of the addresses delivered at the Conference on Classical Studies in Liberal Education held at Princeton University in June, 1917, together with 316 pages of statements from men in all walks of professional and business life testifying to the value of the classics. Elaborate statistics were marshaled to show that the classical studies were not dying out and that classical students were far superior to other students in their college entrance examinations and college studies.[2]

The interested reader who may wish to follow more references on this subject is referred to a bibliography compiled in 1921 at the University of Pennsylvania containing many titles concerning the value of the classics.[3]

To summarize in detail the arguments for the classics contained in these symposia and in the references to which they refer would be to repeat highly familiar arguments which have been in constant use by conservative college educators in America ever since the days of the Yale Faculty Report of 1828. However, it may be profitable to review in very brief form the forces that the twentieth century classicists felt they were fighting and the values that they thought the classics served. They raised their voices *against* specialization; the elective system; the encroach-

[1] FRANCIS W. KELSEY, ed., *Latin and Greek in American Education* (The Macmillan Company, New York, 1911).

[2] ANDREW F. WEST, ed., *Value of the Classics* (Princeton University Press, Princeton, 1917); see also, American Classical League, *The Classical Investigation*, Part I (Princeton University Press, Princeton, 1924).

[3] G. D. HADZITS and L. R. HARLEY, *A Bibliographic Monograph on the Value of the Classics* (University of Pennsylvania, Philadelphia, 1921).

ment of the physical and social sciences; the Thorndike school of psychology which claimed that learning was specific; the encroachment of practical and useful studies; the emphasis upon interests and freedom of students; the decline of morality and discipline; and the poor teaching that had accompanied a good deal of classical study.

On the other hand, they stoutly maintained that a thorough study of the classics would achieve the following ends: give a broad liberal and cultural education for students no matter what occupation they were to enter; give the proper discipline and sense of duty to immature minds; cultivate the intellectual faculties and transfer that training to other fields of activity; provide a sound basis for later specialization and for study of modern languages, science, and the arts; give insight into the foundations of western civilization; cultivate the constructive imagination; clarify moral ideals and stimulate to right conduct in all fields; and furnish a means of recreation for leisure time and an escape from the pressing problems of the present.

In the light of these arguments, many, if not most, classicists insisted that surely Latin and possibly Greek should remain the central core of study for a liberal education and for a B.A. degree. From such confidence as expressed by Shorey, that "Classical education is not an academic superstition, an irrational survival of the Renaissance. It is a universal phenomenon of civilization,"[1] the classicist often arrived at a conclusion such as West's, that not only Latin should be prescribed but also "[Greek] should be provided in all our considerable secondary schools and has a moral right to its historic place as a requirement for the Bachelor of Arts degree in all our colleges."[2]

Not only from the Humanists and classicists but also from high college administrators have come steady pronouncements deploring the decline of traditional and classical studies and urging their rehabilitation. President Angell of Yale has said:

Furthermore, in almost all collegiate institutions the A. B. degree is now given for work of the most varied and unorthodox sort. Greek, Latin, mathematics and philosophy, which used to figure as the foundation of the arts curriculum, are at present almost wholly extinct as specific requirements and Greek has unhappily well-nigh reached the absolute vanishing point.[3]

The whole tenor of the proposals of President Hutchins is to conserve and preserve the linguistic, rhetorical, mathematical, and philosophical studies of the traditional education. President Wriston finds very discouraging the abuse that has been heaped upon mathematics and the

[1] KELSEY, op. cit., p. 319.

[2] WEST, op. cit., p. 32.

[3] J. R. ANGELL, American Education (Yale University Press, New Haven, 1937), pp. 156–157.

languages and asserts that they both deserve a permanent place in the college curriculum because of their permanent validity for a liberal education. Albert Jay Nock has insisted that the traditional studies *mean* education and that newer studies have no right to be called educational. Hartley Burr Alexander struck the same note when he stated that Scripps College would center its attention upon preserving traditional culture through traditional studies.

In his annual reports and public statements, President Butler of Columbia University has repeatedly deplored the decline of the classics and has predicted dire social and cultural consequences if they are allowed to die out. In 1916, he said:

The decline in the number of those American students who study Greek and Latin and who have a reasonable familiarity with the history and literature of Greece and Rome is greatly to be deplored. No educational substitute for Greek and Latin has ever been found, and none will be found so long as our present civilization endures, for the simple reason that to study Greek and Latin under wise and inspiring guidance is to study the embryology of the civilization which we call European and American.[1]

Again, in 1930, Butler expressed similar sentiments:

It is hard to imagine anything more sad than the decline and fall of classical scholarship and classical teaching in American education, with the resultant paralysis in the development of our national understanding and our national cultivation. . . . The Greek language and literature, Greek history, Greek eloquence, Greek philosophy and Greek institutional life, a knowledge of all of which is a *sine qua non* to an understanding of the intellectual and spiritual life of today and to preparation for full participation in that life, have passed quite outside the range either of knowledge or of interest of the present generation of American students and their teachers. . . . The effects of all this are apparent on every hand. They reveal themselves in a lack of historical knowledge and perspective, in a lack of acquaintance with what is the very best and most fruitful of human experience, and in a lack of understanding of the significance of those literally colossal achievements of the mind and spirit which made ancient Greece and Rome immortal. . . . With all these have come also an increasing carelessness of good manners and a sorry lowering of literary and artistic standards.[2]

Thus, with very much the same arguments as were used by the conservatives of the nineteenth century, the conservatives of the twentieth century have tried to hold out against the encroachment of newer studies.

[1] E. C. ELLIOTT, ed., *The Rise of a University*, Vol. II, *The University in Action* (Columbia University Press, New York, 1937), pp. 220–221; yet when Columbia dropped Greek and Latin as requirements for the B.A. degree in 1905, President Butler defended the move: *ibid.*, pp. 215–217.

[2] *Ibid.*, pp. 351–352; for other forceful statements by Butler, see *ibid.*, pp. 150–151, 176 177.

That they have been quite successful in many respects is doubtless true, despite outward appearances which seem to show that the newer studies have been decidedly more popular among students.   The liberal arts colleges still attract the greatest number of college-going students, and the older academic departments very often dominate the faculty policy of a great many institutions.   Even many advocates of the newer studies have often tried to ape the style and methods of the older ones and to justify themselves with a good many of the arguments with which the traditional studies have been fortified.   That this is true is supported by the evidence concerning the liberal arts tradition provided by the recent survey of the North Central institutions:

It is also true, although this fact may not be fully apparent from these tables, that the older subjects rather than the newer occupational courses occupy the central place in most institutions.   In most cases they claim the major portion of student time; to a great extent they determine the content of the libraries; they provide the subject matter that is required of all students; the instructors who teach them constitute the controlling power of the faculty; and they enjoy an academic respectability not accorded to other subjects.[1]

Many conservative college educators hope that the new program at St. John's College (see next chapter) will usher in a renaissance of the classical languages and traditional studies.   Other conservative educators see hope in the reports from some colleges in recent years that the number of students taking courses in the Greek and Latin classics was increasing.   Such reports have come, for example, from Bates, Trinity, New York University, Holy Cross, and the College of Our Lady of Good Counsel.

Despite the determined stand of the traditional studies noted above, the physical and social sciences have rapidly gained greater and greater recognition and during the last twenty years have climbed to a place of equality and even superiority in the field of liberal education on the college level.   The battles waged by Eliot and White and C. K. Adams and Gilman and Jordan and many others of the nineteenth century began to bear the fruits of victory in the twentieth century.   A whole host of energetic and capable scholars in the fields of physics, chemistry, astronomy, biology, physiology, psychology, history, political science, economics, sociology, and anthropology were carving out fields of knowledge which soon attracted greater numbers of teachers and students than ever before until, by the second and third decades of the twentieth century, the tide of college popularity had turned definitely in their favor.

Typical names that stand out in these fields are: Pupin, Steinmetz, Millikan, Compton, Osborn, Michelson, Slosson, Richards, Bridgman,

[1] M. E. HAGGERTY, *The Evaluation of Higher Institutions*, Part III, *The Educational Program* (University of Chicago Press, Chicago, 1937), p. 73.

Cannon, and Carrel in the *natural sciences;* Hall, James, Titchener, Thorndike, Dewey, Lashley, and Woodworth in *psychology;* Turner, Andrews, Schlesinger, Robinson, Smith, Shotwell, Paxson, Faulkner Beard, and Nevins in *history;* Ross, Sumner, Giddings, Cooley, Hobhouse, Ellwood, and McIver in *sociology;* Veblen, Commons, Mitchell, Jevons, Perlman, and Douglas in *economics;* Laski, Beard, Merriam, Ogg, Pound, Cardozo, and Frankfurter in *political science;* and Boas, Mead, and Linton in *anthropology.* As a result of the efforts of scores such as these, national associations and organizations were formed to pursue scholarly research in these fields, and students began more and more to flock to these studies in an attempt to become better informed and better equipped to cope with the pressing problems of a new and rapidly changing society.

Space will not be taken here to delineate this progress in detail, for the story is too well known and familiar to need retelling. Only one or two personalities will be cited in order to give point to the contrast with the position of the traditionalists. For example, John Dewey has been only one of a great many progressive educators of the twentieth century who have constantly urged that a greater place in the collegiate scheme of studies be given to the physical sciences and to the scientific method.

Dewey's proposals as early as 1916 are shot through with insistence that the separation between humanistic and naturalistic studies must be broken down and that the sciences must be recognized as properly a most important type of subject matter for the study of human affairs. This he justified because modern science had restored the intimate connection between humanity and nature by viewing the knowledge of nature as a means for securing human welfare.[1] For twenty years and more, Dewey has kept returning to this theme, and it appeared stronger than ever in his most recent statement in 1938 when he insisted that science and the methods of science must be the pattern for the progressive and intellectual organization of subject matter and for a genuine philosophy of experience in education.[2]

Typical of the different approaches to this problem of older versus newer studies are some of the articles appearing in a symposium published in 1915. While Shorey was insisting that language and literature should have the prime place in college education, Professor Edwin G. Conklin of Princeton was insisting just as emphatically that a liberal education must include science as well as literature and the humanities, because

[1] DEWEY, *Democracy and Education;* see especially Chap. XVI, "Significance of Geography and History"; Chap. XVII, "Science in the Course of Study"; Chap. XX, "Intellectual and Practical Studies"; Chap. XXI, "Physical and Social Studies: Naturalism and Humanism"; Chap. XXV, "Theories of Knowledge."

[2] DEWEY, *Experience and Education;* see especially Chap. III, "Criteria of Experience"; Chap. VII, "Progressive Organization of Subject-matter"; Chap. VIII, "Experience—The Means and Goal of Education."

science has freed man from slavery to his environment, freed him from superstition and authority, changed our whole point of view as to nature and man, and given us a method that is rapidly being applied to all fields of human activity.[1]

Even more effective than the statements of Shorey and Conklin in this symposium was the article by Dean Charles H. Haskins of Harvard on the place of the social sciences in college education. Haskins' argument for history, economics, political science, and sociology was so effective that it set a standard for all future statements of like kind, and it proved highly prophetic of the future trend that the college curriculum actually took. Haskins pointed out that inasmuch as the social sciences dealt with the study of man and human society, they were particularly appropriate to the historic meaning of a liberal education in the Latin sense of humane, or human, culture. He noted also that the social sciences were expanding most rapidly in the larger universities and less rapidly in the independent colleges where the hand of tradition was strongest.

As Haskins looked at the problem, he decided that the social studies were really intermediate between the older humanities and the newer physical sciences, inasmuch as they dealt with human subjects and used scientific methods. Even before the popular days of survey courses, or "core" curriculums, Haskins was urging that the social studies be made the central group for a liberal education:

If our curriculum is to have a center or core, it may well be sought in this great connecting group of subjects, which, by joining the study of literature to the present and bringing the student of nature into touch with the world of man, furnish a natural corrective to the one-sidedness of a training which is purely literary or purely scientific.[2]

Haskins' other reasons for giving the social sciences a greater part in the curriculum were that they were more interesting to students and were particularly good in a democracy where discussion and knowledge should be put to use. Even more important was the fact that the social studies more than any others provide the necessary preparation for intelligent participation in social and civic activities and thus are eminently practical for life:

Central with respect to the other subjects of the curriculum, the newer humanities are unique in their relation to social action.[3]

[1] *The American College* (Henry Holt & Company, Inc., New York, 1915), Chap. IV, "The Place of Physical and Natural Science in the College Curriculum."

[2] *Ibid.*, p. 45; see all Chap. III, "The Place of the Newer Humanities in the College Curriculum."

[3] *Ibid.*, p. 45.

One great aspect of training for social action was brought to light by the World War to which Haskins referred as evidence that national isolation was over and that Americans more and more in the future would be obliged to make judgments on national and international matters. In this way, the social studies would be most important in creating a sense of international-mindedness among students and help the colleges to exert intelligent leadership upon public opinion. All in all, Haskins served direct notice upon the traditionalists that the central task of liberal education should fall in the future not on the classics but upon history and the social sciences:

The time has come when we might as well admit frankly, however much we may deplore the fact, that for the great body of our college students the classics have lost their hold as the basis of general education, and that for the present generation the chief opportunity for giving the background and breadth of view which our conceptions of culture still demand is to be found in the study of history.[1]

Haskins' foresight is all the more remarkable when it is remembered that he was writing at a time when the classicists were giving great publicity to their subjects and the social sciences had not yet proved their worth. He apparently picked the winning horse when he singled out, as an example of what he meant, the new survey course in social and economic problems that had just been established at Amherst during the administration of President Meiklejohn. That survey courses in the physical and social sciences have since become most popular as required courses throughout the country is a matter of common knowledge.[2] For one of many investigations showing the trend away from traditional and toward newer studies, see a recent book by Merle Kuder who found that within the New England colleges themselves there is less emphasis upon ancient languages, mathematics, and physical sciences and more upon the social sciences, modern languages, fine arts, education, and physical education.[3] One of the most recent and most important indications of the direction that the social studies have taken and should take is described in the reports of the Commission on the Social Studies of the American Historical Association.[4]

The controversy over the social sciences is still being waged vigorously. General conservative reaction against progressive education tends to

[1] *Ibid.*, pp. 49–50.

[2] For a summary of the progress of survey courses, see B. L. JOHNSON, *What About Survey Courses?* (Henry Holt & Company, Inc., New York, 1937).

[3] MERLE KUDER, *Trends of Professional Opportunities in the Liberal Arts College* (Teachers College, Columbia University, New York, 1937).

[4] See especially the summary volume *Conclusions and Recommendations of the Commission* (Charles Scribner's Sons, New York, 1934).

single out the social studies for special attack. For example, Peter A. Carmichael, professor of philosophy at Louisiana State University, recently deplored the too great emphasis upon psychology, sociology, political science, and economics in American colleges. In the style of Flexner, he decried the practicality and "thinness" of courses in the social sciences and recommended that they be reduced to "half a dozen or fewer solid courses."[1] In contrast, Robert S. Lynd, professor of sociology at Columbia University, has recently issued a call to American educators to put more emphasis than ever upon the social sciences as a means of understanding and directing the future of American culture.[2]

FOUR-YEAR COLLEGE VERSUS JUNIOR COLLEGE AND SHORT COURSES

Another phase of the discussions that have centered around the cultural conception of the college has specifically to do with the length of the college course. This conflict over whether or not the college should maintain its traditional four years is no longer so prevalent as it was in the later nineteenth century when Eliot and others were urging the adoption of the elective system in order to shorten the time, but it has often reared its head in college conferences of the twentieth century. Much of the influence of the American Association of Colleges which was organized in 1915 has been in the direction of strengthening the effectiveness of the four-year liberal college. More particularly, this tendency has been expressed by a group of colleges that formed what was known as "The Liberal Arts College Movement," launched at a conference in Chicago in 1930.[3]

Inspired by President Albert Norman Ward of Western Maryland College and working in close conjunction with the American Association of Colleges (especially through Robert L. Kelly and Guy E. Snavely), representatives of 278 colleges met at a conference in Chicago in 1930 to stimulate interest in the liberal arts college and its ideals. Feeling that the liberal colleges had been put on the defensive in recent years, the movement avowed the purpose of publicizing the advantages of the liberal and cultural college as opposed to professional and vocational schools, the small college as opposed to the great university, the independent college as opposed to public institutions, the religious and denominational college as opposed to secular institutions, and the four-

---

[1] PETER A. CARMICHAEL, "Panem et Circenses," *American Association of University Professors, Bulletin*, 25: 191–202 (April, 1939).

[2] ROBERT S. LYND, *Knowledge for What? The Place of Social Science in American Culture* (Princeton University Press, Princeton, 1939).

[3] For the ideals, purposes, and description of this movement, see Archie Palmer, ed., *The Liberal Arts College Movement* (Little and Ives Company, New York, 1930).

year college as opposed to junior colleges or combination courses looking toward specialized purposes. These were the college ideals which the new movement set out to defend and for which it proposed to raise funds, solicit gifts and endowments, and generally bring more effectively to the public's attention. As an aid to publicity, seven issues of *The Liberal Arts College Bulletin* were published beginning in November, 1930, and ending in March, 1932. The depression of those years must have taken its toll of the new movement, because little has been heard of it recently.

Another indication, however, that the debate over the four-year college has not ended is given in the report of the proceedings of the Institute for Administrative Officers of Higher Institutions for 1937 whose conference centered its discussion around "Current Issues in Higher Education." The four-year college was defended by President McConaughy of Wesleyan and by President Carter Davidson of Knox College. McConaughy feared that the four-year college was being overshadowed by the development of junior and senior colleges and by university, professional, and vocational courses which tended to make of liberal education a two-year affair. He urged that the four-year independent liberal college try to publicize itself and improve its program in order to maintain its function as traditionally held, especially in New England.[1]

Davidson's speech directed itself especially to the "Case for the Four-year College" in a debate concerning whether or not the B.A. degree should be granted at the end of the junior college period. He pointed out that four years is none too long for the enrichment and maturing of youth in days when people live longer, have more leisure, and are gradually working less all the time. Believing, in general, in the cultural type of liberal college, Davidson felt that there should be no rush to end the period of general or liberal education before the four-year period was completed.[2]

In these ways, the traditional liberal arts college has sought to preserve its four-year form and tried to defend itself against what seemed to be the disintegrating forces of the junior college and various other schemes whereby it was cut in the middle or at some point short of four years in order to allow greater professional or occupational preparation for the undergraduate. The junior college movement has offered a special challenge to the four-year college. Gaining very rapidly in momentum and popularity since 1915 or so, it has tended to sharpen the break between the general education of the first two years and the more specialized or professional aspect of the last two years of college. This has been true not only of the independent and public junior college but also of the undergraduate college divisions of the larger universities.

[1] W. S. GRAY, ed., *Current Issues in Higher Education* (University of Chicago Press, Chicago, 1937), Part II, "Is the Four-year Liberal Arts College Doomed?"
[2] *Ibid.*, Part I, "The Case for the Four year College."

The efforts of Eliot, Barnard, White, Butler, and especially Harper to enlarge the elective system in the later nineteenth and early twentieth century tended to introduce more flexibility into the four-year college and to break its rigidity for the majority of students. Then, with the great upswing in numbers of junior colleges since the World War, the tendency to end general education with the second year of college and begin concentration upon advanced work in the last two years received even greater impetus. Finally, in very recent years, the so-called "general education" movement has increased the efforts to link the first two years of college with the last two of high school. It would treat these four years as a unit and as a preparation for more specialized work later on or as a common educational experience that all students should have even if they did not go on to advanced study.

The junior college movement has apparently met a definite need which appeared when new thousands of students began to graduate from the public high schools of the country after the turn of the century and especially after the World War. These new graduates made more acute than ever the question of democratic college education, and the junior colleges appeared on the scene to provide a greater measure of democracy in college education when the traditional colleges steadfastly refused to modify their admission standards. Hence, the democratizing and popularizing functions of the junior colleges have given a cheaper education to many more students than ever before. And they began to alarm the traditional four-year colleges whose cultural aim prompted them to be selective and to maintain their high admission requirements in order to keep out the great masses of students flowing out of the high schools. Writers on the junior college have indicated that other aims were to provide occupational and vocational or semiprofessional courses for those students who were not going on to advanced university study. Some junior colleges, however, maintained their preparatory function of cultural as opposed to specialized, or vocational, education.[1]

The "general education" movement, which has taken on larger proportions since about 1930, has in some respects overlapped the earlier junior college idea but has appeared in many different forms, most of which have tended to concentrate on the *first* two years of college life and thus reduce the emphasis upon the four-year college as a unit.[2]

[1] For general references on the junior college, see L. V. Koos, *The Junior College* (University of Minnesota Press, Minneapolis, 1924); W. M. PROCTOR, *The Junior College, Its Organization and Administration* (Stanford University Press, Stanford University, Calif., 1927); W. C. EELLS, *The Junior College* (Houghton Mifflin Company, Boston, 1931).

[2] See *National Society for the Study of Education, General Education in the American College*, Thirty-eighth Yearbook, Part II (Public School Publishing Company, Bloomington, Ill., 1939).

Outstanding examples of this tendency are to be found in the University of Chicago College which has linked its work with the last two years of high school and the University of Minnesota General College which has developed a new type of program parallel to the first two years of the regular undergraduate college. In both cases, there has been a tendency to grant some kind of diploma or recognition to students who do not go on to the last two years of college or university work.

There have even been proposals that the B.A. degree should be given at the end of the junior college period. Such a suggestion was made recently by Professor George A. Works of the University of Chicago in his debate with Carter Davidson at the Institute for Administrative Officers of Higher Institutions.[1] Professor Works believed that the influences of the junior college movement and the need for shortening the period of formal education so that students could marry and begin to earn a living earlier all lead to the conclusion that the B.A. should be given at the end of the junior college period and the M.A. degree after three more years of study.

Besides the junior college and the general education movement, there has been also the recognition on the part of progressive educators that no special or inherent value should be attached to the four-year period. For example, the Rollins Conference (see page 375) insisted that the place of the liberal college should be a growing and ever changing one so that the sharp separation between undergraduate and graduate education might be eliminated. In place of these traditional conceptions, the Rollins Conference would substitute an integrated program beginning with the last year or two of secondary school and continue *through* the completion of professional preparation.[2]

It should be pointed out that the controversy over the junior college and general education does not follow the lines of controversy between conservatives and progressives laid down in former chapters. For example, the proposals for general education on the junior college level suggested by President Hutchins or by Andrew F. West are far more conservative in tone than those proposed by the Rollins Conference and accepted more or less by several progressive junior colleges (such as Sarah Lawrence and the University of Wisconsin Experimental College).

Even in the traditional colleges that have clung to the four-year ideal, the notion has gradually been gaining that the first two years of study should emphasize general and cultural education and that the last two

---

[1] GRAY, *op. cit.*, Part I, "Should a Bachelor's Degree be Granted at the End of the Junior College Period?" President Hutchins has also recently suggested in public addresses that the B.A. degree should be given at the end of the first two years of college.

[2] *Rollins College, The Curriculum for the Liberal Arts College*, pp. 8–9.

should stress greater specialization and preparation for advanced university or professional work. As the matter stands at present, and despite the inroads of the junior colleges and the general education movements, the predictions of the progressives of the late nineteenth century and of conservatives in recent years have not entirely come true. Throughout the country as a whole, the college as a four-year institution has remained and has not yet been swallowed up by the secondary school, on the one hand, or the university, on the other, even though its aspect may have changed greatly since the palmy days of the prescribed curriculum and the cultural ideal.

RELIGIOUS VERSUS SECULAR CONCEPTION OF THE COLLEGE

The last set of opposing points of view that remains to be mentioned here concerns whether the college should maintain a fundamental religious atmosphere in its curricular and extracurricular life or should concentrate on secular aspects and leave religious instruction and observance to informal and noncollege agencies. This conflict does not today present the controversial proportions that it assumed in the nineteenth century, but the two points of view still tend to oppose one another. Much evidence exists that the small denominational and religious college leans toward conservative and traditional conceptions of a liberal education, whereas the secular college is more often likely to be free to adopt more progressive notions of college education. An abundant literature during the period since the World War has asserted that the college should be predominately religious, and this view is commonly associated with the cultural ideal. Newspaper headlines on almost any Monday morning will testify that sermons on the preceding day have attacked the "godless," or "atheistic," college and eulogized the religious college.

Typical among the many religious statements of the college ideal is the small book published in 1916 entitled *The Christian College* containing the addresses given at the one hundredth anniversary of Alleghany College.[1] Here the emphasis is upon culture as opposed to practical education and upon inculcation of qualities of character, morals, reverence, humility, and evangelism through Christian ideals. Striking the same note for the Presbyterians was the volume of addresses published in 1920 by John Henry MacCracken, president of Lafayette College.[2] In his inaugural address, MacCracken insisted that the denominational college should remain free to be onesided, ignore whole fields of knowledge

[1] HERBERT WELCH, HENRY C. KING, and THOMAS NICHOLSON, *The Christian College* (Methodist Book Concern, New York, 1916). Welch was president of Ohio Wesleyan, King was president of Oberlin, and Nicholson was secretary of the Board of Education of the Methodist Episcopal Church.

[2] JOHN HENRY MACCRACKEN, *College and Commonwealth* (D. Appleton-Century Company, Inc., New York, 1920).

if it chose, pick and choose students and teachers carefully, remain small, train leaders, and emphasize religion. In other addresses, MacCracken has asserted that the churches have long been in the teaching business and should assert their right to remain in it.

More recently, a large part of college literature has maintained the same point of view. For example, in 1928, the dean of Ohio Wesleyan, William E. Smyser, stated that the denominational college had the obligation to maintain a positive Christian influence in general spirit and specific policy in order to develop in students a Christian character and the Christian way of life.[1] This must be done by a definite program of religious instruction and inspiration and should not be left to extra-institutional agencies such as the Y.M.C.A. or Y.W.C.A.

At his induction as president of Muhlenberg College, in 1937, Levering Tyson reaffirmed in these words his adherence to the religious conception of the college:

Muhlenberg was founded by the Ministerium of the Lutheran Church in Eastern Pennsylvania. Its chief purpose was not only to make it possible for young men . . . to be trained as ministers, or as laymen under auspices thoroughly consistent with the ideals of the church and of the community of which that church was an active part, but also to be witness, to bear vital testimony, that a living religion must be an active force in the life of an educated man. . . . There has been no deviation from this original concept. . . . I would be recreant to my trust if I did not state here and now, unequivocally, that I will continue this fundamental purpose. All my predecessors have been ministers of the gospel. As the first layman you have chosen to be president of your College, I want particularly to express my determination to uphold this policy, my belief in its soundness, and my pride and confidence in making this public declaration.[2]

Hundreds of baccalaureate sermons in all kinds of colleges bear witness to the same adherence to the values of religious influence upon college students.

The Liberal Arts College Movement of the early 1930's showed itself closely associated with the religious conception of the college. Also, many statements showed that the sponsors felt that they had divine guidance and that the religious colleges would be special beneficiaries of the campaign for funds and publicity being carried on. For example, an editorial in the first bulletin states:

The Liberal Arts College Movement is now under way. Its ultimate success is certain. We believe it is a movement born of God.[3]

[1] R. L. KELLY, *The Effective College*, Chap. XX, "Religion in the Denominational College."

[2] *Muhlenberg College, Induction to the Presidency of Levering Tyson, October 2, 1937* (Allentown, Pa., 1938), pp. 29–30.

[3] *The Liberal Arts College Bulletin*, 1:11 (November, 1930).

Again:

This is an adventure of faith. The resources of God are promised to those who undertake the program of God. The colleges of liberal arts belong to a divine order.[1]

Furthermore, the bulletins published by his movement contained many articles reprinted from the periodical *Christian Education* (which, incidentally, is a good source for statements of this point of view) and many with such titles as "The Case of the Church-related College" and "The Influence of the Small Denominational College upon the Ideals and Standards of Conduct of Students."

In addition to the Protestant church-related colleges which adhere to their own religious doctrines, the Catholic Church, of course, maintains many institutions of higher education all of which are devoted to giving correct religious training to their students. In explaining the Catholic position with reference to higher education, James H. Ryan has said that the Catholic college does not draw a line between secular and religious knowledge or between morality and religion. Thus, the unity among science, religion, and morality is considered an unchanging truth laid down authoritatively by the church to be accepted by Catholic students:

Now, the Church proposes a definite set of religious truths for our belief and a no less definite set of moral principles for our life, and it does so authoritatively. . . . The well-informed Catholic feels no intellectual restraints because of the authoritative character of religious beliefs which he accepts. On the contrary, he experiences the utmost freedom in the discussion of every problem not directly concerned with matters of faith and morals.[2]

There are, of course, many statements of the Catholic conception of the college, but none draws more clearly the traditional outlook than a recent book by J. J. Walsh in which he stated that the proper philosophic position of the Catholic college is the scholasticism of the Middle Ages.[3] Walsh described how strong scholasticism had been in the colonial colleges and showed the continuity of that philosophy in Catholic colleges down to the present.

In opposition to the strictly religious conception of the college, the secular point of view has been gaining steadily in collegiate theory as well

[1] *Ibid.*, p. 1.

[2] R. L. KELLY, *The Effective College* (Association of American Colleges, New York, 1928), Chap. XXI, "Religion in the Catholic College," p. 224.

[3] J. J. WALSH, *Education of the Founding Fathers of the Republic; Scholasticism in the Colonial College* (Fordham University Press, New York, 1935), esp. Chaps. IX, XI, XII. For a good statement of the Jesuit philosophy of education in practice, see catalogue of Fordham College (Bronx, N. Y.) for 1936–1937, pp. 26–29. Mental training is considered more important than the acquisition of knowledge, and special importance is attributed to the Greek and Latin classics and scholastic philosophy.

as in all of American life. The conflict has not taken the form of direct controversy, because few if any college educators have directly attacked the religious colleges; they have been content to leave out of their statements any mention that secular colleges should emphasize religion in their teachings. The secular point of view has been expressed by those who have urged acceptance of the scientific method and of the implications of modern science in collegiate theory and practice. To avoid repetition, the reader is referred to statements in previous chapters or sections dealing with the underlying philosophy of experience, experimental naturalism, scientific method, organismic psychology, social responsibility, and union of liberal with practical studies.

Likewise, the dominating social, economic, and intellectual trends of the twentieth century have tended to impress upon progressive educators the necessity of recognizing and understanding the implications of industrialism, democracy, social planning, cooperation, and modern conceptions of science. These new social and intellectual trends have led to new conceptions of the universe, human nature, truth, knowledge, and learning, many of which come into conflict with the corresponding conceptions of traditional philosophy, orthodox religion, and economic conservatism.

Altogether, these dominating secular trends in American society of the twentieth century have left their mark upon American higher education, especially the state universities, the larger private universities, and the more progressive of the smaller colleges. Whereas earlier statements of the aims of college education put religious ideals in a prominent place, the weight of more modern statements seems increasingly to neglect the religious emphasis. For example, the study of college aims made in 1921 shows that the preponderance of statements made in the nineteenth century mentioned the religious aims, whereas that preponderance had dwindled by at least half in the statements made in the second decade of the twentieth century.[1] Moreover, the actual decline in religious studies and religious emphasis in the curriculum of colleges throughout the country during the twentieth century has tended to parallel the corresponding decline in the authority of the churches over the social and personal life of the people.[2]

Thus, it has been not so much the arguments for or against the religious conception of the college that have swung the balance against

[1] Koos and CRAWFORD, "College Aims Past and Present," *School and Society*, 14: 499–509 (December 3, 1921).

[2] See, for example, *Recent Social Trends in the United States* (McGraw-Hill Book Company, Inc., New York, 1933), Chap. VIII; BEARD and BEARD, *The Rise of American Civilization*, Vol. II, pp. 778–784; H. E. BARNES, *An Intellectual and Cultural History of the Western World* (The Cordon Company, New York, 1037), pp. 1118–1128.

the religious ideal but rather the trend of the times, political, economic, social, scientific, and psychological. As the temper of experimentalist philosophy and organismic psychology, with their denials of dualism between spirit and body, has gained influence over educational theory and practice, so has the secular temper gained in the colleges. As people have come to accept natural and social bases for morality and good character, they have increasingly accepted the idea that persons can be good individuals and good citizens without orthodox religious precepts to guide them. So, increasingly, many colleges have been led either to maintain *official* connections with the religious denominations that founded and support them while not forcing denominational doctrines upon students or to forswear the doctrines of any *particular* denomination and allow the churches to work unofficially with those of the students who are interested.[1]

The progressive position has by no means tried to belittle religious, or spiritual, values in human life, but it has tried to divorce those values from narrow and sectarian creeds and make them much more pertinent to the actual personal and social life of modern persons. Progressives have deplored the frequency with which religious attitudes have become compartmentalized and separated from actual living in the business or social world. They would put uppermost in education a keen regard for understanding and fostering human values in actual operation. The most all-inclusive purposes of which human beings are capable must become a legitimate concern of college education, and this is what progressives sometimes identify as religious.[2]

[1] W. A. MacDonald, writing in the *New York Times* for Mar. 26, 1939, saw an increasing interest on the part of college students in religious questions. He cited Tufts and Boston University.

[2] See, for example, Edward H. Reisner, *Faith in an Age of Fact* (Farrar & Rinehart, Inc., New York, 1937).

CHAPTER XXI

NEW PRESCRIPTIONS ARISE FROM THE CHAOS
OF THE ELECTIVE SYSTEM

All the conflicting points of view described in foregoing chapters have their implications for the reform of the elective system. Some of these were mentioned as the discussion progressed; hence this chapter will be devoted, first, to summarizing the meaning of the various controversies as they affect the elective system and, second, to a very brief summary of some of the actual experimentation and changes that have been introduced into the college curriculum in the last 20 or 30 years. Much of the actual experimentation has not been based upon a well-defined or well-thought-out philosophy of higher education. Much of it has taken the form of tinkering and juggling course requirements or patching up old types of courses in the fervent hope that somehow the worst evils of the elective system would be reformed. Of recent years, however, there has been a much more noticeable effort to formulate clearer theoretical positions to be used as a basis for reform of the elective system and of the college curriculum as a whole. As pointed out several times in previous chapters, these theoretical positions have tended to group themselves into opposing positions which have been identified as conservative and progressive.

It may be worth while to note again here that, whereas the elective system in the nineteenth century was progressive and the prescribed curriculum was conservative, the lines of battle in the twentieth century have changed. Now, both the conservatives and the progressives agree that the free elective system as it developed with highly specialized courses of narrow subject matter is educationally bad, but they differ in their proposals for reform. Both conservatives and progressives are suggesting more prescription, but they differ radically concerning the kinds of studies that they would prescribe. They both agree that the *common* elements in education and life should receive greater emphasis in the prescribed studies, but they differ as to what those common qualities are. They both favor greater integration and correlation of knowledge, but they differ as to how that should be done and what studies best show the interrelationships of knowledge. For example, the "general education movement" which proposes to provide greater integration through stressing common bodies of knowledge ranges all the way from the conservative proposals of President Hutchins to the experimentalist proposals of the group working at Teachers College, Columbia University.

We might very well say that today there are all sorts of proposals for the reform of the elective system, all the way from "conservative prescription" to "progressive prescription." In between these two extremes, the majority of college educators seem to be trying to patch up the college curriculum with compromises between the principles of election and prescription, taking inspiration now from the conservatives and again from the progressives. In order to evaluate more intelligently the differing directions in which modern experiments are leading us, we must look more carefully at typical suggestions for reform of the elective system as they emanate from these opposing intellectual camps.

CONSERVATIVE PRESCRIPTION RESURRECTS THE PAST

With reference to the foregoing controversies, the conservative type of prescription in general looks to the Great Tradition and to the traditional liberal arts for inspiration, and thus it is likely to favor the prescription of traditional studies in order to provide the common fund of knowledge that is deemed so important. The reasons for this approach are usually couched in terms of culture, development of the intellect, and inculcation of mental and moral discipline. Along with this approach, emphasis is often put upon prescribed books or encyclopedic survey courses, upon rigid selection of only the best students, and upon study *removed* from the pressing problems of the present. Here, again, as in the foregoing controversies, the Humanists provide a good example of the extreme conservative position. Babbitt insisted that the need of discipline and common ideas was more important for human nature than the free play of one's individual faculties through the elective system. Hence he urged that the college should recapture its original purpose of coordinating and integrating knowledge by returning to the humane tradition of the past and by prescribing the humanistic liberal arts.[1]

Likewise, Foerster has attacked the elective system and has proposed that integration be given to students by prescribing studies that will give them a common fund of knowledge: "Arbitrary or not, a selection of studies pursued in common must always form the heart of a liberal curriculum. If the university is to be an intellectual community, its members must have much in common."[2] Foerster is certain that this "commonness" cannot be achieved by providing a different curriculum for each student or by letting students plan, execute, or judge the curriculum. It can be achieved only by a prescription of the best books,

[1] BABBITT, *Literature and the American College*, Chap. IV, "Literature and the College."
[2] FOERSTER, *The American State University*, p. 250.

or "human masterpieces," which are capable of transmitting the knowledge, wisdom, and beauty of the tradition.[1]

President Butler's attitude toward the elective system represents admirably the change that came over a great many college educators as the elective system did not fulfill all that was hoped of it in the nineteenth century. Butler was definitely with the progressives of the nineteenth century in advocating the adoption of the system and attacking the rigid scheme of prescribed studies that overemphasized languages and mathematics. In 1898, he spoke of "The blessings of the principle of choice, which in higher education is known as the elective system"; and in 1900, he spoke of the "wonder-working elective system."[2] The whole weight of his influence in the earlier days of his administration at Columbia was in the direction of breaking up the rigid prescribed curriculum of the past, but soon he was deploring the effects of free election and urging that unity should be restored to the curriculum by exercising greater control over student choices and prescribing a greater number of studies. Thus, Butler gave his support to the establishment of such prescribed survey courses at Columbia as the well-known "Contemporary Civilization." In this way, he felt that the damage done to the unity of knowledge by the elective system could be repaired.

In 1937, President Butler praised the fact that Columbia College had instituted four survey courses and that the freshman's time would be virtually taken up with Contemporary Civilization, Modern Science, Humanities, and Modern Foreign Languages.[3] This he felt was a result of a long-term program at Columbia to get away from the old prescribed curriculum and also from the elective system. In another statement to the press in 1937, Butler indicated that the common qualities in a curriculum were the most important part of the educational process:

It does not matter how varied the types of students may be or how their individualities may differ . . . education fails entirely unless it provides them all with a common denominator. The practice and policy of permitting the student, who is a mere child, to choose his own subjects of study or to pursue those and only those which appeal to his taste and fancy is a complete denial of the whole educational process.

Those who call this type of school progressive reveal themselves as afloat on a sea of inexperience without chart or compass or even rudder. Young people

[1] As noted previously, Foerster quotes approvingly the emphasis made upon great books of the past by G. R. Elliott, "President Hyde and the American College," *American Review*, 2: 143–169 (December, 1933); Robert Shafer, "University and College," *Bookman*, 73: 225–240, 387–400, 503–521 (May, June, July, 1931).

[2] N. M. BUTLER, *The Meaning of Education* (Charles Scribner's Sons, New York, 1915), pp. 159–160, 315.

[3] Article in the education section of the Sunday *New York Times* (Jan. 10, 1937).

thus deprived of the privilege of real instruction and real discipline are sent into the world bereft of their great intellectual and moral inheritance.[1]

President Hutchins' proposals for greater prescription have fitted in nicely with the revised curriculum of St. John's College in Annapolis, Md. We have described earlier at some length the proposals Hutchins made to destroy the elective system by prescribing permanent studies that will give common ideas to students, train their intellects, and develop their common human nature. In March, 1938, he was elected chairman of the Board of Visitors and Governors of St. John's. Several of the leading men on the staff of the college have long been interested in reviving the traditional liberal arts through a completely prescribed course of study. The streams of influence that have determined the character of the college have, of course, not come entirely from Hutchins, but his election as chairman of the board served to identify the college program rather closely with his proposals. He has helped to give a philosophical justification for the program and to provide theoretical foundations for the great interest that the college has developed in prescribing a long list of human masterpieces and classic books.

The college has eradicated the elective system in its "new" program and replaced it with a four-year all-required program of studies centering about the reading and study of the prescribed list of books. Statements of policy from the college indicate that several sources have contributed to this emphasis. John Erskine devised a book list for the American Expeditionary Force in France in 1918; and when the war ended, he took it to Columbia and taught an honors course centering about the reading and discussion of the books. In the twenties, Scott Buchanan developed a similar idea in adult education in New York City and continued this idea when he went to the University of Virginia and joined Stringfellow Barr, where both emphasized the reading of great books. Meanwhile, Mortimer Adler had gone to the University of Chicago, where he and Hutchins collaborated on a course in the great books of the past. All four men formed the nucleus of a committee on the liberal arts appointed by Hutchins at Chicago to restudy the place of the traditional liberal arts in the college curriculum. Not only did St. John's College receive inspiration and aid from this committee, but, in addition, Barr was elected president, Buchanan appointed dean, Hutchins made president of the board, and Adler assists in the teaching. The "new" program was launched in September, 1937.

The written statements that have been prepared at St. John's emphasize the fact that they have rediscovered the liberal arts of the past and that liberal education has been rededicated to the purposes stated so well

[1] *New York Times Magazine* (Jan. 3, 1937), p. 7.

in such great periods of history as the thirteenth century and the early national period in America following the Revolution: "Ultimately, the ends of liberal education are the intellectual virtues."[1] The liberal arts are defined in terms of symbols, and on this basis the traditional emphasis of liberal education upon language and mathematics is justified:

The liberal arts are the arts of thinking, and we human animals think through symbols. The liberal arts are therefore the arts of handling symbols. Since the symbols through which we think are of two general sorts, words and numbers, it is not hard to see why for many centuries the liberal arts have been practised primarily on languages and mathematics.[2]

In other words:

In general the liberal arts are the three R's, reading, writing, and reckoning. So they still appear in our primary schools; it is their integrity and power that still lure us back to the little red school houses where our fathers and grand-fathers studied and practised them. . . . For fifteen hundred years they were called the Seven Liberal Arts, and before that they were called the Encyclopedia, the "circle for the training of boys."[3]

Thus, the St. John's program would try to recapture this continuous tradition through which and only through which it is held that the students may be trained in a liberal education:

But all these traditions are parts of the great liberal tradition of Europe and America, which for a period of two thousand years has kept watch over and guided all other Occidental traditions. The liberal college is concerned with transmitting this rich heritage and with continually restating it in fresh and contemporary terms. The tools which it requires, in order to do this well, are the liberal arts. The most tangible and available embodiments of the tradition itself are the classics.[2]

The St. John's program points out that the classics were until recently Greek, Latin, and mathematics but that now that the integrity of the old liberal arts has been destroyed by the elective system, they must be replaced with prescribed books that are "classics." Classic books are defined as those books of the past which have been read by the largest number of persons, have the largest number of possible interpretations, raise the persistent unanswerable questions about the great themes in European thought, are in themselves great works of art, and are master-pieces of the liberal arts. Hence, in the college catalogue is published a list of great books that St. John's feels embodies these five principles. The emphasis is easily seen to be upon the languages and literature of the

---

[1] *Catalogue of St. John's College* (Annapolis, Md., July, 1938), p. 21.
[2] *Ibid.*, p. 22.
[3] *Ibid.*, pp. 23–28.

past, mathematical science of the past, and liberal arts of the past.[1] Progressives would doubtless point out the fact that the list almost entirely neglects the tremendous additions to knowledge of the last 50 years in the physical sciences of all kinds, in psychology, in history, in political science, in economics, in sociology, and in anthropology.

Although the basic requirement of the St. John's program is the reading of these prescribed books, there are several aids in accomplishing this: seminars, or discussion groups; formal lectures; laboratories; and tutorial classes for drill in the original languages and mathematics. Since drill in language and mathematics alone takes 10 of the 18½ hours of formal meetings a week, it can easily be seen that the whole program is weighted on the linguistic and mathematical side:

In the interest of speed, all the books are read in English translation, but the student is required to master enough Greek in his freshman year, enough Latin in his sophomore year, and enough French and German in his last two years to refer intelligently to the original text for doubtful meanings.[2]

The stated requirements for the B.A. degree show again the tremendous emphasis upon book reading and knowledge of language and mathematics:

Knowledge of the contents of the required books [more than 120] in the course.
Competence in the liberal arts [language and mathematics].
A reading knowledge in at least two foreign languages.
Competence in mathematics through the elementary calculus.
Three hundred hours of laboratory science [in four years].
Satisfactory work in the course in hygiene and in physical training [two years].[3]

PROGRESSIVE PRESCRIPTION BUILDS
FOR THE PRESENT AND FUTURE

In contrast to the road to reform of the elective system proposed by the conservatives, the progressive position is likely to stress the prescription of a much broader range of activities, with the emphasis upon scientific and social studies. With reference to the foregoing controversies, the progressives are likely to emphasize an underlying philosophy of experience, the scientific method of thinking, adaptation of the curriculum to the freedom and interests of students, activities to develop the student's whole personality, and group activities in the study of

---

[1] For the list of books see *ibid.*, pp. 26–27, 30.
[2] STRINGFELLOW BARR, *The St. John's Program*, mimeographed material obtained from the college itself.
[3] *St. John's Catalogue*, p. 73.

community and society to bring out the social responsibility of citizens in a changing democracy.

The progressives also tend to stress the importance of common elements in the curriculum; but rather than achieving commonness through prescribed books of the tradition, they favor achieving common qualities by having students engage together in trying to solve common problems which face all persons in a democracy. Commonness is thus reached not by giving finished answers to students but by requiring them to grapple with the pressing problems presented by modern life and to seek answers based upon the best evidence available from the past and the present and the best prognostications of what should be done in the future. They believe that this knowledge needs to be reorganized into broader fields so that interrelationships among the different fields of knowledge can be understood and used more easily in the solving of important problems.

Furthermore, the problems and the organized knowledge in the progressive point of view must be adjusted not only to the demands of a changing society but also to the level of ability and interests of the students and to their realm of experience. Whereas the conservative position plays up the importance of tradition and plays down the point of view of the students and the importance of present-day society, the progressives stress both the individual and society. Progressive colleges start either with the experience of the individual student or with a reorganization of knowledge that will help him integrate his experience and see knowledge and action as connected parts of the process of intelligent thinking. To achieve these ends, the scientific and the social studies have increasingly played a larger part in progressive curriculum building, and formal language study and formal mathematics have tended to play a smaller part.

Reference will be made here very briefly to a few progressive educators in order to focus their ideas more specifically upon the controversy of elective versus prescribed studies. Alexander Meiklejohn heads the list, partly because he has attacked the elective system in colleges ever since his inauguration as president of Amherst in 1912, partly because under his influence one of the first survey courses in the problems of "Social and Economic Institutions" was established at Amherst in 1914, and partly because he has consistently advocated a thoroughgoing reorganization of the college curriculum to remedy the elective system, a reorganization that culminated in the prescribed course of study of the Experimental College at the University of Wisconsin.

It may be said that President Lowell at Harvard was earlier in his attack upon the free elective system, but his proposed remedies as expressed in the principle of "concentration and distribution" led not so much to a thoroughgoing revamping of the college curriculum as it did toward a reshuffling of requirements and electives on the basis of the older type of rather narrow subject-matter course. In his inaugural of 1912, President Meiklejohn proposed that the college must help the student to unify knowledge and grapple with important human and social problems by plunging him directly into the great significant fields of human knowledge, namely, philosophy, social sciences, physical sciences, history, and the arts and literature (see pages 306–308). This classification of important problems anticipated closely the broad divisions into which the more progressive colleges have tended to organize knowledge ever since the World War period.

It is this insistence that students be *required to struggle* with significant social and human problems that sets off the progressive attack upon the elective position from the conservative emphasis upon acquiring a fixed body of traditional knowledge through the study of classic books or through the more encyclopedic type of survey course which describes a great mass of material and gives all the answers. Thus, the Wisconsin Experimental College took students directly into the broad fields of knowledge and helped them to identify significant problems with which intelligent persons ought to be familiar to such a degree that they could set about solving them. The Experimental College was often criticized as traditional, because it spent a whole year upon the study of ancient Greek civilization, but this was done in order to get students to see as a *whole* the interrelated problems of a complete civilization and thus insure that they have a common basis for mutual study and discussion. Furthermore, it is often forgotten that the last year of the Experimental College concentrated upon contemporary America and its problems in the same way, primarily to bring students face to face with present problems and to bring out vividly the differences involved in a prescientific civilization as contrasted to a highly scientific and industrial one. The Experimental College ranged itself definitely upon the progressive side of reforming the elective system by instituting a new kind of prescription in the form of *significant problems*.

Another example of a college educator who saw in the early twenties the desirability of prescribing more studies that would prepare students for greater social usefulness was Jay William Hudson of the University of Missouri. Hudson insisted that colleges needed more orientation courses to give greater perspective to the narrow fields of unreal analysis that the elective system had fostered. He hoped that such courses would bring students much closer to the problems of American life and to a recognition of their obligation to the social order. In other words, the college must disclose to students what America means in such terms as the recognition of the worth of individuals, the social basis of individual expression, equality of opportunity, freedom, and ability of individuals to become intelligent. The college must institute more prescribed courses and must strive to correlate knowledge much more than heretofore, so that students will get a vital conception of the problems of politics; economics; the industrial order; social groupings and their significance; and the implications of American life as expressed in literature, fine arts, and religion.

James Harvey Robinson and Charles H. Haskins have been cited earlier as typifying the newer emphasis upon the social studies not only as a means of correlating and synthesizing knowledge but also as a means of leading students more directly into a consideration of modern social problems and preparation for solving them. The story told by A. Monroe Stowe has also been cited (see page 344) as an example of the difficulty with which the problems of modern society were introduced into a college curriculum against the opposition and antagonism of traditionalists who called down intellectual discipline and the classics to witness that the colleges would be devoured by the unholy fires of "social usefulness." Yet Stowe showed himself to be no slight prophet when he forecast in 1926 that the college of tomorrow would be putting more emphasis upon civic and social purposes by requiring students to be familiar with and competent in the realms of health, scientific thinking, means of expression, and orientation in the modern world of science, economics, political science, sociology, literature, and philosophy.

Another example of the broader approach to the problem of progressive prescription as a way out of the evils of the elective system is found in the statement of the Rollins College Conference in 1931. It was felt there that the student at the end of his college career should show not only an effective mastery in his chosen field of accomplishment but also a reasonable acquaintance with the subject matter and appreciation of the problems involved in the world in which we live, both organic and inorganic; the realm of personal and social relationships; the literary, linguistic, and artistic products of our civilization; and the tools necessarily involved in the acquisition of these. The conference felt that a creative synthesis of the present interests of the students, the problems of civilization, and the traditional classifications of knowledge was necessary and somehow possible.

A more recent discussion shows that the problem of elective versus prescribed studies is still with us. In 1937, one of the subjects of debate before the Institute for Administrative Officers of Higher Institutions concerned the question "Should election or prescription be given the greater emphasis in the organization of college programs?" In outlining the case for prescription, A. J. Brumbaugh of the University of Chicago maintained that the predominance of common needs among students supported the conclusion that prescription should receive the greater emphasis. He mentioned such basic common needs of all students as the relation of the individual to government, civic enterprises, home life, leisure time, mental and physical health, exploring the possibilities of a vocation, command of the processes of communication, and a guiding philosophy of life:

. . . an understanding and appreciation of certain basic facts and principles are essential to living in contemporary society, no matter who the individual or where he is found. They constitute the basic curriculum that should be pre-scribed—a curriculum embodying principles and values in the natural sciences, in the social sciences, in the humanities, in the use of spoken and written language, in the critical evaluation of decisions and actions.[1]

Finally, such outstanding leaders in the progressive position as Dewey and Bode have both recently chided so-called "Progressives" who have gone too far in letting student interests guide the development of the curriculum and not far enough in directing the curriculum toward socially useful ends. In his *Experience and Education*, Dewey indicated that more, not less, planning was necessary in constructing the curriculum; and although he insists that students shall have a part, nevertheless the teacher must assert enough guidance to give direction to the educational process, and this means prescription of a progressive kind: "The planning must be flexible enough to permit free play for individuality of experience and yet firm enough to give direction towards continuous development of power."[2]

Dewey asserted his opposition to the conservative notion of prescrib-ing fixed studies when he stated that "A single course of studies for all progressive schools is out of the question" because "it would mean abandoning the fundamental principle of connection with life-experi-ences," but he insisted, nevertheless, that educators must see to it that the problems that arise out of present experience must lead ever onward and outward toward new problems, new experiences, and new solutions.[3] The important thing is that the principles of intellectual organization must take their cue not from traditional philosophy or theology but from modern science and the scientific method. In a sense, then, prescription occurs when students are led *by cooperative efforts to understand and use the scientific method of thinking as a tool for solving human and social problems.*

[1] W. S. GRAY, *Current Issues in Higher Education* (University of Chicago Press, Chicago, 1937), p. 43.

[2] JOHN DEWEY, *Experience and Education* (The Macmillan Company, New York, 1938), p. 65.

[3] *Ibid.*, p. 102. For Dewey's conception of the use of the past in solving present problems, see pp. 297-298.

In his *Progressive Education at the Crossroads*, Bode made even more explicit his position that the newer conceptions of students' interests and freedom still leave room for prescription. He pointed out that *interests are not inherent* in students but are conditioned by the surrounding physical and social environment. Hence, progressive educators must drop their earlier reverence for *immediate* student interests and so shape the environment of the schools (by prescription) that the interests of students will be directed along lines appropriate to scientific thinking and to the problems of democratic social living. Likewise, student needs are nothing inherently sacred but must be determined with reference to the democratic way of life, which means that at least enough prescription is necessary to insure that students develop their critical capacities for thinking and action through democratic social relationships rather than through a traditional or authoritative method.

Furthermore, a mistaken notion of freedom, Bode said, cannot be allowed to define freedom so loosely that students are left free to be unintelligent. Since freedom is to be gained only through the development of intelligence, and the development of intelligence is gained primarily through adherence to the scientific method of thinking, students must somehow be guided to scientific thinking through prescription, if necessary, unless mere guesswork is to replace scientifically organized material: "In terms of Dewey's conception of freedom it is not at all evident that there is no place for compulsion or prescription. Any device is justified if it actually promotes thinking."[1] Mere prescription just for the sake of compulsion or discipline would not, of course, in Bode's conception, lead to good thinking, because it would be too authoritative; and authority and absolutism are the twin enemies of science, intelligence, and democracy.

The emphasis upon prescription, both conservative and progressive, that has been described in this chapter does not, of course, mean that the principle of election has completely vanished from collegiate theory and practice. As has been indicated several times already, the most customary practice in colleges today includes that of allowing students to elect a good many of their courses in order to major, or specialize, or concentrate their work, in one more or less narrow field. This practice grew out of the first efforts to reform the free elective system as represented by the plan of "concentration and distribution" instituted at Harvard by Lowell. It is still supported by such college educators as E. J. McGrath of the University of Buffalo who upheld the "Case for Election" against Brumbaugh before the Institute for Administrative

---

[1] BODE, *Progressive Education at the Crossroads* (Newson and Company, New York, 1938), p. 99.

Officers of Higher Institutions in 1937.[1] Thus, the University of Buffalo and most other colleges allow a good many courses to be elected and submitted for the bachelor's degree in order to allow students to serve their own needs and interests. This kind of compromise rests upon a psychology of learning that assumes the existence of discrete and independent mental traits each of which can be developed by different students through studying different subjects.

The more progressive and organismic approach to the problem of election is not to allow students to elect a number of rather fixed and isolated "courses" but rather allow them to engage in appropriate "projects," or activities, which center about an interest as a core and then lead to all sorts of related problems which cut across traditional subject-matter lines. For example, such progressive colleges as Sarah Lawrence, Bennington, and Bard allow students to work out from a center of interest and embrace other fields of knowledge, using their own experience as a means of arriving at more general social and human problems. Thus, whether they start with prescribed problems, as at the Wisconsin Experimental College, Minnesota General College, or Stephens College, or with student interests, as at Sarah Lawrence, Bennington, or Bard, the progressives are trying to lead students to a better understanding of modern civilization as a means of preparing them to participate more intelligently in the life of modern society.

SUMMARY OF EFFORTS TO REFORM THE ELECTIVE SYSTEM

In order to round out our story of the reaction against the free elective system that has taken place in the past 20 or 30 years, a brief summary will be given of some of the more important steps that have actually been taken in many colleges to reform it. The summary will be brief because a good many books are available that describe these changes in greater detail than can be undertaken here.[2] It should be said at the outset that the identifying terms used here are applied in all sorts of different ways by different colleges and that the same names used by different colleges often have very different meanings. A complete survey of all the experiments that have been carried on and are now being carried

---

[1] GRAY, *op. cit.*, Part III.

[2] See, for example, such books as the following: *National Society for the Study of Education,* "Changes and Experiments in Liberal Arts Education," 31st Yearbook, Part II (Public School Publishing Company, Bloomington, Ill., 1932); *National Society for the Study of Education,* "General Education in the American College," 38th Yearbook, Part II (Public School Publishing Company, Bloomington, Ill., 1939); *American Association of University Women,* "Newer Aspects of Collegiate Education; a Study Guide," (Washington, D. C., 1936); B. L. JOHNSON, *What about Survey Courses?* (Henry Holt & Company, Inc., New York, 1937); MOWAT FRASER, *The College of Tomorrow* (Columbia University Press, New York, 1937). See also bibliographies of these books and bibliography of this book, pages 435–442.

on in the colleges of the country would require large resources and a large investigating staff. Also, an attempt to judge all of the new procedures on the basis of conservative and progressive as defined in this book would take several years and a new book or two. This book has merely tried to clarify the arguments; each educator and layman must try to judge for himself among the various plans and procedures that he knows about. If this book has indicated the need for such judgments and has helped in any way to make those judgments rest upon a more sound historical basis, it will have served its purpose.

The attempt has been made not merely to list a large number of new plans but to give greater clarity to this discussion by grouping the efforts for reform of the elective system into three general types: (1) attempts to shuffle course requirements; (2) efforts to give greater attention to the individual students; and (3) efforts to break down narrow subject-matter fields and to prescribe more material in larger and more interrelated fields of knowledge.

1. **Administrative Shuffling of Course Requirements.** One of the earliest and ultimately the most common method of reforming the elective system (already described in Chap. XIII) has been the administrative approach, whereby certain studies are prescribed and others are left to student choice. Most commonly this has accepted as valuable the customary type of subject-matter course dealing with a relatively narrow segment of knowledge, and it has retained the traditional reliance upon lectures, assignments, and recitation or "quiz sections." On the whole, this method has been perhaps better than the *free* elective system; but in most cases, it still has shown only a relatively small adaptation to the new social and intellectual trends of the times, except in so far as the physical sciences, social sciences, and vocational studies of a vital sort have played a larger part in prescription or election. The following terms have been among those which represent this approach to the elective system:

a. Concentration and Distribution. Stemming out of the efforts of President Lowell when he became president of Harvard in 1909, this principle of concentration and distribution struck a compromise between prescription and election. It has become very popular throughout the country as a means of requiring students to make selections from a more orderly range of studies than would probably be the case if they were left entirely to their own devices. In this way, they are required to concentrate enough to get a better grasp of one field of knowledge and at the same time to distribute their other selections so that they will be somewhat acquainted with other important fields of knowledge. As President Lowell put it, the student should know "a little of everything, and something well." Customarily, the student is required, for purposes of "concentration," to take so many "credits," or "units," either in specific studies or in a certain department, and then he is given an opportunity, for purposes of "distribution," to select a certain number of studies in other specified or unspecified departments.

b. Majors and Minors. A variant of this administrative juggling is to be found in the method that requires the student to take enough credits within one department to count as a major and then to take fewer credits in one or more other departments to make up a minor or minors in those fields. In this way, another compromise between prescription and election has been struck, especially as applied to the last two years of the college course.

c. Group System. Another variant of the administrative tinkering with course requirements has been obtained by grouping required studies within a few large classifications and requiring students to select a certain number of them from each group. It often made no difference which studies were selected within the group just so long as the students had taken enough credits within a group to satisfy the group requirements. This arrangement allowed slightly more freedom of choice, inasmuch as the student was allowed to select specific courses of his own choice from within the general prescribed area.

2. Individualized Instruction. A second kind of general approach intended to break the "academic lockstep" of credits and units has involved special provisions whereby each student will receive more individual attention to his interests and learning needs. Some of these special provisions have been instituted only for the better students who, by various means, have indicated that they could be trusted and could profit by pushing out more directly on their own. The feeling has doubtless grown in recent years that the average and poorer students should also be given the advantage of individual attention, but financial difficulties and an aristocratic conception of college education have often combined to assert that only the brilliant students should be given these advantages. Among the efforts to individualize college instruction are the following:

a. Tutorial and Preceptorial Plans. At such colleges as Princeton, Harvard, and Vassar, students have been assigned to tutors, or preceptors, whose function is to advise and help them with their classwork or in preparation for their final or comprehensive examinations. Thus the individual abilities or disabilities of students may more easily be discovered, and appropriate measures taken to give them special work better adapted to their own peculiar needs than would be possible in large lecture or recitation classes. Also, the more informal character of the discussions with the tutor are intended to relieve the impersonal elements of large classes and stimulate the student to do better and more

sustained work.   Such plans have often been criticized, because they
may begin to concentrate merely upon helping the student "get through."
Many progressive educators are urging that guidance must be put upon
a much broader and deeper basis through well-organized programs of
counseling for students.   In this respect, the "guidance and personnel"
movement has been making notable headway in recent years.

b. *Honors and Independent Study Plans.*   The honors plan is most
customarily identified with Swarthmore; and the independent study plan,
with Stanford.   In both cases, the main intention is to give the more able
students a chance to branch out for themselves and to go more rapidly
than the speed of the average classes would allow them.   In conjunction
with a faculty member, the student is directed to an individual plan of
study which he follows on his own without being held down by the usual
requirements and class obligations of his less fortunate companions.
These plans have had a great vogue in American colleges, especially
through the efforts of those who admire the English system upon which
they are modeled, but increasing attention is being called to the fact that
students often specialize excessively and concentrate too much upon the
reading of books.

c. *Reading Periods and Flexible Attendance Requirements.*   Taking a
cue from the honors plan of reading, some colleges have so arranged their
programs that students may be relieved from class attendance during
some parts of the year so that they may concentrate upon a period of
reading and study uninterrupted by the necessities of class attendance.
The days or weeks before and after holiday recesses or at the end of
academic terms are often utilized in this way.   Some variation of this
plan may be found at Harvard, Yale, Columbia, Dartmouth, Chicago,
Rollins, Swarthmore, Bennington, and many others.

d. *Individual Conferences, Discussion Groups, and Seminars.*   Some
colleges have applied the technique of individual conferences or small
discussion groups for use among all students rather than for just a few.
Informality becomes the keynote, and spirited discussions and group
activities have a better chance of flourishing than in the traditional rather
stiff and formal atmosphere of the recitation room.   Rollins, Reed,
Sarah Lawrence, and the Wisconsin Experimental College are outstanding
examples in which these methods have been used effectively.

e. *Field Activities.*   The formal atmosphere of large classes has also
been broken up by some colleges through their emphasis upon excursions
into the surrounding community or state, individual study during
vacations, a year of study abroad and other traveling plans, and periods
of work or study in community activities.   Students in the Wisconsin
Experimental College made extensive studies of the regions from which
they came; students at Antioch go out to work in various jobs during

parts of the year; and students in the arts college of the University of Cincinnati work part time in the City Hall and with other social agencies of the community. Students at Reed, Black Mountain, Berea, and Commonwealth work closely in connection with some of the industrial and agricultural agencies in the study and solution of problems that confront the surrounding community. Vassar students have created a "social museum" to show how their work is correlated with the life of the surrounding region. Bryn Mawr has recently expanded its program of fieldwork. Goucher tries to give students a realistic approach to various life activities.

f. House Plans. To regain some of the advantages of communal life that were characteristic of the smaller college of the past, a few large universities have started out upon a large-scale plan of dividing students into houses, or "colleges." Thus, at Harvard, Yale, and Wisconsin, students are being given a chance to build up a spirit of morale and community interest with other students of their house in a way that is impossible where students with the same intellectual interests see each other only in regularly stated class time and where those in dormitories or fraternity houses have only a superficial, or "social," community of interest among them.

g. Student Interests and Experiences as a Starting Point. The most thoroughgoing efforts to individualize instruction are probably found in the few progressive colleges that consciously try to begin with the student's own interests and to develop an appropriate course of study for him that grows out of his own experience and purposes. Thus, at Bennington, Sarah Lawrence, and Bard, students have a great deal of freedom to work out their own programs of study along with instructors, plan what they are going to do, and criticize their own efforts and activities in an effort to judge the value of their work for others and for themselves. Despite the great emphasis put by the progressive colleges upon individual interests, there is evident a growing tendency to see that the student's interests not only serve as a starting point for the projects, or activities, program, or "experience curriculum" but also that they lead him to ever widening implications of his activity for social welfare. Some progressive colleges have urged that the genuine interest shown by students in extracurricular activities should give a cue to the way in which colleges might make their curricular activities more interesting and vital. In this way, extracurricular activities have been made respectable and have been taken properly into the realm of legitimate teaching functions of the college.

3. **Greater Prescription to Increase Integration and Afford Common Funds of Knowledge.** The third and most direct method of reforming the elective system has been the formation of several kinds of new pre-

scribed courses which it is hoped (a) will break down the customary narrow divisions of subject matter, (b) by showing the interrelationships of knowledge will help to provide a more integrated approach to knowledge and society, and (c) will afford students the common funds of knowledge necessary to intelligent activity in modern society. Not all of the new prescribed courses have achieved these purposes with equal success, because some of them have merely reshuffled old materials into an even more encyclopedic mass of material to be "covered" and mastered. Some of the various aspects of this general type of approach are as follows:

a. *Broader Fields of Knowledge.* Some colleges have abolished the narrow departments and created in their place a relatively few broad divisions or groups of departments that offer fewer and broader courses of study. Typical reorganizations have created such broad divisions of knowledge as social sciences, natural sciences, languages and literature, philosophy and religion, and fine arts. Thus, for example, the college of the University of Chicago has grouped all of its course offerings under the four divisions of natural sciences, biological sciences, social sciences, and the humanities. Students are then required to become reasonably proficient in each of these four major areas. In this way, the former sharp lines between departments are eradicated, and the divisions sometimes try to meet the needs not only of students who are going to be specialists in that field but also the needs of students who are just exploring or who have decided to specialize in other fields.

b. *Comprehensive Examinations.* Another technique for breaking down narrow departmental lines and still providing for a certain measure of prescription has been the comprehensive examination which has often accompanied the process described above. In other words, students are required for graduation to pass a certain number of comprehensive examinations in various fields of knowledge, and a relatively large amount of flexibility is allowed in preparing for the examinations. Prescription is stated not in terms of courses taken and passed but in terms of examinations passed, and the student may attend classes, listen to lectures, engage in discussion groups or laboratory work, study on his own initiative, or, in general, make any combination of these activities that he feels will best prepare him to pass. Harvard was early engaged in this field of comprehensive examinations; Chicago has developed them to a great extent; and a number of other colleges have adopted them in greater or lesser degree. In recent years, many educators have urged that the factual nature of tests and measurements should give way to a greater emphasis upon "evaluation" techniques of a broader kind to help the student develop more genuinely in all aspects of his personal and social life.

c. Survey Courses.   One of the most popular methods for inserting a greater degree of prescription into the college curriculum has been the survey course.   Survey courses have been framed with many different purposes in view and with many different names attached to them.   The last 10 years has seen a great mushroom growth of "orientation courses," "correlated courses," "coordinated courses," "integrated courses," and "cooperating courses."   Some have aimed at giving freshmen an orientation into college study or into the various fields of knowledge. Some have aimed at giving a bird's-eye view for all beginners in any particular field.   Some have been devised particularly as an introduction to a field for students who will never take more work in that field.   And some have been required as a first course for all who intend to specialize further in that field.   Frequently, all of these aims have been combined, and a single course has been given the burden of achieving these different aims for different students.   These courses have ranged all the way in their effectiveness from mere encyclopedism to a real emphasis upon problem solving and the acquiring of essential skills and principles necessary for intelligent action within the field.   Amherst and Columbia have been pioneers in this area, and many other colleges, such as Dartmouth, Minnesota, Stephens, and others too numerous to mention, have followed suit.

d. Culture Epochs and Needs of Living.   A less popular but perhaps more effective technique for reforming the elective system has been the centering of study around a whole culture epoch, or civilization.   Thus, the Wisconsin Experimental College focused its study upon ancient Greek and contemporary American civilization, emphasizing significant problems with which intelligent citizens ought to be ready to deal.   As a whole people is viewed in its efforts to solve its major problems of political and social control, industry, science, wealth, war, unemployment, leisure, and fundamental world view, the student has a good chance to integrate his knowledge and to focus it upon social action.   Other techniques involve the study of pressing personal needs that face the individual, such as physical health, sex, marriage and home relationships, vocation, leisure, social and civic relationships, and religious attitudes.   Whittier, Minnesota General College, Florida, Stephens, and others have adopted some version of this latter method.

e. Prescribed Books.   A final approach to the problem of prescription has been made, particularly in the case of St. John's College, by centering the curriculum around the required reading of specified "great" books. This method has been described at some length in earlier pages, and the reader is referred to them for further elucidation of this approach. Suffice it to say here that, from the point of view of this writer, the method of prescribed books as set forth by President Hutchins and the St. John's program has a great deal in common with the intellectual outlook and the curricular content of the traditional prescribed curriculum of the past.

Whatever the name given to such revisions or reforms, and whatever the specific aims and details with which they are worked out, at least two aims commonly stand out in the more progressive of these experimental colleges and courses. One is to give more attention to the needs of the individual student and greater meaning to his college study than was possible in the large impersonal courses and lectures of the elective system. Another tries to relate college study more closely to the needs of present-day society and to give students a more integrated approach to their study of and participation in modern life than was given by the highly specialized and academic courses that came to characterize the elective system. Hence, the prescribed courses are coming back into favor as the college tries to make certain that all students will gain a more common understanding of the problems of man, society, and the world at large. However, the aims of the more progressive of the new prescribed courses are far different from the traditional prescribed curriculum of the past or the conservative prescribed courses of the present.

The distinguishing characteristic that makes a prescribed course progressive lies in the fact that it tends to recognize more adequately modern theories of science, human individuality, and society. Whereas the traditional, prescribed curriculum was based upon a conception of truth that assumed a fixed and unchanging body of knowledge for the understanding of which only certain permanent studies were pertinent, the new, progressive prescribed curriculum should look upon truth as continually subject to experimental revision and as understandable through different avenues for different individuals. Whereas the traditional, prescribed curriculum looked upon the development of intellectual power apart from specific problems as the highest aim of college training, the progressive prescribed curriculum should look upon the development of active intelligence in a social situation as the paramount aim of college education.

Whereas the traditional, prescribed curriculum concentrated upon classical and mathematical studies, the recent, progressive prescribed curriculum should emphasize the major problems of society through the study of the social and natural sciences. Whereas the traditional, prescribed curriculum was devoted largely to the reading of books, the new, progressive prescribed curriculum should emphasize the development of the whole personality and creative expression for the hand-minded as well as for the book-minded. Whereas the traditional, prescribed curriculum conceived a liberal education as essentially literary in character and as opposed to a useful or practical education, the modern, progressive prescribed courses should conceive a liberal education as supremely useful and practical for the art of living in modern society.

To sum up the evidence of history, it seems reasonable to indicate that the theoretical position represented by the conservatives of today not only follows closely the traditional conception of a liberal education and the traditional arguments for a prescribed curriculum but also is geared to a social and intellectual milieu that has largely passed out of existence.   The elective system arose to replace the traditional prescribed curriculum as a result of rapid changes in American society which had to be met rapidly; and if there are today confusion and excessive compartmentalization in the college curriculum, they doubtless reflect corresponding conditions in present-day society.   But from the historical perspective, the remedy seems to lie *not* in justifying a conception of a liberal education that was destroyed by the social changes of the nineteenth and twentieth centuries or in trying to go back to a prescribed curriculum similar to the one that was destroyed by the elective system.

The more adequate remedy of the elective system seems to rest in the hands of those experimental colleges and integrated courses which are consciously based upon a progressive philosophy of experimentalism and experience.   Whatever the difference among them, *they* seem to be moving in a direction more nearly appropriate to modern society than do the proposals for a return to a curriculum that would prescribe an exclusively bookish and intellectual education.   This is not to say that everything labeled conservative is bad or that everything labeled progressive is good; but on the whole, it is firmly believed here that the approach that is at heart progressive will be most fruitful and most appropriate to modern times.

CHAPTER XXII

AS THE CONTROVERSIES CONTINUE

This book has attempted to provide a scheme of reference with which to judge the controversies that have charactized and will doubtless continue to characterize discussions of college policy making. It has attempted to present an interpretation of history that will improve judgments concerning proposed plans for the college of the future. As higher education in many European countries becomes increasingly warped and stultified, the condition and nature of college education in the United States becomes an increasingly important concern of public policy. In an admirably forceful way, Charles A. Beard states the relation of history to public policy as follows: "Since any formulation of a large public policy is at bottom an interpretation of all history, it follows that a judgment upon such a policy is also an interpretation of all history —frightful as the thought is to contemplate."[1]

The upshot of this book is that any acceptable theory of college education in America must take adequate account of the best historical and scholarly evidence concerning modern society, modern science, and modern conceptions of human nature and the learning process. As the serious-minded citizen reads about the continuing controversies in the newspapers or listens to speeches over the radio or at commencements, he must try to separate the wheat from the chaff. As the educator studies the problems of college education or reads the professional periodicals and books or engages in disputes at educational conventions and in faculty meetings, he must try to clarify his own assumptions and burrow beneath the glittering generalities of his colleagues.

With as much fairness as possible, this book has tried to point up typical conflicting points of view that have appeared in answer to several persistent controversies in the field of college education. This has been done in the hope that it will aid citizen and educator alike to judge more adequately among the various proposals and to engage more intelligently in making policy. Each individual must, of course, decide for himself what the historical evidence means for policy making in his own circumstances. This last chapter will summarize and interpret very briefly and in very general terms what the evidence means to the writer. Each

[1] CHARLES A. BEARD, *The Open Door at Home* (The Macmillan Company, New York, 1934), p. vii.

of the controversies listed in Chap. I will be discussed, but the order will be somewhat modified.

THE GREAT TRADITION VERSUS EXPERIMENTAL NATURALISM

At the heart of most of the controversies is a fundamental opposition between underlying philosophical positions. The question that faces modern education is this: Shall our modern philosophy of education be based upon a philosophy of idealism that stems from the absolutes of Plato and the medieval church, or shall it be based upon a philosophy of experimentalism that stems from modern science? The Great Tradition answers that the only real philosophy is the idealistic philosophy of the past which looks upon reality, ideas, and truth as essentially spiritual, fixed, and authoritative. Therefore, it says that modern education must reenforce the education of the past because it has unique power to lead students to ideas and truths that are not subject to the vagaries of human experience. Experimental naturalism answers that philosophy must be reshaped in the light of modern scientific evidence which views reality, ideas, and truth as essentially changing and dependent in large part upon human experience. Therefore, since ideas and truth change in the light of the consequences produced when they are acted upon, modern education must also change, as old ideas are found to be inadequate when put to the test of human experience.

The historical evidence indicates that all societies in the past have really changed their educational procedures to fit the philosophy that they have considered final. It is only modern experimentalism that has *consciously* recognized that philosophy is a *method* of revising our ideas and truths to meet changed circumstances. It is time, therefore, for modern education to accept a frankly experimental philosophy that will do for our own day what the philosophies of past ages did for their education. Our way out is *not* to hold to philosophies that were formulated and appropriate to ages existing before the scientific techniques were devised.

Our way out is to put into practice in the educational and social spheres the methods of scientific inquiry that have proved so fruitful in the realms of physical science. This is not to say that the specialized techniques of the laboratory are wholly applicable to social affairs, but it *is* to say that we can criticize past assumptions and experiment with new procedures until we devise a college education more adequately attuned to the stubborn necessities of modern life and to the best considered plans for improving it. This willingness to criticize, to experiment, and to change in accordance with the consequences of criticism and experimentation is the essence of the progressive approach to education. It has been tried fruitfully on the lower levels of education. It should now be tried wholeheartedly on the college level.

INTELLECTUALISM VERSUS SOCIAL INTELLIGENCE

This controversy focuses attention upon the learning process. The Great Tradition tends to interpret the learning process in terms of the rationalism of Plato, Aristotle, and Thomas Aquinas. The individual is conceived to have a faculty of reason, or intellect, which somehow reaches out and grasps the ideal truths which in some manner exist out there waiting to be attained. Higher learning is thus a process whereby the student is trained in the methods of arriving at ideal truth and knowledge; and the study of certain books is taken as the best means of cultivating the intellect and acquiring intellectual ideas. Experimental naturalism, on the other hand, tends to look upon learning as an empirical process whereby the human organism as a whole interacts with the external conditions of experience. Intellect thus becomes merely the superior way in which human beings solve problems of all kinds, and the name usually given by experimentalists to this process is intelligence. In this way, intelligence is closely associated with the *way people act* in a social situation, and much more attention is given to the *social processes* involved in learning and in the building of intelligent behavior.

The progressive approach to college learning would seem to demand that the newer evidence of science and psychology should be assimilated into the actual practice of learning in college. It would seem to indicate that we should discard conceptions of learning that were formulated before modern science came on to the scene to revise the older notions of intellectual learning. Modern conceptions, of course, do not rule out the importance of learning through books, but they do insist that learning through actual experience is a method which must be given greater attention if college education is to be brought up to date.

Modern conceptions also insist that the physiological and emotional processes cannot be disregarded in learning; they are integral parts of any learning process adequately conceived. Hence, older conceptions that try to separate the intellectual from bodily functions in accordance with a rationalistic theory of learning must give way to newer conceptions more in line with the best evidence concerning human experience and the development of broader ranges of human personality. This means that a progressive theory of college education would try to reshape the college in such a way that students have more opportunity to develop the broader and deeper reaches of their personalities through social and creative activities of all sorts.

DISCIPLINE VERSUS FREEDOM

Historically, the conception of discipline has been associated with the philosophies of idealism and rationalism. "Discipline" is a method found appropriate by any philosophy or institution that seeks to maintain its authority through relatively unquestioning obedience.   It is a conception that has gained great support in the past from the various churches which felt that higher education was a particularly effective way of training young people in the correct doctrines of their beliefs.   Whenever truth in the past or present has been considered fixed and authoritative, the educational doctrine of discipline has been strong; and conservative educators of today, whether they be intellectualistic, humanistic, or religious in their allegiance, urge that modern education must revive the older notions of discipline.   Some educators still insist that the college must exert strict control over the whole life of the student in order to see that he acquires the correct moral discipline as well as the correct intellectual discipline.

Since the eighteenth century, however, the idea of freedom in education has been steadily growing, and it received particular emphasis when the experimentalist doctrines of science began to encourage criticism of older social ideas as well as older physical science.   When truth came to be looked upon as subject to change, and when learning came to be associated with actual human experience, educators began to realize that students learned best when they were relatively free to learn from the activities that interested them.   It was realized that different individuals learn effectively in different ways and that no *one* method of discipline is appropriate to all.

Discipline has been redefined by experimentalists so that it no longer means merely doing a task that the teacher sets out because *he* feels it is important; the best discipline is considered to be attained when the *student* feels that the task is important.   Students will discipline themselves when they have had a share in defining a task to aid them in solving a problem that seems important to them.   To be sure, the teacher should not allow students to be free to do anything that occurs to them on the spur of the moment; but teacher and students should cooperate in defining problems, setting tasks, and judging the results.   A progressive theory of college education would consciously try to incorporate the best evidence of modern psychology into college procedures.

THE IVORY TOWER VERSUS THE WATCHTOWER

Educators are divided in their attitudes concerning how directly the college should engage in preparing its students for the society in which they will live.   Certain conservative educators hold to a conception of academic retreat formulated in the days of Plato and found appropriate by the medieval church.   The ivory tower conception of higher education was doubtless appropriate in a time when philosophy looked upon the intellectual life as the only means of arriving at truth and when it believed that a life of action would seriously interfere with intellectual or spiritual contemplation. When it was believed that the perceptions of the bodily senses gave only an incorrect picture of reality, it was natural that higher education should try to shut out all knowledge of life except that which came through books. Modern conservative educators have tried to hold on to this older conception of higher education which was formulated in days when life moved slowly and when centuries passed without fundamental social changes occurring every few decades.

In more recent times, the rapidly changing character of society has brought home to progressive educators the fact that higher education must try to be in the vanguard of change in order to see that society moves in socially useful instead of socially harmful directions. Modern science and modern industrialism have created a society whose very essence is rapid change; and unless higher education takes account of the *direction* of change, it is easily possible that social and economic forces will outrun the forces of social welfare. Progressive educators point to the recent German universities as examples of ivory towers where the most highly educated persons were hiding out in ignorance of and indifference to the disastrous results of the direction in which dictatorship was leading the German people.

In other words, the intellectual life must not be and cannot really be separated from the life of action, and therefore the higher education in the United States must prepare its students directly to take part in the social life in which they will live. The progressive philosophy of education insists that the college must become fully aware that new times demand new measures, and it must see that college students understand the fundamental forces that are at work and that make our times quite different from any of the past. The watchtower conception of the college insists that American society cannot afford to let its best people hide in isolation from the pressures of society but must see that its faculty members and students alike are constantly engaged in studies and activities that will be useful in solving persistent social and personal problems.

CULTURE VERSUS CASH

The cultural conception of the college was formulated in ancient times when the great masses of the people did the work and received no education and when the few at the top who did not work for a living were thereby enabled to play with education. Thus, culture became a matter which the intellectual elite could enjoy and from which the masses of people were forever excluded. Whenever one was wealthy enough or fortunate enough not to be obliged to depend upon his own efforts to earn a living, he could afford to become cultured, but everyone else had to be concerned with the practical business of earning a living. So a distinction grew up between cultural affairs and practical affairs, and that tradition has lived on in our own day when conservative educators insist that the college must be devoted to cultural and liberal studies but must assiduously avoid the practical and the vocational. The real question is whether or not modern society is so constructed that it is still appropriate to use conceptions devised many centuries ago.

Progressive educators insist that it is no longer appropriate to hold to a conception of liberal education that fitted an essentially slave society. Modern democracy and modern industrialism have created a society in which it is no longer fitting that we should divide so rigidly the cultural from the practical. Times have so changed that the cultural and practical must be brought into a working union so that the values of both kinds of studies can be realized by the majority of people. A democratic society cannot rest upon the stratified class basis of ancient and medieval times; and the highly industrialized society of today requires technological skills of a practical nature which were never dreamed of in former agrarian societies.

Cultural studies need to be brought down to earth and made effective for actual living, and practical studies need to be broadened and shorn of their narrow intent merely to aid students in earning more money by teaching them to learn quickly the tricks of a trade. It is significant that, although colleges have grudgingly given in to the social demand for more practical studies, they have often claimed that their prime function is to hold to the cultural ideal of the past. If they are to embrace a progressive philosophy of education, they must try to reinterpret the function of cultural and practical studies in the light of modern society. It may be that they will decide that so-called cultural studies should be focused upon the solving of actual problems and that so-called practical studies should be so revised that they will help the student to solve problems on an ever broader and more socially useful level.

If the term cultural education is to continue in use among college educators, it should drop its connotation of effete acquaintance with the languages and literature of the past. It should be used in the sociological sense of culture to refer to the whole man-made environment of a people at a given time. Thus, cultural education would embrace the most fundamental and most important activities, ideas, and purposes that a society has inherited from the past *and* has produced for itself. Likewise, the term liberal education must be made practical again for our day, just as it was practical in free Athens, in the thirteenth century universities, and in the most vital and vigorous days of the Renaissance and Reformation. But *our* liberal education must liberate persons to live intelligently in *our* society, and thus it must be different from the education that was appropriate to different eras in the past, just as medieval education was different from Greek education and Renaissance education was different from medieval education.   Liberal education must be appropriate to its own culture.

ARISTOCRATIC VERSUS DEMOCRATIC CONCEPTION OF THE COLLEGE

Another residue from times past is the belief that college education should be reserved for the few.   In ancient and medieval times, the higher education was largely a function of the upper social classes; and in more recent times, it has been largely a function of wealth.   To be sure, some countries such as the United States have made it relatively easier for less fortunate students to attend the higher institutions; but by and large, university training in Europe and America has been largely reserved for the favored classes.   Over a period of many centuries, a psychological defense for this custom has been built up which assumes that only the few are intellectually *capable* of higher education and that therefore all others should not be admitted to colleges and universities. In a sense, the aristocratic argument in higher education runs in a vicious circle.   It says that only certain subjects are appropriate to a cultural and intellectual education; only a few persons can pursue profitably those subjects; and therefore, by definition, only a few are intellectually capable of going to college.   The aristocratic conception of college, then, objects to the great numbers of students who have flooded the colleges of America in the last 50 years and says that the great majority of them should be shunted into technical or vocational schools where the intellectual work is not so difficult.

The progressive approach insists that college education must not only reexamine the kind of studies that it offers but must also reexamine the assumption that only a few superior individuals should be given a college education in a democracy.   The progressive argument says that we must revise the kind of subject that is offered in colleges and then see if we cannot profitably educate the great majority of young people to become better democratic citizens.   Democracy requires that we give our best attention not only to the superior individuals but also to developing more intelligent methods of problem solving among the masses of the people.   We need more and better leaders and experts, but we also need vast numbers of people who can judge more adequately among the proposals and plans that are presented to the electorate.

Unless we are to rely upon the dictatorial rule of a minority, the sole resource of a democracy lies in the intelligence of the people as a whole. A Regent's commission in New York State has recommended that the public high schools of New York should extend their courses of study by two years.   This movement, along with the junior college movement and public higher education in general, indicates a trend that seems in line with the requirements of democracy, but it is opposed by many conservative educators who hold to the older aristocratic notions. In the long view, it seems obvious that a democratic society must put forth ever greater efforts to make some measure of college education effectively free for far greater numbers of the population than is now possible. The question that progressive educators must now answer is not Who shall we keep out of college? but What can the college do for all of these different kinds of individuals?

TRADITIONAL STUDIES VERSUS MODERN STUDIES

The strength of tradition is easily recognized in the studies that occupy the privileged position in the average college. The extreme conservatives cling to the traditional liberal arts in the belief that the study of languages, literature, mathematics, and traditional philosophy is uniquely effective in producing cultured persons. They attack violently the inroads that practical and vocational subjects have made upon the college curriculum; and they often resent the attention paid to the physical and social sciences. Progressives, on the other hand, insist that each age must redefine for itself what studies are of most worth. They argue that, although the seven liberal arts may have been appropriate to the Middle Ages, modern times must concentrate upon the studies that will most effectively help to solve the problems of modern times.

Inasmuch as the physical and social sciences as we know them were not even imagined by the best scholars of past centuries, the fact remains that the methods of science (broadly considered) are the best resources that modern man has for solving his complicated social problems. It is only the better part of wisdom, therefore, for the modern college resolutely to adopt the methods and implications of the sciences, both physical and social. That is not to say that the older liberal arts are not valuable, provided they are used not as the revelation of eternal truths or as a means of worshiping the past but as means of improving our own social and aesthetic life. We need to study the past in order to solve our own problems more intelligently, but the *focus* is not upon the past; it should be upon *contemporary* problems, whether economic or political, social or individual, intellectual or artistic.

RELIGIOUS VERSUS SECULAR CONCEPTION OF THE COLLEGE

The strength of tradition is perhaps seen most clearly of all in the religiously inspired colleges. The church, of course, was closely associated with the very origin of the college and university type of organization in the Middle Ages; and ever since that time, all of the larger religious denominations have supported institutions of higher education. Only within the last century have state universities and private secular universities begun to challenge the religious conception of the college.

By and large, this challenge has been by means of competition for students rather than by attack upon the religious doctrines of the denominational colleges.

Students have doubtless flocked to the secular colleges not only because the fees were smaller but also because they more closely reflected the growing secular temper of the times. In great measure, the religious colleges have been most rigid in adhering to the Great Tradition and its implications as described in the conservative arguments above. Progressive theory, resting as it does upon the implications of science, plainly is moving with the times in the direction of greater secularization of college education. In the long view, if the church-related colleges hope to continue to compete with the secular and public colleges, they may be obliged to take some cues from the progressive approach to education, as some churches have done in their elementary and lower schools.

GENERAL EDUCATION VERSUS SPECIALIZATION

Prior to the nineteenth century, it was quite unanimously agreed that colleges should be devoted to general and broad education rather than to specialities for earning a living. But with the growing technological demands of the nineteenth and twentieth centuries, most colleges have accepted the principle that they should divide their time between general and specialized education. The more extreme conservative colleges have not agreed to this compromise; but in the main, most of them now insist that students devote the first two years of their college career to general education and then specialize in fields of their own choosing during the last two years.

The junior college movement and the general education movement seem to be advancing in somewhat this same direction, but there is no complete agreement as to what shall make up the general part of the program, and this is the point on which conservative and progressive educators most heartily disagree. Conservatives would redirect attention to the liberal studies of the past, and progressives would redefine what liberal must mean for modern times. Some of the experimental colleges suggest that the whole compromise of the nineteenth century must be reexamined and that the way out is to make the curriculum much more flexible so that general and specialized values may be more closely integrated according to the needs of different students. Perhaps some students should start with specialties and progress into broader areas; perhaps some flexible means of alternating between the general and the special is what is needed.

THE ELECTIVE SYSTEM VERSUS THE PRESCRIBED CURRICULUM

Before the nineteenth century, the prescribed curriculum was seldom challenged in the American college. But vigorous controversies appeared in the nineteenth century when new studies arose out of new knowledge that had never been conceived before and began to clamor for admittance to the college curriculum. It was then that conservatives of the nineteenth century began to defend the old and oppose the new, whereas the progressives (by definition) were the ones who insisted that the colleges should adapt themselves to the new times and accept the new studies by using the device of the elective system. The elective system was progressive in the nineteenth century; it was needed in order to bring the colleges up to date in a swiftly moving society. However, in the twentieth century, it became rigid and unwieldy; the quantitative credits that it devised became ends in themselves; its courses became narrow, specialized, and unrelated to each other; a good many other evils arose which have been discussed at length in earlier chapters. A great part of the difficulty grew out of the fact that events moved so rapidly that a clear-cut educational philosophy was not developed to guide collegiate policy.

Gradually, however, in recent decades, clearer philosophies of college education have been emerging, and these philosophies have been called in this book conservative and progressive. The issues have been joined in terms of the persistent controversies defined at length in earlier chapters. The opposing kinds of answer have become clearer; but the final answers, of course, have not been given. Indeed, the thesis of this book has been that *final* answers cannot be given, and that is the reason why the conservative proposals have not been considered so appropriate to modern life as have the progressive proposals.

Conservative plans for reform of the college look to the past for final answers, whereas the progressive attitude looks to the past, present, and future for guides to aid in continuous revision as new conditions point to new changes. For example, conservatives would reform the elective system by reestablishing the prescribed curriculum of old, whereas the progressives would try to preserve only the values of both systems that are appropriate to present-day society.

The emphasis that the elective principle put upon science, freedom for the student and teacher, and usefulness of college studies for actual living in an industrial democracy should be incorporated into a wider and deeper philosophy of education rather than discarded in favor of a philosophy that looks for its assumptions to prescientific, preindustrial, and predemocratic societies. The final blueprints cannot be given, but the historical evidence would lead this writer to indicate that the appropriate way out of present college confusions lies in the acceptance by educators and laymen of an attitude that is frankly critical, experimental, and progressive.

BIBLIOGRAPHY OF HIGHER EDUCATION

The following references have been selected and annotated in order to provide a working bibliography in the history and current problems of higher education. They have been divided into four sections on the basis of their general interest to those who may wish to investigate further the underlying assumptions and opposing points of view that have been guiding college developments in the past and in the present.

Section I provides a list of studies in the history of various phases of American higher education. Only a few of the most outstanding histories of individual institutions have been included, because such histories are so easily found through library card catalogues.

Section II gathers into one place a representative list of firsthand materials from the great amount of college literature that appeared prior to 1910. These references, largely in pamphlet and periodical form, are focused mainly upon the fundamental purposes and nature of college education as raised by the controversies over the elective system.

Section III lists some of the more important recent statements and studies that illustrate present trends and current proposals for the improvement of college education. The periodical literature since 1910 has become so vast that this section has been confined largely to material appearing in book form. *The Reader's Guide to Periodical Literature* and *The Education Index* provide easy access to recent periodical literature.

Section IV gives a short list of bibliographies that may be of value to students who are undertaking research in the foundational areas of higher education.

I. STUDIES IN THE HISTORY OF AMERICAN HIGHER EDUCATION

ADAMS, HERBERT B., ed.: "Contributions to American Educational History," *U. S. Bureau of Education, Circulars of Information*, 1887–1903, Nos. 1–36. Histories of colleges and universities in 35 states; some good, some indifferent.

BOAS, LOUISE S.: *Women's Education Begins; the Rise of the Women's Colleges* (Wheaton College Press, Norton, Mass., 1935). A recent and valuable addition to the history of higher education for women.

BRONSON, WALTER C.: *The History of Brown University*, 1764–1914 (Brown University, Providence, 1914). One of the better histories of individual institutions, based largely on original sources.

BROOME, EDWIN C.: *A Historical and Critical Discussion of College Admission Requirements* (Columbia University, New York, 1902). Historical development and problems of administration from colonial times to the beginning of the twentieth century.

BROWN, E. E.: *The Origin of American State Universities* (University of California Press, Berkeley, 1903). Traces the earlier development of state control of higher education.

BRUCE, P. A.: *History of the University of Virginia*, 1819–1919 (The Macmillan Company, New York, 1920–1922), 5 vols. A comprehensive and detailed study.

BUTLER, V. M.: *Education as Revealed by New England Newspapers Prior to 1850* (Majestic Press, Philadelphia, 1935). Based entirely on source material from early newspapers, this study contains much on college education.

427

BUTTS, R. FREEMAN: "A Liberal Education and the Prescribed Curriculum in the American College," *Educational Record*, 18: 548–564 (October, 1937). A short historical survey of some of the material contained in this book.

CANBY, HENRY SEIDEL: *Alma Mater; The Gothic Age of the American College* (Farrar & Rinehart, Inc., New York, 1936). "A critical memoir of a long college experience."

CASSIDY, FRANCIS PATRICK: *Catholic College Foundations and Development in the United States*, 1677–1850 (Catholic University of America, Washington, D. C., 1924). A dissertation written at the Catholic University of America.

COULTER, E. M.: *College Life in the Old South* (The Macmillan Company, New York, 1928). Interesting comments on the methods and courses of early colleges, especially the University of Georgia.

COWIE, ALEXANDER: *Educational Problems at Yale College in the Eighteenth Century* (Yale University Press, New Haven, 1936). Short description of instruction and discipline in early days.

COWLEY, W. H.: "European Influences upon American Higher Education," *Educational Record*, 20: 165–190 (April, 1939). Brief historical survey of English, Scotch, French, and German influence from colonial times to the present.

DEMAREST, WILLIAM H. S.: *A History of Rutgers College* (Rutgers College, New Brunswick, N. J., 1924). A president of Rutgers wrote this rather thorough history of the college with quotations from much documentary material; bibliography.

DUFFUS, R. L.: *Democracy Enters College; A Study of the Rise and Decline of the Academic Lockstep* (Charles Scribner's Sons, New York, 1936). An interesting and valuable study of the history and recent trends in college entrance requirements.

ECKELBERRY, R. H.: "The History of the Municipal University in the United States," *U. S. Office of Education, Bulletin*, 1932, No. 2. The most complete survey of this aspect of higher education, with a long bibliography.

ELLIOTT, EDWARD C., and M. M. CHAMBERS, ed.: *Charters and Basic Laws of Selected American Universities and Colleges* (Carnegie Foundation for the Advancement of Teaching, New York, 1934). A compilation of source documents for 51 institutions.

ERBACHER, S. A.: *Catholic Higher Education for Men in the United States*, 1850–1866 (Catholic University of America, Washington, D. C., 1931). A dissertation describing the aims, administration, teaching staff, students, curriculum, and methods; with a bibliography.

FOSTER, WILLIAM T.: *Administration of the College Curriculum* (Houghton Mifflin Company, Boston, 1911). A president of Reed College deals with the historical and critical aspects of the elective system.

HARRIMAN, PHILIP L.: "The Bachelor's Degree," *Journal of Higher Education*, 7: 301–307 (June, 1936). Historical summary of new types of bachelor's degrees.

HINSDALE, B. A.: "Notes on the History of Foreign Influence upon Education in the United States," *U. S. Commissioner of Education, Annual Report*, 1897–1898, No. 1, pp. 597 *ff.* Lists many American scholars who studied in German universities.

HOLMES, D. O. W.: *The Evolution of the Negro College* (Teachers College, Columbia University, New York, 1934). A good historical summary by the dean of the graduate school of Howard University; a dissertation with bibliography.

HOWE, M. A. DEW.: *Classic Shades; Five Leaders of Learning and Their Colleges* (Little, Brown & Company, Boston, 1928). Interesting sketches of Timothy

Dwight of Yale, Mary Lyon of Mount Holyoke, Mark Hopkins of Williams, James McCosh of Princeton, and Charles W. Eliot of Harvard.

JAMES, HENRY: *Charles W. Eliot, President of Harvard University*, 1869–1909 (Houghton Mifflin Company, Boston, 1930). A comprehensive study of Harvard's famous president.

KELLY, FREDERICK J., and E. B. RATCLIFFE: "Privately Controlled Higher Education in the United States," *U. S. Office of Education, Bulletin*, 1934, No. 12. A brief summary of colonial colleges and the current status of higher education under Protestant, Catholic, and other private auspices.

KIRKPATRICK, J. E.: *Academic Organization and Control* (Antioch College Press, Yellow Springs, Ohio, 1931). Historical and critical study showing how American methods of control differed from those in Europe.

KOLBE, PARKE R.: *Urban Influences on Higher Education in England and the United States* (The Macmillan Company, New York, 1928). The president of Brooklyn Polytechnic Institute describes adult education and workingmen's problems in relation to higher education and especially the municipal university.

KOOS, LEONARD V., and C. C. CRAWFORD: "College Aims Past and Present," *School and Society*, 14: 499–509 (Dec. 3, 1921). Comparison of aims as stated in early writings and in more recent times.

MERIWETHER, COLYER: *Our Colonial Curriculum*, 1706–1776 (Capital Publishing Company, Washington, D. C., 1907). A convenient drawing together of materials illustrating methods and subject matter fields; bibliography.

MONTGOMERY, THOMAS H.: *History of the University of Pennsylvania from Its Foundation to A. D.* 1770 (George W. Jacobs Company, Philadelphia, 1900). A detailed and documented account with considerable source material of Franklin's academy and college.

MORISON, SAMUEL ELIOT: "American Colonial Colleges," *Rice Institute Pamphlet*, 23: 246–282 (October, 1936). One of the best short discussions of the colonial colleges.

———: *The Founding of Harvard College* (Harvard University Press, Cambridge, 1935). The first volume in a projected series of five on Harvard; a scholarly, well-documented story of the historical and European backgrounds of Harvard and its development to 1650.

———: *Harvard College in the Seventeenth Century* (Harvard University Press, Cambridge, 1936), 2 vols. One of the finest examples of historical writing in higher education; detailed descriptions of all phases of Harvard's development; with bright pictures of individuals, humorous sidelights, and solid contributions to the intellectual and educational history of America.

———: *Three Centuries of Harvard*, 1636–1936 (Harvard University Press, Cambridge, 1936). A condensed account of the larger history written for Harvard's tercentenary celebration.

———: ed.: *The Development of Harvard University Since the Inauguration of President Eliot*, 1869–1929 (Harvard University Press, Cambridge, 1930). Accounts of the various departments of study written by Harvard professors with an introduction by Morison.

PATERSON, WILLIAM: *Glimpses of Colonial Society and the Life at Princeton College*, 1766–1773, ed. by W. Jay Mills (J. B. Lippincott Company, Philadelphia, 1903). The letters of a graduate of 1763 give an illuminating and interesting picture of what the college students did, thought about, the love letters and poems they wrote, and the songs they sang in the eighteenth century.

PATTON, LESLIE K.: *The Purposes of Church-related Colleges* (Teachers College, Columbia University, New York, 1939). A dissertation study of the aims of denominational colleges as found in catalogues, publications, and letters from college presidents to the author; bibliography.

PERRY, CHARLES M.: *Henry Philip Tappan—Philosopher and University President* (University of Michigan Press, Ann Arbor, 1933). A capable study of Michigan's early president; bibliography.

RICHARDSON, LEON BURR: *History of Dartmouth College* (Hanover, N. H., 1932), 2 vols. A running account for the general reader.

ROBINSON, JAMES HARVEY: "The Elective System (Historically Considered)," *International Quarterly*, 6: 191–201 (September-December, 1902). Brief historical survey by the eminent Columbia University historian.

ROBINSON, MABEL LOUISE: "The Curriculum of the Women's College," *U. S. Bureau of Education, Bulletin*, 1918, No. 6. A survey of some of the more prominent women's colleges.

SCHMIDT, GEORGE PAUL: "Intellectual Crosscurrents in American Colleges," *American Historical Review*, 42: 46–67 (October, 1936). The controversies in the early nineteenth century are well pictured and documented.

————: *The Old Time College President* (Columbia University Press, New York, 1930). A valuable and lively portrait of typical attitudes and problems facing college educators especially in the early nineteenth century; good bibliography.

SEARS, JESSE B.: "Philanthropy in the History of American Higher Education," *U. S. Bureau of Education, Bulletin*, 1922, No. 26. A convenient summary of an important phase of higher education.

SMALLWOOD, MARY L.: *An Historical Study of Examinations and Grading Systems in Early American Universities* (Harvard University Press, Cambridge, 1935). Scholarly treatment of source materials of all kinds.

SNOW, LOUIS F.: *The College Curriculum in the United States* (Teachers College, Columbia University, New York, 1907). One of the earliest general studies of the college curriculum; valuable chiefly for the colonial period.

TEWKSBURY, DONALD G.: *The Founding of American Colleges and Universities before the Civil War* (Teachers College, Columbia University, New York, 1932). An excellent general study with a complete list of the denominational and state institutions founded in the United States up to the middle of the nineteenth century; bibliography.

THWING, CHARLES F.: *A History of Higher Education in America* (D. Appleton-Century Company, Inc., New York, 1906). An old study, but still the most complete general history of American higher education in one volume.

WALSH, JAMES JOSEPH: *Education of the Founding Fathers of the Republic; Scholasticism in the Colonial Colleges; A Neglected Chapter in the History of Education* (Fordham University Press, New York, 1935). Historical and critical study from the Jesuit point of view.

WOODY, THOMAS: *A History of Women's Education in the United States* (The Science Press, New York, 1929), 2 vols. The standard work in this field; scholarly and well-documented material on the women's colleges; extensive bibliography.

II. EARLY POINTS OF VIEW AND CONTROVERSIES (PRIOR TO 1910)

ADAMS, CHARLES FRANCIS: *A College Fetich* (Lee and Shepard, Boston, 1883). A prominent noneducator opposes over-emphasis upon the classics and favors the elective system and practical studies.

ADAMS, CHARLES KENDALL: *The University and the State* (Madison, Wis., 1896). The president of the University of Wisconsin recites the various ways in which a state university may serve the state.

American Institute of Instruction: Addresses and Proceedings, Vols. 1–78 (1831–1908). Fruitful source of early controversies; prior to 1882 the title reads *Lectures*.

ANGELL, JAMES BURRILL: *Higher Education; A Plea for Making It Accessible to All* (Ann Arbor, Mich., 1879). The president of the University of Michigan urges greater democracy in higher education.

ASHMORE, SIDNEY G.: *The Classics and Modern Training* (Knickerbocker Press, New York, 1905). A professor of Latin insists that the classics provide the proper "brain work" for enlarging "reasoning powers" by developing certain nerve centers.

ATKINSON, WILLIAM P.: *The Liberal Education of the Nineteenth Century* (D. Appleton-Century Company, Inc., New York, 1873). Influential address favoring election and modern studies by a professor at the Massachusetts Institute of Technology.

BARNARD, FREDERICK A. P.: *Analysis of Some Statistics of College Education* (New York, 1870). The president of Columbia is forced to recognize that the elective system is popular with students and public.

—— and JOHN W. PRATT: *Report on a Proposition to Modify the Plan of Instruction in the University of Alabama* (New York, 1855). A defense of the prescribed curriculum and classics against the elective system and modern studies.

BARNARD, HENRY, ed.: *American Journal of Education*, Vols. 1–32 (1856–1882). Fruitful source of early controversies; see cumulative index.

BARTLETT, S. C.: "Shortening the College Course," *Education*, 11: 585–590 (June, 1891). The president of Dartmouth urges that the four-year college course be maintained, even if the secondary school must be shortened.

BIGELOW, JACOB: *An Address on the Limits of Education read before the Massachusetts Institute of Technology* (Boston, 1865). An effective plea for the elective system and more attention to scientific studies.

BIRDSEYE, CLARENCE F.: *Individual Training in Our Colleges* (The Macmillan Company, New York, 1907). A description of student life and a plea for giving more attention to the students' point of view.

BOONE, RICHARD G.: "Results under an Elective System," *Educational Review*, 4: 53–73 (June, 1892). The president of the University of Indiana describes favorably the working of the elective system in his institution.

BREARLEY, SAMUEL: "The System of Instruction and Government at Harvard College," *New Englander*, 45: 359–372 (April, 1886). An attack upon the elective system as instituted at Harvard.

BRIGGS, LEB. R.: "Some Old-fashioned Doubts about New-fashioned Education," *Atlantic Monthly*, 86: 463–470 (October, 1900). Harvard's dean criticizes the free elective system.

BRIGHAM, ALBERT PERRY: "Present Status of the Elective System in American Colleges," *Educational Review*, 14: 360–369 (November, 1897). Descriptive study of 25 college catalogues.

BURGESS, JOHN W.: *The American University. When Shall It Be? Where Shall It Be? What Shall It Be?* (Ginn and Company, Boston, 1884). Urges the establishment of the German type of university instruction with large use of the elective system.

CANFIELD, JAMES H.: "Wide Election and Minute Courses," *National Education Association, Proceedings*, 1905, pp. 495–501. Pros and cons received from many institutions.

CHAMBERLAIN, D. H.: "The Elective Policy," *New Englander*, 45: 459–461 (May, 1886). Withering blasts at Eliot, his reports, and the elective system.

——: *Not a "College Fetish"; Address in Reply to the Address of C. F. Adams* (Willard Small, Boston, 1884). Defense of the classics against the "practical" men.

CLAP, THOMAS: *Religious Constitution of Colleges, Especially Yale-College in New-Haven, in the Colony of Connecticut* (T. Green, New London, Conn., 1754). A famous statement by a president of Yale.

"Conservative View of College Electives," *National Education Association, Proceedings*, 1895, pp. 657–661. Pros and cons in discussion.

CORBIN, JOHN: "Harking Back to the Humanities," *Atlantic Monthly*, 101: 482–490 (April, 1908). Links rise of the elective system and decline of the humanities as correlative evils.

———: "Is the Elective System Elective?" *Forum*, 31: 599–608 (July, 1901). Claims that the offer of elective study is specious because of the weight of administrative machinery.

COULTER, JOHN M.: "The University Spirit," *Educational Review*, 4: 366–371 (November, 1892). Insists that when universities abandoned the prescribed curriculum and adopted the elective system they changed from a false to a true theory of higher education.

DEWING, A. S.: "Neglected Values in the Elective System," *Education*, 30: 442–447 (March, 1910). A Harvard professor says that the moral value of the elective system is high because it develops a sense of responsibility in students.

"Discipline in the American College," *North American Review*, 149: 1–29 (July, 1889). A symposium of many points of view: Bartlett of Dartmouth, Angell of Michigan, Shaler of Harvard, Adams of Cornell, Hyde of Bowdoin, Dawson of McGill, and Davis of California.

"Dr. Hedge's Address to the Alumni of Harvard," *New Englander*, 25: 695–710 (October, 1866). An editorial comment insists that colleges overestimate the value of knowledge and underestimate the value of training.

DWIGHT, TIMOTHY: *Addresses at the Induction of Professor Timothy Dwight as President of Yale College* (New Haven, 1886). Continues the Yale tradition by opposing the elective system, but hints at the possibility of being forced to yield to events of the twentieth century.

ELIOT, CHARLES WILLIAM: *Educational Reform* (D. Appleton-Century Company, Inc., New York, 1898). A collection of some of Eliot's most effective addresses and articles in his long fight for changes in the college.

———: "The New Education," *Atlantic Monthly*, 23: 203–220, 358–367 (February, March, 1869). Articles that drew attention to Eliot just before he was elected president of Harvard.

———: *University Administration* (Houghton Mifflin Company, Boston, 1908). A restatement of Eliot's point of view on various topics near the end of his long administration at Harvard.

GARNETT, J. M.: "The Elective System of the University of Virginia," *U. S. Bureau of Education, Circular of Information*, 1888, No. 1. Detailed study of the theory and practice of electives in the South.

GILMAN, DANIEL COIT: *The Launching of a University and Other Papers* (Dodd, Mead & Company, Inc., New York, 1906). Remembrances of the early days of Johns Hopkins University and other articles concerning higher education.

———: *University Problems in the United States* (D. Appleton-Century Company, Inc., New York, 1898). An early collection of addresses and articles on a variety of topics by the president of Johns Hopkins.

GOODWIN, WILLIAM WATSON: *The Present and Future of Harvard College* (Boston, 1891). Vigorous plea for progressive changes at Harvard and interesting sidelights on why change was difficult.

"Greek and Latin against Nature and Science," *Popular Science Monthly*, 22: 116–120 (May, 1883). An editorial states the issues bluntly and calls for more science and election of studies.

HANUS, PAUL: "Graduate Testimony on the Elective System," *Harvard Graduates' Magazine*, 10: 354–363 (March, 1902).   Questionnaire study favorable to elective system.

HARPER, WILLIAM RAINEY: *The Prospects of the Small College* (University of Chicago Press, Chicago, 1900).   A warning to the liberal arts college to improve itself.

———: *The Trend in Higher Education* (University of Chicago Press, Chicago, 1905). A collection of addresses and papers by the president of the University of Chicago.

HARRIS, SAMUEL S.: *Complete Education* (Ann Arbor, Mich., 1880).   A bishop opposes utilitarian and elective studies.

HARRIS, WILLIAM T.: "Equivalents in a Liberal Course of Studies," *National Education Association, Proceedings*, 1880, pp. 167–175.   The U. S. Commissioner of Education opposes election.

Harvard University: Annual Report of the President, 1883–1884.   Eliot's history of the elective system at Harvard is presented on pp. 5–30.

HEDGE, F. H.: "University Reform," *Atlantic Monthly*, 18: 296–307 (September, 1866).   An early statement by a Harvard professor favoring election.

HOWISON, G. H.: "The Harvard 'New Education,'" *Andover Review*, 5: 577–589 (June, 1886).   A University of California professor takes issue with Palmer and his defense of Harvard's elective system.

HYDE, WILLIAM DEWITT: "The Policy of the Small College," *Educational Review*, 2: 313–321 (November, 1891).   The president of Bowdoin would allow only a small amount of election in the undergraduate college.

JORDAN, DAVID STARR: *The Care and Culture of Men; a Series of Addresses on the Higher Education* (The Whitaker and Ray Company, San Francisco, 1896). A collection of early addresses and articles by the president of Leland Stanford Junior University.

———: *The Voice of the Scholar; with Other Addresses on the Problems of Higher Education* (Paul Elder and Company, San Francisco, 1903).   A summing-up of Jordan's theory of higher education on various topics.

JOYNES, EDWARD S.: "Classical Studies," *National Education Association, Proceedings*, 1873, pp. 131–140.   Favors election to save the classics.

LADD, GEORGE T.: "Education, New and Old," *Andover Review*, 5: 1–18 (January, 1886).   A famous Yale professor answers and criticizes the article by Palmer.

———: "The Recent Change in the Academic Curriculum at Yale," *New Englander*, 44: 114–127 (January, 1885).   Although some election was allowed to upper-classmen at Yale, it is made plain that Yale will not follow Harvard further.

LEVERSON, MONTAGUE R.: *Thoughts on Institutions of the Higher Education, with a Chapter on Classical Studies* (New York, 1893).   A most vitriolic and unusual attack upon the classics and classicists.

LINDSLEY, PHILIP: *Address in Nashville . . . at the Inauguration of the President of Cumberland College* (Nashville, Tenn., 1825).   An early plea for making higher education serve all classes in the community.

McCOSH, JAMES: *Inauguration of James McCosh as President of the College of New Jersey* (New York, 1868).   A famous president of Princeton indicates that the free elective system will not be favored in his time.

———: *The New Departure in College Education* (New York, 1885).   A point-for-point reply in opposition to Eliot's advocacy of more freedom for students.

MILLS, CALEB: *New Departures in Collegiate Control and Culture* (New York, 1880). A professor of Greek vents his spleen upon all the changes in higher education that threaten the classics.

MOORE, CHARLES S.: "The Elective System at Harvard," *Harvard Graduates' Magazine*, 11: 530–534 (June, 1903).   Descriptive study of 448 senior programs to illustrate the variety of choices by students.

National Education Association: Addresses and Proceedings, 1871–1939. Fruitful source of early controversies; see also *National Teachers' Association*, 1857–1870.

ORDAHL, GEORGE: *The College Curricula; A Study of Required and Elective Courses in American Colleges and Universities* (Nevada State University, Reno, 1910). A descriptive and interpretive study of college catalogues.

PAINTER, F. V. N.: *The Modern Languages versus the Ancient Languages in the College Curriculum* (Salem, Va., 1883). Favors the elective system to give greater place to the modern languages.

PALMER, GEORGE HERBERT: "The New Education," *Andover Review*, 4: 393–407 (November, 1885). A famous Harvard professor makes a strong case for the elective system and provokes considerable controversy.

———: "Possible Limitations of the Elective System," *Andover Review*, 6: 569–590 (December, 1886); 7: 1–18 (January, 1887). Not a retraction from his earlier position, but an expanded statement of wise and unwise ways to limit election.

PHILLIPS, E. D.: "The Elective System in American Education," *Pedagogical Seminary*, 8: 206–230 (June, 1901). Extensive questionnaire study of the status and opinion of elective studies in secondary schools and colleges.

PORTER, NOAH: *American Colleges and the American Public; with After-thoughts on College and School Education* (Charles Scribner's Sons, New York, 1890). A most effective defense of the prescribed curriculum, the classics, the "class system," and the religious character of college by the famous president of Yale; bibliography.

Present College Questions (D. Appleton-Century Company, Inc., New York, 1903). Eliot, West, Harper, and Butler debate the advisability of shortening the college course through use of the elective system; addresses before the National Education Association.

PRITCHETT, HENRY SMITH: "The College of Discipline and the College of Freedom," *Atlantic Monthly*, 102: 603–611 (November, 1908). A plea for preserving the values of both kinds of colleges.

QUINCY, JOSIAH: *Remarks on the Nature and Probable Effects of Introducing the Voluntary System in the Studies of Greek and Latin* (Cambridge, 1841). A prominent Harvard president urges elective studies to improve the college and the classics.

RUSSELL, WILLIAM F., ed.: *The Rise of a University, Vol. I, The Later Days of Old Columbia College* (Columbia University Press, New York, 1937). An excellent compilation of selections from the annual reports of President Frederick A. P. Barnard.

SILL, E. R.: "Herbert Spencer's Theory of Education," *Atlantic Monthly*, 51: 171–179 (February, 1883). Attacks Spencer, scientific, and elective studies as inferior to classical studies.

SMITH, CHARLES SPRAGUE: *The American University* (New York, 1887). Startles a Phi Beta Kappa audience by suggesting that the university ideal ought to replace the college; some colleges should become universities and others secondary schools.

STEVENSON, J. J.: "The College Course," *Popular Science Monthly*, 64: 202–209 (January, 1904). Attacks Jordan and urges a return to the college of 25 years earlier with its strict discipline and severity.

TAFT, CHARLES PHELPS: *The German University and the American College* (Cincinnati, 1871). Berates Porter for defending the traditional college and cites the advantages in scholarship, specialization, and freedom found in the German university ideal.

TAPPAN, HENRY PHILIP: *University Education* (New York, 1851). Admiration of the Prussian system by Michigan's president.

TICKNOR, GEORGE: *Remarks on Changes Lately Proposed or Adopted in Harvard College* (Boston, 1825). One of the earliest and most effective arguments for reform of the college curriculum to meet new times.

U. S. *Commissioner of Education, Annual Report*, 1888–1889, No. 2, pp. 1224–1361. A complete list of studies offered in 101 colleges and universities with elective subjects in italics.

VAN HISE, CHARLES RICHARD: *Inaugural Address* (Madison, Wis., 1904). The president of the University of Wisconsin makes a memorable statement of the democratic theory of higher education for a state university.

WAYLAND, FRANCIS: *Report to the Corporation of Brown University, on Changes in the System of Collegiate Education* (Providence, 1850). A radical program for the times by the president of Brown.

——: *Thoughts on the Present Collegiate System in the United States* (Boston, 1842). An early statement that provoked much discussion.

WEST, ANDREW F.: "Must the Classics Go?" *North American Review*, 138: 151–162 (February, 1884). The graduate dean at Princeton defends the classics for their value as mental discipline and opposes election.

——: *A Review of President Eliot's Report on Elective Studies* (New York, 1886). Questions Eliot's arguments for the elective system, his statistics, and his conclusions.

WHITE, ANDREW D.: "The Need of Another University," *Forum*, 6: 465–473 (January, 1889). The president of Cornell favors election as proper in a university.

WHITE, EMERSON E.: "Election in General Education," *National Education Association, Proceedings*, 1897, pp. 373–384. Believes that election has little place in nonspecialized education.

WILSON, WOODROW: "What Is a College For?" *Scribner's Magazine*, 46: 570–577 (November, 1909). Intellectual discipline is paramount, but some form of the "group system" should give alternative routes.

WOOLSEY, THEODORE DWIGHT: *Discourses and Addresses at the Ordination of Theodore Dwight Woolsey to the Ministry of the Gospel and His Inauguration as President of Yale College* (New Haven, 1846). Typical early expression of the Yale emphasis upon mental discipline as more important than knowledge and religious aims as more important than practical aims.

WRIGHT, H. B.: "The American College Course," *Educational Review*, 27: 384–394 (April, 1904). A Yale graduate insists that the public should be included in discussions of higher education and that students too should be heard.

Yale Faculty: "Original Papers in Relation to a Course of Liberal Education," *American Journal of Science and Arts*, 15: 297–351 (January, 1829). The famous Yale report of 1828 which defended the prescribed curriculum and the classics as integral to a liberal arts college.

III. RECENT TRENDS AND CURRENT PROPOSALS (SINCE 1910)

The American College; a Series of Papers Setting Forth the Program, Achievements, Present Status and Probable Future of the American College, with introduction by W. H. Crawford (Henry Holt & Company, New York, 1915). A symposium presenting several different points of view.

ANGELL, JAMES ROWLAND: *American Education; Addresses and Articles* (Yale University Press, New Haven, 1937). The president emeritus of Yale sums up his point of view on various phases of higher education.

AYDELOTTE, FRANK: "Honors Courses in American Colleges and Universities," *National Research Council of the National Academy of Sciences, Bulletin*, Vol.

X, Part 2, No. 52 (Washington, D. C., 1925). The president of Swarthmore describes the aims and methods of an influential trend in college education.

BABBITT, IRVING: *Literature and the American College; Essays in Defense of the Humanities* (Houghton Mifflin Company, Boston, 1908). One of the most extreme statements of the humanist position.

BAKER, JAMES HUTCHINS: *American University Progress and College Reform Relative to School and Society* (Longmans, Green & Company, New York, 1916). Forward looking proposals by the president emeritus of the University of Colorado.

BEASLEY, PATRICIA: *The Revival of the Humanities in American Education* (Teachers College, Columbia University, New York, 1939). Unpublished manuscript. A dissertation study of the history of Humanism and the recent interest in humanities courses; bibliography of different kinds of Humanism.

BIXLER, EVELYN TRUTH: *A Study of Electives in the Liberal Arts Colleges of Certain Universities in Forty-two States* (University of Maryland, Baltimore, 1933). An unpublished dissertation study of catalogues and questionnaires.

BODE, BOYD H.: *Progressive Education at the Crossroads* (Newson and Company, New York, 1938). Short critique of traditional and earlier "Progressive" points of view.

BUTLER, NICHOLAS MURRAY: *The Meaning of Education; Contributions to a Philosophy of Education* (Charles Scribner's Sons, New York, 1915). Collection of essays, some of which deal with higher education, by the president of Columbia University.

———: *Scholarship and Service; the Policies of a National University in a Modern Democracy* (Charles Scribner's Sons, New York, 1921). Another collection focused largely upon several aspects of higher education.

COFFMAN, LOTUS D.: *The State University—Its Work and Problems* (University of Minnesota Press, Minneapolis, 1934). Selected addresses delivered between 1921 and 1933 by the president of the University of Minnesota.

COSS, JOHN J., ed.: *Five College Plans* (Columbia University Press, New York, 1931). New developments at Columbia, Chicago, Swarthmore, Harvard, and Wabash.

DEWEY, JOHN: *The Educational Situation* (University of Chicago Press, Chicago, 1902). An early statement of the progressive point of view.

———: *Experience and Education* (The Macmillan Company, New York, 1938). An effective restatement of Dewey's philosophy in brief form, much of which applies to college education.

———: *The Way Out of Educational Confusion* (Harvard University Press, Cambridge, 1931). This Inglis Lecture has pertinence for many current controversies in college education.

DONNELLY, FRANCIS P.: *Literature the Leading Educator* (Longmans, Green & Company, New York, 1938). A Jesuit defense of classical literature and an attack upon the experimental sciences in college education.

EELLS, WALTER CROSBY: *The Junior College* (Houghton Mifflin Company, Boston, 1931). A comprehensive textbook with extensive bibliographies.

———: *Surveys of American Higher Education* (Carnegie Foundation for the Advancement of Teaching, New York, 1937). Description and analysis of over 200 surveys of colleges and universities made during the last 30 years.

ELLIOTT, EDWARD C., ed.: *The Rise of a University*, Vol. II, *The University in Action* (Columbia University Press, New York, 1937). An excellent selection from the annual reports, 1902–1935, of President Butler of Columbia University.

FAIRCHILD, HENRY PRATT, ed.: *The Obligation of the Universities to the Social Order* (New York University Press, New York, 1933). Symposium of addresses delivered at a conference on higher education held at New York University in 1932.

FLEXNER, ABRAHAM: *The American College* (D. Appleton-Century Company, Inc., New York, 1908). A plea for the undergraduate college and an elaborate attack upon the elective system.

————: *A Modern College and a Modern School* (Doubleday, Doran & Company, Garden City, N. Y., 1923). An early criticism which stirred up the conservatives.

————: *Universities, American, English, German* (Oxford University Press, New York, 1930). An attack upon certain outstanding universities which created much controversy both pro and con.

FOERSTER, NORMAN: *The American State University; Its Relation to Democracy* (University of North Carolina Press, Chapel Hill, N. C., 1937). Comprehensive critique of higher education from the Humanist point of view.

————: *The Future of the Liberal College* (D. Appleton-Century Company, Inc., New York, 1938). A more caustic collection of addresses and articles.

FOSTER, GRACE RUTH: *Social Change in Relation to Curricular Development in Collegiate Education for Women* (The Galahad Press, Fairfield, Maine, 1934). Dissertation study of questionnaires, interviews with college alumnae, and analysis of curriculums; bibliography.

FRASER, MOWAT G.: *The College of the Future; an Appraisal of Fundamental Plans and Trends in American Higher Education* (Columbia University Press, New York, 1937). Description of various new plans for college education; elaboration of a philosophy of higher education; and an extensive bibliography of recent changes.

GALLAGHER, B. G.: *American Caste and the Negro College* (Columbia University Press, New York, 1938). An effective appraisal and suggested program.

GAVIT, J. P.: *College* (Harcourt, Brace & Company, New York, 1925). A staff writer of the *New York Evening Post* describes what he found during two years visiting 30 colleges.

GIDEONSE, HARRY D.: *The Higher Learning in a Democracy* (Farrar & Rinehart, Inc., New York, 1937). A specific reply to President Hutchins.

GRATTAN, C. HARTLEY, ed.: *The Critique of Humanism; a Symposium* (Brewer, Warren & Putnam, Inc., New York, 1930). Criticism of Humanism by such men as Grattan, Henry Hazlitt, Malcolm Cowley, and Lewis Mumford.

GRAY, WILLIAM S., ed.: *Current Issues in Higher Education* (University of Chicago Press, Chicago, 1937). Debates on various topics before the Institute for Administrative Officers of Higher Institutions.

————: *General Education: Its Nature, Scope, and Essential Elements* (University of Chicago Press, Chicago, 1934). Various experiments in organization and subject matter.

————: *The Junior College Curriculum* (University of Chicago Press, Chicago, 1929). Experimental procedures in different kinds of institutions.

————: *Needed Readjustments in Higher Education* (University of Chicago Press, Chicago, 1933). Readjustments affecting instruction, organization, curriculum, student life in the light of the depression.

————: *Provision for the Individual in College Education* (University of Chicago Press, Chicago, 1932). Various methods of adapting instruction and the curriculum to individual students.

————: *Recent Trends in American College Education* (University of Chicago Press, Chicago, 1931). Reorganizations on the junior college level, senior college level, and examination and measurement procedures.

HAGGERTY, MELVIN E.: *The Evaluation of Higher Institutions*, Vol. III, *The Educational Program* (University of Chicago Press, Chicago, 1937). An investigation of college aims and curriculum for the North Central Association of Colleges and Secondary Schools.

HARTSHORNE, HUGH, HELEN R. STEARNS, and WILLARD E. UPHAUS: *Standards and Trends in Religious Education* (Yale University Press, New Haven, 1933). Part II describes and appraises what the churches do for their young members when students leave home for college.

Higher Education and Society; a Symposium (University of Oklahoma Press, Norman, Okla., 1936). A collection of addresses on widely varied topics.

HOLLIS, ERNEST VICTOR: *Philanthropic Foundations and Higher Education* (Columbia University Press, New York, 1938). The most comprehensive description and evaluation of the relation of the philanthropic foundations to higher education; annotated bibliography.

HUDELSON, EARL, ed.: *Problems of College Education; Studies in Administration, Student Personnel, Curriculum, and Instruction* (University of Minnesota Press, Minneapolis, 1928). Many reports of new programs and investigations of new procedures; bibliography.

HUDSON, JAY WILLIAM: *The College and New America* (D. Appleton-Century Company, Inc., New York, 1920). An early progressive statement by a University of Missouri professor of philosophy.

HUTCHINS, ROBERT M.: *The Higher Learning in America* (Yale University Press, New Haven, 1936). Recent proposals which have rocked the educational world and precipitated much controversial discussion.

———: *No Friendly Voice* (University of Chicago Press, Chicago, 1936). A collection of addresses and articles by the president of the University of Chicago.

JOHN, WALTON C.: "Requirements for the Bachelor's Degree," *U. S. Bureau of Education, Bulletin*, 1920, No. 7. Study of prescriptions and electives in 101 institutions.

JOHNSON, B. LAMAR: *What About Survey Courses?* (Henry Holt & Company, New York, 1937). Comprehensive study of the development of different kinds of survey courses in various subject matter fields.

JOHNSTON, JOHN B.: *The Liberal College in a Changing Society* (D. Appleton-Century Company, Inc., New York, 1930). A penetrating analysis of college life by the dean of the College of Science, Literature, and the Arts at the University of Minnesota.

JONES, EDWARD S.: *Comprehensive Examinations in American Colleges* (The Macmillan Company, New York, 1933). Historical and descriptive account of the uses and varieties of comprehensive examinations; selected bibliography.

KELLY, FREDERICK J.: *The American Arts College; a Limited Survey* (The Macmillan Company, New York, 1925). Description of the aims, curriculum, guidance, methods of instruction, measurement of achievement, and extracurricular life of a dozen typical arts colleges.

KELLY, ROBERT L., ed.: *The Effective College; by a Group of American Students of Higher Education* (Association of American Colleges, New York, 1928). Symposium by several educators on various topics.

KELSEY, FRANCIS E., ed.: *Latin and Greek in American Education; with Symposia on the Value of Humanistic Studies* (The Macmillan Company, New York, 1911). Articles on the educational value of the classics for general education and as preparation for the professional and business pursuits.

KENT, RAYMOND A., ed.: *Higher Education in America* (Ginn and Company, Boston, 1930). A textbook with chapters by different individuals on the various aspects of higher education with bibliographies.

KILPATRICK, WILLIAM H., ed.: *The Educational Frontier* (D. Appleton-Century Company, Inc., New York, 1933). One of the best composite statements of the progressive point of view with many implications for higher education.

KIRKPATRICK, J. E.: *The American College and Its Rulers* (New Republic, Inc., New York, 1926). A study of the business and lay control of higher education.

KOOS, LEONARD V.: *The Junior College* (University of Minnesota Press, Minneapolis, 1924), 2 vols. A comprehensive series of studies on all aspects of the junior college.

KUDER, MERLE: *Trends of Professional Opportunities in the Liberal Arts College* (Teachers College, Columbia University, New York, 1937). Dissertation study of the "practical" courses offered in certain New England liberal arts colleges.

LIMBERT, PAUL M.: *Denominational Policies in the Support and Supervision of Higher Education* (Teachers College, Columbia University, New York, 1929). Dissertation study of the relation of organized religion to higher education as illustrated through eight denominational boards of higher education.

LOWELL, A. LAWRENCE: *At War with Academic Traditions in America* (Harvard University Press, Cambridge, 1934). A collection of articles, addresses, and excerpts from the annual reports of Harvard's noted president.

LYND, ROBERT S.: *Knowledge for What? The Place of Social Science in American Culture* (Princeton University Press, Princeton, N. J., 1939). An outstanding sociologist calls for a reinterpretation of the part that social science should play in higher education.

McCONN, CHARLES M.: *College or Kindergarten?* (New Republic, Inc., New York, 1928). A lively critique and program for the college.

MacCRACKEN, JOHN HENRY: *College and Commonwealth; and Other Educational Papers and Addresses* (D. Appleton-Century Company, Inc., New York, 1920). Especially interesting for the religious point of view in college education by the president of Lafayette College.

McKOWN, H. C.: "The Trend of College Entrance Requirements, 1913–1922," *U. S. Bureau of Education, Bulletin*, 1924, No. 35. Analysis of the changes in prescribed and elective courses over the period of a decade.

MacLEAN, MALCOLM: *Scholars, Workers, and Gentlemen* (Harvard University Press, Cambridge, 1938). In the Inglis Lecture for 1938 the dean of Minnesota's General College indicates that higher education must give appropriate attention to all three aims cited in the title.

MARKS, PERCY: *Which Way Parnassus?* (Harcourt, Brace & Company, New York, 1926). An answer to what he calls the "muckraking" of Upton Sinclair, and a defense of the college.

MEIKLEJOHN, ALEXANDER: *The Experimental College* (Harper & Brothers, New York, 1932). Description of the Experimental College at the University of Wisconsin and an excellent statement of a philosophy of college education.

————: *The Liberal College* (Marshall Jones Company, Boston, 1920). A collection of articles and addresses by the president of Amherst College.

MORE, PAUL ELMER: *On Being Human* (Princeton University Press, Princeton, N. J., 1936). An outstanding Humanist gives the grounds of his faith.

National Society for the Study of Education: "Changes and Experiments in Liberal Arts Education," 31st Yearbook, Part II (Public School Publishing Company, Bloomington, Ill., 1932). Descriptions of many new plans and programs in various areas of college education; bibliography.

————: "General Education in the American College," 38th Yearbook, Part II (Public School Publishing Company, Bloomington, Ill., 1939). Discussion of the underlying philosophy of general education and descriptions of various approaches in several institutions; short bibliography.

National Society of College Teachers of Education: "Improving College Instruction," 1939 Yearbook (University of Chicago Press, Chicago, 1939). Historical and current problems facing college educators in their efforts to improve instruction.

NOCK, ALBERT JAY: *The Theory of Education in the United States* (Harcourt, Brace & Company, New York, 1932). Defense of tradition in higher education.

O'CONNELL, GEOFFREY: *Naturalism in American Education* (Benziger Brothers, New York, 1938). Attack upon Dewey, Kilpatrick, Rugg, and Thorndike from a Catholic point of view.

On Going to College; a Symposium (Oxford University Press, New York, 1938). Essays by several educators on the values of their fields of knowledge; written for students.

PALMER, ARCHIE M., ed.: *The Liberal Arts College Movement* (Little and Ives Company, New York, 1930). Proceedings of a conference held in Chicago in 1930 to stimulate interest and financial support for the small liberal arts colleges of the country.

PATTON, LESLIE K.: "Undergraduate Student Reports," *Journal of Higher Education.* 3: 285–293 (June, 1932). Description and analysis of reports on curriculum and organization made by student committees in several colleges.

The Relation of the Liberal College to Urban Life (Evansville College, Evansville, Ind., 1938). Addresses by Edward S. Jones, R. A. Kent, William H. Kilpatrick, and President F. M. Smith.

RICHARDS, PHILIP S.: *Belief in Man* (Farrar & Rinehart, Inc., New York, 1932). One of the most forthright and uncompromising of the statements by Humanists.

RICHARDSON, LEON B.: *A Study of the Liberal College; a Report to the President of Dartmouth College* (Dartmouth College, Hanover, N. H., 1924). A theory of college education and a program based upon considerable travel and study of institutions in England Canada, and the United States.

Rollins College: The Curriculum for the Liberal Arts College; Being the Report of the Curriculum Conference Held at Rollins College, Jan. 19–24, 1931 (Rollins College, Winter Park, Fla., n. d.). A forward-looking and progressive theory of higher education formulated by a conference of which John Dewey was chairman.

SANTAYANA, GEORGE: *The Genteel Tradition at Bay* (Charles Scribner's Sons, New York, 1931). A notable attack by a famous philosopher upon the supernatural basis of the Humanist point of view.

SCHILLP, PAUL ARTHUR: *Higher Education Faces the Future; a Symposium on College and University Education in the United States of America* (Liveright Publishing Company, New York, 1930). Points of view ranging from the extremely conservative to the extremely progressive.

SHOREY, PAUL: *The Assault on Humanism* (Atlantic Monthly Press Publications, Boston, 1917). A defense of Humanism by a noted Humanist and classicist.

SINCLAIR, UPTON: *The Goose-Step; a Study of American Education* (Private printing, Pasadena, Calif., 1923). A well-known American author traveled among many institutions and wrote a scathing indictment of them.

STOWE, A. MONROE: *Modernizing the College* (F. S. Crofts & Company, New York, 1926). The difficulties of reorganizing a college in the face of traditional conceptions and attitudes.

STUART, HENRY WALDGRAVE: *Liberal and Vocational Studies in the College* (Stanford University Press, Stanford University, Calif., 1918). A plea for both types of studies in the college curriculum.

The Students Speak Out! a Symposium from Twenty-Two Colleges (New Republic, Inc., New York, 1929). Essays written by students for a contest sponsored by the *New Republic* on the topic "College As It Might Be."

Value of the Classics; Classical Investigation Conducted by the Princeton University Advisory Committee (Princeton University Press, Princeton, N. J., 1917). Extensive statistics and testimonials to prove the value and vitality of study in the classics in high school and college.

VEBLEN, THORSTEIN: *The Higher Learning in America; a Memorandum on the Conduct of Universities by Business Men* (B. W. Huebsch, New York, 1918). Pictures and deplores the excessive control of university policies and methods by capitalistic ideals.

WECHSLER, JAMES: *Revolt on the Campus* (Covici Friede, Inc., New York, 1935). Concerned with the new currents of thought and feeling that have been stirring among students in many colleges and universities.

WEEKS, HELEN FOSS: *Factors Influencing the Choice of Courses by Students in Certain Liberal Arts Colleges* (Teachers College, Columbia University, New York, 1931). Dissertation study of the reasons students gave for selecting their courses in college.

WELCH, HERBERT, HENRY C. KING, and THOMAS NICHOLSON: *The Christian College* (Methodist Book Concern, New York, 1916). Addresses at the 100th anniversary of Alleghany College emphasizing the purposes of the religious college.

WILKINS, ERNEST HATCH: *The College and Society; Proposals for Changes in the American Plan of Higher Education* (D. Appleton-Century Company, Inc., New York, 1932). The president of Oberlin College presents his specifications for a general college to meet nonprofessional needs.

WRISTON, HENRY M.: *The Nature of a Liberal College* (Lawrence College Press, Appleton, Wis., 1937). A distinctive approach to the liberal ideal of a college by the president of Lawrence College.

IV. BIBLIOGRAPHIES

American Association of University Professors. Committee G: "A Bibliography of Methods of Increasing the Intellectual Interests and Raising the Intellectual Standards of Undergraduates," *American Association of University Professors, Bulletin,* 9: 385–418 (December, 1923). Alphabetical and topical list of 255 book and periodical references which appeared from 1901 to 1922.

American Association of University Women: "Newer Aspects of Collegiate Education; Outline and Bibliography," (Washington, D. C., 1932). Includes topical bibliographies on the changing curriculum, the liberal arts college and professional objectives, effective teaching, rise of the junior college, and others; a supplement with additional references appeared in 1933.

————: "Newer Aspects of Collegiate Education; a Study Guide," (Washington, D. C., 1936). Includes references on general trends, curriculum, better teaching and learning, liberal arts college and professional objectives, rise of the junior college, and other topics; compiled by Kathryn McHale and Frances V. Speek.

————: "The Student Goes to College; Outline and Bibliography," (Washington, D. C., 1932). Periodical and book references on such topics as who should go to college, religion and the student. value of a college education, and student life and opinion.

"Books on Education in the Libraries of Columbia University," *Columbia University Library Bulletins,* No. 2 (Columbia University, New York, 1901). A convenient compilation of hundreds of books, pamphlets, articles, addresses, and selections on higher education for the eighteenth and nineteenth centuries.

EELLS, WALTER CROSBY: "Bibliography on Junior Colleges," *U. S. Office of Education, Bulletin,* 1930, No. 2. Several hundred references on all phases of junior colleges

GOOD, CARTER V.: *Teaching in College and University; a Survey of the Problems and Literature in Higher Education* (Warwick and York, Baltimore, 1929). Extensive and comprehensive bibliographies on various sources of information concerning higher education, objectives, curriculum, psychology of learning, methods of teaching, measurement, administration, and twelve subject matter fields; reports all kinds of experiments, research investigations, and plans.

HADZITS, G. D., and L. R. HARLEY: *A Bibliographic Monograph on the Value of the Classics* (University of Pennsylvania, Philadelphia, 1921). Outlines various arguments in favor of the classics and contains annotated references illustrating the arguments.

MONROE, WALTER S., and LOUIS SHORES: *Bibliographies and Summaries in Education* (H. W. Wilson Company, New York, 1936). "A catalog of more than 4000 annotated bibliographies and summaries listed under author and subject in one alphabet," covers the period from 1910 to 1935 and includes many subject headings on higher education.

PEIK, W. E.: "Curriculum Investigations at the Teacher-training, College, and University Levels," *Review of Educational Research*, 4: 199–213, 244–252 (April, 1934). Review of literature from November, 1930, to November, 1933.

RATCLIFFE, E. B., and M. R. McCABE: "Good References on Changing Philosophies in Higher Education," *U. S. Office of Education, Bibliography* No. 53, 1937. A list of periodical and book references from 1931 to 1937; especially good for lists of associations, yearbooks, reports, proceedings, and periodicals which commonly contain material on higher education.

SEEGER, RUTH E.: *Orientation Courses; an Annotated Bibliography* (Bureau of Educational Research, Ohio State University, Columbus, 1931). Contains books and articles pertaining to orientation courses of all kinds, and textbooks and course outlines used in various colleges; covers the period from about 1920 to 1930.

STOWE, A. MONROE: *Studies in Collegiate Education; a Bibliography on Recent Literature on Collegiate Education* (Bulletin of Lynchburg College, Lynchburg, Va., 1930). A list of 1,040 titles; a supplement in 1931 adds 418 titles.

Teachers College Bulletins on Higher Education; Classified References from Current Literature (Teachers College, Columbia University, 1930–1932). Three volumes containing 7,589 book and periodical references from 1929 to 1932; alphabetical and topical arrangement covering all phases of higher education.

WOLCOTT, J. D.: "List of References on Higher Education," *U. S. Bureau of Education, Library Leaflet*, 1927, No. 35. Includes general references, history of higher education, academic freedom, curriculum, junior colleges, liberal arts colleges, municipal universities, and value of higher education; covers the period 1887–1927.

INDEX

AMERICAN EDUCATION:
ITS MEN, IDEAS, AND INSTITUTIONS
An Arno Press/New York Times Collection

Series I

Adams, Francis. **The Free School System of the United States.** 1875.

Alcott, William A. **Confessions of a School Master.** 1839.

American Unitarian Association. **From Servitude to Service.** 1905.

Bagley, William C. **Determinism in Education.** 1925.

Barnard, Henry, editor. **Memoirs of Teachers, Educators, and Promoters and Benefactors of Education, Literature, and Science.** 1861.

Bell, Sadie. **The Church, the State, and Education in Virginia.** 1930.

Belting, Paul Everett. **The Development of the Free Public High School in Illinois to 1860.** 1919.

Berkson, Isaac B. **Theories of Americanization: A Critical Study.** 1920.

Blauch, Lloyd E. **Federal Cooperation in Agricultural Extension Work, Vocational Education, and Vocational Rehabilitation.** 1935.

Bloomfield, Meyer. **Vocational Guidance of Youth.** 1911.

Brewer, Clifton Hartwell. **A History of Religious Education in the Episcopal Church to 1835.** 1924.

Brown, Elmer Ellsworth. **The Making of Our Middle Schools.** 1902.

Brumbaugh, M. G. **Life and Works of Christopher Dock.** 1908.

Burns, Reverend J. A. **The Catholic School System in the United States.** 1908.

Burns, Reverend J. A. **The Growth and Development of the Catholic School System in the United States.** 1912.

Burton, Warren. **The District School as It Was.** 1850.

Butler, Nicholas Murray, editor. **Education in the United States.** 1900.

Butler, Vera M. **Education as Revealed By New England Newspapers prior to 1850.** 1935.

Campbell, Thomas Monroe. **The Movable School Goes to the Negro Farmer.** 1936.

Carter, James G. **Essays upon Popular Education.** 1826.

Carter, James G. **Letters to the Hon. William Prescott, LL.D., on the Free Schools of New England.** 1824.

Channing, William Ellery. **Self-Culture.** 1842.

Coe, George A. **A Social Theory of Religious Education.** 1917.

Committee on Secondary School Studies. **Report of the Committee on Secondary School Studies, Appointed at the Meeting of the National Education Association.** 1893.

Counts, George S. **Dare the School Build a New Social Order?** 1932.

Counts, George S. **The Selective Character of American Secondary Education.** 1922.

Counts, George S. **The Social Composition of Boards of Education.** 1927.

Culver, Raymond B. **Horace Mann and Religion in the Massachusetts Public Schools.** 1929.

Curoe, Philip R. V. **Educational Attitudes and Policies of Organized Labor in the United States.** 1926.

Dabney, Charles William. **Universal Education in the South.** 1936.

Dearborn, Ned Harland. **The Oswego Movement in American Education.** 1925.

De Lima, Agnes. **Our Enemy the Child.** 1926.

Dewey, John. **The Educational Situation.** 1902.

Dexter, Franklin B., editor. **Documentary History of Yale University.** 1916.

Eliot, Charles William. **Educational Reform: Essays and Addresses.** 1898.

Ensign, Forest Chester. **Compulsory School Attendance and Child Labor.** 1921.

Fitzpatrick, Edward Augustus. **The Educational Views and Influence of De Witt Clinton.** 1911.

Fleming, Sanford. **Children & Puritanism.** 1933.

Flexner, Abraham. **The American College: A Criticism.** 1908.

Foerster, Norman. **The Future of the Liberal College.** 1938.

Gilman, Daniel Coit. **University Problems in the United States.** 1898.

Hall, Samuel R. **Lectures on School-Keeping.** 1829.

Hall, Stanley G. **Adolescence: Its Psychology and Its Relations to Physiology, Anthropology, Sociology, Sex, Crime, Religion, and Education.** 1905. 2 vols.

Hansen, Allen Oscar. **Early Educational Leadership in the Ohio Valley.** 1923.

Harris, William T. **Psychologic Foundations of Education.** 1899.

Harris, William T. **Report of the Committee of Fifteen on the Elementary School.** 1895.

Harveson, Mae Elizabeth. **Catharine Esther Beecher: Pioneer Educator.** 1932.

Jackson, George Leroy. **The Development of School Support in Colonial Massachusetts.** 1909.

Kandel, I. L., editor. **Twenty-five Years of American Education.** 1924.

Kemp, William Webb. **The Support of Schools in Colonial New York by the Society for the Propagation of the Gospel in Foreign Parts.** 1913.

Kilpatrick, William Heard. **The Dutch Schools of New Netherland and Colonial New York.** 1912.

Kilpatrick, William Heard. **The Educational Frontier.** 1933.

Knight, Edgar Wallace. **The Influence of Reconstruction on Education in the South.** 1913.

Le Duc, Thomas. **Piety and Intellect at Amherst College, 1865-1912.** 1946.

Maclean, John. **History of the College of New Jersey from Its Origin in 1746 to the Commencement of 1854.** 1877.

Maddox, William Arthur. **The Free School Idea in Virginia before the Civil War.** 1918.

Mann, Horace. **Lectures on Education.** 1855.

McCadden, Joseph J. **Education in Pennsylvania, 1801-1835, and Its Debt to Roberts Vaux.** 1855.

McCallum, James Dow. **Eleazar Wheelock.** 1939.

McCuskey, Dorothy. **Bronson Alcott, Teacher.** 1940.

Meiklejohn, Alexander. **The Liberal College.** 1920.

Miller, Edward Alanson. **The History of Educational Legislation in Ohio from 1803 to 1850.** 1918.

Miller, George Frederick. **The Academy System of the State of New York.** 1922.

Monroe, Will S. **History of the Pestalozzian Movement in the United States.** 1907.

Mosely Education Commission. **Reports of the Mosely Education Commission to the United States of America October-December, 1903.** 1904.

Mowry, William A. **Recollections of a New England Educator.** 1908.

Mulhern, James. **A History of Secondary Education in Pennsylvania.** 1933.

National Herbart Society. **National Herbart Society Yearbooks 1-5, 1895-1899.** 1895-1899.

Nearing, Scott. **The New Education: A Review of Progressive Educational Movements of the Day.** 1915.

Neef, Joseph. **Sketches of a Plan and Method of Education.** 1808.

Nock, Albert Jay. **The Theory of Education in the United States.** 1932.

Norton, A. O., editor. **The First State Normal School in America: The Journals of Cyrus Pierce and Mary Swift.** 1926.

Oviatt, Edwin. **The Beginnings of Yale, 1701-1726.** 1916.

Packard, Frederic Adolphus. **The Daily Public School in the United States.** 1866.

Page, David P. **Theory and Practice of Teaching.** 1848.

Parker, Francis W. **Talks on Pedagogics: An Outline of the Theory of Concentration.** 1894.

Peabody, Elizabeth Palmer. **Record of a School.** 1835.

Porter, Noah. **The American Colleges and the American Public.** 1870.

Reigart, John Franklin. **The Lancasterian System of Instruction in the Schools of New York City.** 1916.

Reilly, Daniel F. **The School Controversy (1891-1893).** 1943.

Rice, Dr. J. M. **The Public-School System of the United States.** 1893.

Rice, Dr. J. M. **Scientific Management in Education.** 1912.

Ross, Early D. **Democracy's College: The Land-Grant Movement in the Formative Stage.** 1942.

Rugg, Harold, et al. **Curriculum-Making: Past and Present.** 1926.

Rugg, Harold, et al. **The Foundations of Curriculum-Making.** 1926.

Rugg, Harold and Shumaker, Ann. **The Child-Centered School.** 1928.

Seybolt, Robert Francis. **Apprenticeship and Apprenticeship Education in Colonial New England and New York.** 1917.

Seybolt, Robert Francis. **The Private Schools of Colonial Boston.** 1935.

Seybolt, Robert Francis. **The Public Schools of Colonial Boston.** 1935.

Sheldon, Henry D. **Student Life and Customs.** 1901.

Sherrill, Lewis Joseph. **Presbyterian Parochial Schools, 1846-1870.** 1932 .

Siljestrom, P. A. **Educational Institutions of the United States.** 1853.

Small, Walter Herbert. **Early New England Schools.** 1914.

Soltes, Mordecai. **The Yiddish Press: An Americanizing Agency.** 1925.

Stewart, George, Jr. **A History of Religious Education in Connecticut to the Middle of the Nineteenth Century.** 1924.

Storr, Richard J. **The Beginnings of Graduate Education in America.** 1953.

Stout, John Elbert. **The Development of High-School Curricula in the North Central States from 1860 to 1918.** 1921.

Suzzallo, Henry. **The Rise of Local School Supervision in Massachusetts.** 1906.

Swett, John. **Public Education in California.** 1911.

Tappan, Henry P. **University Education.** 1851.

Taylor, Howard Cromwell. **The Educational Significance of the Early Federal Land Ordinances.** 1921.

Taylor, J. Orville. **The District School.** 1834.

Tewksbury, Donald G. **The Founding of American Colleges and Universities before the Civil War.** 1932.

Thorndike, Edward L. **Educational Psychology.** 1913-1914.

True, Alfred Charles. **A History of Agricultural Education in the United States, 1785-1925.** 1929.

True, Alfred Charles. **A History of Agricultural Extension Work in the United States, 1785-1923.** 1928.

Updegraff, Harlan. **The Origin of the Moving School in Massachusetts.** 1908.

Wayland, Francis. **Thoughts on the Present Collegiate System in the United States.** 1842.

Weber, Samuel Edwin. **The Charity School Movement in Colonial Pennsylvania.** 1905.

Wells, Guy Fred. **Parish Education in Colonial Virginia.** 1923.

Wickersham, J. P. **The History of Education in Pennsylvania.** 1885.

Woodward, Calvin M. **The Manual Training School.** 1887.

Woody, Thomas. **Early Quaker Education in Pennsylvania.** 1920.

Woody, Thomas. **Quaker Education in the Colony and State of New Jersey.** 1923.

Wroth, Lawrence C. **An American Bookshelf, 1755.** 1934.

Series II

Adams, Evelyn C. **American Indian Education.** 1946.

Bailey, Joseph Cannon. **Seaman A. Knapp: Schoolmaster of American Agriculture.** 1945.

Beecher, Catharine and Harriet Beecher Stowe. **The American Woman's Home.** 1869.

Benezet, Louis T. **General Education in the Progressive College.** 1943.

Boas, Louise Schutz. **Woman's Education Begins.** 1935.

Bobbitt, Franklin. **The Curriculum.** 1918.

Bode, Boyd H. **Progressive Education at the Crossroads.** 1938.

Bourne, William Oland. **History of the Public School Society of the City of New York.** 1870.

Bronson, Walter C. **The History of Brown University, 1764-1914.** 1914.

Burstall, Sara A. **The Education of Girls in the United States.** 1894.

Butts, R. Freeman. **The College Charts Its Course.** 1939.

Caldwell, Otis W. and Stuart A. Courtis. **Then & Now in Education, 1845-1923.** 1923.

Calverton, V. F. & Samuel D. Schmalhausen, editors. **The New Generation: The Intimate Problems of Modern Parents and Children.** 1930.

Charters, W. W. **Curriculum Construction.** 1923.

Childs, John L. **Education and Morals.** 1950.

Childs, John L. **Education and the Philosophy of Experimentalism.** 1931.

Clapp, Elsie Ripley. **Community Schools in Action.** 1939.

Counts, George S. **The American Road to Culture: A Social Interpretation of Education in the United States.** 1930.

Counts, George S. **School and Society in Chicago.** 1928.

Finegan, Thomas E. **Free Schools.** 1921.

Fletcher, Robert Samuel. **A History of Oberlin College.** 1943.

Grattan, C. Hartley. **In Quest of Knowledge: A Historical Perspective on Adult Education.** 1955.

Hartman, Gertrude & Ann Shumaker, editors. **Creative Expression.** 1932.

Kandel, I. L. **The Cult of Uncertainty.** 1943.

Kandel, I. L. **Examinations and Their Substitutes in the United States.** 1936.

Kilpatrick, William Heard. **Education for a Changing Civilization.** 1926.

Kilpatrick, William Heard. **Foundations of Method.** 1925.

Kilpatrick, William Heard. **The Montessori System Examined.** 1914.

Lang, Ossian H., editor. **Educational Creeds of the Nineteenth Century.** 1898.

Learned, William S. **The Quality of the Educational Process in the United States and in Europe.** 1927.

Meiklejohn, Alexander. **The Experimental College.** 1932.

Middlekauff, Robert. **Ancients and Axioms: Secondary Education in Eighteenth-Century New England.** 1963.

Norwood, William Frederick. **Medical Education in the United States Before the Civil War.** 1944.

Parsons, Elsie W. Clews. **Educational Legislation and Administration of the Colonial Governments.** 1899.

Perry, Charles M. **Henry Philip Tappan: Philosopher and University President.** 1933.

Pierce, Bessie Louise. **Civic Attitudes in American School Textbooks.** 1930.

Rice, Edwin Wilbur. **The Sunday-School Movement (1780-1917) and the American Sunday-School Union (1817-1917).** 1917.

Robinson, James Harvey. **The Humanizing of Knowledge.** 1924.

Ryan, W. Carson. **Studies in Early Graduate Education.** 1939.

Seybolt, Robert Francis. **The Evening School in Colonial America.** 1925.

Seybolt, Robert Francis. **Source Studies in American Colonial Education.** 1925.

Todd, Lewis Paul. **Wartime Relations of the Federal Government and the Public Schools, 1917-1918.** 1945.

Vandewalker, Nina C. **The Kindergarten in American Education.** 1908.

Ward, Florence Elizabeth. **The Montessori Method and the American School.** 1913.

West, Andrew Fleming. **Short Papers on American Liberal Education.** 1907.

Wright, Marion M. Thompson. **The Education of Negroes in New Jersey.** 1941.

Supplement

The Social Frontier (Frontiers of Democracy). Vols. 1-10, 1934-1943.